MANY VOICES

MANY VOICES

AN INTRODUCTION TO
SOCIAL ISSUES

Herbert W. Helm, Jr., and Duane C. McBride, Editors

ANDREWS
UNIVERSITY PRESS

BERRIEN SPRINGS, MICHIGAN

Andrews University Press
Sutherland House
Berrien Springs, MI 49104-1700
Telephone: 269-471-6134
Fax: 269-471-6224
Email: aupo@andrews.edu
Website: http://universitypress.andrews.edu

ISBN 978-1-883925-56-7

Printed in the United States of America
11 10 09 08 07   5 4 3 2 1

Library of Congress Cataloging-in-Publication Data

Many voices : an introduction to social issues / Herbert W. Helm, Jr. and Duane C. McBride, editors.
     p. cm.
  ISBN-13: 978-1-883925-56-7 (pbk. : alk. paper)
1. Sociology. 2. Social problems. I. Helm, Herbert W., 1955- II. McBride, Duane C.

  HM586.M36 2007
  301--dc22

                          2006027978

Project Director	Ronald Alan Knott
Line Editors	Michael Rigsby, Penelope Sky, Clifford Goldstein
Copy Editor	Deborah L. Everhart
Typesetters	Thomas Toews, Deborah L. Everhart
Text and Cover Designer	Robert N. Mason

Typeset: 11/14 Adobe Caslon Pro

TABLE OF CONTENTS

SOCIAL INSTITUTIONS

DEVIANCE AND WELL BEING

SOCIAL INEQUALITY

PROBLEMS WITH MODERNIZATION

DEALING WITH SOCIAL ISSUES

PREFACE

by Herbert W. Helm, Jr.

It is hard to visit San Francisco without noticing the plight of the homeless. While homeless people can be found in all large cities, they seem especially noticeable in San Francisco. They can be seen throughout the city, sleeping on the streets (some with their pets) and begging (using techniques from panhandling to holding signs that say things like "Please help: I have AIDS" or "Why lie? I need money for a drink"). Some streets have portable toilets placed for use by the homeless. Besides being homeless, some of these people also appear to have a number of mental disorders, ranging from drug abuse (as evidenced by the alcoholic beverages around their sleeping areas) to schizophrenia (a psychotic disorder in which one is in poor touch with reality). The situation in San Francisco and other cities around the country raises a number of questions:

- Is the plight of the homeless a social problem, or just part of the social structure?
- Is the issue a lack of individual responsibility, a choice of living style, or the failure of some institution?
- Did the education system fail to give these people usable skills or did they fail to take advantage of the education offered them?
- Have mental disorders played a role and how should these disorders be dealt with?
- Has the economy played a role and what is the relationship between homelessness and poverty?
- Is there a relationship between the type of government and the economic system? How has it affected these people?
- Has immigration filled economic niches that affected these individuals?
- Has violence contributed to these people living on the street? Does violence continue to affect them as they live on the street?
- Who should take responsibility—the government (local, state, or federal), the church, or the individual?
- What would be the best way to resolve the problem?

These are just a few of the questions that could be asked. At a broader level we could pose the questions this way:

- What is a social issue?
- Who gets to define social issues?
- How should we deal with social issues?

These are questions we will be looking at as we go through this text. The "Social Problems" or "Social Issues" course is typically taught in the sociology department by sociologists. As a result, almost all textbooks on social issues and problems are written from the view of a sociologist. At one level this makes sense since sociologists study human behaviors, especially as they apply to groups. On the other hand, there are many disciplines that deal with social issues and problems. These disciplines include psychology, anthropology, social work, family studies, economics, political science, theology, and others. The idea for this text came about as an attempt to include the "many voices" which deal with the social issues and problems of our society.

In their book, *Provocative Therapy*, Farrelly and Brandsma (1974) note the following concerning the diversity of views among various disciplines: "President Kennedy once asked his scientific advisor why scientists (who are supposed to 'know') with disturbing frequency arrived at remarkably divergent conclusions regarding the same problem, question, or phenomenon. The answer was that although scientists may study the same phenomenon, they approach it with different kinds of assumptions" (p. 35).

As noted above, many disciplines study human behavior. Each has perspectives on why humans engage in various behaviors, and on the origins of, and solutions to, social issues and problems. While sociologists report some findings and concepts from other fields, they may not do so from the same perspective as individuals within those fields. These individuals are more likely to see the issues from their own set of assumptions. And those assumptions are likely based on what they have learned from the study of their discipline as well as their own personal biases. Each author reflects the training of a discipline and the uniqueness of his or her own personal individuality. A particular author may have viewpoints that vary from others within a discipline. Hence, it is not to be assumed that each author will be "representative" of a discipline; rather, he or she will be a voice within that discipline.

The purpose of our text is to bring in the perspectives of a number of social scientists, as well as those from other disciplines, in order to broaden the student's understanding of how different fields may approach social issues. These differences in approach may include different research methods, various paradigms of the world, and diverse ways of dealing with an issue or problem.

In order to broaden the different perspectives, the social issues chapters in this text include responses by other social scientists. Most of these responses have been written by social scientists of different disciplines, or perspectives, than that of the main author(s), and they serve to give a different or enlarged point of view.

This book cannot provide a comprehensive picture of all the beliefs and perspectives of each discipline as it relates to a given social issue. Instead, the purpose of this text is to give glimpses through various windows (paradigms) of how individuals from various disciplines view social issues and problems. The point of the text is to broaden the student's perspective of social problems by putting forth divergent points, which are discussed within social issues—realizing that not all points will be covered. In that vein, this text can be used as either a reader or a single text for a social problems class. Sociologists who teach from this text will likely not be as conversant in psychology, anthropology, or other disciplines as someone trained in those fields. However, this text gives them the opportunity to note how the "voice" (the traditional sociological paradigms) of a sociologist may compare and contrast to the "voice" of an individual from another perspective or field.

In order to broaden the perspectives in this book, there has been an attempt to include issues of religion and culture. Religion plays a very important part in society. This is demonstrated from the weekly commitments that many make to worship. Culture obviously plays an important role in helping determine the views people hold. As people move around more, cultures interact with one another at an increasing pace, so there is a need to try and understand the perspectives of others if we are to live peacefully. In many places, the roles of culture and religion are entwined, and an understanding of one helps in understanding the other. Considering the importance that culture and religion play in the development of social paradigms, it was felt that students should be exposed to some level of thinking about these concepts in the development of their beliefs about social issues and problems.

Organization of the Text

In order to have meaningful discussions of social issues, it is helpful for students to have some understanding of foundational courses focused on human behavior, such as psychology, sociology, and anthropology. In order to facilitate this understanding, we have organized the text in the following manner:

1) The text begins by considering various views which sociology, psychology, and anthropology have concerning human behavior.
2) Then we consider how we define and study social issues.
3) The "social issues" sections have been grouped as follows: social institutions, deviance and well being, social inequality, and problems with modernization.

4) Finally, we will consider how to deal with social issues.

Pedagogical Features

The following pedagogical features are added to the text:

1) The social issues chapters have a feature called "ISSUES"—a collection of questions—which introduces main sections within each chapter. Not all of the questions raised will be answered within the section, but they are presented to stimulate thinking about those issues. Besides using the text to answer these questions, further study of material from the web, journal articles, and other sources is recommended.
2) Two types of web resources can be found within the chapters. Some authors have incorporated web sites into the main discussion, while at the end of a chapter appears a list of web sites revolving around that chapter's issue. The web sites within the chapters are related to the material being discussed at that point. The web sites at the end of the chapter have information and articles which can help the student answer the "ISSUES" and discussion questions. The professor and student can also use these sites for further and advanced study.
3) For social issues to take on personal relevance, it would be useful to discuss the issues and questions raised in the various social issues chapters. In order to facilitate this exchange, a section called "Discussion Questions" is included at the end of each chapter. Chapters also have related readings and videos that can be used for discussions.

In short, we believe that this text offers a broader and more multi-pluralistic view of "social problems" than most other texts. As a result, the text fits both the traditional social problems class and those classes which seek to broaden the disciplinary perspectives of social issues.

Thanks

As editors of this text, Duane McBride and I would find it nearly impossible to acknowledge and thank all those who have been involved in the development and publishing of this text. But, as always, there are a handful of exceptional people without whom it would have been nearly impossible. To each of the authors we can only express gratitude for the number of times they have adjusted their time and writings to accommodate changes that have occurred along the way. Three student workers—Nisim Estrada, Jonathan Cook, and Jacquelyn Giem—have put in an enormous amount of time structuring and restructuring the text. Beverly Peck, our office manager, has (as usual) kept our paperwork on track. The Office of Scholarly Research provided a grant to make this text a reality. And, finally, thanks to Andrews University Press for publication of the text.

FOUNDATIONS OF SOCIOLOGY

Lionel Matthews, Duane C. McBride, and Marciana Popescu

Chapter Outline

- Introduction: What Is Sociology?
- The Sociological Perspective
- Social Structure as Social Facts
- Theoretical Perspectives: The Varied Lenses of Sociology
- Sociological Perspectives within the Context of Modernism and Postmodernism
- Conclusion

Introduction: What Is Sociology?

Sociology may be defined as the scientific study of society and human relationships (Henslin, 2005). The core position of the sociologist is that human behavior is strongly contingent upon group norms and values as well as social structures. Thus, human beings do not act in isolation but within a larger group and structural context. The interaction between you and your society affects your individual behavior. This concept is one of the main elements that distinguish sociology from other fields, such as psychology and economics. Sociology has a group-based, or interpersonal, perspective, whereas psychology, for example, has an individualistic, or intrapersonal, emphasis.

As an academic discipline, sociology is relatively new. It emerged in France during the nineteenth century as a reaction to several conditions, including the Industrial Revolution, the French Revolution, and the travel of Europeans to the New World. These events ignited the interest and concern of European scholars, who sought to find answers to the turmoil resulting from rapid social change and questions these situations provoked.

While bringing many benefits to society, such as increasing the production of goods and services, the Industrial Revolution also produced many troubling patterns, including the disruption of the village and family harmony often associated with pre-modern society. The rural lifestyle offered a sense of safety and stability to village inhabitants. As individuals migrated to the cities, they were greeted by the kind of estrangement and competitiveness more typical of a modern capitalist economy. Large numbers of people migrated from the rural communities to the industrial towns of Europe in search of jobs. There was thus a huge surplus of labor, and many of those who sought employment were disappointed. This resulted in a number of social problems such as homelessness, vagrancy, prostitution, and a wide variety of crimes. New citizens of the cities came to see themselves as individuals engaged in competition for jobs without significant levels of social support from family or friends. Individualism increased at the expense of community cooperation, and social relationships were devoid of the support and meaning that characterized interaction in the rural areas.

While the Industrial Revolution dislocated families and bred crimes, the French Revolution attacked the established church and monarchial forms of government. The architects of the French Revolution attacked these establishments in the name of liberty, equality, and fraternity. At the height of the revolution, French General Berthier took the Pope captive, thus striking a major blow to the established church and upsetting many people's understanding of what God had created. This course of events proved unsettling to the French, in particular to those scholars who had exercised confidence in the status quo.

Another event that interested scholars was the travel of Europeans to the New World. There travelers found lifestyles very different from the ones they knew, and this needed explanation. But there was hope that the needed answers would be found. Much of this optimism was inspired by the successes that scholars of the natural sciences were realizing.

Auguste Comte, a French scholar, was among the first European thinkers to assert that a discipline was needed for understanding major social changes. He wanted to pattern the new area of study after the methodology of the natural sciences, which focused upon observation, comparison, and prediction. Comte was optimistic that the secret to the social turmoil created by the French and Industrial Revolutions would be unlocked, and a formula for creating a better world found. He named the new area of study "social physics," but when he learned that someone else already had used the term he quickly changed it to "sociology."

In this chapter, not only will we look at sociology as a whole, but we will evaluate some of the ideas of the main contributors to the discipline and discover how these ideas still affect the way we view social issues.

The Sociological Perspective

Emile Durkheim, like Comte, was troubled by the disorder resulting from the French and Industrial Revolutions. He was especially interested in understanding **social solidarity**, or the nature of societal order, and how it changes over time. Specifically, Durkheim wanted to trace the relationship between individuals and society and determine how consensus among different parts of society was generated. As Durkheim contemplated these questions, the intellectual traditions of psychologism and biologism caught his attention. These traditions suggest that human behavior is traceable to either psychological principles, such as drives and personality, or to such biological factors as genes and hormones. Durkheim rejected their view of human behavior and the sort of reductionism they implied. For him, social phenomena (human behavior and related social patterns) are caused by wider social forces. This circular approach is largely due to Durkheim's determination to shy away from non-social explanations for social action. Durkheim would argue that only the wider social world produced human social behavior.

Durkheim (1950) was convinced that social facts lie at the base of all events in society. He described social facts as "Every way of acting, fixed or not, capable of exercising on the individual external constraint" (p. 13) and suggested that social facts should be the subject matter of sociology. Accordingly, the sociologist will say that people think, feel, and act the way they do because these ways of thinking, feeling, and acting are already present in their society. But this suggestion that social facts frame the actions of individuals raised the issue of determinism and free will.

Scholars who argue for determinism believe that human action is influenced by forces other than personal choice. For example, from a biologically deterministic perspective, it is the level of testosterone, not free will, that produces aggressive acts more in men than in women. Or from the social determinist's viewpoint, it is being part of a particular social/cultural group, and not free will, that determines, for example, how women conduct themselves in society. Free will proponents, on the other hand, see individual choice as the main source of human conduct. From this point of view, people exercise their freedom to create their own response to environmental stimuli; they are not pawns of their social environment or biological endowments.

Thus, although many sociologists reject the notion of psychological and biological determinism, they have embraced social determinism as the basis of human conduct. However, the idea of a pure social determinism is not common to all sociologists. The sociological perspective does not assume a mutually exclusive relationship between determinism and free will. It sees human conduct on a continuum (see Figure 1.1) from complete determinism on one end to complete free will on the other. Sociologists' views vary in their position along this continuum.

C. Wright Mills (1959) and Michael Schwalbe (1998) have both built on the ideas of Durkheim and offered their own interpretations of the sociological perspective. Whereas Durkheim used the term *social facts*, Mills used *sociological imagination*, and Schwalbe *sociological mindfulness*.

In his landmark work, *The Sociological Imagination*, Mills (1959) made a strong argument for the necessity of being able "to understand the larger historical scene in terms of its meaning for the inner life and the external career of a variety of individuals" (p. 5).

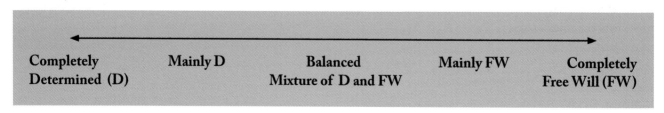

| Completely Determined (D) | Mainly D | Balanced Mixture of D and FW | Mainly FW | Completely Free Will (FW) |

Figure 1.1: The Continuum of Determinism to Free Will

This capacity, which he labels "the sociological imagination," enables one to grasp the connection between history (the wider social structure) and biography (the immediate circumstances of individual lives) as they affect human conduct. Thus, we can make the distinction between social problems and personal problems.

Social problems (or issues) are patterns that affect the lives of a broad cross section of society. Social problems are caused by forces beyond the individual. On the other hand, personal problems afflict individuals and families without being widespread enough to be defined as social issues. If, for example, three people in a labor force of 5,000 are unemployed, or four families among 4,000 families are criminally deviant, the unemployment rate and the tendency to crime may be attributable to personal rather than social causes. To understand the problems of these individuals and families, one may need to look closely at their lives and their private circumstances. Problems of this sort tend to be within the realm of the psychologist, whose prime focus is to understand social patterns by way of the individual's mind. When problems are demographically dispersed (involving a broad cross section of age cohorts, ethnic groups, religious affiliations, etc.), we seek explanation within the broader social context. In other words, we use our sociological lenses to detect the causative or associative factors. This "sociological mindfulness," as Schwalbe calls it, makes us both more objective and more empathetic. For, by "paying attention to the hardships and options other people have and how their circumstances differ from ours we are more likely to grant them the respect they deserve as humans and be less prone to condemn them unfairly" (Schwalbe, 1998, p. 5).

In summary, the sociological perspective is group-focused. It locates social patterns in the social conditions of group interaction while de-emphasizing intrapersonal and biological factors as adequate explanations for human behavior. In this view, the social dimension of life takes precedence over individual intrapersonal causes of behavior. Thus, it is argued that while it is possible to understand the individual from the standpoint of the wider social system, it is not as fruitful to pursue an understanding of the social system by studying the individual lives that constitute it. In this view, sociologists embrace the position that the whole is greater than the sum of its parts.

Social Structure As Social Facts

To more fully understand what Durkheim meant by social facts, we should examine the components of social structure. Social structure is thought to operate at two levels. The macro level is made up of the broad features of a society, such as institutions, cultural norms, and social organizations. The micro level consists of face-to-face interactions among social actors, who constantly assess and interpret their encounters to determine how to act. The micro level is the scene of constant negotiations between people.

One of the implications of Durkheim's view of social facts is that the macro level of social structure pre-exists the micro level. For instance, Henslin (1995) noted that "We came into this world without language, values or morality, with no ideas of religion, war, money, love" (p. 36), yet over time we come to acquire these things through learning within a social environment. These learned ways of seeing and doing things become the basis from which we view the world about us. The culture into which we were born constitutes the chief source of our viewpoint.

Today we live in a society that is increasingly made up of members who were raised in very different social environments, with very different perspectives. The groups that comprise our society often have very different views, for example, on gun use, sexual morality, the role of religion in society, and the roles of men and women. Members of one group may believe very strongly that guns should be banned, that there should be strong separation between church and state, and that there should be no social or legal barriers to either gender playing specific social roles. Conversely, other groups may believe very strongly that religious leaders should control public morality and that there should be a strict separation between the social roles of men and women. To members of both groups, their own perceptions will seem "natural"—the way things should obviously be done. Let us examine some of the elements of culture.

Culture

When sociologists speak of **culture**, they are referring to the blueprint, or system of meaning and technology, by which people live. The system of meaning is rooted in the beliefs, values, and norms of society, and is called its nonmaterial culture. The material culture consists of tangible objects such as buildings, means of transportation, and other physical artifacts.

The nonmaterial aspect of culture is especially important for people's behavior, even if the degree to which it influences behavior is often not fully evident. For example, our language provides us with several benefits without which life as we know it would be vastly different. Not only does it enable us to store our experiences and share our perspectives with each other, but, according to Edward Sapir and Benjamin Whorf, our view of reality is largely determined by our language. These two American researchers argued that through our language we embrace a particular way of thinking about and perceiving the world. This theory has become known as the **Sapir-Whorf Hypothesis** (Sapir, 1921; Whorf, 1956).

Apart from our language, the values of our culture exert a critically determining force in our lives. **Values** are our ideas about what is good or bad, worthy or unworthy, desirable or undesirable. Robin Williams (1965) identified specific core values of American society. They include science and technology, achievements, success, individualism, progress, material comfort, humanitarianism, freedom, democracy, equality, racism, group superiority, activity, and work. Values by themselves do not provide a sufficient guide to action. We must also look at **norms**, or standards of behavior, which can be seen as an extension of values, enforceable by sanctions. Norms thus reflect the expectations that are associated with the values of a society. There are basically two types of norms: folkways and mores. **Folkways** are norms that, when violated, carry relatively light sanctions. The violation of **mores** carries higher penalties than the violation of folkways. There is a special category of norms called taboos. These norms are proscriptive in nature and generally evoke outrage when violated.

For example, we violate a folkway if, instead of using a spoon to eat our soup, we lap it up with our tongue. Those around us may treat our behavior with no more than raised eyebrows or looks of surprise.

On the other hand, if we pilfer food from the plate of our dining companions while they are not looking, we will be guilty of violating a mos (singular for mores). For this behavior, our companions may not invite us to future such gatherings. Yet greater and more severe sanctions may be meted out against us if we declare that our favorite drink is human blood. Such a declaration will most likely be met with feelings and expressions of outrage by our audience, and may lead to us being derided and ostracized from the group as well as potential criminal penalties.

But what is taboo in one society may be acceptable in another. In the United States, it is quite acceptable for women to wear pants or go about with their heads uncovered, practices that would be greeted with severe sanctions in Saudi Arabia. What, then, is appropriate attire? From the standpoint of the sociologist, there can be no blanket answer. The question must be approached from the standpoint of a particular group. However, this principle is not easily followed, as each group, or society, tends to see its own blueprint for living as the most reasonable and desirable. This tendency often leads to **ethnocentrism**, in which we use our own cultural norms and values to determine the rightness or wrongness, appropriateness or inappropriateness, of other peoples' norms and values. Because of the obvious bias inherent in ethnocentrism, sociologists suggest that each culture must be evaluated in terms of its own circumstances. **Cultural relativism**, as the latter practice is described, is therefore thought to be a fairer and more realistic evaluation of norms and values than ethnocentrism.

Statuses and Roles

A society's norms and values become custom as statuses and roles are assigned to various individuals. A **status** is simply a social position that someone occupies in a society. Each of us is enmeshed in a constellation of statuses, referred to as our **status set.** A status set consists of all the positions we hold, from our jobs to the infinite number of relationships we share with others.

Consider all the positions you hold. If you are a woman, that is part of your status. In addition, you are a child of your parents, and you could be a sister, an aunt, a cousin, an American, and so forth. Some of these statuses are ascribed—that is, they are assigned to you by birth or by some other means over which you have no control. Other social positions you occupy have been achieved. For example, if you are a teacher and a mother, you had a part to play in attaining those positions. When people in your group, or environment, come to see one of your statuses as more important than the others, it becomes your **master status**. For example, an individual who is a pastor may have that status overshadow all other statuses he or she may occupy. At the other end of the social status spectrum, a master status may involve deviant behavior. If someone is a drug addict, that status may overshadow all other statuses of the individual.

Whereas statuses reflect social positions that people occupy within groups, **roles** are the expectations, privileges, obligations, and behaviors that are associated with statuses. How individuals dress and travel in a given culture, where they live, and the activities they engage in are, to a large extent, guided by the roles associated with their various statuses. For example, the president of a corporation will engage in certain social activities, dress in a particular way, and have an apparently ideal family because it is expected of him or her. Thus, status incumbents behave in keeping with expectations placed upon them by their roles. Although what is expected of us in a given status does not always match our behavior within that status, our behaviors are generally guided by role expectations if we wish to retain our roles in society.

Theoretical Perspectives: The Varied Lenses of Sociology

Sociologists view social issues from three broad perspectives: **functionalism**, **conflict theory**, and **interactionism**. These perspectives provide a framework for describing various social issues and problems as well as for understanding the etiology (cause) of a problem and its possible solutions.

Functionalism

Functionalism is one of the oldest perspectives in sociology. It focuses on how social institutions work to meet the basic needs of a society by socializing and resocializing its members into expected norms, values, and skills. The functionalist perspective also focuses on how the behaviors of individuals and groups are controlled—how our needs for resources such as housing, food, and clothing are met. Functionalists would argue that when family, educational, political, legal, and economic institutions are working in a consistently integrated fashion, society experiences low rates of poverty, crime, mental illness, alcoholism, and drug abuse. When any of these institutions does not function well, or when they are not integrated, society experiences higher rates of social problems. From a functionalist perspective, the key to preventing social problems is to have well-functioning and integrated institutions that achieve the basic goals of a society.

Functionalist theory focuses on macro-level conceptual development and analysis. This means that functionalists emphasize the effect of more distant institutions (macro), as opposed to smaller group (mezzo) or individual (micro) interactions. They tend to point out the macro institutional effects on human behavior. A basic assumption of functionalism is that it is possible to achieve a basic broad consensus on what the major social institutions are and how they can function for the good of almost everyone in a society. That assumption is largely based on a pragmatic belief that functional institutions are a basic goal—even expectation—of a human society, and that human beings are sufficiently rational to work together to achieve them. Functionalists recognize that no institutional system functions perfectly and that there will always be a significant number of individuals who are not successfully socialized, who do not obtain the skills they need to do well in a social economic system, and who therefore end up in the criminal justice system.

As our society becomes increasingly pluralistic in ethnic, cultural, and religious values, the ability of social institutions to provide common socialization experiences with shared values, a common language, educational and occupational skills, and access to economic opportunities becomes more difficult. In contemporary American society, we have a large public school system, but also private religious schools that often teach very different norms and values. For functionalists, the challenge is to develop institutions that can provide the basic common ground of experience, skills, and values so that society will function with minimal conflict.

The American and French governments have both recently struggled with the role of religious symbols in public. In Alabama, a state Supreme Court judge erected a monument of the Ten Commandments. He was later forced to remove it, despite the objections of many. The French have struggled with the role of religious symbols in public schools. Muslims may sincerely view the female headscarf as an outward symbol of faith, devotion, and modesty; Christians may see the wearing of a cross as a sign of their devotion. Yet the secular French government has the functional concern that such symbols pit one group against another. The fear seems to be that public schools cannot perform their role of common socialization in a shared normative value system if strongly competing views are symbolically present.

From a functionalist perspective, the causes of social problems may be attributable to the peculiar circumstances of individuals who for a variety of reasons may not conform or achieve. The causes can also be institutional and structural; that is, the educational system may not train individuals for roles in the economy, or intergenerational value transmission may not successfully occur if educational and family systems do not function well. From a functionalist perspective, efforts to improve social problems would focus not on individual psychological interventions but on understanding why existing institutions failed in preventing the problem from emerging. It would also seek to develop and implement institutional changes that would reduce the problem.

A functionalist approach to a social issue might focus on poverty and racism in the United States, so clearly identified by social science researchers in the 1960s. These sociologists argued that high rates of poverty emerged from four basic causes: institutional racism, the lack of access to quality education for all ethnic groups, limited access to health care, and few job skills. As a result, the United States developed and implemented a major "War on Poverty" under Lyndon Johnson's administration. Programs under this initiative included busing to improve racial balance in schools, significantly increased federal aid to schools, Medicare to provide health insurance to the elderly and Medicaid to provide state insurance to the poor, affirmative action to improve the job opportunities for all ethnic groups, and a wide variety of economic stimulus packages. Major institutional changes resulted.

The 1960s and 1970s were a time of the most rapid changes in the history of society in the United States. While the success of these institutional changes is much debated (school busing and **affirmative action** have been largely discontinued), they illustrate how a functionalist approach to change in institutional functioning can address social problems. Regarding the reduction in crime rates during the last few years, functionalists might argue that the increased opportunities in an expanding economy, mandatory minimum sentencing for criminal offenders, and increased emphasis on parental and school social bonding all played a major role in crime commission.

Among the more influential sociologists who promoted and embraced this perspective were Auguste Comte, Emile Durkheim, and, more recently, Talcott Parsons (see Box 1.1) and Robert Merton (see Box 1.2). While these sociologists emphasized different theories in their works, they all agree on the following assumptions:

- Social problems should be explained and understood by the causal relationships at the macro level of the social structure.
- Consensus is the basis of social order. This means that societal order is based on the willing compliance of social actors.
- Various social institutions generate consensus. The willingness of people to comply with the norms of society is learned from institutions.
- Change is adaptive rather than radical; a society maintains its basic features over time. For instance, if a society is capitalist or socialist in nature, either of these characteristics will tend to endure; the changes that take place will not alter these features fundamentally.
- Human beings are drawn by reason, and their rational powers enable them to comply with social authority, the basis of societal cohesion.
- Disorder results when the social structures in a society fail to function as they should to meet the goals for which they were established.

8

Box 1.1: Talcott Parsons and the AGIL Matrix

Talcott Parsons (1902–1975) is best known for his contribution to structural functionalist analysis. He combines the systemic (parts as related to the whole) and functionalist approaches, discussing the interdependence of sub-systems in the social realm. The tension between determinism and free will becomes the core for understanding social action. Based on these core concepts, Parsons defines four major functions that guide the relationships between different social systems:

- **A**daptation
- **G**oal attainment
- **I**ntegration of systemic components
- **L**atent maintenance of cultural patterns through which traditions and values are transmitted and preserved

All these functions are integrated by Parsons into a matrix known as AGIL (an acronym of the basic functions presented above). Behaviors are explained as a result of individual choice. The theory of action proposed by Parsons brings together all these elements on the assumption that all systems tend towards stability. When one part of the social system does not properly perform its functions, others will take over and ensure the stability of the whole. In other words, to coexist in harmony, all parts of a social system establish functional relationships among themselves.

For example, consider an immigrant family from a developing country coming to the United States for a better life. They will start learning the language; they will learn the know-hows of the American society—all the do's and don'ts. In short, they will adapt to their new environment. From a purely economic point of view, they must do so to survive (**a**daptation). As they begin life in the States, they develop clear goals that eventually parallel the American dream. They work hard to achieve these goals (**g**oal attainment). Their children are enrolled in mainstream American schools; they participate in the civic American life; they are regular taxpayers and befriend their American neighbors (**i**ntegration). All these functions lead to the internalization of the new lifestyle, with all the values and norms that come with it (**l**atent pattern maintenance).

If any of these functions is disabled, the whole structure of interactions and relationships changes. One possible scenario: The family lives and works in the States, attaining immediate goals, yet the internalization of values does not occur. While apparently adapted and even integrated into their new society, the family faces pressure from within, leading to further inter- and intra-generational and intercultural conflicts.

From a functionalist perspective, the AGIL matrix can be used to explain the interdependence of the basic functions in our society: economic, political, legislative, and ethical.

The AGIL Matrix

Economic function

Adaptation = Social systems have the function of adapting to their external environment from which their physical resources are derived.

Political function

Goal attainment = Social systems have the function of regulating the use of resources, and of ensuring that needs are met.

Legislative function

Integration = Social systems have the capacity to develop legitimate rules or norms, with the purpose of regulating the entire system.

Ethical function

Latent pattern maintenance = Social systems have the capacity to transform internal, personal values into value patterns that will characterize the given systems, being shared and tending towards stability.

Box 1.2: Robert Merton and Anomie Theory

Robert Merton (1910–2003) is credited with major sociological concepts, not only within the functional paradigm, but also as part of establishing sociology in the interdisciplinary world of sciences. His major contribution was to promote concepts such as latent versus manifest functions, theories of the middle range, self-fulfilling prophecy, paradigms, unanticipated consequences of social actions, reference group, and anticipatory socialization. Among his more enduring contributions to the discipline is his **anomie theory** which focuses upon the disjoint between socially recommended goals and the available means to those goals.

Merton defines the functions of any social system from a dichotomist view as either manifest or latent. **Manifest functions** are the consequences of social actions that are intended and expected to occur. It is a manifest function of the family to socialize children into becoming autonomous and functional adults who serve the interests of the society as a whole. **Latent functions** are consequences of social actions that are unintended and unexpected. The latent functions of the family are to raise children who fulfill parents' needs for affection, approval, and control.

Merton goes beyond defining latent and manifest functions to discuss the functions and dysfunctions of social systems. Dysfunctions are those consequences that interfere with the system as a whole. In this connection he introduces the notion of *anomie*. This concept as originally used by Durkheim meant a state of **normlessness**. Merton redefined it to refer to the disjunction between "culturally defined goals and the acceptable modes of reaching those goals" (Merton, 1949, p. 126).

Merton states that any divergence between culturally defined goals and socially acceptable means to achieving them undermines a society's tendency toward conformity. This state of anomie generates certain tensions to which people respond in different ways. Merton discusses five response modes that people adopt to resolve the goals/means dichotomy: conformity, innovation, ritualism, retreatism, and rebellion.

- Conformity is the most accepted mode of adaptation, when an individual or an institutional system accepts the existing, culturally approved norms, internalizes them, and supports the means for reaching them. This is the only adaptation mode that does not involve any form of deviance.

- Innovation is that level of adaptation at which individuals or institutional systems design various means for reaching the goals that are culturally accepted and defined by existing norms. Due to the fact that some do not have access to culturally approved means for reaching the set objectives, they will opt for illegal or socially disapproved means. For example, if success is not easily obtained through the culturally approved means, the individual will find a deviant way to become successful and popular among peers, either by gang-approved activities, or by crime, that will eventually promote him or her as a powerful character on the streets. This mode of adaptation is active, with little or no internalization of institutionalized norms for reaching objectives.

- Ritualism is an adaptation mode that helps individuals and institutional systems to work within the norms, using accepted means, while "abandoning or scaling down" socially valued goals. This kind of adaptation leads to a rigid outlook as people try to live up to standards they do not believe in. They work within the norms just for the sake of fitting in, or because they lack other perspectives. This adaptation mode is mostly passive, promoting the value of a risk-free trip through life, with little aspiration or frustration. However, Merton highlights the fact that prolonged periods of overcompliance with rules and standards that are not necessarily internalized and approved can lead to increased ritualization (e.g., being a workaholic to the extent of neglecting one's family).

- Retreatism is one of the least chosen modes of adaptation. It rejects both goals and means that are culturally accepted. Being a passive response, it involves the actual separation of an individual or institutional system from mainstream society. Individuals usually adopt this mode of adaptation through drugs or alcohol, homelessness or vagrancy, or other expressions of social/individual alienation. While relinquishing all social goals, the individuals in this category also reject all institutional norms and standards, becoming the "aliens" of modern societies. This is a passive mode of adaptation—becoming a silent reproach to social injustice and discrepancies between values and goals.

- Rebellion is the adaptation mode that promotes standards, goals, and means that are not socially approved to replace existing ones that are. Rebellion has the potential of eventually leading to major changes in the social structure. This is an active mode of adaptation, determining forms of deviance that may become normal responses for particular groups. An example is massive social movements (e.g., riots and revolutions) that target those standards, goals, or means which do not express the will of the masses, with the goal of changing them. Toward the negative side of the continuum, we have terrorist movements that use this form of adaptation in a most deviant way for changing the status quo.

While all the adaptation modes except conformity promote deviant/anomic behaviors, the social structure itself is directly questioned only by rebellion. The other modes do little to challenge existing mechanisms or promote change. The focus of the analysis provided by Merton is not social change, but rather a theory for understanding and preventing deviant behaviors, thus preserving the existing social structures.

- When disorder (social disequilibrium) occurs, adjustments are made by the society to restore the order (equilibrium). In other words, society tends toward stability.

Under the functionalist paradigm, society is a system of various interrelated subsystems, each of them performing specific functions that contribute to the operation of the whole (Merton, 1968; Parsons, 1951; Stone, 1998; Sullivan, 1998; Turner & Maryanski, 1979).

In many ways, functionalism is consistent with a "modernist" approach to understanding society. **Modernism** suggests that scientific reasoning and research correctly evaluate what works best in a society. Within this modernist framework, functionalists undertake research that focuses on the best institutional policies and practices—those which result in the most good for the most people and in the fewest social problems that involve the least number of people.

Conflict Theory

Unlike functionalists, **conflict theorists** are skeptical of the idea that social groups can consensually agree on the types of necessary institutions, on how they function, or on whether they equally benefit all social groups. Conflict theorists see society as a series of conflicts between social groups vying for political and social dominance. This perspective does not see consensus governing the socialization of new members or access to economic opportunities; rather, it sees powerful groups controlling socialization mechanisms and economic institutions for their benefit. This control results in the imposition of one group's values onto other social groups. Social problems emerge when groups who do not accept current institutional arrangements, culturally dominant values, or the fairness of their access to economic opportunity strongly react to or even try to change dominant institutional arrangements and cultural values. From a conflict perspective, these issues can be wide-ranging, such as the objection of conservative religious groups to sex education in schools, abortion clinics, and sexually explicit entertainment. Ethnic conflict can emerge over access to quality education and economic opportunities.

At its base, conflict theory views society as an entity that can be subdivided into an almost infinite number of competing social groups. Theorists believe that conflict between those groups over the control of the major social institutions is inevitable. The dominant norms and values reflected in law are seen as the imposition of one group's values over another's. Society is seen neither as static nor as moving toward the best institutional arraignments on the basis of careful logical scientific analysis, but rather as a series of conflicts that result in dynamically changing institutional and social arrangements.

Like functionalists, conflict theorists make certain assumptions about the social world and are united on these grounds. These assumptions can be stated as follows:

- Conflict has been a part of all past and current societies.
- Societal order is based on coercion rather than consensus. The suggestion here is that people will not be compliant if they are not made to be.

- Change is basic to all societies. This is in contrast to the structural functionalist claim that society tends to stabilize.
- Change is born of tension and comes about dialectically. The belief is that while opposing elements, beliefs, and ideas may be resolved at a higher level of synthesis, this resolution becomes a new source of conflict as opposition to the new arrangements emerges.

Modern conflict theory originated with the work of Karl Marx (see Box 1.3), who emphasized class conflict and the consciousness of one's position in a social structure. He believed that conflict will ensue once people become aware of their position in society and understand how it affects access to what is valued in a culture (the means of production, education, economic position, etc.). In classic Marxism, class conflict ends once workers obtain dominant positions in a society. In contrast, modern conflict theorists see conflict as almost an evitable result of a pluralistic society, in which each group seeks the advantage—from value dominance to wealth dominance.

The conflict and structural functionalist paradigms link social issues either to the schemes of the powerful or to the social structure. Conflict theorists, including Marx, call for a redistribution of a society's wealth as a solution for social ills. For these theorists, society's problems are not a reflection of inadequate means. Rather, the unequal distribution of available means lies at the heart of social problems. For conflict theorists, the problem is exemplified by such things as corporate presidents making hundreds of millions of dollars

Box 1.3: Karl Marx and the Sociology of Class Conflict

Karl Marx (1818–1883) is considered by many to be the chief architect of the conflict perspective. He lived at a time when capitalism in Europe and the United States was practiced in an unbridled fashion. Marx was widely read and well-acquainted with past societies. He, along with Friedrich Engels, argued that the history of all past and current societies is the history of class conflict (Marx & Engels, 1969). Marx saw one's class position as determined by one's relationship to the means of production. While he recognized that a plurality of classes was possible in any particular conflict-ridden society, he identified two basic classes of the capitalist society of his day: the bourgeoisie and the proletariat. The bourgeoisie made up the capitalist class—those who owned the means of production (the land and the capital)—while the proletariat were the workers who sold their labor in order to survive. Marx also pointed out that feudalism, the European society preceding capitalism in his scheme, also had two basic classes: the serfs and the feudal lords, which reflected slave society with its basic classes of masters and slaves.

In Marx's view, the tension between these basic classes is the engine of change in society. One group, the workers, seeks to acquire the means for its survival; the other group, the capitalists, is interested only in profits and strives to exact as much as possible from the workers. Marx pointed to the tendency of the capitalists to accumulate wealth at the expense of the workers. He reasoned that this tendency is a growing source of conflict between the two groups, and that the working class would rise up through a revolutionary struggle and overthrow the capitalist system. Thus, for Marx, society's problems are largely rooted in social inequality.

One of Marx's interesting ideas is his basic subdivision of society into substructure and superstructure. He calls the economic institution the **substructure** and all other institutions (e.g., educational institutions and religious institutions) the **superstructure**. It is Marx's contention that the superstructure of society operates in a way that supports and justifies the economic institution and the arrangements associated with it. This is so because social relations between people in the productive process are full of conflict, benefiting one class at the expense of the other. Hence the need for systems of *legitimation* (those that justify and explain) and *coercion* (using physical strength to enforce the policies of the economic institution). These systems include institutions such as education and the mass media as well as legislative councils, military forces, and courts. Since all these institutions function in the interest of the powerful, conflict theorists like Marx reason that these institutions tend to portray social issues as the activities of the powerless. This is the reason conflict theorists will advance for more poor people and marginalized people being in trouble with the criminal justice system than wealthy people.

a year even if their companies are going bankrupt and workers not only lose their jobs but also their pensions and have nothing left when a company dissolves.

On the other hand, theorists embracing structural functionalist assumptions tend to see the solution to social ills in a more efficient functioning of the social structure. Often, in this view, such structures as educational, political, family, and religious institutions are blamed for not operating effectively. Take the social issue of teenage pregnancy. It could be argued that this problem exists because families do not do a good job of parenting, or because educational and religious institutions do not help to inculcate the right values. Political constituents may be blamed for not implementing a legal and policy framework that eliminates this situation.

A modern example of a conflict theory approach might be the debate over national substance use policy. Early in the twentieth century, Congress passed an amendment to the constitution that prohibited (with very few exceptions) the production, distribution, and consumption of alcohol. Many observers saw this as a last attempt by America's Puritan Protestant population to maintain its dominant position in the face of immigrant groups coming from Catholic countries, where alcohol use is part of the culture. Within the democratic processes of the United States, this attempt failed. Candidates who favored eliminating alcohol prohibition won elections at almost every level in 1932. What was illegal one day (the sale and use of alcohol) became legal and respectable the next. Similar debates are now occurring over the legalization or medicalization of marijuana. Very few people over fifty (the age of those who dominate the legal structure) currently use marijuana (though they may have in the past). However, a large number of youth use marijuana. If their values were followed in law and policy, national drug policy might change. Conflict theory reminds us that society is not static; social conflicts are routine and, as a result, there can be fairly dramatic rapid changes in the functioning of social institutions.

Symbolic Interactionism

The interactionist perspective tends to focus on mezzo-level (group) and micro-level (individual) interaction. The proponents of **interactionism** assume that human beings are not inevitably controlled by social institutions

or locked in conflict over institutional control and access to power and economic advantage. Interactionists are critical of the functionalist assumption that institutions are almost superordinate and control human development. They are also critical of conflict theorists' belief in the inevitability of human conflict. The interactionist perspective emphasizes human creativity in the development and modification of human institutions. Institutions are seen not so much as controlling human development but as resulting from human interaction. Values are seen not as being imposed by human institutions on new members of society, but as developing and changing in response to individual and group interaction, including that by new members of society—either new generations or new immigrant groups.

Interactionists argue that human beings have the capacity to order their lives to the extent that they are able to select and create their responses to the various demands of their environments. Their assumptions can be stated as follows:

- Human nature is intentional and voluntary.
- Human nature is characterized by an enduring dualism; it is both sociable and self-assertive.
- Human action is strongly unpredictable.
- Humans act toward things on the basis of the meanings that the things have for them.
- Social meaning is derived from social interaction.
- The way individuals apply meaning is based on what they encounter in the environment.

Interactionist theorists are not likely to see changes in institutional arrangements, laws, or values as the result of one group's dominance over other groups, but rather as a result of dynamic individual and group interaction. We will now focus on aspects of the works of three sociologists—Charles Horton Cooley (Box 1.4), George Herbert Mead (Box 1.5), and Erving Goffman (Box 1.6), each of whom was guided by this perspective and the above assumptions.

Symbolic interactionists tend to view social issues in terms of the meanings constructed by groups in various situations. Because generated meanings are not fixed, but emerge and change continually, social issues will vary accordingly. As Maines (2001) has argued, interactionism can be seen as underlying all perspectives in sociology. The strictest functionalist likely would recognize that human institutions are produced, maintained, and changed by human interaction. Conflict theory is inherently close to the interactionist perspective

Box 1.4: Charles Horton Cooley and the Looking-Glass Self

Charles Horton Cooley (1864–1929) came to the study of sociology with a background in engineering and economics, both of which he studied at the University of Michigan. He formulated his ideas about human beings and society by drawing strategically from the works of Goethe, Darwin, Emerson, and Thoreau (Perdue, 1986). For him, society and the human self are inextricably linked; they are twin-born. It therefore is difficult to conceive of the self without society and vice versa. In terms of the determinism/free will opposition, he resolved the tension somewhere between the two, leaning toward free will. William Perdue (1986) noted that it was Cooley's contention that, although people made choices, they were not completely free in this process, since those choices were somewhat constrained by social forces in the society.

One of Cooley's ideas that is still popular is the **looking-glass self**. According to this notion, the self comes into being through a three-phase process:

- We imagine how we appear to others. (For instance, we may think that others see us as smart.)
- We interpret the reactions of others to us. (That is, we conclude that they like us or dislike us for being smart.)
- We develop a self-concept. Based on how we interpret the reactions of others toward us, we develop feelings and ideas about ourselves. A favorable reflection in the social mirror leads to a positive self-concept (Henslin, 1995).

Box 1.5: George Herbert Mead and Social Role Playing

Like Cooley, George Herbert Mead (1863–1931) could not conceive of a self apart from society. He argued that society must be understood as a structure that emerges through an ongoing process of communicative social acts, through transactions between persons mutually oriented toward each other (Mead, 1934).

The reciprocal nature of social life is accordingly given much emphasis by Mead. Human consciousness should be seen as a stream of thought that results from the interaction between people and their environment. This consciousness, the way we think and are aware, is not a static entity but an evolving quality of the mind based on interaction with others and the general environment around each of us.

Mead contributed greatly to our understanding of how humans acquire their sense of self. He presents the process as extremely social; it consists of role taking, the means by which one person tries to act like another. Mead identified three stages in this process.

- *Imitation stage:* This stage lasts from birth to three years of age. During this stage the child merely mimics what others do, because she or he cannot separate self from others. Strictly speaking, no conscious role taking occurs at this stage.
- *Play stage:* As children grow older, the ability to separate themselves from others develops and they attempt to play the roles of others. Perhaps you can recall times when you played being a firefighter, teacher, farmer, or something else.
- *Game stage:* During this stage, which begins sometime after five years of age, the ability to see the world from the standpoint of multiple others develops. This puts the child in a position to take the role of the **generalized other**. The child is now capable of measuring his or her behavior against that of others and acting according to their expectations. At this stage, the child not only plays a particular role, but is aware of how others react to how well the role is played and if it is played appropriately. It is often at this stage that children learn what roles are appropriate to their gender, ethnicity, or group values.

Box 1.6: Erving Goffman and the Drama of Social Life

Erving Goffman (1922–1982) distinguished himself as a symbolic interactionist with his book *The Presentation of Self in Everyday Life*, which was published in 1959. He sought to present human behavior in terms of a dramatic performance on the stage of life. His theory of dramaturgy suggests that human beings in their behavior are engaged in managing the impressions that others receive of them. For him, in the perpetual impression management game of life, each person is a con artist who seeks to "present himself in a light that is favorable to him" (Goffman, 1959, p. 7).

Goffman defines as "sign vehicles" the means we use to convey the impressions we wish others to have of us. He identified three types of sign vehicles: social settings, our appearance, and our manner. Social settings are the places where we perform our acts of impression management. These are actual places such as the church or the ball park, as well as the furnishings and equipment we use. A teacher's social setting will be the classroom as well as the chalkboard, overhead projector, and other pieces of material or equipment. Appearance is the sign vehicle that determines how we look when we perform our roles. Take the case of a nurse. Appearance includes the uniform worn and the stethoscope and blood pressure apparatus carried. The attitudes we project when we play our roles depict the sign vehicle of manner. This includes how we speak, the eye contact we make, and the ways we sit and walk or stand. Each of these sign vehicles, Goffman argued, makes and reinforces the impressions we desire to create in others.

because it sees conflict emerging in group interaction. Interactionist sociologists see the possibility of reducing conflict through communication, as well as through group interaction that focuses on creating broader, more inclusive values and opportunities for members of society. Interactionists in sociology would likely argue that the American Civil Rights movement and consequent legislation is an example of social interaction that resulted in broader social inclusion. Functionalists would likely agree that social institutions are functioning better because of broader inclusion. But conflict theorists would probably argue that the relatively large differences in educational attainment and income between ethnic groups show that educational and economic institutions are not functioning well and that traditional powerful groups are retaining that power.

Sociological Perspectives within the Context of Modernism and Postmodernism

To a large extent, both functionalism and conflict theory can be considered as parts of a modernist approach to social issues; that is, they both claim to be based on a scientific understanding of society and the use of empirical scientific research to address social problems. **Postmodernism** rests on the premise that at least many, if not all, values, norms, and beliefs have equal value and cannot be verified by empirical scientific analysis. Such a perspective, it is argued, reflects the dynamic interaction between many social groups in a pluralistic society.

From a postmodernist perspective, social institutions do not function or develop to impose a narrow range of common values but rather to teach the existence of different perspectives and values and the importance of respect for those differences. At a macro level this may involve teaching different perspectives on history and values without emphasizing a "correct" one.

Postmodernism has emerged in two stages. It first took root during the social, political, and cultural tumults of the 1960s and 1970s. It was greatly facilitated by rapid developments in the economy, technology, and culture. During the re-emergence of conservatism in the 1980s and through the beginning of the 21st century, a second wave of postmodernism has emphasized a sort of conservative individualism.

For example, let's compare the postmodernist approach to religion to more traditional approaches. Marx's prediction that religion would disappear in modern society did not come true, but many traditional churches are facing challenges from at least two directions. New non-denominational churches or religious groups have emerged that do not focus on traditional beliefs or doctrinal differences but on general spirituality and interpersonal relationships. Furthermore, even conservative religions go through a time of revival, redefining their purpose according to new "market" demands. The marketplace of ideas has clearly shown that human beings are still interested in the spiritual.

Berger (1967) describes the contemporary religious environment as a response to modern social needs. First, he mentions choice as the mode of some modern world religions, noting the rise of a "privatized" religion based on individual preference and not on generally accepted rituals and traditions. Second, in an era of diversity, religion has to face the challenges posed by pluralism. If we adopted a Marxist conceptual framework, adapted to a postmodern paradigm, we could agree with Berger's view that religious institutions are becoming marketing agencies, and religious traditions consumer commodities.

Integrating the adaptation modes described by Merton into this new paradigm, we could say that religious providers are gradually faced with two choices:

- Conformity to the new demands of postmodern society, or adapting the product to the consumer's demand.
- Rebellion against new trends, coupled with an ongoing effort to preserve the old structures and functions of religion.

The whole issue of determinism versus free choice is at the core of the postmodernist reframing of religion, as it shifts from an organizational functional view (promoted by Weber and Durkheim) towards an uninstitutionalized, less structured view, geared primarily towards the satisfaction of individuals. Thus, the new approach to religion has several main characteristics:

- *Individualism:* immanence stressed over transcendence
- *Experientialism:* focus on experience and faith
- *Pragmatism:* questioning religious authority and practice
- *Syncretism, relativism, and tolerance:* truth is polymorphous
- *Holism:* a religious worldview that emphasizes that religion affects one's entire life and perspective
- *Organizational openness* (Dawson, 1998): The organization does not unilaterally impact the lives of people, but remains open to and is shaped by people as well.

Postmodern theorists have put a completely new spin on the sociological perspective. They suggest that we should no longer approach the social world as a given (an objective entity) to be studied in the same fashion as the physical world. They have taken the symbolic interactionist perspective to a new height, emphasizing the temporary, process-driven nature of social reality. As Maines (2001) has noted, interactionism—which emphasizes that meaning emerges from conversations and group interaction—can provide a useful framework for examining the search for and acceptance of meaningful values, norms, and expectations in the postmodern world.

Critics of postmodernism have emphasized that a perspective that assumes the equal worth of all human traditions and values could result in the destruction of society, or could tolerate behaviors such as the oppression of some groups. In other words, all values are not equal. Slavery, the oppression of women, and cruelty toward animals, detractors say, cannot be seen as equal to such values and practices as gender and ethnic equality, democratic processes, and the humane treatment of animals. However, the postmodern view has had a major impact on society; it has made us more accepting of divergent beliefs and practices. Society, to a large extent, accepts the Muslim head scarf and Super Bowl half-time entertainment (within limits!) as parts of the contemporary postmodern social world.

Functionalists would probably be very concerned about how a society would continue without generally acceptable core institutions, laws, and norms. Conflict theorists would probably predict the failure of an equal-value perspective as each social group inevitably tries to perpetuate its own values in law. As Maines (2001) notes, interactionism can provide some expectation that continuing conversation about differences might result in the integration of these differences into a widely acceptable form that allows diverse groups to form an increasingly global society. Most of all, interactionism might allow us to believe that human beings are capable of doing this.

Conclusion

As we have seen, theories provide a framework for describing the various social issues and problems. Understanding the different perspectives helps us conceptualize various discussions about social issues—the theoretical "whys" of human behavior. Are we in conflict as groups? Do institutions help us to function? Does interaction between groups create change? In studying the chapters to come, it is recommended that you understand not only the research methods for analyzing questions, but also the perspective from which each issue is being addressed.

Related Readings

Babbie, E. (1998). *The sociological spirit* (3rd ed.). Belmont, CA: Wadsworth.

Berger, P. L. (1963). *Invitation to sociology.* New York: Doubleday.

Charon, J. M. (2000). *Ten questions: A sociological perspective* (4th ed.). Belmont, CA: Wadsworth.

Charon, J. M. (2002). *The meaning of sociology* (7th ed.). Upper Saddle River, NJ: Prentice Hall.

Gordon, M. M. (1998). *The scope of sociology.* New York: Oxford University Press.

Johnson, A. G. (1997). *The forest and the trees: Sociology as life, practice, and promise.* Philadelphia: Temple University Press.

Mills, C. W. (1959). *The sociological imagination.* New York: Oxford University Press.

Shibyutani, T. (1986). *Social processes: An introduction to sociology.* Berkeley: University of California Press.

Related Web Sites

American Sociological Association: http://www.asanet.org

JSTOR: Contemporary Sociology: http://www.jstor.org/journals/00943061.html

Sociology Central: http://www.sociology.org.uk

The SocioWeb: http://www.sonic.net/~markbl/socioweb

WCSU List: Sociology Internet Resources: http://www.wcsu.edu/socialsci/socres.html

WWW Virtual Library: Sociology: http://socserv2.mcmaster.ca/w3virtsoclib

FOUNDATIONS OF PSYCHOLOGY

Herbert W. Helm, Jr.

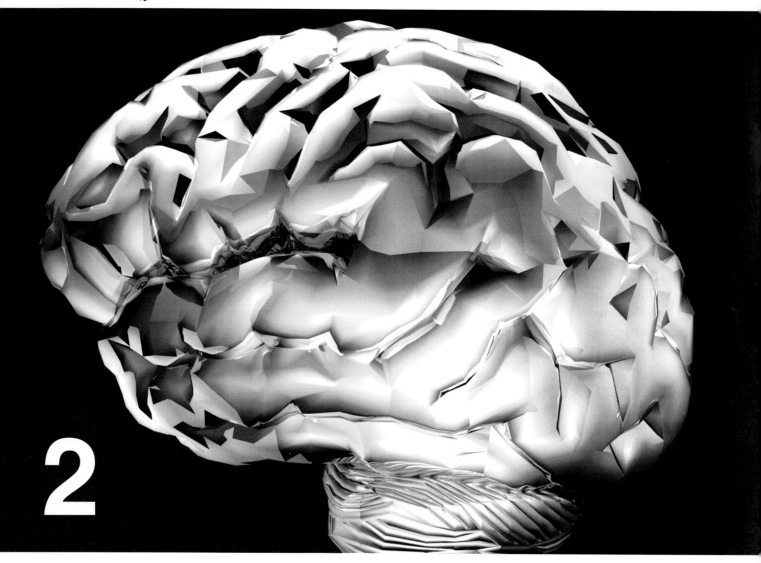

2

Chapter Outline

- Introduction: What Is Psychology?
- The Nature of Motivation
- Personality and/or Social Roles
- Development
- Learning

- Biopsychology
- Conclusion

Introduction: What Is Psychology?

Dreams, loss of consciousness, delirium, and death were four elements that primitive cultures considered evidence of a *soul,* that is, an element different from the body. How else could one explain that a person could travel to various places while his or her body remained immobile (dreams); that a person could be alive but at the same time be oblivious to his or her surroundings (loss of consciousness); that a person could have hallucinations of the dead rising (delirium); or that the body weighs the same before and after death, though something is missing after death? The concept of a soul helped to explain these phenomena (Stagner, 1988).

The word **psychology**, derived from the Greek word *psyche,* can be translated as "breath," "soul," or "mind," thus suggesting an element within humans that is different from the body. The word *logos,* meaning "word" or "study," refers to an area or field of study. So psychology began as a study of the soul or mind. We have always been fascinated by our nature and behavior and from time immemorial have speculated on why we engage in given behaviors. Psychology as a formal discipline is only about a century old. Up to that time, philosophers discussed the types of questions, such as the following, that now concern psychologists.

1. What is human nature?

- Do unconscious elements, such as aggression, determine our behavior? Freud and the psychoanalytic camp would say "yes."
- If forces such as culture did not interfere with development, would people try to maximize their potential and be basically good? Rogers and the humanistic camp would say "yes."
- Are we born neither good nor evil, but simply become the result of the rewards and punishments we experience? Skinner and the behaviorist camp would say "yes."

Also within the purview of human nature is the question of whether we possess free will or whether our behavior is predetermined by other, more powerful forces.

2. What is the basis of true knowledge? Do we gain our knowledge from reasoning or from our experiences?

- **Empiricists** took the position that our knowledge is gained from experience. They saw the mind as a **tabula rasa** (blank slate) on which experience wrote ideas.
- **Rationalists** believed that experiences were not always dependable. Therefore, one had to use reason to understand truth.

Hergenhahn (1992) described the difference between these positions as the active (rationalism) versus passive (empiricism) mind. The passive mind automatically and mechanically acts on sensations, whereas the active mind places meaning on them—even meaning we might not otherwise have.

3. Are mind and body two separate elements or only one element?

- **Monism** takes the view that only mind or only body exists. The two major forms of monism are materialism and mentalism (or immaterialism). Whatever this "substance" is, it is only one entity. The materialist would say that physical element (matter) underlies reality; that is, human behavior is a result of physical and chemical principles. There is no such entity as "the mind." The mentalist, however, sees the mind as the foundation of science and would like to explain everything in terms of consciousness (mental processes), experience, perception, representations, ideas, and awareness. The mind perceives the physical world, which may not even exist. For the monist, there is no mind-body problem; everything is a *uni*verse.
- **Dualism** suggests that there is both a mind and a body—both a mental and a physical reality. Although these differ and are independent of each other, they may interact with each other. The body may be physical, but the mind (or soul) is not. Most

religions demand a dualistic thought process, a place where the soul can affect behavior. The difficulty for the dualist lies in determining where and how mind and body are related. How does the mind (soul) affect the body? To dismiss a religious concept such as "soul," it has been discussed using such concepts as consciousness, thinking, and intentionality.

4. Is our behavior determined by nature (our genes) or by nurture (our environment)?

Although we recognize that both components play a part, how we answer this question can affect our social politics and our perception of others. When Herrnstein and Murray (1994) wrote *The Bell Curve,* they raised the issue of the differences between traditional IQ scores of whites and African Americans. Although they declined to estimate the contribution of genes versus environment, their tone seemed to lean toward the genetic influence. The social implications of a genetic view would cause us to question the value of social or environmental factors with which we attempt to remedy the situation.

Although the preceding list does not include all the issues and areas that psychologists study, it provides examples of the types of issues that psychologists explore. When students enter a psychology course, they expect to study such questions as "What creates our personality?" "Why do people go crazy?" and "What do our dreams mean?" Currently, psychology is defined as the scientific study of mental processes and behavior. Students entering an introductory class may study such topics as memory, perception, learning, human development, intelligence, cognition, personality, psychological disorders, motivation, emotions, biopsychology, language, states of consciousness, and stress and health.

In trying to understand the complexity of the world, psychology has traditionally viewed it from the perspective of the individual and how he or she develops. However, psychology has become a very diverse field that now includes such areas as social psychology—the behavior of people in groups (much like sociology)—and cultural psychology, how ethnic practice and culture affect behavior (much like anthropology). The following section of the text will offer background on some issues of human behavior as seen through the field of psychology. It is hoped that you will begin to integrate the theories presented here with the larger questions posed by some of the social issues and problems presented in the text and life in general.

The Nature of Motivation

In considering why people behave in a given manner, we will begin with the question of what motivates us to engage in specific behavior. It will be helpful to remember that we perform actions for reasons both internal and external. For example, you may eat because you have not eaten in ten hours, and internal factors, such as glucose or brain peptides, are playing a role in your hunger. On the other hand, you may have just eaten and be experiencing satiety when you spot a chocolate chip cookie and decide to eat it despite internal signals of being full.

What determines whether or not you will engage in a particular behavior? People have come up with a plethora of theories on what motivates us, but no single motivational theory will sufficiently answer this question for all behaviors. To begin, take a look at the three photos in Figure 2.1, and answer the question, "What is motivating these people to engage in the behavior shown?"

Instinct Theories

Instinct theories suggest that behavior stems from an organism's instincts—inborn or genetically determined patterns that are rigid, inflexible, and fixed. An organism behaves the way it does because it has no other choice. Geese migrate to the south for the winter, an oriole builds a nest unlike that of a robin, and a female dog will mate if it is in estrus (in heat). Some scholars, such as William McDougall (1908), saw human behavior as instinctive—"an inherited or innate psycho-physical disposition" that determines our perception, attention, and action. Later (in 1923), McDougall listed instincts such as escape, parental overprotectiveness, mating, and gregariousness. Of course, human behavior, which is far too complex and variable to be explained by instinct alone, can also be learned from the environment.

Drive-Reduction Theory

Drive-reduction theory argues that all organisms try to achieve and maintain homeostasis (balance or equilibrium). When an organism's system is out of balance, the organism experiences a drive to return to homeostasis. All organisms have needs—such as food, body temperature, and oxygen—that arise when requirements get too far from an acceptable level. Drive theorists, such as Clark Hull (1943), posit that these needs create drives, which we then try to reduce by engaging in behaviors that will restore homeostasis. For example, if you are thirsty, you are driven to reduce that drive by finding something to drink. Drive theories are based on the premise that we are pushed by an internal factor to engage in a specific behavior.

Incentive or Expectancy Theories

Tolman (1932) stated that behavior is goal-oriented and that we learn to expect "what will lead to what." Repeated interactions with the environment cause us to have various expectations. In contrast to drive-reduction theory, **incentive theory** posits that external factors pull us toward a given goal. Our expectations of reinforcement or reward are incentives for our behavior. For example, you may study hard in school because you realize that this may bring recognition from your teacher, parents, and possibly peers, thus meeting your social need for approval. As Lefton (2000) said, "people learn through their interactions in the environment to have needs for mastery, affiliation, and competition" (p. 292).

Extrinsic vs. Intrinsic Motivation

The internal and external aspects discussed in the preceding sections are also applicable to the topic of extrinsic versus intrinsic motivation. Although this topic has some similarities with others discussed here, it also differs in some ways. **Extrinsic motivation** suggests that organisms behave in certain ways because of what is "out there": money, status, food, praise, and so forth. **Intrinsic motivation** states that organisms engage in certain behaviors for the joy or pleasure they bring; for example, I may draw pictures solely for the enjoyment I receive from doing so.

Though we use extrinsic motivators (grades, gold stars, praise, and so on) to encourage students to learn, some research suggests that at times extrinsic reinforcement may reduce intrinsic motivation. A study by Lepper, Greene, and Nisbett (1973) placed preschool children who showed initial intrinsic interest in drawing into one of three groups. One group was in an expected-award condition: for drawing, students would receive "a certificate with a gold star and ribbon." Another group was in an unexpected-award condition, receiving the same extrinsic reward after the activity but having no prior knowledge of the reward. A final no-award condition had no expectations of a reward and received no reward. Members of the group who knew they were getting a reward subsequently showed a decrease in their interest in drawing and produced pictures of poorer quality than the other two groups.

We can also see this progression with sports figures. At first, they may play for hours just because they love the sport. Later in life, however, they may stop playing because they do not believe they are being paid enough (though their pay is often in the millions). Here again, external reward has hindered internal motivation.

Arousal and Opponent-Process Theories

In a classical experiment, Yerkes and Dodson (1908)

Figure 2.1: What would motivate someone to engage in the activities shown in these photos?

examined the relationship between arousal and performance. They suggested that performance on tasks of varying difficulty was affected by the individual's level of arousal; this became known as the **Yerkes-Dodson Law**. For example, if you do not feel anxious enough, you may not study adequately for a given test and consequently will do poorly. If you feel too much anxiety, though, you may not be able to study effectively, or you may experience test-related anxiety, again resulting in poor performance. However, for some tasks that demand high performance it is better to have low arousal, while tasks that demand low performance may require high arousal. For example, hitting a golf ball correctly is difficult (high performance). Therefore, when doing so, we expect people around us to be quiet, in hopes that this low arousal will help us hit the ball correctly. On the other hand, a person who has entered data for a while may experience boredom, which results in slower work (lower performance). Increasing arousal, such as playing a radio, might help the person enter more data, thus increasing performance of a low-arousal activity.

Hebb (1955) also discussed the relationship of arousal to performance. He tied arousal into the amount of activity occurring in the reticular activating system (RAS). The RAS plays a role in exciting structures of the brain, which enhances alertness. Hergenhahn and Olson (1997) described the process: "When arousal level is too low, such as when the organism is asleep, sensory information transmitted to the brain cannot be utilized. Likewise, when arousal is too high, too much information is being analyzed by the cortex, and often conflicting responses or irrelevant behavior results. Thus a level of arousal that is neither too high nor too low is necessary for optimal cortical functioning and therefore optimal performance" (pp. 404–405). Hebb (1955) believed that effective behavior requires an optimal level of arousal and that individuals will increase or decrease arousal as needed. If a person is bored, he or she may go to an exciting movie or read a thriller to increase arousal.

At what point does excitement take on a negative value, and does that point change? The **arousal theory** says there is an optimal level of arousal (though this does not explain why someone would willingly go over a 60-foot waterfall in a kayak). The **opponent-process theory** of acquired motivation may help to explain such behaviors. Acquired motivation consists of three

processes: 1) affective *contrast*, 2) affective *habituation* (tolerance), and 3) affective *withdrawal* (abstinence). For example, the first time a kayaker goes over a waterfall, he or she may experience fear and its physiological symptoms—the autonomic nervous system turning on, producing sweat, and increasing the breathing and heart rate. After landing in the water below the falls, the kayaker may be stunned and shaking. Within a few minutes, realization of survival sets in, and he or she begins to smile and feel great *(contrast)*. After a few waterfalls, the kayaker becomes accustomed to these feelings *(habituation)* but retains the "thrill" of the fall. This thrill may last a while, but it is eventually followed by a withdrawal syndrome. All of this creates a new and positive way to get reinforcement and motivates our kayaker to do the same thing again, perhaps at higher levels (Solomon, 1980).

The preceding theories help to describe how arousal affects motivation and why we may seek excitement. We may ride a roller coaster, kayak white water, or climb mountains in order to increase our arousal level.

Cognitive Theories

The **cognitive** (thought) **theories** describe motivation as having purpose and being goal-directed. People are actively involved in thinking, explaining, or giving attributions to their behavior. Leon Festinger's (1957) work on **cognitive dissonance** was a motivation theory that attempted to explain cognitive processes and our behavior. Festinger thought that people wanted consistency between their thoughts and behavior. When inconsistency existed between cognition and behavior, or between two cognitions, a person would experience cognitive dissonance—a negative, tension-filled state that most people want to avoid.

If a person abhors racism, discovering that the one he or she has been dating is a racist could create cognitive dissonance. Ending the relationship is one way to reduce this dissonance because it would result in consistency between the individual's behavior and thoughts. However, not all people adjust their behavior to meet their thoughts; many people adjust their thoughts to meet their behavior. For example, having found out that the new love is a bigot, the person may try to justify the other's behavior, rationalizing that the other person's many good qualities outweigh the racism or that the other person's brand of racism is not that bad. As humans, we like to see ourselves as rational, reasonable beings. By restructuring their cognitions, people can reduce their dissonance and feel that they are indeed being reasonable.

Another cognitive factor is the **attributional theory** of motivation, or how we attribute success and failure. The basic principle behind this theory is that people want to understand or discover why an event has occurred (Weiner, 1980). For example, you might want to know why you scored lower on a test than you thought you would. One attribution you could make is whether your test results were due to an internal or external element. Rotter (1954) called this **locus of control**. You can believe that you control your own life (an internal locus of control), or you can believe that your environment, chance, or other people are in control (an external locus of control). Believing that you did poorly on the test because you did not study hard enough is an example of internal locus of control. Believing that your professor created an unfair test is an example of external locus of control.

You might also "attribute" whether this event, or your response to the event, is a stable or passing feature. If you believe that you did poorly on the test because you were temporarily emotionally upset (for example, you had just quarreled with a friend), you might consider your poor test performance as a temporary factor. However, if you believe that you are incapable of comprehending the material being presented, you might consider your poor performance a stable factor. These and other factors determine how we perceive our reality and thereby affect our motivation to behave a certain way.

Field Theory

Kurt Lewin (1935) was a Gestalt psychologist who was interested in topics such as perception, learning, and motivation. His theory of motivation developed around field theory, and his answer to what motivated human behavior was the concept of **life space**. Life space can be defined as all the influences or psychological facts that act upon a person's behavior at a given time. It can include our internal aspects, external events, what we perceive or are consciously aware of, and facets that are unconscious.

Lewin referred to objects or situations that the subject desires or wants to approach as having *positive valance*, whereas objects one wants to avoid or finds frustrating have *negative valance*. Valances are dynamic. If you are starving, food has a positive valance; if you feel nauseated, food may have a negative valance.

Let's say you have a bachelor's degree in psychology and find your current job as a psych tech both low-paying and unrewarding. You tell your friends that you would like to go on to graduate school for reasons such as increased pay, more decision-making power on the job, or more prestige. However, every year around application time you find "reasons" not to apply. Your friends begin to believe that you don't really want to go back to school, but you tell them that you have not yet found the right program. In your life space, you are responding "as if" you do not want to go to school even though you may be convinced that you do. You may fear that you will be rejected or will fail (negative valance), but you may not be conscious of those fears. Conscious awareness is not necessary. As can be seen in this example, many aspects make up life space; these are not static, and they influence and motivate our behavior.

Final Thought on Motivation

Obviously, there are numerous ways to conceptualize what motivates people to engage in a given behavior. No one theory can adequately describe or foretell which behavior a given person will choose in a given situation. It may be that one theory or a combination of theories will work better in one situation than in another. However, these theories provide windows from which to view various aspects of behavior.

Personality and/or Social Roles

Another question we could consider is whether we behave as we do because of our personality type or because of the social roles we play. Let us say that it is the end of the semester, and you are hoping for an extension on a project for this class. (Please note: This is a hypothetical situation. Do not test your professor on this aspect!) You ask for the extension but are denied. Why? You might believe that it is because the professor is authoritarian and controlling. In this case, you have attributed some personality aspects. **Personality**, which comes from the Latin word for "mask," refers to a relatively stable pattern of behavior, thoughts, or feelings that predispose a person to act in a given manner. Therefore, we can expect that this professor will act in an authoritarian and controlling manner in other situations. On the other hand, you might conclude that your plea was denied because of the role your professor has to play. In reality, your professor may have wanted to give you the extension but thought that granting an exception for you would be unfair to the other students. Or perhaps your professor believes it is his or her job to teach you to be responsible for finishing projects on time. In this case, your professor had to play a role that dramatically affected his or her behavior.

We begin this section by considering personality-related explanations for our behavior.

Sigmund Freud and Psychoanalysis

A man goes on a trip to an exotic location and sends a postcard to his wife. The bottom line reads, "Wish you were her." His wife becomes outraged, believing him to be having an affair. He says that it was a simple mistake—that he had forgotten to put an "e" on the end of "her" and had actually meant to say, "Wish you were *here*." Was it a conscious mistake or an unconscious process that led to his behavior? In trying to decide, we will examine a few of the major concepts that Sigmund Freud posited concerning human behavior, including the role of sexual instinct and the motivating force of the unconscious.

Freud's levels of consciousness are comparable to an iceberg. The visible part of the iceberg, or the *conscious* level (see Figure 2.2), consists of thoughts and feelings that one is consciously aware of at any given moment. You can switch your conscious awareness from one aspect to another. That is, you may be consciously aware of what you are reading, but if asked what your mother looks like, you will probably switch from the content of your reading to a conscious mental picture of your mother.

Continuing with the iceberg analogy, we find the *preconscious* just below the water's surface. The preconscious consists of all the concepts, thoughts, and feelings that you have access to but are not consciously aware of at the moment. For example, when asked what your mother looks like, you probably mentally rummaged through the preconscious and brought your mother's image into the conscious.

The largest part of the iceberg is that which you cannot see; this part is analogous to the *unconscious* level. Freud considered the unconscious the motivating force of behavior, or the container of sexual and aggressive instincts. By definition, the unconscious is that of which we are not aware. Besides being an area for instincts, it holds memories that we have repressed because they cause us pain. If we were consciously aware of them, these memories would create anxiety. Although unconscious elements can affect our lives, we gain access to this unconscious level through a process of therapy called **psychoanalysis**.

Later in his life, Freud integrated these concepts into a new conception of personality that featured three psychic structures (conceptual ways of seeing the personality). The **id**, which is the only structure present at birth, is a driving force of the personality. It consists of our drives and instincts and operates on the **pleasure principle**. It wants both immediate gratification of these instincts and immediate removal of any tension without regard for the world around. The id is unconscious and cares nothing about the morals of society.

The next part of the self to develop is the **ego**, which develops from the id to deal with the external environment. The ego operates on the **reality principle**—the idea that it must find ways to satisfy the id that are rational and logical and can be safely secured in the external environment. If you have ever seen a child in a grocery store line taking candy from a rack near the

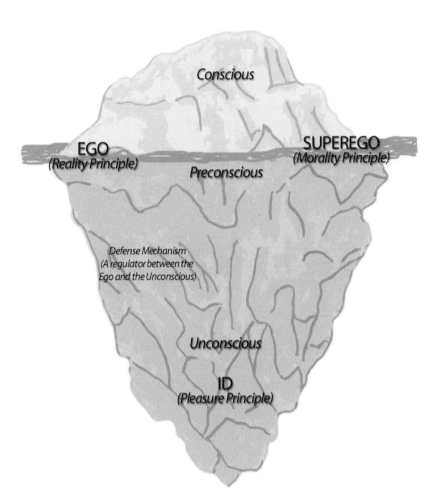

Figure 2.2: Freud's levels of consciousness

Conscious

EGO
(Reality Principle)

SUPEREGO
(Morality Principle)

Preconscious

Defense Mechanism
(A regulator between the
Ego and the Unconscious)

Unconscious

ID
(Pleasure Principle)

checkout counter, you have seen both the id and ego in action. The id demands that it is hungry, and merely fantasizing about food will not satisfy it. (Freud called this "wish-fulfillment.") Therefore, the ego finds a way to get food, and the child takes it from the candy rack.

As we grow, our parents and society teach us that some things are "right" and some "wrong." We are taught that it is "wrong" to take the candy. This part of the self, the **superego**, develops out of the ego and is determined by social and moral codes. The superego's main goal is perfection, and it operates on the **morality principle**, which consists of the ego ideal (tied to the superego, it is an idealized way of seeing oneself, how one should be) and the conscience.

These three psychic structures may or may not be in agreement with each other. Sometimes our needs (id), our planning (ego), and our morals and standards (superego) are in conflict; the result is anxiety. Neurotic anxiety occurs when the id makes irrational demands on the ego; moral anxiety arises when the superego pushes guilt onto the ego. To deal with anxiety, the ego uses

defense mechanisms, which distort our reality so that we are not conscious of the conflicts. There are a number of defense mechanisms. (Table 2.1 gives examples of four of them.) The goal of therapy from a Freudian viewpoint, called **psychoanalysis,** is to discover the unconscious motives behind people's behavior.

Carl Jung's Analytic Psychology and the Collective Unconscious

Carl Jung was part of Freud's inner circle but later broke away and developed his own school of thought called **analytic psychology**. A major point of disagreement between Jung and Freud was the centrality of sexuality in the development of the personality. For Jung, the idea of a sexual energy (called *libido*) dealing with instincts and driving our personality was too narrow. He suggested that the driving force that motivates us was much broader than sexuality and was more of a life energy composed of several instincts.

We used the analogy of an iceberg to describe Freud's concept of personality development; we could

Table 2.1: Examples of Defense Mechanisms

Defense Mechanism	Definition	Example
Denial	Refusal to accept information or external reality	Denying the truth of the warning on the side of a cigarette pack
Rationalization	Justifying or excusing one's behavior	Claiming failure because a test was too hard rather than admitting that you went on a date and didn't study
Reaction Formation	Doing the opposite of one's unacceptable thoughts and impulses even though they are true at an unconscious level	Joining a group to ban "dirty" books from the local library, though in reality you love to look at "dirty" books and now can while believing that you are getting rid of them
Sublimation	Changing unacceptable impulses into constructive and socially appropriate ones	Having a lot of aggression with a desire to hurt someone, and thus becoming a boxer

use that of an island to describe Jung's concept of personality. The part of an island that you can see is above the water—this is the idea of ego. Ego is conscious; it is what we think, perceive, feel, and remember. It helps us with everyday living.

The next part of the island is that which is underwater, yet unique to that island. Jung called it the personal unconscious. It is similar to Freud's ideas of preconscious and unconscious. The personal unconscious may be material that has been repressed or suppressed. The personal unconscious contains complexes. A **complex** is a group or set of ideas, feelings, and memories that hold together and come from both personal experiences and a core behavior pattern that is inherited. "A complex has a disproportionate influence on one's behavior in the sense that the theme around which the complex is organized keeps recurring over and over again in one's life" (Hergenhahn, 1990, p. 67). Both the ego and the personal unconscious are unique to the individual.

Jung believed that the mind has a form, a shape, a structure. Below each individual island (that is, each person) is a base that connects all the islands. Jung referred to this as the **collective unconscious.** The collective unconscious is not personal experience; rather, it is the collected experience of all humans. It is the deepest layer of unconsciousness—that to which we do not have access. Jung theorized that we have collective memories of the common experiences that were shared by all people in the past. These inherited tendencies or images,

called **archetypes,** predispose us in how we shape our experiences. We never directly experience archetypes, but they indirectly affect our consciousness.

There are many types of archetypes. Some of the ones most commonly discussed are the anima and animus, the shadow, the persona, and the self. Other archetypes include the divine child, the wise old man, the hero, and other images that appear in religions and myths of various cultures. For example, the anima is the female archetype in males; the animus is the male archetype in females. Here, the anima helps males in their experiences and relationships with females. A given male's anima is made up of both personal experiences with various females and the collective experience that comes from the archetype. This can help explain why you may meet someone of the opposite sex and feel that you have known him or her for a long time. Obviously, this cannot be true because it is your first meeting. However, it can be true in the sense that you have brought with you the anima or animus, which you have known (although not consciously) for a long time.

The shadow is the darkest side of the personality. It is primitive material that contains animal instincts and is a part of our personality that we do not want the public to see. If we speak of the shadow in mythological terms, we talk of demons, monsters, evil spirits, and such. We may also see the shadow through other people. This animal nature is not all evil, however. It can be a source of creativity or be transformed into something positive. The shadow should be recognized and can be used to help make us whole. If one tries too hard to repress the shadow, it may come out in another way.

The persona, the public mask that each of us wears, helps us maintain the various roles we play in society. The self, which tries to bring unity and harmony to the personality, seeks optimal development or self-actualization.

Jung also distinguished between two attitudes or orientations that people have to their world: **introversion** and extraversion. (We typically spell it **extroversion**.) Introverts are primarily concerned with the inner world and feel that the world of ideas is more important than the world of people. Terms such as self-sufficient, quiet, hesitant, imaginative, reflective, and unsociable often describe an introvert. Extroverts, who are more concerned with the outer world, function better in the world of people and events. Terms such as adaptable, social, outgoing, candid, and accommodating may describe an extrovert. Although each of us has aspects of both orientations, one is likely to be dominant, or at least more dominant in given situations.

In Jung's work, we encounter several concepts concerning human behavior. For instance, Jung spoke of the power of complexes in predisposing our behavior. The concept of a collective unconscious and archetypes was one of his more controversial ideas. However, it does beg the question of whether there is a predisposed structure to our personality and how much the experiences of previous generations predispose our behavior. Jung also addressed the question of whether people have different orientations to the world. Of course, if differences exist, then one may need to use different methods to motivate, punish, or train these individuals.

Alfred Adler's Individual Psychology

Alfred Adler, another "defector" from Freud, developed a school of thought called **individual psychology.** Individual psychology might better be called "indivisible psychology" because it focuses on unity and inner harmony. Rather than seeing the mind as consisting of warring parts, Adler saw it as a whole that strove for perfection for both the individual and the goals of society. Goal setting was central to Adler; it was what motivated and influenced us. Consciousness, not the unconscious, was what motivated us; it was the center of our personality.

Adler, who received his M.D. from the University of Vienna, later developed the notion of organ inferiority: that the body breaks down in its weakest spot. For one person, this might be the heart; for another, the eyes or some other organ. A person can compensate for this weakness, however. For example, a blind person often becomes more attuned to his or her auditory system. A person also might overcompensate, as in the case of Demosthenes, who overcame a speech impediment to become one of Greece's great orators.

As Adler became more psychologically oriented, he altered this idea of the physical and placed more emphasis on feelings of inferiority. These feelings typically arise during infancy and childhood when we are inadequate, inferior, and helpless in almost every way. Whether these feelings are due to physical disabilities or arise from a sense of psychological or social inferiority, they lay the groundwork for many of our goals. At that point, these feelings of inferiority can result in compensation, overcompensation, the will to power, or **striving for superiority**. The latter two concepts involve taking feelings of inferiority and striving to become superior or perfect. Seen from another angle, this would mean to become a fully functioning person who is in control of his or her life. Although feelings of inferiority can lead to growth, some people become fixated or overwhelmed by these feelings and, as a result, their growth is blocked. Adler described these people as having an inferiority complex.

Adler was influenced by Hans Vaihinger's book *The Psychology of "As If"* (1924). Vaihinger suggested that people lead their lives based on various **fictions**, or subjective beliefs that guide them in their attempts to reach an ideal. If you live "as if" a Higher Power will judge your life, you might choose different behaviors than you would otherwise. If you live "as if" getting good grades will bring success later in life, you will strive hard to do well in class. So Adler developed the concept of **functional finalism**, which suggests that we have an ideal that we want ultimately to reach (a final functional goal). For example, a person who might want to become a famous actor will organize his or her personality and behavior to maximize the chances of reaching that goal. This concept places importance on the future, which Adler considered more important than the past.

Adler has presented several other important concepts in addition to the theories discussed earlier in this section. For instance, he perceives people not as automatons leading predetermined lives, but as active beings who have the ability to act upon their environment and choose their own life goals. People may have feelings of inferiority, but their attitudes determine whether they are overwhelmed by them or use them to create goals, such as in the case of Demosthenes noted above. Rather than focus narrowly on the goals of individuals, Adler has also examined the importance of goals in society.

Karen Horney and Feminine Psychology

Freud, with his psychosexual stages, focused heavily on sex and the biological forces of personality formation and the effect these differences had on men and women. Although Karen Horney (pronounced "horn-eye") was trained in the psychoanalytic tradition, she disagreed with Freud on many points. She considered the Freudian psychoanalytic tradition largely a masculine psychology that did not deal with the development of women and their issues.

Horney disagreed with a number of Freud's concepts about sexuality. For example, she did not believe that "biology is destiny" (sometimes noted as "anatomy is destiny"). This means that biology, which determines your sex, also determines your personality. She believed that culture had a stronger effect than biology on the development of differences between the sexes. In addition, Horney thought that people struggled more with various cultural, environmental, and social issues, such as caring for their children and earning enough money, than with gender differences. Women did not have a desire to be men per se; rather, they desired the privileges, such as independence and success, that culture offered to men.

Horney believed that people develop neuroses because of basic anxiety—the feeling of being lonely, isolated, and helpless. Anxiety occurred if one's parents, who should have provided for their child's basic needs and safety, failed to do so. As children, we are not powerful enough to show our hostility toward our parents for their indifference and rejection; as a result, we turn this hostility into anxiety.

To minimize our anxiety (and neurotic trends) and to search for security, we tend to focus on three neurotic patterns of adjustment. First, we can *move toward people*. A person who does this is submissive or compliant and has strong needs for love and acceptance, along with the need to be taken care of and to live in a manner that could be described as self-effacing. If you comply with others, then they should not hurt you. Second, we can *move against people*. A person who does this can be described as hostile or aggressive. Power is an important issue to this person, because the most powerful one with the most money and prestige is the one least likely to get hurt. Finally, we can *move away from people*. Those who do this are detached, withdrawn, or self-sufficient. Their reasoning is as follows: If you stay far enough away from people and do not become emotionally involved with others, then they cannot hurt you.

Horney felt that all of us use all three of these methods. However, the neurotic person would focus on one of these methods regardless of whether it was appropriate for his or her particular situation. Of course, it would be better if an individual were raised in an environment in which basic needs were met. In such a case, there would be no need to develop a neurotic style.

Horney confronts us with the issues of how much "anatomy determines destiny." If our biology does not determine our personality, then personality may be influenced more by cultural and social factors. If society has different roles and developmental issues for each gender, then differences are not likely to be related to one gender being inferior to another, as Freud would have believed.

Humanistic-Existential Theories

Psychology is sometimes seen as having three movements or forces: 1) psychoanalysis; 2) behaviorism; and 3) **humanism** and **existentialism**. Both existentialists and humanists tend to focus on issues such as human freedom, choice, and responsibility.

Humanistic psychology views individuals as having a drive toward self-fulfillment or actualization. Characteristics of self-actualization include being spontaneous, humorous, creative, and democratic; enjoying satisfying interpersonal relationships; and having "peak experiences." In short, self-actualization means reaching our potential despite our imperfections.

However, most of us do not live by these innermost feelings and characteristics, because we have grown up in situations (family and society) in which we experienced conditional love or conditions of worth. **Conditional**

positive regard means that to receive love, one must engage in ways of thinking and acting of which parents and society approve. In this situation, the parent essentially says, "I will love you if…[your grades are better, you dress more appropriately, you do not use that cuss word, etc.]." Rogers (1966) said that because the parent withholds love unless the child meets the parent's terms, the child's "self-concept contains false elements that are not based on what he is experiencing" (p. 192). These conditions of worth can cause a person to feel guilty or unworthy, which in turn can result in the person's living with such defenses as denial and distortion. By trying to live up to the conditions of significant others, ultimately one can lose his or her sense of self.

Rogers believed that to develop a more positive self-image, one should receive empathy, genuineness, and unconditional positive regard. Empathy is shown through active listening, which demonstrates the listener's sensitivity and sincere desire to understand the speaker. Genuineness is the ability to show our real or authentic selves and not live behind a facade. **Unconditional positive regard** means that we should accept, love, and value other people, even when their behavior is disagreeable to us. However, Rogers did not intend to suggest that no behavior was undesirable or that there should be no constraint on behavior. However, there is a difference in the type of atmosphere, conditional or unconditional, in which right behavior can be learned. As one experiences unconditional positive regard, he or she feels less of a need to be defensive. As a result, that person becomes open to new experiences and becomes better able to recognize and value his or her inherent potential, and thus develops into a more fully functioning person.

Another humanist, Abraham Maslow (1970), suggested the existence of a hierarchy of needs (see Figure 2.3) and further stated that we are first motivated to meet the needs that are at lower levels in the hierarchy. When these needs have been met, we move to higher levels of needs. In Maslow's hierarchy, physiological needs rank lower than safety needs; therefore, the organism should first meet its basic physiological needs (such as food, water, and sleep) before addressing safety concerns.

Maslow's theory divided human needs into different categories and placed them into a hierarchy. Wahba and Bridwell's literature review (1976) found "that Maslow's Need Hierarchy Theory has received little clear or consistent support from the available research findings" (p. 233). Several unresolved issues exist: 1) how exactly to define a "need," 2) how "needs" can be placed into hierarchies, and 3) how the deficiency and growth concepts form this hierarchy. By the time they finish college, most students have had the experience of giving up sleep (a physiological need) in order to do well on an examination (an esteem need). Perhaps the issue is closer to what Kalat (2002) noted in his *Introduction to Psychology* text: "Depending on the circumstances, almost any motivation may take priority over the others, at least temporarily" (p. 413).

Existentialism comes from a diverse group of individuals. Fogiel (1994, c1980) describes the existentialist view of personality development as follows: "One of the most important themes to the existential psychologist is the human struggle between being and nonbeing. This struggle involves not only life and death but full acceptance of oneself versus partial acceptance or rejection of parts of oneself. Being authentic versus being fraudulent is seen to be another major conflict

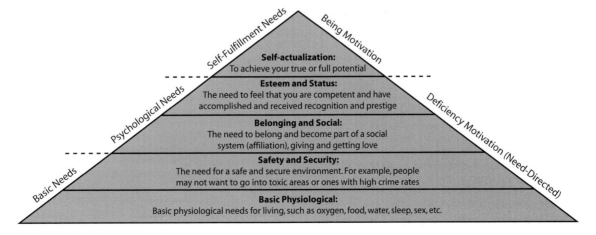

Figure 2.3: Maslow's hierarchy of needs

for humans. To be authentic a person needs to be able to be honest with himself, to make commitments to life and to accept the risks and suffering involved in actualizing his full potential. Should a person not do this he will be phony, he will suffer a loss of meaning or alienation from himself. This is seen to be a major source for mental and personality disorders by the existentialist school" (p. 499).

For Victor Frankl (1984), the search for meaning in life is our primary motivator. What people need is not equilibrium (a homeostasis tensionless state), but a desire to strive for a worthwhile goal of our own choosing. The lack of meaning in one's life can create a void, an "existential vacuum." Without meaning in their lives, people live in a state of boredom. So, then, what is the meaning of life? "One should not search for an abstract meaning of life. Everyone has his own specific vocation or mission in life to carry out a concrete assignment which demands fulfillment. Therein he cannot be replaced, nor can his life be repeated. Thus, everyone's task is as unique as is his specific opportunity to implement it.…Ultimately, man should not ask what the meaning of his life is, but rather he must recognize that it is *he* who is asked. In a word, each man is questioned by life; and he can only answer to life by *answering for* his own life; to life he can only respond by being responsible" (p. 131). Being human ultimately points beyond oneself to something or someone else; it is by giving oneself that one becomes self-actualized. It is through self-transcendence that self-actualization may be possible.

The Trait Theorists

Think for a minute about how you define yourself or your personality. Did any of these words come to your mind: *quiet, self-reliant, outgoing, aggressive, rigid, practical, dominant, passive, agreeable*? If so, you were trying to describe yourself based on what are called traits. **Traits** are relatively enduring aspects of personality. In psychology, there are a number of trait theories.

As early as Greek medicine there were attempts to explain what affected our traits. Galen (130–200 A.D.) borrowed on Hippocrates's four-humor theory to describe how humors affected the four temperaments (traits): phlegmatic, sanguine, choleric, and melancholic. The phlegmatic person was apathetic, controlled, and unemotional; the sanguine person was cheerful, social,

and outgoing; the choleric person was quick-tempered, insensitive, and bold; and the melancholic person was sad, reserved, and moody. Some of these words are still used to describe behavior. There are a number of trait theories; in this section, we will consider one called the **Big Five**.

The Big Five is a model which views domains that are descriptive at the highest level of behavior. They do not attempt "to reduce the rich tapestry of personality to a mere five traits" (Goldberg, 1993, p. 27) but set up a framework from which to organize individual differences. When reducing a complex concept like personality to something more understandable, one must always strike a balance between complexity, which makes the concept harder to understand, and oversimplification, which strips away all but the most obvious points. Although a couple of other five-factor models exist, for our purposes we will focus on the one developed by McCrae and Costa (1987). They see the research pointing to the following five personality traits (to help remember these, think of the acronym OCEAN): openness, conscientiousness, extraversion, agreeableness, and neuroticism. Each of these traits has two dimensions:

- *Neuroticism vs. Emotional Stability.* People who have neuroses are perceived as insecure, worrying, temperamental, and impulse-ridden. They not only have irrational beliefs, but negative feelings and disturbed behavior can accompany their thoughts.
- *Extraversion or Surgency.* The core aspect here would be sociability. Such people are friendly, talkative, and sociable.
- *Openness to Experience.* This is distinguished by having broad interests and being original, daring, and imaginative. It can display itself in ideas, feelings, fantasy, and actions.
- *Agreeableness vs. Antagonism.* Antagonistic people are mistrustful, unsympathetic, uncooperative, and rude. They have trouble attaching themselves to others and are seen as setting themselves up against others.
- *Conscientiousness vs. Undirectedness.* Conscientious people have self-control and are hard-working, ambitious, and persevering, whereas undirected people have trouble living up to their standards since they are lazy and lack energy.

Although trait theories of personality help describe actions, they often do not explain them.

Social Role, Not Personality

Trait theories suggest that people have a certain amount of consistency to their personality; others claim that people are not all that consistent. More important than the characteristics or traits of people are the situations in which they find themselves. This is the theory of **social roles**: the behaviors that we expect from someone who holds a given social position. You may know of a person with whom you worked who seemed to change in personality upon becoming a boss or director. Social role theory would say that your friend's traits did not change, but that he or she was expected to act a certain way in that position and did. The theory does not deny that people have individual differences, but notes that situation has a powerful influence on behavior.

A classical study on how roles shape behavior is shown in the Stanford Prison Experiment (Haney, Banks, & Zimbardo, 1973). Philip Zimbardo, at Stanford University, took 24 males (of 75 respondents) judged to be the most mature, least anti-social, and most mentally and physically stable. He randomly assigned half of them the role of "guard" and half the role of "prisoner." The study was designed to look at the effects of playing the "guard" and "prisoner" roles. The prisoners were told that their basic civil rights would be suspended and that they would be under surveillance. The guards were allowed the use of humiliation and other methods to "control" the prisoners, but they were not allowed the use of physical violence.

Following the first day, the guards redefined most of the prisoners' rights as "privileges." Aspects such as time and conditions of eating, talking, going to the bathroom, and sleeping were earned by complying behavior; as the experiment wore on, the guards escalated their harassment. Their behavior was described as follows: "Despite the fact that guards and prisoners were essentially free to engage in any form of interaction (positive or negative, supportive or affrontive, etc.), the characteristic nature of their encounters tended to be negative, hostile, affrontive, and dehumanizing. Prisoners immediately adopted a generally passive response mode while guards assumed a very active initiating role in all interactions....In lieu of physical violence, verbal affronts were used as one of the most frequent forms of interpersonal contact between guards and prisoners" (pp. 80–81).

Five prisoners had to be released due to extreme emotional responses. Because of growing problems, the experiment was ended after only six days. The prisoners were delighted by the experiment ending; most of the guards, in contrast, were distressed. They did not want to give up their power and control. Both groups appeared to play their roles. While there were individual differences, both groups showed pathological reactions, indicating the power of social forces. For more information on this experiment, see the documentary video "Quiet Rage: The Stanford Prison Experiment" distributed by Harper Collins *CollegePublishers*.

Development

Developmental psychology is concerned with behavioral changes and capacities which occur as people go through the life cycle. Not only are psychologists interested in our intellectual, moral, cognitive, and physical development, but they want to know whether these changes are stable, due to nature or nurture, and whether they occur in stages or follow a gradual process.

Erik Erikson and Psychosocial Theory

One of the issues in development is whether the changes we make are in stages (sometimes called discontinuous change) or whether change is continuous. Continuous change would say that we change gradually and add to what was there. We become different because we build on earlier levels. Stage theories suggest that we develop in different stages, and that they are qualitatively different. Two of the major stage theories of development are by Freud and by Erikson. Since Erikson's theory covers more stages of life, especially adulthood, we will use his theory as an example. (A good introductory text on psychology will give you the basics of Freud's developmental stages.) Freud's stage theory relates to psychosexual development, while Erikson's stage theory talks in terms of psychosocial development.

Erikson believed that Freud placed too much emphasis on sex and how it motivated our behavior. He thought that, as we developed, society confronted us with different issues or conflicts at different time periods. How we dealt with these conflicts affected how healthy or maladjusted of an outcome we had in our personality development, and whether we moved on to the next stage. Each stage builds on the foundations of the earlier ones; for example, one must have *trust* in order to develop *self-sufficiency*. Erikson's stages are as noted (Erikson, 1963):

- *Basic Trust vs. Basic Mistrust* (birth to one year). In early life, a baby can develop a sense of trust from the quality of the relationship it has with its mother. If trust does not develop, then one could see schizoid and depressive states in adulthood. It was not frustration per se during this time that caused problems (neurosis), but frustrations that lacked social meaning. Erikson thought that in organized religion one must show this childlike surrender or trust. Because many religions require that the individual surrender to a "Provider" that disbursed health and possessions, it was mistrust that formulated evil. "Trust born of care is, in fact, the touchstone of the *actuality* of a given religion" (p. 250).

- *Autonomy vs. Shame and Doubt* (1 to 3 years). At this stage, the child wants to experiment with both holding on and letting go. These two aspects can either be destructive or enhance our development as we need to learn when to let go and when to hold on. If children have a "well-guided experience" of free choice, they can learn to stand on their own (autonomy or self-sufficiency); they develop a will. One can see this assertion of autonomy in a two-year-old who says "No" to situations in life. A child too restricted or overprotected may develop shame and doubt.

- *Initiative vs. Guilt* (3 to 6 years). Here initiative adds to autonomy. Through play and other activities, the child begins to initiate, to have the wish or ability to follow through with a task, to have ambition and commitment. The problem at this stage is also that of regulation. The parent may stifle this "exuberant enjoyment of new locomotor and mental power" (p. 255), which can lead to guilt about the activities which are initiated.

- *Industry vs. Inferiority* (6 to 11 years). The earlier stages have set up the stage for entrance into life. For those in the industrial world, that "entrance into life" is school. Now, instead of wishing to play, the child begins to work toward completing various tasks (industry). In school, the child must first become literate (a task) before taking on more specialized tasks. The danger of this stage is that the child may become discouraged or fail at these tasks and develop a sense of inferiority and inadequacy.

- *Identity vs. Role Confusion* (adolescence). People need a sense of competence (industry) in order to have a sense of identity—knowing who they are and understanding their place in society. As youth see adult tasks confronting them, they begin to focus on what others think of them instead of what they think of themselves. As they test various societal roles, the danger is that of role confusion, the inability to focus on an occupational identity. For adolescents in our society, this may be a time of moratorium—a time that they look at various alternatives without making a commitment.

- *Intimacy vs. Isolation* (young adulthood). Having a sense of who he or she is, the young adult is ready to merge his or her own identity with others. "He is ready for intimacy, that is, the capacity to commit himself to concrete affiliations and partnerships and to develop the ethical strength to abide by such commitments, even though they may call for significant sacrifices and compromises" (p. 263). The counterpart is isolation, the avoidance and combativeness against people who could commit to intimacy.

- *Generativity vs. Stagnation* (middle adulthood). With maturity comes both the need to be needed and the need to guide the next generation (generativity). Here you may see middle-aged adults taking on the role of mentors or doing other activities that help those younger than they are. Erikson noted that while not replacing the idea of generativity, the words *productivity* and *creativity* have been used to describe it. When this enrichment does not take place, the person stagnates into self-indulgence and self-concern.

- *Ego Integrity vs. Despair* (late adulthood). As one looks back at life, ego integrity implies integration. This does not mean that things were perfect, but perhaps it does bring the realization that one had a good life and that life was worth living. Despair is the realization that by now life is too short to start living a different life.

With Erikson, we have the issue of how socialization and developmental tasks affect our behavior. Issues of the individual and society need to be balanced in order for healthy development to occur. Resolution at one stage sets the foundation for the next stage.

Piaget and Stages of Cognitive Development

Jean Piaget's (1970) theory is described as genetic epistemology. Epistemology looks at the nature of knowledge, and what Piaget meant by "genetic" was close to our term for development. In his theory, we gain knowledge as we mature and interact with our environment. In attempting to describe development, Piaget used the concept of equilibrium, which he called equilibration. He did not mean a type of equilibrium that was a single structure for all situations, but a process of progressive states of equilibrium that went from lesser to higher states. Thus, as children interact with their environment, they run into problems. As they correct these problems (achieve equilibrium), they learn more and develop new ways of thinking and reacting. These new ways of thinking and responding are different stages, or ways, for dealing with the environment. Each stage is a more in-depth way of perceiving the world. Piaget delineated four of these stages:

- *Sensory-Motor Stage* (birth to 1½ to 2 years). Here, the child goes from being unaware of the world, except for the core self, to recognizing that he or she is part of a larger family and world. At this stage, children respond to the world with sensory and motor activity—perhaps putting things into their mouths or banging pots and pans together. By the end of this stage, the child has developed **object permanence**, the idea that the object is still there even when it cannot be seen, and the ability to grope "mentally rather than physically" (Pulaski, 1980, p. 24), or to think.

- *Preoperational Thinking* (2 to 7 years). At this stage, a child is not yet capable of the mental actions of organized, logical thinking—what Piaget called an *operation* (a thought)—but has faulty thinking. During this stage, children begin to use symbols (e.g., words that stand for things) in their thinking. Instead of actually having to do something, they can imagine it. They are egocentric, and see the world from their point of view. The development of language is an important achievement.

- *Concrete Operations* (7 to 11 or 12 years). This is "a period characterized by the ability to reason logically, to organize thoughts into coherent, total structures, and to arrange them in hierarchic or sequential relationships" (Pulaski, 1980, p. 55). Although children at this stage can "reason logically" or think logically, it is at the concrete level—dealing with the tangible (actual problems) rather than the abstract.

- *Formal Operations* (beyond 11 or 12 years). Here, Piaget presents **hypothetico-deductive thinking**, the ability to set up a hypothesis and deduce, through logical consequences, whether it is true. At this stage, children's thinking need not be tied to only concrete examples; they can now work with abstractions, such as advanced math. Their thinking becomes more logical and idealistic, and they are able to see a number of ways to solve a problem.

This is only a brief sampling of Piaget's ideas of cognitive development. He saw our style of thinking as changing, maturing, and learning as we interact with the world. We not only know more as we move from stage to stage, but our style, complexity, and manner of thinking changes as well. He would have said that our thinking develops as we **accommodate** to new experiences; so one determinant of our behavior is the stage of thinking of which we are capable.

Learning

Jeanne Omrod (1999) noted the importance of **learning** to humans: "The learning process allows the human race a greater degree of flexibility and adaptability than is true for any other species on the planet. Because so little of our behavior is instinctive and so much of it is learned, we are able to benefit from our experiences.

We know which actions are likely to lead to successful outcomes and which are not, and we modify our behavior accordingly. And as adults pass on to children the wisdom gleaned from their ancestors and from their own experiences, each generation is just that much more capable of behaving intelligently" (p. 2).

It would be hard to argue that learning does not affect our behavior. A change in behavior is actually one way in which we can determine that learning has occurred. Though we all have an idea of what learning is, it is hard to define it very specifically. For example, how would you respond to the following questions?

- Does overt behavior (behavior that you can see) have to be demonstrated for learning to have occurred?
- How permanent a change has to occur before you know you have learned something?
- Are cognitions (thoughts or mental associations) necessary for learning to occur?

Which research and theory you examine will determine how you answer these questions. In this section, we will examine four theories of learning. This is not a comprehensive view of the field of learning, but it will give some idea of how we think our behavior is affected by what we learn.

Classical Conditioning

Classical conditioning (conditioning can be viewed as learning) is sometimes called *Pavlovian conditioning* because we contribute its discovery to Ivan Petrovich Pavlov. Pavlov (1927) was studying reflexes as they related to digestion when he began to have trouble with his dogs. The dogs were salivating to a number of stimuli, not just the food. Pavlov decided that timing was the principal condition for new connections in the nerves. He noted that "any external stimulus which is to become the signal in a conditioned reflex must overlap in point of time with the action of an unconditioned stimulus" (p. 26). In one experiment, it was found that a dog could be made to salivate at the sound of a metronome by stimulating the dog to both the metronome and an immediate presentation of food. This phenomenon was demonstrated with a number of other stimuli as well.

Pavlov found that a neutral stimulus (called a **conditioned stimulus** because the dog has to learn to respond to a metronome), when paired with an **unconditioned stimulus** (in this case, food), will produce salivation. In this scenario, salivating to food is called an **unconditioned response** (the dog does it "naturally"), but salivating to a metronome is called a **conditioned response** (the dog has learned to connect this response to the metronome). This is called **stimulus-response (S-R) learning**.

You may find that your own dog has become classically conditioned to different stimuli. The dog may have learned to respond to the sound of you rattling a can in the cupboard, the click of a can opener, or any other stimulus that consistently takes place shortly before the dog is fed. When the dog recognizes the stimulus, it runs to its usual feeding place before the food is presented. Learning has occurred by stimuli being close together in time before the reinforcement.

Operant Conditioning

If you have ever gone to a theme park, such as Sea World, and watched dolphins perform tricks, you have seen behavior that has been shaped by **operant conditioning**. When Skinner, a major behaviorist and proponent of operant conditioning (1938), talked of an operant, he meant a behavior that was not normally associated with a particular stimulus. For example, a dolphin does not normally flip to a given hand signal. Skinner's *Law of Conditioning* stated: "If the occurrence of an operant is followed by presentation of a reinforcing stimulus, the strength is increased" (p. 21). In other words, if an organism *operates* on its environment and is rewarded for that behavior, it will increase the odds that the organism will repeat the behavior. Feeding your dog when it whines while you are eating increases the odds that your dog will again whine for food while you are eating.

While classical conditioning does not imply that the subject chooses to engage in a behavior (there is merely a timing association between the metronome and the food), operant conditioning does suggest that the organism may be working toward a goal: the dog does want your food. Thus, operant behavior is behavior you have learned as a result of the rewards and punishments that you have received as you operate on your environment.

Social Learning Theory

Children imitate behavior—Albert Bandura called this **observational learning**. Bandura and Walters (1963) thought that such learning especially occurred in the attainment of novel responses and that learning theories failed to take into adequate account the influence of social variables. In several studies, Bandura and his associates looked at the effects of modeling, or observational learning. In a typical experiment, a child would observe a person's (model's) behavior, and then the child would be tested to see how much his or her behavior would mimic that of the model. For example, one group of children might see a model act physically and verbally aggressive toward an inflated plastic doll, whereas a second group would see the model ignore the doll (the nonaggressive condition). When these groups were compared, the children in the aggressive condition would demonstrate more imitative aggressive behavior.

Most people are aware of the power of observational learning. When you find yourself in an unfamiliar setting, you might look around to see what other people are doing in terms of both acceptable and unacceptable behavior. Television commercials use favorable models, such as sports figures, in the hope that you will imitate the model's behavior by buying the sponsor's product. Imitation is a strong motivation for much of our social behavior.

Gestalt Theory

Gestalt, a German word that can be interpreted as "form" or "shape," is used to describe the whole of something. The Gestaltist would say that the whole is greater than the sum of the parts. A marquee, the set of lights outside a movie theater, is a demonstration of a Gestalt concept called the *phi phenomenon*. Even though the stimulus is one light coming on after another, followed by another, you experience it as movement—something beyond the actual stimuli. When listening to an orchestra, you experience more than just one note following another. In fact, you may not even be able to hear a specific note from a given instrument. Instead, you experience a "whole" musical selection. The Gestaltists argued against an S-R style of learning. Not only did they attack such concepts as classical and operant conditioning, but they asserted that we all try to organize our learning and world. Their *Law of Prägnanz* states that "psychological organization will always be as 'good' as the prevailing conditions allow" (Koffka, 1935, p. 110). Although "good" is not defined, it embraces the concept of making our perceptions as simple, regular, symmetrical, and organized as possible. People bring meaning and thought to their perceptions, and perceptions are understood within a given context. Everyone has a mind and uses it.

Biopsychology

Early in this chapter, a question was raised: Is our behavior determined by nature or nurture? This last section briefly examines behavior from the biological (nature-oriented) viewpoint. You have probably met someone who was smarter, more athletic, or more musically inclined than you. If you believe that differences in genetic makeup gave that person an advantage, then you believe in the power of nature (biology) to affect behavior. We have long been interested in how our minds and bodies are connected. We believe that there must be some kind of biological underpinning, process, or system for our behaviors.

In biopsychology we study the human body from the perspective of a number of systems and subsystems. We may begin by looking at what neurons are and how they communicate. Then we move into the central and peripheral nervous systems. We try to understand how neurotransmitters, neuromodulators, and hormones convey messages and govern various cells and organs. We look at the development of the brain and how its structures and functions affect our behavior and communication. Biological processes—such as hearing, seeing, and tasting—are studied to see how we interpret our environment. Researchers in the field of psychophysics study the relationships between stimuli and how we experience them. For example, how much weight has to be added to something before you notice the difference? Most biopsychology texts cover the biological aspects of movement, sleep and wakefulness, drinking, eating, sex, emotions, learning and memory, language, and mental illness.

Examples of the types of questions that biopsychology attempts to answer are as follows:
- What effect does cutting the corpus callosum (a large bundle of nerves connecting the right and left hemispheres of your brain) have on brain functioning?
- What effect does pheromone (a chemical released outside the body to affect members of the same

species in specific situations, such as when an animal comes into heat) have on human sexual behavior?

- What is the function of sleep, and what will happen if one is deprived of sleep?
- How does learning occur at a cellular level?
- Why are women more likely to suffer from depression than men?

As with other sections of this chapter, this one should be seen in its reciprocal context. Biological structures and their functions affect our behavior, and what happens in our environment can modify our biological structures. We no longer question whether a phenomenon is caused solely by nature or solely by nurture; rather, we now try to discover the ways in which they interact and influence each other.

Conclusion

In this chapter, we have examined some of the ways in which psychology, the scientific study of mental processes and behavior, helps us evaluate human behavior. We have briefly touched on issues of motivation, learning, personality, social roles, development, and biopsychology. Had another person written this chapter, the emphasis may have been different; he or she may have seen some topics as more, or less, important in the development of human behavior.

The important issue, however, is how this material is interpreted and applied to social issues. How does the development of your personality, however it occurred, affect your views? Maybe it is not your personality but your roles that affect your decisions and views. Then there is the question of motivation. As you read the chapters on social issues, what elements are behind your decisions? Are you motivated just to "learn" about the issues, or will you be moved to take some type of social action?

Related Readings

Hergenhahn, B. R. (2004). *An introduction to the history of psychology* (5th ed.). Belmont, CA: Wadsworth.
Hunt, M. (1993). *The story of psychology.* New York: Anchor Books.
Plotnik, R. (2005). *Introduction to psychology* (7th ed.). Belmont, CA: Wadsworth.
Wood, S. E., & Wood, E. G. (2004). *The world of psychology* (5th ed.). Boston: Allyn & Bacon.

Related Web Sites

American Psychological Association (APA): http://www.apa.org
American Psychological Society (APS): http://www.psychologicalscience.org
Encyclopedia of Psychology: http://www.psychology.org
PsychCrawler indexing the web for the best in psychology: http://www.psychcrawler.com
Psychology World Wide Web Virtual Library: http://www.dialogical.net/psychology
Social Psychology Network: http://www.socialpsychology.org

FOUNDATIONS OF ANTHROPOLOGY

Steve Helm

3

Chapter Outline

- Introduction: What Is Anthropology?
- Common Methodologies for the Study of Behavior

- The Study of Behavior as Approached by Anthropology's Four Core Areas
- Conclusion

Introduction: What Is Anthropology?

In the anthropological pursuit to study the science of human beings, anthropologists seek to find order amid the untidy heap of behaviors demonstrated by peoples of various cultures throughout the world. If this sounds easy, consider the following case involving zombies and voodoo. For many years, conventional wisdom held that zombies were complete fabrications, the stuff of primitive folk tales. Then, after decades of "knowing the truth about zombies," anthropologist Wade Davis was given documentation indicating that a Haitian man who had been buried as dead was, indeed, found to be alive (although he was a psychological shell of his former self). Wade traveled to Haiti, where he interviewed a number of individuals including the man, a woman who had met a similar fate, and a voodoo witchdoctor who had given the man a potion that claimed to be able to turn a human into a zombie. After having the potion analyzed, Wade discovered that it contained a drug that slows bodily functions to the point that the victim appears to be dead. He learned that when formal Haitian social controls are insufficient for controlling the behavior of a particularly difficult individual, a voodoo priest may, unbeknownst to the individual, administer the potion. The night after burial, the priest unearths the victim and keeps him or her as a drugged slave. The experience, attitudes, and expectations of the victims keep them from ever recovering psychologically (Davis, 1985).

Wade essentially reached into the "untidy heap" and pulled out something that resembled a zombie, a feat considered impossible. This discovery is not an isolated event, however. Anthropologists and other students of human behavior have repeatedly broken through conventional wisdom to discover the real stories of human behavior. This task requires us to set aside our personal agendas and learn about the larger world.

As seen from the above, **anthropology** is the study of human beings. In this aspect one could say that it is similar to sociology and psychology. However, anthropologists study the human condition across time

(past, present, and future) and across place, giving it a cross-cultural outlook.

For anthropologists, the study of behavior is beset with three particular problems:

- Each behavioral act may have multiple causes. This problem is compounded by hidden personal agendas.
- A tremendous amount of variation exists among individuals in a society (even small societies).
- Our ability to detect patterns is diminished by the infrequency of certain events, and by our limited ability to force repetition through experimentation. Also, many experiments that might help answer anthropological questions are unethical or difficult to perform. For example, we would not start a war for the purpose of studying behavior (although this appears to have happened once in New Guinea).

To understand how anthropologists have approached these problems, and to more fully appreciate their contribution, we must journey back to the 19th century when Europeans were expanding into parts of the world they knew very little about. At that time, Europeans and their descendents were trying to understand the new peoples they met. As always, advances in knowledge were slowed and muddied by selfish and biased agendas. The relative success of the more legitimate attempts may be exemplified by Charles Linnaeus's placement of humankind into his biological taxonomy. He correctly classified all humans as a single species: *Homo sapiens*. However, some of his methods and details were incorrect. He stated that there are five kinds of *Homo sapiens*, which vary by education and situation: Wild Man, American, European, Asiatic, and African.

The early anthropologists held misconceptions that were not unlike those of Linnaeus. They were, however, at the forefront of research and discussion on the nature and behaviors of these misunderstood peoples. Their research had flaws, yet the anthropologists studied "primitive" peoples in great detail and from a position of respect. (The word "primitive" was used to describe illiterate societies that had simple technology; simple social and political organizations; and few class, ethnic, or occupational divisions. It was not meant to be pejorative.) They used their detailed knowledge of primitive cultures to debunk traditional wisdom. The general theories that were developed in Western societies were typically found to be limited in scope. They usually did not apply to these newly-studied societies. Some of the methods and models of the early anthropologists have been rightfully swept into the dustbin of failed attempts. However, others were gems that laid the groundwork for modern anthropology.

Common Methodologies for the Study of Behavior

The early anthropologists addressed the three problems discussed in the preceding section through a number of methodologies. Two of these methodologies, fieldwork and the comparative method, remain central to anthropology. Before we discuss these methodologies, a brief note about the limit of our anthropological investigation will be made, and some of anthropology's building blocks require mention. These building blocks include anthropology's attention to detail, culture, cultural relativism, manifest and latent functions, fieldwork, and the comparative method.

Anthropology is primarily a behavioral science, although its scope extends beyond human behavior. In this chapter we will focus only on the parts of anthropology that deal with human behavior.

Detail-Oriented

Anthropologists are interested in the rich diversity of human behavior, with all of its associated needs, desires, and customs. They tend to analyze behavioral patterns in great detail. A common approach by economists, for example, has been to simplify behavior by focusing on specific behavioral aspects and creating a generic profile of a "representative" individual. Some studies might look only at the economic aspects of a society, while ignoring other cultural and personal elements of behavior. While such studies can be useful, anthropologists are rarely content to reduce the diversity and detail of behavior into simplistic behavioral models such as "economic man" or "socially controlled robot."

Culture

Culture is one of anthropology's most important constructs. At its most basic level, culture consists of symbols that describe and organize our sense of reality (e.g., our system of meaning, values, sense of beauty, and rules of conduct), and help us to experience the world. Knowledge, belief, techniques, and material objects are integrated into culture. For example, blue jeans, jazz music, and the metal plow are part of American culture.

Culture also provides rules and norms aimed at guiding behavior. These should be complementary, maintain a logical consistency, and contain sufficient flexibility to permit change. Behavior is not part of culture; but one's behavior does reveal something about one's culture. The interplay between culture and behavior is so important to the study of behavior that one of anthropology's primary goals is to find and describe patterns of meaning, values, and style within the cultures being studied.

Cultural Relativism

The principle of **cultural relativism** is one of anthropology's finest intellectual contributions to twentieth-century thought. It is based upon the fact that every society experiences a distinct set of social and environmental conditions, adaptations, inventions, and acquisitions. These experiences provide each culture with a unique development and perspective. This reality implies that one's behavior must be judged by one's own culture. For example, the relatively sweeping gestures an Italian makes in conversation must be judged by Italian culture. A traditional Navajo, who would be expected to perform minimal gestures, would misunderstand sweeping gestures if he judged them by the standards of Navajo culture.

The principle of cultural relativism requires that we set aside personal feelings when we study marriage, discipline, murder, sexual standards, religion, and so on. For example, the readers of this book are expected to detest infanticide. However, the principle of cultural relativism would lead someone researching a hunting-gathering society where infanticide was practiced to consider the attitudes, expectations, and constraints of that society. The researcher might look at infanticide in the nomadic society as a cultural solution to the problem of disabled children who would be unable to survive the hardships of travel and hunting.

Manifest and Latent Functions

A behavior has two types of functions: manifest and latent. The **manifest function** is the stated purpose for the behavior, whereas the **latent function** is usually less obvious and may include hidden agendas. A researcher studying a South American community observed a number of wives who grew interested in religion and then became devout church members. These wives then influenced their families to follow suit. This pattern raised a question: What is the function of these conversions? The manifest functions in this situation include the expectation of going to heaven. The latent functions were less clear until the researcher observed a common behavioral pattern. He noted that before a wife's conversion, members of her family spent a good portion of their meager income on gambling, alcohol, and tobacco. After conversion, these same family members stopped gambling, drinking, and smoking, which led to a household increase in savings. After attaining an improved socioeconomic position, members of these same families again started to gamble, drink, and smoke. The evidence suggested that the latent function was an improved socioeconomic status.

Fieldwork

The early anthropologists had few options for gathering accurate information on distant and remote peoples. Most available information was anecdotal, gathered or reported by people unaware of their own **ethnocentrism**—that is, the belief that their own culture was superior to others. As the science grew, anthropologists saw the need to visit and study cultures first-hand. They began to conduct fieldwork, which is comprised of first-hand observations and interviews.

Interviews involve gathering information from other individuals, while observation allows the researcher to examine events and the behaviors of those being studied. The two information sets—interviews and observations—are combined and compared to obtain a more complete picture. The first picture to develop may not be consistent. Conflicts may be found between the two information sets which could result from informants misunderstanding parts of their own cultures, having taboos against giving correct answers, possessing an overly strong desire to portray an ideal picture, and so on. When mismatches are found, the anthropologist may need to spend additional time in interview and observation to determine the cause.

Napoleon Chagnon's study of the social organization of a South American tribe called Yanomano (Chagnon, 1977) illustrates the value of in-depth fieldwork. Chagnon began his research by learning kinship terms, since kinship is the basis of primitive social organization. However, after finding Yanomano kinship terms to be vague and uninformative, he tried to learn the kinship rules by reconstructing the village's genealogy. After several months of trying to learn everyone's name, he discovered that his subjects had provided false names. At the time, Chagnon did not know the Yanomano have a taboo against uttering the name of someone who has died and, out of fear and respect, had extended the taboo to the living. The Yanomano had enjoyed making up colorful and sometimes vulgar names simply to avoid giving the real names. Chagnon was eventually able to learn the names of the living inhabitants, even though his best informants always lied about the names of their own close relatives and the dead. Chagnon was eventually able to understand Yanomano social organization because he used fieldwork.

Fieldwork typically lasts one to two years. This period usually gives an anthropologist time to learn the society's language, observe changes and events that occur throughout the annual cycle, shed some of his or her misperceptions and biases, and develop some understanding of his or her influence upon the subjects' behavior.

The Comparative Method

Fieldwork was an excellent solution to some of the problems associated with studying distant and relatively unknown societies. However, it does little, in and of itself, to advance general rules that apply to all, or even most, peoples. The **comparative method** can assist fieldwork in determining the general behavioral patterns by placing what would otherwise be an isolated case into a more general context.

Anthropologists use the comparative method to compare and contrast customs and practices found in different societies. The origin of male circumcision is a particularly suitable example of the use of this method, since we cannot (and should not) use experimentation to understand the practice's origins. We start with the knowledge that the practice of male circumcision is found in Muslim, Jewish, and certain New Guinea societies. Given the geographical proximity, we may postulate that borrowing occurred between Muslim and Jewish societies. We may also postulate that borrowing occurred between the New Guinea societies. However, the geographical distance and the lengthy history of the practice suggest that the practice began independently in the Middle East and in New Guinea. We then apply the comparative method in attempts to demonstrate that the practice arose independently out of similar conditions. To do this, we show a necessary interdependence between variables (i.e., we discover which variables are necessary for the practice to occur). We look at all societies that are characterized by A, B, and C (circumcision in this example) to see what they have in common. We can then go on to examine groups that have A and B, but not C, to see how they differ.

A brief review of the historical treatment of Abraham Lincoln's father, Thomas, can similarly act as an illustration. Thomas Lincoln has been considered a failure. He moved from one place to another, perhaps in part because he did not use correct agricultural methods. This limited view of Thomas reflects the type of treatment that can be obtained when an individual or society are studied in relation only to one's own society.

The farming methods of Thomas Lincoln and his neighbors were eventually compared to those of contemporary swidden (slash-and-burn) farmers around the world. Since slash-and-burn farming depletes soil nutrients, farmers must periodically move to new, more fertile areas. But this style of farming also yields higher returns with less effort than more intensive farming methods. As a result, swidden techniques are usually preferred in areas where population density is low in relation to available arable land. Where population density is higher, farmers adopt more intensive farming methods.

In the area where the Lincolns lived, farmers were beginning to use more intensive methods at about the time that Abraham was becoming a man. The increasing population density warranted the extra labor needed for intensive agriculture. The traditional historical accounts have ignored the fact that Thomas used the right methods for the times.

The comparative method relies upon studies from many societies. As might be expected given the history of Anthropology, primitive societies provide the bulk of the diversity, practices, and social institutions. This rich diversity of behavior and the principle of cultural relativism help to prevent overly ethnocentric interpretations. The comparative method has been an effective tool for challenging those who make gross generalizations or abstractions about humankind as a whole. It reminds us that the human experience is not uniquely Western.

Anthropologists tend to be (or at least should be) cautious when interpreting results obtained through the comparative method. They pay attention to exceptions, and are unlikely to form a theory that cannot explain them. Anthropologists also recognize a pitfall of the comparative method and other research methods that use correlations. When two customs or practices are always found together, they may not be directly related. In fact, the two are frequently found to be part of a larger phenomenon.

Other Methods

As anthropologists extended their studies into peasant, urban, and complex modern societies, and as they learned that small, distant societies are not as isolated as once thought to be, they found the need to develop additional methods. While fieldwork and the comparative method are valuable and necessary, they are best suited for small societies or small groups within larger societies. These two traditional methods are limited in their ability to explain behavior in complex societies with huge populations and great internal diversity.

An understanding of behaviors in large, complex social systems requires techniques that make it possible to take a subset of selected individuals within that population and infer what is happening to the larger population. In other words, we take a representative sample of people and judge, or surmise, what is happening in a larger group. Anthropologists adopted survey and statistical techniques designed to make those inferences with a reasonable degree of accuracy.

The Study of Behavior as Approached by Anthropology's Four Core Areas

The study of diverse and previously unknown peoples helped shape the development of anthropology's four core areas. The early anthropologists studied peoples who looked different. Their interest in anatomical variation and human evolution led to the development of **physical anthropology**. They also encountered a wide variety of rules and norms of behavior. The studies of these rules, norms, and the behavior itself became known as **cultural and social anthropology**. Many of the societies lacked written records. Their histories were partly reconstructed by unearthing and analyzing material remains such as pottery, arrow points, ruins of houses, and old campfire sites. These activities formed **archaeology**. The early anthropologists also encountered numerous unwritten and unknown languages, which they catalogued and analyzed. Their efforts led to the compilation of dictionaries and grammars, and eventually to modern anthropological **linguistics**.

These four core areas remain important. Contemporary anthropologists still study the four traditional areas of the societies that they research. However, a study will tend to focus upon a few select areas. For example, a study of San (formerly known as the Bushmen) subsistence may concentrate upon the social and cultural areas of food procurement and distribution, social organization (including the division of labor), and the area of nutrition in physical anthropology. Linguistics may be limited to a review of the few words that are directly connected to San subsistence, and archaeology may be ignored.

Specialization has occurred at the same time that the discipline as a whole has expanded and branched out into new areas.

Physical Anthropology

The study of physical anthropology extends far beyond the study of behavior. Anthropologists have tended toward caution when linking biology and behavior. They are ideologically opposed to the unsubstantiated and damaging claims that race is a basis for behavior. Anthropologists have been at the forefront in providing evidence that one's race does not make one more romantic, rhythmic, greedy, entrepreneurial, violent, and so on.

When the prevalence and frequency of behavioral traits varies between cultures, it is culture, not biology, which plays the directing role. Common behavioral patterns found within a society are often attributed to common child rearing and socialization practices, universals in childhood experience, and societal expectations of adults. Some key patterns are attributed to variations in child-rearing practices, particularly the implementation of basic disciplines such as weaning and toilet training. Children in more primitive societies are often breastfed for relatively lengthy periods (up to three to five years). Toilet training is similarly more relaxed, and children may simply be admonished to perform their functions outside the dwelling when they are old enough to understand. These more lenient practices are associated with more relaxed discipline toward adults. They stand in contrast to practices of societies that enforce harsh discipline upon adults and are organized in rigid hierarchies.

This is not to suggest that physical anthropologists have little to say about behavior. In fact, their studies reveal much about human behavior. However, many anthropologists believe that human behaviors that are nearly, or totally, universal involve biological factors. These factors may either be directly biological or may result from a common experience of living in a human body.

Our Biological Endowment

Humans have a biological endowment that permits some behaviors and denies others. This biological endowment includes arms, hands, fingers, and opposable thumbs. These features permit the ability to grasp, yet they don't allow us to fly even if we flap our appendages very quickly. The influence of biology upon our behavior affects a variety of other physiological features. Anthropologists have tried to increase their understanding by studying the areas of genetics, growth, and development.

For physical anthropologists, an understanding of the biological basis of our behavior begins with the study of human origins and change. These biological changes have occurred using the following mechanisms: 1) hybridization; 2) mutation, which is the sole source of new genes; 3) natural selection; and 4) genetic drift. Genetic drift occurs in small populations as one gene eliminates another. For example, due to genetic dominance, a small, isolated population with multiple blood types can expect the eventual elimination of the O blood type from their descendents.

The human upright posture has received substantial attention. It allows for a larger brain without requiring a corresponding muscle-density increase in the back of the neck. (A muscle increase would be required for animals with brains positioned in front of their bodies, such as dogs and horses.) It also permits speech, and a style of walking that frees the hands for other uses. For a variety of reasons, an upright posture permits a relatively high level of symbolic thought, learning, memory, and communication that make elaborate cultural detail possible.

Anthropologists study primates to learn about humans, because we are genetically very similar. Humans and chimpanzees are 98.4% genetically identical, which makes our two species genetically as close as horses and donkeys (Gribbin & Cherfas, 2003). Primate studies have been informative, among other things, in explaining the significance of a variety of bone and muscle systems.

Genetics

Early anthropologists were intrigued by physical variation and studied peoples with general physical appearances different from their own. They quickly found qualitative descriptions of physical differences to be insufficient, and began to take quantitative measurements of such anatomical features as the head, trunk, limbs, stature, and breadth. These measurement techniques of physiological features grew into anthropometry, the branch of anthropology concerned with measurements of the human body (especially for cross-cultural comparisons).

The study of human variation went through a revolutionary change in 1900 when ABO blood types were discovered and Gregor Mendel's genetic studies were rediscovered. The study of genes, which are the building blocks of our biological endowment, came to the forefront. Genes are involved in behavioral ability traits such as intelligence and factors that influence behaviors associated with life in a human body (e.g., stature, weight, features of adaptability, and features of homeostatic mechanisms). However, while genes affect the variation of a single characteristic, a gene's immediate expression is remote from the characteristic. Characteristics that anthropologists have studied include hair form, pigmentation, blood groups, proteins, finger and palm prints, and certain mental attributes.

One of the primary aims of genetics is to determine the genes responsible for a particular trait variation. These studies must be performed in conjunction with an understanding of the effect of environmental factors, since both are necessary for the development of a characteristic. These studies could be completed more quickly and easily if experiments used large breeding programs with known genotypes; this, however, would be unethical.

Growth and Development

Our biological endowment permits and directs growth when environmental factors provide the appropriate triggers at the right time in a child's development. The form that the development takes is limited to the allowed settings of the biological endowment. This is primarily a biological process, since the development cannot be gained through learning or training. However, social factors such as inadequate nutrition and smoking may alter the rate and timing of the changes.

Imagine, for a moment, how our behavior would differ if we lacked language. The ability to learn a language as a child is made possible by the language faculty, a biological endowment. When a child hears speech, a number of triggers will occur that direct (not dictate) the formation of a language skill. The process by which a child learns a language is analogous to the setting of a series of on/off switches. One sequence of settings represents English, another sequence represents German, and so on. Of course, a child's language faculty can retain multiple switch settings that accommodate multiple languages. The switches seem to be set around puberty, after which time people learn new languages in a different way. If language is not communicated to a child up through puberty, the absence of the trigger will distort or stunt language and cognitive development. The mental abilities will not allow particular behaviors, such as the ability to use more than a little grammar (if that much), for the brain will not have developed sufficiently. A non-human example may help illustrate the development of biological endowments. A kitten that is blindfolded and only allowed to see diffuse light (but never patterns) will not be able to see objects as an adult. The environmental stimulation that triggers the genetically determined process which develops this system of computation was absent at the needed time.

Human Adaptability

The study of **human adaptability** links humans and their physical environments. Studies of human adaptability take one of two forms. The first is related to physiological changes. The second may be thought of as the study of behaviors associated with the experience of living in a human body.

In regard to physiological changes, humans have an unusual adaptive response that permits the transfer of large quantities of information from one individual to another without the use of genetic coding, allowing for a rapid expansion in knowledge. This adaptive response is particularly important, since humans differ from other animals by being biologically "uncommitted." That is, our anatomical features don't commit us to a specific and constrained way of life. For example, we are not exceptionally good at running and climbing, at least in comparison to some animals. Gibbons are an example of an animal biologically committed to a particular way of life. Their disproportionately long arms permit brachiation (hand-over-hand swinging) to rapidly move through trees. But this commitment puts them at a disadvantage when they are out of their ecological zone. Their long arms make walking awkward, and are usually held up high.

Some human adaptability studies focus upon the complex set of physiological, neurological, and behavioral mechanisms that play a role in our homeostatic process. The maintenance of our homeostasis requires that certain needs (e.g., water, food, oxygen, appropriate temperature) be met. These needs are diffuse in form and few in number. When the environment is found to be part of a homeostatic change, the difference is considered to be adaptive. For example, it is adaptive to have a greater lung capacity when living at high altitudes. Of course, not all differences are advantageous. Studying genetically similar populations living in different environments helps researchers separate genetic from environmental factors. An example of this might be a population where some members have recently emigrated from the lowlands to the highlands.

Anthropologists sometimes assume that human-environment interaction takes the form of an optimization of one's environment. If this assumption is true, then many behavioral patterns will be direct outcomes of people extracting benefits from their environments. Of course, two things must be kept in mind. First, some adaptations are not optimal or even beneficial. And second, the environment limits possibilities, but is not deterministic.

Many studies of human adaptability have focused upon gender roles because biological differences between men and women make for profound differences. In primitive societies, the female role has been limited by anatomy since size, strength, and endurance are important factors in the division of labor. In these societies, women usually perform the central economic tasks near the group's home base, such as caring for the house, tending the fire, cooking, caring for children, and gathering roots and seeds. In horticultural societies, women do much of the garden work for similar reasons. In more modern societies, changes in technology, demographics, and economics lessen these anatomical restrictions, freeing women to take on other roles. In our own society, for example, most jobs do not require great strength. We have a relatively low birthrate, and mothers have more options for childcare. The statuses of women and the roles available to them have expanded as a result.

Other studies of human adaptability focus on interactions in which there is a central biological component, such as infectious disease. For example, a population with a low mortality rate in the face of a particular disease may have genetic or cultural adaptations that lessen their vulnerability to that disease. In such studies, researchers must take care to consider all the possible variables. In the above instance, a low mortality rate might be due, instead, to population density, methods of food production, the physical environment, or contact with other groups.

Social and Cultural Anthropology

Social and cultural anthropologists have developed techniques that help them address the problems of overwhelming behavioral variation. These techniques define least-common denominators of behavior by referencing norms that should guide behavior. This moves our focus from individual variation of behavior to the relationship of the behavior to social expectation. We may learn much about the public aspects of people while remaining uninformed about particular individuals.

Schools of Thought

The anthropological study of social systems has been pursued from three primary schools of thought: functionalist, structuralist, and Marxist. None of these approaches is necessarily right or always optimal. But each has particular strengths suitable for answering particular questions.

The early anthropologists were true functionalists. They viewed systems, such as societies, as organisms that exist in a state of equilibrium. They attempted to understand how a behavior works, how it affects other parts of the social organism, and how it affects the overall system. They focused upon norms and behaviors aimed at keeping systems in balance, and attempted to produce universal and objective ideas.

Contemporary anthropologists in the tradition of the functionalists have long abandoned the idea of systems as organisms. They have also realized their limitations in being able to produce universal concepts, and have recognized that tensions (e.g., racism, insufficient resources, differences in power) pull systems away from an equilibrium state, and eventually will change and replace the forms of the systems. These tensions make rules and norms necessary since rules and norms define and guide acceptable behavior. When anthropologists use the concept of equilibrium, they do so simply to provide an easy-to-understand framework.

Structuralist approaches are based upon the work of Claude Levi-Strauss and his theory of the mind

(Levi-Strauss, 1963). In structural theory, the mind continuously sorts perceptions into paired opposites. These opposites create contradictions that the mind then resolves. For example, when one associates with others, a contradiction is created since one's desires are delayed in order to satisfy the needs and desires of others. One resolves this contradiction by expecting similar treatment from his or her associates.

The Marxist approach is not an outdated vestige of a collapsed Soviet social system. In fact, a number of Marxist researchers have provided informative ethnographies of social systems. The Marxist approach is the counter to the functionalist approach. Where the functionalist approach focuses upon equilibrium and balance, the Marxist approach focuses upon conflict. According to some Marxists, conflicts move a social system from one stage to another.

Social Systems

The interplay between social systems (e.g., the family, the household, the village, the clan, the society) and their rules and norms creates an opportunity for understanding behavioral patterns. The society, which has received special attention, is a social group that has some economic and political autonomy and recruits most of its new members through the procreation of its own members. Social systems have sets of rules and norms to regulate behavior through such measures as positioning people within the social system, assigning them tasks, scheduling their acts relative to each other, and so on. Rules and norms, though, do not always have this desired effect. They also promote conflict, duplicated effort, and ambivalence. When the rules and regulations of a cultural system are expressed in real social life and behavior, they produce the social system.

This interplay makes the seemingly random and endless variety of behaviors more intelligible, meaningful, and predictable. However, these rules and norms are not deterministic. In the traditional Bozo culture of West Africa, cultural norms guide most men to become fishermen. A Bozo man can, and probably will, fish for a living. But a Bozo man may also choose to pursue some of the other possibilities available to him, such as wage labor and cultivation, instead of, or in addition to, fishing.

A social system's rules and norms include elements that typically fall within some general categories: economics, ecology, marriage, family, order, authority, and

Many Voices: An Introduction to Social Issues

religion. Most rules and norms fall into more than one of these categories. Elements rooted in the various categories interweave and influence each other. The Potlatch of the Northwest Coast Indians illustrates the intertwining elements. The Potlatch was a system of feast and gift giving that included the trading of wealth for prestige. Each noble hosted feasts for guests from other villages and his rivals (e.g., his in-laws) in order to revalidate his titles of rank. The feasts reached grandiose excess as each noble (and his fellow villagers) tried to outrank other nobles through excessive generosity. Gift giving was not only a simple economic transaction, but also became a display of wealth that carried social implications of prestige and power.

Social Actors

Social positions (e.g., child, student, father, or boss) are the basis for another method of reducing variation. Anthropologists refer to these positions as *statuses*—a term that makes no direct reference to rank or prestige (although some statuses have higher rankings than others). A status may be either ascribed or achieved. Ascribed statuses are few in number and largely unavoidable. Examples include sex, age, kinship, and race in American society, and caste membership in India. Achieved statuses, which cover every occupation and activity in which people may engage, can be more easily adopted and avoided. Examples include student, king, skin diver, and Presbyterian. Many social statuses are a combination of achieved and ascribed statuses. For example, a coal miner is an achieved status, yet there are very few female miners in this country. The ascribed status of male acts as a gateway for the achieved status of coal miner.

Social systems use statuses to categorize individuals, to assign rights and responsibilities, and to shape expected behavior. Each status has roles that signify expected behavior. For example, the status of teacher has roles that include instruction and grading. Anthropologists regard people holding a particular status as actors playing the role of that status. If an actor conforms to the expected behavior, he or she may expect to receive rewards; likewise, he or she may expect punishment for dramatic deviation.

Statuses and their roles vary widely from one society to another. In fact, one measure of a society's evolution is the number of achieved statuses. Primitive societies tend to organize groups around ascribed statuses. Social groups are typically organized by kinship, and the primary division of labor is by gender and age. Many behaviors are restricted to certain statuses, with little opportunity for change. Achieved statuses increase in number when technology and the division of labor become more complex.

Each person holds multiple social positions. An individual may simultaneously be a woman, manager, Caucasian, mother, Catholic, and surfer. However, one needs to perform the roles of a given status at the right time so as to manage consistent behavior and personality integration. We learn this lesson as children when our friend roles conflict with son or daughter roles. The tension between conflicting roles increases as we grow up, and may involve career demands, family obligations, religious duties, and so on. When one plays multiple roles before the same audience, one's behavior must be consistent and congruous with the self-image one attempts to project. However, credibility only requires that one's behavior is consistent with each role set (a role set includes all of the actors associated with a particular role). For example, a teenage girl may successfully play the sweet, innocent daughter to her parents and the foul-mouthed tramp to her friends. This separation is called "segregation of the role set."

Archaeology

Archaeologists study artifacts (i.e., material remains such as pottery and bones) to understand—among other things—the behavior of the people associated with those remains. The linking of material remains and behavior places the focus upon things that people have made or altered, which typically sheds the most light upon art and technology. Other areas that have also been better understood are society, economics, and religion.

The archaeologist may need to begin a study by searching for material remains. This search may consist of researching records, studying distribution maps of artifacts, aerial photography, and reconnaissance. Reconnaissance may include tapping the ground to detect sound differences that suggest substructures and subsoil inequalities, deep probes, study of the degree of electrical conductivity in the soil, and detection of magnetic disturbances caused by underground features.

Once the location of an **artifact**, or set of artifacts, has been identified, the archaeologist excavates the site to extract the artifact(s). The archaeologist may use a

Archaeologists study material remains to better understand the behavior of the people originally associated with those remains.

variety of methods and tools, including recorder, survey, photography, and careful work with trowel, penknife, and brush. Of course, not all excavations start the same way, since some will begin with accidental finds. Also, the rate of excavation and the methods used will vary. Under ideal conditions, excavations are carefully planned. But under some circumstances, such as when an archaeological site is about to be demolished, archaeologists must try to rescue what remains they can. At larger archaeological sites, the archaeologist will excavate only a part of the site, leaving the other areas for future excavation that, as new methods and tools are developed, will provide additional information.

In studying an artifact, an archaeologist performs four basic steps:

1. The artifact is described.
2. The artifact is classified according to an objective and reasonable taxonomy. This step may require the help of colleagues with other skill sets, such as geology or metallurgy.
3. The artifact is analyzed. An analysis should consider the form, material, biological association, and dating. An artifact may be dated through the following methods:
   a. Cross dating: An artifact from an undated culture is dated according to artifacts found with it that are from a dated culture.
   b. Relative dating: An artifact is dated relative to the date of other objects in its immediate vicinity.
   c. Absolute dating: A date is determined via a physical science method such as counting the layers of clay left by melting glaciers, radioactive carbon, or potassium-argon.
4. The archaeologist will provide an interpretation that places the artifact(s) into historical context. This step frequently requires the archaeologist to draw from written texts and other disciplines.

More recent developments in archaeology include the study of modern cultures. Some archaeologists study material remains of contemporary groups (e.g., materials found in garbage cans) to understand their behavior. Another relatively recent development is ethnoarchaeology. Ethnoarchaeologists study material remains of modern cultures in order to understand ancient artifacts and the people associated with them. For example, the construction and use of pottery may be better understood by studying groups that use traditional methods to make pottery.

Linguistics

Language is the most orderly and systematized part of the systems of symbols that form a culture (as you will recall, culture provides the rules and norms that

Many Voices: An Introduction to Social Issues

should guide behavior). In particular, language helps us to discriminate, generalize, organize, and articulate our thoughts, emotions, and experiences. Moreover, language provides access to experiences that are necessary for intellectual and social development.

The Basic Components of Language

To better understand behavior, anthropologists study the three parts of language: it is vocal; it uses words arranged in sequences that make up strings and sentences; and it assigns meaning to words. Each of these parts is highly adaptable and tends to reflect societal needs and desires. Individuals manipulate the three parts of language to their advantage (or disadvantage) to better express thought and emotion and influence behavior. Of course, cultural factors play a role, and the meaning of a given word, phrase, or sentence may differ depending on how it is used and in which context it is spoken.

Differences in vocal sounds are sometimes studied, since they are used to distinguish and reinforce societal differences. The perpetuation of caste membership in India has been aided by sound shifts that differ between castes. While different vocal sounds do not directly influence people's behavior, they do make it easy to classify individuals into their respective castes. Similarly, some upper-class Britons speak stylishly "bad" English to separate themselves from non-upper-class social climbers.

Words are arbitrary representations that help us to categorize and classify. As such, word-meaning concepts help anthropologists understand the categorizations that affect our rules of behavior. For example, Americans of African descent have undergone categorization changes. Many people who were called Negroes welcomed a name change. They preferred being called Black, which they viewed as holding a different rank in American society. However, others clung to the old term because they did not like the image portrayed by the new term. These same dynamics occurred when the term Black was replaced with African American. The success of a categorization change may not be predictable.

Anthropologists also study vocabularies to learn about behavior. For example, vocabularies increase when critical judgments require fine distinctions. The Eskimos have 17 words to describe various types of snow, and the Hanuoo (a Filipino tribe) have a taxonomy of at least 822 plants. By comparison, the Hopi Indians of the American Southwest used to have two words for things that fly—one for birds, and one for everything else. While they were certainly capable of making finer distinctions, these two words, and the context in which they were spoken, were sufficient for their normal communication.

To see how the arrangement of words in sequences influences cultural norms and rules of behavior, one simply needs to listen to the media or, really, to anyone with an opinion. Words are arranged to portray images that reflect our biases and our intentions to influence others. For example, the U.S. media habitually refers to the Hezbollah of southern Lebanon as the Iranian-backed Hezbollah. The Hezbollah appear to be framed as our enemy, or as irrational extremists who cannot be reasoned with, because some Americans have this unfortunate perception of Iranians and want the rest of us to have it as well.

The Sapir-Whorf Hypothesis

The extent to which language molds our perception and orders our experience has been intensely debated. Some believe that a society's language is a major influence in its members' thought processes and culture (both of which influence behavior). The idea that language directs our thoughts is called **linguistic determinism**. The idea that different languages frame relativity differently is **linguistic relativity**.

The controversial Sapir-Whorf hypothesis presents a case for linguistic determinism and linguistic relativity. Benjamin Whorf, who built upon the work of his teacher Edward Sapir, postulated that one's grasp of reality is determined, in part, by one's native language (Whorf, 1941). He believed that because the native speakers of a given language punctuate and categorize reality in a particular way, they will be more aware of some segments of reality and less aware of others. Essentially, people think like they talk. Opponents of this view believe that the Sapir-Whorf hypothesis simplistically reduces much of our thought to language. These opponents point out that meanings can also be expressed by context and by a nonlinguistic understanding of the world. Other opponents, such as Steven Pinker, have successfully criticized Whorf's analysis of the Hopi language and people (Pinker, 1994). He has found that some of Whorf's facts are not correct. This, however, does not necessarily invalidate the hypothesis.

A synopsis of Whorf's case for linguistic relativity follows. It compares some key differences between English and Hopi (Hopi is the name of the indigenous language spoken by the Hopi Indians), and their effects upon behavior.

Whorf found that native speakers of English routinely impose spatial forms upon the non-spatial, which gives the non-spatial the appearance of form, motion, and continuity. For example, speakers of English use metaphors of spatial extension (e.g., size, number, shape, position, and motion), imaginary plurals to objectify time (e.g., days, weeks, months), and mass nouns which reference objects without specifying amount or quantity (e.g., water and sugar).

Whorf found that this lineal perception of reality affected behavior. According to him, an evenly scaled and limitless timeline influences native speakers of English to perceive of the world as routine and to behave as though events are more monotonous than they really are. This has two consequences: individuals behave in relatively routine ways, but also act more recklessly (e.g., engaging in careless driving or throwing cigarette butts into wastebaskets). Their timeline also motivates them to define goals that display linearity in purposefulness, which is favorable to recording history, accounting, scheduling, calendars, clocks, romanticism, archaeology, and an economy based on time-prorated values (e.g., time wages, rent, credit, interest, and insurance premiums).

In contrast, Hopi does not apply spatial forms to non-spatial existents. Traditional Hopi thought does not perceive of time as a line or length. As a result, it lacks the associated linguistic forms, including metaphors, analogies, imaginary plurals, and mass nouns (all Hopi words include a certain mass or quantity). Instead, native speakers of Hopi make frequent use of tensors to directly express duration, intensity, tendency, and sequence. For example, day and night are tensors that are formed on a root (day for light and night for sleep).

Traditional Hopi perceives of time in terms of lateness. Objects pass through time (age), or get later, in several different ways. Some objects get later in a manner similar to plant growth, others diffuse and vanish like a scent, others undergo stages of metamorphoses, and others maintain their shape until changed by violent forces. The manner in which an existent gets later (e.g., its growth, decline, stability, cyclicity, creativeness) is in its nature. For example, one would not state *ten days is greater than nine days*, but instead would say *ten days is*

later than nine days. Summer does not fall within a well-defined annual cycle, but rather is noted as continuously getting later. Similarly, a new day is not *just another day* or *a new start*, but rather *the return of a friend who retains traces of the previous day and has aged a little*.

According to Whorf, the Hopi language and the associated flow of time affect Hopi behavior. Native speakers of Hopi emphasize preparation because they believe that their words and actions leave impressions that influence the future. Traditional Hopi farmers engage in elaborate preparative behaviors to ensure bountiful corn harvests. They believe a trace of their thoughts, words, and actions remains on the plants and influences the future harvest. These farmers also believe that the more they repeat these thoughts, words, and behaviors, the greater the trace (influence) that remains on the plants. In contrast, speakers of English tend to find this unvarying repetition a waste of time.

Whorf's examples do not provide evidence that one's native language prohibits behaviors. Native speakers of Hopi can and do use all of the institutions (such as banks and calendars) that are associated with a timeline. According to Whorf, the impact to behavior is not in the ability to participate in these institutions but in the origin of these institutions. Institutions that follow timelines were born and developed by speakers of languages, like English, that impose spatial forms on non-spatial existents. Culture and language influence each other. But of the two, language is more rigid in its effects upon development.

Trobriand

Other linguists have attempted to put the Sapir-Whorf hypothesis to the test (Gordon, 2004). Dorothy Lee studied Trobriand (Lee, 1950), the language of the Trobriand Islanders. Lee is only one of the authors who has tested the Sapir-Whorf hypothesis. There are others, including, more recently, Peter Gordon, who studied the language of Brazil's Priaha tribe (Gordon, 2004). Like Hopi, Trobriand lacks lineality. Trobriand words refer to self-contained concepts. One word is used to describe a good object, and an entirely different one is used if the object is bad. Objects are also segmented into different beings as they pass through time. Rather than a fruit being ripe or overripe, one word is used for a fruit when it is ripe, and another for an overripe fruit. In short, there is no linguistic distinction between the past and present, no causation, and no arranging of the events into means and ends.

Lee found no evidence for linguistic determinism. Trobriand does not dictate the behavior or thought processes of the Trobriand Islanders. Despite having a language deprived of lineal connections, the Trobriand Islanders do think and behave in ways that demonstrate some understanding of lineal continuity. They see and have names for constellations, engage in gift giving and gift receiving, and can navigate a course. However, Lee found evidence for limited linguistic relativity. There is organization, or, rather, coherence in Trobriand behavior. Trobriand activity is patterned activity in the same way that making a sweater is patterned activity. One act within this pattern brings into existence a pre-ordained cluster of acts (a causal relationship is part of a patterned whole). Language reflects culture and plays a role in shaping it. It influences, but does not dictate, our thoughts, perceptions, and behavior.

Conclusion

During the Vietnam War, a man applied to the anthropology departments at two different universities. On his application, he wrote that he wanted to obtain a graduate degree in anthropology in order to understand the hill peoples of South Vietnam. Through this understanding he hoped to convince them to support the United States in the war against North Vietnam. After a lengthy and intense discussion, the first school rejected his application. The committee decided not to accept any part of this plan. The second school accepted this application. The man attended the second school and graduated. However, by the time he graduated, his views of the world had changed radically, and he had no interest in his original purpose.

This story (told to the author by a member of the committee at the first school) is not intended to portray anthropologists as anti-war. Anthropology is not pro- or anti-war. The point is that when anthropologists consider war or other activities, they are expected to consider many factors. The second school in this story took the chance that, with an understanding of anthropology, the applicant would take a wider perspective, which is exactly what happened. In the words of a committee member from the first school, "They [the second school] believed in anthropology and we did not." This chapter concludes with the hope that you will draw from the lessons of anthropology to develop a wider perspective, and that you will test whatever method you use to understand behavior—as did the professors at the second school.

Related Readings

Campbell, J. (1988). *The power of myth.* New York: Doubleday Books.
Chomsky, N. (1988). *Language and problems of knowledge: The managua lectures.* Cambridge, MA: MIT Press.
Gould, S. J. (2002). *The structure of evolutionary theory.* Cambridge, MA: Belknap Press of Harvard University Press.
Lee, R. B. (1979). *The Kung San: Men, women, and work in a foraging society.* New York: Cambridge University Press.
Netting, R. (1986). *Cultural ecology.* Prospect Heights, IL: Waveland Press.
Stewart, R. M. (2002). *Archaeology: Basic field methods.* Dubuque, IA: Kendall/Hunt Publishing Company.

Related Web Sites

American Anthropological Association: http://www.aaanet.org
Annual Reviews of Anthropology: http://www.annualreviews.org
Anthropology in the News: http://www.tamu.edu/anthropology/news.html
Anthropology Resources on the Internet: http://www.aaanet.org/resinet.htm
WWW Virtual Library Anthropology: http://vlib.anthrotech.com

RESEARCH METHODS

Herbert W. Helm, Jr., and Lionel Matthews

4

Chapter Outline

- Introduction
- Defining Social Issues
- Identifying Social Problems and the Movements They Create
- Sources of Information and Research Methods
- Conclusion

Introduction

The title of this text indicates that we will be evaluating "social issues." Most textbooks on this topic use the term "social problems." Is there a difference between these concepts? Before we address that issue, we ought to consider the following questions, as they can help to set up some parameters by which to view this chapter.

- What is a social issue?
- Is a social issue different from a social problem? If so, how?
- Who defines a social issue or problem?
- Is a personal problem the same as a social problem? If not, how do they differ?
- What are the various perspectives on social problems?
- How do different disciplines analyze behavior? What research methods are used? How are these methods used in defining or solving social issues and problems?

Most of us have some concept of a social problem. For example, a law passed by Congress in 1882 declared that people who were considered idiots or lunatics would not be allowed entry into the United States. Immigration had reached about a million a year in the early 1900s; with this came concern about the "feeble-minded" entering the country.

Henry Goddard was invited to Ellis Island, an entry point for U.S. immigrants, to deal with this "social problem." Goddard had translated the Binet-Simon scale, an early intelligence test, into English and was the first to use it widely. As a result of his testing, he became concerned about what "morons" (individuals with low-functioning intelligence) would do to society. Fearing that they would become social misfits and criminals, he believed that they would produce feeble-minded children as well, thus perpetuating the situation. His test suggested that around 80% of Jews, Russians, Hungarians, and Italians were feeble-minded. As a result, Congress passed a law in 1924 that reduced the number of immigrants allowed to enter the United States from southern and eastern Europe.

What was Goddard's method? Typically, Goddard or one of his assistants would pick out an immigrant who looked feeble-minded and administer the test through an interpreter. Most candidates failed. No doubt many lacked education, knew little of American culture or English, and were probably tired and afraid. Hothersall (1995), in his *History of Psychology*, noted that even the interpreter "protested that the test was unfair as the questions were unfamiliar" (p. 419). The test contained questions about Crisco and the New York Giants, topics about which few immigrants knew anything.

Goddard was concerned about a potential reduction in the quality of the American gene pool. As a result of his "psychological methods," there was a large increase in deportations in 1913 and 1914. Another of Goddard's solutions to the problem of the mentally deficient was sterilization as a way to reduce pollution of the gene pool. In 1907, Indiana passed the first state sterilization law. Twenty other states would follow, passing laws which permitted eugenic sterilization (Hotherstall, 1995; Hunt, 1993).

This account raises several questions:

- What effect does immigration have on our economy and culture?
- What is a fair way to assess people's intelligence?
- How should we use the results of our assessments?
- Should we create laws to deal with issues that we believe create social problems?
- Are there racial differences in intelligence and, if so, what are the implications?
- How should we deal with people who are mentally defective?
- Should some social groups be targeted more than others?

These social issues continue to be debated. Though not all are specifically addressed in this chapter, a thorough discussion will appear in a chapter on social issues.

Defining Social Issues

We still debate immigration, intelligence, and assessment. Yet we must determine how a social issue should be defined. For example, if AIDS had not hit this country, but was limited to some continent across the ocean, would it be a social issue? Why were we interested when Iraq invaded Kuwait, but barely turn our heads for most wars in Africa? What makes one event or topic a social issue and another not?

To answer these questions, we begin with the concept of **society**, a group of people living in a structured community. It may exist for cultural, religious, political, or other reasons. The society may determine how large groups of people are to live together. It may provide an economy, protection, identity, and a framework for interacting with others. If you see yourself as a middle-class American student, you have classified yourself with regard to a number of social issues. *Middle-class* tells us something about how you live economically, *student* tells us something about your role in society, and *American* tells us that you live in an industrialized, economically prosperous nation. We could probably guess that politically you see democracy as better than communism, socialism, or other systems. You may have grown up with a Protestant work ethic, believing that working hard will pay off in high status and material prosperity. You probably believe that a nuclear family is a better system than an extended family or group living situation. In all of these areas, your society has largely defined how you view the world.

In helping to define your worldview, your society influences you to perceive as issues those points of discussion that are considered important in your society. In the United States, the topic of whether females should go to school is not an issue; yet it was in Taliban Afghanistan, and some females attended secret schools despite the possibility of severe punishment. An issue in the United States might be whether gender equality exists in the school system. Some may see the issue as a problem, while others may believe that overall equality exists. Not all social issues are problems. However, it may be difficult to distinguish between an issue and a problem.

Problems can exist on both personal and societal levels. By definition, a *personal problem* affects the individual. If, as an adult responsible for a family, you lose your job, you may find yourself suffering something between sadness and severe depression. This is a personal problem. Some personal problems are just part of life, and may be seen as challenges to overcome; perhaps they may lead to personal growth. They do not necessarily indicate a mental disorder, although, depending on how severe an effect it has, it may be associated with one. A person may have a problem that affects other people. If one person in a couple has a sexual dysfunction, it will affect both of them. It may even lead to more personal problems, such as arguments, substance abuse, anxiety, or depression. Yet the couple's problems are not likely to affect the whole of society.

Why does the individual have a sexual dysfunction? Does it stem from sexual abuse as a child? Perhaps his or her first sexual experience was negative, and this resulted in sexual aversion or an arousal disorder. Again, this is an individual interpretation of cause, and the treatment would also be individualistic (or perhaps geared toward the couple). It is less likely that we would look at how the diagnoses of sexual aversion or arousal are arrived at from a social basis, the ways that society helps to create these diagnoses, and the social issues that result.

As residents of a country that promotes individualism, we tend to ask why problems are suffered by the individual. Why did someone lose a job? Perhaps he or she did not work hard enough or did not prepare for changes in the economy. If those things had been done, he or she wouldn't be in this predicament. The solution is also frequently seen as individualistic. If this person worked harder, received more training, or searched more diligently for a job, the unemployment problem would be solved.

If a large number of people lose their jobs, resulting in negative effects to the economy, family structure, school system, or in drug use, unemployment is likely to be considered a social problem. We are not very concerned—in fact, we might be happy—if the country's unemployment rate is at 3%. But if the rate goes up to 10%, unemployment may affect how we live together as a group and therefore be considered a social problem. Even in this case we may hold an individual responsible rather than society as a whole.

If the economy is turning downward, we may blame the actions of the Federal Reserve chairperson, or of the president. This type of thinking suggests that one individual may be so powerful that his or her actions affect a whole economy.

While psychologists study the behavior of individuals, sociologists analyze the behavior of a group, or what we have defined as society. While acknowledging that a society is made up of individuals, a sociologist tends to think in groups or categories. For example, instead of focusing on a single person who is physically abusive or addicted to alcohol, the sociologist considers how drug addicts as a group affect society. The issue has switched from a personal problem to a social problem.

Identifying Social Problems and the Movements They Create

Sociologists view social problems and issues as **social constructions**, identified through a process of group definition (Scarpetti et al., 1999). This suggests that what we label a social problem is dependent on the meaning given it by members of various social groups. A social problem arises from the perception a society has of certain events. Thus, what is isolated as a social issue in one social context may not be seen as one in another; the critical element is how people react to particular events.

The way we deal with events varies not only within societies but across societies as well. For example, before the 19th century, husbands had the legal right and marital obligation to discipline and control their wives through corporal punishment (Mooney et al., 2000). Today, however, just mentioning a man having the right to discipline and control his wife, let alone use physical punishment against her, evokes strong resentment in the United States. In fact, a man who used corporal punishment against his wife in our society today could be taken to court.

Another example of how patterns of activities get labeled differently over time is tea drinking. During the 17th and 18th centuries, the practice was disdainfully looked upon in England as "a base Indian practice" (Mooney et al., 2000, p. 4). Today, however, tea drinking is a quite acceptable activity in England. A social issue can thus be seen as having two elements: 1) an objective element, which is the actual activity (tea drinking), and 2) a subjective element, which is how society views the action or event.

How does the objective element of a social condition become viewed as a social problem? While there are a number of ways to define and identify social problems, we will focus on three of the most common: expert opinion, public opinion, and the influence of the media.

Expert Opinion

The scientist who studies social problems and issues is called a sociologist. The word *scientist* here suggests that systematic research methods are used in the work. If you browse sociology textbooks, you will see much agreement regarding the topics to be addressed: health, drugs, crime, sexuality, poverty, racism, gender roles, family, education, economy, and violence. However, it is less likely that you will see a section about food. This makes sense in a country like the United States, because few textbook authors face issues of hunger or see hungry people around them. If hunger were perceived as a big problem in the United States, it would probably be addressed in sociology textbooks.

Sociologists and social psychologists assume a central role in the identification of social problems. They carefully and systematically investigate and order empirical data in an unbiased way, or at least free of the subjective contamination of vested interests. Experts in the field of sociology use several methods to study social phenomena. In broad terms, these methods are either **qualitative**—in which the data is not represented in numerical form, but looks at the qualities of the data, such as gender or ethnicity—or **quantitative**, in which the data can be expressed in a numerical form. As noted, these methods are distinguished from one another by the extent to which they transform data to numerical values, as well as by the assumptions they make about social phenomena.

Sociologists who prefer the qualitative method argue that social phenomena, especially human behavior, cannot be meaningfully reduced to mere numbers. Social phenomena are more than just data collected by a researcher. Qualitative researchers emphasize that phenomena should be investigated both from the viewpoint of an objective investigator (the researcher) and from the standpoint of those being studied (the subjects). Data collection techniques include case studies and participant observation. Case study techniques focus on a specific subject, with the goal of generating as much information as possible. A researcher may be interested in understanding the problem of spousal abuse from the standpoint of an individual who has been abused. In participant observation, the researcher participates in the group he or she is studying in an attempt to obtain data first-hand in as direct a way as possible. A researcher who wants to understand a certain group of people, for example, would live with that group and engage in their customs and festivals, eat the foods they eat, and learn the language they speak.

Current research in the social sciences is largely based in the empirical and quantitative tradition. Researchers who follow this tradition tend to view social phenomena as items that can be meaningfully transformed and measured in numerical terms. These researchers use snapshot data collection procedures (taking a small piece or section of a larger picture, much as a picture is only a small representation of a larger scene) to conduct surveys and experiments. Unlike psychologists, sociologists seldom use experiments as a method for gathering data.

The chief method used by quantitative sociologists is the survey. A survey involves asking people to respond to a questionnaire on some topic. By using a reliable and valid instrument administered to a representative sample of the wider population, sociologists inspire confidence in their findings.

Public Opinion

People often define a social problem on the basis of their perceived self-interest. The expert or the media may say that a certain issue *should* be seen as a problem; but unless enough people feel that the issue affects them, they probably will not regard it as a social problem. If only a few individuals or small groups perceive a problem, society is not likely to institute changes. For example, some people see the destruction of animals by the fur industry as a social issue and problem. They believe that animals have rights (such as the right to life) and that humans should help protect those rights. However, the majority does not see this issue as a problem worthy of a social policy.

The issue of oil supply is an example of perceived self-interest. When filling stations have plenty of gasoline and prices are relatively low, people are not particularly concerned about the issue. They may understand that our country is quite dependent on foreign oil, and may recognize that this could be a problem. However, when things are relatively good, the issue is not perceived as a problem. Once there is a shortage and prices go up, then people see oil as a social problem.

People may also define a social problem as something that violates their beliefs or norms. In mental health classification systems, such as the one outlined in the *Diagnostic and Statistical Manual of Mental Disorders* (DSM), certain types of behavior may be seen as problems during one time period but not another.

For example, some have felt that homosexuality violates both their norms and God's law, and therefore is a perverse sexual deviation. It was classified as a sexual deviation in past editions of the DSM and, as such, was seen as a problem. Since the 1950s, various organizations have attempted to alter people's views on homosexuality and eliminate laws that discriminate against homosexuals. They view homosexuality as an alternative sexual orientation that creates no more pathology than heterosexuality and, therefore, should not be discriminated against. So today, under current DSM-IV-TR classification, homosexuality is no longer considered a sexual deviation (American Psychiatric Association, 2000).

Is homosexuality a social problem? Even if the experts say "no," the people could choose to say "yes," or vice versa. In this case, the people help to define the issue and the degree to which that issue is seen as a problem. Similar arguments could be made for such issues as racism and feminism.

One method of taking the pulse of a population on social issues is polling, in which people are requested to indicate their opinions on matters of public interest. Various polling agencies gauge public moods and attitudes on issues like the decision of the president to commit the country to war, or whether the economy or terrorism is the more significant issue for our society. In 1989, for example, Americans identified violence as the most important social issue facing the nation. Though using polls to identify social issues remains, perhaps, the fastest and least expensive method of gathering data, they can be flawed. Polling can be fickle, manipulated, and based on ill-founded logic. Also, public opinion regarding problems can vary over a six-month period for any number of reasons, ranging from the mood of the respondent to the general social situation at the time of the poll.

The Influence of the Media

The role of the media as an identifier of social problems is being recognized more and more by sociologists. Media elements such as television, radio, newspaper, magazines, and the tabloids constantly bombard our attention and shape our views of life. For example, most people probably have a more tolerant view of homosexuality now than in the past because of the influence of the popular press and sitcoms such as *The Ellen Show* and *Will and Grace*. The media's attention to the bombing of the World Trade Towers altered Americans' views of terrorism as a social problem. Before September 11, few Americans gave real thought to terrorism. Now many can still visualize the pictures provided by the media.

Media come to have lives of their own and often are seen as ends in themselves. Many accept their presentations unquestioningly and savor their claims to "truth." Think, for instance, of the impact of the Oprah Winfrey Show, viewed by over 20 million people on a daily basis. While the media is often a creditable and authentic source of information, it is not without its flaws. Exclusive reliance on the mass media as a sorter of social issues can result in a skewed view as to what constitutes social problems. Often stories and events are exaggerated and sensationalized by vested interests for the effect of appeal. The media also helps to sustain incorrect or incomplete views of social problems. When a television program needs footage for a story about drug use, it may be easier to get a picture of a minority member selling drugs in the inner city than it is to go into a fraternity and get a picture of middle-class white students doing drugs. As a result, people are more likely to perceive drug abuse as a problem among minorities; yet, in the United States, the majority of abusers are white.

Whatever its mode of presentation, the mass media cannot be seen as an interest-free and value-neutral enterprise. TV programs, radio news, and periodicals not only disseminate information, but they also sell products and have hidden agendas such as profit, and lifestyle or policy change. Thus, the extent to which reported events are doctored and modified to capture the attention of consumers is an ongoing concern for social scientists. Consider the following news scenarios from two separate news agencies following the September 11 attack:

Atlanta, Georgia, United States. September 12, 2001. Breaking News: America under Attack

- *Main scene:* the bombing of the Twin Towers, alternating with faces of people crying, in shock, asking about their loved ones, wandering through a city that will never be the same.
- *Problem declared throughout the news:* extremely violent terrorist attacks have been made against civilization.

Islamabad, Pakistan. September 12, 2001. Breaking News: Jihad

- The Holy War was launched against the Western moral and social depravation, strongly represented by the American nation.
- *Main scene:* faces of clerics and religious leaders expressing their concerns about the violence and death involved, while pointing towards the depravation of the West as a cause. Archived images of Americans supporting Israel against Palestine.
- *Problem identified:* America's habit of finding a scapegoat or reason for military attack against Arabic countries.

Same event, different interpretations: Which consumers are the media playing to, what is the real social problem, and who ultimately decides?

Sociologists do not take representations by the mass media for granted. They often probe beyond what appears to be compelling evidence. Thus, consistent with the social facts perspective that ideas, feelings, and behavior are influenced by external forces, sociologists tend to see media portrayals as a function not only of the wider social structure but also of how those with power seek to manipulate our views. This awareness sensitizes sociologists to the limitations of the mass media as a sorter of social issues, and leads them to look to other ways by which social issues may be more objectively identified.

Yet we are left with the knowledge that the media is a powerful force that helps to define social issues. The next time you are watching or reading the news, ask yourself this question: How is the media helping to shape my view of this social issue or problem, and in what direction are they pushing my view?

Social Movements

In 1979, five-and-a-half-month-old Laura Lamb became one of the world's youngest quadriplegics when she and her mother, Cindi, were hit head-on by a repeat drunk driving offender traveling at 120 mph. As a result of the crash, Cindi and her friends waged a war against drunk driving in their home state of Maryland. Less than a year later, in California, 13-year-old Cari Lightner was killed by a drunk driver. Two days earlier, the offender had been released on bail for a hit-and-run drunk driving crash. He already had two drunk driving convictions with a third plea-bargained to "reckless accident." At the time of Cari's death, the drunk driving offender was carrying a valid California driver's license (Lord, 2000).

As a result of their experiences, Cindi Lamb and Cari's mother Candace Lightner joined forces and helped create Mothers Against Drunk Driving (MADD), a nationwide organization whose mission is to help victims of drunk drivers and to stop drunk driving and underage drinking. MADD has helped pass more than 2,300 federal and state anti-drinking and driving laws since 1980. And their fight continues: In 1999, nearly a million people were severely injured in accidents involving drunk drivers, and another 16,000 were killed. Today the organization has over 600 chapters and is one of the country's most popular nonprofit causes.

MADD is an example of a social movement. A social movement consists of people who join together for purposes such as mutual support, raising public awareness of their social issues and problems, and taking actions that will help resolve those issues and problems. As we see in the MADD example, these movements can be effective in making the public aware of a problem and helping to institute social policies and laws.

Social issues may also be addressed by the government and result in social policies. The policies attempt to deal with and resolve the issues. These social policies can range from the local level to the federal. Because of the importance of this subject, the last chapter of this book addresses the topic of how social problems result in social policies.

Sources of Information and Research Methods

How do you know something? If you were taking the class "Sociology of Religion," you might be asked whether prayer is effective. All of us are likely to have some view on this. How did you acquire your particular view? Take a minute and think of all the ways that you "know something." You might decide that you know the answer to a question because of authority (someone of stature told you the answer) or personal experience, or because of experiments run on the question. However, there might be great variance in the answers to the question from the people in your class. This variance might be even greater when your classmates explain

how they know the answer. Therefore, we have to ask whether each of these methods of knowing is equally valid. And of course the answer is "no."

Every discipline has a number of research methods for answering questions and thus acquiring knowledge. Throughout this book, many statements are made about a wide variety of topics. How can the authors make these statements? Is each statement equally valid? Usually, authors make most of their statements on the basis of authoritative research about a topic. However, rarely do authors tell you what type of research was done. The best you usually get is a reference telling

Many Voices: An Introduction to Social Issues

you where to look for more information. Rarely does a student check the reference to see if the information was reported accurately or to determine whether the research was done correctly. One problem is that we have a very broad definition of what constitutes research. Therefore, not all statements rest on equally valid research methods.

In using the "scientific method," we create theories that help to organize and predict the behaviors or events that we are studying. We then put our theories to some type of test, a research method, to see whether or not they are supported. Sometimes we try to describe only what is occurring. Case studies, surveys, interviews, and naturalistic observation are examples of descriptive methods. Sometimes we look for relationships between situations and behavior. Here we use correlations, which can also be used to predict relationships. At other times, we try to determine the cause of a situation or behavior. With experiments we manipulate one factor and study the effect that it has on another factor. This is called the cause-and-effect relationship.

A great number of research methods are used by various social science disciplines. Some methods are used primarily within one social science discipline, and other methods are used in a variety of disciplines. Some have more methodological rigor than others. We will look at a number of research methods used to gain information about social issues. As you read, think about the weaknesses and strengths of each method. Keep different methods in mind so that you can determine which ones were used for the various "scientific statements" throughout this book and others.

Idiographic vs. Nomothetic Techniques

Two techniques can be implemented when determining whether to use a single subject or a large number of subjects when studying the reasons for behavior. The **idiographic** approach involves a longitudinal study—observing a single subject for a long time in order to determine the reason behind his or her *particular* actions. The **nomothetic** approach studies many subjects to determine what is happening to the "average" person in the group. Here social scientists are looking for a *general* reason, a principle, for behavior. Most of the studies cited in this book used the nomothetic approach. Perhaps we could sum up the issue this way: If you study the average of large groups of people, you

may miss the richness and uniqueness of the individual, and may not be prepared to make accurate predictions on the individual level. If you study only the individual, that person may not accurately represent other people.

Naturalistic Observation

When we look around and describe what is happening in our world, we are using what social scientists call **naturalistic observation**. It is often used in early stages of a study when little is known about the subject, and an attempt is being made to describe an event. Imagine that you are sent out to a playground to determine what provokes physical fights. You can observe the children, record what you saw, and categorize the different types of behavior. As observer, you will not try to manipulate the event, but will attempt to remain unobtrusive (this is sometimes called unobtrusive research), allowing the subject to have unrestricted behavioral responses. The advantage of this style of research is that you, the researcher, can observe the natural behavior of the subject. Some subjects will alter their behavior when they know they are being studied. This is called **reactivity**.

Since naturalistic observation can reveal the spontaneous behavior of a subject in a natural setting, why isn't it used more often? One issue is that of **selective perception**, seeing what we want to see. Because there are so many actions that we can focus on, it is difficult to recognize them all. In addition, our bias towards seeing what we are predicting increases the subjective nature of this type of research. Some behaviors, like suicide, happen infrequently, therefore making them unlikely to be seen in a natural setting. When a given behavior is rarely observed, the likelihood of making an inappropriate **generalization** is increased. While naturalistic observation cannot be used in making cause-and-effect statements, it is useful in helping to create theories of behavior that can be studied with another type of research method.

Case Study

The **case study** is an idiographic approach to studying a given subject, or "case." One describes, observes (perhaps using naturalistic observation), and records the behavior of the subject. There is no manipulation of the environment in order to see its effect on the subject. One may want to see the behavior in its natural state, or may consider it unethical to manipulate certain variables. Case studies are used in clinical research for both normal and deviant cases. The method can be used to observe how an individual develops normally, or it can compare the deviant behavior of an individual to "normal" cases so as to determine a disorder's origin. It can be used to develop theories or categories of behavior. It can look at current behavior or **retrospective data**—data from the subject's history. A problem with retrospective data is that it is limited by what a person can remember. Since we do not observe an individual all the time, we may miss relevant information. The subject also might not provide some information if he or she deems it to be too embarrassing, irrelevant, or socially deviant (Myers & Hansen, 2002).

While the case study can give us an accurate description of a given individual's behavior, and may be a good source for creating hypotheses, the information is still limited to a specific individual. If we had studied George Burns and smoking, we might have concluded that smoking increases the life span. The comedian died at the age of 100, still promoting the pleasure of smoking cigars. In other words, we do not know how far we can go in generalizing our information to apply to other people. With the case study, the researcher develops only an in-depth description of the behavior of a given subject.

Survey Research

All of us at some point have probably been exposed to a survey or questionnaire. A **survey** typically contains a list of questions that attempt to reveal your feelings, behavior, characteristics, opinions, expectations, positions, or beliefs about some topic. At most colleges and universities, instructors give students a questionnaire near the end of the semester, asking them to evaluate various aspects of the class. This is a type of survey research. For fields like sociology, surveys are a major way of obtaining information. Surveys and questionnaires are typically done in person (an interview), by mail, in the classroom, or on the telephone. Surveys can use open-ended questions ("What have you found most useful in this class?") or closed-ended questions ("How many dates have you had within the last month?"). Answers to the dating question may be set up as categories: "zero," "one," "two," "three," "four," and "more than four." Yet the question about what is most useful in the class has no categories, so an individual can offer any response, such as "the lectures," "the discussion," or "the view out the

window." Surveys can be used to describe behaviors or beliefs, or they may be used to analyze the relationship between variables. Surveys may be administered only once or they may be repeated a number of times. While it is typical for a survey to be done just once, a researcher may want to look at changes that occur over time and therefore ask the questions again one or more times.

A number of response styles may be triggered by questionnaires, thereby affecting the outcome of the data. A **response style** is the way a subject responds to a question, regardless of its content. The response styles we will study are 1) yea- and nay-saying, 2) position preference, and 3) willingness to respond. If you have ever watched the old television program *Gilligan's Island*, you might have noticed that Gilligan will agree with almost anyone who is talking, even if there is disagreement among those with whom he is conversing. We would call Gilligan a **yea-sayer**—a person who agrees with almost anything appearing on a questionnaire. By contrast, a **nay-sayer** will disagree with almost everything. This doesn't tell you much about what the person believes, except that he or she likes to agree or disagree with whatever is presented.

Position preference indicates that you choose a particular answer because of its location on a list. Complete this statement: "If in doubt on a question, pick the letter ___." You may have said "b," or another letter, in which case you have a position preference. Thus, the response is not to the content of the question but to its position, and this affects the results. Finally, we consider the **willingness to respond**—whether the interview subject will answer. If you have taken a test like the SAT or ACT, you may remember having had to decide whether to guess the answers you were uncertain of. Your willingness either to take a risk or to proceed conservatively is an example of your willingness to respond. This response style is relevant to survey research when it comes to questions about specific knowledge, or very personal issues, such as sexual behavior (Myers & Hansen, 2002).

Compared to other types of research, surveys have an advantage in that they can gather large amounts of data at a reasonable cost in terms of time and money. They also can be used to collect information about opinions and beliefs that may not be readily observable. Surveys are a way of gathering data when it would be unethical to manipulate aspects of the environment in order to see their effect. However, surveys also have a number of disadvantages. One significant problem is that of **response rate**—the number of surveys that are returned. If only 30% of the subjects return your survey, you have no idea how the other 70% would have responded. The differences between people who respond and those who don't could affect your results. Telephone surveys are an example of **representativeness**—how much your sample resembles the general population. If telephone calls are made during the day, people who are at home may represent the unemployed, night workers, and stay-at-home spouses and may not be representative of the whole population. It should be noted that each of these disadvantages could arise with any type of survey or interview.

Interview

The **interview** is a type of survey research method that includes a social component, since the interviewee is addressed directly. The interview may be structured, in which a given set of questions is presented to all subjects, or it can be unstructured, in which the questions reflect a more flexible relationship between the subject and the interviewer. Structured interviews make data analysis easier, since all the subjects have been exposed to all the same questions, and in the same manner. Unstructured interviews make analysis more difficult. Since the questions may have been worded differently, the manner in which they were answered may affect the type of data received from those subjects. On the other

hand, unstructured interviews allow for a wider array of subjects for discussion, which may be relevant to the information being sought. They may involve questions that the interviewer had not considered asking in a structured interview, or questions that are harder to ask in a close-ended form.

Since interviews occur in social settings, one must be aware of the biases that may be present. **Social desirability** is the tendency to respond to questions in ways that make the interviewee look good. While it can be a problem on questionnaires, it is intensified with face-to-face contact. Another issue is the behavior of the interviewer. How interviewers ask questions, their tone, their reactions to answers, how they are dressed, and the setting in which the interview takes place may all affect the respondent's answers.

Statistics

Using statistics is a major part of analyzing data. **Statistics** are mathematically based methods that make data more understandable. **Descriptive statistics** help us clarify characteristics of the data. For example, we could talk about the "average" of something, or how far something deviates from the average, or what the shape of our data might look like on various charts. The normal curve helps describe the "average" and the deviations from the average. Figure 4.1 is a curve of the theoretical distribution of scores in nature (what we assume occurs in the natural setting), with most

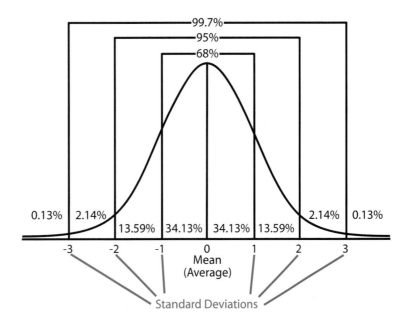

Figure 4.1: Bell-shaped curve of theoretical distribution of scores.

scores falling in the middle, and fewer and fewer scores appearing farther away from the middle. This distribution is called a frequency distribution. **Inferential statistics** allow us to infer or draw a conclusion about a population from a sample. We study a sample of people to estimate what is happening to a larger population.

A **population** is a group of people who have at least one characteristic in common. For example, we might want to know what the people of the United States think about abortion. It would be ideal to survey each person to determine exactly what that population thinks. However, this is impossible. Therefore, we study a **sample** of people, and hope it is representative of the population. By "representative," we mean that the answers or behavior our sample provides reflect how the population would have responded to the same survey. The extent to which our sample is representative is the extent to which we can generalize the information to the population. **Generalization** is our ability to take what is happening in a sample of people (a small group) and make an estimate as to what happens in a population of people (a large group). A bad (unrepresentative) sample is equal to bad data about the population.

When we generalize or infer, we can never be absolutely sure about our results. Therefore, statistics speak in terms of probability and **statistical significance**, both of which refer to the likelihood that the results are correct. For example, it may be generally believed that men are taller than women. Yet you know some women who are taller than some men. What you are really saying is that on average men are taller when you consider the amount of variability between men's and women's heights. To determine this scientifically, you could look at a **p-value**. A p-value indicates the level of probability that our samples have come from the same group (or population). For example, if we had a p-value of .001, we could say there was only a 1 in 1,000 chance we could get results that look like ours. If the results are this rare, we will probably choose to believe that our groups are distinct enough to let us claim that there is a difference. So, while we can never be sure, we assume that our results are unlikely to have occurred by mere chance.

Correlation

One type of statistic used frequently in the social sciences is correlation. A **correlation** looks for co-relations, or associations, between variables. We may want

to know which variables are related and which ones are not. This may help us understand the nature of our theory, or problem, and can help us predict one variable by knowing another. We may find an association between IQ and grades, but not between shoe size and grades. Therefore, IQ would be a better predictor of grades than shoe size. A correlation gives us a score, called a **correlation coefficient**, which describes the relationship of our variables in numerical terms. A correlation of .00 indicates no relationship between our variables, while a correlation of 1.00 indicates a perfect relationship. If we had a perfect relationship, we could perfectly predict the value of one variable by knowing the value of the other variable. So the closer our coefficient is to 1.00, the better the relationship and the better our prediction.

A correlation coefficient also indicates the direction of the relationship between variables. A positive (+) coefficient says that as one variable goes up so does the other. If there was a positive relationship between the educational level achieved by parents and that achieved by their offspring, we could predict that as parents' educational levels go up, so will those of their offspring. A negative (-) coefficient says that as one variable goes up the other goes down. If the old adage "an apple a day keeps the doctor away" is true, we can expect that as one eats more apples (one variable going up), one will have fewer doctor visits (a variable going down).

While correlation is a highly useful statistic, it does not prove cause. It is very tempting to say that because IQ and grades are related, a high IQ produces high grades. However, we do not know if this is true. All we can safely say is that they are related. If there is no correlation, we can be quite sure that one does not cause the other. Why can't we say that one causes the other? For one, we can never be sure which variable causes the other. The second reason is that the relationship may be **spurious**. A good example of a spurious relationship is presented in Morton Hunt's *The Story of Psychology* (1993). Did you know that the longer a man is married, the balder he becomes? Since we have a positive relationship, can we say that marriage causes baldness? This question usually bothers both men and women. Luckily, we can say "no," because there is a third variable called "age" that affects the relationship between the other two variables. So a spurious relationship is one that creates an artificial relationship between variables. Ultimately, we have to say that "correlation does not equal causation."

Many Voices: An Introduction to Social Issues

Experiments

In performing an **experiment**, we manipulate one or more variables and measure the effect on one or more other variables. The variable that we manipulate is called the **independent variable** (I.V.), and the variable that we measure is called the **dependent variable** (D.V.). We hope the variable we are independently manipulating (I.V.) will cause the other variable (D.V.) to change.

We could try to determine whether the amount a person studies (I.V.) affects his or her grade (D.V.). We test the idea that by manipulating the student's study time we can affect the grade. The experiment is the research method used to determine cause and effect.

The true experiment requires us to randomize our subjects into groups. For example, in our research on study time and grades, it may be that one group is brighter than the other, and that it is the level of intelligence, more than study time, that affects the outcome (grades). If **randomization** is in effect, then each person has an equal chance of landing in any of our groups. By randomizing, we are attempting to equally disperse any differences that should exist. Then the only variable that can systematically affect the dependent variable is the variable being studied. When we are studying large groups, randomization should disperse other variables, thereby making them ineffective.

Experiments require that at least two groups are studied. The **experimental group** is the one that receives the treatment. If we were testing whether a new drug worked, we would give it to a group of people and see if their conditions improved. However, some people may improve simply because they believe they will get better by taking the medicine. This is called the **placebo effect**. Therefore, we prescribe a fake drug (one with only inert substances that should not have any effect) to another group of people, the **control group**, and see what happens to them. If both groups get equally better, we can conclude that a placebo effect was responsible. However, if our experimental group does significantly better, we can feel sure that the improvement was due to the drug.

Quasi-Experiments

Quasi-experiments are very like true experiments except that we have no control over who will comprise the experimental and control groups. There is no randomization of subjects for two major reasons. First, it may be impossible. If we are studying gender differences in reading skills, we cannot randomly assign male or female; nature has already done that. If we want to study how a variety of personality variables affects grades, we cannot assign various personality variables. They have already been created by the interaction of genetics and environmental factors. The second reason for not randomizing subjects is that it may not be ethical to randomly assign someone to one of two groups. If we wanted to study the effects of cocaine on reaction time of newborns, it would not be ethical to randomly assign pregnant women to "cocaine" and "no cocaine" groups. Women who used cocaine during pregnancy would be compared with those who did not. The problem with non-randomization is that it is not known whether a preexisting state or condition had already created differences in these groups, and how those differences affected the results. In other words, some pre-existing differences may help determine who will take cocaine and who will not. Therefore, the problem with quasi-experiments is that the independent variable may have been contaminated (confounded) by variables other than the one being studied, and other variables may have affected the dependent variable.

Field Research

One problem with doing experiments in a laboratory setting involves **demand characteristics**. These are aspects of the environment that "demand" that we respond in a given way. These demands are like expectations of which we may not consciously be aware. When you attend a funeral or make a presentation at a convention or church, you are more likely to wear dress clothes than shorts or blue jeans. Probably nobody "demands" such attire, but you know it is expected. When people know they are being studied, they are likely to alter their behavior. This is reactivity. If you are in a laboratory and a person with a white lab coat comes up to you and asks you to do 10 push-ups, you are more likely to do so than if you are out walking on the sidewalk and someone comes up to you with the same request. The idea that we try to do what is requested of us in a study is called **experimenter bias,** or expectancies. Sometimes people try to be so helpful that they attempt to guess the hypothesis (what the researcher believes or claims will occur) and then work to make it come true. Experimenter bias, reactivity, and social desirability are all types of demand characteristics, which make it harder to know how far to generalize a study.

A way to resolve some of the demand characteristic problems is to do a **field experiment**, in which the research is taken out of the laboratory to a natural setting. We can still manipulate the antecedent conditions (our independent variable), and can watch and measure their effects on people. In one social psychology class, students were sent out to try an experiment on campus. Someone from the group lay down in front of the university library, as if passed out, while the others took different positions to see what would occur. The reactions ranged from a nursing student who rushed to help to someone declaring that "it must be those psychology students." While this experiment may not have had all the controls it should have, it did allow for more natural responses. What occurs in a natural setting helps to generalize how others outside a study may behave. Of course, one problem with a field experiment is that there is little control over who participates in the study. Field studies can be done in conjunction with laboratory studies to see if different results are obtained.

Ethnography

Ethnography is a research method used, especially by cultural anthropologists, to describe what is occurring in a culture, or some portion of a culture. In order to understand the group of people being studied, the ethnographer may live among them for a period of time—experiencing their style of life, speaking their language, eating their food, studying their rituals and ceremonies, analyzing their social relationships, and becoming a "participant observer in the culture under study" (Haviland, 1990, p. 13). Bodley (1994) notes the following about the participant observation role: "It involves total immersion in the alien culture and a suspension of one's own cultural judgments about appropriate behavior. However, the participant observer never loses his or her own cultural identity and can never become a full member of the other culture" (p. 5).

The ethnographer may try not only to describe what he or she is observing, but also to explain the customs of the culture. The information may be gained by experience, by asking informal questions and jotting down answers, by formal interviews, or by the use of a **key informant**, someone who acts as a guide to the culture. With ethnographic data, a researcher can compare various cultures and create hypotheses concerning human behavior.

Conclusion

As noted above, there are many research methods from which to choose. Which one is best for the project at hand? This difficult question is likely to be answered differently depending on who is answering and what field that person represents.

In different disciplines some methods are used more than in others, and researchers are usually biased toward those methods with which they feel most comfortable. To a large degree, the method chosen often depends on the hypothesis and the subjects obtained. As a consumer of research, or as a citizen being affected by social policy, you should understand the different methods of research in a particular study, along with their strengths and weaknesses, and decide whether their conclusions are reasonable

or whether other methods will better answer the research question.

Think about it: the method used to study an issue or problem may affect the results and the recommendations made. What you read or hear about different research studies may affect your beliefs and actions toward given groups, issues, or policies. Of the methods discussed in this chapter, the only one that assesses cause-and-effect is the experiment. It should be remembered that all research methods have their weaknesses. In studying the chapters to come, you should seek not only to understand the research methods used for analyzing the various social issues, but also to understand the perspective from which each issue is addressed.

Related Readings

Heiman, G. W. (2002). *Research methods in psychology* (3rd ed.). Boston: Houghton Mifflin.

Myers, A., & Hansen, C. (2006). *Experimental psychology* (6th ed.). Belmont, CA: Thomson Wadsworth.

Rosnow, R. L., & Rosenthal, R. (2002). *Beginning behavioral research: A conceptual primer* (4th ed.). Upper Saddle River, NJ: Prentice Hall.

Related Web Sites

IDEA—A journal of social issues: http://www.ideajournal.com

Social Issues Research Centre: http://www.sirc.org

The Society for the Psychological Study of Social Issues: http://www.spssi.org

EDUCATION

Judy W. Taylor and Loretta B. Johns

5

Chapter Outline

Today's children are living a childhood of firsts. They are the first day-care generation; the first truly multicultural generation; the first generation to grow up in the electronic bubble, the environment defined by computers and new forms of television; the first post-sexual revolution generation; the first generation for which nature is more abstraction than reality; the first generation to grow up in new kinds of dispersed deconcentrated cities, not quite urban, rural, or suburban (Louv, 1990, p. 5).

Introduction

Richard Louv (1990), a columnist for the *San Diego Union*, wrote the preceding description of the "90s child" after traveling across the United States for three years and observing the lives of American families, particularly children. How will the 90s children be affected by these "firsts"? What effect will the above-mentioned influences have on behavior as these children become young adults during the first quarter of the 21st century?

Children experience these firsts in the contexts of home, community, and school. In this chapter, which focuses on the school context, we identify issues that must be addressed. How these issues are resolved or ignored will affect how children are treated and taught in the classrooms and corridors of our schools. Over the years, issues have centered around six major areas of concern:

- Can our educational past teach us about our current educational problems? (Historical and Legal Background)
- What are the financial resources to support school programs? (Budget Issues)
- Who and what should be taught? How should it be taught? How should schools be held accountable? (Academic Issues)
- How can we use technological innovations to enhance learning? (Enhancing Learning Issues)
- How can the nation's schools provide an environment that supports the development of students' mental, physical, and social abilities? (Student-Centered Issues)
- How can educators connect with the home and community in preparing productive citizens? (Parent- and School-Centered Issues)

Historical and Legal Background

ISSUES: How has our historical background affected the direction education has taken? Is it good that education is more the function of the state than the federal government? How has the historical separation of church and state affected education? How should the concept of public education for all students be carried out?

I think by far the most important bill in our whole code is that for the diffusion of knowledge among the people. No other sure foundation can be devised for the preservation of freedom and happiness....Preach, my dear sir, a crusade against ignorance; establish and improve the law for educating the common people.

—Thomas Jefferson, in a letter to George Wythe in 1786 in support of a Bill for General Education (Alexander & Alexander, 2001, p. 24)

Historical Background

Even before 1789, when the U.S. Constitution was ratified, Thomas Jefferson made an appeal for public education to include "commoners." Ultimately, however, the Constitution contained no mention of education at the federal level. Rather, the only provision for education had been delegated to the states through the Tenth Amendment to the U.S. Constitution in 1791. This amendment "provides that '[t]he powers not delegated to the United States by the Constitution, nor prohibited by it to the States, are reserved to the States respectively or to the people.' Education is not mentioned in the Constitution and is, therefore, presumably reserved to the states or to the people" (Alexander & Alexander, 2001, p. 66). Thus, education became a function of the states.

The development of the American educational system was slow and painful. Education was highly valued, but differences of opinion arose regarding who should be responsible for that education. Four educational venues evolved: parochial schools, private schools for the privileged few, parental responsibility at home, and, ultimately, free public schools supported by state taxes; proponents of each tried to define the role of educator.

Parochial schools were established in colonial and early America. Their goal was to advance people's knowledge of the Bible. States generally recognized and supported these efforts, and some states even set aside lands to help church schools (Alexander & Alexander, 2001).

Latin grammar schools were first established for the privileged few in Boston, Massachusetts, in 1635 (O'Shea, O'Shea, & Algozzine, 1998). The primary purpose of these schools was to prepare students for Harvard College. Education for such an elite group reminded early Americans of the class system and the religious persecution that caused them to leave Eng-land. Education was not available to poor or lower-class children; instead, they either received no education or became apprentices to learn trades or manual skills.

Education for others besides the so-called elite was explored and debated. The first "free" schools in the colonies were called pauper schools. If parents declared themselves paupers, their children could be sent to schools for a "free" education, though the parents were charged a "rate bill," which was a tax that supplemented the school's revenues. Colonists explored the concept of free education and argued that "[c]lass distinctions... would be reduced if all children could be given a free education financed with revenues from taxes levied on everyone" (Alexander & Alexander, 1992, p. 21).

The first legal requirement regarding responsibility for education fell to parents as mandated by a 1642 statute in Massachusetts. However, parents fell short of fulfilling this responsibility, so Massachusetts then passed the School of Law of 1647 "to teach all to read the Scriptures in order to avoid falling prey to 'the old deluder, Satan'" (Alexander & Alexander, 2001, p. 22). This law also required any township that had increased the number of households to 50 to appoint someone in that town to teach all the children (Alexander & Alexander, 2001).

Free public schools were established in the eighteenth century as political philosophy began to identify education as necessary to the welfare of the state. Before this time, the benefits of education were perceived as largely personal. As time went on, however, education became the primary means for obtaining and maintaining freedom as the struggle for independence from England evolved.

The establishment of education in America rivaled only the abolition of slavery in the antagonism it aroused. The educational battle line was drawn between sectarian education and free education—that is, private and parochial schools versus free state schools. Those who supported public schools were typically middle-class liberals, social and religious reformers, organized labor groups, and working classes of northern cities. These people supported public schools because they believed that the development and perpetuation of a democratic society rested upon educated citizens and that secular schools ensured the principle of the separation of church and state. Those opposed to public schools included conservatives, Southern aristocrats, some religious groups, and certain non-English-speaking groups. These groups were against public schools for many reasons: 1) they thought their private interests would be undermined, 2) they opposed taxing the wealthy to provide education to the lower classes, 3) they thought "Godless" schools would destroy society's moral and religious foundation, 4) they were afraid that donations and endowments to existing private and religious schools would be threatened, and 5) they feared that the government could gain control of children's religion and language through the schools (Alexander & Alexander, 1992).

Two types of laws cinched state control of public education: compulsory attendance laws and child labor laws. Compulsory attendance laws were first passed in Massachusetts in 1852 to ensure that all children would attend school. Proponents thought these laws were necessary because not all parents took responsibility for educating their children either at home or at school. Those children not attending school included minorities, poor children, children whose parents made no educational commitment, and working children. Compulsory education was not firmly established until the beginning of the twentieth century; by this time 32 states had such laws (Alexander & Alexander, 2001).

Child labor, a concurrent issue in America during this time, kept many children from attending school, even though compulsory attendance laws had been passed. "In large cities children were virtually enslaved—in factories and shops, from daylight until dark—working for abysmally low wages. In the South, public school advocates and the labor unions crusaded against the abuse of child labor. In 1900 three out of ten mill workers in the South were children under sixteen years of age, and 57.5 percent of those children were between the ages of ten and thirteen.…Thus, a combination of industrial exploitation and the inability of parents to make decisions in the best interest of their own children greatly retarded educational progress for many years. It was not until compulsory attendance laws and child labor laws were enforced, in concert, that public schools became a viable social phenomenon" (Alexander & Alexander, 2001, p. 240).

The responsibility for education shifted from the parents to the state as the idea of public school education gained momentum and acceptance, and people recognized that education should exist not only for individual benefit, but also for the advancement of a civil society. A state system of education required general and direct taxation of a major source of revenue

such as real property. This formed the basis for the educational system that we know today—a free secular school supported by public taxation.

Legal Background

Pennsylvania Association of Retarded Citizens (PARC) v. Pennsylvania (1972): Thirteen school-aged children with mental retardation brought a class-action suit against the Commonwealth of Pennsylvania for its alleged failure to provide a publicly supported education for all of its school-aged children with mental retardation. The PARC suit was resolved by a consent agreement that specified that the state could not apply any law that would postpone, end, or deny children with mental retardation access to a publicly supported education. Furthermore, the agreement required the state to identify all school-aged children with mental retardation who were excluded from the public schools and to place them in "a free, public program of education and training appropriate to their capacity." Finally, the agreement indicated that it was highly desirable to educate these children in programs most like those for children without disabilities.

Mills v. Board of Education (1972): Parents and guardians of seven District of Columbia children brought a class action suit against the DC Board of Education on behalf of all out-of-school children with disabilities. This case was resolved with a judgment against the district school board. The result was a court order that the District of Columbia must provide, to all children with disabilities, a publicly supported education, regardless of the severity of their disabilities (Kupper, 1996, p. 1).

When did public education become available for "all" students? As public education developed—dealing with the social calamities of the Civil War, the Great Depression, World War I, World War II, and the Civil Rights movement—"all" students became redefined through various legal directives that resulted in federal legislative mandates and, ultimately, federal involvement in the public educational system. It was not until 1972 that students with mental retardation were included in the educational system as mandated by the above-mentioned court cases (Turnbull & Turnbull, 2000).

Schools were segregated by race prior to 1954; African American students attended African American schools, and white students attended white schools.

This practice was justified by the philosophy of "separate but equal" (Turnbull & Turnbull, 2000, p. 8), and it was ruled illegal by the U.S. Supreme Court in the first school desegregation case, *Brown v. Board of Education*, in 1954. This was the federal government's first decision about education, and it maintained that "separate but equal" did not hold for racial segregation.

This landmark case laid the legal groundwork for future educational issues that involved interpretation of constitutionality and civil rights. The U.S. Constitution did not guarantee the right to an education, but due process under the Fifth Amendment and equal protection under the Fourteenth Amendment will apply if state educational guidelines deny education to any group for any reason (Yell, Rogers, & Rogers, 1998).

The Civil Rights Act of 1964 directed attention to continued segregation of African American students and equity issues. This federal act made it illegal to discriminate against persons on the basis of race, color, or national origin in any program receiving federal financial assistance. However, the definition of "all" students did not include students with disabilities.

Several federal legislative mandates gave the federal government a foothold in the educational system, even though education had primarily been the responsibility of state government. Advocacy groups like the National Association for Retarded Citizens, the Council for Exceptional Children, and the Association for Persons with Severe Handicaps were organized to

pressure the government to become more involved in education. In addition, some important federal laws have been passed that redefined "all" to include students with disabilities. These changes did not come about voluntarily or easily. More than 45 right-to-education lawsuits were filed on behalf of children with disabilities in 28 states over a two-and-one-half-year period during the mid 1970s. Despite this plethora of litigation, many students with disabilities were still denied appropriate education (Zettel & Ballard, 1982). School districts argued that sufficient funds did not exist even though federal money had been promised, facilities were inadequate, and instructional materials and adequately trained teachers were not available. Public school inaction sparked the first federal intervention for students with disabilities and subsequently resulted in federal mandates to enforce free and appropriate public education for all. These federal mandates are listed in Table 5.1 (adapted from Yell, Rogers, & Rogers, 1998).

Special education has developed an adversarial nature with general education as a result of this litigation because many changes did not occur until lawsuits were filed. IDEA 1997 assisted in alleviating this problem by encouraging mediation as a voluntary means to resolving disputes. Ultimately, however, public education was divided into two camps—general education and special education—each with its own bureaucracy, goals, and problems.

Budget Issues

ISSUES: How "free" is public education? What would you see as a reasonable way to fund public education? How would you ensure that there was equal spending among students, or would you? How much money should be spent on special education as opposed to regular education? How far should the state go in paying for private education? At what level (federal, state, or local) should funding issues be resolved?

The median (average) total expenditure by regular school districts in 2002–2003 was $8,724 per student. Total expenditures do not include money paid to private schools and other school districts. For 90 percent of the school districts, those between the fifth and 95th percentile, the total expenditure per student

ranged from $6,145 to $16,720. Based on the federal range ratio, 172 percent more per student was spent by the district at the 95th percentile than by the district at the fifth percentile. Per student, 13,494 percent more was spent on capital outlay (construction and equipment) for the district at the 95th percentile than

Table 5.1: Federal Laws That Influenced Education

Federal Law	Common Name	Description of Impact on Education of People with Disabilities
Expansion of Teaching in the Education of Mentally Retarded Children Act of 1958		Funds were appropriated for teacher training.
Elementary and Secondary Education Act of 1965	ESEA (created Title I)	Federal funding was provided for educationally and culturally disadvantaged students in both public and private schools. This law became the legal framework for much subsequent legislation.
Section 504 of the Rehabilitation Act of 1973	Section 504	This was the first major effort to protect people with disabilities against discrimination based on their disabilities.
Education Amendments of 1974	Amendment to ESEA, P.L. 93-380	Funding was provided for students who were disadvantaged or disabled. Each state was required to provide full educational opportunities to these children.
Education for All Children Act of 1975	EAHCA P.L. 94-142	Federal funding was provided to states to assist them in educating students with disabilities. • Nondiscriminatory testing, evaluation, and placement procedures • Education in the least restrictive environment • Procedural due process • Free, appropriate public education
Individuals with Disabilities Act of 1990	Reauthorization of Amendments to P.L. 94-142, IDEA 1990	• The language of the law was changed to emphasize the person first, including renaming the law the "Individuals with Disabilities Education Act" and changing the terms "handicapped student" and "handicapped" to "child/student/individual with a disability." • Students with autism and traumatic brain injury were identified as a separate and distinct class entitled to the law's benefits. • A transition plan was required to be included on the IEP of every student by age 16.
ESEA of 1994	Goals 2000 Act (Included Safe Schools Act)	Provided federal assistance to programs preventing violence in schools
Individuals with Disabilities Act Amendments of 1997	IDEA 1997, P.L. 105-17	• IEP should include a statement of measurable and reportable goals. • Alleviate the adversarial nature of special education through mediation. • Discipline
ESEA of 2001	No Child Left Behind Act	Continuation of Title I programs, Safe Schools Act; accountability, flexibility, and local control; parental choice; and "what works" are basic principles of this act.

for the district at the fifth percentile (National Center for Educational Statistics, December, 2005).

Approximately 46.9 million students attended public school and 2.9 million teachers were employed in the 1999–2000 school year. Approximately five million other students were enrolled in private schools not included in this report (U.S. Department of Education, 1999–2000).

Obviously, public education is not actually "free." Public education is the fiscal responsibility of the states and is funded by a combination of local district and intermediate sources at approximately 43 cents per dollar, state revenues at approximately 50 cents per dollar, and federal sources at approximately 7 cents per dollar. Educational expenditures per student vary among states. Some states, including New Jersey, New York, and Connecticut, spend over $9,000 per student, while Utah spends less than $4,500 per student. The average expenditure per pupil was $6,530 (U.S. Department of Education, 2002).

School funding has become increasingly complicated over the last decade. Bell and Whitney (1998) report that most states have school districts that are considered "impoverished" and have been sued at least once in the past 30 years for funding inequities. Lawsuits have been filed in 48 states questioning state funding systems (Park, 2003). Legal conflict can result from funding the local share of a school district when districts with wealthy homeowners can raise more money than districts with poorer taxpayers. It is the responsibility of individual state legislatures to address this equity issue.

Equity, involving equal spending among students and communities, drove school finance litigation, and it was assumed that more money meant better schools and a better education. More recently, however, "adequacy" of money has joined the equity issue. It is not just a question of the disparity of funds between wealthy and poor school districts, but whether the "amount of school funding for each student is sufficient to produce a good education" (Bell & Whitney, 1998, p. 25).

Another fiscal challenge for today's public schools concerns money for declining school facilities. Arnold (1998) quoted a 1994 U.S. General Accounting Office (GAO) report suggesting that "it would take $112 billion over a three-year period to bring the nation's schools into 'good' overall condition" (p. 36). The National Center for Education Statistics (U.S. Department of Education, 2000, June) reported that these costs for school facilities could involve repairs, renovations, modernizing, as well as new construction and additions to existing facilities. Specific repair problems included poor ventilation, plumbing, sagging roofs, and overcrowding. The National Education Association (cited in U.S. Department of Education, 2000, June) reported the estimated cost of school modernization to be $322 billion. However, the NEA included the cost of education technology needs in its estimate, whereas the GAO report did not. The NEA also included a more comprehensive list of facility requirements than those listed in the GAO report and others. The NEA's list included landscaping and paving; purchasing; and fixtures, equipment, and furniture.

Special Education Funding

A local special education administrator observed, "People in general education don't listen to us or even ask us about the kids in our caseloads." A state-level administrator said, "We have consistent problems with some of our districts," explaining that the state deals with such challenges by using legal and administrative sanctions to coerce general educators into "playing ball." General educators voice reciprocal concerns. One administrator spoke for many, saying, "I have all I can handle right now without attending to students with wildly varying educational and behavioral needs." A high school teacher reported similar frustration, relating, "I remember trying to teach history to one kid who had to pass the SOL (Standards of Learning) test, and all he was doing is [sic] sitting there and calling me a bitch. And, because he's in a special education program, there's nothing I can do about it and nothing that anybody else is willing to do about it" (Hess & Brigham, 2001, p. 165).

Hess and Brigham (2001) quoted these teachers and administrators to illustrate that parallel public school systems have resulted from the implementation of federal laws. Only expenditures for general education were previously discussed. Those figures did not include the revenue required for educating students with disabilities, and this rising cost has become another challenge facing the states.

There has been a tremendous growth in the special education population in the last fifteen years. There were 3.7 million children eligible for special education in 1976–77 and 6.1 million children in 1999–2000

(Horn & Tynan, 2001). Horn and Tynan (2001) cited several reasons to explain the 65% increase in this population:

- There was an increase in eligible students, including students from ages three years to 21 years old, and those with autism and traumatic brain injuries.

- More students became eligible due to definition and policy changes: children with Asperger disorder (a mild form of autism) were considered eligible, as were children with attention deficit disorder and attention deficit hyperactivity disorder who may previously have been served as "other health impaired."

- There was an increase in the number of children diagnosed with **specific learning disabilities**," who made up 46% of the total special education population. (This is a 233% increase since 1976–77.)

- Districts placed low-achieving students in special education in order to receive federal funds.

- Districts placed low-achieving students in special education in order to inflate their statewide assessment scores.

- Parents request special education services for their children. Parents may be attracted to accommodations and special programs that special education may provide because the social stigma for having a child in special education has lessened. Accommodations could include a personal tutor or notetaker, laptop computer, extra or unlimited time on tests (classroom and college entrance exams), or immunity from severe discipline.

What are we spending on students with disabilities in special education to ensure their access to a free, appropriate public education? With the passage of the Education for All Children Act of 1975, federal funds were promised to help pay 40% of the extra expenses incurred in educating students with disabilities. However, this amount has not been forthcoming. Instead, Palmaffy (2001) reported that the federal share of special education costs has been only about 12%. Parrish (1999) revealed that national expenditure on special education is unknown at this time because of the complexity of special education finance. Using statistics from the National School Boards Association, Horn and Tynan (2001) ascertained the cost of special education for 6.1 million students to be about $79.3 billion, $41.5 billion more than the cost of regular education.

Because the federal government funded only 12% of this amount, the financial burden of special education has fallen upon the states.

Different states reported varying amounts of special education expenditures. The Prince William County school system in Virginia reported spending more than twice the amount spent on their non-special education students, which was about $6,500 (Palmaffy, 2001). Individual student expenses in Michigan during 1996–1997 were based on students' disabilities. Expense for a student receiving speech therapy was only $1,911, and expense for a visually impaired student was $46,987; both of these figures were above the amount spent on students in regular classrooms (Cullen, 2001). "On average, states pay 56 percent of the costs, with a range of 11 percent to 95 percent. The remaining 32 percent is paid for by local school districts" (Horn & Tynan, 2001).

Other reasons for the increased cost of special education besides increased enrollment should also be considered. Berman, Davis, Koufman-Frederick, and Urion (2001) identified "advances in medical technology, deinstitutionalization and privatization of services, and increases in children in poverty, and families experiencing social and economic stress" (p. 183) as possible causes of increased costs for students with disabilities. However, it is difficult to ascertain any actual increase in special education expenditures at the state or federal level because no uniform data sources currently exist to track this data (U.S. Department of Education, 1997).

The parallel educational systems, general education and special education, blame one other for financial shortages. School districts reported short-changing "their general education programs because they are bound by the courts to fund special education fully, even as general education enjoys no such legal protection" (McGroarty, 2001, p. 5).

Because of the federal mandates that created it, special education faces an interesting financial dilemma—litigation (McGroarty, 2001). Parents may resort to litigation if their children are not receiving the free and appropriate public education they expect. The Individuals with Disabilities Act guaranteed parents this right. However, the lack of uniformity in special education services has made it easy for parents to sue schools in order to gain services for their children. And litigation is placing a burden on school finances.

"Activists, often affluent parents, [are] aggressively 'gaming' the system to obtain special options paid for by the public" (McGroarty, 2001, p. 6). These games can result in public schools reimbursing the parents for hiring lawyers to sue them. This has created two special education systems instead of one: one for affluent parents with "gaming" skills and one for poor, usually minority, parents without such legal resources. The latter's children with disabilities "may be treated like 'non-persons' by the same school system" (McGroarty, 2001, p. 7).

Private Education

Some people see private schools as another drain on funding designated for public schools. "Private and parochial schools already receive significant financial assistance from the government through tax exemptions, book loan programs, free pupil transportation, Title I, school lunch programs, etc." (Stover, 1997, p. 64). This coexistence has been successful for a long time, but objections may arise if public schools are asked to go beyond what they pay private schools now.

What do states currently pay for private education? Stover (1997) reported that the cost varied per state and that 12 states offered little or no support to private schools. The Ohio School Boards Association reported that their private school budget increased from $85.4 million to $91.4 million in one year. The Pennsylvania School Boards Association estimated an expenditure of $200 million for private schools, and the Minnesota School Boards Association estimated $39 million in 1997.

What federal money is currently being spent on private education in a country that has battled church-state constitutional issues in the courts? The U.S. Department of Education (Stover, 1997) reported spending $6.3 billion in 1994–1995 under the Title I program that pays for remedial instruction and assistance to disadvantaged students. Federal funds spent for lunch and breakfast programs in 1996 were $154 million. Federal funds were also available for special education, innovative programs, technology acquisition, teacher training, safe and drug-free schools programs, and bilingual education. Stover (1997) stated that no one currently knows "how much public money is spent to subsidize private education" (p. 66) because complex formulas make tracking federal money difficult. However, it is not that federal money is allocated to private education. Instead, what they currently receive is through entitlement programs.

This may create a symbiotic relationship between public and private schools. What would happen if the nation's five million students in private and parochial schools returned to public schools? Who would be responsible for an average cost of $6,098 per student, a total of about $29 billion? Stover (1997) suggested that public investment in private and parochial schools may be a bargain.

Some states, however, are being asked to go beyond what they are currently paying. These requests often concern programs with vouchers that would help people pay private school tuition. More than 20 states, along with Congress, are looking at school voucher programs (Stover, 1997). Additional requests for state funding for private schools include extensive transportation costs, textbooks, and technology-related expenses.

Those who work in the field of special education provide yet another perspective on private school funding. "Education writer Jonathan Fox reports that public school districts are paying private school tuition for approximately 2 percent of the nation's 5.6 million special-needs students, or about 126,000 children, 'at an estimated cost of $2 billion to taxpayers'" (McGroarty, 2001, p. 292). Private placement ranges from tuition to residential facilities, and costs range from $20,000 to $60,000 per child per year.

Future Funding Sources

Public education is certainly not free, and ultimately it comes down to federal, state, or local tax dollars. Do other funding sources exist, or is it possible to redesign the current finance system?

Thayer and Short (1994) explain that schools cannot downsize like businesses can to save money, and it may be left to individual principals to solicit additional money for their schools beyond tax dollars. The financial needs of schools—which include facility needs, human resources, major capital purchases, instructional materials, and technology—cannot be met merely by sales from fruit, candy, and vending machines. New funding sources should be explored, including public and private grants; multilevel partnerships between schools and businesses; outsourcing for transportation, breakfasts and lunches, and custodial services; and school foundations. Finn and Amis (2001), in their online book, *Making It Count: A Guide to High-Impact Education Philanthropy*, even suggest that individual philanthropists contributing to public schools could influence reform.

Odden (1995) proposed a more radical approach to redesigning school finance. The system now in place in all fifty states is typically "district-driven." Districts raise money and decide how to spend it; states and federal tax dollars are distributed to districts, often through complex, convoluted procedures with strings attached. Odden suggested that school districts receive a lump sum, which would place the decision-making for its expenditure upon the district itself. This was an unusual recommendation in a time when state and federal governments were taking on more significant roles in the educational process. Ultimately, this type of refinancing could pave the way for other school reforms to be implemented, including charter schools, public school choice programs, and home schooling.

School finance is a complicated process. Even though steps have been taken to improve school finance equity and adequacy, it is wrong to have a system that educates some students very well and others very poorly. Arnold (1998) suggested that elected officials apply Garrison Keillor's quotation to financial matters: "Sometimes you have to set your principles aside and do the right thing" (p. 36).

Academic Issues

ISSUES: How should educators determine the "best practices" for teaching, and how should those practices be evaluated? Is it possible to have testing that is equal for all students and groups represented? Is it better to use standardized or norm-referenced tests? Does America do too much testing? How has this been both harmful and helpful? How should the issue of a disproportionate number of minorities in special education programs be handled?

She is a small wisp of a woman, but she is getting gigantic responses from her group of 20 fourth-grade children. The first three weeks of teaching in a large school district was a nightmare, according to her account. She didn't realize it at the time, but she had been assigned the classroom that no other teacher wanted to tackle, as the children were difficult to handle. At the end of her "initiation," she announced to the children that they had been in charge for the first three weeks, but she was going to be in charge from that day forward. She spent some time practicing with them simple things like how to turn in an assignment, how to walk down the corridor, and how to treat their classmates. That day during reading class, the textbook story was about a grandfather who rode his bicycle through Europe, but the children could not relate to his experiences and became restless and bored. She loves drama, so she started telling them a story about a boy who returned home after running away and the responses he received from his family. Suddenly, the children were engrossed in the story. They began discussing the issues involved in the story and were soon writing about their responses. This was the beginning of an entirely different environment in the classroom. A couple of weeks later, the principal walked into her room to observe the class. There was classical music playing in the background, the children were polite to each other and to the teacher, and they were all engrossed in a learning activity. He was thrilled with what he saw and asked her to share with him and the other teachers her special methodology.

Had this fourth-grade teacher chanced upon some magic formula for teaching, or had she matched students' needs with sound learning theory? In the book *Research on Educational Innovations,* Ellis and Fouts (1997) addressed the search for new practices and programs to improve learning and help children reach the highest levels of performance. They raised some interesting questions: How does one know whether a technique or process is a fad or truly an innovation in education? Why does a plan work in one classroom and not in another?

An educational innovation can be defined as a strategy or idea that has wide application across grades and subject matter. Ellis and Fouts (1997) provided a set of questions that can be addressed when evaluating changes in educational plans. The last thirty years have produced an impressive accumulation of research findings regarding teaching and student outcomes. One issue that educators face now is how to synthesize these findings and apply them to the purpose of each school community.

Educational Research and Best Practices

How is the complex system of public education performing? Are students learning? Are teachers teaching? How is progress evaluated, and is anyone held accountable for performance? These questions of accountability have arisen as more money has been poured into the educational system, and budgets have been stretched tighter and tighter. Educational research and proponents of standardized testing are trying to answer these questions.

Carnine (2000) notes that educational research is unlike the quantitative research conducted in the medical profession, which seeks to clarify complex issues. Educational research, which has relied more heavily on qualitative research, rarely provides cause-and-effect results that separate effective from ineffective teaching methods. This has made it difficult to use educational research to develop "best practices," although educators are attempting to do so. It is even more difficult to use educational research to develop effective methodology when educators themselves overlook results that do not support their own philosophies.

A quest for cutting-edge techniques has often led to premature implementation of educational practices regardless of research results. For example, brain research in the 1980s indicated that children might learn to read by using a "whole language" approach instead of the phonics-based one used for the previous 30 years (Carbo, 1996). Many schools jumped on the whole-language bandwagon and insisted that it was the only method that should be used to teach reading. Experienced teach-

ers were not sure that this was the case, but "research" indicated that this was indeed the best method, and phonics did not appear to be based on sound research. Proponents of the phonics approach claimed it also was research-based. Thus, the great debate ensued: whole language versus phonics. In fact, James Collins (October 1997) in a *Time* magazine article noted: "Hundreds of studies from a variety of fields support" the conclusion that "the value of explicit, systematic phonics instruction has been well established" (p. 81).

William Damon summarized this dilemma in his book, *Greater Expectations*, when he observed that our society tends to develop "unnecessary polarization of opinions about education and childrearing. Oppositional thinking rules the day. In education, we argue about whether we should teach children subject matter *or* thinking skills; whether we should make school playful *or* rigorous; whether we should teach reading through phonics *or* whole language; whether we should emphasize character *or* academics; and whether we should encourage children to acquire good habits *or* to develop their capacities for reflection" (1995, p. 95). Damon concluded that these positions are not opposite but are linked, and the truth falls in between and is lost in the gap.

Academic approaches should transcend this archaic style of reasoning and should embrace the philosophy that no one approach works for all children. In education, one size does not fit all. Our understanding of individual learning styles and multiple intelligences should have brought us to this conclusion long ago. Why are educators surprised when they throw successful approaches out the window, replace them with the latest cutting-edge, research-based methodologies, and then discover they do not work for all children? However, education should be lauded for its effort to return to its research to develop "best practices."

Educators have tried to apply brain research in the classroom with the development of materials for students who are right- or left-brain dominant because it helped to explain individual learning differences. Other materials that are linked to brain research can be easily located and purchased for classroom use. Even with the dramatic increase in knowledge about the brain in the past five years, researchers have cautioned educators against applying this research prematurely in our schools. Wolfe and Brandt (1998, p. 8) identified warnings from the scientific community:

- "Much more work needs to be done before the results of scientific studies can be taken into the classroom."
- "There are no quick fixes. These ideas are very easy to sell to the public, but it's too easy to take them beyond their actual basis in science."
- "Our knowledge and understanding of the brain may change within two years."

Benjamin Franklin gave us wise advice 200 years ago that we can apply to education today: "Make haste slowly" (Snider, 1990, p. 12). In other words, "Babies don't talk one week, tie their shoes the next and then work on their emotional development" (Wolfe & Brandt, 1998, p. 10). Incorporating new research into educational application should be done with the aim of focusing on the development of the whole child, not just on the brain.

Education as a profession continues to develop sound research practices for evaluating and implementing effective teaching methodology. Despite these efforts, though, education continues to polarize its methodology. The current "best practices" polarization is **constructivism** (child-centered) vs. **standards-based education** (teacher-directed). The web site for School Improvement in Maryland (http://www.mdk12.org, 1997) identifies both as "best practice" models based on research. A review of the research can be helpful for educators trying to determine which approach is more effective in getting results. Constructivism research tends to be qualitative, whereas research of direct instruction is often quantitative. Douglas Carnine described Project Follow Through, which was conducted in the United States from 1967 to 1976. The results rated direct instruction as more effective than the constructivist approach (Carnine, 2000). Shouldn't educators reach a consensus about effectiveness before materials are marketed to schools and the public?

Testing—Another Educational Debate

- "During the early decades of this century, eugenicists attempted (unfortunately, with success) to institutionalize or sterilize those with 'marginal' IQs, thereby isolating them and preventing them from 'breeding.'
- Tests were grossly misused to rank racial and ethnic groups, which led to the rigging of immigration quotas in the 1920s.

- Deaf children, it was felt, were incapable of any mental processing and so were routinely institutionalized until McCay Vernon (1967) showed the fallacies of testing the deaf with verbally based tests.
- Nowadays, diagnostic labels often follow individuals forever once labels are applied, in many cases creating self-fulfilling prophecies. Today's terms may be kinder than the 'technical' terms used earlier in this century to describe different IQ levels—moron, idiot, and imbecile—but the results are the same…
- Nearly a hundred years after eugenicists began ranking races of people and ethnic groups by test scores, issues of cultural bias in testing remain.
- Even now, the hoary myths of IQ return. Richard Herrnstein, Charles Murray, Daniel Seligman, and others link genes and criminality based on IQ scores. According to Herrnstein, 'If you accept the correlation between crime and IQ, then some people are genetically predisposed to break the law. People on welfare on average have low IQ's. The income of this country is an echo of IQ distribution'" (Zappardino, 1995, pp. 248–249).

Zappardino (1995) cited these historical examples about the abuse of testing in our country, especially IQ tests, which influenced unfair social practices and undermined the productive purpose of assessment. FairTest (2001), a national, nonprofit advocacy organization developed to reform standardized testing, has identified current test abuse and misuse practices. Possible test abuses and problems cited include 1) test score inflation; 2) curriculum narrowing, or "teaching to the test"; 3) emphasis on lower-order thinking skills; 4) declining achievement; 5) unfairness to minorities and women through tracking and program criteria; 6) excessive costs; 7) the fact that other countries do not test students nearly as much as the United States does; 8) opposition of parents, teachers, and students to testing; and 9) high-stakes testing (FairTest, 2001; Phelps, 1999; Fuchs, 1995).

Standardized tests are **norm-referenced tests** designed to produce a spread of scores that allows a comparison between the student's score and the norm group. Test items that permit relative comparisons are those which are answered correctly by about half of the students. Items that are answered correctly by too many or too few are omitted. Therefore, tests are designed to provide a range of scores; a test would be rejected if all students scored high on it (Popham, 2000, 1999).

Consequently, standardized tests are intended to give information about a student's relative strength or weakness in subjects and to measure the student's growth over time, but are *not* intended as a means to compare students or schools with one another or evaluate educational effectiveness or quality (Popham, 1999).

Popham (2000) described three things that standardized tests were created to measure: 1) what a child learns in school, 2) what a child learns outside of school, and 3) the child's inherent intellectual ability. Test items based on out-of-school learning and natural ability are the items that give the test its score spread. It is also the out-of-school learning test items that place students from a lower socioeconomic status (SES) at a disadvantage. Children from a lower SES seldom have the same enriching experiences as their more affluent peers. Popham (2000) suggested that the multiple-choice test items narrowly measure intellectual ability and pointed readers to Howard Gardner's work on multiple intelligences (*The Theory of Multiple Intelligences*, n.d.). Approximately one-third of the test items actually measure school instruction. Those who are opposed to standardized testing advocated using other indicators to evaluate student and school performance, including alternative assessment (authentic or performance assessment) and portfolios (Bizar, 2001; FairTest, 2001).

While critics of testing denounce testing in general, they are particularly passionate in their denouncing of high-stakes testing—testing which has rewards for being successful and consequences for not. Their basic contention is that "instead of leading to stronger academic achievement, it is said to interfere with good teaching and learning. In this contention, the critics embrace a sort of domino theory. Pressure to produce higher scores leads teachers to focus on material that will be covered by the tests and to exclude everything else. The curriculum is thereby narrowed, which means that some subjects are ignored. Within those that are taught, lower order thinking skills are emphasized. As a result, test scores get inflated while real learning suffers" (Phelps, 1999, p. vii).

Proponents of standardized testing have argued against anti-testing criticisms (Phelps, 1999). They recognized test score inflation as a potential problem when teachers become aware of test items and begin teaching to the test. Phelps (1999) suggested that school districts could remedy this problem by not using tests with the same questions year after year or by using unannounced tests or different forms of the test. The fact that teaching to the test results in narrowing the curriculum while eliminating "frills," such as art or music, was conceded to be a problem but was dismissed by the suggestion that "the public wants students to master the basics skills first, before they go on to explore the rest of the possible curriculum" (Farkas, Johnson, & Duffett, 1994, p. 17). Phelps (1999), responding to the criticism that test preparation results in an emphasis on lower-order thinking skills, claimed that teachers in high-stakes testing situations use the most successful instructional practices geared toward students passing the test, which may indeed eliminate higher-order thinking skills. He suggested that teachers may have a misconception about being creative and innovative and may even want to "conform to system wide standards for curriculum, instruction, and testing" because of the "security, convenience, camaraderie, and common professional development" it brings (Phelps, 1999, p. 15).

After examining a number of issues concerning testing, Phelps (1999) concluded that some of the "problems" may not really be problems—some are solvable and others are "inherent and inevitable—but similar problems are also present in the alternatives to standardized tests" (p. 25). High-stakes testing occurs when test scores alone are used to make promotion or graduation decisions, so Phelps suggested that test scores could be "blended" or "moderated" for these important decisions. Other measures, including classroom grades and attendance records, should be used

Many Voices: An Introduction to Social Issues

together with test scores. In addition, two solutions could make comparisons of the scores of rich and poor school districts fairer. The first solution is to let the poorer district set goals based on past performance. The second one uses "value-added" scores that are adjusted for students' background and prior achievement. Ultimately, standardized tests are not perfect; however, neither are teacher testing and grading, which are more idiosyncratic. The non-standardized testing alternative has resulted in social promotion for many students in the past and is not a system worth revisiting. Phelps suggests that we solve the problems with tests because "[w]ithout standardized tests, no one outside the classroom can reliably gauge student progress" (p. 24).

Even though educators know about the problems associated with testing, it is the one method that has been used to answer questions about performance in our schools. Presidents Bill Clinton and George W. Bush have both called for testing and accountability (Clinton, 1997; Jones, 1999). State standards and, possibly, national standards have arrived.

Public School Performance

How are public schools doing? What does the testing data reveal in the era of accountability? In 2000, national mathematics scores increased for students in the fourth, eighth, and twelfth grades. African American and Hispanic students had higher averages in math, but their scores still lagged behind those of white students (National Center for Education Statistics, 2001, September). Cook (2000, July 25) reported rising math scores at state levels. Students are also reading better, according to the National Center for Education Statistics (2003). Since 1982, a greater number of students are taking more mathematics and science courses, and more aspire to attend college (Forgione, 1998a). A school's performance is also evaluated by the number of students who drop out. The U.S. Department of Education (2000) reported that the total high school dropout rate in 1999 was 11.2%, much lower than the 27.2% in 1960.

Performance of Minority Students in Public Education

Minority students approach standardized testing at an inherent disadvantage. It has been previously mentioned that portions of standardized tests measure what the child has learned outside the classroom. George Will notes that children spend 91% of their lives outside of school (Bracey, 1998). Obviously, minority students living in poverty are severely disadvantaged in what they learn outside of the classroom. Shor and Pari (1999) reported: "Black and Hispanic families have a poverty rate nearly three times that of white households. About half of all American families live on less than $42,000 a year while 41 percent of all American families live on less than $35,000; but if these figures are broken down racially we find that more than 60 percent of Black and Hispanic families live on less than $35,000 while only 37 percent of white families are at this low economic level" (p. x).

The way minority students perform on standardized tests reflects this observation. Barber (1997) referred to it as a "caste-like stratification" and says that our schools are dealing with "our nation's oldest and most intractable problem: racism." It appears that public education is not divided into two parts but, actually, into three or even four—special education (one part for those with litigation-savvy parents and another part for those without), general education for white or affluent students, and general education for minority or less socio-economically advantaged students.

The dropout rates for minority students are higher than those of their white peers. Forgione (1998a) reported that the dropout rate for African Americans has declined, but it remains much higher for Hispanic students: 17% for first-generation, U.S.-born Hispanics and 44% for Hispanic immigrants. The U.S. Department of Education (2000) reported the dropout rates as 7.3% for whites, 12.6% for African Americans, and 28.6% for Hispanics. These statistics make it clear: the dropout rate for minority students is too high.

Minorities in Special Education

Ladner and Hammons (2001, p. 15) coined the phrase "special but unequal" (alluding to the phrase "separate but equal" that was used to justify separate school facilities for minorities before the Civil Rights Movement) to illustrate the disproportionate number of minority students placed in special education programs. They report that "African-American students accounted for 16 percent of the total U.S. student population in 1996, but represented 32 percent of students in programs for mild mental retardation, and 24 percent in programs for serious emotional disturbance" (p. 86). They also conclude that "white districts enroll a greater percentage of minority students in special education than majority-minority districts" and "a greater percentage of black students are placed in special education programs than any other racial group," including Hispanics (pp. 102–103). It is interesting that this has occurred under the auspices of federal laws passed specifically to prevent such action.

Performance of Students in Special Education

The U.S. Department of Education reported that 55% of children with disabilities, ages 6 through 21, are not fully included in regular classes even though 71% of the five million students with disabilities had the least severe disabilities: **learning disabilities** (51%) and speech impairments (20%) (Lipsky & Gartner, 1998).

The dropout rate for students with disabilities in 1995 was 14.6%. White youth with disabilities were more likely to drop out than were their nondisabled peers. However, race-ethnicity differences between nondisabled whites and African Americans held true for their peers with disabilities. In summary, students with disabilities were at greater risk of dropping out of school. The severity and nature of the student's disability increased the risk of dropping out, and students with mental or emotional disabilities were at the greatest risk (National Center for Education Statistics, n.d.). Lipsky and Gartner reported in 1997 that the graduation rate for students with disabilities was 57%, as compared with 76% for nondisabled students. These figures helped fuel the inclusion movement for students with disabilities to gain access to general education.

The 1975 Education of All Handicapped Children Act and the reauthorized 1997 Individuals with Disabilities Education Act gave students with disabilities access to a free and appropriate education in the least restrictive environment. How many such students are included in general education classes? President Bill Clinton (1997) discussed the progress of IDEA in his speech at the signing ceremony: "For 22 years now, the IDEA has been the driving force behind the simple idea we have heard restated and symbolized here today, that every American citizen is a person of dignity and worth, having a spirit and a soul, and having the right to develop his or her full capacities. Because of IDEA, disabled children all over America have a better chance to reach that capacity. And through IDEA, we recognize our common obligation to help make the most of their God-given potential."

This sounds as though we have made progress in educating America's students with disabilities, but we must do even more work to provide a free public education to these students. Barclay (1999) reported that many current court cases have been filed, which indicates that many states are still reluctant to comply with IDEA. "This reluctance costs parents and school systems both time and money when compliance would be a much easier and cost-efficient way to resolve the IDEA-related issues" (p. 330).

It has been difficult to track the academic performance of students with disabilities because special education's legal framework has stressed individualization, which is in direct opposition to developing uniform standards for general education students. Students with disabilities have often been excluded or exempted from the standardized testing that their nondisabled peers experience. This might account for the increase in special education enrollment as school districts dealt with the pressures of accountability. However, with the reauthorization of the Individuals with Disabilities Education Act of 1997, students exempt from standardized tests must be given an alternative assessment. Will the number of students identified for special services decrease now?

The Goals 2000: Educate America Act and other federal and state policies are developing standards-based reforms for students with disabilities (McDonnell, McLaughlin, & Morison, 1997). Special education may then have to meet the academic expectations that general education has been meeting for some time. Maybe the joint expectation of standards-based testing will bring these separate public education entities together, eliminating the authoritative nature of special education and replacing it with a cooperative spirit aimed at educating all children.

Technology for Enhancing Learning

ISSUES: How has technology changed or enhanced learning? Are schools keeping up with or training students for the technology they need in today's economy? How much technology should teachers have? How far should technology be incorporated into special education?

Bill and his friend, Paul Allen, were teenagers when they started their software company. They read an article in *Electronics* magazine about Intel's new microprocessor. Up to then (1971) each computer company (e.g., IBM) wrote proprietary software for its own machines. The general-purpose chip would rely on software to make it perform different tasks. There weren't any pure software companies, so the two teenagers decided to start their own company. They called it Microsoft (adapted from Gates, 1999).

The above story refers to Bill Gates. In his 1999 book *Business @ the Speed of Thought,* he makes the following statement: "If the 1980s were about quality and the 1990s were about reengineering, then the 2000s will be about velocity" (p. xiii). He is referring to XML (Extensible Markup Language) and the second-generation web. Developed in the late 1990s, these advancements allow the exchange of information not only between different computer systems but also across national and cultural boundaries. For example, they allow English to be translated into Chinese or documents to be rendered into Braille. They allow mathematicians the ability to insert equations into their web pages. (Previously, mathematical expressions could only be pictures.) Astronomers will probably be able to control their telescopes from any place in the world through browser software. In educational settings, software such as Blackboard or D2L enables students to be anywhere in the world and still communicate with their classmates.

How will individuals and institutions apply new technologies, and how will these technologies impact students' learning? The challenge has been and will continue to be how to integrate technology into the educational environment to maximize learning. The difference today is that changes happen so fast. How will we respond to the swift currents of change?

Schools are responding slowly to the integration of technology into their instructional programs. Watson (2001) urged schools to incorporate technology to prepare students better for their future after graduation. Currently, common workplace computer skills include bookkeeping/invoicing (66%), word processing (57%), communications (47%), analysis/spreadsheets (41%), and calendar/scheduling (38%) (U.S. Department of Education, 2001). Watson (2001) also reported that schools are still using teaching practices developed more than a century ago and are not meeting the needs of today's students to be able to function in the "knowledge society" (p. 1). "Why the delay?" he asks.

Several barriers prevent schools from responding to the technological challenge of the twenty-first century (Watson, 2001):

- About three-fourths of schools have computers and televisions but lack the system or building infrastructure needed to use this technology to its maximum potential. However, the National Center for Education Statistics (2005) reported that 100% of the public schools in the United States had Internet access by the fall of 2003, but only 30% to 58% had access in 1994 (30% for school size of less than 300, 35% for 300 to 999, and 58% for 1,000 or more).
- Half the schools do not have sufficient instructional space.
- Teacher preparation and training are inadequate.
- Not all students have equal access to computers. Inner-city schools and "schools with a 50% or higher minority population are more likely to have

insufficient technological resources" (Watson, 2001, p. 6).

- Funding of technology may come from an already tightly stretched budget.

The issue of racial differentiation in use and knowledge of technology requires further exploration. Bolt and Crawford (2000) have coined the term "digital divide" to identify this increasing phenomenon. Specifically, the U.S. Census Bureau (2001) reported that 77% of white children had access to home computers, compared to 72% of Asians and Pacific Islanders, 43% of African Americans, and 37% of Hispanics. There is an economic "digital divide" as well. The U.S. Census Bureau (2001) also reported that 88% of the households with incomes of $75,000 or more owned at least one computer; only 28% of the households with incomes below $25,000 had a home computer. Who will be left behind in this technological race to the future?

The final topic worth exploring is special education and technology. According to Levinson and Mineo (1998), technology is a double-edged sword for special educators. It makes it possible for students with disabilities to do things they could never do before. On the one hand, technology can help children talk, listen, write, read, and become mobile. It also makes the dreaded paperwork of special education more manageable. On the other hand, however, the cost of such technology is driving up special education expenditures beyond the reach of many school districts. As a result, technology is becoming a special education financial nightmare.

Student-Centered Issues

ISSUES: How would you define a "student-centered issue"? Who should define it—the students, parents, or school system? What can be done to reduce school violence? What kind of disciplinary accommodations should a school make for special education students?

Most of the chapter up to this point has dealt with more "traditional" issues revolving around the running of a school (e.g., budget, educational techniques, etc.), but schools today have much more to deal with than academic issues. The remainder of this chapter will look at some of the struggles that schools deal with, from violence to drinking, which go beyond the academic realm but which can affect schools and their performance.

School Violence

It was lunchtime at Columbine High. Denny Rowe, a 15-year-old sophomore, and some of his classmates were eating their sandwiches and joking around on a knoll outside the cafeteria entrance. Denny noticed Eric and Dylan in their black trench coats walking toward the school. One of them lit a brick of firecrackers and threw it toward the entrance. The other took out a semiautomatic rifle from under his coat and shot a 17-year-old girl. At first, Denny thought they were acting, maybe filming a video, and that the blood was a paintball. He thought, "It's just like Eric to think of some morbid-like senior prank." After all, they were known for their obsession with violence, especially with the video game Doom. Eric and Dylan were part of the "trench coat mafia," a group of students who prided themselves on being social misfits. He remembered when Dylan, always needing someone to follow, hooked up with Eric. They had become especially antagonistic toward jocks, African Americans, and students who professed belief in God. Suddenly, fantasy turned into bloody reality as the gunmen turned on his group of friends. Their shots shattered the knee of one of his friends; another friend was shot in the chest. Denny started running with bullets missing him as he found cover. The boys entered the school door and the massacre continued (adapted from Bai, 1999).

The word *adolescence*, derived from the Latin word *adolescere*, means "to grow into maturity." It is a time of transition—from the dependence of childhood to the independence of adulthood. Typically, a teenager's major challenges revolve around responding to the physical changes that accompany sexual maturation, exercising abstract reasoning powers, and forming an identity separate from his or her parents. Teenagers from the 1990s and later were confronted with a new and frightening challenge—survival.

Student unrest, discipline problems, and drug use are not new phenomena, but cold-blooded violence certainly is. School shootings devastated families and schools during the 1990s and beyond. Here are some examples (Violence in U.S. Schools, n.d.):

- On October 1, 1997, in Pearl, Mississippi, Luke Woodham, age 16, killed his mother and then went to his school, where he killed three and wounded seven.
- Michael Carneal, age 14, from West Paducah, Kentucky, shot three students attending an early-morning high school prayer meeting on December 1, 1997.
- Mitchell Johnson, age 13, and Andrew Golden, age 11, set off a fire alarm and then waited in a wooded area for their fellow students to exit their school in Jonesboro, Arkansas. They killed four students and a teacher on March 24, 1998.
- On May 21, 1998, in Springfield, Oregon, Kip Kinkel, age 15, killed his parents and then went to school, where he shot 24 students. Two died.
- On April 20, 1999, Eric Harris, age 18, and Dylan Klebold, age 17, entered Columbine High School in Littleton, Colorado, where they terrorized students and teachers. The school resembled a war zone by the time it was over, with 12 classmates and a teacher massacred before Harris and Klebold both committed suicide.
- Just one month after the Columbine massacre, a 15-year-old shot six students at Heritage High School in Conyers, Georgia, a suburb of Atlanta.
- A six-year-old boy used his father's .32 semiautomatic to kill his first-grade classmate Kayla Rolland in Mount Morris, Michigan, on February 29, 2000.

Why did these children and teenagers maim and kill their fellow classmates, teachers, and parents? Parenting (or the lack of it), violence in video games and movies, easy access to guns, and several other factors have all been set forth as causes of the epidemic of school shootings during the 1990s. Are these the real causes? Or are they symptoms of a far more serious underlying issue, such as a lack of emotional connection between a child and other people? The authors of the May 10, 1999, *Newsweek* article entitled "Beyond Littleton—How Well Do You Know Your Kid?" may have articulated this underlying problem in the following statement: "In survey after survey, many kids—even those on the honor roll—say they feel increasingly alone and alienated, unable to connect with their parents, teachers and sometimes even classmates. They're desperate for guidance, and when they don't get what they need at home or in school, they cling to cliques or immerse themselves in a universe out of their parents' reach, a world defined by computer games, TV, and movies, where brutality is so common it has become mundane" (Kantrowitz & Wingert, 1999, p. 36).

Connectedness may well be one of the most urgent issues that we must address during the first part of this century. Connection is vital to a child because it provides a strong support system that fosters a sense of belonging—thus fulfilling a basic human need. How can the school work with the home to help a child connect to other people?

Schools' Response to Violence

Most schools were free from serious problems before the 1960s (Townleyk & Martinez, 1995). In fact, before 1960, teachers and administrators identified the most serious discipline problems as talking, chewing gum, making noise, running in halls, cutting in line, wearing improper clothing, and not putting paper in wastebaskets. Things changed after 1960, when discipline problems cited included rape, robbery, assault, burglary, arson, bombings, and murder.

As a result, schools evaluated their security policies more closely and initiated many security measures, including security guards, backpack and locker checks, drug dogs, hotlines, telephones, two-way radios, computers, digitized cameras, scanners, metal detectors (fixed and hand-held), and video cameras. The Safe Schools Act of 1994 allowed school districts to pass more stringent measures for their discipline offenders. Forgione (1998b) reported measures schools developed to deal with serious discipline problems. For example, schools enforced in-school and out-of-school suspension, alternative schools, and expulsion guidelines. Zero-tolerance policies were adopted for firearms and weapons, alcohol and drugs, violence, and tobacco. School "hot spots" for violence were identified and mapped out for better supervision. Such hot spots included bathrooms, locker rooms, hallways, and cafeterias.

Measures to deal with school violence did not stop there. School culture was evaluated and techniques were employed to teach students how to think, act, and manage their anger (Friedland, 1999). Specifically, measures adopted to help schools become warm, supportive communities included cooperative learning, positive attitudes, and parenting education.

It was a shock when on March 5, 2001, 15-year-old Charles Williams shot and killed two students and injured 13 others at Santana High School in Santee, California. This school had employed extensive preventive measures, including anonymous sign-in sheets for students to report threats. The principal had undergone SWAT training, and a part-time sheriff's deputy was assigned to the school. The school had seven full-time campus supervisors walking the school grounds and had installed extra phones, as well as radios and speakers (Randall & Grey, 2001). None of these measures prevented the shooting. What else could have been done?

Special Education and Discipline

"It is a Friday afternoon during the spring semester. The principal walks the halls one last time before the final bell of the day. A boy emerges from the restroom followed by a cloud of cigarette smoke. He has cigarettes and matches in his pockets and obviously has been smoking.

"The principal knows the student [is learning disabled], receives special education services under the Individuals with Disabilities Education Act and has no behavior accommodations in his individual education plan. According to the school district's disciplinary code, possession or use of tobacco on school grounds carries a penalty of 10 school days in an off-campus disciplinary setting. The principal discovers in the student's disciplinary records that he was suspended on three occasions in the fall for a total of 10 days.

"What action can the principal take for the latest violation of rules? Must the student's individual education plan team be involved? Can the student be disciplined at all?" (Horton, 1999, p. 30).

Disciplining students with disabilities is difficult. A principal often deals with two discipline procedures: one for students in general education and one for students with disabilities. The reauthorization of IDEA in 1997 contained statutory requirements for discipline for the first time. These policies provided due process and other safeguards designed to prevent children with disabilities from being suspended or expelled if the behavior in question was a manifestation of their disability. However, "about 27 percent of principals reported that a separate discipline policy for special education students is unfair to the regular student population, and 20 percent reported that the discipline procedures for IDEA are burdensome and time-consuming" (United States General Accounting Office, 2001, p. 7). However, this report also stated that special-education students are being disciplined in the same manner as their nondisabled peers. A dual discipline system holds students in special education to a different standard and is often perceived as unfair and discriminatory.

College Issues

ISSUES: How are issues for college students different from those in earlier grades? What are the risks that college students face as a result of binge drinking? What can be done to reduce date rape? How should schools respond to binge drinking, date rape, and other student issues?

The problems in educating our youth are not confined to their formative years. Binge drinking and date rape are social issues experienced primarily by college-aged students. College-aged students with disabilities continue to face issues of accommodations, specifically in the area of testing. Likewise, funding continues to influence decisions at the level of higher education. Ultimately, funding may determine who gets into colleges and universities.

Binge Drinking

"The new college year was barely underway in 1998 when…a fraternity member at Illinois was discovered…dead as a result of what is believed to be alcohol overdose, a result of binge drinking.…

"An intoxicated Cornell University student fell down a gorge and died. At Michigan State University, a birthday celebration turned tragic after a student down[ed] two dozen shots of booze. A Pennsylvania State University student was found clinging to life on her 21st birthday, her blood-alcohol level nearly seven times Pennsylvania's intoxication limit.

"Although statistics indicate that college drinking is down from a decade ago, several recent studies show that binge drinking—five or more drinks in one sitting for men, four for women—remains a serious problem" (College Binge Drinking Kills, 1999).

These grim statistics about college drinking were reported in 1999 by About.com, available at http://alcoholism.about.com/library/weekly/aa990922.htm (College Binge Drinking Kills, 1999). Others found similar statistics, including Walsh-Sarnecki (1999) and William Sederberg (cited in "Binge drinking high on campuses," 1999). Sederberg, president of Ferris State University in Big Rapids, Michigan, authorized a survey of 600 Michigan young adults ages 17 through 24 between April 15 and 26, 1999, following the deaths of two of their students from drinking and two deaths on other Michigan campuses (Walsh-Sarnecki, 1999). The poll (completed by telephone) reported that "nearly half of Michigan's college students engage in binge drinking" (p. 2). The survey results revealed that binge drinking is more common among college students than among non-college-aged young adults, among men than among women, and among infrequent churchgoers than among those who attend church frequently.

Wechsler (2000) conducted a college alcohol study and reported similar findings. The proportion of students who binge-drink remained consistent from 1993 to 1999; however, the most extreme form of binge drinking increased from 20% to 23%. Wechsler also reported that the number of abstainers increased from 15% to 19% during the same period. Male binge drinkers

typically began binge-drinking in high school. Alcohol abuse on college campuses was linked to fraternities, sororities, and intercollegiate athletics. Young women who binge-drink put themselves at risk for sexual assault. Other risks included a greater chance of vandalizing others' property, poor academic performance, dropping out of college, death by alcohol poisoning, car accidents, drowning, falls, and fights.

Why has this epidemic spread across our country's college campuses, and what can be done to help students find more constructive ways to release stress and cope with life? Most college students are away from home for the first time. They may be forming their own identity and deciding whether they will adopt their parents' value systems, but why should that lead them to drink excessively? Why do college students succumb to peer pressure to do things they wouldn't necessarily do alone or at home? Does parenting matter? Recently, thought has been changing about the influence of parents versus the influence of peers. In an article by Judith Rich Harris in *Psychological Review* (1995), she posits that the influence of peers might be much more than that of parents.

Binge drinking and surrender to negative peer influences are symptoms of a deeper issue: many young adults lack resiliency. Resiliency can be defined as "the ability to bend but not break." It enables us to stand firm for our values, yet be flexible to new ideas.

Are educators more than purveyors of information? Should they also participate in helping their students develop strength of character? Many educators attending recent National Education Association meetings think so, as noted in the following resolution: "The Association also believes that public education is the cornerstone of our social, economic, and political structure and is of utmost significance in the development of our moral, ethical, spiritual, and cultural values" (http://www.nea.org/annualmeeting/raaction/images/resolutions2005-2006.pdf, n.d.). Educators are charged with the responsibility of helping to prepare productive citizens. Educators must find ways to help students become more resilient to negative influences, especially from their peers.

Date Rape

"Alcohol has been the 'date rape drug' of choice for years. Now there are some 'new' drugs out on the market which are being used for date rape. These drugs really aren't new, they're just being used in some 'new' ways. These drugs are Rohypnol…and GHB, or gamma-hydroxy butyrate acid. They're used to 'spike' unsuspecting victim's [sic] drinks" (p. 1).

This warning, quoted on the Rape and Sexual Assault Homepage (http://www.raperesponseservices.com, n.d.), originated from a University of Maine flyer. Hughes and Sandler (1987, April) reported that alcohol and drugs are a significant factor in date rape. It was often too late for women to realize what was going on and respond after drinking too much or taking too many drugs. It was also reported that 60% of the victims knew their sexual assailants, and the majority of victims were women between the ages of 15 and 25 years old. The authors identified four key elements of date rape: socialization, miscommunication, changing sexual mores, and a lack of consideration for a woman's rights and wishes.

College women are at great risk for date rape, especially when they drink. Date rape occurs on virtually all campuses and cannot always be prevented; but the more students know, the more likely they will be to avoid situations where it might occur.

Koss, Gidyez, and Wisniewski (1987) are the authors of the benchmark study that brought statistics about the prevalence of rape among college women to the public. They reported that 15% of college women had been raped during their one-year study. Currently, women ages 16 through 19 have the highest risk of being victimized, and women ages 20 through 24 are in the second-highest risk group (Bureau of Justice Statistics, 1995). Berkowitz (1992) reported that 25% to 60% of college men have participated in "some form of sexually coercive behavior" (p. 165).

Synovitz and Byrne (1998) have identified three behaviors that differentiate victims from nonvictims: having a higher number of lifetime sexual partners, dressing provocatively, and drinking alcohol during or before a date. Having a high number of sexual partners increases a woman's chances of being victimized. Dressing provocatively may contribute to the miscommunication between the victimized woman and the man who misreads her intentions. Provocative dress may communicate "yes" when the woman says "no!" And, once again, alcohol was identified as increasing a woman's vulnerability by decreasing her inhibitions and mental alertness.

Perceptions of the Educational System

ISSUES: How would you perceive the educational system in your country? How does it compare to countries around you? What rights should parents versus the state have in choosing their child's educational experience? Should school become privatized?

"When the Perchemlides family moved from Boston to Amherst, Massachusetts, in 1976, they enrolled their son, Peter, age seven, in second grade. The well-educated parents wanted their 'free, confident child' to have a rewarding educational experience. However, to their great disappointment, Peter became 'shy, unsure, self-conscious, and discouraged over academic achievement by the end of the year.' During the first half of the school year both parents tried to contribute to the school by serving on the parents' council. Finally they resigned

as they felt that the school system did not provide for parental input for discussion regarding school plans. The next September they presented a home education plan to principal Frizzle. The request was denied. The parents filed a lawsuit and after a year of litigious battle, the court ordered the school committee to review the request again" (Bumstead, 1979).

Bumstead (1979) cited the preceding case when compulsory attendance laws were challenged in the state of Massachusetts by nonreligious parents who chose to home-school their son. The court concluded that the parents' alternative form of education should exempt their son from the compulsory attendance statute (Lyman, 1998). Other parents began to choose home-schooling and other alternative educational options when their dissatisfaction with the public school system increased during the 1960s and 1970s. Growing dissatisfaction with the public system and increased accountability measures have caused parents and policy makers to seek reform measures that would provide the best and quickest results for their children. In the 33rd annual Phi Delta Kappan/Gallup Poll (Rose & Gallup, 2001), 51% of Americans said they have a lot of confidence in public schools as an institution; the other 49% said they lack confidence. However, it appears the public school system has come full circle when available educational choices included private schools, parochial schools, public schools, and home-schooling. In reality, these choices have always been part of the American educational system.

Dissatisfaction with public schools grew after *A Nation at Risk* was first published (Goldberg & Harvey, 1983). This controversial document brought the questionable performance of public schools to light and called for reform. The quest for school reform placed increasing demands on educational institutions. Public schools were confronted with accountability while challenged to educate a changing student population: 20% of their children came from poverty (this ratio was even higher in inner cities and minority populations), 25% lived in single-parent households, and the percentage of working mothers doubled (Greenwald, Laine, & Hedges, 1996).

The Center for Education Reform (2000) reported strong disapproval for the public educational system and strong support for school choice from a 1997 survey. "Seventy-eight percent of those polled did not believe that 'children, especially in the inner cities, are receiving the education they need'" (p. 1).

Demitchell (1997) observed that the wave of educational reforms implemented since the release of *A Nation at Risk* occurred through legal initiatives, including federal and state laws, school board policies, and court decisions. He estimated that 700 state laws were passed to meet the first wave of accountability reform and the second wave of professionalism. He concluded that educational goals can best be achieved not by passing laws or filing lawsuits, "but by maintaining high

standards for the people who work in our schools, by putting the interests of children above that of adult special-interest groups, and by becoming more involved in efforts to improve the overall welfare of children in our society. Reform is too important to be left to legal mechanisms" (p. 30).

Glenn (1998) summarized the public school choices that historically have been available to parents. The first school-choice option was based on residency; parents bought houses in "good" school districts. It was less costly for middle-income families to purchase high-priced homes than to pay private school tuition. Low-income families were unable to choose schools based on residency. Ultimately, families with incomes over $50,000 had the most school choices available to them. In 1993, 72% had enrolled their children in private schools, magnet schools, or schools based on residency. In fact, "contrary to a widespread impression, it is the public schools in affluent suburbs, not the private schools (except for prestigious prep schools), that represent the elite option in American education" (p. 10). It is more affordable for some parents to choose non-public schools than to purchase a house in an expensive community.

The choices for educating our children have evolved, but they have not changed. The options still include public schools, private schools, parochial schools, and home-schooling. However, the range of these choices has changed, and the gray areas created by their overlap are uncomfortable for many. Public school options include intradistrict, interdistrict, magnet schools, charter schools, and alternative schools (Cookson & Schroff, 1997). Private school options include private schools, parochial schools, and home-schooling. New options include charter and alternative schools, privatization of schools, vouchers, and tax credits.

Charter schools, sponsored by a public school body, can hire their own teachers and develop their own academic program and are held to a minimum accountability standard (Kolderie, 1998). In comparing charter schools to private schools, Buechler (1997) concluded that if they do not attract students, they will fail. However, unlike private schools, charter schools have to follow some public school procedures. They may not exclude students, charge tuition, or have a religious focus. Most states have charter schools at this time, but the success of such schools has not yet been evaluated. **Alternative schools** were created within the public school system for at-risk students—those at risk for dropping out of school. These schools were established in an effort to reduce the financial burden that results from a high dropout rate.

Privatization programs extend the current practice of hiring vendors for specific services, such as food service, custodial work, and transportation. What is new in this area is the movement of private business into the field of education in order to make a profit. Buchen (1999) explained the attraction for the private sector to enter into the educational market: 1) education is a $600 billion industry; 2) despite efforts to reform itself, "education has received such bad press that confidence in the established system is low" (p. 38); and 3) education is "there for the taking" (p. 38). The jury is still out regarding the effectiveness of for-profit schools.

Abbott (1997) observed that no child in Western society spends more than 20% of his or her time in a classroom. Schooling does not take place solely in educational institutions because children learn everywhere. A lot of "schooling" takes place at home, and home-schooling has, again, become another viable option for parents to consider. In fact, the National Center for Education Statistics (2001) reported that approximately 1.7% of U.S. students ages 5 to 17 were home-schooled in the spring of 1999. Most of these students were white and from households whose parents had higher levels of education than parents of students who were not home-schooled. The three main reasons that parents say they choose home-schooling are religious grounds, a poor learning environment at schools, and the parents' ability to provide a better education.

Vouchers evoke the most emotional response from policy makers, educators, and parents. Vouchers are cash certificates that allow students to attend any school of their choice and may be redeemed at public or private schools, depending upon the state's plan. Opponents of vouchers fear they may take much-needed funds away from public schools. Proponents are often policy makers seeking methods for holding public schools accountable through competition or minority parents who are looking for better and immediate opportunities for their children (Center for Education Reform, 2000).

The Center for Education Reform addressed the criticisms about school choice through an article entitled "Nine Lies about School Choice: Answering the Critics" (2000, September). Maralee Mayberry, in a paper presented at the American Educational Research Association meeting in 1991, suggested that "the decision to homeschool (or seek other forms of privatized education) represents a political response by people who perceive a threat in the current organization and content of public education" (cited in Aiex, 1994, p. 1). Ultimately, public schools fear losing more funding than they can afford, and this fear underlies most of the criticisms about school choice. Throughout the educational history of the United States, school choice has been an option for some parents, but making it available to all students is a new concept.

Conclusion

Currently, educators are primarily concerned with six major issues: 1) connection with the home and community for preparing productive citizens, 2) finances, 3) academic and technological tools to enhance learning, 4) school violence and discipline, 5) college-related problems, and 6) school choice through a historical and legal framework. The questions posed to this generation are difficult, and the answers are elusive. It is a difficult time to be a child.

Balancing budgets has always been a problem and will require careful strategic planning and prioritizing initiatives that most reflect the mission of the educational community. Both general education and special education face funding problems that will require creative financial solutions.

Academic issues involve the difficulties of applying research findings in the classroom and of approaching the educational needs of expanding minority populations. The use of technology can enhance learning, but integrating technology into the educational environment to maximize student learning is still a challenge to educators.

Violence in schools devastated families and schools during the 1990s. In searching for causes of school violence, educators uncovered an important underlying problem: the lack of connection to other people that some children experience. The need to develop resiliency—the ability to stand firm for values, yet be flexible to new ideas—was another student-centered issue that has emerged. In the face of increased violence, educators are concerned about appropriate discipline for students both in general education and in special education.

College students are not exempt from serious social issues. The prevalence of binge drinking and date rape are only two of the problems that students face today. At this time, programs have been created and implemented at the college level to prevent or resolve these problems, but the incidences of binge drinking and date rape are still on the rise.

School reform has been a slow and difficult process. The case of *Perchemledes vs. Frizzle* was one of the earliest opportunities to define educational environments other than formal schooling. The increase in home-schooling is one indicator of parents' lack of confidence in the public school system.

Examining issues in education has revealed the extreme complexity of the educational system in the United States. It is currently an educational system—built on federal, state, and local laws to educate all of our children—that has fallen short of its goal. A disparity exists between the quality of education received by children at the two ends of the socioeconomic scale. This gap exists in general education, special education, testing, discipline, technology, and school choice. Ironically, educators are beginning to realize that the very laws enacted to create many educational opportunities and accountability measures may actually be restricting reform and preventing improvement from occurring. Education policy makers, such as Goodlad and McMannon (1997) and Shor and Pari (1999), refer to Thomas Jefferson's message to educate the common people because education is the foundation of democracy and is essential to its endurance. Let us educate all of our students in the 21st century.

Response

A Look at Testing and Assessment

by Herbert W. Helm, Jr.

The fairness of tests and testing is a common topic in the field of education. From a historical standpoint, testing has created such social issues as the "six-hour retarded child." This phrase, coined in 1969 by the President's Committee on Mental Retardation, described children who were considered to be retarded for five days a week during the hours when they attended school. In this case, a child was considered retarded while in school, and the classification was the result of an IQ test. Not taken into consideration was the behavior of these children outside of school, which may have been considered adaptive for the community in which they lived. This has been called adaptive behavior.

Because of the type of testing administered at the time, larger numbers of minority students were being placed in special education categories, especially into that of mild mental retardation. This error was further exacerbated by the social restrictions on the roles in which citizens with mental retardation could participate. Efforts to address this issue have helped to bring about debate regarding the role of tests in decision-making, the fairness of tests per se, the types of tests that are fair, and even whether we should test at all. Questions arose: Did tests measure what they claimed? Were students being mislabeled as a result?

In a response of this length, it would be impossible to answer the preceding questions. The issues are further complicated by the sheer variety of opinions about what answers are appropriate. Therefore, I would like to consider here some of the foundational issues that people seldom address in their struggle with testing-related questions.

The perceived unfairness of testing procedures has led not only to debate, but also to litigation. In California, *Larry P. v. Riles* raised the issue of using IQ tests, allegedly culturally and racially biased, to put African American children into "dead-end" classes for the educable mentally retarded. In 1979, the judge ruled that the tests were biased, that they discriminated against African American children, and that the scores from these tests were not valid justification for placing African American students into stigmatizing, dead-end educational programs. Just one year later, the case of *PASE v. Hannon*, tried in Chicago, involved essentially the same issues, but the judge said the tests were not biased against African American children (Gregory, 1992). In these cases, two courts gave different judgments with similar arguments. Although we can never be sure of the fairness of the judgment or the judge's level of knowledge concerning assessment and its related issues, we can say one thing: the courts have reduced and limited the roles of testing and assessment, not expanded them.

Let's begin with the issue of test bias versus test fairness. The issue of test bias has its origins in the approximately 15-point discrepancy on standardized IQ tests between whites and African Americans (Gregory, 2004). This gap has traditionally resulted in more African American students being placed in special education, especially for mental retardation. Is this bias? To answer this question, we must address two others: What is test bias? What does not qualify as test bias?

The terms *test bias* and *test fairness* are often used interchangeably. However, they are very different and relate to different issues. Test bias is an objective statistical issue.

Test fairness is a subjective social issue that concerns how just or fair it is for society. (The statistical components are at best contributory.) Gregory (2004) defines test bias in this way: "*[T]est bias* refers to objective statistical indices that examine the patterning of test scores for relevant subpopulations. Although experts might disagree about nuances, on the whole there is a consensus about the statistical criteria that indicate when a test is biased....[A] test would be considered biased if the scores from appropriate subpopulations did not fall upon the same regression line for a relevant criterion" (p. 242).

A regression line helps to define the kind of relationship occurring between variables and is used to help predict that relationship. In our discussion, the relationship in question would be between the test scores and performance in school, as well as whether we could predict school performance based on those test scores. So "in an unbiased test a single regression line can predict performance equally well for all relevant subpopulations, even though the means for the different groups might differ" (Gregory, 2004, p. 244). Under this criterion, it does not matter whether African American students have a mean score 15 points below that of whites. What matters is whether a single regression line can predict equally or whether two separate lines—one for African Americans and one for whites—are required for prediction. If two regression lines (or two different lines of prediction) exist, you have bias.

Jensen (1981) has noted three aspects that are not adequate concepts of test bias. The first is the

egalitarian fallacy, which states that all groups and subgroups should have scores that fall equally on a test or trait being measured. The problem with this fallacy is that it is a social-equality belief, and there is no reason to assume that all groups or subgroups are equal on all elements. For example, on average, men are taller than women. This does not mean that something is wrong with the measuring stick or with trying to create a measuring stick that makes them equal; there simply are differences. The second concept is the *culture-bound fallacy*, which states that all items on a test must be equal for all cultural groups. This concept does not stand up to empirical evidence: "Biased tests or biased items simply cannot be identified by subjective impressions based on the external appearance of the test or item or on judgments of their culture loading" (Jensen, 1981, p. 130). The third concept is the *standardization fallacy*, which states that it is unfair to take a test "normed" on one group and then use it on another group for which it has not been normed. Again, this empirical question cannot just be declared so.

As mentioned earlier in this section, test fairness is a social issue. A test can meet the objective standards of test bias and still be judged unfair. The fairness of a test typically takes into account the group's social values and philosophy of testing. Here, testing decisions cannot be made using statistical values alone but must also take into account society's ethical values (Gregory, 2004). The placement of large numbers of a particular group (or subgroup) in what is considered a less desirable setting may not be acceptable to that subgroup or society.

Many Voices: An Introduction to Social Issues

Three common methods, each with a different underlying belief system, have been used to deal with testing. The first method is *establishing quotas*. The philosophy behind quotas is that society consists of a variety of groups and subgroups, each of which should have equal access to various institutions. For example, if the population of a state like Mississippi is 40% African American and 60% white, then the school systems (including higher education and special education) should have similar ratios. The second method is *unqualified individualism*, in which the "best" person is taken and nothing else is considered. Advocates of this method are unconcerned with race, gender, or school test scores. The philosophy behind unqualified individualism is like that of a sports team: If an individual is the best player and will help the team win, that is all that matters. However, although most people accept this philosophy for sports, many are less likely to accept it for such institutions as colleges. The third method is *qualified individualism*. This type of individualism comes from the philosophy that it is unethical to use such predictors as race and gender, even if they would be useful in prediction. Although this sounds admirable, it can result in a less accurate regression line (a line used for prediction), which in turn may lead to overprediction of some groups. This philosophy lies somewhere between those of quotas and unqualified individualism (Gregory, 2004). Although it is not my intention to say which philosophy I think is best, it should be noted that one's philosophical preference will affect which students are placed in various programs.

When test bias is being discussed, it is usually test fairness that is the actual issue. Often, this is why two judges can look at essentially the same arguments and come up with opposite rulings; they are each most likely using a different philosophy of fairness. Included in these decisions is usually the question of what constitutes intelligence, which is not easy to answer. Because intelligence is defined in a variety of ways, a variety of components are espoused. Two elements often mentioned in definitions of intelligence are the ability to learn from experience and the ability to adapt to the environment (Gregory, 2004). To ensure test fairness, we must decide what we expect students to learn from their experiences and how to measure adaptive behavior.

For the remainder of this response, we will look at three attempts to remedy some of the aforementioned issues: a redefinition of intelligence, the introduction of adaptive behavior, and the determination of what should appear on an IQ test. As noted in the chapter, Howard Gardner (1998) has a theory of multiple intelligences. He defines ten natural intelligences as linguistic, logical-mathematical, spatial, musical, bodily-kinesthetic, interpersonal, intrapersonal, naturalistic, spiritual, and existential. Although such a theory illustrates the complexity of intelligence, it does not indicate how the various intelligences should be measured or suggest why they would be better measurements for a school setting. For example, when deciding whether an individual has a learning disability, which is usually defined as a discrepancy between IQ and achievement, would measuring spiritual or existential intelligence be a

better way of gauging IQ than using a more traditional measurement? If so, why? These types of definitions do not attempt to explain the difference between such concepts as intelligence, skills, talents, and gifts. If everything is defined as intelligence, the concept of intelligence loses any distinctiveness. Should we equate the ability to play basketball with the ability to think logically? Should the discrepancy between body-kinesthetic abilities and achievement define a learning disability?

The concept and assessment of adaptive behavior was established in an effort to deal with the issue of the "six-hour retarded child." In the assessment of retardation, a test of adaptive behavior (that is, how well a person adapted to his or her environment) was administered, along with an IQ test. Two problems with measuring adaptive behavior are knowing what to assess and determining how to gauge it against real-world behavior. For example, how would you create a test that measures the adaptive behaviors of three very different students, such as an African American student living in Queens, a white student of Scandinavian descent living on a farm in northern Minnesota, and a professor's child enrolled in a school system in a city like Palo Alto? What behaviors or knowledge could a test contain that would show how each of these students had adapted to his or her environment? What would be fair?

The question of what should appear on an IQ test cannot adequately be answered here. However, the majority group, because it usually has more political power, has more decision-making clout on this issue. One role of schools is that of transmitting knowledge deemed important by society, something we might call its traditional knowledge. Those who control the flow of information have a larger say in what constitutes those traditions and knowledge. They can assert that some words, typically French-based, are considered part of a more intelligent vocabulary than others. This also partly explains how different judges can look at items on an IQ test and reach different conclusions: One judge might say that the items are common knowledge that all students should know while another judge believes that these items are culturally biased.

One question has yet to be addressed: Why do we engage in testing and assessment? Testing is a standardized method (meaning we treat each individual the same) that educators use to make decisions about the individual being tested. This method usually consists of obtaining a sample of the person's knowledge, behaviors, or both, and using it to assess the level of knowledge the student has achieved or to aid in predicting future performance. For example, you probably took the Iowa Tests of Basic Skills in elementary school to assess your level of achievement. Later, you probably took the SAT or ACT to help predict your performance in college. In summary, although standardized testing can be problematic, without it, each individual assessor might create his or her own standards, which would result in there being no standards at all.

We have addressed only a few of the issues in testing and assessment. However, it is hoped that you have begun to see the complexity of this social issue and the improbability of finding a simple answer that would satisfy all involved. We need to find answers that are both fair and unbiased. However, to date, attempts to create culturally fair tests have not succeeded.

Discussion Questions

1. Discuss the historical background of our educational system, including the role of the federal and state governments, and the relationship between church and state.
2. How should educators determine the "best practices" for teaching, and how should they be evaluated?
3. Testing is a controversial issue in education. Compare and contrast the current uses of testing. Consider issues regarding the reasons for testing, the types of tests used, and whether or not there is an equal representation of students who are tested. What have been the effects of testing? Do the results justify the expenditure?
4. How can we use technology to solve some of the problems in education? Explain how schools can keep up with the rapidly changing field of technology by preparing its students and teachers. Describe the use and effects of technology in educating students with disabilities.
5. Compare binge drinking and date rape, both college issues, by evaluating their causes and prevention measures.
6. Analyze the current school choices that parents have available to them, and explain the reason for school choice. Compare and contrast the school choices available today with the ones that were available during education's historical conception.
7. How do federal educational laws affect reform?

Related Readings

Glasser, W. (1969). *Schools without failure.* New York: Harper & Row.

Kozol, J. (1991). *Savage inequalities: Children in America's schools.* New York: Harper Collins.

Kralovec, E. (2003). *Schools that do too much: How schools waste time and money and what we can do about it.* Boston: Beacon Press.

O'Shea, L. J., O'Shea, D. J., & Algozzine, B. (1998). *Learning disabilities: From theory toward practice.* Columbus, OH: Merrill.

Popham, W. J. (2000). *Testing! Testing! What every parent should know about school tests.* Boston: Allyn & Bacon.

Related Web Sites

The American Council on Education: http://www.acenet.edu
The Chronicle of Higher Education: http://chronicle.com
Education Index: http://www.educationindex.com
Education Planet—The Education Web Guide: http://www.educationplanet.com
Education Virtual Library: http://www.csu.edu.au/education/library.html
Education Week on the Web: http://www.edweek.org
Education World: http://www.educationworld.com
Kathy Schrock's Guide for Educators: http://www.discoveryschool.com
National Center for Education Statistics: http://www.nces.ed.gov
National Education Association: http://www.nea.org
The Ten Best Web Sites for Educational Technology: http://www.fno.org/techtopten1.html
U.S. Department of Education: http://www.ed.gov

Related Movies/Videos

Bowling for Columbine (2002)
Dead Poets Society (1989) with Robin Williams
Mr. Holland's Opus (1996) with Richard Dreyfuss and Glenne Headly
Music of the Heart (1999) with Meryl Streep
The Ron Clark Story (2006) with Matthew Perry
Stand and Deliver (1988) with Edward James Olmos
To Sir, with Love (1967) with Sidney Poitier

MARRIAGE AND FAMILY

Susan E. Murray

6

Chapter Outline

Jeffrey and Tammy Mosser relate this experience:

In August 1995, Jeffrey Mosser, Jr., the second child of Tammy and Jeffrey Mosser, Sr., was diagnosed with acute myelogenous leukemia. Only eight years old, young Jeffrey underwent intensive chemotherapy between the time of the diagnosis and the following January. Mr. and Mrs. Mosser were determined to spend as much time with their son as possible. Mr. Mosser was fortunate to work as a building operator at a Philadelphia-area hospital in close proximity to the hospital where his son was receiving treatment. After spending all night with Jeffrey Jr. in his hospital room, Mr. Mosser would return during his half-hour morning break from work and again at lunch. When his work day ended at 4:30 P.M., he again attended to Jeffrey.

In May 1996, the Mosser family learned that Jeffrey had relapsed. He would again have to enter the hospital, but the doctors admitted that nothing more could be done beyond continued chemotherapy.

Mrs. Mosser, a nurse at a New Jersey hospital, learned of the Family and Medical Leave Act (FMLA) from a social worker at the hospital where her son was receiving treatment. She submitted a request for FMLA leave and was granted it. When her legally-guaranteed 12 weeks expired, her co-workers donated their own personal paid days. Mr. Mosser followed his wife's lead and was also granted FMLA leave. The Mossers spent the summer providing Jeffrey with as many experiences as possible, including trips to the New Jersey shore, the Pennsylvania Dutch country, and the Poconos to fish.

In January 1998, Jeffrey Jr. passed away. The Mossers greatly appreciate the time the FMLA allowed them to spend with their son during his last days of life. Mr. Mosser expresses his gratitude by saying, "It was a joy and a miracle to be home during that period. Being there for him was the best thing I could have done in the whole world" *(National Partnership on Work and Family, 2002).*

This example of one family's journey of caring for their ill son illustrates several things: the love of parents for their child, the ongoing responsibilities of parenting, how unexpected grief comes upon families, how illness affects a family's daily life, governmental policies that aim to protect families, and the enduring strength of one family.

Introduction

Some say the American family is in trouble. Some even say that the American family is disintegrating. Mary Catherine Bateson (2000), an author and anthropologist, believes that while the family is changing, it is not disappearing. She suggests that we have to broaden our understanding of the family and look for new metaphors. The goal of this chapter is to consider some of these important issues for American families.

Since September 11, 2001, the notion of family seems to extend to an ever-widening community embracing coworkers, friends, and even compassionate strangers. Family has been held as central in organizing cultures since the beginning of time. Today it may seem unnecessary to define "family," as almost everyone has one. But the meanings vary among groups and change over time.

Definitions have important consequences for policy decisions. Policies often determine what rights and obligations some legal and social institutions will recognize for family members (Benokraitis, 2002). While some definitions of family are based in theory, others come from the heart. Perhaps you are familiar with some of these definitions:

- A family is two or more persons living together and related by blood, marriage, or adoption (U.S. Bureau of Census, 2000).

- An intimate environment in which two or more people live together in a committed relationship, see their identity as importantly attached to the group, and share close emotional ties and functions (Nijole Benokraitis, 2002).
- A family is where, when you come home at night, they have to let you in.
- A family can be a group of people who simply define themselves as having feelings of love, respect, commitment, and responsibility to and identification with one another (Mary Ann Schwartz & BarBara Scott, 2000).
- It could be said that all marriages are families but not all families are marriages (J. Ross Eshleman, 1997).
- The family is the country of the heart (Giuseppe Mazzini, Italian nationalist leader).
- Happy or unhappy, families are all mysterious (Gloria Steinem).

Not everyone would agree with all of these definitions because they do not explicitly include legalized marriage, procreation, or child rearing. Some would say that definitions should emphasize affection and mutual cooperation.

In this chapter we will look not only at the theoretical perspectives for studying families, but at issues of love and commitment, dating and mate selection, single living, cohabitation and domestic partnerships, gay and lesbian relationships, marriage, and contemporary parenting. In considering the family-life cycle, issues for adult children and their aging parents are also studied. Work and family are explored in terms of macroeconomic changes, family dynamics, balance of time and schedules, and issues of equality. The chapter closes with a discussion of the challenges to and need for creating connected and sustainable families and the importance of commitment in couple and family relationships.

To begin, a discussion of the theories used to study families may assist you in building your beliefs and defining your values about family.

Theoretical Perspectives for Studying Families

ISSUES: Is it important to define what a family is, and why? What are the different perspectives on families and how do they affect roles and functions? On what elements should a family be based (e.g., love, economic security, stability for child raising)? What should be done if some of these elements conflict? How far should one be committed to a given family structure?

The way we look at and understand society and human behavior depends on our theoretical perspective. In sociology there is no one theory of marriages and families; many perspectives exist. Researchers use these theories to build their designs and explain their findings.

Several perspectives will be addressed, all of which are also more broadly used to explain how humans organize themselves. According to Schwartz and Scott (2000), sociologists use three basic perspectives: structural functionalism, conflict theory, and symbolic interaction. Also addressed will be social exchange theory, ecological theory, and developmental theory.

Structural functionalism views society as an organized and stable system and examines the relationships between the family and the larger society. Each structure meets one or several functions. Sociologist Talcott Parsons (1902–1979) was the leading proponent of the structural-functional perspective through the 1950s and into the 1960s (Benokraitis, 2002). Parsons and his colleagues believed that adult family tasks are best accomplished when spouses carry out distinct and specialized roles. These roles can be defined as instrumental and expressive.

The instrumental role is that of providing for the family and, at least theoretically, being hardworking, tough, and competitive. The expressive role provides the emotional support and nurturing qualities that sustain the family unit and support the instrumental role. Today we would recognize this form of family functioning as the **nuclear** or **traditional family**, which will be more fully discussed later in this chapter.

Family members may play other functional roles so as to preserve order, stability, and equilibrium. They provide emotional support and physical shelter, both of which can ensure the health and survival of individuals within the family. The structural functionalist perspective also recognizes that the family affects, and is affected by, other interrelated institutions such as the economy, politics, and laws.

Those relying on a structural-functionalist perspective are also interested in the intended, overt, or manifest functions as well as the unintended, unrecognized, or latent functions. A manifest function would be having children to add to marital satisfaction or to continue the family lineage; a latent function of having children might be a decreasing level of marital satisfaction because children can add stress to a relationship.

The perspective of **conflict theory** has become increasingly popular since the 1960s. Even though there are different approaches to conflict theory, all of them have their roots in the writings of Karl Marx (1818–1883). He did much to revolutionize social and philosophical thinking about human society and came to believe that problems lay in the social organization of industrial societies. From this perspective, marriages and families can be viewed as smaller versions of the larger class system, where the well-being of one class is the result of the exploitation and oppression of another class (Schwartz & Scott, 2000). Historically, women have been oppressed by men. Even though women in the United States are no longer legally defined as men's property, they still continue to have the major responsibility for child rearing and a major portion of housework, though most are in the work force today (Hochschild, 1997; Schwartz & Scott, 2000).

A major source of criticism about conflict theory is its underlying assumption that power is people's main objective and conflict is the major feature of social life. This implies a narrow view of human behavior. Also,

whereas structural functionalists evaluate a system's social patterns in terms of whether they are positive or negative, conflict theorists are purposely critical of society. However, this can be a useful framework when considering how factors such as race, class, gender, age, and ethnicity are linked to unequal distribution of valuable resources (e.g., power, property, money, prestige, and education) in marriages and families.

Unlike structural functionalism and conflict theories, which focus on the large-scale or macro systems, **symbolic interaction theory** focuses on the small-scale or micro patterns of individuals' interaction with one another. This theory looks at subjective, interpersonal meanings and at the ways in which we interact with and influence each other. We do this by communicating through words, gestures, sounds, objects, and events. These are sometimes referred to as symbols, and our symbols must have shared meanings or agreed-upon definitions. Benokraitis (2002) suggests that one of the most important shared meanings is the definition of the situation—that is, the way we perceive reality and react to it. We learn our definitions of a situation through interaction with the significant others in our lives (parents, friends, relatives, and teachers).

Born in 1926, the late family sociologist Ernest Burgess (1948) wrote of the family as a changing society and suggested that the patterns of family life were numerous and varied. Rather than speaking of the American *family* in one **homogeneous** term, he preferred to speak of *families* in the context of a changing entity in the place of a stable one. He held that the family represents a united set of interacting individuals. Unity in family life, therefore, arises because of the interactions among the various family members.

Thus, symbolic interactionism addresses both issues—socialization and social interaction—that are of central concern to the family. It offers a specific theoretical perspective and a rare methodological orientation that focuses on individual social interactions in the real world.

Social exchange or social choice theory rests on the belief that humans attempt to make choices that they expect will maximize their rewards and/or minimize their costs. For example, work, gifts, cards, affection, and ideas are given in hopes of getting something in return. **Social exchange theory** has reflected two differing schools of thought, represented best by George Homans and Peter Blau. Homans (1961) is recognized as the initiator of exchange theory, the concept that humans react to stimuli on the basis of need, reward, and reinforcement. In other words, he focused on actual behavior that is rewarded or punished by the behavior of others. Blau (1964) differed in believing that not all exchange is explained in terms of actual behavior, but is more subjective and interpretive.

A good example of Blau's ideas can be seen in various interracial relationships. An interracial couple might find their relationship mutually beneficial and satisfying, with the benefits outweighing the costs. But social approval of the relationship may be very important to the couple; so if family and friends strongly disapprove, the couple might decide to terminate the relationship. But both Homans and Blau agreed that it is important that each party in the exchange receives something perceived as equivalent to what is given. Family literature is filled with many examples of social exchange. For instance, in arranged marriages, especially in nonindustrialized or traditional societies, labor, gifts, or a bride price are often exchanged for the right to marry (Eshleman, 1997; Schwartz & Scott, 2000).

Social exchange theory shares many of the assumptions of symbolic-interaction theory, and in broad terms is an extension of it. Family sociologists have long used exchange theory to explain dating, mating, and marital behaviors. On the other hand, exchange theory assumes that people are rational and that they consciously weigh the pros and cons (costs versus benefits) of a relationship. But we do not always react rationally (it is even difficult to agree on what defines rational behavior). Perhaps exchange theory is most valuable for explaining people's actions when we want to know and understand the details of their behavior.

When we hear or read the word "ecological," we often think of the study of plants and animals, and how we relate to the earth. But in sociology, **ecological theory** addresses human groups, such as families, in terms of how they adapt to their physical environment. The earliest studies in the United States were conducted from the early 1920s to the late 1940s by sociologists at the University of Chicago. Using the neighborhoods in Chicago as their laboratory, they observed how communities and individuals changed because of urbanization, industrialization, and immigration. Today the University of Chicago is among several universities that offer undergraduate and graduate programs in ecological-community psychology (Council of Program Directors in Community Research and Action, 2001).

Psychologist Urie Bronfenbrenner's work has been important in the field of developmental science. He has been involved in laying out the implications and applications of developmental theory. He has been instrumental in communicating—through articles, lectures, and discussions—the findings of developmental research to undergraduate students, the general public, and decision-makers in the private and public sectors. Bronfenbrenner has also played an active role in the design of developmental programs in the United States and elsewhere. He is one of the founders of Head Start. His widely published contributions have won him honors and distinguished awards at home and abroad. He holds six honorary degrees, three from European universities (Bronfenbrenner, n.d.).

Bronfenbrenner (1979) developed an ecological model of human development. His view is that we are shaped by both the immediate and remote environments (the macrosystem and the microsystem). The ecosystem consists of settings or events that people do not experience directly but that affect their development, such as job flexibility, adequacy of child care, and availability of health services. Any programs for families or individuals within families must take into consideration not only the dynamics of the specific family, but those of the neighborhood and broader community. All of these factors affect the family and the individuals within it. Thus, the major concerns are how family roles and the environmental setting are interrelated and how families can allocate and manage responses to meet their needs (Benokraitis, 2002). Klein and White (1996) point out that while ecological theory explains how growth comes about because of changes in the environment, it does not explain decay or disintegration, which is inevitable in human life.

Developmental theory examines the many ways families change over time. The family life cycle consists of the transitions that a family makes through a series of stages and events. Evelyn Mills Duvall wrote more than twenty books on family development. In 1957 she first published her family life cycle model. It has been the most widely used developmental view. As defined by the original theory, families were formed through marriage, had and reared children, moved to the empty nest, then to retirement, and eventually to death. Each step built upon the previous stage, and life went on. However, distinguishing a "typical" life cycle

Many Voices: An Introduction to Social Issues

is near to impossible, as we now know that issues such as poverty, racial and ethnic issues, and the diversity of family types in our society today mean no family is typical.

The life cycle model, though, gives us important insights into the complexities of family life and the tasks of individuals at various points in time. For example, it can assist researchers and practitioners as they seek to understand and alleviate family stress. Another example is that policy makers could be more sensitive to the needs of families at different stages of development, based on developmental theory (Klein & White, 1996).

Systematic theory construction in **family sociology** did not begin until around 1950, and work from 1950 to 1966 centered on the effort to develop coherent conceptual frameworks. For the next ten years there was great effort in developing theories. Since 1976, the field has become theoretically and methodologically pluralistic, moving toward more interpretive and critical approaches (Klein & White, 1996). Today, researchers and practitioners often combine several of these perspectives to interpret data or decide on intervention strategies. Other theoretical frameworks such as family systems and feminist theory are also employed. Understanding the theories used to study families can help us understand specific issues in marriage and family.

Love and Commitment

ISSUES: What is love? What is commitment? Is it possible to sustain a healthy life-long relationship today? Is it worth the work? What is the role or function of dating? Why are more people choosing a single lifestyle? Why do people choose cohabitation over marriage? What elements strengthen, or destroy, marriages? What should be the role of parents? Why do you think more couples are choosing to be childless? How does having or not having children affect a couple's relationship? How should couples decide what type of discipline to use with their children? What is the effect of the current pace of society on children? What should an adult child's responsibility be toward his or her parents?

Love means many different things to people. The media sends powerful messages about love. A classic TV commercial reminded us that as Americans we "love" baseball, apple pie, and Chevrolets! We all long for love in our lives; yet we can be hurt by it, addicted to it, and enriched by it. But what is it? Books have been written on it. Some people have spent their lives attempting to define love; others spend entire lifetimes searching for it. For the purposes of this study, we begin with some inspirational, clever, and sometimes humorous definitions of love:

- I like not only to be loved, but to be told I am loved. *George Eliot*
- The supreme happiness of life is the conviction of being loved for yourself, or more correctly, being loved in spite of yourself. *Victor Hugo*

- Romance is built on illusion, and when we love someone, we love the illusion they have created for us. *Anonymous*
- Love is like an hourglass, with the heart filling up as the brain empties. *Jules Renard*
- A kiss, when all is said, what is it? A rosy dot placed on the "I" in loving. *Edmond Rostand*
- Loving relationships are a family's best protection against the challenges of the world. *Bernie Wiebe*
- Our heart caves in not because we have lost love, but because we have temporarily stopped loving. *John Gray*
- When two people are under the influence of the most violent, most insane, most delusive, and most transient of passions, they are required to swear

that they will remain in that excited, abnormal, and exhausting condition continuously until death do them part. *George Bernard Shaw*

- What Women Want: To be loved, to be listened to, to be desired, to be respected, to be needed, to be trusted, and sometimes, just to be held. What Men Want: Tickets for the World Series. *Dave Barry*
- Love is not the dying moan of a distant violin; it's the triumphant twang of a bedspring. *S. J. Perelman*
- The first duty of love is to listen. *Paul Tillich*
- Never part without loving words to think of during your absence. It may be that you will not meet again in this life. *Jean Paul Richte*
- Platonic love is love from the neck up. *Thyra Winslow*

In a more serious tone, Olson and DeFrain (2000) make a broader suggestion: "Love and friendship bind society together, providing both emotional support and a buffer against stress and thereby preserving our physical and psychological health" (p. 122). While love in families and friendships binds us together, love can be the outcome of dating and is an important part of mate selection in American culture.

Dating and Mate Selection

Dating, as we know it today, is a practice that developed in the last hundred years in the United States. Before 1900, a century-old system of courtship that had its roots in Europe was practiced in the United States. Until that time, the term "dating" was not even used. Unfortunately, the information that we have tends to be about the practices of the rich and affluent in society, while little is known about the courtship of the poor, as they left few diaries and letters (Cherlin, 2002). However, from what we do know, love, a distrusted emotion to count on in selecting a spouse in earlier times, became more and more favored. Today it is the primary reason for courtship continuing into marriage.

When children lived with or close to their parents, and most social encounters were in groups, parents had an active role in selecting mates for their children. But as people migrated from rural areas (and from overseas) to cities, changes occurred in social and economic domains, such as higher standards of living and a longer adolescence. People had more and more opportunities to meet prospective spouses and make their own choices, even though parents might disagree with their

decisions. In a sense, dating created a power shift from parents to adolescents that is evident in other areas of family living today.

Dating serves several purposes. It provides recreation and companionship; it can be romantic, exciting, and fun. But it is also a serious enterprise. It is usually a step in mate selection. It is an activity in which people learn to socialize and to adapt and adjust their behavior in different situations. Dating also provides social status, fulfills ego needs, and offers opportunities for sexual experimentation and intimacy (Benokraitis, 2002).

Benokraitis describes the dating process as a "*marriage market*, in which prospective spouses compare the assets and liabilities of eligible partners and choose the best available mate" (p. 165, italics added). She suggests that in this sense everyone has a "market value," and whom a person "trades" with depends on the resources each one brings to the exchange. As people have different goals, their objectives differ. The marriage market analogy is an example of social-exchange theory.

Dating can be disappointing and even harmful to individuals. Issues of power, manipulation, and control become apparent in dating relationships; they are danger signs too often ignored in the quest for an intimate relationship. In a cartoon in *Upscale Magazine* (cited in Benokraitis, 2002), a woman says to her friend, "Mine was a marriage of convenience. I wanted desperately to get married and Hank was convenient." There are many bad jokes about relationships between men and women, and these subtly affect individuals' views of love, dating, and marriage.

A wise person will be attentive to ongoing issues. Some examples are an absence of shared basic beliefs and values, personality issues, substance use and abuse, and other compulsive/addictive behaviors. The list of potential problems goes on: few areas of common interest, ineffective communication (which would include frequent arguments and/or avoidance of sensitive issues), jealousy or suspicion, serious emotional disturbances in one's partner, financial irresponsibility, and a lack of inner peace about the relationship.

It is important to be realistic, yet positive, in our quest for love and companionship. David Olson, researcher and developer of several instruments used to measure couples' views of their relationships, has found several attributes of relationships to be highly predictive of couples' marital satisfaction. Couples who reported satisfaction in their relationship on a premarital inventory also reported satisfaction later on in marriage. According to Olson's research (Olson, Russell, & Sprenkle, 1989; Olson & DeFrain, 2000), "Happy premarital couples—who generally become happily married couples—are those who:

- Are realistic about the challenges of marriage.
- Communicate well.
- Resolve conflicts well.
- Feel good about the personality of their partner.
- Agree on religious and ethical issues.
- Have equalitarian role relationships.
- Have a good balance of individual and joint leisure activities" (Olson & DeFrain, 2000; pp. 376–377).

While many people choose the marriage option, many choose single living.

Single Living

The number of single adults in the United States increased from 10.9 million in 1970 to over 26.5 million in 1999—25% of all U.S. households (U.S. Bureau of Census, 2000). These figures represent a significant shift in adult living patterns, reflecting a change in societal attitudes in the United States. Some reasons are these:

- people marrying at a later age
- emphasis on advanced education
- an increase in people choosing not to marry at all
- an increase in couples who live together without marrying
- the current divorce rate
- women placing career objectives ahead of marriage
- women not depending on marriage for economic stability

Although single living has become more acceptable in our society, and single people can enjoy the benefits of growth and independence, most people still choose to enter into a long-term relationship with a partner. Cherlin (2002) suggests that the decline of lifelong marriage as the organizing principle of families has created important changes in the nature of kinship. Kinship used to be easy and automatic, coming into the relationship in the form of extended families and blood relationships. Today singles must sometimes create their own kinship networks with people whom they regard and from whom they find support. Yet "created kinship" presents challenges. It requires continual attention to maintain, whereas relations of blood and marriage are supported by strong social norms.

It has been said that men's classic strategy for support has been to marry and let their wives keep up ties with relatives. The strategy worked well for men as long as most were married for life. With the rise in divorce, and childbearing outside marriage, men often become disconnected from kin. They may be isolated unless they remarry, be distant from their adult children, and be unable to forge links with other kin (Cherlin, 2002).

Cohabitation, in which unmarried couples live together, has been a source of concern and controversy in the United States. While we have historically depended on related kin, today many individuals are creating a sense of "kin" with non-relatives.

Cohabitation

Cohabitation statistics first appeared in the 1990 census. Figures reveal that by 1999 unmarried couples living together in the United States numbered 4.5 million (U.S. Bureau of Census, 2000). In the 1960s, cohabitation was common mainly among the poor and near poor. For many, it served as an acceptable substitute for legal marriage. But beginning around 1970, the proportion of all young adults who lived with partners prior to marriage increased sharply to 1.5 million. Today, cohabitation is most common among adults in their mid-twenties, with about 25% of this age group living together (Waite & Joyner, 2001).

Cohabitation is defined as the sharing of a household by unmarried persons who have a sexual relationship (Cherlin, 2002). Cohabitation has blurred the boundaries between marriage and single living; yet it has distinct characteristics. Compared to married counterparts, those living together have fewer traditional gender-role attitudes, less desire to have children, and more equity in doing household tasks. Cohabiting women have partners with less or as much education as they do, but husbands are likely to be more educated than their wives (Blackwell & Lichter, 2000).

Though cohabiting couples have less desire to have children than do their married counterparts, a surprising number of cohabiting couples do have children. According to the March 2000 U.S. Census, 40.9% of unmarried partners had children present in the home, as compared to 45.6% of married couples (Fields & Casper, 2001). About 40% of the births listed in official statistics as occurring outside of marriage are births to cohabiting couples. In recent years, most of the rise in childbearing outside marriage has been the result of births to cohabiting couples rather than births to women living alone (Bumpass & Lu, 1998).

Cherlin (2002) suggests that this transformation in living arrangements has technological, economic, and cultural roots. The technological change is improvement in birth control; economic changes include women investing more time and effort in establishing job skills and experience, thus resulting in a later age of marriage. Oppenheimer (cited in Cherlin, 2002) suggests that the stagnant earning prospects for young men may encourage some to cohabit rather than marry, for it involves less commitment and responsibility. The cultural change involves the greater acceptance and practice of sex outside marriage and the reduced moral stigma of living with a partner without marrying. Oppenheimer further states that happiness in marriage is now culturally defined more in terms of individual satisfaction and less in terms of how well one performs roles as parent or spouse, an ethic that lends itself to cohabitation.

Two major perspectives on the meaning of cohabitation can be identified as cohabitation as a substitute for marriage, and cohabitation as part of the marriage process (Cherlin, 2002). If cohabitation were truly seen as a substitute for marriage, we could expect to see more long-term cohabitation relationships and more individuals who never marry but do cohabit one or more times during their lives. Bumpass and Lu (1998) find that half of all cohabiting relationships last only a year or less, and only one out of ten lasts as long as five years. For some African Americans, cohabitation may be more of a substitute for marriage, as black women who cohabit are much less likely to marry than are white women (Manning & Smock, 1995; Brien, Lillard, & Waite, 1997).

Cherlin (2002) suggests that in terms of the marriage process, women may use cohabitation as a way of determining whether their male partners will be steady wage earners and whether they will share the work at home.

Domestic Partnerships

Couples and other individuals who have long-term committed relationships and share a home and household duties have become increasingly noticed in American society in the past three decades. The term by which unmarried partners in relationship have come to be known is "domestic partners."

These relationships challenge the traditional view of the family and traditional family law, and they produce a collection of novel legal issues in numerous situations: 1) the distribution of property or the custody of children upon dissolution of the partners' relationship; 2) the relationship of one partner with the other's family members upon the death or disability of the other partner; and 3) the resolution of disputes with third parties (for example, when one partner seeks benefits traditionally accorded to married couples or when a creditor attempts to hold one partner liable for the other partner's debts) (Fowlkes, 1994).

In response to pressure from gay rights advocates and other concerned parties, some cities and businesses have begun to recognize such partnerships by passing municipal domestic partner legislation and developing corporate benefits programs for domestic partners (Amer et al., 1992; Gewertz, 1994).

Gay and Lesbian Relationships

Just after midnight on Sunday, April 1, 2001, six men and two women became the first same-sex couples to be legally married anywhere in the world. The ceremony took place in the Netherlands, which opened the institution of marriage to gays and lesbians. Other countries such as Belgium, Spain, and Canada have also since decided to allow same-sex marriages (Demian, 2005; Johnston, 2005; Roman, 2005).

Of course, the European decisions have not seemed to have any legal impact in the United States, where there has been debate over adding amendments to the Constitution to restrict gay and lesbian marriage. The United States currently allows states to decide their own policies concerning same-sex marriages. Same-sex marriage legislation has been passed in Massachusetts, same-sex civil unions are allowed in Connecticut and Vermont, and domestic partnerships are legal in California. However, even in these states, further gay and lesbian demands have been checked, as seen in California Governor Arnold Schwarzenegger's veto of a Religious Freedom and Civil Marriage Protection Act, thereby continuing limits for same-sex couples in California (Curtis, 2005; Equality for All, 2005). Some same-sex couples from the United States have begun moving to other countries, such as Canada, where same-sex marriage is allowed, in order to have the legal rights afforded to married partners (Same Sex Marriage in Canada, n.d.). There is no question whether gay and lesbian marriage is a hot topic in civil rights and human sexuality.

Often issues of homosexuality are discussed in terms of sexuality. As cultural beliefs and attitudes about sexuality have changed, so have some beliefs and attitudes about gay and lesbian relationships. Social scientists have been studying homosexual couples only since the late 1970s, and early research tended to focus on individual sexual orientation and behavior. Early research emphasized the sexual component of homosexual relationships and ignored other dimensions, such as love and commitment. Even today, much of the information available is based on nonrepresentative samples and is therefore subject to bias (Shehan & Kammeyer, 1997).

Gay and lesbian couples feel as strongly about their own relationships as heterosexual couples do about theirs. A major social concern has been the effects on children of living with or having homosexual parents. While space does not allow for a full discussion of gay and lesbian relationships and families, it is important that you gather legitimate information rather than accept stereotypes and myths that surround gay and lesbian individuals, couples, and families. Often, to "come out" means saying "good-bye" to one's family. This is particularly difficult, as homosexuals love their families and generally want to continue being an active part of their immediate and extended families. It is important to remember that once you learn that someone is homosexual, that person is still the same person you knew and enjoyed before you knew of his or her sexual orientation.

Marriage

After considering the lifestyle choices above, it is important to study the institution of marriage. In our society, marriage generally grows out of a dating relationship and a continuing commitment to another person. While the concept of marriage may seem simple, it is full of paradoxes. Though most people want to get married and assume their marriage will last a lifetime, few couples prepare themselves in any meaningful way for marriage (Olson & DeFrain, 2000). Montaigne, one of the greatest intellectuals of 16th-century Europe, is quoted as saying, "It [marriage] happens as with cages: The birds without despair to get in, and those within despair of getting out" (Wikipedia, n.d.a).

Here are some other thoughts on marriage to consider:

- Marriage is a shared stroll of two living souls. *Neuenschwander*
- Marriage is the beautiful blending of two lives, two loves, two hearts. It's the wonderful, mystical moment when a beautiful love story starts. *Unknown*
- Marriage is the alliance of two people, one of whom never remembers birthdays and the other who never forgets. *Ogden Nash*
- A good marriage is the union of two good forgivers. *Ruth Bell Graham*
- Marriage is an unconditional commitment to the total person for total life. *H. Norman Wright*

Marriage is found in every society throughout history. In Western society we have had our own marriage ideals. Marriage used to be a necessity. It legitimized a relationship. It represented sexual and emotional exclusivity and assumed monogamy. People didn't necessarily marry for love. They married in order to have an acceptable place in society, to provide a legitimate environment for having and rearing children, and to carry on societal values. This perspective was followed by a more romantic view of marriage. The old saying, "First comes love, then comes marriage, then comes Baby in a baby carriage," reflected the way many did it. But now people hold even higher expectations for personal happiness and desire passionate companionship in a time when marriages are dissolving, either by separation or divorce.

Linda Waite, a professor of sociology, and Maggie Gallagher, a nationally syndicated columnist and director of the Marriage Program at the Institute of American Values, are authors of *The Case for Marriage* (2000). They make a compelling defense of what historically many in our country have defined as a sacred union. Waite and Gallagher attack the anti-marriage movement and propose that marriage brings many benefits to individuals—emotional, physical, economic, and sexual—and that these in turn benefit society. While their book is not one of moral exhortation, these authors argue that marriage, in order to do its beneficial work, must be treated as a socially preferred option. "In America over the last thirty years, we've done something unprecedented. We have managed to transform marriage, the most basic and universal of human institutions, into something controversial" (p. 1).

While some are asking, "Is marriage worth it?" or "Is it just another lifestyle choice today?" others are searching to understand "how to do it successfully." David Olson and his associates (Olson & DeFrain, 2000); Howard Markman, Scott Stanley, and Susan Blumberg (1996)—college professors, researchers, and authors of *Fighting for Your Marriage*; and John Gottman (1994) have all devoted much of their professional lives to studying how couple relationships can be successful and sustaining. Their work has added substantially to our understanding of how couples relate and negotiate and what makes a marriage work in the United States today.

Markman, Stanley, and Blumberg's (1996) point is that good marriages take work. They suggest that marriage is the most risky undertaking routinely taken on by the greatest number of people in society. While marriage can be the most ecstatic relationship filled with great joy and promise, it can also be the most frustrating, painful, and miserable relationship in life.

These authors suggest that the damaging effects of destructive relationships take a toll on our families, and on society as a whole. Their research has been able to predict, with 82% to 93% accuracy, which marriages will end in divorce and which ones will be healthy. They suggest that it is not how much you love someone, but how you handle conflict and disagreements, that has the greatest impact. As a result of their extensive research with couples, the authors have identified four patterns that harm relationships: escalation, invalidation, withdrawal and avoidance, and negative interpretations.

- *Escalation* occurs when negative comments spiral into increasing frustration and anger; the things people say threaten the very lifeblood of the marriage.
- *Invalidation* involves subtle or direct "put downs." The authors call invalidation a "highly toxic poison" to the well-being of a relationship.
- *Withdrawal* happens when one or both partners avoid important discussions. It can be as obvious as getting up and leaving during conversation or as subtle as shutting down emotionally but staying physically present. *Avoidance* reflects the same reluctance, but more emphasis is placed on preventing a conversation from happening in the first place.

Either way, the couple loses opportunities to build intimacy.
- *Negative interpretations* arise when one partner consistently believes that the motives of the other are more negative than is the case. This can be very destructive, and a sense of hopelessness and demoralization can set in. People tend to see what they expect to see in others.

Gottman (1994; Gottman & Silver, 2000) and his research team have used a multi-method model for collecting extensive data drawn from 20 different studies of more than 2,000 couples. Patterns have emerged that predict, with more than 90% accuracy, whether a couple will separate within the first five years of marriage:
- the ratio of positive to negative comments
- facial expressions of disgust, fear, or misery
- high levels of heart rate
- defensive behaviors such as making excuses and denying responsibility for disagreements
- verbal expressions of contempt by the wife, and stonewalling by the husband (showing no response when his wife expresses her concerns).

An important variable in predicting duration and happiness in marriage was found to be the number of positive interactions compared to negative emotional interactions. People satisfied with their marriages demonstrated a ratio of at least five positive interactions to one negative interaction. "It is the balance between positive and negative emotional interactions in a marriage that determines its well being—whether the good moments of mutual pleasure, passion, humor, support, kindness and generosity outweigh the bad moments of complaining, criticism, anger, disgust, contempt, defensiveness and coldness" (Markman, Stanley, & Blumberg, 1996, p. 44).

Markman, Stanley, and Blumberg's (1996) research has shown that the way partners in a couple respond to one another in the areas of recreation and entertainment is vital in achieving and maintaining marital satisfaction. All too often, the recreational pleasures and romantic affections of courtship end after marriage.

Frank Pittman, a marriage and family therapist, holds that marriage is not about being in love but about agreeing to love one another. He believes that the relationship between love and marriage is oblique: "Marriage is not supposed to make you *happy*. It is supposed to make you *married*, and once you are safely and totally married, then you have the structure of security and support from which you are free to make yourself happy, rather than wasting your adulthood looking for a structure" (1998, p. 160).

Pittman (1998) suggests that falling in love is something people cannot do without first learning the skills of friendship: "Lonely people who look around for someone with whom to fall in love are comparable to friendless, unemployed, starving people who spend their last dollar on a lottery ticket rather than a meal or a bath" (p. 175).

The element of friendship and the ways couples are involved with one another and have fun together have been found to be important aspects of a healthy, functioning marriage. Of course, it is not that simple. Many couples can identify factors that are tearing down rather than building up their relationship. However, they can also learn to use skills to communicate more effectively so as to build healthy, sustaining couple and family relationships. Divorce does not have to be the only option.

Parents and Children

A couple's relationship has an impact on children who may be born into a family as well. Parenthood involves both costs and benefits that vary over the family life cycle. The best-case scenario is that two adults consider these costs and benefits in light of their individual and mutual values before conceiving a child. However, that does not always happen. On one hand, parenthood is viewed in a rather romantic way: babies gurgling, laughing, smelling sweet after a bath, or sleeping peacefully. Toddlers do clever and cute things, and elementary-aged children are smart and community-minded. On the other hand, parenthood is billed as "hard work." Difficulties present in childrearing can include balancing work and parenting, urging children to eat and sleep, and dealing with children's behavioral problems. And then there's adolescence!

Jane Brooks (1998), an author of college-level textbooks on parenting, defines parenting as a cooperative venture. "Parenthood transforms people. After a baby comes, parents are no longer the same individuals they were. A whole new role begins, and they start a new way of life" (p. 1). Brooks (1999) further identifies parenting in terms of "parenting as a process." It can be described as a series of actions and interactions by parents to promote the development of children. It's not a

one-way street in which the parent influences the child day after day. It is a process of interaction influenced by cultural and social institutions.

Jay Belsky (1984), a professor, author, and researcher in the areas of parent-child relationships, marriage relationships, and related social policy issues, has identified three major influences on parenting: 1) the child's characteristics and individuality, 2) the parents' personal history and psychological resources, and 3) stresses and supports.

Six basic functions of parents and families are described by David Blankenhorn (1990), founder and president of the Institute of American Values: 1) procreating; 2) providing basic resources like food, shelter, and clothing; 3) giving affection and caring; 4) teaching society's core values; 5) linking the individual to the larger society; and 6) controlling the individual's sexual behavior.

The processes Belsky identifies and the parenting and family functions described by Blankenhorn and colleagues will be explored later.

To Parent or Not

Now, as no time in the past, adults have options regarding parenthood. Not only is it more socially acceptable not to have children, but contraception methods are in abundance. Elizabeth Anscome (cited in Houlgate, 1999), a professor of philosophy at Cambridge and one of the leading British philosophers of the twentieth century, suggests that the question "Why have a child?" would not have been asked prior to the twentieth century.

More than ever before, couples are choosing to be "kid-free." According to the U.S. Census Bureau, 28% of marriages in 2003 were childless marriages. This amounts to 30,621 married couples with no related children. While this includes empty nesters, the numbers are still significant. To better understand the impact of these changes, we can compare the situation in 1975 to that of 1997. In 1975, close to 9% of 40-year-old women did not have children; in 1997, almost 17% were childless (Clark, 2000). A national probability sample of 16- to 29-year-olds found that 14% were very sure and another 14% were moderately sure that they would not have children (Schoen, 1999).

Increased career choices for women, birth control, the expense of raising a child, and concern for overpopulation and the environment help explain the childfree trend. Some childfree couples do not wish to have children because they never have had parental feelings or do not believe they would make good parents. Organizations such as the ChildFree Network and No Kidding! promote not having children.

Several terms are used to describe childfree marriages: non-parenthood, voluntary childlessness, and the childfree alternative. A review of 22 studies (Veevers, 1980) of childfree marriages revealed some interesting answers to common questions about childlessness. The review looked at four questions:

- What long-term effects does voluntary childlessness have?
- Is there something wrong with people who don't wish to have children?
- Do people without children do better in their careers?
- Is the quality of a childfree marriage as good as that of a marriage with children?

Rempel (1985, cited in Olson & DeFrain, 2000) found that without children, adults often prepare for their later years by developing a network of friends and family and do quite well. Statistics show that a disproportionate number of high-ranking businesswomen and professionals are childless (Olson & DeFrain, 2000).

Veevers (1980) found that the majority of studies looking at possible problems in people who don't wish to have children showed that those who are not parents exhibit no more **psychopathology** or deviance than a control group of randomly sampled parents. Two studies found more vital and happy relationships among childfree couples than among those with children. This is due partially to the fact that childless couples can devote more time to their marriages and are more likely to divorce if they do not have a good relationship (Olson, McCubbin, et al., 1989; Somers, 1993; all as cited in Olson & DeFrain, 2000).

"No Kidding!," "The Child Free Network," and "Childfree and Happy" are all online networks established to provide support and social networks for couples without children. No Kidding!'s website defines itself as "an all-volunteer, non-profit social club for adult couples and singles who, for whatever reason, have never had children. It is not a business or a dating service" (NoKidding!, n.d.).

Many of the individuals involved in these types of clubs say that they face social stigma for not having children and are sometimes labeled as "selfish, immature and having a hedonistic lifestyle" (Arenofsky, 1996, para. 5). Childfree couples state that this is simply not true, as they contribute to society in many other ways, and have more time and energy to do so. Many childfree couples say that they in fact enjoy children. They may volunteer with Sunday Schools and organizations such as Big Brothers and Big Sisters, or participate in other activities that involve kids, but have simply decided not to have children themselves. The web sites and childfree clubs provide them with an opportunity to interact with other couples who may be experiencing some of the same societal challenges that come with deciding to be childfree.

Though some people prefer to be childless, others find great fulfillment in parenthood. Children give us love and receive our love. Their presence may enhance the love between married partners as they share in the experiences of parenting. Successfully managing the challenges of parenthood can provide a sense of accomplishment. Parents report that they discover new and untapped dimensions of themselves that give them greater meaning and life satisfaction. Children offer ongoing stimulation and change; they challenge us to be our best. Clarke and Dawson begin their book, *Growing Up Again: Parenting Ourselves, Parenting Our Children* (1998), with a thought from Joyce Maynard, a journalist and novelist, who once said, "Like every parent, I want nothing so much as my children's well-being. I want it so badly I may actually succeed in turning myself into a contented and well-adjusted person, if only for my children's sake" (p. 3).

There are no guarantees in regards to the benefits of rearing children, nor for life satisfaction in childfree living. Still, it is important to consciously consider the options beforehand, because parenthood is a permanent and major life decision. Besides recognizing the costs and benefits of parenting, and generally being contented and well adjusted, parents need an understanding of human development, particularly child development.

This author recalls: "I will never forget the day I was standing in a grocery store near Lansing, Michigan, waiting in a long check-out lane. I glanced over at the newspaper rack and saw in print the anguished face of a young man. I went over and picked up the paper and read about this young nineteen-year-old father who was being charged with the death of his young daughter. As she had repeatedly dropped something

Many Voices: An Introduction to Social Issues

on the floor from her highchair, he repeatedly picked it up and returned it to her, telling her not to do it again. Finally, in his frustration, he picked her up out of her chair and to make his point shook her harshly. In his misguided, yet well-meaning attempts to teach her about obedience and responsibility, he broke his daughter's neck, killing her."

As can be seen from this illustration, parents should have a working knowledge of developmental issues in parenting and learning skills in order to meet the challenges of parenting in today's society. Otherwise they will not be able to relate positively to their children.

Contemporary Parenting Issues for Growing Families

Discipline and disciplinary measures are an important part of parenting, with a plethora of books available to assist parents in this important task. Some hold to a "cookbook" approach to parenting, believing that following the "recipe" (a set of disciplinary measures) will assure that children will flourish. But children are individuals; while it is important to have an understanding of disciplinary measures that will assist a child in becoming a person capable of self-regulating behaviors, it is also important to realize that just following a set of rules will not guarantee that one's child will grow up healthy and well-adjusted.

Many parents want to give their children what they did not have growing up. They want their children to feel the love they perhaps didn't experience, or maybe they want to give them all the love and nurturing they *did* experience. What parents bring from their families of origin has a strong impact on what they bring to their own family. Clarke (1978) suggests that "the family is the first place we decide who we are and observe and practice how to be that way. To the extent that we decide we are lovable and capable, we build positive self-esteem. Therefore, the parenting or nurturing that we give and receive in the family is important" (p. 4). Parents who had their own needs for stimulation, recognition, and certainty met during childhood will find it easier to balance their own lives and meet those needs for their children.

Some parents cannot just step in and take the lead in assisting the development of self-regulation in their children. These parents are either too preoccupied to monitor their children because their stress levels are overwhelming, or they do not understand child development (Kopp, 1989, cited in Brooks, 1999).

Parents' emotional states determine the type, consistency, and effectiveness of their discipline. Theodore Dix, a professor at the University of Texas at Austin who specializes in parenting and parent-child interaction, presents a model of parenting that gives a central role to emotions in organizing parents' behavior with children. Children arouse parents' warmth and love, but they also trigger conflicts that can occur as many as fifteen times in an hour when children are young. According to Dix (cited in Brooks, 1999), these feelings determine whether parents will view children's behavior in a positive or negative light.

Daniel Goleman—a psychologist, journalist, and author of *Emotional Intelligence* (1995), and John Gottman—a psychologist, university professor, and author of *Raising an Emotionally Intelligent Child* (1997), are both concerned with the need for children to master their emotions, and they promote parents' responsibilities in teaching children to understand and regulate their emotional world. While he does not discount the importance of IQ, Goleman (1995) believes it is not the sole measure of what it means to be smart and successful. According to Goleman, emotional intelligence (EI)—which involves emotional balance, persistence, motivation, empathy, and social finesse—is a critically important predictor of success in life. Although shaped by childhood experience, EI can be improved and developed by learning throughout life.

Affluenza, or the Rich Kids Syndrome, is a term coined by Ralph E. Minear and William Proctor in their book, *Kids Who Have Too Much* (1989). Minear is a Harvard Medical School pediatrician and Proctor is author or co-author of more than 80 non-fiction books. They believe a social epidemic is endangering the physical and emotional health of America's children. They suggest that there are many ways in which parents give children too much: too much freedom, too many material goods, too much pressure to perform, too much information (and not enough instruction about how to use that information), too much protection and too little preparation for the difficult challenges of real work, too much independence, too much food, and too much parental sacrifice. These authors believe that the most important keys to eliminating this problem are summarized in two words: time and values. They encourage parents to set aside adequate time to interact on an intimate level with their children—interaction that should occur in the context of a clear-cut set of moral or spiritual standards.

The media have a powerful effect on parenting, influencing children's beliefs and values and sometimes confusing parents in their quest to understand what their children really need. The National Institute on Media and the Family provides resources for parents, educators, and children to assist them in managing the multiple opportunities of the media. David Walsh, the director of the institute, serves as a watchdog alerting parents to specific media concerns. He wrote a column entitled, "Our Brains Are Built for One Thing at a Time" for MediaWise, an online newsletter published by the institute.

"Kids are wired like never before. Cell phones, instant messaging, pagers, faxes, CD players, video games, and the Internet have all become as common as TV and the radio for this generation of kids. It is common for kids to be listening to music, watching TV, and talking on the phone at the same time. Pop culture says that if you aren't doing a couple of things at once, you're slacking off.

"Some try to tell us that because kids are so wired today they are excellent multi-taskers. But it turns out that 'one thing at a time' is not old-fashioned advice. It's backed up by cutting edge brain research.

"Common sense tells us multi-tasking should increase brain activity, but scientists found out it doesn't. Our brains are built to pay attention to one thing at a time. That's the finding of Carnegie Mellon University scientists using the latest brain imaging technology. As a matter of fact, they discovered multi-tasking actually decreases brain activity. Neither task is done as well as if each is performed individually.

"It's not that we can't do some tasks simultaneously. We can all chew gum while walking, and most of us can drive a car and carry on a conversation. But if we are lost in heavy traffic in an unfamiliar part of town, the radio goes off and the talking stops. If two tasks are performed at once, one of the tasks has to be familiar. We perform a familiar task on 'automatic pilot' while really paying attention to the other one. If they both require attention, we're in trouble. The brain can only do so much at one time. That's why insurance companies consider talking on a cell phone and driving as dangerous as driving while drunk"(Walsh, 2002).

In Ellen Galinsky's book, *Ask the Children* (1999), a number of parenting skills were identified from research. They include raising the child with good values, making the child feel important and loved, knowing what is going on in the child's life, spending time talking with the child, being involved in the child's school or child care, encouraging the child to want to learn and to love learning, establishing family routines and rituals, not losing control when the child makes the parent angry, and attending the important events in the child's life. According to Galinsky, "There are two essential ingredients of parenting: warmth/caring (in other words, love) and responsiveness (reading and responding to the child's cues and clues). Everything else we do falls under these two important parenting skills" (Families and Work, n.d.). Though society continues to change, these basic needs of children will not. Parents need to balance their own lives in order to provide these crucial components for their growing children.

This chapter has considered only a few of today's issues facing parents, such as discipline dilemmas, the affluence of our culture, and the benefits and adverse effects of the media. Other areas to explore include chronic illness, disabilities, issues of abuse and neglect, fertility, adoption, how poverty affects parenting, and issues for immigrant families. Examining one's beliefs and values as they relate to children and parenting within the context of contemporary society is important. While the focus thus far has been on choices related to having and rearing children, another important issue within the context of parenting is adult children and aging parents.

Adult Children and Aging Parents

In U.S. society many people accept the conventional wisdom about old age, most of which is negative. A form of prejudice known as *ageism* is common. It prejudges an older person negatively, solely on the basis of age. An example of how our society looks upon aging is the popular color of black for decorations at the 40th birthday party. Actually, 40 is early middle age, as middle age by definition roughly spans ages 35-65. The assumption that 65 is the beginning of "old age" arose with the U.S. government arbitrarily selecting this age, in 1935, as the time when a worker could receive full social security retirement benefits. Actually "old age" is more complicated to define.

Perhaps a more useful term is "functional age," measured by an individual's psychological, intellectual, and social capacities, as well as accomplishments (Schwartz & Scott, 2000). People grow old at different rates, with one person being "old" at 60 whereas another is "young" at 75. Including everyone over 65 in a single category obscures significant differences in the social realities of older people.

Because of the economic realities of today, some middle-aged adults have had to put their own expectations aside. People in their middle years may find themselves in the "sandwich" generation, responsible for managing adolescents, dealing with their "boomerang" children (adult children who have returned to the parental nest), and caring for their own aging parents. The results can be both positive and negative. Closer relationships between the caregivers and aging parents can develop, but there may be too much stress (Olson & DeFrain, 2000). The situation of young adults still living with their parents is termed the "cluttered nest." In the United States, one of every four adults between the ages of 18 and 34 is still living with his or her middle-aged parents (Schwartz & Scott, 2000). However, the majority of those in this group are ages 18 to 24, with 55% of males in that range living at home and 46% of females living at home (Fields, 2004).

Men of the "boomerang generation" are almost twice as likely as women to live with their parents. As our culture fosters independence in young adulthood, it would not be surprising if both generations reported dissatisfaction (these living arrangements can be stressful). Conflicts between lifestyles and values are not uncommon, and both generations complain about a lack of privacy. We know marital and parental satisfaction can decline for adults living with their boomerang kids (Schwartz & Scott, 2000). However, some parents claim to enjoy spending time with their co-resident adult children, especially daughters. In a national study of parents with children ages 19 to 34 living at home, researchers found a high degree of satisfaction among the parents. Three factors were found to affect the level of parental satisfaction: the presence or absence of younger siblings in the home, the employment status of the adult child, and the presence or absence of grandchildren in the home (Aquilino & Supple, 1991).

Carol Abaya is a nationally syndicated newspaper columnist and nationally recognized expert on the issues of aging, elder/parent care issues, and the sandwich generation. She suggests that there are three types of "sandwiches":

- Traditional: those sandwiched between aging parents, who need care and/or help, and their own children.
- Club: those in their 50s or 60s sandwiched between aging parents and adult children and grandchildren, or those in their 30s and 40s with young children and aging parents and grandparents.
- Open Faced: anyone else involved in elder care.

Abaya writes, "It's not easy to become elderly or a parent to your parent(s). After all, our society 'says' adults should be able to take care of themselves. But, as more live well into their 80s and 90s and families are dispersed across the country, everyone is going to be involved somehow, some way, in elder care. If not today, then tomorrow" (2001).

Historians of the family note that a persistent myth in Western societies claims that before the twentieth century, older people always lived with their grown children and were lovingly cared for by them (Houlgate, 1999). However, the older generation of the past lived in circumstances remarkably similar to those of the elderly today. They either lived alone, with other elderly people, or with a married couple to whom they may or may not have been related. There is a greater percentage of elderly people in the current population than ever before, and today these elderly are more likely to live in institutions than with their adult children or with other families.

John Locke, a 17th-century philosopher and professor at Oxford University in England, argued in 1690 that grown children have a "perpetual obligation" to honor their parents. He said it was a God-given duty. He believed that we should be grateful for the benefits received from our parents and show our gratitude by honoring them, accepting what he called the "duty to defend, relieve, assist, and comfort them" (Locke, as quoted in Houlgate, 1999).

Jane English (cited in Houlgate, 1999) wrote several essays on contemporary moral problems and addressed the difficult question, "What do grown children owe their parents?" She believes that there are many things which children ought to do for their parents, but it is inappropriate and misleading to describe them as things "owed." Voluntary sacrifices of parents should not be considered debts to be repaid, but should create love or friendship (which she describes as characterized by mutuality rather than reciprocity). Thus, what children choose to do for their parents (and vice versa) should depend on their respective needs, abilities, and resources, as well as the extent to which there is an ongoing friendship between them.

In discussing intergenerational relationships, Schwartz and Scott (2000) report that the majority of the elderly live alone or with a spouse. Many older citizens fear ending their lives in a nursing home, but only about 5% of them are in such institutions, and most of these are over the age of eighty-five. Eighty percent of older adults who are sick and need long-term care receive such attention from their families (Olson & DeFrain, 2000). Studies have found that 50% to 60% of older people have at least one child living within a ten-minute drive of their home. Many adult children talk to their parents on a regular basis, and older people are not primarily dependent on their adult children. Older parents often remain a resource to their children, sharing child-care services and providing financial assistance.

However, social class has been shown to influence the direction of tangible aid by parents to adult children. It has been found that wealthier older people are likely to continue giving financial assistance to middle-aged children, while working-class parents are more likely to be receiving assistance from their adult children. Elderly men are more likely to live with their spouses, while a greater percentage of elderly women live alone. White elderly parents are less likely to live with their adult children than are parents of other ethnicities (Bengtson & Harootyan, 1994; Hogan & Farkas, 1995).

Families and individuals relate to aging and family responsibilities in many ways. Some elderly suffer in difficult situations that make them a burden to their families; others add a richness and stability.

It is important to consider other issues such as poverty, living arrangements, general health issues and illnesses, mental health issues, grief and loss, and retirement in determining whether aging parents will be seen as a blessing or a burden. Adult children will have many opportunities to explore and act on their beliefs and values as they deal with the important and sometimes very difficult challenge of aging parents.

Work and Family

ISSUES: What is the relationship between work and family stability? How is the average family doing financially? Why would an expanding economy hurt some families? How should one balance family and work? What should families expect from employers in terms of concessions for family issues? What is meant by the concept of "equal partners" in a marriage? What is the relationship between marital satisfaction and involvement in domestic labor? What solutions do you have for couples as they face the challenges of meeting work demands and caring for their homes and children?

Because of changing economic and social conditions, it is important to consider the interconnection between work and families. The quality and stability of family life are, in a large part, dependent on the type of work available for family members. Work provides income that determines a family's standard of living.

In describing the world of her grandparents in the early 1900s, Mary Pipher (1996), author of *The Shelter of Each Other*, explained that the family was the source of everything in her grandparents' lives. They were up before dawn to milk the cows, everyone had favorite chores, and they lived and worked in the "natural

Many Voices: An Introduction to Social Issues

world." She recalls the work was physical and that it was "good work," connected to real benefits for the people involved. The work made sense and produced concrete results—calves were branded, kraut chopped and put in jars, gardens weeded, and hogs butchered. People were busy, not hurried. Farmers scheduled their lives according to weather and the needs of the day.

With the introduction of wage labor, men's and women's work roles changed, although men's more than women's (Cherlin, 1999). Husbands began trading their labor in factories or shops for wages, while wives worked mainly in the home, although they often earned money there by producing goods on a piecework basis, taking in lodgers, or doing laundry. By the second half of the twentieth century, married women were entering the labor force in large numbers; now a majority of women with young children are employed outside the home.

Today workers are concerned about meshing their jobs with their family responsibilities, and corporations and government have a growing role in responding to this current dilemma. What is the relationship between work and family living, and how does each influence the other? One might consider these questions: To what degree does an adequate income contribute to marital satisfaction? If one spouse earns substantially more than the other, which one should do more of the housework or childcare? Are government and employer benefits really helping, or are they creating unfair situations for families? If children learn patterns of work and industry from their own family of origin, what are today's children learning?

Macroeconomic Changes Affecting the Family

Macroeconomics, a term coined in 1948, is defined as "a study of economics in terms of whole systems especially with reference to general levels of output and income and to the interrelations among sectors of the economy" (Merriam-Webster Collegiate Dictionary at http://www.m-w.com).

Macro-level activity influences the general society, which in turn affects individual families. Bottom line? The economy is changing and it has a big impact on the family.

While the expansion in the U.S. economy during the last 25 years has benefited our country overall, it has not helped all families. An increase in income inequality, poverty, and homelessness has created complex and troubling situations. The rich have gotten richer, and the poor poorer. The average poor person fell further below the poverty line in 2000 than at any time since 1979. Those who remained poor in 2000 fell as far below the poverty line as in 1999, further than in any other year in more than two decades. Declining participation among poor households in programs such as food stamps and cash assistance, along with reductions instituted in these programs in the latter part of the 1990s, contributed to this development (National Partnership on Work & Family, n.d.).

Median household income is the point at which half the households have higher incomes and half have lower incomes. In 2000 it was $42,148, statistically unchanged from $42,187 in 1999 and tied with the level in 1999 for the highest median income on record (data available back to 1952). While median household income did not increase among the population as a whole, it did rise among African Americans, Hispanics, and female-headed households. Among African American households, the median income was $30,439 in 2000, more than $15,000 below median household income among non-Hispanic whites (which was $45,904), but nearly $1,600 above the 1999 level for African Americans, a significant gain for a single year. Similarly, among Hispanics, the median household income rose to $33,447, about $1,700 above the 1999 level (National Partnership on Work & Family, n.d.).

While median household income generally remained the same or increased among certain groups, median earnings fell modestly among one group— men who work full-time year-round. Median earnings declined one percent (or $362) for this group (National Partnership on Work & Family, n.d.). A nonpartisan research group, The Center on Budget and Policy Priorities, has found that income inequality in the United States is greater than in any other Western, industrialized country (Center on Budget and Policy Priorities, 1997).

Poverty rates increased by 1.1 million people from 2003 to 2004, which shows a consecutive rise in the poverty rate for the last four years (DeNavas-Walt, Proctor, & Lee, 2005). Many economic indicators had pointed to this slowing economy even before September 11. The monthly unemployment rate, which averaged 4.0% for 2000, climbed to 5.5% by 2004 (Bureau of Labor Statistics, 2005). However, natural disasters—such as Hurricane Katrina in the Gulf Coast region, which damaged the area's economy by lowering revenues, interrupting the oil supply and exports of grain, costing billions in insured and uninsured damages, and increasing the unemployment rate in the area—are predicted to impact the economy and unemployment rates (Wikipedia, n.d.b).

In addition to the unemployment rate and events such as natural disasters, other macro factors that affect individual families can be identified, including welfare reform (begun in 1996), U.S. trade policies, medical and health care issues, interest and mortgage rates, tax policies, and the increasing aging population.

A particularly relevant issue for families is welfare reform and how it affects the poor, especially women. While caseloads fell and employment rose, most women who left welfare now work in low-wage jobs without benefits. Large numbers of minority populations report material hardships and face barriers to work, such as depression, low skills, or no transportation. Disposable income decreased among the poorest female-headed families.

Among the important challenges for the future are that of differentiating between the effects of welfare reform, the economy, and other policies on women's work, and of assessing how variations in state welfare programs affect caseloads and employment outcomes of recipients (Corcoran, Danziger, Kalil, & Seefeldt, 2000).

It is important to be knowledgeable about the macroeconomic influences on American families. We also need to be aware of the work being done, and what still needs to be done, on behalf of these families.

Effects of Work on Family Dynamics

Work, stress, and the family are all interconnected. Finances are among the most common stressors for families across the life cycle, regardless of how much money they make (Bowen, Pittman, Pleck, Haas, & Voydanoff, 1995; Voydanoff, 1991, as cited in Olson & DeFrain, 2000). For some, finances are more difficult to talk about than sex. There are other issues related to work and family dynamics. Job schedules create barriers to family closeness; the choices couples make in how to use their income, as well as how to use their free time, can create barriers as well.

Researchers have documented what families report informally: that job stress affects marriages and parents' relationship with their children (Kinnunen, Gerris, & Vermulst, 1996). Stressful jobs have been identified as those that require periods of separation, those that are so consuming that they sap the energy of the employee, and those that are so difficult that the employee feels constant strain.

When a partner's ongoing job stress is great, the other partner is likely to experience as much psychological distress as if it were his or her own job. It was found that women in untroubled marriages feel the greatest concern and suffer more from their spouses' job issues than women in troubled marriages. Men with commitments to both their families and jobs, who perceive their wives as very supportive of their work and parenting activities, report less role strain than men with less supportive wives (Rook, Doley, & Catalano, 1991, as cited in DeGenova & Rice, 2002; O'Neil & Greenberger, 1994).

Balancing Time and Schedules

Balancing work and family has become a major theme in the United States. Managing work and family in a 24/7 world is one of the biggest challenges individuals face. Ellen Galinsky, president and cofounder of the Families and Work Institute, gave the keynote address for the Working Mother Work-Life Congress in October 2001, discussing the challenges of working, motherhood, family life, and personal life. The following is an excerpt from her address (reprinted with permission, http://familiesandwork.org):

"Family life? Personal life? It was seen as a distraction to work. It was seen as an interference to work. I remember a meeting that I had with an executive almost 20 years ago. He said to me, 'There are competent people and incompetent people. The competent people can manage their work and family lives. The incompetent people can't. And there is nothing, NOTHING at all you or anyone else can do to help them.'

"On September 13th, two days after the terrorist attacks, a young woman I know was at work in her office in New York City when there were bomb threats in the neighborhood. She heard the authorities on bull horns advising people to evacuate. She has an eight-year old, she is a single parent, she was frightened, and she wanted to be with her son. She asked her boss if she could leave, like the employees she saw streaming out of nearby building [sic] and hurrying home. Her boss said, 'NO. I don't care if there are bombs. We have work to finish.'

"We know, of course, that this kind of exchange between a boss and an employees [sic] does take place, even in the best of our companies and even over issues that are less life-threatening than a bomb scare.

"But it is increasingly rare. At the Families and Work Institute, we know this empirically from the studies (our National Study of the Changing Workforce) we do that keep tabs on how nationally representative groups of employees feel they are treated when a personal or family issue emerges. It has changed, changed even over the past five years.…

"I would contend, however, that the changes that we are seeing in employees and feeling in ourselves are not so new. They have been there, latent. The events of the past few weeks have simply brought them forward into clearer view.

"What do I mean? I mean the desire among us all to do work that is meaningful and to be able to focus on the people who are important in our lives.…

"My own grown daughter says that among her colleagues at work people are asking themselves, 'what's of value, what's core?'

"I hear this among other employees too. If we are going to leave our loved ones to go to work everyday, we want what we do to mean something.

"This focus is not, as I said, new. Our research has increasingly shown that good quality jobs where people feel that their work is meaningful, is challenging, and makes a difference is critical to how they manage their work lives and home lives" (Galinsky, 2001).

A strategy some couples are using in their attempt to balance their lives is called "scaling back." They put limits on how long they will work, they reduce expectations for career advancement, and they make compromises with regard to the time and effort they put in at work in order to achieve success at home. This is not an easy task in a competitive society, but it is an option.

As the emphasis on meaningful work has become stronger in the workplace, Galinsky (2001) has this advice for employers:

- Continue to ask employees what they need.
- Destigmatize the need that we all have to ask for help and support and provide opportunities for employees to do so.

- Create new traditions or uphold old ones at work… and help employees do so at home.
- Help employees help the people who are close to them.
- Help managers help others.
- Continue to support your CEO and other leaders in having ongoing communication with employees.
- Help those who help others.
- Continue your work redesign efforts to make work meaningful.
- Focus on diversity.
- Continue to offer employees opportunities to be connected to their communities.

As Galinsky encouraged employers to ask employees what they need, she also asked children what they needed from their parents. The research by Galinsky (2001) indicates that what we believe children think and what they actually think can be quite different. She asked the question, "If you were granted one wish that could change the way your mother's or your father's work affects your life, what would that wish be?" She also asked parents to guess what their children would wish; the majority guessed that their children would wish for more time together. The largest proportion of children wished that their parents would be less tired and stressed. She clarifies that this response doesn't mean that time is unimportant to children. It means that if they were given just *one* wish, they would like to see their parents less stressed out.

She also found that, while three in five parents say they like their jobs a lot, only two in five children think their parents do. Parents often come home and complain, or they tell their children that they don't want to leave them to go to work, and thus do not tell them that they do like their jobs. Galinsky (2002) notes, "They don't want us to love our work more than we love them, but they can get it."

Equality and Inequity in the Home and Workplace

Over the past twenty-five years, social scientists have been telling a grim story of inequality (Deutsch, 1999). Literally hundreds of studies have examined the roles of women and men at home. Initially, when women started to flood into the paid workforce, some researchers assumed the roles at home would change dramatically. Men and women would become equal partners in marriage, sharing the responsibilities of both breadwinning and domestic labor.

Bianchi and Spain (cited in Deutsch, 1999), both college professors and researchers, reported that between 1970 and 1995 the percentage of women ages 25 to 54 who worked outside the home climbed from 50% to 76%. Although women were in paid employment, their husbands' roles were not changing. Studies of domestic life in the 1970s and 1980s showed that men whose wives worked outside the home did not seem to be doing any more than the men whose wives were still full-time homemakers. A few studies did show that the percentage of men's contribution to domestic labor increased, but closer examination often revealed that it was not because men were doing more but because women were doing less (Blood & Wolfe, 1960; Bird, Bird, & Scruggs, 1984; Young & Wilmott, 1973; Barnett & Barusch, 1978, as cited in Deutsch, 1999).

Francine Deutsch, a professor of psychology at Holyoke College, spent over a year talking to "equal sharers" and other dual-earner couples. In her book, *Halving It All: How Equally Shared Parenting Works* (1999), Deutsch shows that, with the best of intentions, people perpetuate inequalities and injustices on the home front. But also, and more importantly, they can devise more equal arrangements out of explicit principles or simply out of fairness and love.

Arlie Hochschild's (1989) work popularized the term "second shift," which defines what many women do, in that the mother and father both work in the paid labor force, but the mother also works a "second shift" at home—a shift not shared equally by her husband. Marriages suffer from the unspoken and spoken resentments of a highly unequal workload. "Households in which men aren't frying the bacon are highly problematic in an age in which women are working harder and harder to bring it home" (Deutsch, 1999, p. 4).

There is no simple equation between women's happiness or marital satisfaction and their husbands' involvement in domestic labor. But it has been said that the involvement of husbands in domestic labor may result in increased marital conflict or in compromising their wives' cherished identities as women. According to Deutsch (1999), the perception of inequity is tied to what women see as their legitimate role. She describes Perry-Jenkins, Seer, and Crofter's research (1992) in which they examined reactions to husbands' domestic help among women who could be characterized as co-providers—those who were employed and believed they held equal responsibility for the financial support of the family. They also considered ambivalent providers, those who worked but preferred to be home, and secondary co-providers, who were employed but viewed their husbands' jobs as primary. The co-providers, whose husbands were doing twice as much household labor as the husbands of secondary providers, were less depressed and harried than other women. The ambivalent providers were considerably less happy, despite having husbands who did just as much at home.

Men's contributions can have a strong effect on women's happiness; yet it is not simply the work done, but the meaning attached to it, that makes the difference (Deutsch, 1999). "Perhaps the gender gap does not exist for all groups of men and women. In fact, women who are housewives may work fewer total hours than their husbands. But it is clear that among parents with young children who work at full-time jobs, women are working a lot harder than their husbands" (pp. 257–258). There are many ways to move toward achieving equality in a home, says Deutsch. She suggests that couples create equality by the accumulation of large and small decisions and acts that make up their daily lives as parents.

Social scientists have also been studying the changing ways in which men combine and prioritize their work and family responsibilities. The question is often asked, "Are men doing more in the family now than they did in the past?" Today's American men spend less of their lives working than their predecessors did. In comparison to men of the early 20th century, they now enter the labor force later and retire earlier. The average number of hours men work each week decreased substantially during the first half of the century, but now there is controversy about whether the trend has continued (Pleck, 1999).

Fathers who live with their families are spending more time with their children. At the same time, more fathers are not living with their families. Although men still perform less childcare than women, the participation of men in family activities, including child and home care, is increasing.

Reed Larsen and David Almeida's (1998) research on the transmission of emotions in families showed that a father's mood at the end of a workday influences a mother's mood when they are together at home far more than her prior mood affects him. In fact, a father's mood at work more strongly influences a mother's mood at home than her own mood at work affects her mood at home. Larsen and Almeida's findings suggest an important difference in the place of work and family in fathers' and mothers' personalities. Fathers carry their workplace emotions home with them, but mothers keep workplace pressures separate from their home experience (Pleck, 1999).

The way men and women experience conflicts between work and family, and of inequality in the home and workplace, have great implications for individuals, couples, families, and society. Parents desire more flexible workplace policies, and some companies are listening. Employing organizations are considering what policies and practices make them "family-friendly." Companies are asking, "What is the responsibility of the workplace to meet the personal needs and desires of working parents today?" A resource for those concerned with work-life issues is the Families and Work Institute (FWI). It is dedicated to providing information on work-life issues and concerns confronting workers and employers. This organization conducts its own research studies and supports the field of work-life research by bringing researchers together, sharing information, and collaborating on projects (Families and Work Institute, n.d.).

Issues of equality and inequality are complex and very personal within couples' relationships. Mary Pipher (1996) suggests that some of the solutions may be in relying on truths from earlier generations. She says that in working with clients today, she relies on truths from her grandparents' generation. She suggests that families can find more time by working together. "Rather than divide chores, everyone can help with the dishes, yard work, laundry and home repair. Children like communal work that's genuinely useful. They learn things with this work. And while they work, they can visit with adults. Many of my clients grew up on farms and they talk of working in the fields with their families. There is often pride and a sense of community in their descriptions of the plantings and the harvests. Their families' survival depended on their efforts" (pp. 232–233).

Creating Connected and Sustainable Families

ISSUES: What are the differences between an intentional and an entropic family? What qualities sustain a family? How would you make a family stronger? How should one deal with a changing family structure? What structures in families do you think need changing? How should family and community life interact?

Bill Doherty, a college professor, marriage and family therapist, and author, explains in his book, *The Intentional Family* (1997), that as he saw contemporary family life drift toward less closeness, less meaning, and less community, he was increasingly concerned. He believes families are nourished and enriched by shared rituals and that only an "intentional family" has a "fighting chance to maintain and increase its sense of connection, meaning, and community over the years" (p. 8).

He identifies the *entropic* family as the opposite of an intentional family. This is a term for the tendency of a physical system to lose energy and coherence over time. "[A] family, through lack of conscious attention to its inner life and community ties, gradually loses a sense of cohesion over the years.…Individual family members may have active lives in the world, but the energy of the family itself slowly seeps away" (p. 9). He believes that society creates entropic families in two ways. One is the lack of support for couples to make marriage work and for parents to make childrearing work. The second is the way we collectively put up barriers to sustaining family rituals. He suggests that cars, TV, busy work schedules, consumerism, and many other forces propel family members along fast-moving diverging tracks. While there may be no less love and no less desire for meaning and connection than in intentional families, members gradually drift apart because of a lack of bonding, intimacy, and community. A key to being intentional is to create and sustain family rituals, which can provide predictability, connection, identity, and a way to enact values.

Connected relationships are sustainable relationships. Herbert G. Lingren (1983), an Extension Family scientist, believes that, "Regardless of structure, a family that sustains, supports, and nourishes its members across its life cycle seems imperative" (p. 1). He defines a sustainable family as one that "creates a safe, positive, and supportive environment allowing all family members to thrive and develop their fullest potential over the family life cycle" (p. 1). Sustainable families can efficiently access and use needed resources, including money, and can live together in a reasonably healthy manner. They effectively manage the many crises and opportunities thrust at them. They avoid high-risk behaviors and situations (e.g., drug and alcohol abuse) and work to make a supportive and safe community environment. The adults in the family are good role models and "practice what they preach" by showing respect for and caring about others. Sustainable families have the power to make their workplace and their community more "family friendly." They are resilient enough to cope with hardships and to bounce back from adversity. Sustainable families work together with neighbors, friends, and extended family to solve problems and meet the demands of unanticipated change, as well as to assist each other in times of hardship.

Sustainable families need skills and support in three major areas: resources, relationships, and a sense of community. If a family has a deficit in one of these areas, the other two are impacted. Lingren is concerned that families must be empowered in ways that can be transferred to the next generation.

Qualities of Strong, Sustainable Families

Doherty's views of rituals and resulting connections, and Levine's concern for sustainable families, are closely related to David Olson and John DeFrain's descriptions of successful families and Rick Stinnet and John DeFrain's concept of strong families. Olson and DeFrain (1994, p. 564) suggest four major systems in society to consider when describing successful families. The *social system* includes national, state, and community policies, laws, government programs, and traditions. The *belief system* includes family members' values, attitudes, behavior patterns, and expectations about parenting, relationships, management practices, and decision-making. The *extended family system* refers to the interaction of the family with relatives, friends, and support networks. The *family system* includes three dimensions of healthy family functioning: 1) family cohesion, 2) family flexibility, and 3) family communication (Olson et al., 1989).

Family cohesion is defined as a feeling of emotional closeness among people. In families, it is an experience of being nurtured and loved. When cohesion is low, a person experiences the sense of being disengaged—not feeling close to or connected with other family members. When cohesion is high, a person feels enmeshed. Personal lives are too intertwined and family members feel "stuck together," even smothered. A balance between separateness and togetherness is most functional across the family life cycle. The right balance allows family members to fully develop their potential as individuals. While in theory it may seem simple to suggest that families need to balance time between individual and couple or family needs, in practice it is difficult. Members often give each other "left-over" time; if an individual is "too tired" or "too busy," or if everybody is "doing their own thing," it is difficult to spend quality time together.

Family flexibility is defined as the ability to change the power structure, roles, and rules of a family as necessary. If a family is unwilling, or unable, to change, it becomes rigid; if leadership, authority, and family rules are lacking, the family will become chaotic. When the family is flexible, leadership is more democratic and less authoritarian. Adults share equitably in the decision-making. Jobs are not based on age or gender, and any person can fill in for another during a period of family hardship. Two qualities related to family flexibility are 1) the ability to cope with stress and crisis, and 2) spiritual well being.

Family communication is a major key in creating, supporting, maintaining, or destroying a family. It is the "facilitating dimension," which promotes an environment of self-esteem and support—or of pain and blame. Ironically, many family members don't spend much time talking to each other. Often they lack the time, energy, or skill to listen and talk. The family may not be an open, safe environment in which people are encouraged to express their feelings and ideas. Many topics may be taboo.

Positive communication and expression of appreciation and affection are related to this third dimension. Family members talk and listen to each other in a non-critical, non-judgmental, and non-threatening manner. They "listen with their hearts as well as their ears." They can talk about what made them angry, sad, hurt, or pleased. Strong families do have conflicts, and members do argue, but they take time to talk out their differences and share feelings to reach understanding. Strong families like to laugh and use humor to reduce tension, lessen anxiety, express warmth, and put people at ease. Appreciation and affection are expressions of how family members show their feelings for each other. They say "Thank you," "Please," "I love you," and "You are important in my life" with both words and deeds. They intentionally give positive strokes and avoid negative ones. Each promotes the self-esteem of the others, and believes and acts as if "I'm OK and you're OK." Positive, caring interaction can be learned and practiced on a daily basis. In the hurry of everyday responsibilities, it is easy to take each other for granted.

Extensive studies of family strengths have been conducted, with data gathered from more than 17,000 families in 28 countries, including the United States. Nick Stinnet, expert in family life who retired from the University of Nebraska, and John DeFrain, professor and extension specialist in family and consumer sciences, propose that six major qualities are commonly present in strong families, especially in Western industrial societies and in more developed countries (1985):

- Commitment
- Appreciation and affection
- Positive communication
- Time together
- Spiritual wellbeing (some define this as faith in God or optimism about life)
- Ability to cope with stress

These qualities are interrelated and overlap to some degree, meaning that each trait positively affects the others.

Changing Family Relationships and Structures

Issues related to love and commitment, parents and children, work and families, and strengths of sustainable and strong families have been discussed. Within each of these areas are issues that can be more fully explored. For example, the effects of marital separation, divorce, remarriage, and blended and step-family relationships are all important. Added to these are issues regarding sibling relationships, extended family members, grandparents raising grandchildren, homosexual and lesbian relationships, poverty and homelessness, grief and loss, culture and ethnicity, family law, and public policies.

Conclusion

The importance of strong families and the impact they have on the quality of life is becoming more obvious. The home sets up a pattern that spills over into all other aspects of our society. A sustainable family is a critical national resource (Lingren, 1983). The home should be a place where people feel comfortable and secure. The home base should provide the grounding needed to face the challenges and stressors of living. Olson and DeFrain (2000) suggest, "The future of families in the United States and around the world begins with each of us as we create the future in our own family....Life inevitably brings challenges; the key to life in a strong family is to work together to meet these challenges" (pp. 565–566).

Clarke (1978) points out that "however we live, we can find better ways to build strong, functioning families. No matter who we are, while we do whatever we can to make our institutions more supportive and humane and to find new networks to replace extended family ties, we can each start, right now, to assess and improve the quality of living experiences we offer to ourselves and the other people in our immediate families" (p. 5).

Call it a clan, call it a network,
call it a tribe, call it a family.
Whatever you call it, whoever you are,
you need it. (Howard, 1978)

2 Portraits of Children of Divorce: Rosy and Dark

by Mary Duenwald (**New York Times**, 3-26-02)

Divorce often hurts children, everyone agrees. It can cause great pain, anger, anxiety, confusion and behavior problems in the first couple of years of the breakup. And for some it leads to lasting anxiety, insecurity and fear of having close relationships with other people.

Most children recover, though it may take years, and go on to find happiness and success in marriage, work and life. Experts agree about that, too.

But from this general accord arises a heated dispute between those who emphasize the pain and those who think more attention should be paid to children's recovery.

Dr. E. Mavis Hetherington, emeritus professor of psychology at the University of Virginia, has recently accentuated the more positive prognosis for children of divorce with the publication of her new book, "For Better or for Worse: Divorce Reconsidered," written with John Kelly and published in January [2002] by Norton.

And in doing so, she has brought this long-running argument among social scientists back into the public spotlight.

"Divorcing is a high-risk situation," Dr. Hetherington said. "But most kids are able to adapt. They're resilient in the long run."

Her studies over the past 30 years have found that 20 percent to 25 percent of children whose parents divorce are at risk for lifelong emotional or behavioral problems, compared with only 10 percent of children whose parents stay married.

"Now, that twofold increase is not to be taken lightly," Dr. Hetherington said. "It's larger than the association between smoking and cancer. But it also means that 75 to 80 percent are functioning in the normal range, and some are functioning remarkably well."

The other side of the debate is represented by Dr. Judith S. Wallerstein, a co-author of "The Unexpected Legacy of Divorce: A 25-Year Landmark Study" (Hyperion, 2000), written with Dr. Julia M. Lewis and Sandra Blakeslee, a contributing science writer for *The New York Times*. The book concentrates on how children of divorce struggle with loneliness and anxiety, especially over love and commitment.

Dr. Wallerstein found that children of divorce, after suffering the breakups and then growing up in fragmented families, end up ill prepared to form their own intimate relationships.

"I am not saying these young people don't recover," Dr. Wallerstein said. "I'm saying they come to

adulthood burdened, frightened and worried about failure. They want love. They want commitment. They want what everybody else wants. But they're very afraid they'll never get it."

The differences between the two researchers are partly of the half-full or half-empty kind. "We're not against each other," Dr. Hetherington said. "When I read Judy's books, I always learn something. But you know Judy has a gloom and doom approach to divorce."

"I don't have a gloom and doom approach," Dr. Wallerstein responded, "but I do think we've underestimated the cost on the child."

Their differences also have to do with how the researchers went about their work. Each spent the past three decades studying white middle-class families, mainly those that broke apart in the early 1970's, when the divorce rate was taking its last giant step to 50 percent of all marriages.

But Dr. Wallerstein, a clinical psychologist, did her own interviews with children and parents, while Dr. Hetherington, assisted by a cadre of researchers, interviewed the children and parents and observed the families interacting in their homes.

Dr. Hetherington's subjects kept journals of their actions and feelings and were given standardized personality tests. Reports were gathered from parents and peers.

Dr. Wallerstein's study involved 59 divorced families. She interviewed the children and parents five times over 25 years, and she compared them with 44 adults who had grown up in intact families.

Dr. Hetherington looked at more than 1,400 families, roughly half divorced and half not divorced. For many, data were collected seven different times over the course of 24 years.

Critics have often said that Dr. Wallerstein examined too few families.

Her work, said Dr. Andrew Cherlin, professor of sociology at John Hopkins University, "is a very valuable exposition of what can happen when divorce goes bad."

"But where I have a problem," he said, "is where she claims that her 60 families are representative of all divorces."

Dr. Hetherington's sample is considered more representative of white middle-class families, and her standards of data collection are viewed as more scientifically rigorous. Still, some argue that Dr. Hetherington's study could not have exposed as much anguish as Dr. Wallerstein found.

But Dr. Norval D. Glenn, professor of sociology at the University of Texas, said he believed that Dr. Wallerstein dug much more deeply. "She got at something I think the standardized instruments wouldn't necessarily pick up on," he said.

The two researchers did arrive at certain similar conclusions. Each found, for example, that children of divorce, especially girls, often took responsibility for other family members' comfort. But each put her own spin on the story of how that happened.

Dr. Hetherington describes 8-year-old Jeannie, who does the laundry and the cooking when her mother is disabled by chronic fatigue syndrome just after her divorce. She also bathes her little brother and reads a story to him each night before bed. Jeannie is able to cope, Dr. Hetherington finds, because her mother does not lean too hard on her, for too long, and she provides love all the while.

Eventually Jeannie grows up happy, well-adjusted and enhanced by her experience.

"As long as the child has some support, divorce can have a steeling effect," Dr. Hetherington said. "Girls become stronger and more able to cope with future challenges." Dr. Wallerstein tells the story of Karen, who, as a 12-year-old, becomes the substitute parent for her younger siblings. She stays home from school to console her depressed mother, and she does the shopping for her father.

Karen, too, ends up happy, but not until after she suffers through a rocky period in her early adulthood, when she lives with a man she does not love or respect, because she knows he will not leave her. Even years later, after she has married someone else, she avoids all conflict with her husband.

"Karen was a child of high integrity, and so eventually she pulls away and becomes a happy and loving mother of her own children and a very good wife," Dr. Wallerstein said. "But what doesn't leave her ever is the fear that when she goes to sleep at night, she won't have it all in the morning."

With divorced fathers, each researcher observed behavior varying from total abandonment of the children to strong bonding. But Dr. Hetherington calls attention to fathers she describes as "divorce-activated," those who are jolted into realizing how much their children mean to them. These fathers, Dr. Hetherington believes, end up forging closer ties with their children than they might have built if they had stayed married and relegated the parental duties to their wives.

Dr. Wallerstein found that most divorced fathers, 70 percent of those she studied, did not pay their children's college expenses. Only 10 percent of the fathers who remained married declined to pay. This lack of support, she said, was a big reason why just 70 percent of the children of divorce went to college at all, compared with 85 percent of their high school classmates.

"The fathers said, Look, I did everything the law expected me to do, but this is where the road ends," Dr. Wallerstein said, noting that most support obligations expire when a child turns 18.

Dr. Hetherington found a similar lack of support, but not as widespread.

Only 35 percent of her divorced fathers paid absolutely nothing for their children's higher education. "Of course, you get much less financial support from a divorced father," she said. "The ones who stay in there are the ones who have felt they have some control over the decision making in their kids' lives."

She finds reason for optimism, however, in her observation that today, about a third of divorced fathers are seeing their children at least once a week, compared with only a fourth of fathers in the

1970's. "They could do a lot better," Dr. Hetherington said, "but there is a trend in a good direction."

Children of divorce have more than the average difficulty with marriages of their own. Women in this group are twice as likely as other women to end up divorced, according to Dr. Glenn of the University of Texas. For men, the risk is 30 percent higher.

The reason for this increased risk, Dr. Wallerstein maintains, is that children of divorce have grown up without good role models.

When they, too, face divorce, she said, "It's the nightmare they've worried about come to life."

Dr. Hetherington questions whether the children's problems with marriage are entirely attributable to the parents' divorces. Perhaps the memories of the strife before the divorces also have an effect, she said. Or, perhaps the children are predisposed to unstable unions.

"I don't mean that there might be a divorce gene lurking somewhere," Dr. Hetherington said, "but that characteristics such as antisocial behavior, irritability, impulsivity, lack of adaptability, which we know have to some extent a genetic basis, contribute to divorce."

Other experts pay tribute to both Dr. Wallerstein and Dr. Hetherington, even as they line up on opposite sides of the argument.

"Mavis Hetherington is an outstanding scholar," said Dr. David Popenoe, director of the National Marriage Project at Rutgers University. "Nobody is saying that her data is off. But just because you are functioning seemingly well in later life, does that mean you still haven't been hurt and maybe hurt badly in some psychological way by divorce?"

Dr. Kyle D. Pruett, a psychiatrist at the Yale Child Study Center, said: "I don't think one of these people is right and one is wrong. But I believe that the public would find it reassuring to have somebody of Mavis's stature say, 'Look, divorce is a process, and you have some control in how it works out.' There are some good ways and bad ways of doing it, but it is not a relational death sentence to the children or to the adults."

Discussion Questions

1. How would you define "family"?
2. What theory of studying families is most useful to you?
3. In your opinion, what are some important elements of a dating relationship?
4. What is the most important—love or commitment?
5. Choose a quotation on family, love, or marriage from the chapter and give an example of how you have seen what it says illustrated in real life.
6. In your opinion, why do marriages end?
7. What are three important elements in a marriage relationship?
8. What have you seen couples do successfully in balancing work and family?
9. What are some governmental and/or corporation policies in place that benefit families?
10. Would you want to work outside the home as a parent of young children? Why or why not?
11. How would it be for you to assume care of your aging parents?
12. Identify some qualities of strong, connected, and sustainable families.
13. Clark (2000) suggests that we can find better ways to build strong, functioning families. Identify some approaches you would recommend.

Related Readings

Christensen, A., & Jacobson, N. S. (2000). *Reconcilable differences.* New York: The Guilford Press.
Covey, S. R. (1997). *The 7 habits of highly effective families.* New York: Golden Books.
Jackson, M. (2002). *What's happening to home? Balancing work, life, and refuge in the Information Age.* Notre Dame, IN: Sorin Books.

Many Voices: An Introduction to Social Issues

Larson, J. H. (2000). *Should we stay together? A scientifically proven method for evaluating your relationship and improving its chances for long-term success.* San Francisco: Jossey-Bass.

Markman, H. J., Stanley, S. M., & Blumberg, S. L. (2001). *Fighting for your marriage: Positive steps for preventing divorce and preserving a lasting love, new and revised.* San Francisco: Jossey-Bass.

McGraw, P. C. (2000). *Relationship rescue: A seven-step strategy for reconnecting with your partner.* New York: Hyperion.

Pittman, F. (1998). *Grow up: How taking responsibility can make you a happy adult.* New York: St. Martin's Griffin.

Small, M. F. (2001). *Kids: How biology and culture shape the way we raise our children.* New York: Doubleday.

Waite, L. J., & Gallagher, M. (2000). *The case for marriage: Why married people are happier, healthier, and better off financially.* New York: Doubleday.

Related Web Sites

Center for the Ethnography of Everyday Life: http://www.ethno.isr.umich.edu

Center for Working Families: http://www.bc.edu/bc_org/avp/wfnetwork/berkeley

The Child and Family Resiliency Research Programme: http://www.quasar.ualberta.ca/cfrrp/cfrrp.html

The Coalition for Marriage, Family, and Couples Education (Smart Marriages/Happy Families): http://www.smartmarriages.com

Cornell Employment and Family Careers Institute: http://www.blcc.cornell.edu/cci/default.html

The Couples Place: http://www.couples-place.com

DivorceSource: http://www.divorcesource.com

Family Information Services: Resources for parenting, couple and family education: http://www.familyinfoserv.com

Fatherhood Project: http://www.fatherhoodproject.org

The Future of Children: http://www.futureofchildren.org

Marriage Alive International, Inc. (MAI): http://www.marriagealive.org

MARRIAGE magazine: Enrich, Enhance & Enliven Your Relationship!: http://www.marriagemagazine.org

National Children, Youth and Families at Risk (CYFAR) Program: http://www.csrees.usda.gov/nea/family/cyfar/cyfar.html

NIH (National Institutes of Health) Work and Family Life Center: http://wflc.od.nih.gov

No Kidding!: http://www.nokidding.net

ParentSoup: http://www.parentsoup.org

SmarterKids: http://www.smarterkids.org

Smart Marriages: http://www.smartmarriages.com

Step Family Association of America: http://www.saafamilies.org

Related Movies/Videos

Dad (1989) with Jack Lemmon and Ted Danson

The Great Santini (1979) with Robert Duvall and Blythe Danner

Kramer vs. Kramer (1979) with Dustin Hoffman and Meryl Streep

Mrs. Doubtfire (1993) with Robin Williams and Sally Field

My Big Fat Greek Wedding (2002) with Nia Vardalos and John Corbett

Ordinary People (1980) with Donald Sutherland and Mary Tyler Moore

The Story of Us (1999) with Michelle Pfeiffer and Bruce Willis

When Harry Met Sally (1989) with Billy Crystal and Meg Ryan

PUBLIC HEALTH AND HEALTH CARE

Nancy L. Farrell, Sharon A. Gillespie, Alina M. Baltazar, and Gary L. Hopkins

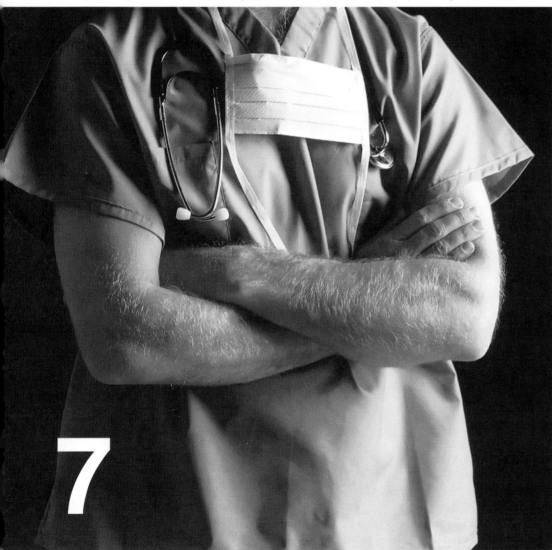

7

Chapter Outline

- Introduction
- What Is Public Health?
- Public Health's Break from Medicine
- Public Health Agencies

- Public Health Concerns
- Health Care
- Conclusion

Cholera death begins with an infection. At first, the infected person doesn't feel particularly ill. Then comes the diarrhea, which soon gets out of control; so much fluid is lost that the blood appears thick. In over half the cases, death occurs within a short time—often after only two or three days, mainly because of dehydration.

In London, in 1854, a terrible and devastating outbreak of cholera killed 600 people within a quarter of a mile from each other in the course of a few days. A striking incident during this epidemic has become legendary. In one particular neighborhood, the intersection of Cambridge Street and Broad Street, the concentration of cholera cases was so great that the number of deaths reached over 500

in 10 days. Dr. John Snow, a local physician and public health's first disease detective, investigated the situation and concluded that the cause was sewage-contaminated water from the Broad Street pump. He advised a disbelieving but fear-struck assembly of officials to have the pump handle removed in order to deny access to the contaminated water. When this was done, the epidemic was controlled. The pump handle has remained a symbol of effective epidemiology, and today the John Snow Pub, located near the site of the former pump, boasts of having the original handle. A John Snow Society honors the memory of the epidemiologist (the only requirement for membership being that one visit the John Snow Pub while in London).

Introduction

In this chapter we examine the roles of public health and health care and how they affect our lives and the lives of our loved ones. The issues discussed reflect these questions:

- What are public health and health care? Are they different? Do they work together, and if so how?

- How do various agencies work together to address public health problems? What is the delivery system for health service in the United States?

- How has public health dealt with concerns such as bioterrorism, HIV/AIDS, tobacco and substance use, and children's health?

- How should problems of health care access among various populations be handled, including the uninsured, the immigrants, older Americans, those living in poverty, and those living in certain areas of the country?

- Where are all the health care dollars going and should we consider national health care?

- Can health care and public health work together?

Public health and health care are often on the opposite ends of a health continuum, due to the nature of their service delivery systems and philosophical approaches. Public health is shaped by numerous forces, which range from the molecular to the socioeconomic. Early intervention and prevention are key aspects of the public health domain. Public health's orientation to health care is geared toward a "population" rather than an "individual" perspective.

Health care has a different focus than public health. In the medical model of health care, the individual receives **acute** (severe but of short duration) or **chronic** (lasting a long time or recurring often) treatments after a medical problem or disease is discovered. For a very long time, medical tradition has focused on health in terms of the individual. Advances in medical knowledge have resulted because of a better grasp of the physiology and psychology of the individual. Interventions attempt to prevent or cure illness in the body.

Another health policy tradition considers the environment as more important to an individual's health than medical intervention. This idea lies behind public initiatives like sanitation, mass vaccination, and health promotion campaigns designed to alter unhealthy behavior. A final approach recognizes a dynamic interplay between the individual and the environment. It contends that a key contributor to health is the interaction between the individual and his or her social context. Negative interactions are associated with lower health status and positive interactions lead to higher health status. Due to the complex nature of health, it is necessary to consider health policy from a complex point of view (Glouberman, 2001). As you will see, there are no easy answers to the challenges of public health and health care. Concern about health care costs continues, as does the debate about access to health care. It is important to know how public health and health care affect the health of this nation and what areas need improvement. We will take a thorough look at how the two areas are different and how they work together.

What Is Public Health?

ISSUES: What are public health and health care? How are they different? In what areas of your life is public health involved? What is epidemiology, and how does it contribute to public health? Why don't more people understand the role of public health?

Few people know what "public health" actually means. In a Harris Poll from December 1996, approximately 1,000 people across the United States were asked, "What is public health?" Ninety percent of those questioned did not know. Only 3% responded with correct answers like "health education," "health promotion," and "immunization." Many of the respondents believed that public health is health care for the indigent, those with no means of paying (Levy, 1998).

Perhaps people do not know about public health because its activities are mostly carried out behind the scenes. The American Public Health Association describes public health as "a whole series of individuals, communities, activities and programs working to promote health, to prevent disease and injury, to prevent premature death—to ensure conditions in which we all can be safe and healthy" (American Public Health Association, http://www.apha.org/membership/aphamem.htm). While public health activities may not be noticed, the results are found throughout the day. Examples include:

- Getting up in the morning and turning on the water, expecting it to be safe.
- Using water that is fluoridated.
- Reading "Nutrition Facts" on the box while eating enriched breakfast cereal.
- Driving to work or to school in low-polluting and safer cars, equipped with air bags, seat belts, and child restraints.
- Spending the day in work and school environments that are continually monitored for hazard and safety threats.

Public health departments implement strategies to enforce safety measures in these areas and many more. Everyone uses the public health system daily, whether they know it or not (Levy, 1998).

The Institute of Medicine's definition from "The Future of Public Health" states: "Public health is what we, as a society, do collectively to assure the conditions in which people can be healthy" (p. 189, as cited in Levy, 1998). This includes 1) access to comprehensive high-quality health care, which provides diagnosis, treatment, rehabilitation, and preventive services; 2) community-based preventive services that are involved in preventing disease while promoting and protecting health; 3) education, research, policy analysis, and development; and 4) organizational infrastructure that supports it all.

Public health is involved in many aspects of daily life. Specializations include biostatistics, environmental and occupational health, epidemiology, health administration, international health, and public health nutrition. Public health activities are designed to prevent disease and injury, and to prevent premature death by assuring conditions in which individuals can be safe and healthy. Public health is also an investigating body for infectious diseases, food-borne disease outbreaks, and threats of bioterrorism (Levy, 1998). Careers for public health professionals include medicine, hospital administration, dentistry, education, and theology.

Health promotion and health education are major areas of concern for public health professionals. Promoting a balanced diet to reduce the risk of disease, attempting to prevent injuries, and spreading the word that exercise promotes health are all public health activities. Public health professionals attempt to prevent disease and increase life expectancy by educating the public about the benefits of exercise and physical activity (Eaton & Lapane, 1999).

Public health professionals are involved with controlling youth access to tobacco and reducing underage drinking and driving. Local public health professionals, who must work together with state and national health officials, are virtually the first to recognize every health problem in the communities—infectious disease outbreaks, chemical hazards, chronic diseases, birth defects, and injuries. The President's fiscal year 2002 budget allowed public health officials to address public health challenges through increased funding in areas such as birth defects and disability; environmental health; epidemic services; health statistics; prevention of HIV/AIDS, sexually transmitted diseases, and tuberculosis; immunization; control of infectious diseases; injury prevention; occupational safety and health; and public health improvement (Koplan, 2001).

Public health faces challenges that are not only complex and challenging, but also enmeshed in politics. Risk reduction through preventive and health promotion activities has been the primary focus of public health; however, the future of public health incorporates resilience, community lifestyle, and multisectoral "healthy public policy" (Levy & McBeath, 1991; Shannon, 1990). While only 3% of those surveyed actually knew what public health is, almost everyone supports its goals, values, and principles (Levy, 1998).

History of Public Health

John Snow, a 19th-century epidemiologist and anesthesiologist, achieved legendary status in the public-health field when he solved London's deadly cholera epidemic of 1854 by removing a pump handle and thereby for-

bidding access to contaminated water that he found to be the culprit. As you will recall from the story at the beginning of this chapter, closing the Broad Street pump put an end to one of the last cholera epidemics (Frerichs, 2000).

Snow was among the first doctors to use anesthesia; he administered chloroform to Queen Victoria during the births of two of her children. His resulting fame was a major reason authorities took notice of his theory on disease transmission. Snow believed that the main, although not only, means of transmission of cholera was water contaminated with an infecting organism or bacteria (the infecting organism produces poisonous substances). This analysis differed from a commonly held "miasma" theory that diseases are transmitted by inhalation of vapors; in other words, infection is due to contagion by airborne transmission. Snow was able to prove his theory in 1854 through painstaking documentation of cholera cases and correlation of the comparative incidence of cholera among subscribers to the city's two water companies (Center for Disease Control and Prevention, n.d.).

Snow was a skilled practitioner as well as an epidemiologist, and his creative use of the scientific information of his time is an appropriate example for those interested in disease prevention and control. The importance of John Snow is his recognition of the power of statistics and his influence on the field of epidemiology. He did not know what organism caused cholera, so he instead gathered what might have been thought of as anecdotal evidence, or stories. However, the cumulative effect of his meticulously gathered data put an end to the devastating cholera epidemic (CDC, n.d.).

What Is Epidemiology?

Modern **epidemiology** has become the backbone of public health and preventive medicine. It is simply defined as "the study of epidemics." This research science began with investigations of infectious disease outbreaks (as seen in the case of cholera and John Snow), which remain one focus of the epidemiologist's investigations. Modern epidemics include plagues of chronic illnesses such as heart disease, cancer, and stroke, as well as injuries. This relatively young science has become an indispensable component of public health, medicine, nursing, and allied health fields. Epidemiologic methods are used to investigate the natural histories of long- and short-duration infectious and non-contagious diseases. The public health approach to management of disease involves control through prevention and intervention. Epidemiological inquiry uses scientific methods to discover the origins of disease in human populations. Emphasis on **etiology**, or cause, has inspired some to describe the epidemiologist as a "medical detective" (Morgan, 1996).

Public Health's Break from Medicine

ISSUES: Why did public health break away from medicine? Was this a good idea? How do you think the two should be related to each other?

Initially, in the 19th century, public health and medicine were aligned and working together. In the early decades of the 20th century, however, this relationship began to dissolve. According to public health historians (Mathew & Meckel, 1990; Brandt & Gardner, 2000), when the medical profession became more solidly organized in defense of its collective interests it came to see an ambitious and increasingly independent public health profession as a threat. Rather than spend time solving the problems of poverty and ill health, public health practitioners began to count numbers of cases and publish the results. This shift toward scientific models of research and training created a separation of public health schools from public health practice. Public health schools built modern epidemiology and public health faculty adopted statistic and economic analyses. Students of public health moved into research positions or took jobs in federal, state, or municipal agencies, private foundations, insurance companies, or hospitals and clinics in a diverse and dispersed health care system. This led to a rapid increase in the number of statisticians in the 1950s and 1960s. In the 1970s and 1980s public health economists began calculating reimbursement rates and cost-effectiveness measures. In the 1990s there was a focus on evaluating clinical health services, managed care and medical care effectiveness, outcomes, and measures of quality (Fee & Brown, 2000).

In the 21st century, public health is renewing a previous philosophy—to put the public back into public health. Public health professionals are promoting measures to protect the public rather than providing health care. This involves disengagement from individual service provisions to focus again on the health of groups and populations. A good example of this is considering the needs of victims of second-hand smoke rather than treating individual smokers (J. Hopp, personal communication, September 27, 2001).

Public Health Agencies

ISSUES: What types of public health agencies are in the United States, and what role do they play? How is energy an issue of public health? Where should the balance be between the economy and health issues?

Many Voices: An Introduction to Social Issues

"Public health" is a very broad umbrella term for many agencies and departments. These include global as well as national organizations. In the United States there are federal, state, and local agencies.

Department of Health and Human Services (HHS)

Public health services include the Department of Health and Human Services (HHS, http://www.hhs.gov), which has various agencies and program offices. The department's mission is to protect health and help those who need assistance. Heading the HHS is a cabinet secretary who works under the President of the United States.

The HHS is responsible for public health in the United States. It supports the world's largest medical research effort, assures the safety of foods and health care products, and fights against the detrimental effects of drug and alcohol abuse. It is also responsible for providing support and protection to older Americans, infants and children, and people with disabilities. In times of crisis, the HHS services can save lives and rescue families. The HHS reaches citizens on important personal levels as well. For example, it works with state and local government and with private organizations to vaccinate children against disease, aid poor families who need income assistance or medical care, and help collect child support from absent parents.

National Institutes of Health (NIH)

The National Institutes of Health (NIH, http://www.hih.gov) is a public health service agency encompassing 17 separate institutes. It is the world's premier medical research organization, supporting nationwide some 37,000 research projects in diseases like cancer, Alzheimer's, diabetes, arthritis, heart ailments, and AIDS. From early experimentation on cancer in the 1930s, the institutes grew in number and importance. The bulk of the research is contracted out to universities and academic medical centers. In 1980, the NIH had a budget of $3.4 billion for nine institutes and affiliated activities, compared with $7.6 billion for 13 institutes and affiliated activities in 1990, and $14.9 billion (52% of the budget) in 2004.

Center for Disease Control and Prevention (CDC)

The Center for Disease Control and Prevention (CDC) operates under the direction of the Department of Health and Human Services. The CDC is a major force in national and international health. Its mission is to promote health and quality of life by preventing and controlling disease, injury, and disability (CDC, 2005). The CDC is a leading federal agency for protecting the health and safety of people in the United States and abroad. It serves the nation by developing and applying methods for disease prevention and control and environmental health; it also sponsors health promotion and education activities. In health emergencies, the initials "CDC" mean an answer to SOS calls from anywhere in the world.

The CDC plays a critical role in controlling infectious diseases, such as HIV and tuberculosis, but its work in protecting the public's health is not limited to mysterious disease outbreaks. In the 21st century the CDC has been involved in many major public health achievements, including healthier mothers and babies, safer and healthier foods, fluoridated drinking water, control of infectious disease, decline in deaths from heart disease and stroke, recognition of tobacco use as a health hazard, motor vehicle safety, and training global partners in HIV education and outreach. AIDS research and prevention activities at the CDC continue to this day. The CDC also evaluates family violence prevention programs, conducts research on the prevention of workplace injury and disease, and protects children from preventable diseases through immunizations. One of its major prevention achievements has been the National Childhood Immunization campaign. All of these activities protect public health and safety (Koplan, 2001).

The CDC has a rich history in disease investigation and public health protection. For example, in 1946 when it first opened, its mission was to work with state and local health officials in the fight against malaria, typhus, and other communicable diseases. In 1951, the CDC assumed responsibility for the control of polio and by 1991 the disease had almost disappeared from the Western Hemisphere. Using the Epidemic Intelligence Service (EIS) as a quick response team, the CDC is able to investigate and respond to a wide range of health emergencies. The EIS was sent out when outbreaks occurred of Legionnaire's disease, smallpox, and acquired immunodeficiency syndrome (AIDS).

Through the CDC's efforts, smallpox was eradicated from the world in 1977. This disease had killed millions of people over the centuries. Supposedly, only a few vials of smallpox exist today for research purposes in labs in Russia and the United States. Smallpox is back in the news as a possible biochemical terrorist threat. Are those who were vaccinated for smallpox in the 1950s and 1960s still immune today? Experts do not know for sure. It is doubtful and there is no need to take the chance. The United States is quickly producing smallpox vaccinations in case terrorists attack with smallpox.

Another important goal for the CDC and public health professionals is to provide credible information to enhance health decisions. The agency accomplishes this through health tracking and monitoring to reduce disease, disability, and premature death. Health surveys are employed, such as the National Health and Nutrition Examination Survey (NHANES, http://www.cdc.gov/nchs/nhanes.htm). This survey helps identify critical, potentially hidden dangers, such as the effects of lead exposure on children.

Environmental Protection Agency (EPA)

The nation needs a balanced energy policy that meets requirements for public health protection and environmental quality controls. Issues facing the Environmental Protection Agency (EPA, http://www.epa.gov) include America's freight needs, plant emissions, and home energy supplies and costs. Providing enough energy for America is a chronic problem. The United States consumes almost one fourth of the world's energy supply even though it contains a mere 5% of the world's population. Energy is needed to heat homes and businesses, power computers and telephone systems, run automobiles and aircraft, drive manufacturing plants and hospitals, and deliver goods. Meeting these demands has meant extracting as much fuel as possible, mostly in fossil form (oil, coal, and natural gas), hoping that demand can be met by supply. However, the future calls for innovation and new technology to meet energy needs while remaining environmentally

responsible (Kassel, 2001).

One area of focus for the EPA is to create cleaner trucks for the movement of goods around the country. Diesel trucks have provided America's freight movement, yet the pollution they emit has created a long-term pollution problem. Diesel trucks and buses use more than 5,000,000 barrels of crude oil per day. They account for more than 40% of the nation's transportation energy use, yet comprise only about 7% of the nation's vehicles. Diesel truck exhaust contains soot particles that have been linked to increased asthma attacks, cancer, and even premature death (Kassel, 2001).

Links have been found between particulate matter and a wide variety of health problems. These include increased asthma attacks, endocrine disruption, numerous cardiopulmonary ailments, cancer, and premature death. The National Resource Defense Council (NRDC) is increasingly concerned about growing evidence that diesel particulates are associated with increased cancer risk. Several national and world organizations have considered diesel exhaust as a probable human carcinogen (Kassel, 2001).

In some urban areas, more than half of the particulate matter comes from diesel tailpipes. In addition, diesel tailpipes are responsible for smog- and acid-rain-causing nitrogen oxides. A very diverse coalition of supporters for a drastic emissions reduction plan joined with public health agencies and professionals to slash soot particles by 90%, starting in the year 2007. This will be done by reducing sulfur in diesel fuel by 97%, which will greatly reduce tailpipe emissions of smog-forming nitrogen oxides. The result of coalition efforts will be diesel vehicles that achieve gasoline-like emissions levels. This program, called the EPA Diesel Rule, is touted as having the ability to remove pollution from 13 million of today's 14 million trucks on the road. The Diesel Rule will aid in the elimination of 2.6 million tons/year of nitrogen oxides, 115,000 tons/year of non-methane hydrocarbons, and 109,000 tons/year of particulates. The public health impact is the avoidance of 8,300 premature deaths, more than 23,000 cases of acute or chronic bronchitis, and 360,000 asthma attacks, along with other health benefits annually (Kassel, 2001).

Public Health Concerns

ISSUES: How should public health deal with an epidemic like AIDS? To reduce the AIDS epidemic, should we focus on prevention, isolation, or other methods? How have tobacco companies targeted young people? How far should the government go to reduce tobacco use? Should a government both subsidize tobacco and try to reduce its use? What can be done about drug use? Should organizations like DanceSafe test illegal drugs for users? Which model makes more sense to you—the disease model of addiction or the harm reduction model? What makes children a vulnerable group in terms of public health? What can public health do for children? How far should genes be studied or manipulated to enhance health? Will the knowledge of disease genes lead to discrimination against some people?

Bioterrorism

Bioterrorism is currently a public health concern. It is especially frightening because a lone terrorist could cause a major disease outbreak in the population, which might not be detected for some time (Health and Human Services, 2003). Since September 11, 2001, and the subsequent anthrax terrorist attacks, a fear of bioterrorism has invaded our culture. People have reacted by shunning flying; demanding more vaccines; buying gas masks, duct tape, and plastic sheeting; and avoiding large gatherings of people. Fears of being chemically attacked have created mass panic; at the E2 nightclub in Chicago on February 17, 2003, 21 people died when there was a mad rush for the door after a security guard used pepper spray to break up a fight (Thigpen, 2003).

Fighting bioterrorism is a good example of various public health agencies at the national, state, and local levels all working together to help improve our safety. The nation's public health workforce consists of 500,000 physicians, nurses, environmental health scientists, health educators, laboratory workers, and managers, supplemented by over three million other professionals, first responders, and volunteers who form the public health front line (Center for Disease Control and Prevention—Bioterrorism, 2003). President Bush named the Federal Emergency Management Agency (FEMA) to coordinate federal response

efforts in the event of bioterrorism. The United States Department of Health and Human Services (HHS) would detect the disease, investigate the outbreak, and provide stockpiled drugs and emergency supplies in the amounts needed (Health and Human Services—Bioterrorism, 2003). The HHS had a $350 million budget for anti-bioterrorism initiatives in 2002. The U.S. committed a total of $1.5 billion in new funding for research on bioterrorism in 2003 (Cassels, 2002).

The CDC website has several sites and links to various plans and information on bioterrorism (Center for Disease Control and Prevention—Bioterrorism, 2003). The CDC has been preparing for bioterrorism since 1998, and plans were put into action in the fall of 2001 with the first bioterrorist attack in the United States. It was proven that rapid identification and communication are essential as the first response. The complexity of the 2001 anthrax investigation and response challenged even experienced field epidemiologists (Perkins et al., 2002). Difficulties arose in trying to identify risks to those exposed to anthrax (Perkins et al., 2002). In response, regional and state laboratories have strengthened their capacity to detect different biological and chemical agents and to communicate the results to the CDC.

There is much room for improvement in our ability to contend with bioterrorism. Formal assessment of national, state, and local public health systems capacities is needed, and there is concern about whether agencies at all these levels will be able to work together in a crisis (http://www.cdc.gov/programs, 2003). The CDC believes the nation's current public health infrastructure is not adequate enough to detect and respond to a large-scale bioterrorist event.

HIV/AIDS

HIV/AIDS has become a very serious public health issue. The first cases of an unusual immune system disease was identified in gay men in 1981; it probably originated in monkeys in Africa. By 1982, the disease was named acquired immunodeficiency syndrome (AIDS). Three modes of transmission were identified: blood transfusion, mother-to-child, and sexual intercourse. At first AIDS appeared to be a problem only for the homosexual community and drug users who shared dirty needles. It soon became apparent that the heterosexual community, especially women, was also at risk. Human immunodeficiency virus (HIV) was identified as the cause of AIDS in 1983. In that same year, a heterosexual AIDS epidemic was revealed in Africa. In sub-Saharan Africa and the Caribbean, heterosexual activity was identified as the most common route of exposure in 2001 (UNAIDS Factsheet, 2004).

Africa has been decimated by AIDS; millions die and millions become orphans every year. The Caribbean has the second highest infection rate. It is a sexual playground for American tourists, and thus a threat to American public health. While drug treatment has come a long way in industrialized countries, it is still expensive, so most people in developing countries cannot afford this option. An AIDS vaccine may not be developed for years (Susser & Stein, 2000). Therefore, prevention has become the way public health and government officials most often attempt to address the epidemic.

But public health concerns and agendas are often complicated by political and international involvement. Southern Africa is engulfed in the tragic AIDS epidemic through heterosexual transmission. It is estimated that one in ten young women in southern Africa will become infected each year.

Prevention programs have become mired in political and cultural debates. Among some groups, a woman can insist that a man use a male condom, and she can withhold sex if he refuses. Among other groups, a woman's request that her partner use a male condom is seen as a challenge to his authority. The female condom that lets women control their protection has shown promise, but there needs to be more education on use and more condoms made available. Each community must be studied in terms of the local situation and preventive strategies must take into account the differences between communities (Susser & Stein, 2000).

The cooperation of world health organizations has placed a focus on HIV/AIDS that has increased remarkably since 1980. As these organizations become more vocal and provide more opportunities for educating the public about this disease, it is providing an impact on the ability to make a significant statement about interest in prevention and treatment.

Tobacco Use

Nearly 3,000 young people across the country begin smoking regularly every day. The CDC helps implement tobacco prevention programs. By not using tobacco, children may be spared a premature death from heart disease or cancer. For example, in California, a comprehensive tobacco prevention program began in 1989. Between 1989 and 1999, per-capita consumption of cigarettes in California declined by more than 50%. As a result, there are reductions in rates of lung and bronchus cancer in California (Koplan, 2001).

Fifty percent of all smokers begin using tobacco before the age of 14, and 90% start smoking before age 20. Each day more than 4,000 kids under 18 try their first cigarette and more than 2,000 become regular, daily smokers, leading to 750,000 new underage smokers every year. To maintain its current U.S. market, the tobacco industry must create some 5,000 new young smokers every day to replace those who either die or quit. Children and adolescents consume more than one billion packs of cigarettes a year (American Heart Association, n.d.). According to DiFranza and Tye (1990), "Although tobacco's victims range in age from the unborn to the elderly, the addiction that fosters tobacco use can be considered a childhood disease" (p. 2,784). The facts are simple: one out of three adolescents in the United States is using tobacco by age 18. Preventing young people from starting to use tobacco is the key to reducing the death and disease caused by tobacco use (Shalala, 1994).

Many Voices: An Introduction to Social Issues

In 1994, the Surgeon General's Report, "Preventing Tobacco Use among Young People," became public. Several important points were made in this report:

- Nearly all first-time tobacco use occurs before high school graduation; this finding suggests that if adolescents can be kept tobacco-free, most will never start using tobacco.
- Most adolescent smokers are addicted to nicotine and report that they want to quit but are unable to do so; they experience relapse rates and withdrawal symptoms similar to those reported by adults.
- Tobacco is often the first drug used by those young people who use alcohol, marijuana, and other drugs.
- Adolescents with lower levels of school achievement, fewer skills to resist pervasive influences to use tobacco, friends who use tobacco, and lower self-images are more likely than their peers to use tobacco.
- Cigarette advertising appears to increase young people's risk of smoking by affecting their perceptions of the image and function of smoking.

How does advertising play into smoking initiation? Do you remember Joe Camel? In the 1960s, R. J. Reynolds (RJR), the manufacturer of Camel cigarettes, was desperate to find a way to compete with Marlboro for the 14- to 24-year-old market. RJR needed to attract minors since, as noted earlier, 90% of all smokers start smoking by age 20 and cigarette users are very loyal to their first brand. In the early 1980s, RJR began using the terms "young adult smokers" and "first usual brand young adult smokers" as innocent catchy phrases for illegal underage smokers. The importance of new smokers is further underscored by RJR's extensive efforts to counteract the Anti-Youth Smoking Movement. The Joe Camel campaign was intentionally developed by RJR to target people younger than 18 years of age. Two years prior to its domestic launch, RJR conducted a focus group with 18- to 24-year-olds. The tobacco company learned that these young people thought Joe Camel was aimed at an even younger audience. Despite its claim that peer pressure is to blame, RJR's internal documents demonstrate that advertising can and does get kids to smoke cigarettes (Coughlin et al., 1998).

The pervasiveness of Joe Camel advertising and promotions was an important ingredient in the character's success with the child market. Contrary to RJR's claims, the Joe Camel campaign was principally designed to attract new users, not to obtain "switchers." Image advertising is more effective with teens than information advertising because teens pay less attention to factual information. Advertising themes of rebelliousness, independence, individuality, and fun are the best themes to motivate teenagers to try cigarettes. The cartoon nature of the Joe Camel ads made the campaign particularly appealing to children.

R. J. Reynolds chose to run Joe Camel advertisements in magazines that were known to be widely read by teens. The company used outdoor advertising as an effective medium for reaching the youth market. Sponsoring sporting events is a powerful method of directing advertising to teenagers. In addition to sporting events, RJR also sponsored local cultural events in order to market its cigarettes to teens. Moreover, RJR identified convenience stores and other locations where teens gather and made sure that the Joe Camel image was strategically displayed. It employed marketing techniques to ensure that teenagers saw the Joe Camel image (Coughlin et al., 1998).

The Joe Camel campaign was extremely successful in addicting teens to cigarettes. Within just three years of its inception, the cartoon character had a remarkable influence on children's smoking behavior. With implementation of the Joe Camel campaign, the brand's popularity with teenagers soared 33- to 66-fold as determined by various studies. In 1991, RJR's share of the illegal teen market surged from .05% in 1988 to an estimated 33% in 1991. Teen smokers accounted for $476 million of Camel sales in 1991 compared with just $6 million before the Camel campaign (DiFranza et al., 1991). Additionally, according to a 1994 study, California's multi-million-dollar anti-smoking television ad campaign had sharply cut smoking by adults and by teenagers until the advent of the Joe Camel campaign, at which time the downward trend for teenagers reversed. This study demonstrated that the increase in teenage smoking was tied to the Joe Camel advertising campaign. It concluded that smoking prevalence among 16- to 18-year-old Californians appeared to be increasing sharply after the introduction of the Joe Camel tobacco advertising campaign (Pierce et al., 1994).

The Journal of the American Medical Association publicly charged RJR Tobacco Company in 1991 with targeting children through its Joe Camel campaign. In the same year, a San Francisco family law attorney,

Janet C. Mangini, brought a suit against RJR to end the Joe Camel campaign. The California Supreme Court agreed that Ms. Mangini should be permitted to prosecute her claims, stating that "the targeting of minors is oppressive and unscrupulous, in that it exploits minors by luring them into unhealthy and potentially life-threatening addiction before they have achieved the maturity necessary to make an informed decision whether to take up smoking despite the health risks" (Mangini v. R. J. Reynolds, 1991, as cited in Coughlin et al., 1998). In May 1997, the City and County of San Francisco, along with the Cities of Los Angeles and San Jose and ten additional California counties, interceded in the suit to help terminate the Joe Camel campaign. As the trial date neared, RJR approached the plaintiffs to decide if the Mangini action could be resolved if the campaign was stopped. Two things happened as a result of this. RJR terminated the Joe Camel campaign and the Mangini settlement provided for the public release of RJR's confidential documents about youth marketing. The RJR documents are now publicly available as a result of the settlement (Coughlin et al., 1998).

Where is Joe now? Joe Camel is now Joe Chemo. He has been in and out of hospitals ever since he developed lung cancer. Although Joe Chemo may seem like a joke, there's nothing funny about chemotherapy. The web site http://www.joechemo.org is dedicated to chemo patients and their family members, with the hope that it will reduce the number of people who smoke cigarettes and have to suffer through medical treatment. Joe Chemo was developed as an antismoking character by Scott Plous, a psychology professor at Wesleyan University, after his father nearly died from smoking. The idea was to present a more honest image of smoking than the Joe Camel character used by R. J. Reynolds.

In Canada, warning labels on cigarette packages are extremely graphic: yellow teeth and swollen, blackened gums; a human heart oozing with blood clots; cancer tumors ballooning out of a lung; a limp cigarette with a message about impotence.

Canadian smokers have a graphic reminder of smoking's possible effects on their bodies each time they pick up a pack. Under a new law, all cigarettes sold in Canada must contain warnings that Canadian health officials tout as the strongest in the world. The goal, said Andrew Swift, spokesperson for Health Canada, the Canadian government's health department, is to get smokers to quit and prevent others from starting. Unlike the U.S. Surgeon General warnings on packs sold in the United States, the Canadian warning labels must cover 50% of the front and back of a pack. And instead of just words, these warnings feature pictures like a newborn baby in an intensive care unit or a young boy pleading not to be poisoned through secondhand smoke.

"Canada's tobacco companies aren't too pleased. They filed a lawsuit in the summer challenging the constitutionality of the law, saying the warnings, among other things, infringe upon their trademarks. That suit is working its way through the court system and could take years to resolve. 'There is no credible evidence whatsoever that these will have any impact on people's decision to smoke,' said John McDonald, spokesman for Rothman, Benson & Hedges, an Ontario-based tobacco company, partly owned by U.S. company Philip Morris. 'It's become more of a harassment of the industry rather than dealing with the issue of smoking.' There are 16 different pack warnings. Each is aimed at a specific group: women, men, nonsmokers, parents" (Wendland-Bowyer, 2000, par. 8–10).

The current war against tobacco has had some positive effects. Smoking among high school seniors is at its lowest level in 27 years (http://www.tobacco-freekids.org, 2002). However, big tobacco companies are still trying to market their products to kids. They spend $9.6 billion a year on advertising, and 25% of high school seniors are smokers. More than 2,000 teenagers become addicted to tobacco every day, leading to 1/3 of them dying prematurely as a result (http://www.tobaccofreekids.org, 2002).

Substance Abuse: The Nation's Number One Health Problem

Legal and illicit drug use is a serious problem in this country. Researchers have found that alcohol and tobacco use is related to increased health problems, greater health service needs, and higher health provision costs (National Institutes of Health, 1997; Meyers, 2000). Unfortunately, drug use is especially popular among teens and young adults. Every generation of teens seems to have its illegal drug of choice. In the 1960s it was LSD, in the 1970s it was marijuana and hashish, in the 1980s it was cocaine, and during the 1990s methamphetamine was favored. Now the drug in the forefront is ecstasy, a chemical cousin to amphetamine and hallucinogens.

The club drug ecstasy (i.e., XTC, MDMA, Adam, etc.) was popular at first because it was seen as providing a safe and enjoyable sensory experience at parties. Research has proven this impression wrong. Initial use of MDMA can cause a significant increase in heart rate, blood pressure, and body temperature and can result in dehydration and heart irregularities. These conditions also may result in liver, kidney, and cardiovascular system failure. A few cases have resulted in user deaths. In animal studies, repeated doses of MDMA have produced long-lasting damage to the neurons that release serotonin. Serotonin is a critical **neurochemical** that regulates mood, emotion, learning, memory, and sleep. Studies on human beings have consistently reported consequences including depression, anxiety, and sleep deprivation that can last for days or weeks after using MDMA (National Institute on Drug Abuse, http://www.drugabuse.gov/ClubAlert/ClubDrugAlert.html).

The Monitoring the Future survey found in 2002 that ecstasy use was down among teens after several years of increasing use. Monitoring the Future is a survey that has been conducted since 1980 by The University of Michigan's Institute for Social Research through a series of grants made by the National Institute on Drug Abuse (Monitoring the Future, 2005). The 2002 survey results were based on nationally representative samples of 8th, 10th, and 12th graders attending public and private schools in the United States. In all, 44,000 students completed the survey. Among high school seniors, annual use rates dropped by 24%, with only 7.4% using ecstasy. The message is getting across that ecstasy use can be dangerous. In 2000, only 38% of high school seniors thought there was a "great risk" in using ecstasy once or twice. By 2002 that number grew to 52%.

In fact, all drug use has declined among teens, except for methamphetamine use, which has remained stable among 10th and 12th graders, but not 8th graders. Dr. Lloyd D. Johnston, program director and research scientist at the University of Michigan's Institute for Social Research, believes this age cohort is simply using drugs less than an age cohort in the 1990s that had higher drug use rates (The Nation's Health, 2003). Peer influence is very powerful. For more information on Monitoring the Future, see http://www.isr.umich.edu, http://www.monitoringthefuture.org, and http://www.nida.nih.gov.

What about Abstention?

With the disease model, complete abstinence is necessary to arrest drug addiction. One drink or one drug will lead the "ill" person to potentially lose control and become an addict (DanceSafe, 2005). This view has been controversial since it was introduced by E. M. Jellinek in 1960. The disease model proposes that alcohol and drug addiction is the primary diagnosis, not a secondary diagnosis. It views addiction as a treatable disease with a genetic link (Page, 1997). Whether this view is helpful or not, one fact is clear: Abstention is the only way to avoid all the harms associated with drug use. This has been the official view of the U.S. government for decades. Prevention programs have been developed with abstention in mind. However, such programs have not been very successful.

The National Center on Addiction and Substance Abuse at New York's Columbia University found that children are beginning to smoke cigarettes daily, drink alcohol, and use marijuana at younger and younger ages. Public health attempts to reduce the rates of substance use and abuse but, more importantly, it designs prevention programs and strategies. In general, most teenagers understand quite a bit about the health and social consequences of drug use, and are not easily fooled by exaggerated claims of danger. Research has found that prevention programs which attempt to scare adolescents straight with exaggerated warnings have virtually no impact. In other words, lack of knowledge is not the problem, although it is one of the many factors that lead to substance abuse. Part of the problem with drug abuse prevention to date is that schools are not using programs that have been tested. The best prevention approaches are developed by researchers, generally in universities, but there is a wide gap between research and practice. Helping schools learn about and use the proven approaches is one of the biggest challenges to the prevention effort (Institute for Social Research, n.d.; Firshein, n.d.).

What Is Harm Reduction?

Harm reduction begins with the observation that despite all our efforts as a society to prevent the use of illicit drugs, people are using them anyway, and it seems unlikely that this situation is going to change soon. This necessitates a practical response to reduce the harm that is taking place right now. And this response is called, appropriately enough, harm reduction (DanceSafe, 2005).

The various harm reduction models contend that individuals must be engaged at the point where they are and moved from there in small manageable steps to increasing levels of improved self-care, health, and well-being; in other words, the goal is not necessarily complete abstinence. For example, rather than attempting to stop the use of heroin altogether, harm reductionists would advocate reducing the threat of diseases by providing clean needles.

The harm reduction movement chooses health and personal responsibility over punishment for behavioral misadventures. It chooses treatment of all varieties, including abstinence-based approaches, over incarceration of the addicted, and the method is less costly. The miserable lack of results from the current "war on drugs" makes one wonder why other approaches are not seriously considered (Marlatt, 1998).

Harm reduction is not likely to be the focus of the current war on drugs anytime soon. Government officials believe it is a dangerous approach and fear it will encourage more young people to start or continue using drugs. Harm reduction cannot get rid of all the damage associated with drug use; it merely reduces the level of danger in increments. There is strong public sentiment in favor of harm reduction, especially among the recreational drug using community. Volunteer organizations have developed harm reduction programs of their own.

DanceSafe is a nonprofit, mostly volunteer organization that uses harm reduction and popular education to address the drug problem in the U.S. and Canada. Educated volunteers who are part of the electronic dance community put up booths at raves, nightclubs, and other dance events. They provide information on drugs, safer sex, driving home safely, and drug treatment referral information, and they also test drugs for added potentially harmful substances. The DanceSafe website, http://www.dancesafe.org, provides additional information geared towards non-addicted, recreational drug users, who are an underserved population despite the fact that they comprise the vast majority of drug users in our society (DanceSafe, 2005).

Child and Adolescent Health

Children are the future and represent the potential for a healthy society. The U.S. Bureau of the Census (2000) estimates that children under the age of 18 comprise 25.7% of the nation's population. There are urgent challenges for public health professionals who are concerned with this important and vulnerable group. At the very least, there is a dire need to ensure that children reach adulthood as healthy and contributing members of society (Schneider & Northridge, 1999).

In 1994, over 47,000 children younger than 15 years old died in the United States, most from preventable causes. The ones who survived developed into adolescence with 32% diagnosed with one or more chronic health problems, including asthma, depression, and frequent headaches. In addition, at least two million children in the nation are classified as learning disabled. Public health can help improve (lower) these numbers by providing research, prevention programs, participation in children's advocacy, and social and political solutions. Problematic childhood conditions have direct and indirect causes. Direct causes may include genetic defects, infectious agents, and violence. Indirect causes may include poverty, negative environmental effects, and poor access to medical care (Schneider & Northridge, 1999).

Public health programs often target populations and age groups at special risk (e.g., toddlers for lead screening, adolescents for safe sex practices). In addition to individual interventions, public health officials may intervene at a community-based level. To increase the health and well-being of all children, public health must address community and societal threats, as well as individual ones. For example, infant injuries from traffic accidents have been reduced since the introduction of infant car seats (Schneider & Northridge, 1999).

When it comes to children, public health programs can and do make a difference. A good illustration is injury prevention. In the United States, the problem of injuries is enormous. Although most childhood injuries are not fatal, injury is the primary killer of U.S. children, accounting for more deaths than all childhood diseases combined. These injuries include falls, traffic, assault, and near drownings. A prevention strategy to reduce disabling and fatal brain injuries is the mandatory use of helmets for bicyclists. This is one of public health's success stories. Others are immunization programs for children, preventing debilitating and killer diseases such as diphtheria, hepatitis B, measles, mumps, pertussis, poliomyelitis, and rubella. Unfortunately, large numbers of children in the United States are still not properly vaccinated, especially recent immigrants.

A children's health problem that has not declined in recent years is asthma. Indeed, the rate of asthma has increased by 42% over the last 10 years (CDC, 1996). Nearly 7% of children under the age of 18 are affected, and for certain urban Latino populations the rates are as high as 18%. In some urban areas, childhood asthma rates are three times the national rate. Children who die from asthma and its complications usually live in cities. Black children are four times more likely than white children to die from asthma (Schneider & Northridge, 1999).

Asthma is costly. From 1993 to 1999, over three billion dollars in medical costs were incurred due to asthma and its complications (Marwick, 1997). Every year, over 10.1 million school days are lost due to asthma (Taylor & Newacheck, 1992). Interventions designed to help children suffering from this disease target deteriorated and substandard housing projects, with a focus on cockroach allergen as a possible precipitating factor. In the South Bronx of New York there is a program to reduce cockroaches in the homes of children with asthma. It is not known whether this strategy will reduce the symptoms of asthma; however, public health is educating the community about asthma and cockroach infestation reduction. This public health challenge involves not only children and their families, but also landlords, their property, and the burden of cost and possible loss of homes (Schneider & Northridge, 1999).

Childhood obesity has become an ever increasing problem in the United States and worldwide, especially in industrialized countries. Thirteen percent of children in the United States are overweight (Tanne, 2002). There are a couple of potential causes for this. Children are not as active as they used to be, with several sedentary activities occupying them: television, video games, and the internet. U.S. children ages 8 to 16 who watch four or more hours of television per day had higher rates of obesity than children who watched less than two hours of television per day (Ogden et al., 1997). High-energy, high-fat foods have become increasingly prevalent in today's culture. It is difficult to ignore the bright containers, good taste, and entertaining commercials tempting impressionable young taste buds and minds. The food industry spends enormous amounts of money to promote high-calorie processed foods of poor nutritional quality. Not only are we eating more junk food, but we are eating more calories than in decades past, an increase of 200 calories a day between 1977 and 1994. Parents are busier than ever and may not have time to cook nutritious meals. More meals are eaten out and the portions are larger today than 30 years ago (Young & Nestle, 2002). When meals are cooked at home, often they are only refined foods from a box to which a few ingredients are added. Although the obesity epidemic has affected a wide age range, most ethnic groups, and people of every socioeconomic status, certain groups have a greater difficulty with this problem. In industrialized countries, obesity is more common among minority groups and those of lower socioeconomic status because of poor diet and less access to physical activities (Ebbeling, Pawlak, & Ludwig, 2002).

Several negative side effects accompany obesity in children. There can be a severe emotional toll when there is excessive teasing. Family members may give an obese child a hard time. This can lead to low self-esteem, depression, and even suicidal thoughts. The mind and emotions are not the only areas affected by extra weight; the body suffers as well. With the increase in obese children there has also been an increase of type 2 diabetes, **hyperlipidemia** (an excess of fats or lips in the blood), and **hypertension** (abnormally high blood pressure), all associated with excess weight. Such conditions used to occur only in adults; now children have to deal with these potentially debilitating and deadly diseases.

Childhood obesity often leads to adult obesity, which carries such additional health hazards as heart disease (the leading cause of death in the United States), diabetes, orthopedic problems, and many other chronic diseases (DeOnis and Blossner, 2000). Currently, more than 61% of U.S. adults are overweight and 20% are extremely overweight (Tanne, 2002; Flegal, Carroll, Kuczmarski, & Johnson, 1998). There was an increase in obesity by 50% between 1991 and 1998 (Mokdad et al., 1999). In the United States, 280,000 deaths a year are attributable to obesity (Allison, Fontaine, Manson, Stevens, & Vanitallie, 1999). All these statistics add up to obesity being responsible for about 7% of the United States' total health care costs (Colditz, 1999). Childhood obesity has been calculated to cost $127 million in annual hospital costs alone (Wang & Dietz, 2002).

It is imperative that childhood obesity be tackled now to prevent a health care crisis in future generations (Laing, 2002). Public health's role is to educate and produce potential solutions, but the solutions have been tentative so far (Bauman, 2002). Increasing activity, improving diet, and limiting television are key. Beyond these simple solutions, public health workers must examine the economic, social, and cultural context of childhood obesity (Laing, 2002). Our culture encourages consumption of high-energy foods and encourages sedentary entertainment (Bauman, 2002). Even institutions that are supposed to help children can contribute to this problem. In order for schools to balance their budgets, physical education and after-school activities have been cut (Andersen, 2000).

Unfortunately, no weight reduction program has been found effective in curbing the obesity epidemic (Visscher & Seidell, 2001). Prevention works better than treating those who are already overweight (Russell, Williamson, & Byers, 1995). Just encouraging minimal changes in the energy balance could help in the long run (Visscher & Seidell, 2001). The food industry must be held accountable for larger portion sizes and the public educated as to appropriate amounts to eat when out or at home (Young & Nestle, 2002). Weight gain prevention programs must be seen as important in the scientific and political arenas (Visscher & Siedell, 2001). In 2002, three senators in the U.S. introduced the Improved Nutrition and Physical Activity Acts, which would provide up to $217 million a year to federal and state agencies (Tanne, 2002). The money would be used to identify obesity risk factors, analyze food assistance programs, and improve exercise and nutrition programs.

Genetics and Gene Therapy

The future of public health may depend partly on the identification of genes that make us susceptible to common diseases such as diabetes, asthma, and cancer. Knowledge of human genome sequences may also lead to the identification of genetic variants that define a patient's response to a particular drug. Fulfilling the promise of the genome sequence even partially may move genetics beyond specialist centers and impact the diagnosis and management of common disorders in primary care. This will in turn impact public health (Mathew, 2001).

Epidemiological evidence suggests that common diseases that are thought to be determined largely by environment and lifestyle may also have a genetic link to risk. Multiple sclerosis is an example of a complex disorder in which both genes and environment contribute to pathogenesis.

There is evidence for complex disease or susceptibility genes that may help determine which people are at risk for a particular disorder. Knowledge of risk would help people avoid the environmental triggers that convert genetic susceptibility into disease. In identifying these genes, scientists could also learn about the molecular pathways that lead to the disease state, and identify new important targets for drug treatment (Mathew, 2001).

Although progress in finding disease genes has been slow, some disorders are associated with promising findings. An increased risk for Alzheimer's disease has been linked to human chromosome 19. This type of knowledge may help guide treatment while a cure is sought. In the future, perhaps within the next 10 years, genotyping may become part of routine disease management. Knowledge of susceptibility genes for complex disorders might be applied in various clinical settings (Mathew, 2001).

Health Care

ISSUES: Should health care focus more on the individual or on the environment? What do you think would be the best way to deliver health care? How should access be improved? Do you favor national health care programs? Is health care a "right" for individuals in the United States? What should be done to bring health care costs down? Should the market determine what is fair?

Health care is the total societal effort to guarantee, provide, finance, and promote health. It can be organized or unorganized, private or public. Health services, provided by medical practitioners and organizations, are the delivery component of health care. Health care and health services developed significantly during the 20th century, moving toward an ideal of wellness and prevention of disease and disability, in comparison with acute restorative care. Public policy initiatives were increasingly interventionist. These changes were smooth at times and turbulent at others (Rakich, Longest, & Darr, 1998).

Concepts of health can be categorized into three categories: those that focus on the body as an organism, those that stress the environment, and those that recognize the importance of the interaction between the two. As stated earlier, the quality of the interaction between individuals and their social contexts is a major contributor to health. This allows for a dynamic picture of health and recognizes that positive interactions, such as those in good parenting, improve health, and that negative ones, such as those in poor work environments, harm it. Health care is part of a complex health system that covers a broad spectrum, including public health, health services, health promotion, and inequalities in health (Glouberman, 2001).

Brief History of Health Services

In the mid-19th century, public health ensured the availability of pure food and water during the "great sanitary awakening" (Schoenbach, 1999). This led to the establishment of state and local health departments. Major contributions to medical knowledge by Pasteur, Lister, and Koch resulted at about the same time. Louis Pasteur identified **bacillus anthracis** (a well-known species pathogenic to humans) as the cause of anthrax, and moved the scientific world into what has become known as "the golden age of microbiology." Pasteur's work established the science of microbiology and led to the development of many sophisticated methods for culturing and isolating microorganisms. He paved the way for later researchers who applied his methods to the understanding, treatment, and prevention of human diseases. Robert Koch was a German microbiologist who introduced scientific rigor to the study of disease causation. His findings led to a model that bacteriologists continue to use today (Morgan, 1996;

Rakich et al., 1998). The efforts of these men led to **antisepsis** (destruction of disease, causing microorganisms to prevent infection) and later **asepsis** (the process of removing pathogenic microorganisms or protecting against infection by such organisms), and to such technologies as radiographs, inhalation anesthesia, and blood typing. Clinical laboratories improved in the late 19th century, permitting significant surgical interventions that greatly reduced morbidity and mortality.

With these developments came the need for organization, personnel, and systems to deliver the new wonders that medicine had to offer. Acute hospitals were an obvious innovation. These hospitals were sponsored by private, not-for-profit corporations that had been formed by concerned citizens and wealthy benefactors; local governments sponsored others. Individual physicians often established smaller hospitals for their patients. Long-term care facilities or nursing homes were rare because extended families assisted their relatives. People with mental illness were warehoused and isolated from society in facilities owned almost exclusively by state governments. Effective, large-scale treatment for them was not available until after World War II, with the development of psychoactive drugs. Public health departments were another type of **health service organization** (HSO), sponsored by local governments (Rakich et al., 1998).

There has been a drastic change in the causes of mortality since the 19th century. Health problems common at the middle of the 19th century were largely solved through preventive measures undertaken by public health departments. Pure food and water and improved sanitation were major contributors. There were few chronic diseases before the 20th century in the United States. Primarily, people died at younger ages of acute gastrointestinal and respiratory tract infections that usually occurred before they developed a chronic disease. Mortality rates have been declining due to technology and scientific discoveries. People are living longer, and with longevity comes the likelihood of more chronic diseases. Acute services have increased and so have the costs of medical care. Chronic diseases often reflect a link between lifestyle and medical problems. If prevention is to be effective, behavior must be changed. Such efforts raise questions of individual choice and free will that are far more complex than purifying water and protecting food supplies. What should be the limits of society's efforts to force people to live healthfully? What is society's obligation to aid people whose illnesses result from unhealthy activities? Consider the following paraphrased story from the *Washington Post* (November 21, 2001).

The Montgomery Council voted to set $750 fines for people who smoke in their homes if it offends their neighbors. This is part of the county's new indoor air quality standards. Tobacco smoke was put on the list with asbestos, radon, molds, and pesticides—potentially harmful pollutants. This legislation was originally meant to protect residents; for example, protecting children in day care from fumes that came from an auto body shop next door. The legislation also gives people bothered by their neighbor's smoking a place to complain, the county's Department of Environmental Protection. First the department will educate the offenders on how to better ventilate their homes to prevent the smoke from bothering neighbors. If they do not cooperate, they will have to pay the fine. Responsible parties could also be landlords and condominium associations that fail to properly ventilate buildings. The legislation does not specify at what levels second-hand smoke is considered potentially harmful. The council members felt an asthmatic kid should not be subjected to irritating smoke coming through their window (Duncan, 2001).

There has been strong reaction to this legislation, the first of its kind in the country. The American Civil Liberties Union and tobacco companies are threatening a challenge. There is concern that it unfairly targets apartment dwellers, since they are more likely to offend their neighbors who live close by. There is no proof that there is any damage to a person's health from this type of smoke exposure, and there have never been any complaints in Montgomery County (Duncan, 2001). In cities and counties across the country, there have been restrictions on smoking in bars, restaurants, workplaces, and even outdoor public areas such as parks and sports arenas. What is next? Could people complain about the smell of garlic coming from their neighbor's cooking? What about strong colognes and perfumes?

These are the types of health controversies we are forced to deal with today. What do you think? Should non-smoking neighbors be able to prevent others from allowing smoke to enter their homes?

Health Service Delivery

Delivery of health service occurs in a variety of organizational settings. Historically, hospitals and nursing facilities have been the most common and dominant health service organizations (HSOs). They are prominent today as well, but other HSOs have achieved importance. Among them are outpatient clinics, imaging centers, free-standing urgent care and surgical centers, large group practices, and home health agencies. Inpatient hospital days have decreased over the past few decades while outpatient procedures have increased significantly. In 1999, 62.4% of all surgeries were done on an outpatient basis compared to 16.3% in 1980 (Eberhardt et al., 2001). Multiorganizational systems are widespread. In the 1980s, **health maintenance organizations** (HMOs), **preferred provider organizations** (PPOs), and **managed care systems** became prominent (Rakich et al., 1998). Managed care systems developed as a need to reduce consumption of unnecessary or inappropriate health care services (Wickizer & Lessler, 2002).

There are problems with the current form of health care delivery in the United States. The system rewards inefficiency by slanting services towards acute care rather than caring for chronic conditions (Marwick, 2001). If the health care system spent more time and money on prevention and successfully managing chronic conditions, there would be fewer visits to doctors and inpatient hospital stays. However, this acute care is where the system receives its money, so the focus is not likely to change. One study of 13,000 diabetic patients showed there could have been a savings of $10 million if the focus had been on improving the patients' health instead of treating acute problems as they occurred (Marwick, 2001).

Why be an informed health care consumer? First, you have only one body. Just as you care for your car or your hair, you must make your health a priority. Your ability to work, go to school, even enjoy activities depends on how good you feel. A second reason to be an active health consumer is that as a citizen or resident of the United States, you have no constitutional right to health care. In U.S. society, health care is treated as a private-consumption good or as services to be bought and sold, rather than as a social good to which everyone is entitled. For that reason, one needs to become proactive in making decisions that affect health and health care, and attempt to obtain optimal care at an affordable cost. However, medical and health care services are much harder to evaluate for need, availability, cost, and quality than, for example, clothing or food. The U.S. health system is a myriad of health care providers, payers, and products. It involves insurance, government, and individuals. Products include prescription and over-the-counter drugs, health aids and devices, vitamins, and herbs. Marketing specialists armed with an arsenal of gimmicks, subtle persuaders, and sophisticated strategies make many claims. Some advertisements play on fears and insecurities, appeal to hidden desires, or present the product as a status symbol (Donatelle & Davis, 1994).

Health Care Access

The Uninsured

For many people, it is difficult to access health care providers. Traditionally, the uninsured have had the greatest difficulty accessing health care. The U.S. Census Bureau reports that about 45.8 million Americans lacked insurance for the year 2004 (The Nation's Health, 2005). Either the uninsured do not qualify for federal and state insurance like Medicare and Medicaid, or private insurance is not provided through their employment, or they cannot afford to buy the benefits offered. About 80% of the uninsured either work or live in a family where someone works. Insurance could be purchased privately when employers do not provide it as a benefit, but the average annual premium is $6,000 for a family and more than $3,000 for an individual; this is too expensive for most workers. The uninsured are either denied care or avoid seeking care in anticipation of the costs. Nearly 25% of uninsured children and 40% of uninsured adults have no regular source for medical care (Oberlander, 2002). Consequently, they may allow their health problems to fester and often end up in the emergency room, where most people are not turned away due to lack of insurance. Some uninsured people use the emergency room as their primary health care provider for minor procedures such as simple cuts or hemorrhoids. This type of emergency room use costs the health care system billions of dollars a year (Thompson & Glick, 1999). This is a concern to the public because emergency rooms are very expensive to operate and the uninsured are far less likely to pay their expensive bill.

The cost of medical treatment is cited as the cause in about 50% of the bankruptcies in the United States (Oberlander, 2002). Thus, hospitals have great difficulty balancing their budgets. Some hospitals have closed their emergency rooms or offer fewer services to make up the difference. Other hospitals have developed a triage system in which emergency room patients are evaluated as they enter to see if their problem really is an emergency or whether they could be treated elsewhere (Thompson & Glick, 1999).

Poverty

Poverty has been identified as the greatest barrier to accessing health care (Ahmed, Lemkau, Nealeigh, & Mann, 2001). People with low incomes cannot afford to pay for insurance privately and are more likely to have lower-paying jobs that do not include insurance as a benefit. Having a low income does help a person qualify for Medicaid, a jointly funded federal-state program, but it reaches only about 40% of the poor (Oberlander, 2002). In order to qualify for many Medicaid programs, a person can have only a few thousand dollars in assets (not counting one house and one car) and must have a disability that affects the ability to work.

Lower income has also been associated with higher rates of medical morbidity and premature mortality; people with low incomes receive less medical care than the more affluent (Ahmed et al., 2001). Those with lower incomes are more likely to make poor health decisions and lifestyle choices, such as not using a seat belt, smoking, consuming large amounts of alcohol, and having diets higher in fat and lower in fiber. These choices alone increase the possibility of health problems. When compounded with decreased primary care access, it increases the risk of problems. Poverty is a stronger factor in affecting health outcomes than race (Qureshi, Thacker, Litaker, & Kippes, 2000).

Poverty can lead to homelessness, which makes health care access extremely difficult. This is a growing problem, with 13.5 million individuals experiencing homelessness in their lifetimes (Link et al., 1994). Not all of the homeless are unemployed transients: in a survey of 30 cities in 1998, 37% of adults requesting emergency food assistance were employed (United States Conference of Mayors, 1998). Those who are homeless experience different types of health problems, such as higher rates of injuries, heart disease, liver disease, poisoning, and ill-defined conditions that caused 73% of deaths among homeless individuals in Philadelphia in the early 1990s (Hibbs et al., 1994).

Living Areas

Poorer neighborhoods have been identified as problematic for health care, no matter what an individual's personal income is. Problems include disorganized communities; residents experiencing higher rates of stress; living closer to polluting factories and toxic waste sites that are related to higher cancer rates; older homes with lead paint that has been linked to neurological damage in children under the age of six; children born underweight; increased cockroaches (correlated with childhood asthma); and higher rates of heart disease, respiratory ailments, and overall mortality (Ellen, Mijanovich, & Dillman, 2001).

Urban areas experience unique problems. Though young men are typically healthy, young African American men living in inner cities have higher rates of violence, sexually transmitted diseases, mental health problems, substance abuse, sexually transmitted diseases, and HIV infection than Hispanics or Caucasians. Living in inner cities provides the environment for experiencing financial barriers and a mistrust of the system due to years of racism and historical oppression, leading to a decreased use of health care services. Unemployment levels in inner cities affect African American men disproportionately more than any other group, as evidenced by higher rates of poverty and unemployment (Rich, 2001). African American men are not the only ones with difficulties. Ahmed et al. (2001) studied 413 non-elderly poor adults of various races in an urban area and found additional barriers, including difficulty accessing child care and lack of information about free or reduced-cost health care. This provides a reminder that these social issues affect all groups of people who experience poverty and the resulting conditions.

While rural areas share some of the same problems as inner cities—such as unemployment, lack of child care, and poverty—they also have other problems. Public transportation is more fragmented or not available, there are fewer local free medical clinics, and there are fewer doctors per person.

Immigrants

Newcomers to the United States have some of the same problems as those mentioned above, and have additional difficulties as well. These include language barriers, lack of knowledge of the health care system, differing cultural health practices, a higher likelihood of being employed at workplaces where health risks are high, a lower likelihood of being insured (nearly 45%), and fear of authorities (if in the country illegally). Immigrants to this country experience higher levels of stress and consequently often turn to drinking and smoking (Smith, 2001). Sometimes there are additional barriers to health care access. In 1994, California voters passed proposition 187, which denied health care to undocumented newcomers (Noble, 1994). This prohibited regular access to basic medical care, and visits to health care clinics decreased as much as 90% (Voelker, 1995), replaced by an increase in emergency room visits.

Older Americans

Older Americans are less likely to be uninsured since Medicare is available to most people over 65, those declared disabled by the Social Security administration, and persons with **end-stage renal disease.** But the quality of Medicare coverage has declined in recent years. Doctors often refuse to accept Medicare because reimbursement rate increases do not keep pace with the rise in health care costs. In fact, reimbursement rates decreased 17% in 2005. Many seniors signed up with health maintenance organizations (HMOs) in the 1990s to get additional benefits through Medicare, but many of these HMOs lost money being in Medicare and declined to continue treating Medicare patients. Organizations handle this problem by passing on the cost differential to the consumer through higher premiums, deductibles, and co-payments (Charatan, 2002).

Other access problems for older adults include difficulties finding transportation and the costs of prescription drugs. Older Americans with health problems may not be able to drive themselves and sometimes have difficulty managing public transportation systems. People who live in rural areas often do not have access to public transportation. Consequently, seniors may be dependent on others to transport them, and ride providers may either charge high fees or may be unavailable or unreliable.

Prescription drugs have become more and more necessary to treat chronic illness in order to sustain and improve quality of life. Some seniors have had to choose between buying food and filling their prescriptions. Many dispute the need for prescriptions to be so expensive. The American Association of Retired

Persons (AARP) believes that direct advertising to the consumer has driven drug prices up. In 2000, drug companies spent $2.5 billion in advertising and also worked to keep generic drugs out of the marketplace (Charatan, 2002). Prescription assistance is available to people with low income through Medicaid, from some short-term assistance programs through states, or from pharmaceutical companies themselves. These programs are not easy to access. Legislation to consider prescription drug benefits for Medicare recipients was suspended while Congress dealt with the aftermath of the September 11th terrorist attacks. The programs being considered mainly included using HMOs, which have their own disadvantages, including more restrictions and a limited number of doctors who accept them. With the final passage of a prescription drug bill and the signature of the President, some prescription assistance will be phased in during 2006.

After decades of debate on how to improve access to medical care, we are no closer to a solution. It is doubtful that small changes will eliminate the problems. Various programs and changes to the system are being considered. The first approach to helping the uninsured would be to expand existing public insurance programs, including Medicaid and the State Children Health Insurance Program, which provides insurance to children living in families with incomes up to double the federal poverty line. Various proposals are being considered, but improvements will probably not be made in the foreseeable future since many state budgets are in debt. In 2002, President Bush proposed tax credits of $2,000 for a family or $1,000 for an individual to buy private insurance; but this does little to help defray the cost (Oberlander, 2002).

National Health Care Expenditures

Up until the terrorists attacked the World Trade Center and the United States started a war campaign, health care was hotly debated. It was a major agenda item for the president and other politicians. Unfortunately, the problem of increased health care spending is not going away. Spending in 2004 was at $1.9 trillion, an average of $6,280 per person in the United States. There has been rate decline in health care costs and good news in health care spending. In 2002 health care spending increased 9.1%, in 2003 it was 8.2%, and in 2004 it was a 7.9% increase, part of an overall

50% rate difference during a five-year span (Centers for Medicare and Medicaid Services, 2006). In dollar volume, the U.S. health care industry is second only to the manufacturing sector. For personal consumption, Americans spend more on food and housing than they do on medical care. Furthermore, health care is by far the largest service industry in the country. In fact, the U.S. health care system is the world's eighth largest economy, second to that of France, and larger than the total economy of Italy. Between 1993 and 1999, health spending averaged increases of 0.5 percentage points less than the gross domestic product (GDP) as the shift to managed care and impacts from the Balanced Budget Act of 1997 resulted in one-time savings. Coupled with faster real growth in the economy, this resulted in a slight decline in health spending's share of GDP, from 13.4% in 1993 to 13.0% in both 1998 and 1999 (Health Care Financing Administration, 2001).

The relatively higher growth in private spending is expected to continue, in large part because of rapid spending growth for prescription drugs. Growth in spending for prescription drugs continued to outpace spending growth for other health services in 1999, as a steady shift toward health insurance plans with small out-of-pocket requirements for drugs raised consumer demand. Between 1990 and 1999, spending on prescription drugs increased by 141%, while spending on hospital care and doctor's visits grew by 54% and 71%, respectively. Between 1999 and 2010, there is an expected 237% increase in spending on prescription drugs (Health Care Financing Administration, 2001). Unlike Canada and much of Europe, where the cost of prescriptions is regulated by the government, in the U.S. drug companies can charge as much as they want (Josefson, 2002). An increase in the number of prescriptions filled; a larger number of new, high-priced drugs in the marketplace; and an increase in advertising expenditures also contributed to the higher spending growth rate for drugs. Prescription drugs, accounting for 9.4% of personal health spending in 1999, continued to lead all other health care services in cost growth with increases of 16.9% (Health Care Financing Administration, 2001).

What is being done to curb this increase in health care spending? The easiest plan would be for the government to lower reimbursement rates for government insurance programs. Medicaid was identified as an area to cut in the 1997 federal budget (Smith, 2001). Payments by the federal government towards state Medicaid programs were reduced, so services declined. About $13 billion was saved due to decreased payments to hospitals (Kraut, 1997). Annual growth in Medicare spending remains low: only 0.1% in 1998, and 1.0% in 1999. This is well below the average recorded for the 1993–1997 period of 9.2%. The dramatic two-year slowdown is attributed primarily to the effects of changing payment systems for home health care facilities and nursing homes and continuing federal government efforts to detect and reduce fraud and abuse.

Medicaid and Medicare have had difficulty with fraud where charges were submitted for medical services that were not given or care was substandard, thus wasting resources. Various levels of government have initiated legislation to deal with this problem (Matthew, 2001). In Figure 7.1, note where funds are received to provide health services and how those dollars are distributed in the population. Are there opportunities for adjustment in distribution of health care dollars that might be more equitable?

With the high cost of health care, the United States faces many difficult decisions in the years ahead.

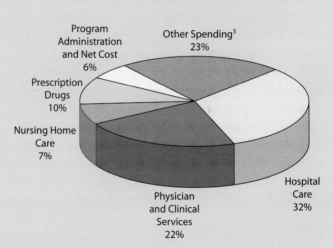

Where It Came From

Other Public[1]
13%

Other Private[2]
5%

Medicaid and SCHIP
16%

Medicare
17%

Out-of-pocket
14%

Private Insurance
35%

Where It Went

Program Administration and Net Cost
6%

Prescription Drugs
10%

Nursing Home Care
7%

Other Spending[3]
23%

Hospital Care
32%

Physician and Clinical Services
22%

1. "Other Public" includes programs such as workers' compensation, public health activity, Department of Defense, Department of Veterans Affairs, Indian Health Service, state and local hospital subsidies, and school health.

2. "Other Private" includes industrial in-plant, privately funded construction, and non-patient revenues, including philanthropy.

3. "Other Spending" includes dental services, other professional services, home health care, durable medical products, over-the-counter medicines and sundries, public health activities, research, and construction.

Figure 7.1: The Nation's Dollar, 1999. Source: Centers for Medicare & Medicaid Services, Office of the Actuary, National Health Statistics Group. http://hcfa.gov/stats/nhe-oact/tables/chart.htm

Many Voices: An Introduction to Social Issues

Citizens will have to decide what benefits there may be for a plan with universal coverage and address what they consider to be the disadvantages as the United States seeks to deal with this important health issue.

What about National Health Care?

Federally sponsored national health insurance programs were proposed and seriously considered at various times during the 20th century, most notably in the late 1940s and late 1960s. However, in the 1960s, momentum for a universal scheme dwindled after Medicare and Medicaid were enacted and provided significant coverage for millions who had inadequate access. National programs were considered again in the early 1990s. Former President Bill Clinton appointed his wife, Hillary Rodham Clinton, to develop a proposal for universal health care coverage. It never had much support from any group. National health care attempts covered the gamut from all-encompassing federal programs to modest interventions. However, they were potentially very expensive programs. Opposition to proposals came from organized medicine, insurance companies, and lack of voter interest as most people had private hospitalization insurance, usually supplied by their employers. National healthcare in the United States was not politically feasible.

Interest in national health is once again active as high costs of health insurance and concern for the uninsured remain in force. One of the major concerns is for the rapidly increasing population of the elderly. In 1990, 12.7% of the population was 65 or older; by 2030 it is projected this proportion will grow to 22.9%. These data suggest that there will be greatly increased demand for health services in geriatrics, chronic diseases, rehabilitation, and institutional long-term care. Unanswered is how these needs will be financed (Rakich et al., 1998). These issues may not seem relevant to a young adult now, but by 2030 they will be very relevant. Long-term care for a parent or one's personal health concerns or expenditures will be at the forefront.

Most developed countries have national health insurance. Western Europe, notably Germany and England, had government involvement in financing health services much earlier than the United States did. Generally, western European and Canadian health services systems have much more governmental control and financing than do those in the United States. It is interesting to note that in the past, despite greater government involvement in planning and financing, many of these countries experienced inflation in health services costs similar to that in the United States. However, since about 1985, increases in the U.S. have been well ahead of those in all other countries. Countries where budgetary allocations to health services are determined prospectively spend substantially less than the United States. An important reason for the difference is that far less is spent on high technology in the United Kingdom and Canada; for example, computed tomography scans and renal dialysis units are less available. In addition, elective procedures are less readily available and there are often long waiting periods (Rakich et al., 1998).

In the past, the best national plans for health programs have emphasized disease prevention and health promotion. This has been true since the 1974 Canadian Lalonde Report, which introduced an important new idea about going beyond medical care to improve the health of Canadians. It led to the introduction and development of health promotion, at first encouraging people to take more responsibility for their own health, and later recognizing the contribution of health communities and environments to health.

In the 1960s, after years of debate, the U.S. government decided to create a mixed private and public system. At that time, most Americans received their health insurance through their employers. Two groups were left out—the nonworking poor and the aged. For that reason, Medicare and Medicaid were passed in 1965 as amendments to the 1935 Social Security Act. The two programs are very different. Medicare is a federal health insurance program for the elderly and the permanently disabled, and Medicaid is a federal-state health insurance program for the poor. In California, this program is known as Medi-Cal (Donatelle & Davis, 1994).

In 1983, the federal government set up a payment system based on Diagnosis Related Groups (DRGs) for Medicare. Nearly 500 groupings of diagnoses were created to establish in advance how much a hospital would be reimbursed for a particular patient. If a hospital can treat the patient for less than that amount, it can keep the difference. If a patient's care costs more than the set amount, the hospital must absorb the difference. This system gives hospitals the incentive to discharge patients quickly after completion of a medical procedure, to provide more ambulatory care, and to admit only patients with favorable (profitable) DRGs. Private health insurance companies have followed the federal government in using this type of reimbursement (Donatelle & Davis, 1994).

Dramatic changes have occurred in health care during the last 30 years. These include changes in the financing of health care and in the delivery patterns of care. Originally, insurance was not supposed to influence how care was provided. However, that has not been the case. Insurance not only determines whether a person receives care, but where, how much, and by whom. This system is known as managed care. It includes health maintenance organizations, preferred provider organizations, exclusive provider organizations, and fee-for-service plans.

By 2000, 90% of persons who received insurance benefits through work were in a managed care plan (Oberlander, 2002). Patients enrolled in a preferred provider organization (PPO) are given a list of "preferred providers" from which to choose practitioners. If they use these practitioners, they are reimbursed at a higher rate than if they choose to "go out of plan" and use **nonparticipating providers**. For example, a patient who uses a physician on the PPO list may be reimbursed for 80% to 90% of the cost of the service, whereas one who uses a nonlisted physician may be reimbursed only 50% to 60%. Doctors may, however, arrange more follow-up visits than necessary to make up the difference for discounted fees (Donatelle & Davis, 1994). Not only is cost reimbursement a consideration, but a physician's clinical decisions are subject to external review (Oberlander, 2002).

Has managed care helped or hurt the health care system? Health care expenditures did slow down for most of the 1990s, but by 1999 and 2000 they rose at higher rates. Most studies do not show much of a difference in quality of care in managed care plans and traditional plans, though there is some evidence that older adults with chronic illness had worse outcomes. Regardless of what studies show, there have been strong reactions from both physicians and patients to the level of interference managed care programs have assumed in health care decisions and access to specialists. Almost all 50 states have enacted laws providing a patient's bill of rights and other laws that regulate the decision making of managed care plans (Oberlander, 2002). If managed care is to continue, there needs to be some improvement in patient and physician relationships with these companies. Insurance companies that practice utilization management to control costs have received the message to improve carrier and provider relations.

The national health care debate may still go on, but a workable plan is far in the future. The failed Clinton plan showed us the following: there was not enough public support since the majority of Americans have insurance; insurance companies had a powerful lobby that did not support the plan; health care professions do not want limits on health care spending; Americans do not want to pay more taxes; and national health care will limit choices and expediency, both important in American culture. The cultural climate may change in the future as more and more companies cut health insurance benefits, and the government continues to cut Medicare and Medicaid budgets. Wessler (1998) suggests that a national health program needs a more coherent message. True national health care promoters prefer the "single payer" system that would eliminate the highly profitable middlemen, the insurance companies. With a strong insurance lobby this may be difficult to achieve. Some states, such as Montana and Hawaii, are trying their own version of universal coverage by mandating managed care for Medicaid beneficiaries (Wessler, 1998).

Conclusion

Changes in health care are continuing rapidly. Most of the forces reshaping the system are basically economic in nature; however, changes affect every facet of health care, from the education of providers to the terminal care of patients. Within both the public health and health care domains there is a unique interplay of technology, work force, research findings, financing regulation, and personal and professional behaviors, values, and assumptions that determine what, how, why, where, and at what cost health care is delivered. The increasing size, complexity, and technological sophistication of the health care system in the United States have further complicated its long-standing problems of limited consumer access, inconsistent quality of services, and uncontrolled costs. Furthermore, changes in the health care system have done little to address the unnecessary and wasteful duplication of certain services in some areas and the absence of essential services in others. These problems have worried political and medical leaders for decades and have motivated legislative proposals aimed at reform by seven successive U.S. presidents. Health care is undergoing a revolution.

Complex and fragmented as public health and health care may seem, professionals are attempting to find common ground and address the problems and challenges of the future. The two systems are dependent on one another. Since most personal health care in the United States is paid by insurance companies, public health agencies depend on the private sector to provide patient-level data to the public health system. Citizens of the United States enjoy an abundance of services, programs, technologies, and well-educated, dedicated professionals within its health care delivery system. Yet many people still suffer from drug addiction, the effects on health of violence, and chronic preventable lifestyle diseases. Much of the overall poor health status is the direct and indirect result of poverty. These are challenges for the United States; however, public health and health care are today a global concern as well. Partnerships are being developed to teach and practice effective public health strategies all over the world. We are all interconnected as a whole, and what happens to one affects another in some way. As Mahatma Gandhi once said, "Be the change you want to see in the world." Individually and collectively, we are all affected by public health and health care.

Response

Public Health—Does It Have a Role?

by Duane C. McBride

Perhaps the most significant point to make about this chapter is that the authors have captured very well the history, definition, activities, and priority struggles of public health. In addition, they have done an admirable job of contrasting the population approach to public health with the individual focus of the modern health care system. They also accurately note the tensions between a population-based preventative health approach and an individual curative care approach.

For me, as the chair of a public health board, one of the most interesting statistics in the chapter is that well over 90% of the U.S. population does not know what public health is or does. In our board discussions, we often say that we are "the best story never told." In fact, if public health is working well there is no news about it. That is, if we are immunizing the population, preventing the outbreak of highly infectious diseases, and ensuring clean water and appropriate sewage disposal, there is no story and no one knows what public health has done. If, on the other hand, public health fails to sufficiently monitor food distributors or handlers and a major hepatitis outbreak occurs, or if a beach is severely contaminated by the runoff of untreated sewage waste water and we do not close it, there will be a story. As a result of public health's inaction, human beings would become very ill, some would possibly die, and there would be extensive media coverage. Public health food inspectors, environmental health workers, prevention educators, and immunization specialists have never had their own TV shows and only rarely has a major motion picture focused on their adventures. They truly are background people whom we take for granted every time we drink water, breathe the air, swim at a local beach, or eat in a restaurant.

As documented by the chapter's authors, much of the progress that our society has made in extending the average life span, improving the health of our citizens, and generally improving the quality of life has not been from individual disease cures but rather from population-based disease prevention. Public health has educated the population (with some success) about the risks of smoking, drug use, and teen pregnancy, and claims some of the success in the reduction of a wide variety of health problems, from decreased heart disease to lower smoking rates. However, for a number of years public health has seen serious erosion of its financial base and frequently questions itself about its purpose. For example, is public health about immunizations or disease control? Is it even necessary as a department?

One of the classic critiques of public health's population-based approach has been that it is unnecessary. In the 1980s, U.S. society became enamored with the power of the marketplace to provide all that was needed in a society. The argument essentially was that if a product or service was needed the market would provide it, and if the market did not provide the product or service it was not really needed by a given population. The idea was that if a broad society, compared to a local community, concluded that it needed clean water, sewage disposal, or immunization for their children, that service would emerge in the free market. In fact, it was noted that the free market provision of health care already existed and that providers could easily immunize children.

The state of Michigan in the 1990s was one of the major advocates of that approach. In 2000, Michigan had an immunization rate of 74% for two-year-olds. This was higher than the 71% national rate. However, as a result of cutting funds for outreach services to "risk" populations, in just one year Michigan's immunization rate dropped to 66% while the national average remained the same. This placed Michigan at the level of states with historically low rates of child immunization.

As the rate of immunization of children drops, an increasingly large proportion of children become susceptible to childhood diseases such as measles and mumps, providing a population base for the incubation of these highly infectious diseases. The free market may eventually respond to epidemics of infectious diseases and environmental health problems, but the response may not occur until there has been a lot of illness and death. The market tends not to engage until clear problems and needs have been identified. Public health's major goal is to ensure there is not an epidemic that threatens a large population's health or existence. Public health seeks to prevent a market-based need to respond to a disaster.

Traditionally, public health has also been a provider of health services of last resort for those without access to traditional health care services—in other words, the uninsured. Such services have included not only immunization, but also prenatal and postnatal care, and treatment for highly infectious sexually transmitted diseases, including HIV infection. Decreased Medicaid funding means increased pressure on public health departments to provide prenatal care and services to women, infants, and children. Public health traditionally has also been very active in working with community members to facilitate access to needed services. For example, many health departments help the poor negotiate the complexities of obtaining Medicaid coverage.

Public health also competes for resources with other public agencies like education and Medicare and Medicaid programs. The infrastructure of public health has significantly suffered in the last decade with consistent decreases in expenditures (controlling for inflation) for public health. It has been expected that the private sector would take over some of the functions of public health, from immunization to aspects of environmental health. In addition, most states have faced very severe reductions in revenue. Immediate needs tend to be seen by policy makers, such as providing police protection, prisons for violent criminals, teachers, and health care for the indigent who appear in hospital emergency rooms. The media and the public at large have a higher priority than disease prevention that will not have significant health care costs for 20 years. Immediate needs tend to overwhelm us in a time of resource scarcity, and it is hard to think of needs that have not developed yet or have a low probability of developing. We often defer costs to the future to meet the tyranny of immediate needs.

The one exception to the preceding picture has been the role of public health in anti-terrorism campaigns. The fear of biological weapons has refocused policy makers and the general public interest on population-based disease prevention. The fear of smallpox has dramatically renewed the public's interest in mass immunization, and the fear of such bio-terror agents as anthrax has significantly increased support for the role of public health in infectious disease monitoring.

Many health departments across the United States have been provided new funds to coordinate disaster preparedness. This has provided some renewal of the role of public health in disease prevention in the United States.

Amidst all of this, it is crucial to remember that states are still cutting back other elements of the public health infrastructure. There is little optimism about being able to continue the current level of involvement by public health in the quality of life in our communities. For example, in the state of Michigan, budget cuts have eliminated funding for the following health department activities:

- Outreach efforts to enroll the poor in the Medicaid health insurance program.

- Worksite wellness programs that help employers with programs such as exercise, smoking cessation, weight control, and preventive care.
- Community health needs assessments that can tell us where spikes are in disease (e.g., a spike in breast cancer rates might be indicative of a toxic problem in the environment).
- Public health staff training budgets.

In addition, significant budget cuts have been made in the treatment of sexually transmitted diseases, teen pregnancy prevention, and basic public health department funding. As a result of budget cuts, your county public health board may have to literally choose between services for the elderly and services for women, infants, and children.

Most health departments are dipping into very limited reserves just to maintain basic services. The thinking seems to be that if we do not know the state of the community's health, there will be less pressure to spend money addressing health problems. For example, if we do not actively enroll the poor in Medicaid so that they and their children can receive basic health services, a lot of money will be saved in the next few years. As a society we do not seem to recognize that limiting access now significantly increases the probability of higher costs in the future. But when states are trying to balance the budget this year, it is hard for governors or legislatures to think of the costs that will be incurred in 10 to 20 years.

Discussion Questions

1. What should the role of law and policy be toward the tobacco industry? Knowing that there is no therapeutic value for any tobacco products, should the government act by legislating complete closure of this industry or do people have the right to use tobacco?
2. Considering the high cost of clinical care, should public health organizations stop screening diseases such as HIV, sexually transmitted diseases, and tuberculosis; move exclusively into education and prevention of such diseases; and leave screening and treatment up to the private medical sector?
3. Is land mine eradication an area in which public health departments should be involved?
4. What areas do you suggest might be included in public health efforts as we move further into the 21st century?
5. How can the health care delivery system be simplified?
6. What are some ways access can be improved?
7. Should health care providers be given easier access to a person's medical records in order to improve quality of care? What about privacy?
8. How can health care expenditures be reduced without affecting quality and access?
9. Is national health care in America's future?

Related Readings

Anderson, R. M., Rice, T. H., & Kominski, G. F. (Eds.). (1996). *Changing the U.S. health care system: Key issues in health services, policy, and management.* San Francisco: Jossey-Bass Publishers.

Beauchamp, T. L., & Walters, L. (Eds.) (1999). *Contemporary issues in bioethics.* Belmont, CA: Wadsworth Publishers.

Crossing the quality chasm: A new health system for the 21st century. (2001). U.S. Institute of Medicine, National Academy of Sciences, http://nationalacademies.org.

Related Web Sites

Agency for Healthcare Research and Quality (AHRQ): http://www.ahcpr.gov

American Medical Association (AMA): http://www.ama-assn.org

American Public Health Association (APHA): http://www.apha.org/index.cfm

Centers for Disease Control and Prevention (CDC): http://www.cdc.gov

Club Drugs: http://www.clubdrugs.org

Dance Safe: http://www.dancesafe.org

http://www.health.gov

Institute of Social Research: http://www.isr.umich.edu

Joe Chemo: http://www.joechemo.org

Monitoring the Future: http://www.monitoringthefuture.org

National Health and Nutrition Examination Survey (NHANES): http://www.cdc.gov/nchs/nhanes.htm

National Institute on Drug Abuse: http://www.nida.nih.gov

National Institutes of Health (NIH): http://www.nih.gov

Office of Public Health and Science (OPHS): http://www.osophs.dhhs.gov/ophs

Public Health Foundation (PHF): http://www.phf.org

Tobacco Free Kids: http://www.tobaccofreekids.org

U.S. Department of Health & Human Services: http://www.os.dhhs.gov

WWW Virtual Library—Public Health: http://www.ldb.org/vl

Related Movies/Videos

The Andromeda Strain (1971) with Arthur Hill and James Olsen
The Insider (1999) with Al Pacino and Russell Crowe
John Q. (2002) with Denzel Washington and Robert Duvall
Outbreak (1995) with Patrick Dempsey, Rene Russo, and Dustin Hoffman
Patch Adams (1998) with Robin Williams
Silkwood (1983) with Meryl Streep and Kurt Russell

RELIGION

Lionel Matthews, Elvin S. Gabriel, and Joseph W. Warren

8

Chapter Outline

In December 1992, several thousand fundamentalist Hindus, armed with picks and shovels, attacked a 350-year-old Muslim mosque in India. Before long, the entire structure was destroyed as the local Hindu police looked on, unable to save the building. Pitched battles followed between Muslims and Hindus in India, resulting in 1,000 deaths. Elsewhere, in Pakistan and Great Britain, Hindu temples were attacked and more than 30 were destroyed by Muslims bent upon avenging the desecration of their mosque. The first mosque was attacked because fundamentalist Hindus believed that it was constructed on the site of a Hindu temple that was destroyed by Muslims. Whether this is so there is not evidence, but what is of importance is that it was widely believed among fundamentalist Hindus (adapted from Farley, 1998).

Introduction

For many, **religion** is the great panacea for social ills. Recent studies, as well as the position taken by the classical sociological theorists on religion, lend strong support to such a view. Patrick Fagan (1996), in his review of the social sciences literature that examined the impact of religion, concluded that religion is the force that most powerfully addresses the major social problems. He noted that many of the goals of social policy and social work can be achieved, indirectly yet powerfully, through the practice of religion. This optimistic position regarding the role of religion is consistent with the views advanced by some of the classical social theorists. Auguste Comte (see Doyle, 1981), one of the earliest of the theorists, rejected most of religion as irrational. Still he was convinced through his own studies that religion, because of its integrative role, was a necessary element of human society.

French scholar Emile Durkheim (1965) thought religion was nothing more than a human construction made sacred. In spite of this position, Durkheim was among the foremost social theorists to underscore the value of religion in society. He noted that religion not only provided a barrier against suicide but was also a potent source of social integration. In contrast, Karl Marx (see Jordan, 1971) declared religion to be "the sigh of the oppressed creature, the sentiment of a heartless world…and the opium of the people" (p. 74). Max Weber (1958), on the other hand, argued for a positive role for religion and suggested that the Protestant ethic was one of the under girding principles that facilitated the emergence of capitalism.

Sigmund Freud, founder of the psychoanalytic movement, was overtly critical of religion. He contended that intelligence offers an alternative to religion because commandments such as "do not kill" are universally rational prohibitions. Religious dogmas, according to Freud, are illusions, and not open to demonstration or refutation. He rationalized that human religion attempts to make sense of things that cannot be logically explained. Yet he noted that without religion, death would be overwhelming, because of the helplessness and frustration that one feels when facing the reality of death (Kernberg, 2000).

More recently, the importance of religion to Americans has been underscored by Kammeyer, Ritzer, and Yetman (1992). These authors noted that the results of several surveys demonstrate that of the industrialized nations, Americans are among the most religious people in the world. Based on public opinion polls between 1952 and 1992, 90% of people surveyed in the United States claimed to exercise some belief in the existence of God. Kammeyer, Ritzer, and Yetman further pointed out that when asked how important religion was in their lives, more than 87% of Americans indicated that it was "very important" or "fairly important."

This chapter addresses the concept of religion and its impact on social issues. In the ensuing sections, we will examine the nature of religion, elaborate on its positive features, identify and discuss specific cases of religious conflict, delineate the features of religion that account for its ambivalent role in society, and speculate on the future of religion. At various junctures of the discussion, the religion/social issues connection will be noted and discussed.

The Nature of Religion

ISSUES: How should one define religion? Is belief in God a necessary element for a religion? How are the concepts of "truth" and religion related? What are the social implications of truth? Of religion?

It is common to regard religion as some form of belief in God or a deity. This, however, is a limited view. Durkheim (1965), one of the early pioneers of the sociology of religion, said that the distinction between the **sacred** and the **profane** is the most important feature common to all religions. By the sacred, Durkheim meant anything that pertains to the supernatural rather than the ordinary world. The profane, on the other hand, is anything that is regarded as part of the ordinary world. Thus, Durkheim defined religion as "a unified system of beliefs and practices relative to sacred things, that is to say, things set apart, and forbidden—beliefs and practices which unite into one single moral community, called a church, all those who adhere to them" (1965, p. 62).

Durkheim's definition is rather useful for its clear depiction of the salient structural elements of religion. It presents four basic elements of religion: an adherence to a system of truth, a system of beliefs, a set of **rituals**, and a moral community. Each of these elements, it must be remembered, contributes to the meaning of religion only and insofar as each is seen to be oriented to the sacred.

The Nature of Truth

Any meaningful discussion on the nature of religion must ultimately address issues concerning the nature of truth. Vroom (1989) said that "the issue of religious truth is raised implicitly, whenever religion and knowledge are spoken of, for the problem of what one understands by 'truth' always entails the question: When is it permissible to speak of 'real' knowledge? Related to this is the problem of criteria by which truth claims must be assessed" (p. 24). This section is a limited discussion of the "absoluteness" and "relativeness" of religious truth as a belief system.

Andrzej Bronk (2003), in his article "Truth and Religion Reconsidered: An Analytical Approach," offers a clear and cogent explanation of "absoluteness": "There is such an understanding of truth of religion which connects it with uniqueness and exclusiveness. A religion which sees itself as absolute takes other religions to be false, i.e. as pseudo-religions. This type of exclusiveness characterizes Christianity and to even a greater degree Judaism and Islam" (p. 6).

Burch (2000) extended this explanation further by using the term "exclusive truth" which, as she emphasized, projects claims that are "couched in terms of polarities," meaning that such claims are either true or false. She wrote: "A belief system that is based on the truth as defined by believers is right. A belief system that is based on any other understanding of what is true is wrong. People who believe in the truth claims are saved. People who do not are damned" (p. 2).

Douglas Groothius (2002)—in his article "What is Truth?"—clearly revealed the essence of "relativeness." He emphasized that relativism appears in many forms, but its central theme is that the truth is a product of the perceptions of individuals and/or cultural groups. There is no correspondence to objective reality. He advanced this argument further by using the following example: "If I say 'Jesus is Lord' and you say 'Allah is Lord' both statements cannot be objectively true because they describe mutually exclusive realities. Jesus is known by Christians as God made flesh (John 1:14), while Muslims deny that Allah incarnates. If 'Lord' means a position of unrivaled metaphysical and spiritual supremacy, then Jesus and Allah cannot be both Lord because 'Jesus' and 'Allah' are not two words that mean the same thing" (p. 3).

What then are the social implications for adherence to these two dimensions of truth? Duke (2003), in expressing his views on "The Nature of Right and Wrong," alluded to implications for embracing the tenets of Absolute Truth. He said: "it means that we aren't the authors of right or wrong, something above us is. It means that we are all subject to the same standard of morality, one that won't bend to suit our whims, justify our sins, or ease our conscience" (p. 2).

David Quinn (1993), in his discourse "What the Secular Humanists Are Up To," noted that relativism is a "two-edged sword," meaning that those who live by it must die by it. He further formulated the "two-edged sword" theory by stating: "This is because relativism not only undermines religious-based value systems, it undermines all value systems. Relativism annihilates everything it touches, and it touches everything. The reason is to be found in the nature of atheism. There is a brute logic to atheism. Its attendant materialism does away with any source of values apart from the human mind" (p. 2). For additional information on the implications of relative and absolute truths, you may go to the following web site: http://www.religioustolerance.org/chr_poll5.htm.

Review the essay "My Absolute Truth" by Nicole Higgins (Box 8.1) and consider the following questions: What was her dilemma? How did she resolve it?

Box 8.1: "My Absolute Truth" by Nicole J. Higgins

I used to be a chemistry major. Science and math classes revolve around givens and constants. Avogadro's number is 6.022×10^{23}. My life in the sciences was nice. It was sure (for the most part) and it was comfortable. I knew what I needed to know. I didn't feel lost, because there were always constants. My spiritual life reflected the same. I knew the facts I needed for my religion. I just love those absolutes!

Soon after I started college, I began to be bombarded by postmodern thoughts. In a world where things were black and white, gray began to seep in. That is a scary thing for me. Anytime I am unsure of what my givens and constants are, I become anxious. Not only that, but the very things that had brought me the greatest comfort, like my denomination and its beliefs, seemed to be in direct contradiction to my new belief in the "world of grays." For a time, I really did not have any clue as to what direction I was going to take. It seemed to be a choice between one or the other.

I am now a journalism/Spanish major. In my Communication Theory class, I learned about cognitive dissonance. The main idea is that our behavior and beliefs must correlate; if they do not, we experience turmoil. This would happen when I tried to live a Christian life, but was entrenched in postmodern philosophy. According to the cognitive dissonance theory, to avoid this philosophical quandary, I would have to either 1) avoid information likely to increase my dissonance, 2) choose to believe one or the other, or 3) adapt both to fit each other. Considering that I am in college, am required to read texts by postmodern thinkers, and am surrounded by fellow students as influenced by postmodernism as I am, the first option would not work. I really value both of my viewpoints, so I could not choose between the two. That left me with option three. I needed to figure out some way to integrate postmodernism with my Christian beliefs—aye, there's the rub.

After much struggle, spiritually and mentally, and through talking to others who were going through the same life experience, I came to a conclusion. Because I believe that there is no absolute truth that can be known by humans, I have to rely on what is most meaningful in my life to determine what is my truth. I cannot be sure whether God makes truths meaningful to my life, or if what I deem meaningful creates my own truths. For me, I have to trust it is the former. I believe God cares immensely for me, and is running the world as He sees fit. That is my truth. It is my absolute.

We live in a postmodern world. We also live in a world with people who need absolutes. I need absolutes. Whether they are truths or absolutes is irrelevant, because we live them out in our daily lives as if they were such. That is what is important. Find what is the most meaningful in your life and live in such a manner.

What are the implications involved in integrating post-modern ideas with theistic Christian beliefs? Read and compare the ideas expressed in the essays by Alexander Carpenter (Box 8.2) and Daniel Pickett (Box 8.3) with those of Higgins. What differences do you see?

Religion and Central Beliefs about the Sacred

Within the Christian theistic belief system, the sacred exists as an objective reality. However, opinions vary among human societies as to what is deemed sacred. In this regard, the sacred can include objects, plants, buildings, animals, or persons—indeed, various objects have been used to represent the sacred. Religious bodies differ with respect to the particular objects which are assigned sacred qualities. McGee (1975) has identified four kinds of religion based on their central belief about the sacred: simple supernaturalism, animism, theism, and transcendent idealism.

Box 8.2: "A Confessing, Cultural Christian" by Alexander Carpenter

I am part of my faith community because it is my story. My religion is not rooted in the Bible or in official church decisions, although each does form my culture. I remain a Christian because no person is an island. I am made up of my family, friends, education, hopes, values, and traditions, and they are all Christian. This is how most later-generational members of a religion are. What keeps us connected is not necessarily true belief, but a deeper pragmatic connection to the culture. For me, beliefs achieve an existential significance that reaches beyond proof texts and the attraction of other religions or sects.

The philosopher George Berkeley summarized his idealism by stating that being is to be perceived (*A Treatise Concerning the Principles of Human Knowledge*, 1710). In a sense, our very existence is a social construct—who I am is made up of those around me. No Christian is one entire of itself. To the communion table, an individual brings private irony and exchanges it for the hope provided by solidarity.

Some will object, sadly shaking their heads at the thought of an admitted cultural Christian. But I suggest that everyone's religion is primarily cultural, even the devout seminarian who quotes lists of texts to support each belief. I say read more and find that not just the canon and the choice of texts, but also the hermeneutic, are all historically contingent. This does not mean that there is nothing transcendent. The sense of the divine transcends, but even this we filter through our times to give meaning. To point out this social influence is just to emphasize the obvious: who we are and the questions we ask arise from the culture. That is what religion does; it consolidates the story of the culture and then provides significance through solidarity. The more people who believe, the more we have hope for the future.

As I am graduating from university, I realize that much of my identity is created by those with whom I've associated. Perhaps that is one reason why it is difficult to leave a place. I am departing a structure that has given me much meaning. And in doing so, I am losing some of my being.

Exploring this idea, John Donne writes: "any man's death diminishes me, because I am involved in mankind" ("Meditation XVII," *Devotions upon Emergent Occasions*, 1624). The convicted Rwandan father-son genocidal duo, professed Christians, clearly never got that last point. Helping to kill hundreds of their fellow believers, they showed that sometimes behind shared beliefs lurks no common care. But having that concern requires a soul.

Most of the time religion in action transcends this soulless evil. I saw that while writing grants for a faith-based relief agency in Bangladesh. The starving pregnant women probably didn't want answers about the nature of Christ. They needed safe water, food, literacy, and health education. And Christians from Australia, Canada, and Sweden gave money, which the agency used to employ Hindus, Muslims, and Christians to make several thousand lives better. That, to me, demonstrates the power of a confessing culture in action.

I heard John Adams's biographer, David McCullough, say that without story we have no soul. Certainly religious stories are one of the most powerful motivators and equalizers of humans, even transcending, at times, nationalism and materialism. And so, in an epistemologically messy world, what can I really confess? Only what gives me hope: that the shared story of my culture will create in me a better soul.

Many Voices: An Introduction to Social Issues

Box 8.3: "A Confirmation of Religious View" by Daniel Pickett

I need to make sense of the world—at least most of it, most of the time. It bothers me when people can't give good reasons for their beliefs or practices. Maybe that's just because I was raised that way, but it has served me well. While my high school classmates were getting high or getting pregnant, I saw no good reason for living that way. I had been taught that there is a God who exists, and He cares about the way we live our lives. He has standards—absolutes based on principles—that will help us to be happier than we can be if we choose to live without them. These standards make sense to me, and most of my friends who do not follow these standards are not as happy as I am. I have been taught to live my life according to principle, and it bothers me when other people can't give good reasons for their beliefs or practices.

But can I give good reasons for why I believe what I believe, or why I do what I do? Maybe that's why I am now a theology major in college: I want to figure out why I believe what I believe, or more accurately, I want to figure out what to believe and what to do. I believe that there is a God who has revealed Himself in the Bible, and by studying the Bible I will discover the truth about what I should believe and how I should live.

I also believe that the Bible teaches the ultimate truth about the universe. No, it doesn't tell us about the speed of light or how old the stars are, but it does tell us why we're here and where we're going, and that helps me make sense of the world—at least most of it, most of the time.

But what about the rest of it, the rest of the time? There are a lot of things that don't make sense to me. I might like my Christian worldview to be perfect, but it's not. For example, if the Bible says the earth was created in six days a few thousand years ago, why does the common interpretation of the geological record suggest long ages of life and death and gradual change? That must bother me, right? Of course it does, but that doesn't mean I should abandon my beliefs. It just means that I haven't gotten it figured out. A scientist doesn't abandon a model because it doesn't explain all the data. Instead, he or she retains the model that explains the largest portion of the data because it is the most useful one. Then the scientist tries to develop the model to accommodate the rest of the data in an attempt to determine the truth.

I believe that the Christian worldview more closely reflects universal, absolute truth than does any other worldview, and that a life lived according to the principles found in the Bible will be a better life than one lived according to any other "truth" system—no matter the person, no matter the context. The Christian God created all life, and all life is lived better when it is lived under the authority of that same God. This gives me purpose, it gives me hope for a better life, and it helps me to make sense of the world I see.

Persons who subscribe to **simple supernaturalism** believe in neither gods nor spirits. They view the ultimate form of the sacred as the diffuse, impersonal, supernatural force of nature. This force is believed to influence the events of life for better or for worse. Though this form of religious belief is typical of simple, pre-industrial societies, Robertson (1989) pointed out that vestiges of it persist in contemporary American society. He argued that beliefs exercised in luck, charms, and certain rituals as sources of achievement and success are evidences of simple supernaturalism in today's culture. For example, some people believe that having a rabbit's foot in their possession serves to attract good luck and thus leads to their success. Another instance of this belief is the practice of some professional athletes wearing special pieces of clothing or performing certain rituals before they compete. Football superstar Barry Sanders is reputed to have worn the same pair of pants over and again with hopes of duplicating past achievements.

Animism is a religious construct that views the central expression of the sacred to be active spirits that pervade nature. These spirits are benevolent or malevolent, and both can be controlled by the shaman. Though animistic beliefs are not widely practiced in modern-day America, exorcisms carried out by priests and other "spiritual" persons are similar in purpose and practice to what shamans do.

The third religious definition of the supernatural, according to McGee, is **theism**. Adherents of theistic religions see God as the ultimate source of the sacred. Monotheists claim there is only one God, while polytheists contend there are many gods. The predominant religious belief system in America is **monotheism** as practiced in Judaism, Islam, and Christianity.

The fourth classification of religion in McGee's typology, **transcendent idealism,** holds that values such as honesty, truth, justice, peace, and even life itself are sacred. Buddhists, as transcendent idealists, for example, seek oneness with the universe and escape from suffering through self-denial. Self-denial, Buddhists believe, is achieved through the following noble eightfold path: 1) skillful understanding, 2) skillful thinking (the renouncing of carnal pleasure and wanting), 3) skillful speech, 4) skillful action, 5) skillful livelihood, 6) skillful effort, 7) skillful mindfulness, and 8) skillful concentration (see Henepola Gunaratana, 2001). The Dalai Lama, the so-called Buddha of Compassion, has been instrumental in drawing the attention of many Americans to Buddhism and its transcendent idealist views. McGee's classification of religion by central beliefs about the sacred is, of course, not the only such classification system. It is included in this chapter because it is believed to be sufficiently broad as to represent a variety of religious phenomena and practices in the United States and many other nations.

Classification of Religion by Level of Inclusiveness and Structure of Organization

The sacred, however it is perceived, is believed to have extraordinary qualities and powers, and therefore exerts powerful influences upon the general views and conduct of believers. Most religions have set social norms by and through which they approach and celebrate the sacred at both the personal and interpersonal (communal) levels. These rules and the associated rituals are expressed through a range of behaviors that vary from simple prayers and singing to human sacrifice. The specific social norms and rituals embraced by religious groups serve to define two central dimensions of their characteristics. These dimensions, in turn, determine the relative prestige of these groups in the larger society and their capacity to deal with several issues. Yinger (1970) summarizes these dimensions as norms regarding degree of inclusion (the degree to which a group's policy regarding membership is selective and exclusive or open and inclusive) and norms regarding organizational structure (how much the group accepts or rejects

the secular values and structures of the surrounding society and reflects this in its own governance). Based on these criteria, religious groups may be classified into three types: churches, sects, and cults.

Churches

According to Troeltsch (1960), a **church** is a formal religious organization that is well integrated into the larger society. Religious groups with church-like structures are generally highly organized, operate by a set of formal rules and regulations, and are managed by highly trained leaders whose functions are hierarchically arranged. Religious organizations of this sort tend to endure for centuries. One other noticeable characteristic of this type of religious organization is the tendency for its membership to include several generations from the same family.

There are really two kinds of church-like organizations, namely, ecclesiae and denominations. **Ecclesiae** are formally connected to the state and tend to exercise influence over, and claim as members, everyone in a given society. In contemporary societies, the Islamic religion in Iran perhaps comes closest to being an ecclesia. **Denominations** are typical of societies such as the United States where there is a formal separation between "church and state," and where religious organizations exist with high tolerance for one another. But not all religious groups are denominations. Some, as indicated above, are sects or cults.

Sects

Macionis (1999) acknowledged that though the church tends to persist for centuries, it is not without its moments of instability. Every now and then, elements emerge within its fold to challenge the legitimacy of its operation and to point out its heresies. Such elements tend over time to become separated from the parent body and to assume their own independent operations. Religious organizations that come into being this way are called **sects**. Unlike the larger, more enduring religious bodies from which they have defected, sects are generally loosely organized and tend to be at variance with the wider society. In fact, the formation of a sectarian group often results from disagreements of critical members with the parent body over the latter's overidentification with the world. Thus, a sect can be interpreted as a religious organization that stands apart from the larger denomination. Independent ministries which break off from organized denominations often mature into sects.

Cults

Perhaps the type of religious organization that evokes the strongest reaction from the public is the **cult**. Tragic incidents involving members of this religious subculture usually attract national attention and widespread disapproval. While the cult shares most of the organizational characteristics of the sect, its emphasis on the "new" puts it in contrast to the sect's focus on calling attention to the waning standards of the "old path." Cults are further distinguished from both the church and the sect in that the former draw their inspiration and guidance from charismatic leaders rather than scriptures. Jim Jones and the People's Temple (Jonestown) and David Koresh and the Branch Davidians were well documented cults. As a rule, cults in America are held in very low esteem and are generally suspect of immoral and unnatural human relationships.

So far, we have discussed the nature of religion, identified its main elements, and delineated its various forms on the basis of central beliefs about the sacred, degree of structural organization, and level of inclusiveness. In the section that follows, we will direct our attention to some of the social merits of religion, and in this connection point out how religious groups are affected by Yinger's two distinguishing characteristics in their capacity to deal with the social ills.

The Church/Sect Continuum and Social Issues

Both the levels of inclusiveness and the organizational structures that characterize religious groups hold strong implications for their ability to deal with social ills. Church-like groups, because of their high tolerance for the wider social system and their often close identification with it, are especially prone to inaction in the face of the "evils" of the system. In particular, ecclesias, because their interests are seen to be similar to those of the politically and economically powerful, can hardly be expected to be critical of the latter. Therefore,

ecclesias are less likely to adopt measures aimed at correcting social ills that result from the policies and operations of these institutions. It is generally recognized by historians that the Russian Orthodox Church was active in the former Soviet Union, and yet remained silent in the face of blatant human rights violation by the communist governments. Also the Islamic "church" in Iran aided and abetted the Ayatollah regime in its insufferable acts of violence against the Iranian people during the 1980s. It is perhaps in this sense that Marx saw religion as the handmaiden of the powerful (Marx & Engels, 2002).

Yet religious organizations with a church-like posture are sometimes among the first to give attention to social issues when they pose a threat to the social order and human dignity. For example, the Roman Catholic Church in El Salvador and Guatemala maintains a firm position in defending the rights of the poor against the protectors of the status quo. However, this raises the important question as to what gets defined and treated as relevant social issues by religious groups that exist in high harmony with the political status quo.

Because sectarian groups tend to exist in high tension with the wider social system, they are more likely to challenge the status quo on social issues. Yet their other-worldly orientation may lead to their refusal to deal with these issues. Cultic groups, which are generally not tradition-bound and exhibit a strong emphasis on "new truth," seem ideally suited to take up arms against the "ills" of society. But because these groups often arise in reaction to the strain and stress of the social system, they tend to seek solutions for their powerlessness and unease in a "better world" beyond the present society. A fair representation of this would be the deceased members of the Heaven's Gate Temple cult who sought escape from the problems of this life through suicide. Their hope was to join a comet that would take them to paradise. Though cults generally create legal, moral, and image problems for the free exercise of religion, the free practice of religion has an overwhelmingly positive impact on American society.

Religion and Its Positive Consequences upon Some Central Issues

ISSUES: What types of positive and negative effects does religion have? Why do you think this is so? How does religion play a role in the order of society and the meaning of life? What are other systems that play similar roles? What is the difference between these systems? Is it possible for religion not to be divisive? How?

Religion is changeable and multifaceted, not only in terms of its ideological orientations and structural arrangements, but more so in its functions and impact upon social systems. McGuire (1997) argues that religion is one of the most powerful and deeply felt forces in human society, with consequences for our familial, communal, economic, and political lives. Evidence of this impact is given in the fact that close to 70% of Americans hold membership in some religious group (Henslin, 1995). Contrary to the rigid, reactionary image with which some have characterized religion, there is now sufficient evidence to support a progressive view of this phenomenon in terms of its capacity to deal with social issues. In his extensive review document on religion and its effects on various social issues, Fagan (1996) has distilled the following benefits:

- "The strength of the family unit is intertwined with the practice of religion. Churchgoers are more likely to be married, less likely to be divorced or single, and more likely to manifest high levels of satisfaction in marriage.
- "Church attendance is the most important predictor of marital stability and happiness.
- "The regular practice of religion helps poor persons move out of poverty. Regular church attendance, for example, is particularly instrumental in helping young people to escape the poverty of inner-city life.
- "Religious belief and practice contribute substantially to the formation of personal moral criteria and sound moral judgment.

- "Regular religious practice generally inoculates individuals against a host of social problems, including suicide, drug abuse, out-of-wedlock births, crime, and divorce.
- "The regular practice of religion also encourages such beneficial effects on mental health as less depression (a modern epidemic), more self-esteem, and greater family and marital happiness.
- "In repairing damage caused by alcoholism, drug addiction, and marital breakdown, religious belief and practice are a major source of strength and recovery.
- "Regular practice of religion is good for personal physical health: It increases longevity, improves one's chances of recovery from illness, and lessens the incidence of many killer diseases."

Religion as a Change Agent

Among the positive aspects of religion that have been identified is the effectiveness of this institution as a change agent. As pointed out earlier, Max Weber identified the Protestant religious ethic as one of the driving forces behind the development of capitalism. He pointed out that the tendency for Protestants of the Calvinistic orientation to regard hard work, frugality, and postponed gratification as indicators of salvation corresponded with the spirit and mindset needed for the development of capitalism.

Furthermore, the value of religion as an agent of social change has been underscored by the Black civil rights movement in the United States. Gunnar Myrdal

(1944) captured the point well when he noted that the African American church functions as a "community center par excellence" (p. 938). During the period of slavery it was the religious sentiment and fervor, incarnated in songs, that kept African Americans buoyant and enabled them to cope. After emancipation, religion became the heartbeat of their communities. Accordingly, Roberts (1994) identified several post-emancipation impacts of the African American church. He noted that it sponsored social and cultural affairs, including political debates; set up insurance programs for those who could not qualify for coverage under the white-controlled corporations; started schools for education of the young; and organized economic recovery and growth programs. The additional importance of religion to the African American civil rights movement can be seen in its leaders. Andrew Young, Jessie Jackson, and the late Martin Luther King Jr. all had their beginnings in the black church and were ministers of congregations before starting their civil rights crusades. King, in particular, was well known for utilizing religious verbiage and the characteristic African American preaching style to present his civil rights messages with much effect. His famous "I Have a Dream" speech is an outstanding case in point.

Beyond the American scene, in the protracted struggle engaged against the now dismantled apartheid system in South Africa, the contribution of religion is unmistakable. Against a system that pitted race against race, the voice of the church, epitomized by Archbishop Desmond Tutu, was heard loud and clear. From his vantage point in his South African home, Archbishop Tutu was persistent in clarifying the issues as they related to the operation of the apartheid system and kept them before the international community. The impressive and impartial way in which he championed this and other human rights causes earned him the Noble Peace Prize in 1984. When the apartheid system was overthrown, Archbishop Tutu was again involved in the reconciliation and healing process in the Reconciliation and Truth Commission which he spearheaded. In this role, he led South Africa to embrace the Christian concept of forgiveness which became the guiding principle of the commission and prevented a continuing cycle of wholesale racial atrocities.

Another example that has served to mainstream the role of religion as facilitator of social change and highlighted its relevance to social issues is the reinterpretation of the gospel by the Reformist Catholic movement in the form of liberation theology. This intellectual movement, pioneered by Father Gustavo Gutierrez in his book *A Theology of Liberation* (1973), represents a merger between aspects of Marxian ideas and the liberation theme of the gospel. According to this perspective, even the violent overthrow of oppressive governments is justifiable if it will lead to the liberation of the oppressed.

Yet another positive feature of religion is its integrative role. Whether in a large group, or in a small twosome such as a marriage, religion is known for its cementing power. As a source of group loyalty and solidarity it stands out. This unifying dimension of religion flows from its ritualistic practices in bringing people together to celebrate their shared understanding of the structure of the world (Hargrove, 1979). Hargrove points out that rituals inspire an appreciation of the social order and help to maintain a society's equilibrium.

Religion and the Family Institution

Further evidence of the integrative nature of religion can be seen in its impact upon the family institution. Levinger (1965), in his study of the factors that relate to marital stability and dissolution, noted that religiously homogenous couples, that is, couples whose partners were of the same religion, stood a better chance of preventing divorce than those who did not embrace a religion. Stinnett (1992) and Lauer and Lauer (1992) did separate interviews with families in order to discover the factors that hold families together and promote their sense of contentment and happiness. Lauer and Lauer found that, among the 360 families interviewed, those with a religious orientation, despite the quality of their marital experience, had lower divorce rates than non-religious families. Stinnett, on the other hand, focused on factors that made for happy families and found that religious families were happier than non-religious families. Fowers and Olson (1989), with a sample of over 5,000 married couples, employed ten factors to describe a well-adjusted family. Their research confirmed that religion was the most important predictor as reported by over 73% of the families.

Thus, the evidence strongly supports the truism that religion not only keeps families together, but it also has demonstrated a capacity to help them strive. In an age when domestic abuse is on the increase and the rate of divorce remains over 50%, the contribution of the religious institution to marital and family life quality certainly deserves further and more thorough investigation.

Religion as a Source of Meaning

As a source of meaning and purpose, the religious phenomenon is unique. At times situations arise that pose a threat to the way we generally make sense of life. Experiences of suffering and death, natural disasters, failures, and unforeseen difficulties often pave the way to personal confusion and hopelessness. Without a frame of reference that transcends the mundane, life hangs precariously unstable in face of these realities. Religion can rescue us from such an outcome by anchoring our uncertainties and instabilities in an ultimate reality. In the light of such an anchor, the senseless becomes meaningful and the chaotic orderly. Pargament and Brant (1998) proposed that religion provides a response to the problems of our insufficiencies. These researchers validated the notion that religion provides support where it is lacking with explanations and a sense of control when life seems out of control. Moreover, religion adds new symbols of significance when old ones are no longer compelling. In summary, religion serves as a social support system and buffer to the psychological stressors for people as they cope with life's unfortunate and often mysterious events.

The maintenance of order in society apart from social measures rests ultimately upon a belief in the sacred. Emile Durkheim (1965) was clear in his assessment that the cause of much of the social disorder in modern society is due to the fact "that the old gods are growing old or are already dead, and others are not yet born" (p. 475). Durkheim was here referring to the decline of traditional religious values and norms and their non-replacement by new ones. Religion aids in the maintenance of the social order by teaching norms and values that are consistent with the demands of such an order. Also, through the legitimation and sacralization of the powers that be, religion lends to the measures of social control.

However, despite the foregoing positive picture on religion, one must be cautioned against expecting the same benefits from all forms of religion. Religious groups vary not only in the extent to which they may become involved in the social ills of society, as pointed out earlier, but also in terms of their specific input on social life, and the degree to which they become sources of concern in the society. Pescosolido and Georgiana (1989) noted the differential effects of religion on suicide rates across denominations. They reported that those U.S. counties in which Catholics and Evangelical Protestants (examples of the latter being Churches of God, Seventh-day Adventists, and Southern Baptists) were in greater proportions demonstrated lower suicide rates than those with greater concentration of mainline Protestant denominations (e.g., Episcopalians, Lutherans, Presbyterians). Because of the positive aspects of religion discussed above, some social critics argue that religion will always remain a force in society. Others have underscored the dysfunctional role of religion, noting its divisive and conflicting nature.

The Divisive Nature of Religion

ISSUES: Is it possible for religion not to be divisive, especially if different religions claim "truth"? If so, how? If not, how should society handle that divisiveness? What kinds of divisions do various religions help propagate? Many past and current wars have been and are being waged in the name of religion. Current conflicts include the Palestinian/Israeli protracted disturbance and the persecution of Christians by Muslims in the Sudan. Because of these wars, and other such conflicts, many social theorists and researchers argue that the elimination of religion would make for a better world. What do you think? How can religion be used to bring peace to society?

While the previous section highlighted the positive value of religion on society, this section identifies the contributory role religion plays in creating, promoting, and resolving longstanding conflicts. Many of the persistent problems in the United States and the world have a religious face. In many cases, issues of racial conflict, gender inequality, and prejudice are rooted in religious sentiment and ideology. We now examine some of these problems and the degree to which religion contributes to their emergence and persistence.

Religion and Racial Conflict

Of the many conflicts that plague human society, none seem as pervasive and entrenched as those in which racial animosity draws on religious sentiments. The annals of these conflicts go back in time to include the Crusades and the Inquisitions among others. The Crusades were so-called "holy wars" fought between Muslims and Christians during the Middle Ages. Christians of that era thought it their God-given duty to defeat the Muslim infidels and drive them out of Palestine, a land they considered sacred. However, this conflict was not one in which the Christians were the sole aggressors and the Muslims the passive sufferers. Muslims also perpetrated great acts of cruelty against Christians in those places where they were the conquerors. The Crusades lasted for many decades and cost countless lives because of religious hatred and prejudice.

The Inquisitions were no less costly in human lives and spirit. By this formal means of the trial of heretics, the Roman Catholic Church of the sixteenth century sought to punish its defectors, whose only faults consisted of their disagreement with the Mother Church over doctrines. By employing the support of the secular authorities, the Roman Catholic Church unleashed a reign of terror and violence against the Waldenses and Albigenssians of France, almost to the point of their extinction. More recently, examples of religiously driven conflicts can be found in the open-ended religious wars in Iraq, the Middle East, and the former Yugoslavia.

The seemingly unending antagonism between Catholics and Protestants of Northern Ireland dates back to the early half of the seventeenth century when Ireland was colonized by England. The decision by the colonial power to dispossess Irish Catholics of their land and award them to Anglican and Presbyterian Protestants ignited a strife that continues to the present. Catholics reacted to the injustice and waged a war for almost eight years beginning in 1641. More than 12,000 Protestants were killed. The Protestants struck back in 1649 when Oliver Cromwell led 1,200 troops into Ireland and avenged the Protestant lives that were lost as a result of the Catholic rebellion. Thousands of Catholics were killed and their land confiscated. Since then several battles have been fought between the two rival sides. According to O'Malley (1983), the eleven-year period between 1971 and 1982 was especially violent. During that period of time there were "over 28,500 shootings, 7,500 bomb explosions with 2,300 lives lost" (Johnstone, 1997). Despite the 1998 ceasefire agreed upon by both sides, it is wondered whether the centuries-old animosity between these two religious factions will erupt in sectarian violence again.

Aguirre and Turner (1998) noted that the present conflict between the Palestinians and the Israelis goes back at least two thousand years. When Jews were driven from Palestine as a result of Ottoman Empire expansion, Palestine came under the control of Muslims. During World War I the Turks were driven out of Palestine by the British, who encouraged the Jews

Praying at the Western Wall in Jerusalem.

to create a Zionist state in Palestine. The creation of the state of Israel in 1948 by the British provoked the protective instinct of the Arab world. The surrounding Arab nations compacted to return the control of Palestine to the Palestinians. This led, among other things, to the six-day war of 1969 in which Israel defeated Egypt and Syria. This course of events served to intensify anger on both sides, and contributed, in no small way, to the animosity that remains between the Arabs (the Muslim world) and the Israelis (the Jewish state). The 2006 election of the Hamass party to power in the West Bank further exacerbated the struggle for land and resources. The Hamass party believes that Israel is an illegal nation and all lands must be returned to the Palestinians.

In the summer of 1999 another religiously fueled conflict was ignited. Tens of thousands of Albanian Muslims were driven from their homes in Serbia at the hand of Kosovar Christians. Many incidents were reported of parents being shot in front of their children, and children being taken from their parents and killed. The events have been described as among the worst of human tragedies in which one religious group inspired by hate sought the dislocation and elimination of another faith-based group.

It seems that these racio-religious conflicts may be attributed, in part, to the psychological and cultural phenomenon of *identity formation and maintenance.* This phenomenon is an intricate and complex facet of human development which influences an individual's thought patterns, behaviors, and attitudes through the lifelong processes of conditioning, modeling, and learning. Over time each individual develops a cultural

group ideology that is destined to shape and maintain one's socio-religious worldview. Any attempt by others to disrupt or redefine this psycho-cultural balance may ultimately lead to violent confrontations. Within the context of religion as a form of identity formation and maintenance, Beit-Hallahmi (1991) stated: "The uniqueness of religion as a system of beliefs and attitudes is often alleged to be its high degree of resistance to change, and its high degree of emotionality. Both can best be explained in terms of the identity system. Religion as an individual belief system is so resistant to change, because it is tied to a sense of identity. Every challenge to a religious belief is a threat to the personal identity system, and people react strongly to such threats" (p. 185).

Religion can, therefore, become the catalyst for hatred, war, and violence if there are perceived threats to a group's social identity and its communal existence. Waging war in the name of religion can be a mask for a perceived fragmentation of a group's social and ethnic cohesiveness. Pope John Paul II, in an address to representatives of the world's faith in October 1999, cautioned that religion should not be a motive for conflict. He stated: "Religion is not, and must not become a pretext for conflict, particularly when religious, cultural, and ethnic identity coincides. Religious leaders must clearly show that they are pledged to promote peace, precisely because of their religious beliefs" (Pope John Paul II, 1999).

Wentz (1993) offers another interesting perspective on why religious groups resort to violent confrontations with other faith-based groups. He indicated that "there are those people who in their religious transcendence of their biological nature, are willing to live with moving horizons, knowing the truth without certainty. But there are also those who cannot live with uncertainty, and this often leads them to defensive and hostile attitudes, even violence. They may use science or religion to support their violent need for certainty" (p. 21).

In summary, we have pointed out that religion, despite its pacific nature, has been the source of conflict and wards. In the following section, religion is discussed as a source of social inequality.

Gender Inequality and Religion

The unequal distribution of the resources of income, power, and prestige between males and females is a social issue that continually attracts a good deal of scholarly attention. Despite the American ideal that all men and women are created equal, subtle and sometimes open acts of discrimination are being perpetrated against women in our society. Figure 8.1 illustrates that women as a group enjoy far less of the three resources mentioned above than men do. The reason for this disparity is not without the legitimating role of religion. Sadly, many systems of inequality are shored up ideologies based on religious explanations.

Gender inequality, in particular, is sustained centrally by the ideology of sexism—the belief that one sex (the female, in the case of most, if not all, societies)

is inferior to the other (the male). In some religious traditions, this notion of the woman's inferiority is at least implied if not expressly stated in relevant sacred writings and rituals.

The Koran, according to Smith (1991), clearly states that men are a step above women and that they are the protectors of women; therefore, God has given preference to men over women. In keeping with this view, Mernissi (1987) noted that Muslim men and women are socialized within religious institutions that keep women repressed and perceived as enemies. The repression of women is, ironically, a heavy burden on men and denies them freedom to actualize themselves in creative ways. In a very real sense, power over any group of people enslaves those exercising power.

Despite the more positive imagery of womanhood painted within the scriptural texts of Hinduism, there are notions promoted in other influential sources which suggest that women are inferior to men. Johnstone (1997) noted that by 500 B.C., Hindu women had clearly been relegated to second class status in the common belief that they could not attain salvation, except as they were reincarnated as men in a future life. Moreover, the practice of suttee, widow burning, speaks to the inferior status imposed on women within Hinduism. In this ritual (a tradition not now widely followed), the widow of a deceased Hindu man submits herself to be

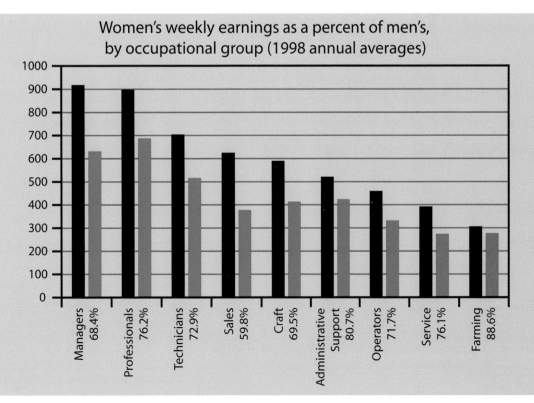

**Figure 8.1: Gender Pay Gap.
Source: Bureau of Labor
Statistics**

cremated on the funeral pyre with her husband. This act was regarded by the Hindu community as an indication of her devotion. However, the implication in this self-sacrifice, in the Hindu community, afforded no sense of devotion to widows in their time of need.

Views on women expressed in the holy writings of Judaism are no more favorable than are those expressed by the Islamic and Hindu sacred texts. Whether it is Biblical, Talmudic Medieval, or modern Judaism, it has always been clear that men were to read, teach, and legislate and that women should be followers of men (Carmody, 1979). Additionally, women were excluded from the privilege of daily religious duties expected of men, since it was believed that this would interfere with their domestic duties for which they were more naturally suited.

Within the sacred writings of the Christian religion there are also examples of men being preferred by God to exercise authority over women in the home. The Pauline account seems clear: "Now I want you to realize that the head of every man is Christ, and the head of the woman is man, and the head of Christ is God" (1 Corinthians 11:3).

However, Christian, Judaic, Hindu, and Islamic apologists have defended their respective religions against the indictment of prejudice against women. It is argued, and perhaps rightly so, that it is not the views expressed in sacred writings by themselves that constitute the problem of gender discrimination, but rather how they are interpreted by those who exercise authority over women. Indeed, within all of the sacred texts referred to above can be found equally convincing passages that speak to the equality of the genders. For example, despite the fact that the Apostle Paul's work is often quoted to support the subordination of women, he also said that "…there is neither bond nor free, there is neither male nor female: for ye are all one in Christ Jesus" (Romans 3:28). Therefore, some have argued that it is the selective reading of sacred texts that make for the construction of sacred-text-based ideologies that are supportive of gender inequality. Be that as it may, social inequalities and gender inequality in particular are strongly shored up by biased interpretations of sacred writings.

Religion and Prejudice

To a large extent, religiously fueled conflicts (and discriminations) trace their origin to some form of prejudice. This seems paradoxical in light of the universalistic appeal of religion. Peterson, Wunder, and Mueller (1999) observed: "Without exception all of the great religions and all of their founders taught the unity of mankind (not racism or separatism of any sort) and without exception these great religions teach love and compassion to others…[and] condemn the ideas and practices of hate groups as wrong…" (p. 91).

Yet the practice of religion over time, despite its stabilizing and positive contribution, has been marked by intolerance, conflict, discrimination, and violence, as evidenced in the previous section. Allport (1954), in his classic discussion, *The Nature of Prejudice*, observed that the role of religion in society is paradoxical, in that "religion makes prejudice and it unmakes prejudice," and that while "church-goers are more prejudiced than the average, they also are less prejudiced than the average." One needs, therefore, to proceed with caution in any attempt to evaluate the relationships between religion and prejudice. Subtle interactions between intervening variables can serve to artificially mask or exaggerate the effect of religion on personal attitudes and the wider social systems.

The question then becomes "what about religion makes it such a Janus-faced phenomenon?" (Janus was the god of gates, doors, beginnings, and endings in Roman mythology. He is characterized by two faces, which look in opposite directions.) The answer to this question resides partly in the tendency of religion to dichotomize and frame the world in dualistic terms. Dualisms such as evil and good, sacred and profane, holy and unholy are basic to religious perspectives. These terms refer not only to ideas but also to objects and people. It is on the basis of these dualisms that people develop the "we-they" mentality and make judgments, often without due process about other persons who do not share their world view. The predisposition of persons to make judgments about others without first examining the facts is the essence of what it means to be prejudiced. In order to understand the social nature of prejudice formation and to appreciate how otherwise decent, noble human beings come to possess prejudice, it is necessary to review the process by which we make sense of the world about us and our membership/affiliation in religious collectivities.

To facilitate our understanding of the world about us, we categorize the world and make generalizations about it. In categorizing the world we isolate chunks out of it, distinguish these chunks from all other parts of the world, give names to these chunks, and associate certain ideas with the assigned names (see Charon, 1998). This process of dissecting and subdividing the world, associating labels with each resulting element, and making generalizations about these is basic to the ease and comfort with which we interact with the world (people, things, and generated ideas). In some ways, therefore, once these categories and their meanings have been created, they tend to become fundamental to the way we sort and respond to the people and ideas we encounter. Either consciously or unconsciously, our religious community sets or changes the values we place on ideas, objects, and people not yet categorized.

But useful as these categories and their meanings are, it becomes problematic when we use them in rigid, inflexible, and judgmental ways to form stereotypes. Stereotypically, we assume that wealthy people drive expensive cars, such as the Mercedes-Benz or Lexus. Whenever we see persons driving luxury vehicles, we automatically conclude, without a passing critical thought, that they are wealthy. Prejudice feeds on this non-thinking process that may be set by personal experiences, religious affiliations, and birth cultures.

Because religious institutions tend to ground their symbolic order (values, rituals, etc.), including the meanings attributed to mundane events, in a transcendent reality, categories and generalization used by religious institutions tend to have a compelling effect on their members. Religious persons are especially prone to perpetuate the same prejudices promoted by their religions. However, religious categories and generalizations do not influence the conduct of people independent of other factors. This explains why different races, genders, and nationalities in a single denomination can have radically different biases and prejudices.

Allport (1954), for example, argued that a prejudicial outlook varies by religiosity type. He concluded from his studies that devoutly religious persons, those personally absorbed in their religion, tended to be far less prejudiced than institutionally religious persons. Understandably, those whose attachment to religion was external and based on political and utilitarian motivations viewed prejudice apart from religious values. What Allport concluded many years ago still rings true: "We cannot speak sensibly of the relation between religion and prejudice without specifying the sort of religion we mean and the role it plays in the personal life" (p. 425). In addition to type of religiosity, prejudice formation and exercise among the religious vary by age, education, region, and ethnicity.

Religion, Social Issues, and the Future

The discussion thus far demonstrates that there is a clear relationship between religion and social issues. It is, however, not predictable what direction that relationship will take in various situations. We have noted the divergent ways in which religion impacts social issues and pointed out the integrative, meaning-providing, change-agent, as well as the conflictful and discriminatory roles of religion in society. In these ways religion proves to be a powerful force in society. However, in light of the secularizing trend evident in our society, it seems reasonable to inquire whether religion will continue to have an influence on social issues in the future. And if so, what will likely be the nature of that impact?

The secularization thesis argues that, as modern society advances in science and technology, religion will eventually recede to the point of non-functionality. Yet there is evidence, to the contrary, that religion is and will likely continue to be functional. The question, however, is how functional? A brief examination of major modernism and postmodernism processes should help us find reasonable answers. The processes of modernism, according to McGuire (1997), include institutional differentiation, changing patterns of legitimization and authority, and rationalization, among others. Postmodernism, on the other hand, rejects any notion of a universal standard of knowing, believing, and behaving. It argues that everything is relative, especially truth and universal principles. The following section examines the processes of modernism and postmodernism with the intent of estimating what roles religion will likely play in the future.

Institutional Differentiation

ISSUES: During the 2000 presidential election campaign, George W. Bush spoke repeatedly about compassionate charity. After being elected and taking office as President of the United States of America, among the first things he did was to put into place measures that made it possible for religious organizations engaging in charitable work to receive federal funding for their programs. Is this a violation of the separation of church and state principle upheld in the constitution? What are the implications of this policy? In reflecting upon this issue, try to apply the notions of the "differentiation of institutions" and "religious pluralism."

One of the features that distinguish a modern society from a traditional one is the process of **institutional differentiation**. In this process, institutions, including religious institutions, become separate in function from one another and take on specialized roles. No longer does a single institution exert complete control over the lives of people. In traditional societies, religious institutions affected many aspects of society's operation, but in a modern society their effect is limited to specific spheres. In traditional societies, the priest or pastor served as the mediator of disputes, career and marriage counselor, education advisor, and in many other capacities that are now under the separate control of highly trained professionals. This has the net corresponding effect of constraining people to keep religion separate from other aspects of their lives. Also, because institutions tend to pursue separate goals, and because values of one institution do not necessarily match values of another, it becomes increasingly difficult for society to mobilize and control its members through the broad acceptance of shared core values and beliefs.

Moreover, the segmented nature of modern society and the increasing trend of postmodernism present real difficulties for those seeking to chart a balanced course of life based on a stable and consistent meaning order. This search is made especially difficult because of the divergent and contrasting relationships persons are forced to have with the differentiating institutions of society. Furthermore, the postmodernist view that there is really no universal rule of right and wrong compounds the situation and leads to a sense of disconnect for individuals who search in vain for moral certitude and social moorings. This discomfort has had and will continue to have the effect of driving many people to privatize their religious experiences in search for meaning.

Changing Sources of Legitimization

One of the means by which order is maintained in a democracy is linked to the source from which individuals and groups derive their right to exercise authority over others. McGuire (1997) theorized that in traditional societies, religion functions as a legitimate authority that directly and indirectly impacts most aspects of social life. He further noted that myths and rituals buttress all areas of life in traditional societies, and that leaders exercise authority to the extent that their roles are sustained by these myths and rituals. However, this widespread effect of religion as a source of justification is undermined by the differentiation process and pluralism prevalent in postmodern societies.

Pluralism, by definition, allows no single position or worldview. The various perspectives embraced by different groups in society are seen as socially valid. The predictability and stability that flow from an overarching order of shared meanings and consensus, typical of a traditional society, continue to erode. The absence of traditional order not only weakens the basis of public morality but also leaves individuals in a state of confusion as to what to believe. Further, in the light of Luckmann's (1967) view that the worldview embraced by individuals tends to become an important part of their personal identity, individuals are likely to drift into identity confusion as they confront the postmodern devaluation of traditional values and mores.

Another way in which modern and postmodern philosophies impact the relationship between religion and the wider society is through the ethical-free application of technology. This approach is characterized by an openness to accept new ideas and give up old ways of thinking and of methodologies in the interest of efficiency, effectiveness, reduced cost, and increased yields. Additional features of the rational approach include a reward system based upon objective criteria, such as academic qualifications and the technical skills and knowledge of individuals, rather than personal and subjective considerations. This means-end focus values things and people only to the extent that they are instrumental in facilitating the realization of given goals in the most efficient, cost-effective way possible. As Weber remarked, the operation of such a system gives us "specialists without spirit and sensualists without heart" (Weber, 1958). Within this scheme of things, nonfunctional values such as kindness, honesty, beauty, and meaningfulness are increasingly irrelevant (McGuire, 1997), and we find ourselves in Weber's proverbial "iron cage" of cold and impersonal instrumentality. These conditions have contributed in no small measure to the proliferation of fundamentalist, cultic, and new age groups that search for answers to the emptiness, social detachment, and sense of loss generated by the calculating processes of modernism and postmodernism. Henslin (1995) reported that with the exception of Roman Catholics, fundamentalist groups, when compared with liberal religious groups, realized the greatest growth in membership between 1965 and 1989.

Some fundamentalist religious groups, as pointed out before, can be sect-like. They aim at recapturing the certitude and sense of identity once guaranteed by traditional religion. In addition, strict doctrine faith systems attract individuals who seek the purity inherent in established values and norms. Fundamentalists generally insist on the literal interpretation of sacred writings, and put up stout resistance to innovative ideas and practices that run counter to long-held values and practice.

Cultic groups, on the other hand, seek solace from the impersonality and detachment of modern society in small, close-knit, family-like communes. Tim Stoen, former member of the ill-fated Jonestown People's Temple commune, stated: "For many in our throwaway, hedonistic society, life has become empty. Anything that involves a family—which is what a cult is—can be very appealing. People want simplicity; a cult provides ready-made answers" (Stoen, 1997, p. 44). What is implied here is that the uncertainty of our modern world creates a deeper longing for a sense of belonging.

The New Age cultic groups draw on the monistic emphasis of Eastern religions in their reaction to the uncertainties of modernism and postmodernism. According to the monistic worldview, the ultimate goal of life is an absorption into the unity of all things (Hargrove, 1979). In light of this view, the pluralities of world views appear less threatening to "New Agers," since all things compose a basic unity. New Age religious worldviews are now experiencing a resurgence precisely because they seem to get around the pluralism question and the uncertainty it generates. If all things, despite their apparent divergent nature, constitute a unity, then we have no need to fear. All we need to do is await the unfolding and enfolding of this cosmic unity.

Conclusion

Despite its shifting emphases and changing forms, religion remains a relevant force in modern society. In fact, issues with which individuals grapple in the wake of modernism and in the face of postmodernism have themselves generated, surprisingly, a new appetite for religion. As one form of religion becomes disenchanting, it seems, new forms are generated to take its place. Human beings are meaning-driven creatures and are

thrown into a state of unease and confusion without a symbolic order, a meaning structure by which to understand the shifting fortunes of life.

In this connection, it is believed that every known society in human history has practiced some form of religion. Some researchers claim that humans are hard-wired to pursue the spiritual and are left unfulfilled without a spiritual/religious orientation. Therefore, despite the eroding distinctiveness between the sacred and the profane, and the effects of societal globalization on the marginalization of the transcendent, human beings will continually seek out religion to meet their needs. It seems reasonable to expect in the future that religious sentiment and practice are likely to expand in non-traditional ways.

Response

A Christian Theological Explanation of Religion

by William Richardson

The chapter begins with the observation that religion is both a blessing and a curse, a boon and a bane. The populace overwhelmingly believes that a faith in God is important. At the same time, history bears out that religion has been the driving force behind some of the truly horrific atrocities that have marred the past. While the authors juxtapose the good and the evil that religion has helped foster, they do not leave them evenly balanced. They make quite clear that the good outweighs the evil, that religion provides more help than hostility in society, more direction than confusion. However, little time is spent attempting to explain how a faith phenomenon purported to bring peace has at times done the reverse with vengeance. Instead, the authors spend the early part of the chapter detailing a variety of both positive and negative contributions that religion has bequeathed to us. They include no real attempt to harmonize the seeming paradox. They simply list several positive and several negative contributions that had their origin in some form of religious worldview. Presumably, the balanced presentation is designed to draw the reader into a position of thinking about and weighing the issues.

The chapter, working primarily from a sociological perspective, points out that for many sociologists, religion may be viewed as a rather utilitarian phenomenon that humans need so that they can cope with the vicissitudes of life. In other words, for them, it serves the necessary function of enabling humans to find a system of beliefs and practices that helps them to function reasonably well. While the chapter does not deny a connection between religion and the supernatural, it sharpens the focus on the psychological underpinnings of so much that is done in the name of religion—an emphasis too often muted or even denied by many.

In contrast, a more strictly theological explanation of religion stresses the self-revelation of God. In other words, religious sentiment is created by God, not by humans. To put it another way, the theological approach takes seriously the biblical statement that humans were made in the image of God and not vice versa. Thus religion is not a phenomenon whereby humans create their own gods according to their various needs. If religion were simply a human creation, there should not be such widespread unhappiness and dissatisfaction—so much complaining about why God doesn't run things better. But behind all the carping about God's seeming inability to control the evil in this world and all its attendant suffering is the implication that somewhere behind all the mysteries and unknowns stands some sort of God figure. He may not seem to be doing His job, but the complaint implies that He exists.

The theological approach asserts that God doesn't just stand behind the scenes, refusing to get involved. Rather, He is a self-limiting God who created beings who could think and react and say "no." In fact, He made humans His crowning act of creation, giving them the capacity to procreate like the animals but also setting them apart by giving them reflective capacities more developed than those of any other creatures on earth. Humans alone were enabled to understand moral categories of right and wrong and make choices accordingly. Furthermore, the theological approach asserts that that ability to choose was prostituted by the first humans, with the result that sin and its attendant alienation from God plunged the race into a tragic state of gradual disintegration that can never be reversed by merely human genius. Instead, God remains at the center of any hope for the "saving" of the race.

Some philosophers have maintained that humans are innately good—that given time, the good influences will ultimately and finally trump the evil and peace will break out everywhere. But the passing centuries have not brought us to such a conclusion. The most we can say is that between serious wars, society has lurched along with an uneasy tension between good and evil, peace and unrest. In fact, today's society seems more dangerous and insecure than ever.

But it is not that religion has failed. Christian theology does not deny the evils of such aberrations as the Inquisition, or the Crusades, or other "religious" extremists. Rather, it maintains that evil and alienation are so pervasive in our society that all kinds of atrocities will be perpetrated in the guise of religion. But it also holds to the faith premise that the presence of good and altruism and compassion and caring for one another are simply dim glimpses of divinity shining through humanity. Of course, Christianity gives a human face to these characteristics by putting Christ and His story at the center. When that is the focus, His teachings will help put down racial injustice, ethnic cleansing, hatred of those who are "different," and all other such attitudes. Hence, Christian theology does not disdain social issues but it clearly gives them new priorities.

Discussion Questions

1. What evidences in your society suggest that religion, contrary to the Marxian position that religion is an opium, is supportive of change and development?
2. What do you think attracts people to join mainstream denominations, sects, or cults? Are there advantages to being in one classification over another? Why are some people not attracted to religion at all?
3. Why do you think fundamentalist groups are increasing as fast as they have been compared to their more liberal counterparts?
4. What creates religious conflicts when most religions advocate peace? Why do religious conflicts last as long as they do?
5. What would it take for religion to be non-divisive?
6. Choose any two social issues and list and discuss ways by which religion contributes to or helps to resolve these issues.
7. List and discuss the factors that account for the longevity of religion and those that can lead to its demise.
8. What is your view of the sacred and how it is created?
9. How are truth and religion related?
10. Is theology liberalizing?

Related Readings

Berger, P. L. (1990). *The sacred canopy: Elements of a sociological theory of religion.* Garden City, NY: Doubleday.

Gutierrez, G. (1973). *A theology of liberation: History, politics, and salvation.* Maryknoll, NY: Orbis Books.

Johnstone, R. L. (2001). *Religion in society: A sociology of religion* (6th ed.). Upper Saddle River, NJ: Prentice Hall.

McGuire, M. B. (1997). *Religion: The social context* (4th ed.). Belmont, CA: Wadsworth Publishing.

Stark, R., & Bainbridge, W. S. (1985). *The future of religion: Secularization, revival, and cult formation.* Berkeley, CA: University of California Press.

Wuthnow, R. (1978). *Experimentation in American religion.* Berkeley, CA: University of California Press.

Related Web Sites

American Religion Data Archive (ARDA): http://www.thearda.com
Christianity.com: http://www.christianity.com
Full texts by recognized religious scholars: http://www.religion-online.org
Religion Today—Crosswalk.com NewsChannel: http://www.religiontoday.com
Virtual Religion Index—Rutgers University, Department of Religion: http://virtualreligion.net/vri

Related Movies/Videos

Agnes of God (1985) with Jane Fonda and Anne Bancroft
The Apostle (1997) with Robert Duvall
Keeping the Faith (2000) with Edward Norton and Ben Stiller
Leap of Faith (1992) with Steve Martin and Debra Winger
The Mission (1986) with Robert De Niro and Jeremy Irons

SEXUALITY

Talin Babikian and M. Catherin Freier

9

Chapter Outline

"Sex has no history. It is a natural fact, grounded in the functioning of the body, and, as such, it lies outside of history and culture....Unlike sex, sexuality is a cultural production: it represents the appropriation of the human body and of its physiological capacities by an ideological discourse."

- David M. Halperin (1989)

"Genitals are the given: what we do with them is a matter of creative invention; how we interpret what we do with them is what we call sexuality."

- Michele Aina Barale

Introduction

Consider the following questions: What does it mean if two men are walking down the street holding hands? How many sexual partners should a person have during a lifetime and what determines this? Who should decide on actions concerning issues such as masturbation or abortion? How you answer these questions is largely determined by demographics such as your age, religion, and cultural and ethnic background. Since people vary so much in their understandings of what is considered "right and wrong" concerning sexuality, it can create a lot of conflict.

The American culture seems fascinated, if not obsessed, with sexuality. It is used to sell everything from toothpaste to automobiles. Yet many consumers also seem upset if too much sex is shown on television. Scenes of sexuality may raise more concern than those of violence. Where did these attitudes originate? It is hoped that the critical issues raised in this chapter will help you think about your own attitudes concerning sexuality and how they affect and are affected by the society around you.

Historical Perspectives on Sexuality

ISSUES: How have different cultures in different times viewed sexuality? How have these views affected our current view of sexuality? How have they, in your opinion, helped to define the various roles males and females play?

In order to better understand the issues related to sex and sexuality in contemporary societies, it is important to examine their historical roots. Gathering accurate data from ancient civilizations has posed great challenges to historians primarily because these societies rarely kept written records of sexual practices. Yet we

have sufficient information from early civilizations to allow us to glimpse the historical aspects of this topic. Such information gathered through time traces the development of attitudes regarding sexuality and reveals that cultural influences have been core to the acceptability or unacceptability of sexual behaviors.

Early Civilizations

One of the earliest cultures in documented history is that of Mesopotamia. Originating around 3500 B.C. in the area now known as Iraq and continuing through the conquest of Alexander the Great, Mesopotamia had a significant influence on the later Greek and Roman civilizations and therefore is important from a historical perspective in our understanding of human sexuality. Although **monogamy**, the marriage of a man to only one woman, was strongly encouraged, as opposed to **polygamy**, where a man could lawfully marry more than one woman, a man could keep a concubine if his wife was infertile or sick. Also, men were sometimes allowed to sell their wives as slaves or as payment for debts. However, **adultery**, having sexual intercourse outside of marriage, was strongly discouraged for both men and women, although women who committed adultery were more likely to face grave punishments (Turner & Rubinson, 1993).

Like other Mesopotamian societies, the Hebrew civilization, dating back to around 1900 B.C., was generally a **patriarchal** society, in which men dominated and women were considered socially inferior. Adultery could cost a woman her life, but it was not clear if the same penalty applied to men (Knight, 1982). In Hebrew civilization, polygamy was culturally acceptable and men had the power to sell their children and divorce their wives (Knight, 1982). While men were dominant in ancient Hebrew civilization, it is important to note that the Book of Psalms frequently describes the value of women and the important roles they played in society (see Monda, 2004). In general, public health and sexual behaviors that fostered the survival and expansion of Hebrew civilization and enabled a close relationship with God were required on the basis of the understanding of the Hebrew Bible (see the codes as enumerated in Leviticus, Numbers, and Deuteronomy). Such practices as incest and homosexuality were condemned because of biblical interpretations that these behaviors separated individuals from God and were specifically condemned in these codes (Pritchard, 1969).

The Greek civilization that emerged about 2,000 years ago was also a **patriarchal** society. Marriage was valued as a system fostering propagation. Because of the sexual double standard, women were expected to remain virgins until marriage, but the same rule did not apply to men (Turner & Rubinson, 1993). The

Greeks regarded beauty very highly. Their glorification of human physical beauty came to signify a new era of sexuality, marked by eroticism and sexual exploration. This led to a proliferation of nudity and eroticism in Greek art and literature beginning with the male form and then extending to the female form (Cahill, 2003).

While prostitution was common in Greece, prostitutes were not all treated with respect. The profession had a unique social hierarchy. The lowest ranking prostitutes were known as the **dicteriades**, literally the whores of the brothel. They lived in special houses and served the sexual needs of the lower class. The **auletrides**, a class higher than the dicteriades, were entertainers. They were acrobats or flute players who gave seductive performances and often engaged in sexual activities with audience members. The highest class of Greek prostitutes, often compared to the Japanese geisha girls, was known as the **hetaerae** and included women who were very educated, talented, able to discuss philosophy, and respected in their communities. They offered more than sexual pleasure and often engaged in intellectual conversations with their clients (Schnurnberger, 1991).

During this time, the practices of **bisexuality**, having sexual relations with both opposite and same gender partners, and **homosexuality**, having sexual relations with same gender partners, were prevalent in Greece and considered to be alternate expressions of sexuality. Female homosexuality was common and acceptable primarily on the Greek island of Lesbos, which provided the root for the word **lesbian** (Cahill, 2003). In Athens, sexual intercourse or penetration was considered a mutual enterprise in which two or more people consensually engaged in the activity with the understanding that the act symbolized the social superiority of one over another. Under these auspices, adult Athenian men could engage in legitimate sexual intercourse with minors or individuals with an inferior political or social status. This included sex with women of any age, sex with pubescent boys who were not old enough to be free citizens, and sex with male and female foreigners and slaves (Halperin, 1989). In essence, Greek men married their wives for the purpose of procreation, but they engaged in sexual intercourse with minor boys for love (Scarpitti, Andersen, & O'Toole, 1997).

The Roman Empire, which included significant portions of what we consider Europe, the Middle East, and northern Africa, saw the homosexual practices of the Greeks as unmasculine. Although prostitution was customary, Roman prostitutes did not represent a variety of classes and social standings, as did Greek prostitutes. Most Roman prostitutes were either brothel workers, who were often mistreated and enslaved, or entertainers and musicians (Turner & Rubinson, 1993). Historians such as Gibbons (1993) consider the sexual excesses as well as the violence associated with Roman culture to be a part of the broad context of the fall of Rome. The early Christian Church arose often in comprehensive opposition to the sexual practices and patriarchal nature of the Roman world. Stark (1997) argues that the rise of Christianity in the Roman Empire was directly related to the way Christians treated women. He argued that Christian belief in monogamy and its doctrines that wives could not simply be cast aside at the whim of husbands was crucial to the growth of the Christian Church among women. Secondly, he argues that the Church's opposition to forced abortions and female infanticide significantly increased the value and status of women in Roman society. That is, it was the Christian Church, Stark argues, that gave women an equal stature with men (see Galatians 3:28) and that taught the Roman world the value of female life.

The Middle Ages

The Middle Ages is the period from the fall of the Roman Empire (c. 400 A.D.) to the sixteenth century. During this time period, monogamous marriage remained important to the Church and society. Sexual intercourse that encouraged procreation and family practices that focused on childrearing within a family setting were the norm. Many parts of the early Christian Church continued to encourage an equal status between men and women (Harrington, 2002). However, during the 11th and 12th centuries, relationships between men and women changed. A woman's feminine qualities and a man's gallantry became the foundation for love and attraction (Turner & Rubinson, 1993). As the early Christian influence faded during the Middle Ages and the society became more hierarchical in secular and religious authority, women were considered to be second-class citizens. The work of St. Augustine (1994) has been interpreted as defining women as less in the image of God than males. Thus the female form and biological functions were often seen as not reflecting the divine image. That had major consequences for

society that likely remain with us to this day. The medieval church views of marriage were pervasive in this period since Christianity was the official religion of the Roman Empire and remained dominant throughout the Middle Ages. Masturbation, homosexuality, and abortion were strongly condemned. Ironically, prostitution was widespread, especially among the Christian Crusaders, and was commonly found in public bathhouses. During the time of the Crusades (1100 to 1300 A.D.), Christian soldiers set out to reclaim their holy land from the Muslims and were away from their wives and families for long periods. Military leaders made prostitutes available for their soldiers in acknowledgement of their hardships (Turner & Rubinson, 1993).

The Renaissance and the Reformation

The Renaissance and Reformation occurred in Europe between the 14th and 17th centuries. Great changes in culture and society took place during this period, which affected attitudes toward sexuality. Among the significant changes was the fractioning of Christianity, and significant differences of religious belief were evidenced between the Catholic and Protestant churches. Although marriage continued to be a valued institution, the weakening of the Catholic Church due to the emergence of Protestantism resulted in the questioning of many commonly held values, including celibacy. The notion of individual freedom and accountability reached its culmination (Weber, 1930) within the framework of the Reformation. Each individual was held accountable for achieving a high level of sexual morality. Although prostitution was severely attacked, sexually transmitted infections were primarily passed on in the context of these relationships and took a severe toll on the population. One of the major medical concerns of this period was the transmission of syphilis, and the perception of that risk provided a strong motivation for strict sexual morality (Turner & Rubinson, 1993).

Colonial America

The Puritans, in search of a better life during the 17th and early 18th centuries, established their families in America and separated themselves from the English Church. They encouraged their children to marry early and have large families. Although prearranged marriages were less common in this society than ever before, traditional views on patriarchy and the inferiority of women continued to prevail. Puritans tried to live a very strict moral lifestyle. This included intolerance of adultery, which was legally punishable by death. Sexual repression was exemplified by the color of the Puritans' clothes. They wore only black, gray, or white, believing that bright clothing had seductive and lustful qualities. Sexual activity was strictly reserved for the purpose of procreation, and both men and women were expected to be virgins before marriage. But it is important to note that within marriage sexual intercourse was expected and it was considered immoral or illegal for one partner to deny the other conjugal rights (Godbeer, 2002).

The Victorian Era

Under Queen Victoria in England in the 19th century, strict and conservative moral codes were established that monitored attitudes and behaviors related to sexuality. Queen Victoria is known for coining "the phrases 'white' and 'dark' meat for chicken and other fowl because of her belief that the words 'breast' and 'leg' would cause men to be overcome by lust and women to faint" (Scarpitti, Andersen, & O'Toole, 1997, p. 252). Furthermore, medical doctors did not look at the bodies of the women they were examining, male homosexuality was outlawed (no mention was made of female homosexuality in order not to embarrass the queen), bland Graham crackers were invented to decrease sexual thoughts, and men were discouraged from "excess ejaculation," which was believed to cause vision problems and vertigo (Scarpitti, Andersen, & O'Toole, 1997). During this period, sexual deviance was related to pathology and authority figures used this point to prosecute many sex crimes.

Sigmund Freud (1856–1939) revolutionized the strict moral values that dominated the Victorian period. His theories suggested that sexuality was a biological factor present at birth that developed throughout infancy, childhood, and early adolescence. His views on sexuality, especially his emphasis on biological drives, brought about a cultural acceptance of sexuality and its expression, particularly in the West. Although his work and theories are highly criticized and considered comparatively primitive by modern experts on sexuality and its development, Freud's influence on how sexuality is viewed in western culture has been significant (Scarpitti, Andersen, & O'Toole, 1997).

The Twentieth Century

While historians have associated the Victorian era with sexual repression and purity, they have determined "…their successors, the Freudian modernists, as liberators of a healthy sex drive" (Duggan, 1990, p. 96). Even so, much of what was written before the 1960s and 1970s reflected the assumption that sexuality occurred within a marital bond and that "…sex was biologically based, heterosexually organized, and rooted in natural gender roles" (Duggan, 1990, p. 96). The study of sex and sexuality took on a different perspective with the development of new research methodologies and a shift from measuring attitudes regarding sex to measuring behaviors. Furthermore, sexuality as a social phenomenon took a completely different turn with two important developments during the 1970s: the "coming out" of the homosexual population and the mass distribution of contraceptives (Duggan, 1990).

Social Norms and Religious and Cultural Aspects of Sexuality

ISSUES: What do you think the difference is between normal and abnormal sexuality? If sexuality is culturally defined, is there any sexual behavior that can be defined as universally abnormal? How have various religions dealt with sexuality? What is their impact today?

What is and is not "normal" is largely determined by a culture and those factors that have created that culture. One of those factors is religion. In this section we will briefly look at some views which three major religions have contributed to the area of sexuality.

Normal vs. Abnormal Sexual Behaviors

Sexual behavior is a social behavior, and thus what is considered normal or abnormal differs from one society and ultimately from one individual to another. The attitudes of a given society's members and their subcultures (i.e., ethnic groups, religious groups, etc.) regarding such aspects of sexuality as homosexuality, extramarital affairs, and monogamy determine what normal and abnormal sexual behaviors are. These attitudes change in relation to the social and/or political climate of the time. For instance, as late as 1969 in the United States, 77% of the population considered sex between unmarried individuals to be abnormal; this figure had dropped to only 35% by 1994 (Lauer, 1998). However, a change of behavior toward indiscriminate sex has not been significant, due to factors that include the threat of disease. Historically, the threat of disease very seldom contributed to a significant change in sexual behavior until the emergence of HIV/AIDS. Importantly, however, as alluded to in the historical perspectives discussed above, religious teachings have greatly influenced societal attitudes regarding sexuality, acceptable sexual practices, and institutional frameworks for these behaviors.

Historical Christianity

Christianity was considered the official religion of the Roman Empire around 300 A.D. Although Judaic tradition called for a "joyful appreciation of sexuality," the teaching of the Medieval Christian church preached otherwise (Crooks & Bauer, 1999).

Toward the end of the Roman Empire, social instability and an increase in contact with citizens of neighboring regions, who provided ample sexual entertainment, led Christians to desire to protect their identity and cultural values. The Medieval Christian church chose to focus on one major delineation—its more conservative views of sexuality. This intense focus resulted in the association of sin with sexuality (Crooks & Bauer, 1999). From the Christian perspective at that time, sexuality was viewed as a "necessary evil" tolerated solely for the purpose of reproduction within the marital institution. As such, sexual pleasure in and of itself was not acceptable and all non-procreative sexual behaviors such as homosexuality, masturbation, and contraception were condemned. Within this societal context, **celibacy** (abstinence from any form of sexual activity) became a high virtue, and leaders of the Medieval Church took vows of celibacy. The Medieval Church also attempted to more vigorously condone the institution of marriage by outlawing divorce and severely punishing adultery.

No understanding of sexuality from a historical, cultural, or religious perspective is complete without reference to St. Augustine, a fourth-century theologian famous for his writings on ethics. His work reflects a very strong Christian perspective and has continually introduced the classical world to Western culture. He has been referred to as the "master of medieval thought" (Fuchs, 1983, p. 115). Up until the 12th century, theologians, moralists, and jurists used his writing as a reference for religion and sexuality. According to St. Augustine, the "goods of marriage" include ordained procreation, guarantee of chastity, and the bond of union (Ramsey, 1991).

Historical concepts which continue to influence some Christians' position on sexuality have included viewpoints such as these: "sexuality is good as long as God ordains it" and "sexual pleasure is considered to be evil." However, Christian doctrine and the Bible speak of sexuality, emphasizing that the primary purpose of marriage is to bring "oneness" to the partners, who become "one spirit with Him [God]" (1 Corinthians 6:16). This view would suggest that sexuality is very relational rather than being purely for purposes of procreation.

Monogamy and the institution of marriage are strongly encouraged in the Bible, which stresses that sexual relations are reserved solely for those in such commitments. Christian sex ethics are based on the premises that humans are sexual beings, and that they were created as such by God. The principles introduced in biblical passages regarding human sexuality and conduct are reflected in the cultural views of Western society today. Furthermore, discussions of love and sexuality continue to carry a religious tone. A clergyman and counselor in the 1940s wrote: "Falling in love ought to be a very religious matter, for love is not only within the sphere of religion, but the center of religion....When love is raised to its highest power because another human being is loved supremely so that the whole personality is consecrated with unselfish, out-going love for another, then the lover is not only at this best, but he shares, as never before, the very nature of God" (Weatherhead, 1942, p. 48).

Hinduism

Dating back to 1500 B.C., Hinduism, shaped over several centuries by various cultures and peoples, is the major religion of India. While most of the country's inhabitants practice Hinduism today, this religion has also migrated to other areas of the world—primarily Africa, Southeast Asia, England, and the East Indies—and is currently practiced by approximately 700 million followers (O'Flaherty, 2003). Hindus believe that sex is an important part of human life. More than just individual passion, sexuality is considered to be an expression of oneness with nature and God. It is an act to be enjoyed by men and women. The **Kama Sutra** (a Sanskrit phrase meaning the "thread of love") is a testament to this perspective. The Kama Sutra, a first-century Hindu text about erotic pleasure and related topics, was seen as "a revelation of the gods" (Turner & Rubinson, 1993, p. 16).

Islam

In the religion of Islam, sexual practices are reserved for the pleasure of a man and a woman within a marital bond. "Since the purpose of **marriage** is to be a mutual source of comfort, peace, and enjoyment of each other, like a garment that protects and covers, the sexual aspect of marriage is an extension of this" (Zaitoun, n.d.). Although both husbands and wives are expected to serve the needs of each other, the latter are held responsible for making themselves attractive to their partners.

The Quran, the Islamic holy book, strongly prohibits a man from having sexual intercourse with his wife until her menses is finished and she has taken a bath. Islam also forbids **sodomy**, any form of "abnormal" sexual behavior including anal intercourse, claiming that Allah condemns anyone who engages in this act. According to interpretations of passages in the Quran, any form of sexual activity that does not potentially result in reproduction is also condemned (Zaitoun, n.d.). From an Islamic perspective, women are inherently sexual beings, and thus it is customary in most Islamic societies for women to wear veils designed to conceal their sexual expression.

Historical Perspectives Summary

Examining historical perspectives on sexuality from various religious and cultural traditions helps us understand how contemporary society's attitudes and beliefs have developed. While the industrial revolution has significantly affected views on sexuality, more traditional views on gender relations, premarital sex, and the role of marriage prevail. Nonetheless, scholars from the social and behavioral sciences consider sexuality to be a socially constructed phenomenon and not merely a biological instinct or drive solely for the purposes of procreation. The following sections highlight these developing and differing perspectives.

Sexual Practices

ISSUES: Assuming that the human sex drive is powerful, how do you view celibacy or abstinence? How does sexual orientation develop? Would a society or religion view sexual orientation differently depending on whether it is seen as being genetic or environmental? What kind of rights should gays have in society?

Sex is an area that speaks to our identity. We may choose to marry, remain celibate, or adopt some other status. There is the issue of whether our gender identity matches our biological sex and how comfortable we are with that. Issues of how much of our sex lives are determined by our environment, our genetics, and our choices are still being debated. This section looks at some of these issues and the complexities that surround them.

Celibacy and Abstinence

Celibacy is historically defined as the state of being unmarried. Yet the term is currently used to refer to complete voluntary or involuntary sexual abstinence. There is relatively little empirical literature on celibacy. However, public emphasis on celibacy, especially through school and media-related programs, has increased since the early 1990s. The focus has been not only on teenage pregnancy but primarily on the prevention efforts related to increases in sexually transmitted infections and HIV/AIDS in youth.

There are several reasons why some people choose to be celibate. The most commonly recognized reason has to do with religious devotion and an effort to uphold ideal morality and leadership. Celibacy has been practiced in many religions, including Buddhism, Hinduism, Judaism, and Christianity. Others remain celibate because they consider sex outside of marriage to be immoral or because they have not found a partner with whom they would like to engage in an intimate act. Still others adopt a celibate lifestyle due to fear of sexually transmitted infections, including AIDS. In a study on gay men's fear of HIV/AIDS, Siegel and Raveis (1993) identified several reasons for remaining celibate, including the potential risks of sexual activity, the emotionally distressing nature of such activity, and the desire to gain more from a relationship than just sex. Finally, celibacy is often recommended for individuals who are recovering from alcohol and/or drug abuse since it allows them to learn about their sexual feelings without compulsively acting on urges (Crooks & Bauer, 1999). It also allows individuals going through the recovery process to acquire and strengthen skills for handling stressful and difficult situations without turning to substances (Pinhas, 1989).

Researchers are often faced with difficulty when attempting to describe or quantify celibacy because people are reluctant to report it, especially if they experience celibacy within a marital context (Donnelly, 1993). Using the National Survey of Families and Households (NSFH), Donnelly (1993) reported a marital celibacy rate of 16%. If neither partner experiences discomfort with the celibacy, then it is typically not considered problematic. Discomfort arises when only one of the two individuals involved insists on remaining celibate. There are several reasons why people remain in celibate marriages. Although divorce is relatively commonplace in our society, couples often choose to stay married for the sake of their children. Furthermore, economic situations, religious beliefs that do not condone divorce, and mutual fondness also cause people to remain in celibate marriages.

In a study conducted within the United Kingdom, Kiernan (1988) investigated characteristics of celibate males and females in their mid thirties. Her findings indicated that a significant number of the participants were disabled and tended to be introverted and ambitious. As compared with the single men, the women were more educated and had higher status occupations.

Sexual Orientation

Sexual orientation has typically been described in terms of categories that include heterosexuality, homosexuality, and bisexuality. However, there is less consensus as to where bisexuality fits within the context of sexual orientation. **Heterosexuality** can be defined as the attraction to and/or the sexual engagement with individuals who are of different genders. Heterosexuality has historically been the acceptable norm of sexual expression. Heterosexuality has also benefited cultures, societies, and individuals with religious beliefs that have regarded the purpose of sexual activity to be procreation. This belief limits sexuality to the ability to have a child and thus restricts sexuality to heterosexuality. Although **homosexuality**, the act of engaging in sexual acts with or being attracted to members of the same sex, has always existed, it has begun to be openly discussed only within the past few decades. The term **bisexual** is used to refer to individuals who are sexually active with or attracted to both males and females. However, it is often used as a catchall for individuals who do not neatly fit into either the homosexual or heterosexual categories.

In recent decades, researchers describing sexual orientation have gradually refrained from using the terms "heterosexual," "homosexual," and "bisexual" as categories, using instead a continuum for sexual orientation with exclusive heterosexuality and exclusive homosexuality at opposing poles. Many social scientists believe that sexual orientation falls along this scale. The Kinsey scale represents this perspective and has been used by many researchers to study degrees of sexuality (see Figure 9.1). There has been a push to modify the scale to account not only for behavior, but also to consider love, sexual attraction, fantasy, and self-identification (Kinsey, Pomeroy, & Martin, 1948). According to this scale, exclusive homosexuality is a 1, heterosexuality is a 7, and bisexuality falls in the middle. However, criticisms of this approach have suggested that sexual orientations are not at opposite poles but are independent dimensions.

Historically, sexual orientation has been missing from empirical studies of human development. Within the past few decades, especially with the advent of gay and lesbian rights and the feminist movement, the origins of sexual orientation have been fiercely debated. Researchers have sought to determine why or how orientation occurs and develops and have examined the components of nature and nurture, questioning whether orientation is something we are born with, whether it is learned from the environment, or whether it involves an interaction of the two. Current research, however, has moved away from this dichotomy. Modern statistical tools have allowed for complex multivariate analyses looking at the interaction of several contributing variables. Furthermore, modern advances in DNA technology have made it possible to examine specific contributions of genetic material instead of merely working with statistical percentages.

The issue of sexual orientation is complex and can be approached from several different theoretical perspectives. Historically, among the primary perspectives have been the biological model (including genetic and hormonal theories) and the psychological model (including psychodynamic and psychosocial/environmental theories). Many contemporary authors and researchers promote the interactionist perspective, or the biopsychosocial model, in which the particular combination of an individual's genetic, hormonal, psychological, and psychosocial makeup during early development is believed to be responsible for determining an individual's sexual orientation. Yet there is still no single unifying theory that fully explains the origins of sexual orientation.

Homosexuality

Because homosexuality as a social issue has propagated a significant amount of research and is often discussed in the current literature, lay and professional, it will be considered in greater depth to further illustrate the issues of sexual orientation. Historically, homosexuality was considered a principal sexual abnormality in the eighteenth and nineteenth centuries (Laumann, Gagnon, Michael, & Michaels, 1994). The American Psychiatric Association removed homosexuality from its list of mental disorders in 1973. Since then, homosexuality has been viewed as yet another variant of sexual behavior, and any emotional discomfort on the part of the homosexual individual has been seen as a consequence of society's biases (Brill, 1998). This, however, has not resolved questions and strong emotions aroused in some individuals who claim that normality is not determined by how comfortable society is with a certain act (Brill, 1998). Also not addressed is the assertion that an abnormality in a sexual behavior does not qualify it as a mental disorder. "Current views tend to be quite tolerant of a variety of sexual expressions, even if they are unusual, unless the behavior is associated with a substantial impairment in functioning" and is seen as a disorder (Barlow & Durand, 1999, p. 299).

There are two dominant perspectives on homosexuality. Some view homosexuals as psychologically damaging and dangerous individuals who wish to gain special rights. Others take the "uniqueness position" and believe homosexuals are simply different (Savin-Williams & Diamond, 1997). Those who view homosexuality as a disorder believe that treating it as normal robs the homosexual patient of an adequate diagnosis and will "compromise the psychoanalytic process" (Brill, 1998). However, others (Altman, 1989) have attempted to demonstrate that many of the negative associations of homosexuality and homophobia are deeply rooted in the challenges to the stereotypical roles of males and females in a given society. These stereotypical roles are seen as socially learned.

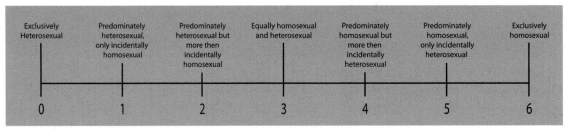

Figure 9.1: Kinsey's Continuum of Sexual Orientation (adapted from Kinsey et al., 1948, p. 638).

0	1	2	3	4	5	6
Exclusively Heterosexual	Predominately heterosexual, only incidentally homosexual	Predominately heterosexual but more then incidentally homosexual	Equally homosexual and heterosexual	Predominately homosexual but more then incidentally heterosexual	Predominately homosexual, only incidentally heterosexual	Exclusively homosexual

Many Voices: An Introduction to Social Issues

The earlier studies of homosexuality are typically drawn from case histories. Brill (1998), through his clinical experience, identified the following characteristics among most of his male homosexual clients: an overattachment to the mother (sometimes sleeping with her throughout adolescence), an absent father or disturbed relationship with the father, fear of sexual inferiority and sexual intercourse, avoidance of physical sports, fearfulness as a child, and having been called a "sissy" as a child. These proposed reasons for homosexual orientation stem from the psychoanalytic perspective, dating back to as early as 1962, which identified a strong dominant mother and a detached father as critical in determining sexual orientation (Bieber et al., 1962).

In addition to the psychodynamic and social learning theories of homosexuality, genetic as well as other biological factors have also been considered as contributors to sexual orientation (Money, Schwarz, & Lewis, 1984). There is a higher rate of homosexuality in monozygotic twins (identical twins who share 100% of their genetic material) than in dizygotic (fraternal) twins. Bailey and Pillard (1991) recruited male homosexuals, either gay or bisexual, and assessed the sexual identification of their co-twin or non-twin biological siblings. Among male co-twins, 52% of monozygotic and 22% of dizygotic twins identified themselves as homosexual. However, only 9.2% of the non-twin biological siblings were homosexual. This number is much lower than would be explained purely by genetics (Brill, 1998). Furthermore, studies attempting to identify factors in the fetal environment have linked high levels of prenatal androgenization with traditionally masculine gender characteristics (Zuker, 1994). However, these findings have not been consistently replicated. The mixed results of prenatal hormonal environment studies are inconclusive since indications of non-genetic factors are still present (Savin-Williams & Diamond, 1997). The question is not whether genes are important, but the extent of their contribution (Pattatucci, 1998).

Although researchers have failed to concur on the nature of the development of sexual orientation, they do agree on one point: no one explanation can adequately cover the many different reasons for sexual orientation. Examples from other cultures reveal that a homosexual orientation is not necessarily due to learned behavior. In one tribe in New Guinea, boys after the age of eight are involved in male-male sexual activities believed to be critical for their development into manhood. Ninety-five percent of these boys grow up to engage in heterosexual activities only. This example illustrates that early sexual experiences do not necessarily determine the course of development. The early Kinsey reports (1948) indicate that only 4% of the men in the United States were exclusively homosexual throughout their lifetimes; 62% to 70% of the men labeling themselves as homosexual had at some point engaged in sex with a woman. Modern western societies seem to demonstrate an increasing tolerance for homosexuality. However, when asked, parents report the desire to have heterosexual children (Brill, 1998). Nonetheless, homosexuality is now more often accepted as a variant of normal and healthy sexual behavior.

Gay Rights

The gay liberation movement that emerged in the 1960s promoted equal rights and civil liberties for homosexuals. The National Gay and Lesbian Task Force (NGLTF, 2006) was formed in 1973 to fight against the American Psychiatric Association's categorization of homosexuality as a mental disorder. The primary mission of this group is to ensure that societies accept gays and lesbians and that they are not discriminated against in their everyday endeavors and activities.

Proponents of gay and lesbian rights consider antidiscrimination to be a civil liberties issue. As such, the Gay and Lesbian Rights Projects of the American Civil Liberties Union (ACLU) have as their goal to fight for "equal dignity for lesbian, gay, bisexual and transgender people. That means even-handed treatment by the government, protection from discrimination in jobs, housing, hotels, restaurants and other public places, and fair and equal treatment for lesbian and gay couples and families" (ACLU, 2001). In half of all states, nearly all forms of homosexuality are still considered to be criminal, although very few people are prosecuted. For example, Illinois was the first state to overturn legislation that outlawed sodomy (1962). It was followed by California (1976) and Nevada (1993). Most recently, Alaska repealed its sodomy laws through legislative action in 2001 (ACLU, 2001). Some states have enacted laws that prohibit discrimination on the basis of sexual orientation.

Sex and Society

ISSUES: How would you define pornography? Does it differ from art, and how so? How should you evaluate the effects of pornography? How should it be decided which laws regulate pornography? Why does prostitution exist? Should prostitution be legal, and what are the pros and cons? Who does prostitution hurt?

While sex is an activity which occurs between individuals, it has ramifications which affect society. It can be viewed as a type of commerce, such as the money made through pornography and prostitution, or be seen for the negative social and psychological effects it may have on users and victims. This section will look at some of the issues which surround three major topics: pornography, prostitution, and sexual victimization.

Pornography

The word **pornography** is derived from the Greek word "pornographos," which literally means "the writing of harlots," and so, by its original definition, refers to a "...description of the life, manners and customs of prostitutes and their patrons" (Hyde, 1964, p. 1). The contemporary definition of pornography is somewhat different and refers to "Materials (such as writings, photographs, or movies) depicting sexual activity or erotic behavior in a way that is designed to arouse sexual excitement" (Garner, 2004, p. 1,199).

Researchers have identified three general categories for pornography: 1) material containing sexual violence in which rape and aggression are portrayed as having favorable effects, 2) sexually dehumanizing but nonviolent material in which women are often portrayed as submissive or inferior to men and experience verbal abuse and degradation, and 3) erotica where a man and a woman are portrayed as having a mutually pleasurable sexual experience (Russell, 1998). However, there are numerous other ways of categorizing pornography, including the medium used to disseminate the material, the age and gender of the individuals who are portrayed, and the type of consumers.

Legal Issues and Perspectives

From a historical perspective, by far the greatest censor on pornographic materials has been the Roman Catholic Church, dating from a 1564 ban. Pope Paul IV added pornographic materials, if they were works "...combined with heresy or a satire or an attack upon the Church," to the "Index Librorum Prohibitorum" (Hyde, 1964, p. 153). The last version of this index was published in 1948, by which time 4,126 books were forbidden for lay people to read or possess (Index Librorum Prohibitorum, 1999). The 1662 Licensing Act of England was aimed at obscene publications, and government agents known as "Messengers of the Press" were held responsible for "...discovering and reporting unauthorized or undesirable printing to a Secretary of State" (Hyde, 1964, p. 155).

Each country has different laws regarding the making, possession, and sale of pornography. Some countries have a complete ban on all aspects of pornography. In 1989, lawmakers in China won much public support and passed a resolution punishable with up to lifetime in prison, and even the death penalty in some cases, for the serious infringement of laws banning the smuggling, producing, selling, or distribution of pornographic materials (Caron, 1998). Similarly, according to Iranian law, capital punishment may be used in extreme cases. Other countries have more lenient laws. For example, there are no laws regarding the production of pornographic materials in Brazil, and both the heterosexual and homosexual pornographic industry thrives in Greece (Caron, 1998). Most countries, however, hold a middle ground and have separate laws regarding the making, distribution, and sale of pornographic materials. For instance, although the Australian government does not impose regulations on what is filmed, there are specific laws restricting the commercial sales and transport of pornographic materials (Caron, 1998). Although a country might have laws against pornography, they may not be enforced. This is the case in South Africa. Most countries have laws prohibiting the use of children in pornographic materials and impose fines and jail time for those breaking the law, even if pornography per se is not illegal in the country.

The legal issues regarding the production and distribution of pornographic materials can be challenging at times. Part of the difficulty in enforcing such laws is the lack of a clear definition of what constitutes pornography. In societies that enforce a ban on pornographic materials, production often takes place clandestinely and the product is distributed on the black market, making it difficult for law enforcement agencies to find, accuse, and sentence offenders.

In the United States, each state has been free since 1973 to write laws regarding pornography. However, the Protection of Children Against Sexual Exploitation Act of 1977 strictly enforces national laws against child pornography and seriously prosecutes those who are in violation of the act. Furthermore, possession of child pornography has been punishable in the United States since a 1990 Supreme Court case (Caron, 1998).

Pornographic material in the United States is protected under the First Amendment except in two cases: pornography involving children (minors under the age of 18) and material that is legally considered obscene. As Justice Potter Steward stated, "perhaps I could never succeed in intelligibly [defining obscenity], but I know it when I see it" (*Jacobellis v. Ohio*, 378 U.S. 184, 197 [1964], as cited in Garner, 1995, p. 610). A three-part test determines as obscene materials that appeal to the "prurient" interest in sex (as assessed by the average person in a contemporary community) and that portray sexual acts in an offensive way, lacking serious literary, political, scientific, or artistic value (Garner, 1995). Thus, what is considered "pornography" by legal sanction may differ from society to society depending upon how they categorize such material.

The Presidential Commission on Obscenity and Pornography reported in 1970 that pornography is harmless and may have some beneficial effects (Scott, 1986). This period was marked by an increase in pornographic material, including hard-core pornography which became more violent, degrading, and sexually explicit. This was followed by an even harder fight on the part of opponents who, in general, believed that pornography "...distort[s] perceptions about what constitutes real-life [and] wholesome sex, ruin[s] relationships with spouses and children (to say nothing of child and spousal abuse), raising guilt and plunging self-esteem" (Scott, 1986, p. 117; Oddone-Paolucci, Genuis, & Violato, 2000). The porn industry's defense against such accusations is primarily based on the flaws associated with much of the scientific literature in the social sciences, namely, the lack of experimental control. Obviously, assigning persons to view or not view pornography and assessing the effects would be contrary to human rights and therefore cannot be studied in this way. As such, since a true cause-and-effect relationship between pornography and its negative effects cannot be declared without a formal experimental procedure, opposing sides continue to defend their position on the effects of pornography on its audience.

The Nature and Extent of the Problem

Pornography in the United States and in many other places in the world is a multibillion-dollar industry. With the advent of the Internet, profits have further increased, making pornography a very profitable form of e-commerce. Consequently, the top five sex sites on the Internet have more visitors than the websites for CNN and MSNBC combined (Webb, 2001).

As part of the 1997 circulation of printed pornography in the United States alone, *Playboy* magazine, designed to appeal to middle-class men, had over four million copies circulated, followed by *Penthouse* and *Hustler* with a little over two million each. However, these rates are far lower than the circulation rates in the 1970s, probably due to the increasing appeal of the video porn industry (Russell, 1998). U.S.-based pornography is also in great demand elsewhere, including Western and Eastern Europe, South America, and parts of Africa. It is important to realize that magazine circulation rates do not include the number of readers who do not buy their own copies. Therefore, the "pass around rates" for *Playboy* are much higher than those reported above and, according to some estimates, are multiple times more. Surveys reviewed by the National Coalition for the Protection of Children and Families revealed that 27.5 million Americans (72% men and 28% female) visited pornographic web sites in January 2002 (NCPCF, 2003). Consumers of fee-based Internet pornography spent approximately $220 million in 2001 (NCPCF, 2003). In addition, 28% of children below the age of 18 reported viewing a pornographic website, 21% of whom were 14 years of age or younger and 40% of whom were females (NCPCF, 2003).

Effects of Sexually Explicit Material on Adults

Those who believe pornography to be harmful claim that "…pornography is the theory; rape is the practice" (Dobson, 1986, p. 40). The Surgeon General's report in 1985 pulled together the social science research and literature of the time and summarized the negative effects of pornographic material: prolonged exposure to pornography strengthens beliefs that unusual sexual practices are more common than they actually are; child pornography has enduring and adverse effects on those who participate; there is an increase in the acceptance of force and coercion in sexual relations; there is a link between coercive sexual activity and sexual aggression; and laboratory studies show that exposure to violent pornography increases abusive behavior toward women (Minnery, 1986). Some reports emphasize that "…when addressing the question of whether or not pornography causes rape, as well as other forms of sexual assault and violence, many people fail to acknowledge that the actual making of pornography sometimes involves, or even requires, violence and sexual assault" (Russell, 1998, p. 113).

Some researchers have claimed that pornography is a cause of rape. However, since not every male who is exposed to pornographic material engages in rape, those who defend the porn industry use this as a factor to disprove the theory. This argument is much like the one used by the tobacco industry. Just as not every individual who smokes tobacco will get lung cancer, so not every individual who is exposed to pornography will commit a sexual assault (Russell, 1998).

Russell (1998) takes a theory used to predict child sexual abuse and attempts to apply it to rape as it relates to pornography. She claims that in order for a rape to occur, four factors must be present: 1) someone must want to commit a sexual assault, 2) the individual's internal inhibitions against acting out are undermined, 3) the individual's social inhibitions against acting out are undermined, and 4) the individual undermines his or her victim's capacity to resist the assault. Russell concludes that these four factors are propagated through pornography.

To date, studies have demonstrated that material showing sexual violence against women encourages males to be aggressive towards women, even though the exact mechanism of this phenomenon is not understood. Nonetheless, some researchers have indicated that men who are at a higher risk for sexual violence tend to be more attracted to and aroused by sexually violent media and are more likely to be influenced by them (Malamuth, 1998). However, sexually non-violent material has not been linked with aggression toward women. Therefore, more research is needed in this area, not only to understand the effects of the different types of pornographic material across times and exposures, but also to understand the role of pornography in our society.

Effects of Sexually Explicit Material on Children

The issue of children as consumers of pornography raises different questions than those concerning adults. However, there is little to no empirical research in this area. Due to the ethical questions arising from the deliberate exposure of children to pornography, the literature on this topic is limited to only a few reports and case studies (Freier, 1998).

In large part, children who are consumers of pornography are in their early and middle adolescence. This period is biologically associated with puberty and naturally marked by curiosity about one's body, sexuality, and sexual practices. Therefore, although a healthy curiosity about sexuality is encouraged during this stage of one's development, including more questioning and interest in the opposite gender, it is important to realize that children, especially young children, do not have the maturity or proper judgment to evaluate materials that influence their behaviors and views on healthy sexuality.

Sexually explicit materials have several significant effects on children. First, since children imitate what they see as part of their natural development, and since they often make demands on other children over whom they have power, there is an increased danger for children exposed to pornographic material to sexually abuse other children. Constant exposure of young children to child pornography can result in imitation or build-up of emotional tension that may find release in action. This can result in harmful acts toward other children (Freier, 1998).

Exposure to pornography, as opposed to addiction to it, in general has not been strongly linked with psychological harm in adolescents as consumers. This is not the case with children younger than 13 or 14 years of age, since these children may have no context in which to deal with exposure. These younger children are unable to differentiate between the real world and the fantasy world, as with material that is presented to them in movies (Freier, 1998).

An important part of understanding the long-term effects of pornography on children (and adults) is the societal context in which exposure occurs. Hawkins and Zimring (1988) discuss how an environment that has instilled an immaturity of judgment may be associated with vulnerability to deviant lifestyles, perverse or misguided attitudes, poor impulse controls, and distorted values. Thus, the effects on children as consumers appear to be developmentally and socially based.

Prostitution

Prostitution as discussed above dates back to the earliest recorded history. Prostitution is illegal everywhere in the United States except for certain counties in the state of Nevada. The exact numbers are difficult to identify because prostitution often operates underground, and figures are often based on arrest records. Reynolds (1986, as cited in Lauer, 1998) estimated that 100,000 to 500,000 American women are involved in prostitution. A nearly two-decade-long study of female prostitutes in Colorado Springs estimated the prevalence of full-time equivalent prostitutes to be approximately 23 per a population of 100,000 (Potterat, Woodhouse, Muth, & Muth, 1990).

Characteristics of Commercial Sex Workers

Although there are rare instances of male prostitutes (usually adolescents who have been sexually abused and primarily "serve" the gay community), most prostitutes or commercial sex workers are young women. Data on over 1,900 female prostitutes in New York City revealed the following: the average age was 29½ years old and they had worked an average of at least four years as a street prostitute, over two-thirds (69.4%) had at least one child, as a group they had an extensive STI history (only 41.8% indicated no STIs or HIV positive), there was wide use of illegal drugs (crack was the most used, at 68.3%), and nearly half had not completed high school (Weiner, 1996). A study of the Chicago metropolitan area suggests that between 1,000 and 4,000 girls and women are involved in both on and off street prostitution. However, when factoring in the ones who are exchanging sex for drugs, the number jumps to 11,500 (O'Leary & Howard, 2001). While Satchell (1986, as cited in Lauer, 1998) estimated that approximately 100,000 to 200,000 of the prostitutes are adolescent girls with a median age of 15, the Chicago study found that the "bulk of females arrested for prostitution in the city of Chicago fall within the ages of 18 and 39. In contrast to social service providers, who state that many girls are involved in exchanging sex for money, law enforcement officers in Chicago report finding few female juveniles involved in prostitution" (O'Leary & Howard, 2001, p. 8). As noted earlier, exact numbers in these areas are difficult to obtain.

There are different kinds of prostitutes. Streetwalkers make up the lower end of the profession. These women operate on the streets and are most often associated with a pimp—usually a male who offers protection, housing, and clients in return for up to 90% of a prostitute's earnings. Other prostitutes choose to work out of **brothels**—derived from the Middle English word "brethen," which means "to go to ruin" (American Heritage Editors, 2000)—which is a place where clients go to attain the services of a prostitute. Still others function out of massage parlors or escort services, which sometimes act as fronts for prostitution.

Characteristics of Clients

It is estimated that a substantial percentage of the male population visits prostitutes at some point in their lives (Scarpitti, Andersen, & O'Toole, 1997). Kinsey et al. (1948) indicate that two-thirds of white males reported having visited a prostitute. Although the typical client of a prostitute is a white, married, middle-aged man, high school and college-age students are also common clients. On average, these men are estimated to visit the same prostitute or same group of prostitutes twice a week or more over a period of about five years (Lauer, 1998). In one study, it was estimated that adult prostitutes see an average of 868 male partners a year (Brewer et al., 2000).

Physical and Psychological Profiles of Prostitutes

On average, prostitutes, now also called commercial sex workers, suffer greatly in several aspects of their personal lives as a result of their work. Problems include venereal disease, AIDS, intravenous drug use, and physical abuse, including abuse from pimps. They also age more quickly because of irregular sleeping and eating patterns, lack of adequate medical attention, drug use, smoking and drug habits, and frequent abortions (Lauer, 1998). Aside from these physical symptoms, prostitutes also suffer from psychological and emotional problems associated with negative social stigma, the lack of true intimacy, and the loss of human dignity. They may become dehumanized and take refuge in drugs or other forms of self-medication. Farley and Barkan (1998) found that 57% of the 130 prostitutes studied in San Francisco (ranging in age from 14 to 61) reported a history of sexual assault. Forty-nine percent were physically assaulted as children.

In this sample, the severity of post-traumatic stress disorder (PTSD) was related to the types and frequency of violence, including childhood abuse and childhood rape. The prevalence of violence in the life of a prostitute is not limited to a specific culture or society. Farley, Baral, Kiremire, and Sezgin (1998) studied PTSD among 475 prostitutes in South Africa, Thailand, Turkey, Zambia, and the United States. Seventy-three percent reported physical assault and 62% met the criteria for a PTSD diagnosis.

Prostitution and Risk

Several studies have attempted to evaluate the risk behaviors of prostitutes and their behavioral antecedents. Consequently, various theoretical models have been applied to the study of prostitution (Sneed & Morisky, 1998). The results of a study by Fritz (1998) indicated that although prostitutes rarely use condoms, they are nonetheless more likely to use condoms with their clients than they are with their love partners. Similar results were observed in a study of Nevada sex workers (Albert, Warner, & Hatcher, 1998) in which the behaviors of 40 prostitutes and 3,290 of their clients were surveyed. Furthermore, Fritz (1998) attributed the use of condoms in female sex workers to their knowledge of AIDS transmission and desire for self-protection; condom use was also enhanced by self-esteem and personal awareness of HIV infection. Various studies have linked prostitution and other high-risk sexual behaviors to drugs and alcohol (Potterat, Rothenberg, Muth, Darrow, & Phillips-Plummer, 1998). However, the "pathway" to prostitution seems to be more complex than simply engaging in drug use. Potterat et al. (1998) surveyed female prostitutes in Colorado who voluntarily and involuntarily (through arrests) visited clinics for sexually transmitted infections (STIs). They found that 66% of the prostitutes had used drugs before entering into prostitution, 18% used drugs concurrently, and 17% began using drugs

afterwards. Furthermore, while early sexual experience or abuse is often reported by prostitutes, in this study it was not a direct predictor of prostitution in later life.

The International Problem

Prostitution is a widespread concern internationally since it is estimated to be a 5.5 billion dollar business annually. There are approximately 30 million prostitutes worldwide, mostly in eastern and central European countries (Marks, 1999). Reports from around the world indicate that the sex industry is on the rise, especially in Southeast Asia. Although unofficial reports indicate that there are approximately 200,000 to 300,000 sex workers in Thailand, these figures are hard to track since sex workers are widely represented in the country's tourist agencies, escort services, hotel room services, saunas, health clinics, brothels, and bars (International Labour Organization, 1998). Since women in these countries face grave financial difficulties, they are attracted to prostitution because it provides them with a substantial amount of money compared to pay for any other kind of unskilled labor. The average prostitute in China makes approximately $30 a customer versus the $4 per day that she would make in a factory (Otchet, 1998).

Although illegal in most countries, prostitution has become an "economic motor" for some of them. There is concern that keeping prostitution illegal is to the detriment of the women involved since their human rights and status cannot be improved (Otchet, 1998). Consequently, there are two views on this subject. Some want to completely eradicate prostitution, while others wish to promote human rights and legalize it. Various countries have taken different stances on the legalization of prostitution across the three dimensions of the law, including prohibition, criminalization, and regulation.

Why the Problem Exists

Historically, prostitution flourished in medieval Europe through to the Victorian era for what are believed to be primarily economic reasons. Prostitution has remained in our culture due to norms about non-marital sex and the lack of open discussions about sexuality (Lauer, 1998). It has been suggested that lack of sexual gratification, men's "need" to experience sexual variety, and avoidance of pregnancy all contribute to what is thought to be a more emotionless and less-complicated

Many Voices: An Introduction to Social Issues

habit of visiting prostitutes. Since women were traditionally considered to have less sexual appetite, visiting prostitutes was a common way to accommodate the sexual appetites of men (Lauer, 1998).

Visiting prostitutes has served different functions for men; for some it has been a rite of initiation, and for others it is a habit. Societal factors, such as migration of males in search of employment and discrimination against women travelers, have historically contributed to this problem. And this phenomenon is still often seen in developing countries. Tolerance for prostitution is based on the ideology that male sexuality, as opposed to female sexuality, must find an outlet (Lauer, 1998). Regardless of why prostitution is maintained in our culture, it is important to recognize that it is very present and has significant implications. The number of men who visit prostitutes, however, decreased from 20% of college-educated men being initiated into sex by a prostitute in the 1940s (Kinsey et al., 1948) to 10% in the 1960s and 1970s (Hunt, 1974). This decrease may be attributed to the sexual revolution, the lessening of the sexual double standard, and the threat of AIDS. Further, the increase in more interactive pornography available today on the Internet may also be impacting prostitution.

Sexual Victimization

ISSUES: What are the causes of rape? What are the effects of rape on the victim? How can child prostitution be eliminated when there is an economic base to it? Are Western societies partially to blame for child prostitution? What effects does child pornography have on victims and consumers?

Sexual victimization includes any sexual act against an individual who has been denied his or her right to voluntarily engage in the behavior. Such an act may happen to adults (e.g., rape), to children (e.g., incest, abuse, or prostitution), and to individuals of legal adult age who are in some way impaired and incapable of deciding whether they wish to engage in the sexual act.

Rape

Rape has been described as the most severe invasion of privacy an individual can suffer; it is not only a physical insult but also a trauma to the self or spirit. Historically, rape was legally defined as when "a man…engages in intercourse with a woman not his wife; by force or threat of force; against her will and without her consent" (Garner, 1995, p. 733). In the eyes of the law, rape has traditionally been separated from seduction, where consent is unfairly obtained either through false promises or affection.

Rape is an international problem. Contrary to what many people believe, most rapes are perpetrated by individuals who are known to the victim. This type of rape is considered "acquaintance rape" or can be "marital rape." Such rape is characterized by non-consensual or forced genital contact or intercourse. Another, less commonly distinguished, form of rape is called "punitive rape," using forced and non-consensual genital contact for punitive or disciplinary purposes. A third form of rape, one that is often overlooked, is rape within the context of war. This type of rape is used to demoralize the enemy and is prominent in ethnic conflicts and wars around the world. More recently, war rapes have been documented in the ethnic conflicts in Cambodia, Uganda, Bosnia, and Bangladesh (Koss, Heise, & Felipe Russo, 1997).

In one national study, 27.5% of female college students reported having been raped or been a victim of a rape attempt at least once since age 14. Only 5% of these women filed a police report (CDC, 1999). Data from the National Women's Study revealed that approximately 683,000 women at least 18 years of age reported forcibly being raped each year, and approximately 84% of these remain unreported to law enforcement officials (CDC, 1998). Privacy is one of the main reasons why an alarming number of rapes are not reported. For this reason, several law enforcement agencies have enacted privacy protection laws that do not allow identifying information about rape victims to be made public (U.S. Department of Justice, 2001).

According to the Uniform Crime Report of the Bureau of Justice, 40% of those who reported being forcibly raped were under the age of 18, and 15% were younger than 12 (CDC, 1998). Approximately nine out of ten rapes are instigated by a single known perpetrator—a family member, intimate partner, friend, or acquaintance (U.S. Department of Justice, 2001). This is particularly true for rapes occurring on college campuses. Forty-three percent of all rapes or sexual assaults were found to occur between 6 P.M. and midnight, and six out of every ten rapes or sexual assaults occurred in the home of the victim, family members, or friends (U.S. Department of Justice, 2001).

The problem of rape has challenged both feminist scholars and criminologists for the past few decades (O'Toole, 1997). Two primary theories attempt to describe rape in the context of our society. These include the gender role socialization theory, which emphasizes the "...dominant culture indoctrinat[ing] males to be sexual aggressors," and the political-economic theory of rape, which is based on "...women's historical powerlessness and their legal definition as the property of the men" (O'Toole, 1997, pp. 215–216). Current thinking on rape attempts to integrate these two theories and understand the problem within the traditional models of deviant behavior and biological sexuality.

Several studies have attempted to identify characteristics of the perpetrators of rape within the context of acquaintance rape and stranger rape. Perpetrators of sexual assault are usually males with sexually aggressive peers who typically engage in heavy alcohol or drug use. Furthermore, these males usually accept violence in the context of dating and desire control in a dating relationship. For example, they prefer to initiate the date, control the parameters of the date (the time and place of meeting), and act as driver. Other variables identified as related to rape are miscommunication about sex, differing expectations, previous sexual relations with the victim, interpersonal violence, and adherence to traditional sex roles. Early sexual initiation (both forced and voluntary) is also a risk factor, as is acceptance of rape myths. Furthermore, perpetrators of sexual assault often have a family history of aggression, violence, and physical abuse (CDC, 1998).

Victims of rape often experience severe psychological and physical injuries. The psychological tolls of rape are many and varied but include chronic headaches, fatigue, sleep disturbance, nausea, loss of appetite, eating disorders, menstrual pain, sexual dysfunction, and, in extreme cases, severe post-traumatic stress symptoms and suicide attempts. Substance abuse is also a common aftermath of sexual victimization. Furthermore, approximately 5% of the rapes in the United States result in a pregnancy. According to the U.S. Census, this suggests an annual rate of 32,000 rape-related pregnancies among American women. Approximately 3% of rapes require overnight hospitalization. Sexually transmitted infections are also suffered by victims of rape and are reported for 4% to 30% of the victims. Consequently, the HIV transmission risk rate in rape victims is estimated to be 1 in 500 (U.S. Department of Justice, 2001).

Use of Drugs in Rape

The use of legal or illegal drugs by rapists to subdue their victims is a matter of increasing concern. Drugs are usually placed in alcoholic or non-alcoholic drinks in social settings and used to involuntarily sedate victims. The survivors of drug-related rapes often do not remember the exact details of the sexual encounter; as a result of their fragmented memories, victims often face even more severe psychological difficulties as an aftermath. In 1996, Congress passed the Drug-Induced Rape Prevention Act to address the emerging concerns related to drug-related rapes. This act sets forth prison terms of up to 20 years for anyone convicted of using controlled substances with the intent to commit a violent crime, including rape.

Sexual Abuse and Incest

Both child sexual abuse and incest are called **pedophilia**, which, ironically, means a "love of children." Child **sexual abuse** is sexual contact between a child and an unrelated adult. **Incest** refers to sexual contact between an adult and a child who are close blood relatives. The legal definition of incest refers only to heterosexual intercourse among immediate family members and grandparents (Garner, 1995, p. 429). Some have argued that this definition is too limiting and should include all types of sexual interaction (oral, anal, or vaginal) among members of a family, regardless of gender.

Child sexual abuse and incest drew rapid attention in the 1970s within the clinical, political, social work, and public policy domains. It is estimated that approximately 20 million individuals (almost 10% of the population) in the United States will be victims of incest

188

(Turner & Rubinson, 1993). Although most offenders initiate the relationship when a child is between five and eight years of age, a full-scale assault usually happens around 11 years of age within the full range of socioeconomic groups (Weinstein & Rosen, 1988). Most incestuous relationships are between fathers and daughters (or stepfathers and stepdaughters), although other forms of incest also occur. Like other sexual assaults, child sexual abuse and incest are unfortunately significantly underreported, especially sibling incest.

The effects of child sexual abuse and incest are countless for the victims of such crimes and include traumatic sexualization, "…the shaping of a child's sexuality in developmentally inappropriate and interpersonally dysfunctional ways" (Turner & Rubinson, 1993, p. 572). Researchers have indicated that traumatic sexualization can result in promiscuity in later years, orgasmic or other dysfunctional problems as adults (Briere, 1984), sexual aggressiveness, and compulsive masturbation (Turner & Rubinson, 1993).

Abused children are usually given negative or punitive messages such as "you have been a bad girl," and are frequently asked, often in the form of a threat of harm to themselves or their family, to "keep the secret," which can cause stress and anxiety. It is also common for the victimizers to convince the children that they are "special" and thus are attaining such attention. Betrayal is intensely experienced in these situations, especially when the perpetrator is a family member or a known individual whom the rest of the family trusts. In these cases, the perpetrator, who is supposed to be a trusted individual, might have been the person in whom the child would have confided the abuse. However, since that person is the perpetrator, the child is now left with no one to turn to. Betrayal is also intense when a child realizes that the non-abusive parent knows about the abuse of the other parent but does not put a stop to it. An abused child feels powerless over the environment, which affects his or her capacity for intimacy in relationships throughout life.

Child Prostitution and Pornography

Of particular concern are sexual acts which involve children. Sex with children is coercive. Even if children "cooperate," we do not consider them capable of making informed decisions or being emotionally and intellectually mature enough to offer consent to something which can affect the rest of their lives. In this section we consider the issues of child prostitution and pornography.

Child Prostitution

It is estimated that one million children are drawn into child prostitution globally each year, making it a multimillion-dollar industry that is rapidly growing, especially in areas with political and economic instability (such as the former republics of the Soviet Union and some Eastern European countries). Most of this industry targets young teenage girls by promising them a better life. It also thrives in Asian countries such as Thailand, Sri Lanka, and the Philippines, where it attracts international clients, some of the most frequent being visitors from the United States, Germany, and Japan (Crooks & Bauer, 1999). The HIV/AIDS epidemic has increased and further impacted child prostitution. With growing concerns regarding the transmission of HIV, clients increasingly seek younger prostitutes in order to protect themselves from acquiring the virus.

In some areas, prostitution for the participating children seems like a viable option for survival for several reasons. They suffer from poverty due to famine and war, they may be orphans from families killed in tribal wars, or their situation may involve HIV/AIDS. The sub-Saharan African countries are home to over 12 million children who are orphaned because of AIDS. The global total is just over 13 million (UNAIDS, 2000). Thousands of children are bought, sold (even by their own parents), beaten, and abused each year while profiting the multimillion-dollar child prostitution industry.

Child Pornography

Child pornography laws specifically prohibit the production, transportation, receipt, and distribution of such visual depictions of minors. Legislation has been written by Congress to protect children from materials that are considered to be harmful. The Child Online Protection Act (COPA) restricts the distribution of such materials over the Internet. Despite its many benefits, the Internet has unfortunately provided pedophiles with a new tool. Offering continuous access and relative anonymity for sophisticated users, the Internet has made it easy for child pornographers to distribute their materials and for pedophiles to lure and prey on children. Child pornography thus is provided free of charge, 24 hours a day, and typically anonymously.

The prosecution of Internet-related child pornography cases, many of them international in scope, has increased by 10% every year since 1995, as reported by the Department of Justice. However, these cases are difficult to pursue and prosecute due to the relative ease by which sophisticated Internet users utilize encryption to mask unlawful materials. Prosecutions are also hampered by the need to effectively coordinate international teams who are capable of pursuing offenders (U.S. Department of Justice, 2001).

Pornography affects children both as victims and as consumers (Freier, 1998). However, since it is universally agreed that children should be protected against pornography by law, there are no empirical studies that address the use of children in pornography. For this reason, little is available about the potential harm of children's participation in pornography (Hawkins & Zimring, 1988). The most consistent finding, however, is that they develop a sense of "psychological paralysis," which results in their feeling victimized, raped, hopeless, and unable to change (Freier, 1998).

It has been argued that the depiction of children in pornographic material increases viewers' desire for children as sex objects. The Child Protection Act of 1984 was written to protect everyone younger than 18. The Child Pornography Prevention Act of 1996 augments the previous act and includes pornographic material that, through the use of computer technology, depicts or appears to depict minor children.

Sexual Disorders

ISSUES: How would you define a sexual disorder? Is there such a thing as sex addiction? What do you think creates paraphilias? What is the difference between normal methods of sexual arousal and arousal via paraphilias? Why are paraphilias almost exclusively male-oriented?

Whether a behavior is considered normal or abnormal is determined by prevailing political and social views. The label of abnormal behavior or deviance has significant implications in society, in clinical practice, and in the medical and research world. Society must face certain questions whenever confronting these issues: If a form of sexual behavior is considered clinically abnormal, does the scientific community attempt to "cure" it? What are the bases of such a disorder? What are its implications? Since its first publication in 1952, The American Psychiatric Association's *Diagnostic and Statistical Manual of Mental Disorders* (DSM) has been faced with the challenge of classifying human behaviors under the rubric of normality or abnormality, where "neither deviant behavior (e.g., political, religious, or sexual) nor conflicts that are primarily between the individual and society are mental disorders unless the deviance or conflict is a symptom of a dysfunction in the individual…" (American Psychiatric Association, 1994). Sexual variants include homosexuality, prostitution, hypersexuality and sexual "addiction," and paraphilias such as pedophilia, sadomasochism, voyeurism, and exhibitionism. In this section, the major sexual disorders and paraphilias will be discussed briefly within the context of modern societies.

Sexual Addiction

Hypersexuality is defined as an insatiable desire for sexual activity, which adversely affects everyday functioning. Sex in this context is considered to be emotionless. Diagnostic labels associated with hypersexuality have included sex addiction, sexual compulsivity, and sexual impulsivity (Rinehart & McCabe, 1998; Stock, 1993, as cited in Stock, 1997). Although it is possible to diagnose hypoactive sexual desire disorder as classified in the DSM, hypersexuality is no longer considered a mental disorder (APA, 1994). Researchers have taken two different perspectives when attempting to explain the issue, developing a medical disease model and a social deviance model. Carnes (1989) proposed a model for sexual addiction that is very similar to a drug addiction model, "…develop[ed] in response to genetic and environmental factors which interfere with the development of self-regulatory processes and a sense of self-coherency" (Rinehart & McCabe, 1998). Although the construct of sex addiction has been theoretically linked to dependency and the addictive personality type, Rinehart and McCabe (1998) attempted to study sex addiction under a disease model. These researchers failed to identify characteristics unique to sex addicts. They did not find any marked differences in anxiety, obsessive-compulsivity, impulsiveness, depression, or fear of intimacy in the sex addicts. Their research did show that a desire for excessive sexual behavior was different from the actual excessive behavior.

Saulnier (1996) argued against the disease model of sex addiction, claiming that it excuses the problematic aggressive and violent behaviors under the umbrella of illness. Pathological behaviors are confused with medical problems that would be better treated as social disorders. Furthermore, Saulnier states that empirical evidence for the diagnostic category is lacking, and that diagnostic categories should be used with caution since they have implications of labeling (Saulnier, 1996). The medical disease model removes responsibility from individuals and makes them helpless, so they are not empowered to change.

A number of programs are available to help those who experience sexual addiction. Programs such as Sexual Addicts Anonymous (SAA) and Sex and Love Addicts Anonymous (SLAA) can help individuals but also are important for helping couples rebuild trust, work on communication, and learn to forgive both oneself and one's partner (Schneider & Schneider, 1996). Schneider and Schneider (1996) reported a higher percentage of successful relationships among partners who attend a 12-Step program and commit to ongoing individual therapy for their relationships.

Saulnier (1996) also stated that the genuine problem of hypersexuality should be separated from the contemporary model of sexual normalcy and deviancy; intervention should be sought only if shame and inflexibility are experienced in the particular form or frequency of sexual expression. In other words, instead of being aimed at eradicating excessive behaviors, intervention should be directed toward helping the addict understand the source of discomfort. Much like aggressions, sexual problems are inevitable in humans, but this does not qualify sexual addiction as a disease.

Paraphilias

A common way to determine whether a behavior is normal is to look at statistical norms (Weiner & Rosen, 1999). Paraphilias include behaviors which provide sexual gratification in ways most would consider to be perverted. According to the DSM-IV-R, paraphilias "…are characterized by recurrent, intense sexual urges, fantasies, or behaviors that involve unusual objects, activities, or situations and cause clinically significant distress or impairment in social, occupational, or other important areas of functioning" (p. 493). Paraphilias may range from experiencing sexual arousal from others' worn socks to more extreme cases in which the object of sexual gratification is rape or even murder. Because the wide range of paraphilias is very difficult to define, it is hard to know exactly how many people engage in such behaviors. Paraphilias are not "catching" (Kinsey et al., 1948), which means they are not necessarily learned.

Very little is known about the prevalence of some paraphilias since most people who experience them are reluctant to disclose. Therefore, most of the available data are based on the reports of victims. It is an important clinical note that paraphilias are almost entirely male disorders, except for occasional cases of sadistic and masochistic behaviors that do not meet DSM criteria (Weiner & Rosen, 1999).

There are several theoretical and developmental studies on the etiology of paraphilias, including conditioning and social learning, inherent personality factors, and biological factors. Social learning theorists claim the source of deviant arousal to be classical conditioning, in that by happenstance sexual arousal occurred at the same time as a deviant behavior did and the individual then is aroused whenever this deviant behavior occurs. Other researchers have looked at inherent personality traits and psychopathology as sources of deviant sexual arousal. Although some studies have linked mood disorders with certain paraphilias (McKibben, Proulx, & Lusignan, 1994), causal associations cannot be made since the etiology of these deviant behaviors is not understood. Others have looked at imbalances in the neurochemistry of the brain. The most appealing theory thus far is that of the "love map." Money and Lamacz (1989) believe that a pattern of sexual behavior, or love map, is etched in the brain during development, which determines the types of activities and stimuli that become sexually arousing in adulthood. In the case of paraphilias, love maps are "vandalized" by early traumatic experiences such as molestation, beatings, and other forms of childhood abuse.

Exhibitionism and Voyeurism

Exhibitionism, the need to expose one's genitals to unsuspecting others for the purposes of sexual gratification, is a relatively common paraphilia. A person with this behavior usually has no urge for any other kind of sexual interaction (APA, 1994). A study by Cox (1988) illustrated the widespread prevalence of exhibitionism. One-third of the 846 college students questioned reported having witnessed a "flasher." The typical exhibitionist is thought to be unhappy, unmarried, and sexually repressed. Though the person is usually at least 18 years of age, exhibitionist urges may begin in early adolescence. The few studies that have attempted to study exhibitionists are based on only the 20% who are arrested. Therefore, these findings may not be generalizable.

Another common paraphilia is **voyeurism**, a strong urge to watch unsuspecting individuals when they are undressing or are engaged in sexual activity. This is frequently seen in adolescents less than 15 years of age. Voyeurs are known as "peeping toms" or "peepers." The element of risk involved in voyeurism appears to be part of the sexual excitement. Voyeurs put themselves in positions where they can be easily discovered or where they can potentially experience physical harm, such as hanging in trees and watching from rooftops.

Sadomasochism

Sadism is sexual pleasure derived from inflicting pain upon or humiliating someone else. The term was derived from Frenchman Marquis de Sade (1740–1814) who—after losing his wife's sister, whom he loved, lived with, and wrote a novel about—turned to a life of torturing and physically injuring partners for the sole purpose of deriving sexual pleasure (Hyde, 1964). He died in a Paris "lunatic asylum" where he had been kept for years. He published many works depicting sexual perversions.

Masochism is sexual pleasure derived from pain inflicted upon oneself. The name comes from Austrian Leopold von Sacher-Masoch (1836–1895). As a young boy, von Sacher-Masoch accidentally witnessed an adultery scene, the aftermath of which led to much whipping or flagellation, not only of the parties involved, but also of himself, which he found to be enjoyable. He became a lecturer at a university and wrote many works with a masochistic nature, the most famous of which is the autobiographical *Venus in Furs* (Hyde, 1964). He is said to have believed that masochistic behavior fostered and encouraged his literary abilities.

Sadism and masochism are considered to be sacrificial paraphilias. They involve inflicting or receiving spankings, blindfolding, restraint, cutting, or crawling; participants may be caged or urinated or defecated upon (APA, 1994). These behaviors range in variety from mutual participation to murder. Sadomasochism involves finding sexual gratification in both masochistic and sadistic behaviors. It sometimes involves **hypoxyphilia**, in which sexual pleasure is derived from oxygen deprivation through the use of a noose, mask, chemical, bag, or chest compression.

Other Paraphilias

Other paraphilias include **frotteurism** (from the French root meaning "to rub"), in which sexual pleasure is gained from rubbing up against or touching unsuspecting others, often strangers in crowded places. **Transvestism** is the experience of gaining sexual pleasure by dressing up in the clothes of the opposite sex. **Necrophilia** involves fantasizing about or engaging in sexual behaviors with a corpse. This behavior occurs almost exclusively in males. Some individuals seek employment in mortuaries or cemeteries and gain access to fresh corpses for their sexual gratification. There are also known cases of individuals who have killed another person in order to gain access to a corpse. One such high profile case was that of Jeffrey Dahmer, who murdered and mutilated his victims and whom some experts believed was driven by very strong necrophilic urges (Crooks & Bauer, 1999). **Zoophilia** is fantasizing about or engaging in sexual activity with a non-human animal. **Coprophilia** and **urophilia** involve gaining sexual gratification or excitement from contact with feces and urine, respectively. Most of these paraphilias are considered to be rare; as such, the societal or psychological factors associated with them are not well researched or understood.

Treatment

ISSUES: What types of treatments are used for sexual disorders? Do some treatments work better than others? Why is so little done to treat sex offenders? Do you believe they can be treated? Would you want a sex offender living in your neighborhood? How can victims be helped? What should be done with children who are perpetrators?

The treatment of sexually atypical behaviors is multi-faceted and varies to some degree in relation to several important factors. These include whether a person is voluntarily or involuntarily (i.e., court appointed) seeking treatment, whether a patient is a child or an adult, and whether a patient is a perpetrator or a victim.

Four important factors highlighted by Wincze (2000) must be taken into account when formalizing a treatment plan. First, it is important to reduce danger both for the patient (e.g., suicide) and for potential victims. Second, it is important to suppress behavior by using pharmacological and psychological methods. At this stage, the patient is asked to refrain from exposure to all sexually stimulating materials in order to reduce episodes of sexual acting out. Third, maintenance and control are important once suppression of the behavior is achieved. This involves relapse prevention and is achieved by identifying alternate "safe" behaviors for the patient to engage in when confronted with unwanted sexual desires and by identifying a positive support system in the case that unwanted desires do arise. Finally, it is important to treat comorbid problems, any dysfunctions the patients may have in conjunction with their atypical sexual behaviors. Most often comorbid with sexual problems are depression and/or anxiety, and these should be treated to further help alleviate the sexual problems (Wincze, 2000).

With these general principles of treatment in mind, we can now turn to some of the specific methods that have been used, and in some cases continue to be used, with individuals who are either victims of sexual crimes or their perpetrators.

Prison

A large and increasing number of prison inmates are sexual offenders. In 1980, state prisons held 20,500 sex offenders (Finn, 1997). By 2002, of the estimated 624,900 inmates held in state prisons, 142,000 were there for rape and other sexual assaults (U.S. Department of Justice, 2005). Although sex offenders do not make up the largest proportion of offenders in the prison system, they are without doubt the most despised group of offenders, even among other prisoners (Miller, 1998). By the middle of the 20th century, most states had laws that required treatment for sex offenders instead of imprisonment, which was not found to be an effective means of intervention. These laws were ultimately revoked due to the high costs of treatment and lack of data regarding its efficacy (Miller, 1998). However, interest in the treatment of sexual offenders re-emerged in the 1980s and 1990s, not only in psychotherapeutic interventions for incarcerated sex offenders, but also for providing medical interventions.

Medical Treatments

Pharmacological treatments are recommended as a form of intervention to be started as quickly as possible (Wincze, 2000). In general, antiandrogens are used to decrease testosterone levels and thus reduce sexual aggressiveness. Both Lupron and Depo Provera are generally known to reduce sexual desire and acting-out in men (Bradford & Pawlak, 1993) and are recommended for use with male sexual offenders such as rapists or child molesters, even though the exact mechanism of action is not known (Robinson & Valcour, 1995). Sexual desire is also decreased by the use of selective serotonin reuptake inhibitors such as Zoloft and Prozac. Medical treatments for paraphilias are quite varied, but the most common include an injection of medroxyprogesterone acetate, which reduces sexual desire. This injection helps bring the behavior under control temporarily, while therapy and counseling are ongoing.

Psychological Treatments

In this section we will consider psychological treatments which attempt to deal with patterns of behavior that have arisen as a result of persons becoming victims or perpetrators of sexual offenses.

Adults as Victims

A sexual assault such as rape results in trauma for most victims that, in some cases, never completely disappears (Turner & Rubinson, 1993). One week after a rape, 98% of victims report post-traumatic stress symptoms. This percentage gradually decreases with the passing of time. However, 67% of rape victims report these symptoms one month after the attack and 43% after three months, after which one is at risk for having chronic symptoms (Solomon, 2000). Several psychological therapeutic techniques are used with victims of sexual assault, some of which are still controversial in the scientific literature. No one form of therapy is considered to be more effective than another. However, regardless of the form of therapy, the psychological issues faced by these individuals often continue not only throughout the period of their therapy, but often throughout their lives.

Adults as Perpetrators

Since as a society we have not successfully identified why an individual becomes a sexual offender, we have no concrete basis for effectively treating perpetrators who either seek help on their own volition or who have a court mandate for treatment. Most convicted sex offenders serve their required prison sentence and are released back into society without much effective intervention (Turner & Rubinson, 1993).

Turner and Rubinson (1993) outline three distinct methods of intervention for sex offenders. These include re-education (basic understanding of human sexuality), resocialization (aggression management and practice forming meaningful relationships), and counseling (group therapy, possibly with victims of sexual assault). Other researchers have assigned the assessment and treatment of sexual offenders to one of two categories, either the sexual addiction model or the cognitive behavioral model. Harnell (1995) suggested that both of these approaches are necessary for an effective intervention since most sex offenders lack skills in the areas of social relationships, interpersonal communication, stress control, and anger management.

Others have stressed the importance of community-based treatment programs that use cognitive-behavioral methods to foster understanding and responsibility while also focusing on relapse prevention (Eccles & Walker, 1998). While many intervention programs have had some immediate success with treatment, little is known about the long-term behavioral changes in sex offenders.

In the United States, the Federal Bureau of Investigation's Unit for Crimes Against Children is responsible for developing and implementing the National Sex Offenders Registry (NSOR). The Lychner Act of 1996 requires that the Attorney General establish a national database with information regarding the whereabouts of convicted sex offenders who are either perpetrators against minor victims, have been convicted of a violent sexual act, or have been labeled violent sexual predators. The Act calls for the registration and verification of current addresses for sex offenders who reside in states that do not have a minimally sufficient sex offender registry (SOR) program. Most states have an internal registry for sex offenders, which is often available through a local law enforcement agency or through the Internet.

Children as Victims

The goal of treatment with abused children is to reduce the stress from the sexual assault and consequent negative reaction, and, if necessary, to modify the child's or the family's chronic dysfunctional emotional and behavioral patterns (Gomes-Schwartz, Horowitz, & Cardarelli, 1990). Although children's reactions to sexual abuse may range from no overt psychopathology to significant emotional problems, most children who have experienced abuse demonstrate behavioral problems and stressful emotional reactions (Gomes-Schwartz, Horowitz, & Cardarelli, 1990). Although there are several reasons why children react differently to sexual abuse, key variables include personal characteristics, type of abuse, and, most importantly, the presence or absence of a reliable supportive individual or network.

Specialized treatment for child sexual abuse and incest is a relatively new field, and therefore most approaches are generic. However, there are some elements that should be taken into account when dealing with child sexual abuse issues. First, it is very important that therapists take great care to provide intervention for the family of a child of sexual victimization. For the child, age, developmental status, and the force and nature of the abuse should be taken into account. For very young children, play therapy is a common form of treatment. For older children and adolescents, treatment is more commonly either individual therapy or group therapy. Furthermore, an important component of treatment is prevention (Turner & Rubinson, 1993).

Research on the long-term consequences of child sexual abuse has not resulted in consensus. Just as the short-term effects of child abuse differ, the long-term effects also vary significantly. However, the way in which the child abuse is handled, both in the immediate environment and with law and social services agencies, has a significant effect on the long-term consequences of abuse (Gomes-Schwartz, Horowitz, & Cardarelli, 1990).

Children as Perpetrators

The outcome of treatment with children is based on many often related variables, including the type and duration of the abuse, reactions to the abuse (both from institutions and from the family), the social environment of the child, and the characteristics and history of the child and of the family. Treatment variables include the time and modality of the treatment and the compliance of the family (Gomes-Schwartz, Horowitz, & Cardarelli, 1990).

The issue of treatment of children who are sex offenders is a relatively recent addition to the scientific literature. Several key issues are involved, including the need for a thorough assessment, the over-identification of children as offenders, and age-appropriate treatment, among others (Johnson, 1998). A quick overview of the general characteristics of a child offender is important. In one study, these children had low IQs, were aggressive, were preoccupied with sex, had a DSM-IV diagnosis of either conduct disorder or oppositional defiant disorder, and had no satisfying relationships within their social networks. Furthermore, most had suffered "severe and erratic physical punishment" and sexual molestation (both boys and girls), and engaged in a variety of sexual behaviors as part of their offense (Johnson, 1998).

Most treatments for child sex offenders are provided by therapists in mental health settings, group homes, or residential facilities. The treatment modality varies, but usually includes group and individual therapy for the child, as well as family therapy. Working with the parents or caregivers of a child who molests is extremely important. Johnson (1998) states that treatment programs that fail to include the parents are doomed since "children who molest are not born this way. The home, and ultimately the community, in which he or she grows up provides the fertile soil for the child to develop the sexually aggressive behavior patterns" (Johnson, 1998, p. 346).

Addendum about HIV/AIDS

A discussion of sex and sexuality in contemporary culture is not complete that does not address HIV/AIDS and its effects on our views and behaviors. HIV/AIDS affects all levels of sexuality and sexual practices, as evidenced in the references to it in many of the different sections of this chapter. While it was once considered a homosexual disease, HIV/AIDS is now equally represented in homosexuals, heterosexuals, and drug-injecting individuals. More than 36 million children and adults are currently living with HIV, with 25 million of these in sub-Saharan Africa alone. AIDS has no environmental boundaries and is a global pandemic. As such, in discussions of sexuality, HIV and AIDS must be seen as critical factors in any society at any level. For more on HIV and AIDS in this book, see the chapter on public health and health care.

Conclusion

In the context of the wide array of topics covered in this chapter, it becomes obvious that sexuality can be very complex as it is an integral part of our humanness. Further, it is central to all parts of our existence with biological, physical, psychological, social, emotional, and spiritual aspects all interacting and influencing what we believe sexuality is, or should be; our intentions related to our own sexuality; and ultimately our own experience. Thus, an understanding of human sexuality is crucial to each of us individually and to society collectively. Even from the brief historical discussion here regarding sexuality and society, we begin to realize that all societies have placed some types of normative parameters around sexuality and sexual intercourse. Further, these have often been done in the context of the religion(s) of that society. While perhaps not openly condoned, many societies have tolerated or accepted a wide variety of sexual practices and behaviors. Overall, however, there have been more similarities than differences throughout history with sexual intercourse consistently having the highest levels of social and religious support for occurring within the context of marriage. Further, even within the context of marriage, culture and religion have perpetuated spoken and unspoken "rules" of what sexuality is (i.e., permissible for procreation and only specific acts of sex permitted).

From a mental health perspective, healthy sexuality is the freedom of sexual expression that is mutually satisfying and acceptable. Currently the prevailing view in American society is that healthy sexuality is recognized as "pleasure bond," representing the most intimate form of long-term bonding and connection between individuals that results in high levels of personal satisfaction, happiness, and social stability. As such, human sexuality is a core part of who we are, and how we understand it and experience it is very important to our sense of well-being.

Response

Societies React to Sex

by Todd Burley

"We are not, have not and do not plan to conduct any sex experiments."

Ed Campion, NASA spokesperson, ridiculing an online story claiming that U.S. astronauts had tried out 10 sexual positions in space (*Time*, **Special Edition, 2000–2001**).

Sexuality occupies a very unique place in the human psyche and society. It is repressed, exalted, legislated, blessed, prohibited, mandated, restricted, sold, given, enjoyed, and abused. I know of no other human activity, with the possible exception of driving, that seems to elicit such elaborate and contradictory controls on the part of society. Sexuality is regulated differently depending on one's gender, age, and even vocation. It is an intensely personal experience under some conditions and totally impersonal under others. So why such intense interest and concern about an experience that is so private and seldom observed by others?

One of the most obvious reasons is that sexuality can culminate in new life. Life is sacred to most societies. It represents the continuity of ourselves, the clan, and the species. The sustenance and nurture of new life in the human species requires tremendous physical, emotional, and financial resources on the part of those responsible for the child. No doubt those responsibilities have something to do with society's belief that it has the right to control private sexual behavior. Such concern has some obvious advantages to the survival of the human race such as ensuring that a parent works to support offspring in the context of a family who can respond to the physical and emotional needs of the child, in addition to providing the tremendous investment in years of training needed to produce a healthy, independent, and socially contributing adult. Failure to accomplish this task is costly to society.

If sexuality is so important to society and its component individuals, and if it inspires and requires such massive regulation, then why is there so little attention to the introduction of sexuality, including its proper care and maintenance? In the United States, any organized attempt to instruct children regarding very basic issues in sexuality evokes massive resistance on the part of the very community that it is intended to assist. The difficulty parents have in instructing children and adolescents about sexuality is a perennial source of jokes for almost any comedian. As a psychologist I frequently hear from adults that their parental instruction on sexuality usually consisted of a few short sentences such as "you can never trust a man," "be sure and use some protection so that you don't end up having to support some girl," or "you just have to endure it, honey."

Restrictions on sexuality are applied much more stringently to women than to men. The feminist explanation is that women are easily dominated by men who do not want to contribute to raising children who are not genetically their own. No wonder sexuality is associated with so many societal difficulties and painful personal experiences. When expectations placed on sexuality are combined with the mystery and ignorance with which it is wrapped, things will certainly go wrong in a terribly amateurish way.

Perversions, coercions, and other signs that healthy sexuality is not possible for many people seem to be rampant. Within Christian communities, one virtually never hears sermons on or readings from the Old Testament Book entitled The Song of Solomon, a distinctly sexual and erotic piece of biblical literature. Imagine someone reading the following words from the pulpit: "Your rounded thighs are like jewels, the work of a skilled craftsman. Your navel is as delicious as a goblet filled with wine. Your belly is lovely, like a heap of wheat set about with lilies. Your breasts are like twin fawns of a gazelle….Oh, how delightful you are, my beloved; how pleasant for utter delight! You are tall and slim like a palm tree, and your breasts are like its clusters of dates. I said, 'I will climb into the palm tree and take hold of its branches.' Now may your breasts be like grape clusters, and the scent of your breath like apples. May your kisses be as exciting as the best wine, smooth and sweet, flowing gently over lips and teeth" (Song of Songs 7:1–3, 6–9, New Living Translation). Now imagine that these verses were presented not in the written medium of 2,500 years ago, but in film, and then try to picture what the congregation's reaction would be.

This chapter has shown that all is not well in the area of sexuality. If society is a self-organizing system, and if we as a culture have some influence on that system, then it seems reasonable that we should give some thought to sexuality and find ways to make it as healthy as any other part of human existence. In fact, it would seem that we should first study sexuality in as detailed a way as we looked at diet and nutrition during the last century. We need to learn much more about sexuality than we know currently. But this would require changing attitudes sufficiently to make such research acceptable.

John Watson, the father of behaviorism, which dominated much 20th-century research in psychology, was fired from his academic position at John Hopkins University when his wife informed the university administration that he was doing research on sexual responses (her interpretation of the facts was that the word "research" was actually a euphemism for an affair with his female lab assistant). He lived out the rest of his life as an advertising executive in New York. Others such as Kinsey et al. (1948, 1953), Hite (1976), Janus and Janus (1993), Masters and Johnson (1966, 1970), and the occasional sex therapist have not always found it easy to investigate areas that seem important to the lives of individuals and to society at large. Even research on sexuality in animal populations has often been incidental to other research projects. Harlow (1962) did research on the effects of mothering in monkeys by raising infant monkeys with their mothers, with wire monkey manikins covered with terry cloth, and lastly with the wire manikins alone. He noted incidentally in describing (in one of the best-turned phrases in the psychological research literature that I have read) the sexual behavior of monkeys "raised" by the wire mothers that "their heart was in the right place but nothing else was."

Clearly there are some things to be learned from research on animal models of sexuality as well as from the behavior of humans. First, imagine what a difference it would make if we simply were able to use what we learned to make sexuality personal rather than impersonal and objectifying. What would be the effects on rape statistics, pornographic exploitation, and child sexual abuse? Imagine what would happen to rates of diseases such as HIV/AIDS if sex were simply made more personal, thus enhancing the sense of responsibility and resulting in less risky approaches to sex.

The second step might be modeling and teaching sexuality. We need to inform, educate, and train. It seems irresponsible and shortsighted on the part of society to try to control that which it does little or nothing to teach. Most human behavior is based on learning that begins with experimentation and/or observation within the normal capabilities of the organism. The variety in sexual behavior seems in some ways random and "self-organizing." I have seen, in my work as a psychologist, behavior ranging from what we would call statistically normal to sex with dogs and cockroaches. In the more unusual situations, it has typically been clear that there was so little training, role modeling, and education that random but gratifying behaviors became the norm for the individual. Society should accept some of the responsibility for more heinous sex crimes rather than placing it entirely on the individual. If we were to take the approach of sharing the responsibility, perhaps we would be more proactive in educating, training, and modeling behavior that benefits both the person's needs and those of society.

This chapter begins with a quote from David Halperin, who stated that "unlike sex, sexuality is a cultural production: it represents the *appropriation* of the human body and of its physiological capacities by an ideological discourse." Perhaps it is time to look at that discourse more carefully. Sexuality should include the whole of society in this very important discourse. It should be based on information and appropriate instruction. In the meantime, society is more careful about teaching its military personnel about the Geneva Convention than its members at large about sexuality.

Discussion Questions

1. How can one determine what sexual behavior is normal or abnormal? Is there or should there be a universal consensus on some behaviors?
2. How can we define pornography? What are the pros and cons of the role of pornography in society? Is some pornography beneficial and, if so, for whom and in what circumstances?
3. How can we define obscenity?
4. How tolerant should societies be of different cultural practices regarding sexuality? For example, is it acceptable for an older family member to rape a 10-year-old girl if it is considered a religious or cultural rite of passage?
5. What is the role of government in influencing individual sexual practices through legislation? Should our government have a say in this regard? If so, to what extent?
6. Some have argued that if prostitution were legalized, both prostitutes and their clients would be safer through regulations designed to protect their safety and health. Others disagree and believe that this would only encourage the practice. Discuss the pros and cons of this issue.
7. Do you think sexual offenders can be cured? Why or why not? If so, at what point should they be released back into society? Would you feel the same if an offender were returning to your neighborhood? Would you feel differently if you were related to the offender?
8. Why do few people report a rape? Discuss the pros and cons of prosecuting a perpetrator.
9. Throughout this chapter, the role of religion is consistently considered as it relates to views on sexuality in general, but also as it is related to acceptable social contexts for its expression. Pick a religious group and discuss what appropriate sexual behaviors are within its belief system.
10. Can a man be raped by a woman? Is there a difference between a man being raped by a woman or by another man? Do you think that the rape of a man is also underreported? Why?
11. How do you think views on sexuality will have changed 25 years from now? How about 100 years from now?

Related Readings

Caron, S. L. (1998). *Cross-cultural perspectives on human sexuality.* Boston: Allyn and Bacon.
Crooks, R., & Bauer, K. (2005). *Our sexuality* (9th ed.). Belmont, CA: Thompson Wadsworth.
Hyde, J. S., & DeLamater, J. D. (2006). *Understanding human sexuality* (9th ed.). Boston: McGraw-Hill.
Laumann, E. O., Gagnon, J. H., Michael, R. T., & Michaels, S. (1994). *The social organization of sexuality.* Chicago: University of Chicago Press.

Related Web Sites

The Electronic Journal of Human Sexuality: http://www.ejhs.org
HS/HSL—Human Sexuality Resources: http://www.hshsl.umaryland.edu/resources/sexuality.html
More About Sex In Islam: http://www.themodernreligion.com/misc/sex/sex_good.htm#more
Sex Information and Education Council of Canada (SIECCAN): http://www.sieccan.org
Sexuality Information and Education Council of the United States (SIECUS): http://www.siecus.org

Related Movies/Videos

The Other Sister (1999) with Juliette Lewis and Diane Keaton
Philadelphia (1993) with Tom Hanks and Denzel Washington
Sleeping with the Enemy (1991) with Julia Roberts and Patrick Bergin
Something to Talk About (1995) with Julia Roberts and Dennis Quaid

DRUGS

Herbert W. Helm, Jr., Duane C. McBride, Gary L. Hopkins, and C. Edward Boyatt

10

Chapter Outline

- Introduction
- Perspectives on Substance Abuse
- Definitions of Substance Use, Abuse, and Dependence
- Drug Mechanisms

- Social Issues
- Treatment of Substance Abuse
- Drug Policy
- Conclusion

He was full of energy, could make you laugh, and was always the most outrageous guy in the room. John Belushi, the comedian from Saturday Night Live, was his idol. Due to his admiration of Belushi he put his energy into creativity as he enrolled in the famed Second City improvisational school in Chicago. Soon he started to be recognized and got a chance to follow his idol's path; he worked for five seasons on SNL. In his movies and skits he played an overbearing character with a sweet side.

This fame apparently couldn't calm the anxiety that came with being accepted. His frame of five-feet six-inches weighed 296 pounds. All the praise and adulation he received for his comedy had only a short-term effect in calming his anxiety. He started to turn to vices and soon became obsessed. Having a strong appetite for alcohol, drugs, food, and women, he always relied on something. Several of his

friends were concerned for him, and his co-workers tried to help him, reminding him that behaviors like his caused Belushi's early death. Surely he did not want to imitate his idol's tragic ending. He enrolled himself in AA, drug rehab clinics, and weight-loss centers, but he had to fight not just one problem daily, but all his demons.

At the end of October he engaged in several food and drinking binges. By Thanksgiving, his relatives noticed that he was even heavier than before. By then he and his two brothers were staying up until 3 A.M. gulping down Jack Daniels with Coke. He continued his excesses until one night it was too much. He was found dead in his Chicago sky-rise apartment at the age of 33. He died of heart failure, which was precipitated by his lifestyle. So went the life of Chris Farley.*

Introduction

Perhaps Maxmen (1986) said it best in his book on psychopathology: "Individuals and religions of every era have sought to suspend people's realities and to alter their moods by the simplest and quickest way possible—'better living through chemistry'" (p. 112).

In this chapter we will address the following major social issues involving the use of substances:

- How should we view the reasons for using substances or the perspectives on substance use?

- How should we define various degrees of using substances, such as abuse, dependency, and addiction?
- What types of treatment are available for substance abuse? Are some better than others, and what assumptions underlie the various modes?
- What are some major social consequences of substance abuse?
- What types of drug policies have developed, and what is the drug-crime relationship?

---

*Written by Nisim Estrada, and adapted from Bellafante, G. (1997, December 29). The suffering of a fool. Time, 150(27), 108. Also Marin, R. (1998, February 16). Spade in America. Newsweek Magazine, 131(7), 73.

Perspectives on Substance Abuse

ISSUES: Is alcohol and drug use a "chosen" behavior? Does substance use or abuse have moral implications? If so, what kind? Is drug use simply a "learned" behavior? What implications does a "disease model" have for drug use?

Throughout most of U.S. history, drug and alcohol use and abuse have been viewed either as sinful behavior or as a disease. In recent decades, the idea of maladaptive, or debilitative, behavior that is "overlearned" has also been added. Today, some may see substance abuse as "a *disease* in which people *learn* to act in *immoral* ways" (Thombs, 1999, p. 1).

The Immoral or Sinful Perspective

The sinful or immoral conduct view suggests that people are not living up to a given ethical or moral standard. They choose to engage in this behavior and as a result may be seen as being on the continuum between irresponsible and evil. This position may be taken by certain religious groups, conservative political groups, and those harmed by addicts/abusers. Since substance use is a "chosen" behavior, those viewing it as immoral often want to deal with it by making tougher penalties and punishing the individual (Thombs, 1999).

Almost all societies have rules regarding alcohol that typically arise from religion. Alcohol has been associated with religion in both the ordinary and the mystical sense. The association of alcohol with the desire for a mystical experience has a long history. The Bible, which influences Judeo-Christian cultures, has some 687 references to wine. While it does not specifically forbid its use, the Bible does prohibit drunkenness, which it sees as a moral sin. The protestant movement toward abstinence started with the Anabaptists of the Reformation. During the 1800s a number of temperance societies shifted the emphasis from temperance to abstinence. A focus was placed on the substance, and alcohol became the "demon rum." Most saw the person involved as depraved and weak-willed. Temperance became associated with total abstinence and no distinction was made between use and abuse. Royce (1985) notes: "…we have many paradoxes in the relations between religion and alcohol. Wine is good, but

drunkenness is bad. As Jellinek once said, it gladdens the heart but puts to sleep the soul. Is it a creature of God, or 'demon rum'? Alcoholism came to be seen as a disease, yet the most successful treatment to date is the intensely spiritual program of Alcoholics Anonymous. And A.A. itself grew out of the failure of a religiously inspired movement, Prohibition" (p. 58).

The Disease Perspective

The disease model suggests that there is an underlying process that causes compulsive use. The disease model is advocated by the medical field and the alcohol industry (both of which have much to gain financially from this position), and by individuals recovering from addictions. This position does not emphasize moral judgment, but urges the individual to focus on what is necessary to live a substance-free life (Thombs, 1999).

It should be noted that within the disease model are more than one approach, emphasizing different components. Different sub-models focus on components such as these:

- The role of genetics in making people susceptible or vulnerable to substance abuse.
- The role of the substance in exposing the brain to chemicals and actions that result in addiction.
- The significance of biological factors like dependence and withdrawal, liver disease, and brain abnormalities as symptoms of the disease.
- The feeling of illness an individual may have from struggling with compulsive chemical use.

A large amount of controversy surrounds the disease model. Researchers have suggested that there may be multiple types of alcoholisms (Thombs, 1999).

The Maladaptive Perspective

The maladaptive model suggests that addiction is learned by the same laws that shape all other behaviors. As with the disease model, the individual is seen as a victim, but of poor learning conditions (e.g., the family, environment, and other social conditions). Advocates of this position are usually within the behavioral sciences, especially psychology. Treatment consists of teaching learning principles, because one needs to learn different responses (Thombs, 1999).

Definitions of Substance Use, Abuse, and Dependence

ISSUES: How should one define levels of substance use and abuse? Are some levels of use/abuse acceptable? How would you know if someone had an addiction?

Before proceeding, we should look at how professionals classify the use and misuse of substances. While there may be some differences in definitions, based upon the classification system used, we will adapt information from the *Diagnostic and Statistical Manual of Mental Disorders* (4th edition, text revision), known as the DSM-IV-TR (2000). In defining the Substance-Related Disorders, the DSM-IV-TR uses the word **substance** to mean a medication, an abused drug, or a toxin. The substances are placed into 11 classes: alcohol; amphetamine (or amphetamine-like); caffeine; cannabis; cocaine; hallucinogen; inhalant; nicotine; opioid; phencyclidine (or phencyclidine-like); and sedative, hypnotic, or anxiolytic. See Box 10.1, "Classes of Substances," for descriptions of these drugs. Applicable across all these substance classes are the concepts of dependence, abuse, intoxication, and withdrawal. As Schuckit (1995) points out, most people in Western society have used a psychoactive substance and the majority have had an adverse experience (e.g, heartburn from coffee). However, substance use, even with temporary problems, is not the same as a diagnosable disorder.

Substance **intoxication** is a reversible substance-specific syndrome that results from exposure to a substance. It is associated with clinically significant maladaptive behaviors or physiological changes. Intoxication typically affects moods, thinking, judgment, psychomotor skills, and interpersonal behavior. Substance **withdrawal** is a substance-specific syndrome that occurs after the cessation or reduction in use of a substance that has been used heavily for a long time. It also affects important areas such as social and occupational functioning. Individuals who are withdrawing desire to take the substance again in order to reduce the withdrawal symptoms, which for most substances are the opposite of those observed in intoxication.

Substance withdrawal is often associated with substance dependence. **Substance dependence** involves a maladaptive pattern of use that includes cognitive, behavioral, and physiological symptoms. The individual continues the use despite the problems and can experience tolerance, as well as withdrawal, to the substance. **Tolerance** involves becoming habituated to the substance, which means that an individual must increase the amount taken in order to have the original effect. A person in a substance dependence pattern may compulsively use the substance despite knowing the psychological and physical problems it causes.

The word **addiction** is not a diagnostic term in the DSM-IV-TR, but is often used in the field to describe the condition of a person who is dependent on a substance and uses it compulsively. But there is not a rigorous and consensual definition of the term. For example, Barlow and Durand (1999), in discussing Fahey's research, note that by standard psychiatric definition, LSD would fail an addictiveness test; but if the same test were applied to activities such as work, running, and mountain climbing, they could qualify. However, the last three activities are hardly viewed as destructive and are seen as qualitatively different from the use of heroin, alcohol, or LSD.

So what is an addiction? Evans and Sullivan (1990) speak of the "disease of addiction." However, Peele (1995), in his book *Diseasing of America,* is against the concept of addiction as a disease and notes: "The label *addiction* does not obviate either the meaning of the addictive involvement within people's lives, or their responsibility for their misbehavior or for their choices in continuing the addiction" (p. 3). He views people as active agents in their addictions. Regardless of how active or passive individuals are seen to be in this process, the concept of addiction is often tied into the disease model.

Substance abuse is a maladaptive pattern of substance use that leads to significant adverse consequences within a 12-month period. The impairment is recurrent or persistent and can result in legal difficulties, lead to dangerous situations such as driving drunk, or result in failure to meet social, home, or work obligations. Unlike substance dependence, abuse does not include compulsive use, withdrawal, or tolerance, but does involve harmful consequences. Substance abuse does not apply to caffeine or nicotine.

Box 10.1: Classes of Substances

Alcohol: Produced through distillation or fermentation, it is usually consumed in the forms of beer, wine, and hard liquor. Alcohol depresses the central nervous system (CNS) and reduces the effectiveness of neural transmission. Alcohol impairs sensorimotor skills and is a major contributor to auto accidents. Heavy, chronic drinking is associated with damage to both the liver and brain, and with impaired sexual functioning.

Amphetamine (or amphetamine-like): A class of synthetic drugs, which have declined in medical use due to their high abuse potential. The effects are similar to cocaine except that they are longer acting. The effects of amphetamines typically persist 4 to 12 hours, while cocaine is effective for between 20 and 80 minutes. These stimulants have been used to reduce boredom and fatigue and to suppress the appetite. High doses can induce stimulant psychosis (a paranoid state) or death.

Caffeine: The most popular drug in the world, with coffee, tea, and soft drinks being common sources. The popularity of the drug is likely due to its stimulation of the CNS, which has mood-enhancing effects. Overall, caffeine seems relatively safe. However, at 600(+) mg one may experience acute caffeine intoxication. At 1000(+) mg one may experience severe toxic symptoms including psychomotor agitation and cardiac arrhythmia.

Cannabis: The cannabis plant produces a psychoactive substance, THC (delta-9-tetrahydrocannabids), which effects neurotransmitters, and smoking is the most effective and rapid method of absorption. Marijuana comes from the top leafy part of the marijuana plant and hashish from the dust of the resin. A decreased level of motor activity is reported as being relaxing and tranquil. Marijuana has been used medically to treat glaucoma and to counter the nausea and vomiting of cancer chemotherapies. Cannabis can impair short-term memory, and marijuana smoking may cause irreversible lung damage.

Cocaine: A powerful stimulant from the leaves of the coca bush. A drug that has probably been used for thousands of years, cocaine became popular in the 1980s in the smokable form of crack. Thought to affect the dopamine-containing neurons of the brain, it is a shortcut to the reward system. At high doses cocaine can cause convulsions, irregular heartbeats including fibrillation, heart attack, and stroke.

Hallucinogen: A group of drugs which can profoundly alter consciousness. There are a variety of drugs in this group, such as the serotonergic hallucinogens like LSD, which induce vivid hallucinations, methylated amphetamines like MDMA (ecstasy) which alter mood and consciousness, and anticholinergic hallucinogens like atropine and scopolamine that produce a stupor or dreamlike trance. Adverse effects of LSD include psychotic reactions (bad trips), a re-experiencing of some aspect of the trip at a later date (flashbacks), and resulting long-term psychiatric disorders.

Inhalant: A group of substances that includes glue, fuel gas, paint thinner, corrective fluid, and many others. Inhalants have less to do with their pharmacology and more to do with their method of administration. Because of the large number of substances and their varying pharmacology, it is difficult to characterize the hazards. Chronic use has been associated with brain damage.

Nicotine: Naturally it occurs only in the tobacco plant, and cigarette smoking is the most common method of use. Nicotine is highly addictive; it has stimulant effects at lower doses and retards neural transmission at higher doses. Major diseases associated with it are various types of cancer, heart disease, and chronic obstructive lung disease. Users experience a calming effect with use, and, especially for women, it is used for its weight-suppressing effect.

Opioid: A group of drugs that includes opium, heroin, morphine, and related compounds. Opiate drugs are used medically as painkillers. Opiates mimic the endorphins in the brain, which help regulate pain and pleasure. The downside is the severe dependency that opiates can cause. With chronic use tolerance develops and the individual must take more to re-experience the rush. After prolonged use a person may continue using the substance in order not to experience the symptoms of withdrawal.

Phencyclidine (or phencyclidine-like): Phencyclidine (PCP, angel dust) and ketamine are the most used drugs in this category; they are known as dissociative anesthetics hallucinogens. At moderate doses phencyclidine produces a potent intoxication and feelings of euphoria. PCP can cause toxic psychosis (paranoia and violence) and long-term psychotic episodes, and it creates more psychiatric emergencies than any other drug. At overdose levels (over 20 mg) it can cause coma, seizures, and death.

Sedative, Hypnotic, or Anxiolytic: This class of drugs includes barbiturates, barbiturate–like hypnotics, benzodiazepines, the carbamates, all prescription sleeping medications, and most prescription antianxiety medications. These substances are brain depressants and at high doses can be lethal, especially if mixed with alcohol. The barbiturates and benzodiazepines have been used to reduce anxiety.

Adapted from Maisto, Galizio, and Connors (1995), with help from the DSM-IV-TR (2000) on class 11 (Sedative, Hypnotic, or Anxiolytic).

Drug Mechanisms

ISSUES: What makes drugs rewarding and/or reinforcing? How do an agonist and antagonist work? Why not use natural reinforcers to counteract the effect of drugs?

In this section we will look at how drugs work and why they can be appealing. Considering that the life of a drug addict may lead to the loss of employment, the destruction of important personal relationships, chaos in finances, degradation of personal happiness, and, in some, death, why would one chose to use addictive substances? One of the hallmarks of addiction is that even while people are using drugs they realize that their lives are completely out of control, they understand that important relationships are deteriorating, and

they know that bad things are happing to all that was good in their lives. Yet they continue to use drugs. The syndrome of addiction is often characterized by compulsive drug seeking and use despite serious negative consequences.

In laboratory settings, normal animals with access to addictive drugs typically engage in self-administration of various substances. This has led researchers to conclude that some neurobiological or neurochemical process in the brain makes animals, including humans, vulnerable to regulation by addictive drugs. Addiction from this view appears to be a brain abnormality.

Addictive drugs are both rewarding and reinforcing. A reward is a stimulus that the brain interprets as positive. A reinforcing stimulus is one that increases the likelihood that the behaviors associated with the use of the particular drug will be repeated. It is important to understand that not all reinforcers are rewarding. For example, a punishment might result in avoidance behaviors.

The brain properties that participate in the perception of reward and positive reinforcement are a set of interconnected structures often called brain reward pathways. These include the nucleus accumbens, the basal forebrain, and regions of the medial prefrontal cortex. All of these structures are intimately innervated by brain material, which promotes the secretion or stops the destruction of dopamine, a neurochemical responsible for the sensation of pleasure.

The chemistry of the brain responsible for sensations of reward and reinforcement has to do with neurotransmitters. The brain is a complex arrangement of cells. Some of these, glial cells, provide structural support and enable the metabolic functions of the nervous system. Other cells, called neurons, are excitable. Neurons transmit and analyze information. When neurons receive sensory information from the outside, they integrate this information and store it, and neurons then control the action of muscles and glands, which results in everything that we understand as behavior. Simply said, what happens at the level of the neuron results in what happens behaviorally in animals, including humans.

Neurons have many forms and shapes. When a nervous impulse (a positive electrical charge) travels down the axon (the long tail attached to the cell body), it eventually branches into a number of small fibers or filaments. At the end of a filament is a terminal button (or end bulb); these do not connect to other neurons. Each neuron is essentially a small set of structures that work in conjunction with other neurons without making physical contact. A nervous impulse does not end in the terminal button. It jumps to the next cell body. The process of passing the electrical charge from the terminal button to the next cell body is a chemical process.

At the terminal membrane are small synaptic vesicles. These vesicles, located very close to the synaptic cleft (the space between neurons), store neurotransmitters—chemicals that will, when stimulated by an electrical charge, flood the space between the terminal membrane (presynaptic terminal) and the postsynaptic membrane, allowing the electrical charge to pass on to the next cell body. The neurotransmitter is what allows an electrical impulse to travel from neuron to neuron.

Embedded in the membrane of the postsynaptic cell (the surface of the cell body, or dendrite, where the electrical charge will pass to after moving across the synaptic cleft) are many different types of receptors. The chemical process of neurotransmission, the passage of a nervous impulse from one nerve to another, occurs at the synapse, where drugs have the opportunity to interfere. Some drugs block the receptor sites so that neurotransmitters will have no effect (called **antagonism**), some drugs can mimic neurotransmitters by occupying receptor sites (this is called **agonism**), and other drugs can alter the synaptic transmission in other ways.

One important feature of neurotransmission is what happens to neurotransmitters after they are released from the vesicles into the neurosynaptic cleft. In review, an electrical charge travels down the axon of the neuron and reaches the wall of a vesicle, causing a neurotransmitter to be released that floods the neurosynaptic cleft, allowing the impulse to pass on to the next neuron. The chemical flooding the cleft will now either be deactivated or will return to the vesicle from which it came. If an experimental drug XYZ blocks neurotransmitters from reentering a vesicle so that the chemical transmitter stays in the cleft longer, it could be said that this neurotransmitter causes euphoria, and would explain how XYZ is responsible for causing a sense of well-being.

Psychomotor Stimulants

Drugs known as **psychomotor stimulants** have one effect in common: they stimulate transmission at synapses that use norepinephrine, dopamine, or serotonin as a transmitter. Some psychomotor stimulants occur naturally in nature (i.e., cocaine) while others (i.e., amphetamine) do not.

The psychomotor stimulants work like this: when an individual introduces cocaine or amphetamine into the body, after absorption the drugs work directly on the synaptic vesicles causing dopamine (and other neurochemicals) to leak from the vesicle into the synaptic cleft. A second effect is that under the influence of either of these drugs, there is an increase in the amount of dopamine that is usually released. Thirdly, the cocaine blocks the dopamine from re-entering the vesicle after it has flooded the cleft. More dopamine is released and then blocked from going back to its storage vesicle, causing prolonged duration and intensity of its effect on the brain.

How cocaine and/or amphetamine influences the neurobiological properties of the synapse leads us closer to understanding why people use drugs. Animal experiments have demonstrated that non-human subjects self-administer psychomotor stimulants in search of the reinforcing properties characteristic of these drugs. In a laboratory setting an animal may learn that it will receive an injection of cocaine every time it presses a lever. By definition, the injected cocaine acts as a reinforcer if it increases the behavior of lever-pressing in the cage. The strength of the reinforcement is measured by how many times the animal will press the lever in order to receive the drug.

Experiments performed on monkeys, rats, rabbits, and other animals have shown that all tested species abuse cocaine. For example, in one experiment an intravenous catheter was introduced into a monkey. The solution passing into the catheter was a mixture of a saline solution and cocaine. The monkey learned that when it pressed the lever it was rewarded with a sensation of pleasure (the effects of the cocaine). The monkey continued to press the lever over and over, and again and again was rewarded with pleasure.

Researchers designed a method by which the monkey would have to press the lever a few thousand times in order to receive a single dose of cocaine. Strikingly, all of the monkeys tested pressed the lever over and over again in order to get the "high" and continued to press the lever to the extent that they avoided feedings, water, and rest (McKim, 1997). They became aggressive toward other animals in the same cage and eventually started to self-mutilate. The monkeys continued to press the lever in many cases until death. They performed incredible work in order to receive the pleasurable effects of the cocaine. Cocaine is a powerful behavioral reinforcer (Nestler, Hyman, & Malenka, 2001).

The brain reward circuitry is targeted by addictive substances to cause pleasure and strengthen natural reinforcers such as food, water, sexual contact, and even a touch or smile. Substances such as cocaine tap into brain networks and interfere with them, thereby causing a person to develop an unnatural desire to seek reward continually. The powerful control over behavior exerted by addictive drugs may be due to the brain's inability to distinguish between the activation of its reward circuitry by drugs and natural activation of the same circuitry by useful behaviors.

It is important to note that any activation of the brain's neurobiological reward system is regarded by the brain as something that should be repeated in order to reproduce the associated pleasant sensations. A problem with stimulating the reward system with drugs is that the sensations and feelings produced are often much more powerful than those that come from natural reinforcers. The powerful influence that drugs have over our brain's reward mechanism is associated with our survival (need to feel good), and makes us vulnerable to addiction.

MDMA (3,4-methylenedioxymethamphetamine), also known as ecstasy or E, is a relatively new synthetic drug with some properties similar to other psychomotor stimulants. The use of MDMA by young people is increasing at a significant rate. MDMA appears to cause addiction because of its close chemical relationship with amphetamine. It increases heart rate and blood pressure, and can disable the body's temperature regulation ability. MDMA increases the activity of three neurotransmitters, including serotonin (an inhibitor of activity and behavior), dopamine (previously described), and norepinephrine (a brain stimulant) (Leshner, 2001).

Even a small dose of MDMA in rats can decrease serotonin levels for up to two weeks. MDMA is toxic to the brain and actually damages brain cells. Use of this substance will cause a reduction in serotonin-producing cells in only two weeks of use. In many cases, this damage may be permanent.

It is beyond the scope of this chapter to describe the neurobiological effects of all substances of abuse, but what should be remembered is that all of them (e.g., alcohol, marijuana, and LSD) have behavioral reinforcing properties. The ways each substance of abuse influences neurotransmitters and the reward systems of the brain may differ and are often complex, but all of them have the potential for addiction or compulsive use.

Social Issues

ISSUES: How many social issues do you see drug use or abuse affecting? How can your country bring down the cost of drug abuse? What cultural components of your country may increase or decrease the use of drugs in your society? What cultural misperceptions of drug use occur in your country or society? What is the role of religion to drug use or abuse?

In a chapter of this length it would be difficult to address all the social issues that are associated with substance use and abuse. Even if one or two were examined, it would be in an arbitrary manner and would not do justice to the large number of issues. Below are examples of the kinds of topics that could be addressed:

- Violence (domestic relationships, within the drug trade, etc.)
- Effect on infants (addicted babies, fetal alcohol effects and syndrome, etc.)
- Driving and induced impairment (effects of driving under the influence, etc.)
- Crime (organized, narco-terrorism—the selling of drugs to finance terrorism; drug trafficking to pay for the habit; etc.)
- Health (cancer, hepatitis, cirrhosis, AIDS, mental health, risk taking, etc.)
- Sex (association of sex and drugs, date rape drugs, etc.)

The Cost of Drug Abuse

The actual cost of drug abuse to a society is difficult to determine. Not only is the data difficult to gather, but one also has to determine what is considered to be a "cost." In this section we will look at a number of estimated costs such as of drug abuse to schools, health care, and loss of productivity. Figures on these costs are usually a number of years old as it takes awhile to collect and analyze such data.

A study by the Lewin Group estimated that the total economic cost of alcohol and drug abuse for the nation in 1992 was $245.7 billion. This was up 50% from the cost estimate for 1985. The major contributors to the increase were epidemics of heavy cocaine use and HIV, an eight-fold increase in incarcerations (both state and federal), and a three-fold increase in crimes related to drug use. More than half of the estimated costs were due to drug-related crime (http://www.nida.gov/Infofax/costs.html, 2003).

As a comparison, a publication by the Office of National Drug Control Policy (2001) estimated the overall cost of drug abuse to be $102.2 billion for 1992. Three categories were used for this estimate: health care costs, productivity losses, and other costs. From 1992 to 1998 there was an annual 5.9% increase, so estimated costs for 1998 were $143.4 billion. Between 1992 and 1998 there was an annual 2.9% rise in health care costs. In 1992 the largest cost element in this category was treatment related to drug abuse of HIV/AIDS patients. New treatments for HIV/AIDS helped to moderate health care costs between 1992 and 1998. However, community-based specialty treatment rose an annual 6.3% during the same period. Productivity losses between 1992 and 1998 rose from $69.4 billion to $98.5 billion, an annual increase of 6%. The primary sources of this increase were drug-abuse-related illnesses and incarceration. During the same period, crime-related costs rose an annual 6.5% and were estimated to have cost society more than $32 million in 1998. During the same time there was only a combined 3.5% increase in population growth and general price inflation.

For school systems it is estimated that $41 billion is associated with the costs of drug, alcohol, and tobacco abuse. This is an added 10% to already strained budgets. One piece of good news is that a student who reaches age 21 without taking illicit drugs, smoking, or abusing alcohol is unlikely ever to start. This means that school systems could have a critical influence on drug abuse (http://www.health.org/govpubs/prevalert/v5/5.aspx).

On the positive side, it does appear that substance abuse treatment is cost effective. An analysis of 154 publications shows that most of the savings come from reductions in one or more of the following areas: crime, health care services, victimization, criminal justice expenses, and loss of work due to illness. Savings also came from improvements in clients' employment/productivity. For example, studies on state treatment systems in California and Ohio suggest a return of about seven dollars for every dollar spent (http://www.neds.calib.com/products/pdfs/fs/140_economic_benefits.pdf). Regardless of the numbers used, the costs of substance abuse to society are large.

Monitoring Drug Use among Teenagers

The Monitoring the Future Survey has been tracking illicit drug use and attitudes of 12th graders since 1975. In 1991, 8th and 10th graders were added to the survey. In 2001, over 44,000 students were surveyed. The 2001 Survey found the following:

- Use of most illicit drugs remained stable from 2000 to 2001.
- For all three grades the rise in MDMA (ecstasy) use slowed; there were still increases, but not as severe as seen for the previous couple of years.
- For 10th and 12th graders the rates of heroin use decreased; there was a significant decrease in inhalant use for 12th graders and a decrease in cocaine powder and crack use for 10th graders.
- The most notable change in this survey was a decrease in smoking for 8th and 10th graders (http://www.nida.nih.gov/MedAdv/01/NR12-19.html, 2003).

Culture and Substance Abuse

Culture can be defined as the values, beliefs, traditions, attitudes, and practices that get passed along from one generation to the next. Culture and ethnicity affect a person's health, beliefs, and practices. Addictions are often manifested differently among the major ethnocultural groups in the United States. For example, whites drink more than blacks do; however, blacks often drink more heavily. White youth smoke more than black youth do. Blacks use intravenous drugs more than do whites. Factors associated with Latino substance abuse typically include acculturation and intergenerational stress and conflict. Substance abuse for Latino youth rarely occurs by itself, but is associated with problems such as truancy, teen pregnancy, and delinquency. Asian Americans drink less than any other ethnic group; part of this may be due to the **flushing response** (following alcohol consumption a flushing of the face, neck, and upper chest, along with symptoms such as dizziness, pounding of the head, and nausea) that is common in some Asian American groups. On the whole, as a group they do not seek out mental health services, but deal with problems within the community or family. For Native Americans, alcoholism is considered epidemic, and they may have a genetic susceptibility to it (Rasmussen, 2000).

There are cultures in which what we define as a problem substance is viewed as part of normal or idealized behavior; this is true for some of the hallucinogenic drugs. Some psychotropic drugs are used for spiritual rather than hedonistic purposes. Early American Indians used smoking as a spiritual aid that was done communally and helped cement agreements (Pihl, 1999). From a sociocultural standpoint, Thombs (1999) points out four functions of substance use:

- It enhances social bonds. Barriers are often lowered and self-disclosure becomes easier.
- It releases people from their social responsibilities and obligations. Thus, it gives people a temporary escape from stress.
- It may promote cohesion among members of a social or ethnic group. Whether used or not, a substance may be identified with a particular group. For example, it is part of Jewish cultural tradition to drink moderately.
- Substance use is a way to renounce established, often "middle class" values. Members of drug subcultures are often rejecting the moral and economic productivity of conventional norms.

The same cultural beliefs, values, attitudes, and practices that influence substance use can also influence individual treatment decisions and their effectiveness. Too often cultural awareness is limited to seeing how others are different from oneself, without incorporating this into a better appreciation of another culture and individuals from that culture. We may fail to understand how culture can be used to encourage the seeking of treatment and to improve its outcomes. The therapist should find out what clients think and feel about etiological factors, the pros and cons of their substance use, their goals, what would be effective treatment, and what would motivate them towards reaching their goals. By assessing a client's values and beliefs, the therapist can better identify the best approach to therapy. A client may be more receptive to a therapist who is seen as not trying to impose values, and this may improve the relationship between them (Baxter et al., 1998).

Religion and Substance Abuse

Drugs and religion have an interesting interplay. On the one hand many religions attempt to control drug use by either abstinence or limitation; on the other hand, individuals (or religious groups) use drugs in order to facilitate a religious mystical experience.

Drugs, mostly psychedelic, have been used to bring on mystical or ecstatic states. Drugs such as LSD, psilocybin, mescaline, and peyote have the ability to create perceptual changes (Wulff, 1991). These drugs seem to encourage illumination, and they can "intensify mental associations, imagery, and symbolic thought; the mind is alive with new combinations of sensations, ideas, and memories" (Batson et al., 1993, p. 121). LSD, for example, works on a neuromodulatory system of serotonin-using neurons that send their axons to almost all areas of the brain, including the neocortex. This system modulates our awareness of the environment and filters out a good amount of information, but leaves enough information for our survival. LSD works to open this filter, thus allowing an abnormal amount of information (somatosensory) to be processed by the brain. It may also be that the mystic is able to reduce the inhibitory action of the serotonergic system, thus creating distortions of cognition, senses, emotions, and perceptions. If this is true, the effects of LSD would seem similar to non-drug-induced mystical experiences (Goodman, 2002). While not conclusive, when Batson et al. (1993) reviewed the research, they thought that it does suggest that psychedelic drugs could and do facilitate religious experience by "disrupting the individual's current way of thinking about one or more existential concerns…and by stimulating the imaginal process, making cognitive reorganization more likely" (p. 132).

Psychedelics appear to disrupt the usual way that an individual views one or more existential concerns, and to stimulate the imaginal process, making it more likely that the person will reorganize his or her thoughts. However, if the individual is not already struggling with existential issues, it is unlikely that psychedelics will evoke a religious transformation.

Koenig et al. (2001) notes that to date there are nearly a hundred studies supporting the idea that religion may be a deterrent to substance abuse for children, adolescents, and adults. The greater their participation in religion, the less likely it is that they will either start using substances or, if they do use a substance, that they will have an associated problem. It is thought that participation in religion may reduce substance use by instilling moral values, increasing coping skills, reducing the odds of choosing substances during times of stress, and by the presence of friends who are less likely to use or abuse substances. Religious and spiritual factors also play an important role in treatment (Booth & Martin, 1998). However, religion is multifaceted and religious organizations have varying norms in regards to substance use. Also, individuals may vary in their commitment to their denomination's beliefs and practices (Koenig, 1998).

Treatment of Substance Abuse

ISSUES: What models of treatment do you consider the best and why? Are there political agendas behind various treatment modes? If so, why do you think this is? Should abstinence be a goal for drug/alcohol treatment? Why or why not? What do you see as the benefits and problems of a 12-Step program such as AA?

This section considers some types of treatments that are used with individuals who have substance abuse problems and will address a couple of issues that affect our views of substance abuse and how they can and do affect treatment. While a large number of philosophical and research issues affect our views of substance abuse and its treatment, only two will be addressed here: Is alcoholism a disease, and should abstinence be the goal for alcohol treatment? Although alcohol is the drug of focus in these discussions, similar arguments can be made about a number of other drugs.

Is Alcoholism a Disease or Part of a Political Agenda?

Does it matter which perspective you use to view substance abuse? If you were basing a treatment on your perspective(s) of etiology, or cause, then of course the answer is "yes." However, the purpose of this section is to broaden the question and evaluate how perspectives may be driven more by power and political agenda than by etiology and treatment. As our example, we will consider the controversy as to whether alcoholism is a disease.

You are likely to hear that alcoholism is a disease in advertisements on radio and television for treatments of the disorder. The disease model is the predominant one in the U.S. and was the major paradigm guiding science and treatment during most of the 20th century. However, outside the U.S. many have discredited it and use other models, like social learning (Bride & Nackerud, 2002).

Whether you consider alcoholism a disease depends on your definition of reality, science, and disease. Hartmann and Millea (1996) view "reality" as a product of social consensus that is reinforced by social power. While there were many steps in the historical process of defining alcoholism as a disease, they tie the concept into the movement and philosophy of Alcoholics Anonymous (AA). AA embraced the flawed work of Jellinek, who in his 1960 book *The Disease Concept of Alcoholism* promoted the disease model as a "fact." During the 1960s, opposition arose to the disease concept of alcoholism as scientific studies suggested that alcoholics could control their drinking and that alcoholism was not necessarily progressive. In a similar paper, Bride and Nackerud (2002) discuss the view of alcoholism through a Kuhnian paradigm of science. Kuhn's model (1996) suggests that a number of schools of thought compete and that in order for one theory to become a paradigm, it has to seem better than its competitors. For alcoholism this pre-paradigm period was during the 19th and early 20th centuries when disease and moral views were in competition. Following Jellinek's

work, the disease concept of alcoholism became firmly established. Normal science for alcoholism became the disease model. The anomaly for this model was the issue of whether alcoholics could return to controlled patterns of drinking (Heather & Robertson, 1997).

In dealing with the concept of addiction as a disease, Peele (1995) discusses the difference between what was previously seen as illness and what it means today. In doing so, he discusses three generations of disease: physical, mental, and addictions. Physical ailments (the first generation) like cancer, AIDS, and malaria have been known and *"defined by their measurable physical effects"* (p. 5). They are known to affect the functioning of the body. The mental illnesses (second generation) are known more by their effect on feelings, thoughts, and behavior. They are usually diagnosed in response to the individual's behavior and reports of suffering. Addictions (third generation) stray even further from the concept of disease first used in modern medicine. Addictions *"are known by the behaviors they describe"* (p. 6), and cultural beliefs and contexts define whether a given behavior or appetite reflects an addiction.

If substance use is seen as a "disease," this label determines who treats the individual and who benefits. As Thombs (1999) notes: "It gives credibility to physicians' efforts to control, manage, and supervise the care given to addicted persons. It makes legitimate such potentially lucrative endeavors as hospital admissions, insurance company billings, expansion of the patient pool, consulting fees, and so forth. It also serves to restrict the number and type of nonmedical treatment providers (e.g., professional counselors, psychologists, social workers, nurses, marriage and family counselors) who could independently provide care for substance-abusing clients. As a result, much of the treatment of such clients in the United States is carried out under physicians' supervision. In fact, the acceptance of the term 'treatment' in the substance abuse field reflects the dominant influence of medicine" (p. 239).

How would you answer the following questions?

- Should we view alcoholics as people with an inherited deficit who, once they begin drinking, are going to follow a downward course, and even if they stop drinking are only "dry alcoholics"? A "dry alcoholic" is an individual who does not drink but displays the thinking and behavior of an alcoholic.
- Should third parties, like insurance companies, have to pay for the treatment of non-disease conditions?

- What roles and advantages does the medical establishment have for continuing to use a disease model for alcoholism?
- Are people less responsible for their behavior if it is the product of a disease?
- Should the current view, whatever it is at the time, determine who gets federal monies to study substance abuse?
- How should we determine who has the power to make these decisions, realizing that benefits will occur to some group(s) on the basis of those decisions?

More than a cognitive exercise, answering questions like these helps determine social policy, views of science, and perceptions of others and ourselves.

Should Abstinence Be the Goal for Alcohol Treatment?

When we look at people with a substance dependency problem like alcoholism, we realize they have three choices: they can quit, they can reduce the amount of substance they are using, or they can continue substance dependency (Marlatt, 2001). In this section we will summarize a debate article in *The American Journal on Addictions* that looked at the issue of whether abstinence should be the goal of alcohol treatment (Owen & Marlatt, 2001). Similar arguments could be made for other substances.

Points from the affirmative viewpoint:

- It is logical. A person with a dependency problem has probably had the problem for awhile and has tried a number of ways to quit. Eliminating the behavior makes sense.
- Studies suggest that about half of those who try can achieve abstinence. With abstinence there is generally improvement in a number of life quality indicators (such as work, relationships, and health).
- For the dependent person, control instead of abstinence is difficult. Studies suggest that brain changes and sensitization issues make the dependent person more likely to relapse.

Points from the negative viewpoint:

- If the only treatment option we have is abstinence, we may set the goal too high for some people, and this may discourage them from seeking help.

- We should not take away a client's major coping method (e.g., drinking) until another coping method has been developed.
- **Harm reduction methods** (methods or techniques that place an emphasis on reducing behaviors that are causing harm to the individual, without focusing on total abstinence) may be a treatment option for those who do not pursue abstinence goals.

In a rebuttal to the negative viewpoints, Dr. Owen questions the effectiveness of harm reduction programs and noted that it is the role of the professional to make the treatment plan relevant to the diagnosis, even if the client wishes to continue drinking. In a rebuttal to the affirmative viewpoints, Dr. Marlatt notes that while abstinence is the best goal, harm reduction techniques should be seen as part of a continuum of strategies to help with problem drinking. Many problem drinkers are not getting help and efforts should be made to develop user-friendly alternatives to abstinence. Finally, he calls into question studies suggesting that about half of individuals achieve abstinence. Using data from Project Match, he suggests that on average less than 20% achieve abstinence.

In this debate it should be remembered that there are many types of substance users such as binge users, social users, moderate users, and individuals with dependency. It is likely that how one addresses the question of abstinence is not only related to the type of substance used, but also to one's philosophical belief system. If at best only around half of those who try actually achieve abstinence, should other treatment approaches (such as harm reduction) be used? If so, what should they be?

Models of Treatment

There are numerous models on how to treat addictions or substance use disorders, and many have components that vary or conflict with each other. These models are affected by the beliefs one has towards addictions. Besides the perspectives already noted in this chapter, one could consider a number of other issues:
- Are drugs an individual problem or should societal elements such as the justice system be involved?
- Does motivation to change come from internal elements or external pressures?
- Should we treat only the individual, or a system such as the family, community, or social network?

- Should treatment focus on education, the restructuring of behavioral-cognitive components, the psychopharmacological approach, or a method which focuses on the deficits of the self, such as the psychodynamic approach?
- Does the focus of treatment change depending on the age of the users (e.g., adolescents), whether they are polysubstance abusers/users, or whether they have the dual diagnosis of a major mental or personality disorder along with the substance abuse disorder?

Opinions about these and other issues typically determine the type of treatment offered and lead to approaches as varied as 12-Step recovery programs, family (systems) therapy, behavioral treatment, cognitive models, pharmacotherapy, group treatment, psychodynamic models, social skills training, relapse prevention, groups for adult children of alcoholics, and others. While we will not be able to address each of these treatments, we will take a look at three that are representative of many of the issues noted above: 1) the 12-Step program of Alcoholics Anonymous, 2) the use of the drug disulfiram (Antabuse) as an adversive behavioral method that uses a pharmocotherapeutic measure, and 3) cognitive behavior therapy.

Alcoholics Anonymous (AA): A 12-Step or Self-Help Treatment Program

In a review of 21 studies on the outcome of AA, Kownacki and Shadish (1999) concluded that on randomized trials, or where individuals are coerced into treatment (usually by courts), AA did no better than alternative treatments, and for some people it may have done worse. Their second conclusion was that there was not a lot of good research on AA. For individuals who chose to be in AA there were larger treatment effects. Of course, this may be due to selection bias, where individuals who choose to attend 12-Step meetings are more motivated to change, and where those who begin drinking again do not return to AA. For inpatient treatment there was some weak support. The components that received the best support included using recovered alcoholics as counselors, the honesty inventory, and specific procedures such as the 12-Step program (see Box 10.2). They indicated that there might be aspects of the AA philosophy that were useful in treating alcoholism, but thought that coercion into AA meetings was a bad idea.

In looking at long-term outcomes (over an eight-year period) of alcohol use disorders, Timko et al. (2000) concluded that those who seek and get help for their drinking have better drinking-related outcomes than those who do not. For example, 54% of those who sought help reported abstinence, while only 26% of untreated individuals did. For those who participated in AA, whether or not they were involved with formal treatment, it was found that they did somewhat better in the short term (1–3 years). However, the advantage did not hold out over formal treatment for the eight-year period. In a similar mode, Tonigan's findings

Box 10.2: The Twelve Steps of Alcoholics Anonymous

1. We admitted we were powerless over alcohol—that our lives had become unmanageable.
2. Came to believe that a Power greater than ourselves could restore us to sanity.
3. Made a decision to turn our will and our lives over to the care of God as we understood Him.
4. Made a searching and fearless moral inventory of ourselves.
5. Admitted to God, to ourselves and to another human being the exact nature of our wrongs.
6. Were entirely ready to have God remove all these defects of character.
7. Humbly asked Him to remove our shortcomings.
8. Made a list of all persons we had harmed and became willing to make amends to them all.
9. Made direct amends to such people wherever possible, except when to do so would injure them or others.
10. Continued to take personal inventory and when we were wrong promptly admitted it.
11. Sought through prayer and meditation to improve our conscious contact with God as we understood Him, praying only for knowledge of His will for us and the power to carry that out.
12. Having had a spiritual awakening as the result of these steps, we tried to carry this message to alcoholics, and to practice these principles in all our affairs.

Source: http://www.alcoholics-anonymous.org

(2001) suggested that AA should not be thought of as an alternative to therapy if the individual wanted to go beyond abstinence. He found only a weak gain to reported well-being by those attending AA.

An analysis of the difference between frequent AA attendees (at least three times a week) and non- or infrequent attendees (not attending or attending less than once a week) suggested that the frequent attendees were older, had more prior drug treatment and more arrests, and differed in the type and number of drugs used. However, being older may have affected the other categories. The groups did not differ in optimism/pessimism about their future. Despite the spiritual overtones of 12-Step programs, the groups did not differ in their religious involvement, including church attendance, ascribing religion as significant to their lives, and comfort with church groups (Brown et al., 2001).

Ellis and Schoenfeld (1990) note that the concept of "Divine Intervention by a Higher Power" is a central philosophy of AA, and God is mentioned in six of the twelve steps. While noting that AA has helped millions and is prominent in drug treatment programs, they also note that this emphasis on a Higher Power has turned away millions of addicts. Further, they question the right of a judge to make mandatory the attendance of an addict to a 12-Step program as this violates the separation of church and state. The concept of a Higher Power clearly involves religious principles and treatment often takes place in a public facility (this argument has been upheld by a federal court). Statements such as that in Step 6 indicate that individuals have no control over their growth and development and can therefore undermine addicts' ability to help themselves.

While agreeing with Ellis and Schoenfeld that AA represents a traditional Christian view of God, McCrady (1990) argues that eliminating the God part from AA treatment should be an empirical question. She believes that Ellis and Schoenfeld miss the point that AA primarily sees alcoholism as a "spiritual disease," and therefore sees the solution as spiritual. While not agreeing with the spiritual disease model of AA, she does note a couple of studies on the role of spirituality in behavior change. McCrady believes the problem with AA is not its spiritual emphasis, but its one-dimensional approach: "AA appears to view alcoholism as *a* disease, with certain characteristics, a certain, predictable course, and one route to change. The

model of alcoholism embodied in AA is at variance with contemporary understanding of drinking problems, which suggest that 'alcoholism' is best viewed as an umbrella term for a multivariate set of problems, some of which have classic disease characteristics, and some of which are characterized by different patterns of drinking, courses of the problem, and appropriate routes to change....Were AA members able to accept the notion of a multivariate rather than a univariate disorder, and accept that AA provides one of many routes to change, then the debate would be over" (p. 479).

Pharmacotherapy and Antabuse

While treatment of substance use can include pharmacology, it is generally agreed that it should also include psychosocial interventions (Moss, 1999; O'Brien & McKay, 2002). Typically, three goals motivate a pharmacological approach: 1) to reduce the withdrawal symptoms, 2) to alter the stimulus properties of the drug to reduce the drug-seeking behavior, and 3) to reduce the cravings for the substance. Examples of pharmacological treatment for reducing withdrawal symptoms include using chlordiazepoxide (Librium) for alcohol withdrawal, and nicotine polacrilex (nicotine gum) for nicotine withdrawal. Examples of altering the stimulus properties of drugs include using disulfiram (Antabuse) for alcoholism and methadone for opiate dependence. Examples of attenuation of cravings include the use of naltrexone for alcohol and methadone maintenance for opiate cravings (Moss, 1999). As an example we will focus on Antabuse, a second strategy type that takes an aversive approach to reducing the stimulus-seeking behaviors of the alcoholic.

When people drink alcohol (ethyl alcohol), an enzyme in the liver metabolizes it into a poisonous substance called acetaldehyde. The enzyme acetaldehyde dehydrogenase normally converts the acetaldehyde to acetic acid, which is used as an energy source by the body. The drug Antabuse antagonizes (blocks) the effects of acetaldehyde dehydrogenase, thereby allowing the levels of acetaldehyde to build up and create feelings of illness (Kalat, 2001; Hamilton & Timmons, 1990). As acetaldehyde concentrations rise, an acetaldehyde reaction is triggered that can consist of vasodilatation, throbbing of head and neck, sweating, nausea, vomiting, vertigo, chest pain, hypertension, and respiratory difficulties. This reaction can last between 30 minutes and several hours (Moss, 1999).

The unpleasant feelings associated with Antabuse are why it is used in treatment. The assumption is that the person will want to avoid the unpleasant effects and develop a learned aversion to alcohol consumption. This learned aversion and cessation of drinking will then lead to improvements in other areas of life, such as functioning at work and home (Maisto, Galizio, & Connors, 1995). Of course, the rational for treatment is not to make people sick, but to create a deterrent (Rawson et al., 2000). The goals for Antabuse treatment are 1) to resist obsessive impulses to drink, 2) to reduce the number of drinking days, and 3) to help people change life styles and give internal organs a chance to recuperate (Kristenson, 1995). However, Antabuse does not affect the underlying neurochemistry of cravings and alcohol dependence. With little affect on craving, the individual has to be strongly motivated or under external pressure to stop drinking (Anton, 2001).

Reviews of the effectiveness of Antabuse as a treatment are mixed. O'Brien and McKay (2000) indicate that studies looking at antidipsotropic medications (that create an unpleasant reaction) for alcohol show Antabuse to be no more effective than a placebo at reducing drinking. Yet Brewer et al. (2000) found that with one exception the thirteen controlled studies they reviewed showed Antabuse to have not only a statistical significance over control groups, but a large and obvious clinical one. The one controlled study that did not show significance concerned homeless alcoholics who did not show up regularly for treatment. In the researchers' view, a topic that reviewers did not especially note was the importance of supervision, or making sure the alcoholic took the medication.

Regardless of the effectiveness of Antabuse, many alcoholics are ambivalent about giving up drinking. They can, therefore, also be ambivalent about taking Antabuse (Brewer et al., 2000). If one becomes sick as a result of combining Antabuse and alcohol, one may be just as likely to give up the medication as the alcohol. One recommendation is that some sort of behavioral contracting occur, since poor compliance can be a major obstacle in the effectiveness of Antabuse (O'Brien & McKay, 2002).

Cognitive Behavior Therapy

Traditionally, there has been a separation between behavioral and cognitive approaches to therapy. Behavioral approaches have focused on the behavior of the individual. They evaluated the antecedent conditions (those coming before the behavior), what the behavioral outcome was, and what reinforced or punished the behavior. Classical conditioning, operant conditioning, and modeling are the three basic learning theories that evaluate the initiation, maintenance, and change of behavior. Little concern was given to mental state or consciousness. Cognitive theorists realized that behavior was affected by the person's thoughts and beliefs. The role of cognitive processes and social learning models was studied to see the effect on the initiation and maintenance of behavior (Rogers et al., 1996). Today more therapies reflect the integration of the two elements: that cognitions (thoughts) affect our behavior and that behavior can affect how we think.

From a cognitive-behavior perspective, drug use and abuse are learned like any other behavior. After repeated exposure to a drug one may find that it helps with coping or has pleasurable short-term effects. This is positively reinforcing and leads to repeating the behavior in similar situations. Treatment focuses on addressing the conditions that precipitate and maintain the behavior. This is seen as more effective than focusing on the substance itself. Treatment may also include skills training to help with deficits the individual has and help him or her cope better in high-risk situations (Kadden, 1999).

Drug Policy

ISSUES: How do various cultural traditions affect our drug policies? Which do you see as most useful or powerful? What is the relationship between drugs and crime? What is the relationship between drugs and violence? What issues should determine our drug policies? How helpful are drug policies?

So far, we have presented definitions, the rate of drug use in the population, the psychopharmacology of drugs, the causes of drug use, treatment strategies, and even a discussion of the social functions of substances. All of these topics illustrate the powerful presence of substance use in our society. This powerful presence has resulted in extensive policy debates, widely differing views, and significant policy shifts in how our laws and society in general approach the production, distribution, and use of drugs.*

The Development of American Drug Policy

An understanding of drug policy in the United States begins with three early American cultural traditions that still strongly affect discussions: libertarianism, mercantilism, and Puritan moralism. Libertarianism argues that government must have an extremely compelling motive for interfering in the personal lives of citizens. Such interference legitimately occurs only if a citizen's behavior is a significant risk to others (Mill, 1979). Consistent with libertarianism, early America had a strong tradition of mercantilism (policies designed to increase the wealth and power of a state/ country) and an open-market orientation that emphasized limited government interference in the production and distribution of desired goods and services. Nineteenth-century national drug policy was consistent with both libertarianism and the open market. While the federal government generally regulated the importation of drugs such as opium and cocaine, there were few regulations governing the distribution of these

and other drugs through the patent medicine industry (Belenko, 2000; Inciardi, 2001; Musto, 1999). Patent medicines were extensively advertised, and because they contained drugs such as opium and cocaine, drug use became integrated into routine American cultural behavior patterns (Musto, 1999).

Conflicting with both libertarianism and a mercantile approach is the Puritan moralist point of view. From this perspective, individual behaviors with the potential to negatively affect the community are seen as a social problem, and thus within the legitimate purview of community action (Cherrington, 1920; Schmidt, 1995). Puritan and other religious and moral traditions in early American history often viewed behavior such as substance use as destroying the individual and undermining the whole moral fabric of society, potentially causing the withdrawal of God's blessing from America.

American policy and political practice are often characterized by vigorous debate, strongly differing interests and traditions, and the attempt by one group to impose its views on the whole of a complex society. The historian David Musto (1999) characterized American society of the late nineteenth century as increasingly integrating highly addictive drugs into daily cultural and behavioral patterns. The late nineteenth century and early twentieth century saw major social reform movements focusing on meat packing, child labor, and the patent drug industry. One of the first successes of the early 20th century social reform movement was the passage of the Pure Food and Drug Act of 1906, which required the patent medicine industry to list product

*The Drug Policy section is taken with some adaptations and additions from McBride, D. C., VanderWaal, C. J., & Terry-McElrath, Y. M. (2003). The drugs-crime wars: Past, present and future directions in theory, policy and program interventions. In H. H. Brownstein & C. Crossland (Eds.), *Toward a drugs and crime research agenda for the 21st century* (pp. 97–162) (NCJ 194616). Washington, DC: U.S. Department of Justice, Office of Justice Programs, National Institute of Justice.

ingredients. Reformists argued that opiates, cocaine, marijuana, and alcohol were highly addictive and dangerous substances that caused violent behavior at worst and the abandonment of individual, family, or social responsibilities at best. The reform movement argued that society could never be at its best if citizens were addicted to powerful substances. The social reform movement grew in state legislatures and at the national level. After a number of states banned the sale or possession of many drugs, Congress passed the Harrison Act of 1914 and the Marihuana Tax Act of 1937. Through tax law, these two acts made the manufacture, sale, and possession of a variety of drugs, including opiates, cocaine, and marijuana, virtually illegal and initiated a strong national prohibitionist policy against commonly used over-the-counter medicines. This strongly prohibitionist approach continued through the 1950s with the Boggs Act of 1951 and the Narcotic Control Act of 1956, when mandatory minimum sentences for federal drug trafficking law violations were strengthened and arrests without a warrant for drug charges were made legal. This prohibitionist policy had a broad base of social, media, and political support.

The 1960s and 1970s represented a major cultural shift in the United States. For a wide variety of reasons, American society experienced a "drug revolution" during this era. There appeared to be an increase in the proportion of individuals using substances, as well as in the variety of psychoactive chemicals used. The evidence for this increase is seen in the number of drug-related arrests and the increase in drug use in the general population (Musto, 1999). During this era, drug policy initially shifted to a stronger treatment- and less punishment-oriented stance. In 1966, the Narcotic Addict Rehabilitation Act established the civil commitment system for federal offenders as an alternative to prosecution, and encouraged state and local governments to develop their own treatment programs. In 1970, the Comprehensive Drug Abuse Prevention and Control Act consolidated and replaced the patchwork of previous federal drug laws. The Act created the drug schedules in use today and initiated the so-called "War on Drugs"; it also changed some possession or causal transfer offenses from felonies to misdemeanors. This era may be considered a time when drug use was thought to be not only a legal problem, but also a medical and public health problem that should be addressed by treatment instead of incarceration.

However, due to the apparent increase in drug use evidenced by rising drug overdose cases and drug treatment admissions, a prohibitionist movement swept the nation in the 1970s. New York's so-called Rockefeller Drug Laws were passed in 1973, establishing mandatory prison sentences of up to 20 years for the sale of any amount of heroin or cocaine. The Anti-Drug Abuse Acts of 1986 and 1988 continued to emphasize law enforcement (although the 1988 Act did give more attention to treatment and prevention). In the 1990s yet another policy shift occurred, and treatment (including diversion into treatment from the criminal justice system) and prevention received increasing attention. Further, some states developed policies that basically decriminalized marijuana possession (removing jail/prison penalties) and reduced the harm of injecting drugs through needle exchange programs.

Essentially, the history of drug policy and debates about where it should move in the future can be broken down into five main approaches: prohibition, harm reduction, medicalization, legalization/regulation, and decriminalization (for an in-depth discussion, see McBride, Terry-McElrath, & Inciardi, 1999). Prohibition emphasizes severe penalties for the use, distribution, and production of illicit drugs. The basis of prohibition as a national policy is deterrence theory, which argues that if punishments are severe enough citizens will not use drugs. This view underlies support for mandatory minimum sentencing for the violation of drug laws. Harm reduction takes a public-health approach to reduce the risks and harms associated with illicit drug use. It emphasizes an educational approach, focusing on the risks of drug use, safer use practices, prevention, and treatment. Public health/harm reduction approaches may emphasize such procedures as needle exchange programs—to reduce the risk of infections (including HIV infection)—and offering treatment on demand. Medicalization calls for physician treatment of drug addicts and views substance abuse primarily as a medical issue. It argues that physicians, not politicians, are the best judges of which drugs should be used for the treatment of health problems. The successful public referendum movements to medicalize marijuana are an example of this approach. Legalization/regulation supports increased access to drugs through governmental regulation of these substances, with possible distribution of specific substances through government-controlled distribution channels. This approach argues that prohibition has been an abysmal failure, that current policy is not enforceable, and that illicit drug use continues at a fairly high rate. It holds that prohibition fills jails and prisons with non-violent offenders and corrupts the criminal justice system through bribery and highly selective law enforcement. Finally, decriminalization calls for a complete end to the use of criminal law to address individual drug use. This may (but not necessarily) imply a relatively open market approach to drug availability and use. This approach may recognize the harms drugs cause, but advocates argue that these harms are best dealt with by a public health and medical approach rather than by criminal law.

While the considerable debate about drug policy is heated and often distorted, there are at this time a number of key, and perhaps somewhat contradictory, elements about national policy. These include 1) a basic federal prohibitionist approach, with a recent reaffirmation of mandatory minimum sentencing for the violation of federal drug laws; 2) the medicalization of marijuana by 22 states; 3) the decriminalization of marijuana in at least 11 states; and 4) strong support in most states, and in the federal government, of diversion to treatment for non-violent drug offenders (see Chriqui et al., 2002). While there are certainly those who advocate the decriminalization and legalization of all drugs, state legislatures and voter referendums basically have limited these policies to the possession of small amounts of marijuana. Recent referendums held in some states indicate that voters are not willing to further decriminalize marijuana or define treatment as a constitutional right.

The current national drug policy is characterized by a complex interplay between a basic prohibitionistic approach and one of decriminalization and medicalization, with significant variance by state. While some states and communities have maintained a high prohibitionist (deterrence) approach for all drugs, other states have decriminalized or medicalized marijuana. Many of these states may also offer diversion to treatment for first-time marijuana offenders. On the other hand, many states are also increasing penalties for the possession of other drugs, such as ecstasy. While it is very difficult to predict the future, it is safe to say that the direction of national, and particularly state and local, drug policy is not clear. Drug policy remains a confusing, often contradictory, and very emotional issue for policy makers, legislatures, and the general public.

The Drugs-Crime Basis of National Drug Policy

Many observers have questioned the basis for the prohibitionist deterrence policy that characterized American drug policy during most of the last century. At one level, a strong argument could be made that substances such as alcohol are much more associated with individual and societal consequences than drugs like marijuana. Similarly, tobacco has been shown to be highly addictive and associated with shortened lives and very high costs in health care. In addition, the incidence and prevalence of alcohol and tobacco use is much higher than the use rates of any illicit drug (Johnston et al., 2002).

There may be a number of reasons that drugs less harmful than alcohol and tobacco are illegal. First, it should be noted that alcohol has historically, and fairly universally, been integrated into a wide variety of human cultural patterns. People use alcohol in many rituals, bonding experiences, and personal, group, and national celebrations. It is our longest-used psychoactive substance. While tobacco is of much more recent universal distribution, it has been a part of wide human cultural practices for over four hundred years. The universal availability of such drugs as opiates, cocaine, and marijuana is of much more recent origin. They have not been integrated into a wide variety of cultural and behavioral experiences. A second and perhaps driving reason for current drug policy is the perceived relationship between drug use and criminal behavior in general and violent behavior in particular.

The Drugs and Crime Relationship

The types of crimes that are associated with drug use range from violent (such as murder and aggravated assault) to acquisitive (burglary, forgery, fraud, and deception) to specific drug-law violations. In addition, crimes such as bribery and corruption are often seen as related to drug use as a result of drug policy prohibitions. Traditionally, discussions of the drugs-crime relationship have focused primarily on violent crime; however, it is important to recognize the variety of criminal acts associated with drug use. The general conclusion of almost three decades of research on the relationship between drug use and crime has been that there is a clearly significant statistical relationship between the two phenomena (Austin & Lettieri, 1976; Dorsey & Zawitz, 1999; Gandossy, Williams, Cohen, &

Harwood, 1980; McBride & McCoy, 1993). Research indicates extensive drug use among arrested populations, a high level of criminal behavior among drug users, and fairly high correlations between drug use and delinquency/crime in the general population. Research also indicates significant differences in the relationship in terms of drug type as well as type of crime.

The changes in drug policy from a relatively open market approach in the 19th century to the prohibition policy of the 20th century were driven by concerns for public safety and the perception of a direct drugs-violence relationship (Brownstein, 1996, 2000). For example, the drug policy reform movement (changing from legal markets to strict prohibition) of the early 1900s was accompanied by horror stories. These focused on exaggerated claims of criminal behavior as a consequence of drug use. In this literature, there was a particular emphasis on horrific crime (including rape), with minority group members often portrayed as the drug users engaged in violent behavior. Musto (1999; see also Belenko, 2000; Hickman, 2000) documents the public concern (perhaps obsession) of the time with Chinese opiate use, African American cocaine use, and the use of marijuana by Mexicans. The creation of the Narcotics Bureau in 1930 led to a media distribution industry focused on violence associated with drug use, "documenting" the criminal consequences of such activity (see Anslinger & Tompkins, 1953; Inciardi, 2001). Among the best known of these efforts were the films *The Man with the Golden Arm* in 1955 (purporting to depict the effects of heroin use/injection) and *Reefer Madness* in 1936 (showing the supposed behavioral consequences of marijuana use).

Drugs and Violence

In 1985, Goldstein provided what has become the perspective most commonly used to examine the relationship between drug use and violence. Essentially, he argued for a tripartite scheme, where "psychopharmacological violence" could result directly or indirectly from the biochemical behavior of the drug user; "economic compulsive violence" could relate to behavior/crimes committed to obtain money for drugs; and "systemic violence" could emerge in the context of drug distribution, control of markets, the process of obtaining drugs, and/or the social ecology of drug distribution/use areas.

Some researchers have concluded that there is minimal evidence for the psychopharmacological impact of drugs on violence (Resignato, 2000). However, Pihl and Peterson (1995) reviewed a wide range of studies on the issue and concluded that alcohol and drugs can be psychopharmacologically related to violent acts because the release of dopamine is associated with reductions in inhibitory anxiety about the consequences of aggressive behavior. In addition, they argue that psychopharmacological interference occurs in relation to cognitive processing of the consequences of potentially violent situations. It should be noted that these authors believe that the evidence for psychopharmacological associations of alcohol use with violence are much higher than for other drugs.

Other indications point to the environment as a more powerful explanatory variable than the psychopharmacological properties of drugs in explaining the drugs-violence relationship (Brownstein, 2000; Fishbein, 1998; Parker & Auerhahn, 1998). In terms of economic compulsive and systemic violence, Collins (1990) as well as Fagan and Chin (1990) argue that crack selling is the main contributor to the drugs-violence relationship. Specifically, their research found violence (mostly robbery) emerging from the need to obtain money to purchase drugs (predominately crack). Fagan and Chin suggest that the drugs-violence relationship also emerges as a part of the subculture of violence.

While concern about the drugs-violence relationship may drive policy decisions, research indicates a stronger relationship between drug use and property crime. In a 1994 study, Roth argued that drug users commit more property crime than violent crime. De Li, Priu, and MacKenzie (2000) examined the relationship between drug use and property and violent crime in a population of probationers in Virginia. Results indicated that drug *use* had a positive association with property crime whereas drug *dealing* had an association with both violent and property crime (though the relationship was stronger for property crime). The analysis also showed an interactive effect involving drug use, drug dealing, and violent and property crime. Among juveniles, Linnever and Shoemaker (1995) found that arrests for possessing and selling drugs were related to the rate of property crime arrests. However, juvenile robbery arrest rates were related only to drug sales arrests (not possession). A National Institute of Justice (NIJ) *Research in Brief* supports such research, stating that "illegal drugs and violence are linked primarily through drug marketing" (Roth, 1994, p. 1).

The Direction of the Drugs-Crime Relationship: Searching for a Cause

As White and Gorman (2000) note, there are three main explanatory models for grappling with the drugs-crime relationship:

- Drug use causes or leads to crime.
- Crime causes or leads to drug use.
- The relationship is coincidental or is based in a common etiology.

Based on their evaluations of the research supporting and/or refuting each of the three main models, White and Gorman conclude that "one single model cannot account for the drug-crime relationship. Rather, the drug-using, crime committing population is heterogeneous, and there are multiple paths that lead to drug use and crime" (White and Gorman, 2000, p. 151).

At a popular, and sometimes governmental, level, the drugs-crime relationship is often clearly causal: drug use causes crime. Models such as Goldstein's tripartite scheme (1985) have been used to illustrate this approach, specifying psychopharmacological, economic, and systemic causes of violence. As noted previously, arguments focusing on the psychopharmacological properties of various drugs cite research indicating that stimulants may increase aggressiveness and paranoia, and that many drugs have a strong disinhibiting effect that could seriously interfere with judgment (Pihl & Peterson, 1995). Economic arguments posit that the cost of drugs, coupled with high unemployment among drug users, results in the commission of property crimes to support drug use. Sixteen percent of jail inmates committed their current offense to get money for drugs (Wilson, 2000). Those arguing for a systemic approach maintain that drug use simply has a sub-cultural relationship with criminal behavior: because it is illegal, drug use essentially involves one in criminal subcultures that often lead to future deviance (Fagan & Chin, 1990).

On the other hand, some researchers argue that a level of general delinquency often precedes drug use (Elliott et al., 1989). The sub-cultural explanation is used here as well: involvement in criminal activity and/or subcultures provides "the context, the reference group, and the definitions of a situation that are conducive to

subsequent involvement with drugs" (White & Gorman, 2000, p. 174; see also White, 1990). Individuals with deviant lifestyles and/or personalities may also use substances for the purposes of self-medication (Khantzian, 1985; White & Gorman, 2000) or to provide a "reason" for deviant acts (Collins, 1993; White & Gorman, 2000). While Apospori and associates concluded that the relationship between early delinquency and subsequent drug use was relatively weak (1995), Bui, Ellickson, and Bell (2000) found what they called a modest relationship between delinquency in grade 10 and greater drug use in grade 12 and, importantly, no significant differences by ethnicity. Hser, Anglin, and Powers (1993) found that addicts who stopped using drugs were less likely to engage in criminal behavior over a 24-year follow-up period.

One of the traditions of research on the drugs-crime relationship has emphasized that drug use and crime may not have a direct causal relationship (White & Gorman, 2000), but may emerge in the same contextual milieu and have the same antecedent variables such as poor social support systems, difficulty in school, and membership in a deviant peer group (Hamid, 1998; Inciardi et al., 1993; Lurigio & Swartz, 2000). This issue is best examined by reviewing some of the conceptual models that have focused on the environmental contexts of drug use and other deviant behaviors.

While recognizing the existence of a wide range of theories focusing on human behavior, the ecosystems theory is used as an overall framework for examining the drugs-crime relationship. Within this framework, the concept of social capital has emerged recently as a promising approach to breaking the drugs-crime cycle.

Ecosystems Theory

Human behavior, including participation in drug use or criminal activities, takes place within the broader social context: circumstances, social norms, cultural conditions, and interactions with others (Kirst-Ashman, 2000). Ecosystems theory acts as an organizing framework (as opposed to a definitive theory of behavior or development), calling for an active awareness that the interaction of biology, interpersonal relationships, culture, and legal, economic, organizational, and political forces affects an individual's behavior (Beckett & Johnson, 1995; Kirst-Ashman, 2000).

Social Capital

Social capital is a relatively new theoretical approach with the potential to explain many complex relationships. Today, the concept of social capital is increasingly used to understand the extent of community interaction and its effects. Social capital was originally defined by Coleman (1988) as the quality and depth of relationships between people in a family and community. Putnam (1993) developed the concept to include "the networks, norms and trust that facilitate coordination and cooperation for mutual benefit" (p. 2). The World Bank Group (2000) modified the definition to include "the institutions, relationships, and norms that shape the quality and quantity of a society's interactions" (p. 1). Finally, Rose (2000) emphasized the utility of social capital by defining it as "the stock of networks (relationships between individuals) that are used to produce goods and services in society" (p. 1,422). Increasing evidence shows that social capital, and the social cohesion and normative environment enabling its development, is critical for community and individual quality of life.

The concept of social capital can be applied to breaking the drugs-crime relationship in several ways. First, high levels of social capital in communities may play a role in preventing drug use and other deviant behavior through the presence of strong formal and informal social bonds and networks. The presence of anti-drug use norms within more informal structures (such as family networks, communities of faith, and neighborhoods) may contribute to lower drug use rates. Conversely, lower levels of community social capital may be associated with greater access to drugs, and with more lenient social norms and lowered social controls regarding the use of drugs and association with drug users.

Second, drug users who have recently entered the criminal justice system may find that the presence of high levels of social capital in a community results in a stronger network of diversion options. This could be due, in part, to formal and informal network interest in restorative justice (described in the next section) as opposed to punishment approaches to crime intervention.

Third, once individuals are incarcerated, high levels of social capital within an offender's home community might better preserve networks of support for reintegration upon the offender's release. For example, previous offenders might more easily obtain jobs, receive support for continued sobriety, and/or receive reinforcement for socially appropriate behaviors.

Finally, communities with high levels of social capital might have strong formal (vertical) **social networks** in the form of coalitions or collaboratives working to reduce substance use. Vertical social networks go from local community level to state, regional, or national organizations. Such agency connections may help focus the community on policy development related to drug prevention and treatment systems in homes, schools, and businesses. Such strong, integrated social networks may offer a larger range of services and may also develop more formal horizontal relationships with other service providers, thereby improving the coordinated delivery of services and care to those with drug or alcohol problems. Horizontal social networks go along parallel lines. That is at the same level in a community. Organizations with horizontal relationships can access more local resources to address local problems and therefore increase the probability of progress.

Collaborative Approaches to Breaking the Drugs-Crime Cycle

Social capital concepts can also provide suggestions on strategies for breaking the drugs-crime relationship. The first step may be to develop programmatic interventions designed to ensure that neither community safety nor offender accountability be compromised in any way, particularly for violent and chronic offenders. However, as noted previously, drug-related crimes exist along a continuum of severity from index crimes, such as murder and armed robbery, to comparatively minor offenses, such as non-violent drug possession. As such, interventions such as drug treatment should be provided along a continuum as well. Drug-involved offenders who commit serious crimes might receive drug treatment services in a significantly restrictive prison-based therapeutic community. Non-violent drug-using offenders might receive sentencing and ongoing supervision from a drug court (see below) and participate in minimally restrictive victim-offender mediation, along with mandated attendance in intensive outpatient drug treatment services. Many jurisdictions struggle to integrate substance abuse treatment into their criminal justice systems, which often view such efforts as adjunct services rather than primary, integrated components. Appropriate client selection, assessment, and placement have been identified as critical components of the treatment continuum (Simpson & Curry, 1997–1998; Taxman, 1998; Farabee et al., 1999). Substance abuse problems are usually enmeshed within a wide variety of other issues. Thus, comprehensive assessment is necessary in order to successfully address alcohol and other drug problems.

The treatment plan should be based on the client's identified needs, problems, strengths, and resources as identified in the assessment process, and should use assessment information to match the client with the best treatment modality and level of risk (Inciardi, 1994; McLellan et al., 1997; see also Taxman, 2000). While clients should participate in the planning process to improve treatment compliance, they cannot dictate treatment goals. At the conclusion of intake and assessment, intake officers generally have the option of dismissing the case with no further action, using diversion programs, or referring the client to further justice system processing. If a decision is made to formally refer an offender to court for further processing, judges will generally use the assessment and arrest report as well as other facts to determine disposition and, if necessary, sentencing. In most jurisdictions, fact-finding and adjudication take place in conventional court systems. However, in an attempt to play a more active role in breaking the link between substance use and crime, the judicial system developed the drug court.

A drug court takes responsibility for less serious drug-using offenders, and often uses an intensive supervision and treatment program based on graduated sanctions (described below). Drug courts are partnerships between justice system personnel (prosecution, defense, and judge), treatment specialists, and other social service personnel (National Association of Drug Court Professionals, 2000). Drug courts allow judges to take a more active role than that provided by previous options (such as mandated lengthy sentences) as well as partner with community resources and agencies. Judges draw on a variety of professionals in assessing needs and recommending services and are then actively involved in deciding what services are to be received. Judges also monitor compliance and apply sanctions when a lack of compliance is evident.

Effectiveness of Drug Treatment with Offenders

Drug courts may be an excellent example of the appli-

cation of social capital. They draw on and integrate a wide variety of social, health, and human service agencies and facilitate their cooperative interaction in providing treatment services. Evaluations of drug courts have been mixed. Concern has been expressed over evaluation research methodology, wide variations in populations served, and lack of consistent standards for assessment and referral (Inciardi, McBride, & Rivers, 1996; U.S. General Accounting Office, 1997). Despite these concerns, evidence still points to a positive impact for drug courts: high treatment retention, increased sobriety, and reductions in recidivism have been noted in many drug court locations; in addition, savings in jail costs can be substantial (Drug Strategies, 1997; Cooper, 1997; Harrell, Cavanagh, & Roman, 2000).

To be successful, drug courts do require a long-term outlook, significant initial resource allocation, and available treatment slots (Platt, 2001). Additional research is needed to address the significant issues critics have raised regarding scientific enthusiasm for drug courts. Drug treatment for offenders is being taken seriously by even the strongest advocates of incarceration for drug possession and use. Flooded court dockets, overcrowded prisons, and high recidivism rates of drug-using offenders have convinced even those most skeptical of treatment that it is impossible to incarcerate all the illegal drug users in the nation. Scientific research on the brain is offering clues into the nature of drug dependence, leading most to agree with the conclusions of NIDA: "Prolonged use of these drugs eventually changes the brain in fundamental and long-lasting ways, explaining why people cannot just quit on their own, why treatment is essential" (Leshner, 2001). This view has also been adopted by the Office of National Drug Control Policy (ONDCP), which states that "chronic, hardcore drug use is a disease, and anyone suffering from a disease needs treatment" (ONDCP, 2001, p. 1).

Recognizing both the public safety benefits from breaking the cycle of drug use and crime and the potential safety risks of allowing drug-addicted criminals on the streets (Taxman, 2000), the ONDCP's National Drug Control Strategy advocates a two-pronged approach to the problem: punish criminals for their behaviors while mandating sanctions-based drug treatment. However, questions remain as to which treatment programs are effective, and for which drug users.

Conclusion

Drugs are an interesting social issue because almost everyone uses them and they are embedded within the cultural and religious traditions of many societies. How is society to deal with the negative outcomes of drug use? Do we deal with users by continuing to fill our prisons, or should there be alternative programs? Of course, a list of questions in this area could go on for pages, but we would still have to deal with the concept that humans are pleasure-seeking organisms and drugs provide a biochemical reward. It is hoped that this chapter has broadened your understanding of the concepts that attempt to define what drives drug use and the policies for managing it.

Response

A View from the Front Lines

by Dewey Murdick

I am the chief analyst of the Berrien County Forensic Laboratory, which serves a population of approximately 210,000 people in southwestern Michigan. The laboratory, established in 1972, is unique in that it is a cooperative effort between Andrews University, which operates and manages the laboratory, and the county of Berrien, which is the funding agency. Thus it is one of a handful of U.S. drug analysis laboratories that is not a division within a police department. During the 15 plus years I have been in charge of the laboratory, I have made several hundred court appearances in the local state and federal court systems. The laboratory currently analyzes approximately 7,000 samples a year, originating from 1,800–1,900 police complaints or incidents. Because I am employed by Andrews University and believe that a university has an obligation to engage in the discussion of current relevant topics, I have on numerous occasions taught classes and engaged in debates related to drugs and drug policy. With this background, I have been asked to comment on drugs and drug policy. Several different positions can be taken, including those of ethics, morals, and paternalism. I am going to argue from the position of societal cost.

Since we are discussing the concept of the state attempting to control citizen behavior, one relevant question should be considered: What justification permits those who lead a society to proscribe behaviors on the part of its free citizens? I believe the best answer is based on the concept of the reduction of harm or risk of harm to the citizenry. If you, a member of a segment of the population, engage in a particular type of activity that causes your segment to create more mayhem than your statistical numbers would justify, then it is proper for the society to in some way restrict that activity because your actions place me and others, as non-participants, at greater risk. Drunk driving is an excellent case in point. Consider the following points:

- Approximately 1.4 million drivers were arrested in 2001 for driving under the influence of alcohol or narcotics. This is an arrest rate of 1 for every 137 licensed drivers in the United States.
- There were 17,419 alcohol-related fatalities in the United States in 2002, 41% of the total fatal crashes.
- The 17,419 fatalities in alcohol-related crashes during 2002 represent an average of one alcohol-related fatality every 30 minutes. An average of one person received an alcohol-related traffic injury every two minutes. (http://www.michigan.gov/msp/0,1607,7-123-1589_1711_4587-49577--,00.html)

Drunk drivers create more mayhem than their representation justifies.

With regard to substance abuse the numbers are much more

appalling. According to results from the 2004 National Survey on Drug Use and Health, the numbers of controlled substance users (those who had used drugs in the 30 days prior to the survey interview) in the United States are described this way:

Ecstasy	450,000
Cocaine	2.0 million
Marijuana	14.6 million
Any Illicit drug	**19.1 million**

If we single out cocaine, this would mean that cocaine users represent 0.8% of the adult population (http://oas.samhsa.gov/NSDUH/2k4NSDUH/2k4results/2k4results.htm). Of those arrested for the violent crimes of murder, rape, and assault, these percentages tested positive for recent cocaine usage:

Atlanta, GA	37.1%
Dallas County, TX	24.2%
Denver, CO	27.1%
Detroit, MI	22.2%
Miami, FL	38.1%
Manhattan Borough, NY	36.0%

www.ncjrs.org/pdffiles1/nij/193013.pdf

Note that the arrests were not drug related but were a consequence of violence perpetrated on others. In the case of those arrested for property crimes in these same jurisdictions, recent cocaine use is double the percentages for violent crimes. These data make drug-related use a front and center issue for anyone interested in public safety and property issues. "In 2002, the estimated number of persons aged 12 or older needing treatment for an illicit drug problem was 7.7 million (3.3 percent of the total popula-

tion)....The majority of these costs are productivity losses, particularly those related to incarceration, crime careers, drug abuse related illness, and premature death" (http://www.whitehousedrugpolicy.gov/prevent/workplace/health.html). Moreover, drug abusers are often uninsured or under-insured and as a result place great strain on the health industry. Recent drug usage is a significant factor in domestic violence and child abuse cases, and is implicated in most suicides. With these factors it is easy to see why we have an American war on drugs.

America's War on Drugs is not without its own flaws. One argument is that all wars have as a consequence collateral damage. Collateral damage refers to the fact that as a result of the prosecution of the war, innocent bystanders are unfortunately targeted through either malice or negligence on the part of the combatants, by bad data, or simply by being in the wrong place at the wrong time. In the case of search warrants, police agencies attempt to minimize collateral damage by using an excessive show of force. However, not everyone whose home is invaded by an army of darkly dressed, intimidating individuals is immediately cowed. Hence, there have been cases of individuals shot and killed in their own homes in which no drugs or drug paraphernalia were discovered. Their only crime was a failure to immediately comply with the order to drop their weapons (example: Donald Scott, October 2, 1992, Ventura County, California; for further information on this case, go to http://www.saveourguns.com/scott001.htm). Another argument has to do with cost. Tax dollars are

a zero sum game. Billions of dollars are spent annually on the prosecution of this three-decade-long war with questionable results, taking limited tax dollars away from other important areas of social interest.

A third argument is that as a result of the prosecution of the War on Drugs, the United States has one of the largest prisoner populations as a percentage of the overall population of any nation. As of mid 2004, 2,131,180 prisoners (one of every 243 U.S. residents) were being held in federal or state prisons or in local jails. The War on Drugs appears to some to be racist because when the above data is broken down by race, one of 20 black males but only one of 139 white males are incarcerated (http://www.ojp.usdoj.gov/bjs/prisons.htm).

A fourth argument is that the War on Drugs is corrupting to both the police and the prosecutors who pursue substance abuse. I have winced at some of the civil forfeitures in my own jurisdiction. In at least one case, the victim was shaken down literally for about $2,500 because to fight for the seized $10,000 would cost her $3,300. In another case a defendant's house was seized under a zero tolerance policy. The defendant was never implicated as dealing drugs, but they had inherited a house that had become a debt-free homestead, and it became a target too good for the prosecutor's office to pass up. Those fighting the War on Drugs can come to believe themselves to be the judge, jury, and executioner of those whose behavior they perceive to be out of bounds.

The essential problem with drugs and drug policy for the citizenry is that the two opposing forces—those who are dedicated to the eradication of drugs and those who wish for a more laissez-faire public attitude—alternately occupy the media stage and the public is swayed first by one group and then by the other. Both sets of arguments appear reasonable on their own merit, but when taken together in context the issue is significantly more complex.

In the end I believe the arguments of laissez-faire will lose out because the issue is being abducted by lawyers. The vehicle for this abduction is the increasing risk adverseness in the U.S. population coupled with the tendency to litigate. Nearly all controlled substances distort perceptions of time and space during and sometime after their use. In a society that is increasingly complex and technological, this will always mean that the average substance user is an impaired person when compared with the average non-drug user (i.e., more accident prone). In addition, because of the high recidivism rate among controlled substance abusers, there is always the fear that once a substance abuser, always a substance abuser. Failure to test employees will be considered a prima fascia case of negligence; potential liability will therefore force employers to make random drug tests as part of employment. With the exception of entertainers whose drug habits can sometimes enhance their careers, drug users will of necessity be forced into professions and careers that are usually associated with the under-classes and that pose little or no risk to the population. The uninsurability of these users will make them wards of the state, which will make them appear more and more as parasites.

In conclusion, I believe drugs and drug policy will become moot for policy makers through the process of civil litigation.

Discussion Questions

1. Should people use drugs/substances to help alter their moods? If so, when? How much mood alteration is acceptable? Which drugs are allowable?
2. Besides mood alteration, what reasons do people have for using drugs?
3. Who should determine whether someone has a drug problem?
4. Which perception of drug use (immoral, disease, or maladaptive) makes the most sense to you? Why?
5. Why do you think some drugs are legalized (e.g., alcohol and tobacco) while others are not?
6. Should governments become involved in people's drug use? Why or why not? To what extent?
7. Is it reasonable to expect people to stop using drugs? Why or why not?
8. Should drug offenders get treatment, prison, both, or neither? Why? What should society do if prisons become overcrowded with drug offenders?
9. Who should bear the cost of drug use in America (or other societies)? Consider two examples: 1) the prison sentence of a marijuana user who has committed no crime other than use, and 2) an individual who kills another in a car accident while under the influence of alcohol.
10. What concepts should drive drug policy?

Related Readings

Levinthal, C. F. (2002). *Drugs, behavior, and modern society* (3rd ed.). Boston: Allyn & Bacon.
Maisto, S. A., Galizio, M., & Connors, G. J. (1999). *Drug use and abuse* (3rd ed.). Belmont, CA: Wadsworth.
Peele, S. (1995). *Diseasing of America.* San Francisco: Jossey-Bass Publishers.
Rasmussen, S. (2000). *Addiction treatment: Theory and practice.* Thousand Oaks, CA: Sage Publications.

Related Web Sites

Club Drugs.org: http://www.clubdrugs.org
D.A.R.E. (Drug Abuse Resistance Education): http://www.dare.co
DRCNet Online Library of Drug Policy: http://www.druglibrary.org
National Institutes of Health—National Institute on Alcohol Abuse and Alcoholism: http://www.niaaa.nih.gov
NIDA (National Institute on Drug Abuse): http://www.drugabuse.gov
ONDCP (Office of National Drug Control Policy): http://www.whitehousedrugpolicy.gov
SAMHSA (Substance Abuse & Mental Health Services Administration): http://www.samhsa.gov
Stop Drugs.org: http://www.stopdrugs.org
U.S. Department of Health & Human Services and SAMHSA's National Clearinghouse for Alcohol & Drug Information: http://www.health.org

Related Movies/Videos

28 Days (2000) with Sandra Bullock
Blow (2001) with Johnny Depp and Penelope Cruz
Clean and Sober (1988) with Michael Keaton and Kathy Baker
Traffic (2001) with Benicio Del Toro and Michael Douglas
When a Man Loves a Woman (1994) with Andy Garcia and Meg Ryan

VIOLENCE

Alina M. Baltazar, Duane C. McBride, and Jonathan R. Cook

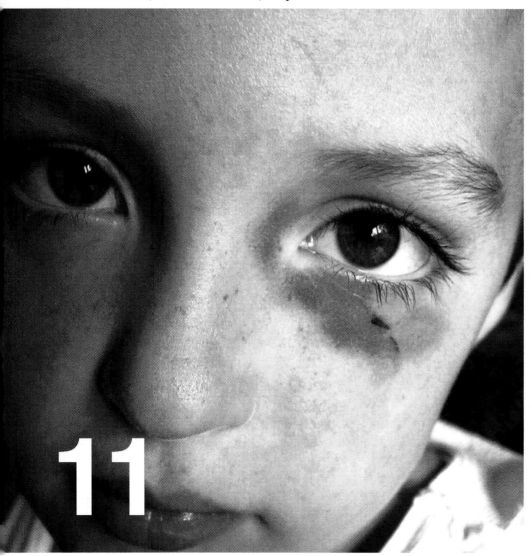

11

Chapter Outline

On November 25, 2001, in Pensacola, Florida, firefighters raced to a house fire where they found Terry Lee King bludgeoned to death in his living room recliner. Meanwhile, Terry's two sons—Alex (12 years old) and Derek (13 years old)—hid in the woods for two nights. The boys then confessed to family friend Ricky Marvin Chavis, a 40-year-old convicted pedophile, that they had beaten their father with a baseball bat and then set the house on fire to cover up the evidence. Chavis had both boys shower and turn themselves in to the police. The boys confessed to murdering their father, but later added that Chavis had been involved as well. Alex said that Chavis was his lover, and that Chavis had told the boys they could live with him if their father wasn't around.

A review of the boys' childhood revealed a life of instability and abandonment. Their parents never married and their father was unable to support them financially, so they were sent to live in a crisis home for children in 1994. The following year the boys were put in foster homes. Alex returned to live with his father a month later. Derek had been taken in by a high school principal who took him to church regularly. After spending six years with his foster parents, Derek became too hard for them to handle and thus also returned to live with his father.

Derek was home for a short time before he got exasperated with how his father was treating Alex, and he promised to protect him from the verbal and physical abuse. Their father told a friend he thought the boys were plotting something and he planned to put them in separate bedrooms and sleep in the living room. Just three hours later, Terry King fell asleep in the recliner in his living room. By his own admission, Derek hit his father in the head 10 times. When firefighters arrived, the fire had not yet spread to the living room where Terry Lee King was found dead. Why did these boys feel their only option was to kill their father? Was it their years of instability or feelings of abandonment? Did they feel Chavis was the only person who could provide them with stability and security? How did the sexual relationship with a 40-year-old man affect the 12-year-old boy? Was the boys' home a violent one? The boys say their father mentally abused them, but they were housed, clothed, and fed by Terry, and were disciplined by him only when they had done something wrong. Were their actions precipitated by immaturity combined with access to a weapon? Or was a combination of all these factors the cause?

What should be done with children who commit the unthinkable crime of murder? The King boys were tried as adults. A jury found them guilty of second-degree murder, declining to convict them of first-degree murder. Alex and Derek did not show any visible reaction to the verdict. Chavis was acquitted of being involved in the murder, but would be tried for molesting Alex King.

A judge later overturned the conviction, reportedly because he did not think the evidence supported a second-degree murder conviction. Rosie O'Donnell—famous comedian, talk show host, and actress—hired lawyers to protest the original verdict. The boys later pled guilty to third-degree murder and arson. Alex King received 7 years and Derek King received 8 years in a juvenile detention center.

The King brothers are not the first early adolescents to serve long prison sentences under Florida law. Lionel Tate was 12 years old when he killed a 6-year-old friend, Tiffany Eunick, by imitating wrestling moves he had seen on television. At 14 he was convicted of first-degree murder and was sentenced to mandatory life in prison. This prompted a national public outcry that this sentence was too harsh for a child.

After Tate's trial, Nathaniel Brazill was tried as an adult at 14 for shooting his teacher Barry Grunow. The jury convicted him of second-degree murder. The judge sentenced Brazill to 28 years.

Above information from Steinhaus (2002).

Introduction

From entertainment to nightly news coverage to politics, violence sells. It increases game sales, media ratings, and movie attendance, and has become an integral part of our daily lives and basic cultural behavioral patterns. We may be appalled by violence, attracted to viewing violence (as suggested by media ratings), or actually participate in violent rituals like hazing. The issue of violence and violent crimes routinely becomes a significant part of political campaigns. Politicians at every level—particularly sheriffs, district attorneys, and judges—campaign on platforms of taking a strong stand against violence and severely punishing those who engage in violent crime. In this chapter, our objective is to provide an overview of violence in contemporary American culture by examining research and theories of violence in sociology and psychology. The issues we address involve three major areas:

- How is violence perceived? How does society help determine what violence is? What are common forms of violence?
- What are some of the etiological views of violence? The chapter covers general cultural issues, socialization into violent behavior, personality variables, **socio-demographic research** on perpetrators and victims of violence, social-cultural explanations, and economics.
- How can violence be reduced? The chapter covers social and cultural change, economic opportunities, punishment, gun control, and programmatic intervention.

What Is Violence?

ISSUES: How is violence defined? What do you think of this definition? Why are some forms of violence socially acceptable and others not?

Philosophers and theologians who have imagined the ideal human society—a paradise or utopia—generally portray human existence as free from conflict (Brunschwig & Lloyd, 2000). While a noble ideal, it has never proven true in a human society. A sampling of human experience shows that conflict is quite prevalent in all aspects of human relationships. A common expression of conflict is violence or aggression. Aggressive behavior is becoming an increasingly prevalent method for resolving conflict. Why are human beings aggressive and violent?

Many religions see human life as a battleground where good and evil continuously conflict. Darwin believed that animals, including humans, compete for space, food, and reproductive access in an environment of scarcity with the strongest or fittest winning access to needed resources and the right to reproduce. Thomas Hobbes, a 17th-century philosopher, believed that human beings, if allowed to exist in their natural state, are essentially brutes. He felt that social law

and order helped curb our natural aggressive instincts. The famous psychologist Sigmund Freud believed that human beings are born with two equally powerful instincts. The first, Eros, is the instinct towards life, and the second, Thanatos, is the instinct towards death. Freud believed that aggressive energy is natural and must be released for healthy functioning.

Approximately a decade ago it was believed that an abusive environment was the cause of violence in individuals. More recent findings suggest that aggressive tendencies are present in infancy, implying a prenatal influence or source (Holden, 2000). We could ask whether aggression is biological—can we trace violent behavior to physiology?—or environmental. However, such a dichotomy would reduce the richness of what is almost certainly a combination of biological and environmental influences.

Human beings living in large complex societies may be socially compelled to limit conflicts, or to resolve them through a series of laws, court systems, and other mediating processes. However, while we may be able to reduce conflict and violence, data consistently show that no human society has been able to eliminate them. It appears that conflict is an unavoidable, although regrettable, circumstance of human life.

Thus, it is important to understand the forms of violence human beings engage in, the causes of this violence, and what society does to ameliorate the levels of violence that exist.

Forms of Violence

ISSUES: How does violence against the self differ from violence directed towards others, or does it? Who is at risk for becoming a victim of violence? Why do you think various groups are more at risk than other groups? Is society as violent as the media portrays?

Violence takes many forms, some of which are parts of other issues discussed in this text, such as school violence in the education chapter, domestic violence and sexual assault in the feminism chapter, and sexual victimization in the sexuality chapter. It is recommended that you refer to those sections as needed. In this chapter we will consider other common forms of violence, such as violence against self, violence directed toward various age groups, hate crimes, and violence in the workplace. These forms have significant consequences for victims and family members. It is hoped that you will look beyond the statistics and facts and begin to see the human faces affected by violence.

Violence against Self

- Suicide was the cause of death for 31,655 Americans in 2002 (National Center for Health Statistics, 2005).
- There are one and a half times more deaths attributable to suicide than to homicide (National Center for Injury Prevention and Control, 2002).
- White males and females accounted for 90% of all suicides (NCHS National Vital Statistics, 1999, as cited by the National Center for Injury Prevention and Control, 2002).
- In 2001, men accounted for 85% of suicides among those over 65 (National Center for Injury Prevention and Control, 2005).

Suicide

While a lifelong risk, suicide can occur as early as 10 years old. Suicide is the third leading cause of death for people ages 15 to 24 years old, followed by unintentional injury and homicide. For children 10 to 14 years old, the suicide rate increased by 109% between 1980 and 1997. The rate for African American males ages 15 to 19 increased 105% from 1980 through 1996. People younger than 25 accounted for 14% of all suicides in 1999 (NCHS National Vital Statistics System, 1999, as cited by the National Center for Injury Prevention and Control, 2002).

The actual number of suicides may be hard to determine. Some who commit suicide try to make the death look natural; conversely, some deaths ruled as suicide may have been murders made to look like suicide. Regardless of the accurate statistic, the rate has tripled since the 1950s (King, 1999). The risk for suicide is highest among white males, who accounted for 72% of all suicides (NCHS National Vital Statistics, 1999, as cited by the National Center for Injury Prevention and Control, 2002). Males are more likely to complete a suicide and females are more likely to make an unsuccessful attempt. This is because males are more likely to use a gun, which is more lethal than the pills women often use (King, 1999). While the vast majority do not follow through, almost all teenagers at some point think of suicide as a solution to a current problem. King (1999) notes that suicidal teens are usually not mentally ill—they just want their psychological pain to stop. Suicide may be used as a cry for help.

Research has identified risk factors and protective factors relating to suicide, as are listed in Table 11.1 (National Center for Injury Prevention and Control, 2005).

Though suicide is usually associated with troubled teens, older Americans have a higher suicide rate than any other age group. We may not be aware of this problem for a couple of reasons. First, the death of an older individual does not shock society like that of a young person. We expect a certain developmental order to life, and we relate death to old age. There is also a social stigma associated with suicide. When the suicide victim is an older individual, the family often does not discuss the facts related to the death.

The high suicide rate among older Americans reflects a fairly recent trend. The decade of the 1980s was the first since the 1940s to have an increase in suicide among older adults (*American Journal of Public Health*, 1991, as cited by the National Center for Injury Prevention and Control, 2002). Over the past two decades, the largest increase has been among those 80 to 84 years of age. People are living longer, but are not always healthier. The suicide rate in 1998 for men in this age group was 52 per 100,000 (NCHS National Vital Statistics System, 1999, as cited by the National Center for Injury Prevention and Control, 2002). Those who have access to a gun are more at risk since 78.5% of males and 35% of females over 65 used a gun to successfully complete the suicide (NCHS National Vital Statistics, 1999, as cited by the National Center for Injury Prevention and Control, 2002). These suicide rates might even be higher if self-neglect (including insufficient fluid and food intake), refusal to follow prescribed medical regimes, and apparent accidents are considered (Morrow-Howell et al., 1998).

Unlike teens and younger adults, most older adults do not attempt suicide as a cry for help. They really intend to die. Though depression is one of the primary causes, social isolation and unmet needs are also to blame (Morrow-Howell et al., 1998). As people age, they suffer multiple losses, including loved ones, support systems, health, roles, and mobility. Loss of health is the primary cause for suicidal thoughts among the elderly. They wish to escape lives of disability and ease the burden they place on loved ones.

Suicide affects society in many ways. Whether or not a person is serious about a suicide attempt, it still requires the attention of medical authorities and

Table 11.1: Factors Relating to Suicide

Risk Factors	Protective Factors
• barriers to accessing mental health treatment • history of mental illness, especially depression • physical illness • history of alcohol and substance abuse • loss (relational, social, work, financial) • unwillingness to ask for help • isolation • family history of child maltreatment • feelings of hopelessness • impulsive or aggressive tendencies • easy access to lethal means • cultural or religious beliefs that support suicide as a viable option and discourage asking for help • local epidemics of suicide • isolation • a previous suicide attempt • family history of suicide	• effective clinical treatment for mental illness, physical illness, and substance abuse • support from an ongoing relationship with medical and mental health professionals • easy access to clinical treatment and support to seek this help • family and community support • skills in problem solving, conflict resolution, and nonviolent handling of disputes • cultural and religious beliefs that discourage suicide and encourage self-preservation

families. If physical damage does occur, a visit to the local emergency room or a doctor's office is likely. In 2002, 116,639 people were treated in the emergency room and released and 132,353 were hospitalized (National Center for Injury Prevention and Control, 2005). A suicide attempt may also involve acute psychiatric assistance. After surviving a suicide attempt, a person may suffer short-term or long-term disability that affects his or her ability to work. This costs the system money, through taxpayer-supported Medicaid and Medicare, insurance, or unpaid hospital bills. Family, friends, and community members suffer an emotional loss and wonder how they could have prevented such a tragedy.

Self-Mutilation

Self-mutilation, also known as deliberate self-harm, is a different form of violence to self. People choose to harm themselves through poisoning, burning, hair pulling, hitting, inserting objects into the body (body piercing *not* included), cutting, scratching at wrists and arms, or other methods (Crowe & Bunclark, 2000; Fowler et al., 2000; Zila & Kiselica, 2001). Self-mutilation has been traditionally associated with autistic children, schizophrenics, and those diagnosed with multiple personality disorders, but recent research has found evidence of it in the general population as well (Zila & Kiselica, 2001). The typical sufferer is female, adolescent or young adult, single, intelligent, and usually from a middle- to upper-middle-class family (Zila & Kiselica, 2001). Self-harmers include those who are **psychotic** or depressed and those who have **personality disorders (**Crowe & Bunclark, 2000). Self-harm usually starts during adolescence or after a traumatic event such as the loss of a loved one, a difficult childbirth, or in the context of a depressive illness (Crowe & Bunclark, 2000).

Ross and Heath (2002) found in a community sample of adolescents that 13.9% of all students reported having engaged in self-mutilating behaviors at one time. Such behaviors should not be confused with suicidal ideation. Self-harmers do not want to die—they just want to release psychological tension (Crowe & Bunclark, 2000). They believe that physical pain will cause psychological pain to go away or at least be reduced. Sufferers also struggle with inner rage or feel they have been victimized by someone else's rage. Self-harm is seen as a primitive defense in dealing with

this rage (Fowler et al., 2000). Often at the heart of these feelings is a childhood of abandonment and abuse (especially sexual). Yaryura-Tobias et al. (1995, as cited in Zila & Kiselica, 2001) found that 70% of the 19 self-mutilators they studied reported childhood sexual abuse and an inability to cope with that level of trauma. Self-mutilation becomes a way to calm down (Zila & Kiselica, 2001). The tension is so strong that the most common component of self-mutilation is lack of pain during the act (Zila & Kiselica, 2001). Self-harmers who have a psychotic cause sometimes cut because of command hallucinations telling them to do so (Crowe & Bunclark, 2000). Treatment usually comes in the form of counseling—either individual, group, outpatient, or inpatient. Crowe and Bunclark (2000) recommend inpatient psychiatric stays of six months to work on a complete cure.

Violence Directed toward Various Age Groups

- In 2000, there were three million referrals to Child Protective Service (CPS) agencies (U.S. Children's Bureau, 2002).
- 1,200 children died as a result of abuse or neglect in the year 2000 (U.S. Children's Bureau, 2002).
- In 1990 it was found that one in 20 elderly persons were victims of abuse, a total of 1.5 million (Rosenblatt, 1990).

Child Abuse

Child abuse and neglect are defined as either causing physical or emotional harm or not preventing harm to a child less than 18 years of age (Kotch & Browne, 1999). When reports are actually investigated, the incident rate was 11.8 per 1,000 children in 2000 (U.S. Children's Bureau, 2002). On the positive side, from 1994 to 2000 there was a decrease of 19.2% in abuse and neglect reports (U.S. Department of Health and Human Services, 2001). However, abuse is usually concealed in silence and many cases are not reported.

Parents are the main perpetrators of child abuse and neglect. Almost nine-tenths (87.3%) of all victims were maltreated by at least one parent. Mothers have been found to be the most common perpetrators of neglect and physical abuse, while fathers are the most common perpetrators of sexual abuse. Mothers are more likely to be the caregivers and to give in to the strain of the responsibility.

Almost three-fifths of all victims (58.4%) suffered neglect, one-fifth (21.3%) suffered physical abuse, and 11.3% were sexually abused (U.S. Department of Health and Human Services, 2001). Victimization rates were the same for males and females with the exception of sexual abuse, in which females have more than double the chance of being victimized. Victimization rates decline as age increases (U.S. Children's Bureau, 2002). No significant racial differences have been observed (Kotch & Browne, 1999).

There are multiple identified risk factors for families that are more likely to engage in violence. Personality disorders may play a part in the onset and continuance of abuse. Maltreating parents are more likely than other parents to be short tempered, inconsistent with discipline, less affectionate, less playful, less responsive, less supportive, and irritable. Depression, anxiety, and antisocial behavior make relationships difficult, leading to social isolation and social support inadequacies, which have been linked to child abuse. A general acceptance of violence in the family and society, including corporal punishment, increases abuse rates. Sexually abusive families also have been shown to have communication problems, lack emotional closeness, and be socially isolated and inflexible. Violence in families can continue for generations, with an estimated 30% (plus or minus 5%) rate of intergenerational transmission (Kotch & Browne, 1999).

Identified risk factors for children in danger of abuse include physical and verbal aggression and health problems early in life. However, the increased aggression could be a reaction to the abuse, and abuse may result from the additional stress a health problem presents to the family unit (Kotch & Browne, 1999).

Poverty can put extra stress on the family and should be considered a major risk factor. Some feel the economically disadvantaged are not necessarily more likely to be abusive, but are more likely to be targeted for investigations by authorities. Impoverished areas are less likely to provide support to parents or encourage social interaction, which has been related to higher rates of abuse (Kotch & Browne, 1999).

The most common intervention for child abuse and maltreatment is alerting the authorities. Certain professionals such as psychologists, teachers, nurses, doctors, social workers, police officers, and school counselors are mandated to report abuse. Generally, over 50% of the reports are made by professionals (U.S. Children's Bureau, 2002). They are often the first to recognize the problem. The remaining reports came from family members, neighbors, and other members of the community. The first call is often to Child Protective Services, a state agency that is usually housed in the county social services department. Social workers investigate the charges and then recommend solutions, which may involve placing a child in foster care or with another family member, counseling for the family, parenting classes, and sometimes prosecution of the abuser. One-fifth of all investigated claims involved a child being removed and placed into foster care (U.S. Children's Bureau, 2002).

Abused children often love their abusive parents, feel they are to blame for the violence, and do not want to leave home. The ultimate goal of Child Protective Services is rehabilitation through treatment and keeping the family together. Many children die in foster homes or soon after they return to their abusive parents (Kotch & Browne, 1999). It is difficult for social service workers to determine if a parent has been properly rehabilitated; hence, there is no easy solution. Also, the system has not always investigated abuse cases thoroughly and has lost track of children who are removed from the home. Unfortunately, the children's services system is overloaded. It is not uncommon for a social worker to have a caseload of 100 children. When problems are pointed out, many social services workers try their best to make corrections and reduce caseloads as they have the budgets to do so. Kotch and Browne (1999) believe that the whole system should be more child-centered.

Child abuse and neglect continue to be significant problems in the United States. Children who have been abused can exhibit a number of psychological and physical reactions. Marans et al. (1998) report chronic symptoms such as regression in toileting, distractibility, inattention, oppositional and aggressive behaviors, and other psychiatric consequences. Major abuse may lead to long-term disability or death (Kotch & Browne, 1999). Withecomb (1997) reports that abuse can result in the child becoming hyper-vigilant toward any slight aggression and perceiving it as threatening, a behavior that may lead to paranoia. Other consequences include decreased academic performance and a tendency toward juvenile delinquency (Kotch & Browne, 1999). Abused children have fewer words to express their feelings and feel less empathy toward others (Withecomb, 1997). Post-traumatic stress disorder is linked with 13% of child abuse cases (Fisher, 1999). The symptoms are similar to those of shell-shocked war veterans, and include recurrent nightmares, flashbacks, and serious emotional and behavioral problems. The consequences of abuse may be victims engaging in abusive behavior with their own children later in life, though most do not.

Elder Abuse

Elder abuse is finally being recognized as a serious form of violence, even though it is not a new problem. Reporting has increased over the past few decades, but under-reporting is still common. Elder abuse takes different forms, such as physical abuse, financial exploitation, neglect, and psychological/emotional abuse. Elder abuse is more likely to occur as a person ages (median age in 1996 was 77.9), becomes depressed, lacks a social support system, becomes dependent on the caregiver, or when the caregiver is emotionally or economically dependent on the older adult (Winnett, 1998). Most victims are women, and the perpetrators are most often their adult sons (Rosenblatt, 1990).

When the caregiver is dependent on the older adult, feelings of resentment, frustration, and stress may result. Often the caregiver is ill-prepared for the responsibility, especially as the elder's health worsens and he or she becomes more dependent. Sometimes there is a cycle of violence in the family, in which a parent who abused a child is now being cared for by that abused child. According to the National Center on Elder Abuse, caregivers who abuse usually are alcoholics, and have mental and emotional disorders, problems with drug addiction, and financial difficulties (National Center on Elder Abuse, 2003). As with domestic violence and child abuse, external factors such as financial problems and job stress have been linked to elder abuse (Woolf, 2003).

In many states, elder abuse is reported to Adult Protective Services, a department of a county's social services department. Other states accept calls at the Area Agency on Aging, the Division of Aging, the Department of Aging, or local law enforcement (http://www.webster.edu, 2002, as cited by Woolf, 2003). Professionals such as social workers, health practitioners, and those within local law enforcement are mandated to report elder abuse. The reporter has a right to privacy. The most common interventions include respite for the caregiver, placement of an older adult into a health care facility or a different health care facility, counseling, setting up agreements between victim and perpetrator (when financial exploitation is involved), and incarceration of the perpetrating caregiver.

Violence in the Workplace

- In 1998, 1.5 million simple assaults, 51,000 rapes and sexual assaults, 84,000 robberies, and 1,000 homicides took place at work (U.S. Department of Justice, Bureau of Justice Statistics, 2001).
- Employees with a higher risk rate include those in retail sales, executives or managers, law enforcement officers, security guards, taxi drivers or chauffeurs, and truck drivers (listed in descending order; McClure, 1999).

Stress at work comes from several sources, including layoffs, accidents, the feeling that a job is not safe, and a disruptive environment (McClure, 1999). Trends for the past few decades show an increase in workplace violence. Most readers have heard stories of disgruntled workers appearing in their workplaces and taking revenge in very pronounced ways. The phrase "going postal" emerged from the highly publicized events of postal workers shooting at co-workers, primarily in the 1980s. A fear in the service industry is that an unsatisfied client or patient might take violent action. This scenario was portrayed by Denzel Washington in the movie "John Q" (2002), in which a distraught father took a hospital hostage, demanding a heart transplant for his son that the hospital had refused to provide because his insurance would not pay for the procedure.

Various risk factors concerning workplace violence have been discussed in the literature. Some forms of mental illness and interpersonal stress have been linked to violence at work, including anxiety, depression, marital problems, family problems, financial problems, and substance abuse (McClure, 1999). A person who comes from a violent background is more likely to act violently at work (McClure, 1999). Those who experience domestic violence can experience further victimization at work. Of women killed at work, 17% were killed by a husband, former husband, or boyfriend (U.S. Department of Labor, 1996).

Employers are also affected by workplace violence. Employers lose about $6 billion a year in income, medical costs, and support costs directly due to workplace violence. For up to two weeks after a violent incident has occurred at work, production decreases by 80%. The residual stress from workplace violence and other work-related concerns lasts longer and costs an additional $200 billion a year to employers (McClure, 1999).

Several interventions have been tried to reduce workplace violence. Many workplaces, as part of the orientation of workers, especially supervisors, provide printed and visual materials with instructions for de-escalating a violent situation. Nicoletti and Spooner (1996) recommend that workplaces form teams to handle reports or threats of violent incidents. The team should actively search for potential problems and respond in a swift and organized manner. Employees also need resources when they are stressed from work or personal responsibilities. Employee Assistance Programs (EAPs) provide in-house counseling for employees and referrals to external counseling resources (McClure, 1999).

Community Violence

Community violence is defined as "crime-related and random acts of violence outside the home and does not include domestic violence or child abuse" (Morrison, 2000, p. 299). Statistics for community violence are not usually considered separately from other forms of violence. Researchers have found that 77 to 95% of youth have witnessed at least one violent crime, but violent acts within families are included in these figures (Weist, 2001 and Scarpa, 2001). Certain communities are more at risk than others. It is well known in the research literature that communities with higher poverty rates will have higher rates of crime. Unfortunately, since more African Americans live in impoverished urban centers, they are disproportionately affected by this type of crime. Inner cities are not the only neighborhoods experiencing community violence. Scarpa (2001) found that 95.6% of rural university students witnessed such violence, and 82% reported being victimized by some form of violence within either the community or their families. Numerous articles have documented the negative effects on youth of exposure to violence. Some of the most common effects are posttraumatic stress, depression, anxiety, aggression, and risk taking. The extent of the impact depends on a few variables. Age, acquaintance with a victim, experience as a victim

of more than one crime, a family background with a high degree of fighting, and removal from family are all linked to more negative emotional responses. There are some gender differences, with girls being more likely to suffer depression as a result of exposure to community violence (Morrison, 2000). Community violence may impact the family as well. Holland et al. (1996) found that mothers of preschoolers living in violent areas focus on basic survival, which creates a more chaotic home life with restrictive and punitive discipline. This type of home life has been associated with higher rates of delinquency and violence.

Hate Crimes

- After the loud roar of civil rights demonstrations died down and was replaced by protests against the Vietnam War, many people believed that racism and hate crimes were no longer a problem (Will, 1993).
- James Byrd, Jr., an African American man, was hitchhiking home after a relative's bridal shower on June 7, 1998, when a truck pulled over. But instead of getting a lift, Byrd was kidnapped, beaten unconscious, chained to the back of the truck, and then dragged several miles. His head and right arm were torn off. His attackers were later identified as three white men with links to racist groups (Hohler, 1998). The whole community reacted in shock since it had been thought that it did not have a problem with racism.

Hate crime, also known as bias-motivated crime, is not a new phenomenon. Since the 1980s and early 1990s, it has actually been defined as a specific type of crime with enhanced punishment, such as additional years in prison, that varies by state and by judicial discretion. Starting in 1990, hate crime statistics were calculated by the Uniform Crime Reporting program. In 2000, 9,430 hate crime offenses were reported. Of those, 65% were crimes against people and 34.4% were against property. Racial bias accounted for 54.5% of the crimes, followed by 17.2% for religion, 15.7% for sexual orientation, 12.3% for ethnicity/national origin, and 1% for physical disability. Anti-black bias accounted for 65.5% of racial bias crimes, anti-Jewish bias represented 74.7% of victims of religious bias, and anti-male homosexual bias composed 68% of sexual-orientation crimes (Federal Bureau of Investigation, 2001). However, it should be noted that there is a great reluctance by many to report hate crimes (Blazak, 2001).

Certain factors can increase the tendency for a person to become prejudiced towards others. A theory by Aronson (1992) suggests some situations that can lead to prejudicial thoughts and actions: 1) When there is a lack of resources, groups will turn against each other, leading the dominant group to exploit minority groups and gain material advantage; 2) an **authoritarian** personality may be linked to racist attitudes; and 3) a conforming personality is more likely to give in to existing prejudiced social norms. A person's attitude towards a group influences his or her behavior.

Hate crimes affect not only the victims but also their families and communities. The crimes may involve damage to property, medical expenses, and loss of wages. On a deeper level, dignity, liberty, and security are negatively affected (Petrosino, 1999). Hate crimes continue to be a problem, though the marches and outcries have died down. While not acceptable, every culture unfortunately includes a human tendency to strike out at minorities.

Terrorism

Until the early 1990s, the United States had been relatively unaffected by the terrorism that had gone on in the world for some time. But several subsequent events are linked to terrorism: the bombing in the basement of the World Trade Center in 1992; the bombing of the federal office building in Oklahoma City in 1995; the attacks of September 11, 2001, on the World Trade Center in New York City and the Pentagon in Washington, DC; anthrax-filled letters following those attacks; and sniper shootings in the Washington, DC, area in 2002.

Those who choose to join a terrorist group are not necessarily violent people (Kramer, 1990). Many terrorists have experienced severe economic challenges and blame "the enemy" for their current problems. They believe violence is a necessary tool to a reasonable end (Kramer, 1990). They see their cause as a "war," and their actions are similar to military confrontation (Powers, 1971). Members of terrorist groups are not unlike members of gangs and religious cults who feel that they must adopt radical thinking in order to feel accepted and find an identity for themselves. Terrorists want to control a group of people by making them constantly fear for their lives. The media aids their cause by making the threats seem larger than they actually are (Colvard, 2002).

After the September 11 attacks in 2001, several ideas for increasing security at airports and international borders were proposed. President George W. Bush and his advisors formed a Department of Homeland Security to oversee security and prevent further terrorism, and increased manpower in the FBI (Federal Bureau of Investigation, 2002a). A military response also followed. Afghanistan's terrorist training camps and the government that supported terrorism were dismantled in 2001 and 2002, and in 2003 coalition troops removed Iraq's Saddam Hussein from power. He was believed to have supported terrorism and to have developed weapons of mass destruction that could have been used against Americans. The research literature has not supported military action as a solution because it has been associated with eroding the legitimacy of the country, requiring its citizens to sacrifice, and multiplying enemies (Colvard, 2002). Decades of restrictions and retaliation have not decreased the number of suicide bombers in Israel and have led human rights organizations to question Israel's actions (Colvard, 2002). McCauley (1991) believes a nation's best response to violence by a small group is to treat it like a regular criminal act and not react politically.

Millions of people have been affected by terrorism around the world, including Americans. Almost every American felt some negative effect on September 11, 2001. There was a sudden fear of airplanes and flying. No longer could we live in security. The economy was negatively affected, further decreasing feelings of security. A heavy burden on domestic police and civil defense intended to prevent further attacks. With many forms of violence, people believe that they will practically eliminate their chances of being victimized if they just avoid certain situations and neighborhoods. But terrorism can strike anyone, anywhere, and at anytime.

Criminal Violence

A major concern about criminal violence has to do with its extent. Every year news headlines tout the rate of criminal violence and trends in violence at the national and local levels. Police chiefs' jobs often depend on these statistics and resulting budget allocations, and prisons and courts are often very dependent on such data. This section is a brief review of recent trends in criminal violence in the United States, based on data from the Federal Bureau of Investigation.

The Federal Bureau of Investigation's Uniform Crime Reporting (UCR) Program is a nationwide, cooperative statistical effort of more than 17,000 city, county, and state law enforcement agencies voluntarily reporting data on crimes brought to their attention. Since 1930, the FBI has administered the program and issued periodic assessments of the nature and type of crime in the nation. It is important to note that these statistics reflect only reported crime, not the actual number of crimes. Unless otherwise stated, the following facts are from the 2004 Uniform Crime Report.

The FBI's Uniform Crime Report shows that 1,367,009 violent crimes were committed in 2004, including murder and non-negligent manslaughter, forcible rape, robbery, and aggravated assault (Federal Bureau of Investigation, 2005). The number of offenses is lower than five and ten years ago by 4.1% and 24.0%, respectively; the decrease of crime in the year 2003 was 1.2%.

Homicide

In 2004, 16,137 murders were reported (a rate of 5.5 murders per 100,000 habitants). This represents the first decrease in homicide rates in four years, down by 2.4% from 2003, and a decrease of 25.3% from 1995. Not included in this count are deaths by negligence, suicide, accident, and justifiable homicides (Federal Bureau of Investigation, 2005).

In 2004, homicide victims were most often male (78.0%) and adult (90.2%). When considering race, 49.8% of murder victims were white, and 47.6% were African American. The vast majority of murders are intraracial: 92.2% of African American homicide victims were killed by African American offenders and 84.8% of white victims were slain by white offenders. When a murder weapon was known, a firearm was used in 70.3% of the homicide cases (Federal Bureau of Investigation, 2005).

Assault

According to the UCR, an aggravated assault is an unlawful attack by one person upon another for the purpose of inflicting severe or aggravated bodily injury. In 2004, 854,911 assaults were committed (a rate of 291.1 per 100,000). This is a 0.5% decrease from 2003, and continues an 11-year decline in aggravated assault rates. Personal weapons (hands, fists, feet, etc.) were used 26.6% of the time, while firearms were used 19.3%

of the time. Aggravated assaults are the most common violent crime (Federal Bureau of Investigation, 2005).

Robbery

Robbery is defined as the taking or an attempt to take anything of value from the care, custody, or control of a person or persons by force, threat of force, violence, and/or frightening the victim. This differs from burglary when threats or violence are not used. In 2004, there were 401,326 robbery offenses (a rate of 136.7 per 100,000 persons), a decrease of 3.1% in number of offenses from 2003. Robbery accounted for 29.4% of all violent crimes in the United States. Robbers strong-armed their victims 41.1% of the time and used firearms 40.6% of the time. Robbers stole more than $525 million from their victims in 2004. Robberies most often occur on the streets and highways at a rate of 42.8%. Robberies of commercial establishments, including gas stations, convenience stores, and banks, accounted for 25.9% (Federal Bureau of Investigation, 2005).

These types of data do not clearly convey the human impact of the experience of violence. But they provide us with the basic knowledge of the sheer number of violent crimes, the rates at which the violent crimes occur, and, most importantly, the trends in violence. These data indicate that rates of violence in the United States may no longer be declining. This makes it even more important that we understand the etiology of violence and possible means of reducing its occurrence.

Police Violence

Police brutality can be a daily occurrence across the U.S., primarily in the form of extra blows, punches, or kicks during arrests (Kirschner, 1997). However, some arrestees die from this violence or of mysterious causes while in police custody. The October 22nd Coalition, a national organization that documents police brutality, estimated that from 1990 to 2000 more than two thousand people were killed by law enforcement officers in the United States (Winslow, 2000). A small proportion of the police are guilty of most of the abuse, but these officers are rarely disciplined or prosecuted. Unfortunately, there is no reliable national data on police brutality.

There is concern that police brutality occurs too frequently and that it is aimed mainly at members of ethnic minorities. Members of the African American community feel unfairly assaulted by the police because of the color of their skin. This has led to a high rate of mistrust of authorities among African Americans, and a feeling that they will not receive justice when cases of police brutality come to trial. When the police were not convicted of a crime for the beating of Rodney King, the riots that followed are an example of a negative effect. Interestingly, Dozier's (1998) dissertation study of 75 Texas patrol officers found that attitudes regarding race or racism were not predictive of use of force towards an ethnic minority.

Why do some police officers behave brutally? Amnesty International reports that young police officers of any race more often shoot in high crime areas (Amnesty USA, 2000). Police officers may strike out from fear for their own personal safety. An "us" versus "them" mentality may guide a police officer to always be on guard. Dozier's (1998) study found a significant relationship between the officers' attitudes towards violence and the self-reported use of force. Violence can also be used by the police to demoralize and subdue arrestees in order to get them to cooperate in an investigation. Coercion is a powerful way to preserve order (Jacobs & O'Brien, 1998).

Etiology: Causes of Violence

ISSUES: How can we explain violence? How can a culture's norms and values socialize individuals into violence? How do childhood experiences help us understand later violence? How does gender and ethnicity relate to violence? What are the roles of drugs, alcohol, and mental illness in violence? What role does economic disparity play in violence?

In this section we will look at the multifaceted causes of violence. Though they are numerous, certain key areas can be researched, and it is hoped that this knowledge can lead to change. The causes will be separated into the following categories:

* *Sociological causal factors* include Americans' violent past, which has led to general cultural factors that have affected certain regions in different ways. We will look at groups and trends to see how society can socialize children to become violent, the role the media plays on violent behaviors, and the roles poverty, racism, and militias play as possible causes.
* *Biological causal factors* include genetics, brain structure, and biochemistry.
* *Psychological causal factors* include personality, the use of drugs, environmental cues, the frustration aggression theory, mental illness, and the role of youth.

Sociological Causal Factors

From America's Violent Past to Its Contemporary Culture

From domestic violence to hate crimes, contemporary society seems willing to act out personal attitudes and **pathologies** in violent expression. Acceptance of certain forms of violent behaviors is ingrained in the American value system. When the pilgrims came to this country they were consumed with the goal of survival. From the colonial era, through the settling of the western frontier, to the waves of immigrant arrivals, Americans have often used violence to establish basic rights. As a result of the past, American culture today considers physical force justifiable when expressing political dissent and protecting self and property, but less so during domestic disputes (Sigler, 1995).

In the 20th century, government policies and capital investment affected crime rates in the inner cities. The New Deal in the 1930s and the early postwar period in the 1940s expanded the consumer economy, boosted wages, and improved educational opportunities. Agriculture was encouraged to be capital-intensive, and millions of small farmers and farm laborers moved from the South into northern cities between 1940 and 1970. At the same time, government policies and corporate investment strategies encouraged flow of capital to nonunion urban centers and suburbs of the South and West where employers could pay lower wages. Mortgage programs favored suburban home-owners over urban renters. Corporate tax code encouraged building new factories overseas or in the suburbs rather than remodeling or upgrading urban factories. Growing international competition led corporations to cut costs, affecting low-wage and minority workers the most. Over the last half of the 20th century, these capital movements destroyed the economic basis of many American cities and pushed up crime rates. Social programs have helped those struggling with poverty to put roofs over their heads and food on the table, but between 1972 and 1992 welfare and food stamp benefits for single mothers declined by an average of 27% nationwide (Winslow, 2000).

Regional Variation

Certain regions in the U.S. have elevated crime rates, and part of this may be due to culture. The UCR defines the South as the most populous region of the United States and having the highest rate of violent acts reported, with 579.9 acts per 100,000 people. The West had a rate of 520.3 per 100,000 people, the Midwest had 432.0 per 100,000, and the Northeast had 429.7 per 100,000 (Federal Bureau of Investigation, 2001). The murder rate in the South is twice as high as in the Northeast (Monahan, 1994). There may be many explanations for the differences, and some have come forward with possible explanations. Whenever a culture encourages the use of firearms to settle disputes or when there is easy access to guns in a community, there may be an increase in violence. For example, Southern newspaper reporters did not respond as negatively to the violence of a husband who kills his wife for having an affair as did reporters in the Northeast (Federal Bureau of Investigation, 1998). Southern and Western institutions have greater sympathy toward a violent perpetrator who had what appeared to be culturally acceptable motives for the behavior (Cohen & Nisbett, 1997).

A wide variety of general geographical, economic, and cultural characteristics also play a significant role in violent acts and trends. Milder climates and longer daylight hours in the West and South may play a significant role in increasing public group interaction and the opportunities for violence. In addition, higher poverty rates may be related to higher violence rates in the South. Within all regions of the country, violence rates are significantly higher in larger cities with greater population densities (Reiss & Roth, 1993). Per capita, all violent crimes occur more often in populous metropolitan areas than rural areas (Federal Bureau of Investigation, 2001). Within cities, research shows that long-term patterns of residential segregation and resulting limits on interaction among members of different groups may be related to higher violence rates among African Americans. All of these data suggest that violence may reflect very basic geographic factors, involving human populations crowded into small spaces, residential segregation, climatic factors that encourage public street interaction, and limited economic opportunity. These basic underlying aspects of violence are powerful factors that make the rate of violence difficult to address.

Socialization

- Even if a family is intact, **transience**, which can lead to social isolation, is known to increase violent tendencies (Dahlberg, 1998).
- Children who are removed from violent or neglectful homes are also at risk. The more foster care placements children have, the greater the likelihood that they will later be arrested for violent crimes (Monahan, 1994).

One of the many tasks of parents is to raise their children with morals and an awareness of society's **norms**. This is not always successfully accomplished. It is rare that those who raise children purposely teach them to be violent. Sometimes it happens unintentionally as a result of a parent or guardian's own violent behavior, arising from a **dysfunctional** childhood and external stressors. According to Winnett (1998), one common cause of violence cited in research literature results from a child witnessing family violence. When children are victims, or witness violence in the home, they are at risk for experiencing both behavioral and emotional problems and for impaired social functioning (Rudo et al., 1998). These children see violence as normal behavior and an acceptable form of handling disputes. Childhood abuse increases not only the chance of hurting another person, but also of violence towards self. Roy (2001) studied 100 male cocaine dependent patients admitted to a substance abuse treatment program. Patients who had attempted suicide had higher rates of childhood emotional abuse, physical abuse, sexual abuse, and emotional and physical neglect than patients who had never attempted suicide. This is not to say that all children who experience or witness violence in the home will become violent, but it increases their chances.

Many research studies have found that a parenting style of harsh, inconsistent punishment also leads to aggressive behavior in children (Withecomb, 1997). Swinford et al. (2000) conducted a longitudinal study on 608 adolescents in 1982 and in 1992–1993. They found that experiencing harsh physical punishment in childhood is directly related to greater perpetration of violence against an intimate partner later in life. National surveys have shown that lack of consistent adult expectations has been linked to violence in youth (White, 1995). Overworked and financially strapped parents come home from work after a long day and vent their frustrations by yelling at their children, sometimes emotionally abusing them (Remboldt, 1998). Busy parents are not only more likely to yell at their kids, but also are not able to provide enough supervision of them, which increases delinquency, including violent delinquency (Monahan, 1994).

Current research into the causes of violence concentrates on males as perpetrators. As teenagers, American adolescent boys behave in a more aggressive and violent manner than adolescent boys from other nations (Tomes, 1995). It is believed that this is because boys in the United States are socialized to be more aggressive. When considering gender, 82.7% of arrestees for violent crimes are male (Federal Bureau of Investigation, 2001). However, Withecomb (1997) notes that delinquency is beginning to spread to girls.

Fewer and fewer children are growing up in two-parent households. The dissolution of the family has led to more aggressive and violent behaviors in children. Carlson (2000) studied the National Longitudinal Survey of Youth for adolescents ages 10 to 14 in 1996 and found that parental involvement of biological fathers has been associated with improved behavioral scores for all adolescents regardless of living arrangements, but larger improvement was more apparent with fathers who are living in the home.

Even parents who live with their children may not have an emotional connection with them. For decades, research has shown that a lack of emotional attachment between parents and children is related to a wide variety of delinquent behaviors among youth, including violence (Hirschi, 1969). Simons et al. (1998), in a study of adolescent boys, support the finding that a lack

of warm, supportive parenting leads children to later develop antisocial patterns of behavior. Some children experience emotional homelessness because their parents do not provide emotional support and unqualified confidence in their ability to invent a promising future. These are often parents who have given up hope (White, 1995). Children whose mothers are incarcerated and thus not available for emotional support typically experience a great many risk factors, including poverty, drug and alcohol problems in their families, multiple changes in caregivers, and community violence. These children experience emotional problems such as fear, withdrawal, depression, and emotional disturbance, as well as behavioral problems such as anger, fighting, stealing, and substance abuse. All too often this leads to higher rates of school failure, eventual criminal activity, and incarceration (Myers et al., 1999).

Social Learning Theory

Children learn appropriate and inappropriate behavior from their parents and other influential adults. According to social learning theory, violence towards others is a learned behavior (Bandura, 1973, 1977). In his classic experiment, Bandura had an adult subject model aggressive behavior for a child by knocking around a plastic air-filled "Bobo" doll. The adult hit, kicked, and yelled aggressively at the doll as the child observed. When the child was allowed to play with the doll, not only was the same aggressive behavior imitated, but the child often improvised to create unique displays of violence against the doll. Bandura's argument is further strengthened by his use of a control group, which consisted of children who observed an adult interacting with the Bobo doll in a non-aggressive way. When allowed to play with the Bobo doll themselves, none of these children beat or attacked the doll as the children in the experimental group had. It would appear that aggression and violence are social behaviors that are learned through observing and then imitating actions that have been modeled (Bandura, Ross, & Ross, 1961, 1963, as cited in Aronson et al., 2002).

If violence is used to handle disputes and to punish misbehavior, then a child will learn that violence is a necessary element in social interactions. Violence between spouses during arguments teaches children to behave violently in relationships. Studies have found harsh physical punishment in childhood or adolescence to be associated with an elevated propensity both to abuse and to be abused in intimate relationships (Alexander et al., 1991; DeMaris, 1987; Kalmuss, 1984, as cited in Swinford et al., 2000). This theory also helps to explain why violence in families can be repeated for several generations.

Class Conflict Theory

Karl Marx developed the concept of class conflict theory. He defined socioeconomic classes in England in the mid-1800s as being the capitalist class, landowner class, and working class. Classes are defined only by their relationship to each other—which classes exploit and which classes are exploited. Most western cultures today have an upper class, middle class, working class, and impoverished class. Marx believed there will always be conflict among these classes for resources, from wealth to housing, food, jobs, power, and status. Class conflict occurs when members of a given social class act together out of shared economic interests and in opposition to members of other social classes contending for those interests (Dugger & Sherman, 1997).

Class, social, and economic conflict can involve ethnicity or religious conflict as disproportionate members of religious groups are in a particular social class. The more people identify with their group, the less likelihood of conflict within the group and the more likelihood of conflict between groups (Hennessy & West, 1999). In class conflict theory, it is this clash of interests that drives both social change and social conflict. The civil rights movement can be used as an example of this theory. From this perspective, in order for the civil rights movement to take place, African Americans had to stop living as scattered sharecroppers throughout the South and become urban workers concentrated in small areas in order to become organized enough to start a movement (Dugger & Sherman, 1997). Considerable violence occurred as attempts for change were made and resisted. These conflicts over change, cultural values, and the perceived imposition of those values through economic and military action also seemed to be part of the violence that was expressed in the attack on the World Trade Center and the Pentagon on September 11, 2001. According to class conflict theory, questing for change is not the only way violence can occur; sustaining the power differential can lead to violence as well. Police officers are seen as instrumental in sustaining economic and racial disparities through coercion

(Jacobs & O'Brien, 1998). The ruling class perceives a threat from the racial and economic underclass, which could lead to violent law enforcement (Jacobs & O'Brien, 1998). Understanding group conflict from its basic origins, its manifestations, and its resolutions is crucial when addressing the form of violence that seems most to threaten our society today.

Media

There has been much discussion about whether violence in the media leads to an increase of violence in our society. Up to this point, all research can say is that it is possible the media plays a role in perpetuating violent behaviors (Tomes, 1995). No one disputes that American television has excessively violent programming and that children and adults watch a lot of television. American television is the most violent in the world, with about 60% of programs containing violence. Among cable programs, 87% contain violence (Federal Communications Commission, 2002). The average American child consumes 40 hours of media per week, an amount of time equivalent to a full-time job (Kaiser Family Foundation, 1999). By the time a child graduates from high school he or she will have seen 200,000 various acts of violence on network television (Federal Communications Commission, 2002). The numbers are higher if the child has access to cable or a DVD player (Bushman & Anderson, 2001).

Scholars have been studying the effects of media on societal violence in the United States since the early 1960s. Societal violence began to increase fairly dramatically in 1965, exactly when the first generation of children who watched television began reaching prime ages for committing violence (Bushman & Anderson, 2001). This phenomenon also occurred in other countries as well (Centerwall, 1989, 1992). The American Medical Association, the American Psychological Association, the American Academy of Pediatrics, and the American Association of Children and Adolescent Psychology conclude that TV violence can lead to aggressive behavior in children (Tristani, 2000). Over 1,000 studies, including reports issued by the federal government, point to a causal connection between aggressive behavior and viewing media violence (Tristani, 2000). Laboratory experiments have found that merely viewing 15 minutes of a program with relatively mild violence increases the aggressiveness of the viewers by 25% (Bushman, 1995). Some experts believe that because violent images have become so common in the media, children have become desensitized to violence in entertainment and to the violence that surrounds us every day (Remboldt, 1998). Thus, as children grow, they are willing and eager to watch entertainment with more thrills and violence. The more violence viewed on television, the more violent incidences at school (Nemecek, 1998).

Video games are also a problem. After playing violent video games, young people show measurable decreases in prosocial and helping behaviors and increases in aggressive thoughts and violent retaliation to provocation (Irwin & Gross, 1995). Learning violence through video games can be more potent than watching violent acts on television because the games are interactive and the player is encouraged to be violent towards others (Pediatrics, 2001).

How much does all this viewing of violent media content actually affect our behavior? Bushman and Anderson's (2001) research indicates that media violence is associated with from 1.2% to 9.6% of the variance in violent behavior. The number may sound small, but suppose 10 million people watch a violent TV program. If only 1% of the viewers become more aggressive afterward, then the program will have made 100,000 viewers more aggressive (Bushman & Anderson, 2001). The strength of the correlation between media exposure and aggressive behavior is equal to calcium intake and bone loss, condom nonuse and HIV, and environmental tobacco smoke and lung cancer (Pediatrics, 2001). The scientific community has generally accepted that viewing violent media increases aggression, but does that lead to violent acts? It is difficult to answer this question through research since it is difficult to isolate the association of media and violence from other potential causes of violence. Also, for ethical reasons people cannot deliberately be put in potentially dangerous situations to see how they will act.

Media consumption does not only increase aggression. The combination of sex and violence can have an even worse effect on viewers than violence alone. Boys who learned about sex from watching pornography on a regular basis were more accepting of rape myths and violence against women. They were also more likely to believe that it is acceptable to force girls to have intercourse (Cowan & Campbell, 1995). Television viewing does not even have to be only violent to have a negative effect on a viewer. Gerbner et al. (1980) found that heavy television viewers 1) overstate crime rates and 2) are more likely to believe the world is unsafe and that they need to look out for themselves and not trust anyone. This is called the mean world syndrome. These people are more likely to support political candidates and policies that are tough on crime, possess guns, and take extra security measures (Nabi & Sullivan, 2001).

Watching violent entertainment is not the only way humans may become more violent because of the media. Media coverage of a horrific violent event watched by a troubled person may inspire copycat violence. The outbreak of mass murders at schools in the mid to late 1990s is an example. The Internet provides easy-to-find information on how to construct a bomb, and helps violent people share ideas with others having violent tendencies. Increased communication among a small violent minority can lead to disastrous results.

The media's response to these studies has been slow. Organizations have put warning labels on various forms of entertainment, though the music industry is lagging (Children Now, 2002). The labels on television shows can be programmed into a V-chip, allowing parents to program their televisions not to allow certain shows to be seen by young viewers. Not all programs or channels have V-chip technology. Labels do not always tell the whole story. Harvard researchers found that 35 of 55 video games labeled E for Everyone (okay for those 6 years and older) have violent scenes 30.7% of the playtime. Injuring other characters was rewarded 60% of the time (Thompson & Haninger, 2001). Only 32% of parents actually use television ratings systems because they are considered too difficult to operate (U.S. Federal Trade Commission, 2000). The movie and video game industries have stopped advertising R-rated films and mature-rated games on television programs for which more than 35% of the viewers are under age 17 (Sanders, 2002). The government is hoping the media will self-regulate itself since the industry claims free speech violations if too many restrictions are imposed (Children Now, 2002).

Research does not show a causal relationship between violent entertainment and violent behavior. Violence is also common in the absence of violent media (Ferguson, 2002). Homicide rates in the 1930s rivaled and even exceeded homicide rates of the late 1980s (U.S. Department of Justice, Bureau of Justice Statistics, 1988). Violent crime records were not complete in the 1800s, but some evidence indicates that there were crime waves in the late 1800s and early 1900s that rivaled or surpassed current rates of violent crime (National Commission on the Causes and Prevention of Violence, 1969). Obviously, television did not exist during these years. The decrease of violence through the 1990s coincides with an increase in media violence (Ferguson, 2002). Media violence accounts for only a small fraction of the variance in violent behavior (Ferguson, 2002). Even if the media may contribute up to 10% of the violence in the U.S., 90% comes from other sources.

Poverty

As has been mentioned several times in this chapter, poverty-stricken areas have higher rates of violence. For example, in 1993, New York City's precincts in the impoverished areas of Harlem, the Bronx, and Brooklyn reported 854 homicides (43.6% of the city's murders), whereas more affluent areas had only 37 homicides (less than 2% of the total)(Winslow, 2000). Poverty affects many areas of our lives. Living in poverty at age eight is the best predictor of later delinquency (Withecomb, 1997). Violent tendencies are more likely in a child who grows up in a neighborhood where there is a sense of uncertainty based on economic insecurity (White, 1995). Families in lower socioeconomic levels are more likely to experience child and domestic violence (Trickett & Schellenback, 1998). The lack of economic opportunities in certain communities leads to increased violence because of frustration and strong desire to acquire riches any way possible. Research has shown that violent people often suffer from low self-esteem, frustration, and hopelessness stemming from poverty (Mason, 1993). Prior to arrest, jail inmates on average had an annual income at the poverty level and about 50% were unemployed (Monahan, 1994). Children living in poverty-stricken areas that usually have high violence rates are more likely to be victimized themselves, witness violence, or know someone who has been victimized. This type of exposure affects a child's adjustment and adaptation (Horn & Trickett, 1998). Higher crime rates can make a place less desirable to live, so those who can afford to do so leave. High robbery rates are associated with African American population growth while stimulating white flight (Liska et al., 1998). Poverty also leads to crowding, which can lead to increased rates of violence (Winnett, 1998). When there is overcrowding, irritability and frustration are the result. Underlying socio-economic deprivation

may predispose a person to both substance abuse and violence (Withecomb, 1997). The problems of poverty and joblessness may reflect corporate investment decisions that have transformed the global economy, making it easier for criminals to launder money, pollute the environment, and expose their employees to dangerous working conditions (Winslow, 2000).

Racism

Two of the most common social predictors of violence are racism and inequality (Winnett, 1998). Racism is discrimination or prejudice based on race and contributes to violence in two primary ways. The racist person or group acts either violently or subtly through segregation or discrimination. The group victimized by this behavior may respond with acts of frustration towards those who are victimizing them or towards each other.

Racism had an early history in the United States. Twenty Africans were brought by a Dutch freighter to be sold as indentured servants in 1619, beating the English Pilgrims who arrived in Massachusetts by one year. Racism became a popular idea among Europeans through the 1700s and 1800s since they considered themselves a purer race; others who came to the new world's shores and those already inhabiting it were believed to be inferior. It helped to justify exploitation. The color of a person's skin was not always the motivating factor. Throughout the history of the United States, new immigrants had violent acts perpetrated against them. These include the Catholic Irish in the late 1840s and the southeastern Europeans in the late 1880s. The West Cost was a focal point of Asian immigration starting in the mid 1840s with the gold rush (Luhman, 1992).

Africans brought to the United States had their lives entirely changed when they were thrust into a slave culture. When slavery ended, then sharecropping began, thus effectively legalizing slavery once again by binding a person to the land regardless of whether it produced food. As free blacks moved out of the South, the Jim Crow laws were enacted in the North as a form of domination. Though those laws are no longer with us, African Americans are more likely than whites to live in the central cities, be poorly educated, be unemployed, work at blue-collar jobs, make less money, and wind up below the poverty level (Luhman, 1992). There were some gains in the 1960s and 1970s, but very few gains since then.

Many Voices: An Introduction to Social Issues

Latino Americans have always been a part of United States history. Their low status was established as a conquest by the dominant Europeans who used them and discarded them as the situation required (Luhman, 1992). As their numbers grow, they continue to experience some of the same growth difficulties as earlier immigrants.

Europeans have a long history of exploitation and control of Native Americans. At first Europeans tried to exploit them as a labor force, but they were too close to home (unlike the Africans) and thus were harder to control and often became sick and died from new European diseases. Native Americans had to be moved to make room for expansion (Luhman, 1992). So Europeans killed them, moved them to undesirable land, and labeled them "dirty" (Smith & Ross, 2004).

There is also the personal side of racism. People who attack others simply based on race do so for various reasons. The psychological profile of a perpetrator actually differs little from those of the general population (Blee, 2002). Racism is a necessary component to perpetrate race crimes, but it is not the only reason. In order to exploit and dominate others, there has to be a culture that allows such conduct. Sibbitt (1997) argues that rates of white racist violence and harassment tend to be highest in socially deprived areas where a high proportion of residents are struggling and thus make ethnic minorities the convenient "scapegoat." There has developed an "us" versus "them" mentality that can be an excuse for all sorts of violent acts.

People sometimes strike out in violence when they feel unfairly treated for any reason or deprived of a chance at the American dream. Systematic disadvantages have led many members of ethnic minorities to be able to afford only cheap housing, to have higher unemployment, and to be more often segregated, leading to unequal opportunities (Commission for Racial Equality, 1993). People who feel the world is against them are more likely to be frustrated and act violently, as discussed in the section on frustration-aggression theory.

Unfortunately, those who are most affected by racism have little political power to change the system. Millions of arrested Americans, with higher proportions from minority communities, have lost their right to vote because of their criminal records (Winslow, 2000). The majority still have the money to spend on lobbyists to sway federal, state, and local officials, while the poor have nothing to spend on the political process.

Militia

The militia was originally an organization of citizens with limited military training which was available for emergency service, usually for local defense. State militias have existed since the United States began, growing out of the Revolutionary War. They slowly died out as Americans became more mobile and the federal government grew stronger. Though not considered to be a large contributor to violence rates, militias are still an increasing violent phenomenon that should be discussed as a causal factor of violence. Militia has become a movement of radical paramilitary groups whose members generally accept highly conspiratorial interpretations of politics and view themselves as defenders of traditional freedoms against government oppression. Now citizen militia activity is a growing concern for the federal government in some regions across the United States. Today's citizen militias grew markedly in the early 1990s after the government's bloody raid in Ruby Ridge, Montana, on a private citizen who was amassing a large gun arsenal and making threats on government officials. Research has shown that militia activity is less likely in states with larger numbers of registered Democratic voters and may be more prevalent in areas where there are polarized ideals and morals. Militia groups are motivated by concerns over a rogue federal government and are composed of larger numbers of Gulf War veterans, zealous gun owners, those with less political representation, and people with a greater inclination toward violence (O'Brien & Haider-Markel, 1998).

Though not mentally ill, militia members often suffer from ignorance, paranoia, and fear. They may be isolated, have had bad personal experiences with the government, and show racist tendencies (Kopel, 1996). Kopel (1996) believes that the militias themselves are not dangerous, but they do attract marginal people and create an atmosphere of crisis. These groups are scattered and vary in purpose. Some are more anti-government and others are motivated more by racism. Similar groups are driven by religious convictions, leading to attacks on abortion clinics.

Biological Causal Factors

Some of our behavior originates in biological factors that affect psychology. Since research ethics are stricter for human subjects, animals have often been used to study the hereditability of aggressive behavior. Studies conducted on human and animal subjects have found evidence for a biological vulnerability towards violence through genetic, neurobiological, and twin studies. Stoff and Cairns (1996) state that "aggression among rodents has been a favorite topic of behavioral genetics and results have consistently found heritability for various definitions of aggression in the mouse and rat" (p. 3). In this section we will search for causes by looking at some genetic, structural, and biochemical views.

Genetic

In humans, twin studies are a primary means of examining genetic influence on violent behavior. There are two types of twins—monozygotic, or identical, twins, and dizygotic, or fraternal, twins. Monozygotic twins come from the same zygote and therefore share the same genetic makeup. Dizygotic twins share only 50% of their genes on average.

Mason and Frick (1994) found that monozygotic twins were more similar to one another than dizygotic twins when aggressive, antisocial, and criminal behavior was compared. Furthermore, they found that the aggressive and criminal behavior of adopted children more closely resembled the behavior of their biological parents than that of their adopted parents. Such findings seem to support the idea that violent and aggressive behavior can be genetically inherited. However, this study does point out that it is difficult, if not impossible, to distinguish between genetic influence and the effects of the prenatal environment—a distinction that is key to showing whether or not genetic influence is truly dominant. A meta-analysis of 24 studies done by Miles and Carey (1997) suggests that up to 50% of the variance in aggression could be explained by genetics. They also noted the following age differences: "The results of our cross-sectional meta-analysis suggest that in youth, genes and common environment equally promote similarity among relatives. For adults, however, the influence of common environment is negligible but that of heritability increases....Common environment has been very important in juvenile delinquency, whereas genes have been relatively more important for adult criminality" (p. 214). This research indicates that environment has a greater impact on juvenile delinquency and genetic influence has more of an impact on long-term criminal behavior.

The Amygdala and Amygdalectomy

The amygdala, located in the anterior portion of the brain's temporal lobe, is thought to play a role in emotion. When stimulated in an animal, attacks on an intruder and other forms of aggressive behavior increase. When this area is damaged or removed, the animal shows placid (calm) behavior. Amygdalectomy, the surgical destruction or removal of the amygdala, has been shown to reduce aggressive behavior for some individuals. However, this may not always be the best approach, since it does not always reduce aggression, and also creates emotional blunting (Pinel, 1997; Kalat, 2001).

Testosterone

In the animal world, males are known to fight for both territory and access to females. At puberty there is an increase in intermale aggression, which can also be induced by repeated injections of testosterone (Carlson, 1998). Higher levels of testosterone are associated with an increase in dominance and violent behavior. Dabbs et al. (1995) found that naturally occurring testosterone levels are significantly higher among prisoners convicted of violent crimes than in those who were convicted of nonviolent crimes. Mazur and Booth (1998) found that higher levels of testosterone encouraged males to exhibit dominant behavior over other people. Su et al. (1993, as cited in Carlson, 1998) found that administering testosterone to a group of males increased sexual arousal, euphoria, irritability, and hostility. However, these were self-reports that did not result in observable behavior, and the effects were minor. Issues of confounding also occur with testosterone studies. It is difficult to say with certainty whether an increased level of testosterone causes more aggression, or whether aggression causes increased levels of testosterone. The problem with many studies of testosterone and aggression is that they are correlational.

Serotonin

Serotonin, a neurotransmitter, has also been linked to increased levels of aggression and violence. Serotonin appears to have an inhibiting effect on aggressive behavior in humans. Hence, low levels of serotonin have been associated with an increase in aggression. This is supported by evidence showing that violent criminals have very low levels of serotonin (Davidson et al., 2000). Depletion of tryptophan, an amino acid that produces serotonin in the brain, has been shown to increase aggressive behavior, furthering evidence that neurotransmitters affect violence (Bjork et al., 1999). Serotonin, however, may not link as strongly with aggression as with something like impulsivity (Brunner & Hen, 1997, as cited in Carlson, 1998). Unfortunately, serotonin and tryptophan are subject to the same issues of confounding as testosterone. So do changes in neurotransmitter levels cause violent behavior, or does violent behavior cause changes in neurotransmitter levels?

The biological associations with violence seem likely, but they do not offer a complete explanation of the origin of such behavior. Furthermore, there is conflicting evidence among scientists concerning biological influences on violent behavior. Research on hormones and neurotransmitter influence does not always yield consistent findings.

Psychological Causal Factors

Personality characteristics

We all remember the neighborhood bully. Why are such children aggressive? Is it the culture surrounding the child, inherited tendencies, or familial patterns? The answer is not always obvious and it probably is a combination of all three. Some children tend to have violent personalities, and certain personality types are linked to violence later in life. Several research studies have shown that young boys who demonstrate certain aggressive, antisocial behaviors are more likely to be arrested for violent crimes when grown (Tomes, 1995). In every culture that was researched, aggression at age eight significantly predicted violent behavior well into the thirties (Monahan, 1994). Hyperactivity by itself has been linked to increased aggression and delinquency later in life. The presence of a conduct disorder, a repeated pattern of behavior that violates others' rights and norms, has an even poorer prognosis (Withecomb, 1997).

Violent children are not all born as more aggressive than other children. Environmental factors also play a role. Failure of a child in school is one of the most cited correlations of later violence (Monahan, 1994). Unsuccessful learning experiences can lead to low self-esteem, which can lead to poor peer choices, and predispose a child to antisocial activity. Children who scored significantly lower on IQ tests and had low intellectual functioning in their daily lives are significantly more violent. Poor communication skills are

also predictors of aggressive behavior because they can result in children perceiving unimportant gestures as provocative (Withecomb, 1997).

Frustration-Aggression Theory

The frustration-aggression theory posits that external circumstances can lead to violence and aggression. This theory maintains that a person who perceives that he or she is being prevented from attaining a goal will have a higher probability of responding aggressively. Bettencourt and Miller (1996) conducted a study that supports this theory. They found that while men are more aggressive than women in everyday situations, women react almost as aggressively as men do when they are subjected to frustration and insult. Proponents maintain that it is not just frustration that induces aggressive and violent behavior, but also the level of perceived deprivation. That is to say, it is the individual's perception that he or she has been deprived, not necessarily the actual level of deprivation, that induces aggression.

The Arousal-Affect Theory

The Arousal-Affect Theory asserts that aggression is influenced by the type and intensity of emotion. Brehm et al. (1999) summarized the relationship of these variables in this way: "…experiences that create negative emotions increase aggression; add high arousal, and the combination could be lethal. Experiences that are emotionally neutral have little impact on aggression, *unless* they are highly arousing. Experiences that create positive emotions and low arousal decrease aggression. Now comes the hard part: experiences that produce positive emotions and high arousal. Will aggression decrease because a positive emotional experience is incompatible with unpleasant angry feelings? Or will aggression increase because there's a lot of arousal available for transfer? It's a tough call and could go either way—depending on the individual, the situation, and the thoughts that come to mind" (p. 407).

Aggression and Stimuli

Some researchers argue that environmental cues stimulate violent behavior. Turner and Leyens (1992) cite the 1967 study done by Leonard Berkowitz and Anthony LePage in which they studied 100 male undergraduate psychology students at the University of Wisconsin. These students were made angry in the presence of a gun and administered more intense electric shocks on their partners in the study than those made angry in the presence of a neutral object, such as a badminton racket. The results were called the "weapons effect." The findings of this study have been replicated many times, but sometimes with mixed results (Toch & Lizotte 1992). Klech (1991) analyzed twenty-one studies that considered the "weapons effect" and theorized that only people with no prior experience with guns were affected.

Drugs and Alcohol

Drug and alcohol use is the second most frequently cited cause for violence in the research literature (Winnett, 1998). Withecomb (1997) reports that drug users tend to fight more, both within and outside of drug-using groups. Alcohol is often present in the perpetrator of violence, the victim, or both (Tomes, 1995). About one-third of all violent offenders are alcoholic. The earlier teenagers start to drink alcohol, the higher the likelihood they will become violent offenders (Monahan, 1994). Having alcohol or drugs in the body often leads to personality changes such as lowered inhibitions, depression, impaired judgment, and/or increased aggression among victims and perpetrators (Winnett, 1998).

The steep rise in inner-city violence in the mid 1980s can be correlated with the introduction of crack cocaine (Rosenberg, 1995), and the later decrease in violence has been attributed to a stabilization of drug markets that reduced violent conflict over drug distribution. Thus, alcohol and drugs affect violent behavior at all levels, from their impact on decision-making to their impact on interpersonal conflict. At a broader marketplace level, they create conflict involving disputes over drug distribution (McBride et al., 2003). There is a definite correlational connection between drug use and violence, not necessarily causal. The nature of the relationship is more complex than it appears. Not everyone who uses drugs or alcohol becomes violent. Kumpfer et al. (1998) found that substance abuse and anti-social behavior may be influenced by genetic and socialization factors.

Psychiatric Disorders

There is a stereotype that violent individuals are often mentally deranged. This is not usually the case. Major mental disorders account for only about 3% of violence in American society (Monahan, 1994). Frontal lobe dysfunction can lead to violent tendencies because of a person's inability to predict potentially violent behaviors and learn from negative experiences. Those who suffer from untreated or poorly treated psychotic illnesses, though small in number, are significant in the study of violence (Withecomb, 1997).

A person with a mental illness is more likely to be a victim of violence than a perpetrator. Goodman et al. (1997) reviewed studies on physical and sexual assault against women with severe mental illness and found they had a lifetime victimization rate from physical or sexual assault of 51% to 97%. These rates are much higher than for the general population (Goodman et al., 2001). Certain risk factors increase the chance of victimization even more. In a convenience sample of men and women with severe mental illness, victims were more likely to be young, never married, recently homeless, and with a history of childhood physical and sexual abuse (Goodman et al., 2001). A person with a mental disability is also much more likely to live in poverty, a known risk factor for victimization.

Youth

Violence is primarily a behavior of the young. People in their late teens and twenties are much more likely to be arrested for violent crimes than younger or older people (Monahan, 1994). This age group shares characteristics that may increase violent behavior: 1) immaturity, 2) more free time, 3) less coping ability to de-escalate arguments, 4) anxiousness about financial security, and 5) better physical fitness.

Younger people not only perpetrate violent acts, but are also victims. Murders of children ages 12 to 17 increased 95% between 1980 and 1994 (Winnett, 1998). Lethal tendencies are occurring in younger and younger people. Violence is the leading cause of death for teens and young adults in America (White, 1995). Between 1987 and 1988, the homicide rate for young African American males increased 38% (Rosenberg, 1995). Homicide is the leading cause of death among African Americans ages 15 to 34 (Tomes, 1995).

Violence Reduction

ISSUES: With violence so apparent everywhere in our culture, is it possible to change our attitudes and behavior toward it? In a free society, how much can new laws affect violent behavior? What programs offer the best hope of violence reduction?

What can be done about violence in America? Some theorize that crime rates declined in the 1990s in part because baby boomers were aging. The majority of crimes are committed by young people, and thus a large aging population is associated with reductions in crime rates.

There are many multifaceted theories being debated today on what creates change and how to further reduce violence. In this last section we will look at the various reduction strategies suggested by research and policy makers: social and cultural change, economic opportunities, punishment, gun control, and programmatic interventions.

Social and Cultural Change

A number of cultural values must be changed if violence is to be reduced. Consider these examples:

- Violence on television should be deglamorized, and more focus put on conflict handling.
- Geographical regions that condone violence for any reason should reevaluate those reasons.
- Child socialization practices should discourage aggression as a way to handle disputes.
- Parents should evaluate their schedules and the importance they are giving to aspects of their lives other than their children.

In order to reduce violence, people should feel valued and see others, both in their group and in other social groups, as valuable (Mason, 1993). Violence in all forms, no matter what the reason, should be shown as harmful to the whole society and not just to an isolated victim.

Economic Opportunities

One accepted theory for the drop in crime levels during the 1990s is that the country experienced an upturn in the economy. Unemployment was very low and there were many employment opportunities. In 2001 there was a very slight increase in some forms of crime and,

coincidentally, the economy was weaker. There must be more commitment by federal, state, and local government to reduce poverty rates further. With more and more states adopting "welfare to work programs," there is a danger that more children will grow up in poverty if there is not enough governmental and community support. This includes good child care for the former welfare recipient who returns to the workforce. There are ways to reduce poverty rates for those trying to get their "heads above water." More business investment opportunities can reduce unemployment in the inner cities. Many government grants encourage development by offering incentives, including lower taxes, to businesses that develop in depressed areas. Having an opportunity to develop job skills and find jobs in one's own community will reduce violence (Mason, 1993).

Educational opportunities are also important to reducing poverty in America. The vast majority of well-paying available jobs in this increasingly complex economy require education and training (Day & Newburger, 2002), which are unfortunately often costly. Government and private industry support scholarships, grants, and loans to assist in meeting this goal. Tutoring must start with the young in order to decrease high school dropout rates and produce graduates ready to enter higher learning.

Punishment

Politicians take credit for reduced crime rates by pointing to an increase in community policing, more jails, stricter sentences, and more stringent gun laws. When communities become fearful of increased violence, the first reaction is to "lock them up" with stricter laws. Yet our prisons are full and overflowing. There are more young men in prison today than at any other time in history (Rosenberg, 1995).

State and federal prison authorities had under their jurisdiction 1,470,045 inmates at year end

2003: 1,296,986 under state jurisdiction and 173,059 under federal jurisdiction (U.S. Department of Justice, Bureau of Justice Statistics, 2005). The United States has the second highest imprisonment rate in the industrialized world, after Russia. Most of the increase in the prison population is due to violent offenders (Van Slambrouck, 1998). The prisons are filled with convicts with little formal education and poor job prospects (Winslow, 2000). When a person enters a prison, dehumanization occurs immediately. He or she is no longer a person, but a number. Guards view prisoners as dehumanized. Most violent offenders are released from prison without rehabilitation and are more violent than ever. There are a limited number of rehabilitation programs, but they are not properly monitored and development of new programs is lacking. The vast majority of prisoners eventually get back out onto the street. Because sending people to prison is not reducing violence rates, law makers should consider stricter limits on young people's access to firearms, alcohol, and illegal drugs, an idea supported by research (Tomes, 1995).

It is unlikely that government policies will change any time soon. Law enforcement is a big business. As of June 2000, state and local law enforcement agencies had 1,019,496 full-time personnel, 11% more than the 921,978 employed in 1996. In the private sector nationally, private police total almost 2 million, far more than the total number of federal, state, and local police (Inciardi, 2002).

A coherent and coordinated federal strategy for studying violence that would set up a long-term national investment in research and development of prevention programs would help lawmakers know where to put tax dollars and votes (Monahan, 1994). There must be more research on the effectiveness of current programs.

Gun Control

Lawmakers on Capitol Hill often consider gun control bills aimed at reducing the violence in our society. The data consistently reports that about 70% of murders and about 40% of robberies are committed with some type of firearm (Federal Bureau of Investigation, 2000). Ferguson (2002) theorizes that Americans' easy access to guns may be why the violence rate is the highest of any industrialized country. When-

ever violence is perceived as increasing, gun purchases increase. Guns are widely available and there is not enough regulatory oversight of ammunition design, manufacturing, marketing, sales, importation, storage, possession, and use (Winnett, 1998). Children and adolescents are finding easier access to guns (Rosenberg, 1995). Youth are often unable to settle arguments without becoming physical; but with the increased availability of guns, fights may become fatal. Guns provide an impersonal, emotionally detached, tidy way of attacking someone, especially for people who do not want close contact with their victims (Kleck & Hogan, 1999). Just owning a gun can increase the chance of becoming victimized. Kellermann et al. (1993) theorized that people in households with guns were 2.7 times more likely to become homicide victims as people in households without guns. Kleck and Hogan (1999) did their own research and believe it is only 1.36 times as likely.

Some researchers have suggested that the presence of a weapon may have an aggression-inhibiting effect. Most perpetrators do not want to kill; they just want to scare the victim into cooperating with them. Without a gun, a robber could not rob without attacking the victim. Thus the presence of a gun may help avoid a physical attack in the perpetration of a crime. Even when someone is actually shot, Kleck and Hogan (1999) found, only 8% of all gun shootings end in a fatality. This is still the highest fatality rate of any weapon, with knives coming in second. There is no doubt that guns are used in many crimes by perpetrators or victims, but the debate questions whether guns influence the frequency and outcomes of violent crimes (Kleck & Hogan, 1999). If they do, then what can be done with all the guns available in this country?

The United States is a long way from enacting very strict gun laws because Americans feel very strongly about the second amendment to the Constitution, which states, "A well regulated Militia, being necessary to the security of a free State, the right of the people to keep and bear Arms, shall not be infringed" (The Constitution of the United States, Amendment 2). The founders of our country fled homelands that allowed only the ruling classes to own guns and they feared this could also happen in their new country. They did not want the ruling classes to use weapons to oppress the common people. The National Rifle Association is a very powerful gun lobby with a large membership and a lot of money to take its case to the public and influence law makers. There are also theorists who associate England's stricter gun laws with an increase in robbery because robbers have less fear of being shot (Faria, 1999). The debate will go on for many years with a lot of compromises that may or may not lead to a reduction in the overall crime rate.

Programmatic Intervention

Prevention programs should be based on the needs of each community (Willis & Silovsky, 1998). Rosenberg (1995) supports prevention programs that focus on changing individuals' knowledge, skills, and attitudes on individual behavior. According to the UCR of 1997, 31% of murders were committed after an argument. There needs to be more development of conflict resolution programs. Such programs can teach behavior modification to model and reinforce skills in conflict resolution, stress and anger management, impulse control, problem-solving, and empathy (Winnett, 1998).

Schools are primary sites for programmatic intervention because violent tendencies begin to develop in the very young. Unfortunately, those most at risk for becoming offenders and victims are not in school because they have dropped out. So schools cannot be the only site for programmatic intervention. Tomes (1995) recommends early childhood interventions designed to help children learn to deal with conflict effectively and nonviolently. Schools that are located in or near major cities have the most success in combating violence because they have been dealing with it the longest (Cloud et al., 1999). The key to preventing violence lies in shaping children's beliefs, attitudes, and behaviors before violence becomes an automatic manifestation of their anger and a seemingly expedient and respectable way to resolve conflict or get what they want (Rembolt, 1998). Schools can also link at-risk boys with positive male mentors in the community (Rosenberg, 1995). The age difference does not have to be large; a 15-year-old could mentor a 12-year-old. Schools are also a likely place to introduce positive interactions with and tolerance of others different than oneself. Some schools have successfully offered classes with various activities geared to reduce prejudice (Salzman & D'Andrea, 2001), increase knowledge of others' cultures, and teach languages (Reese, 2001).

Schools are working harder to reduce violence on their campuses. Researchers have shown that quick fixes like installing metal detectors do not seem to help reduce the violence (Nemecek, 1998). Schlozman (2002) recommends that clinicians and school officials pay attention to threatening journal writing, disturbing art projects, and other students' concerns about a potentially violent student, and that authorities be designated to handle threats. Programs should deal not just with individual students, but with the school as a whole. It is important for all students to know they have a part in decreasing school violence (Schlozman, 2002).

Reseda High School in San Francisco Valley, California, has developed a few programs that show promise. Older students teach younger students the importance of keeping guns out of school and the correctness of reporting any awareness of guns at school (Gergen, 1998). Reseda High School also has a council of 30 students made up of known gang members and popular kids who keep in close contact with the principal as to what is going on among the students. Unfortunately, this method is not always fool-proof (Nemecek, 1998).

Thirty-four states are experimenting with school resource officers—law enforcement officers who are trained to spot troubled teenagers, teach students how to prevent violence, and arrest those who commit crimes. Texas is trying a law that has local law enforcement officials reporting to the school within 24 hours whenever a student is arrested (Gergen, 1998). These programs show signs of positive impact. Small schools also help reduce violence by providing more professionals per student and contributing to a sense of community so that students feel personally vested in their school (Klonsky, 2002). Wolfe et al. (1998) support cooperation among schools, families, community mental health agencies, medical and health organizations, and other social and governmental agencies.

There must also be public education to teach the causes and effects of violence and explain the problems with using certain types of weapons (Winnett, 1998). This is where the media can help. Just as "Just Say No" became a household phrase to reduce drug use and smoking, ads are created to reduce violence, especially the use of guns to settle arguments. Gun owners can also learn through public awareness advertising campaigns the importance of keeping their guns locked up safely.

Funding a prevention program can be very costly, as can researching the program to see if it works. The costs of running a community-based program averages $5,000, but to provide adequate evaluation can run as high as $50,000 (Rosenberg, 1995). Monahan (1994) suggests there should be a partnership between private foundations and community organizations to create and evaluate prevention programs.

Conclusion

Violence is a problem that affects and should concern all Americans. Though violence rates had until recently been steadily going down, America has the highest violence rate of all industrialized nations. Socialization into violence occurs within our culture of aggression and retribution, and in families where violence is used to settle disputes. Parents often do not spend enough time guiding their children. Multiple acts of violence, shown as entertainment, affect the susceptible viewer and make us all numb to real violence. Politicians have been debating for years what they can do to reduce violence. Research has shown that guns are used in a large percentage of violent acts, and these rates are increasing for the young. Marx theorizes that violence is inevitable when there is inequality among the classes, and as long as there is poverty there will be violence because of feelings of inequality and frustration. Programmatic intervention shows some promise within schools and communities, but more money must be made available to help assess how well these programs work and how they can better serve the community. American culture needs to change.

Response

All for the Love of God

Taken from the *New Scientist*, 5/11/2002, Vol. 174, Issue 2,342 (46–50) [used by permission]

Why do people go to war? You can blame inequality, oppression, even greed, but the fact remains that in most recent or current conflicts, religion plays a crucial role: The Middle East, the Balkans, Kashmir, Sri Lanka, Northern Ireland. Aren't irreconcilable beliefs bound to lead to friction? Isn't it too easy for political leaders to exploit religious differences for their own ends? *New Scientist* asked leading figures from several major faiths about the link between belief and violence, and whether organised religion does more harm than good.

Islam
Zaki Badawi, Principal of the Muslim College in London

"Religious differences do not cause conflict. Religion comes in only once the lines of conflict have been drawn, and the people who start the violence may not be religious at *all*. When the Germans were knocking at the gates of Moscow during the Second World War, for instance, Stalin called on the Patriarch to help mobilise public opinion to stand up to the Germans. You cannot believe that Stalin was a particularly pious Christian.

"Religion plays a part in conflict because it has the power to influence people's emotion. Islam runs very deep in Arab societies, it is part of our being, our identity. Hence an appeal to it would be natural, and it would have an echo very quickly.

"As Muslims, we would very much like everybody to be a Muslim, but through dialogue. The Koran tells us to encourage people through dialogue and good manners and gentle words. Conflict can happen if you use methods that are not legal, or not just. Islam has an agreement with the Vatican that we should avoid preaching our religions in each other's territories in Africa. We have a large sea of non-Christians and non-Muslims who are still following the traditional African religions that we can both work and compete for.

"One hopeful outcome of the terrorist attacks on September 11 is that many people have started writing and reading about Islam, and reading the Koran. This will make people realise that the propaganda that has filled Western minds since the Crusades—that Islam has an inherent hostility towards Christians or towards the West in general—has no foundation. Of course there have been wars between Muslims and Christians, but these wars were about territory or property, not about religion. They still are. The Americans are not in Saudi Arabia to try to convert the Saudis to Christianity, or for that matter even to secularism. They are there because of the oil.

"On the question of suicide bombers, they are driven primarily by the physical conditions to which they are subjected. Being subjected to brutal treatment fills them with rage and an urge to inflict harm on anyone, however innocent, who might be connected with their tormentor. The religious element is a minor factor in their behaviour. Suicide bombers are present in every culture. You find them in Japan, Sri Lanka, India and South America. Incidentally, the first Palestinian suicide bomber was a Christian, not a Muslim.

"The Palestinian-Israeli conflict is essentially a question of human rights. The truly religious people treat the Palestinians as human beings. The myths that have been spread about the conflict—that Palestine was a country without

people, for example—have nothing to do with religion. The first step is to treat the Palestinians as human beings. Any Jew who says otherwise would not be a Jew. He would be a politician. The worst politician is the one who uses religion to achieve his objectives. He muddies the name of religion because he uses it in this fashion. Likewise, the religious person who uses his position to achieve his political objectives corrupts politics."

Judaism
Albert Friedlander, Rabbi Emeritus of Westminster Synagogue in London

"I believe in the total separation of church and state because it is too tempting for religions to use the power of the state to propagate their own ends. Abortions are one example. If they are given extra power, most religions try to push their own approach to the detriment of their neighbours. And it is quite true that religious differences, more than anything else, have created evil situations.

"I believe in the basic decency of human beings, and I believe that in most religions the majority of believers want to reach out towards others and that they respect others. When a religious person is sure of what they believe and practise, then they are much more relaxed and they can accept others. Fanatics tend to cling to some smaller aspect of the totality and they ignore the bulk of the religion in which they have been brought up.

"How can religion help resolve conflict? First of *all*, individuals have to acknowledge their own

shortcomings. In the Middle East conflict, Yasser Arafat and Ariel Sharon are totally frozen in their roles as fighters and this has made it almost impossible for reconciliation to take place. There has to be an acknowledgment by both sides of things that have been done wrong. This has to be said at the beginning, not the end, of the bargaining.

"I do a great deal of work in Germany. I do not treat the children of those who have sinned against the Jews during the Second World War as sinners. I do not think that they should have to carry the burden of guilt. But they should carry the burden of responsibility. Most religions hold that you do not carry the burden of the sins that have been committed in the past by your ancestors, but you carry the responsibility to undo the effects of those past actions."

Catholicism
Michael Sabbah, Latin Patriarch of Jerusalem

"Should Catholics try to convert others to Christianity? Every believer must believe that his religion is best for him and for everyone. If he did not, he would be a liar and a hypocrite. What remains of my religion if I don't see that it is the best? And since I believe that my religion is best for everyone, I have a duty to share it with others.

"But while it is my responsibility to give what I have of my religion, it is not my responsibility that the other person takes. When I make the other's taking my responsibility, then it becomes not a sharing but an aggression. Some people do not respect this freedom of taking. But if I impose my faith upon someone who sincerely believes that he has *all* the truth, then I induce him in error, because he sincerely does not believe that my faith is the true one.

"Corruption of faith comes when a political leader gives to the religion other meanings, other ideas, other aims. Religion is my link with *God*, and with the creatures of *God*. Religion is to *love* every creature of *God*. Now if I do not respect other people as creatures of *God*, I have no religion at *all*, whatever tradition I come from.

"There is nothing bad in religion itself. What is bad is the one who uses religion for other purposes, especially for the killing of others. That evil is not in the religion, it is in the man."

Anglicanism

Michael Nazir-Ali, Bishop of Rochester

"Religion is sometimes a defining character in conflict between groups because it can be so fundamental to a people's identity and culture. When that identity is threatened then religion becomes a factor. In this, it is no different from politics or economics. It is something quite basic to human society.

"In the 20th century, most of the mega conflicts in the world were caused by secular rather than religious ideologies. National socialism, for example, and Stalinism, and on a smaller scale Pol Pot in Kampuchea. Many of the tribal conflicts in Africa have been caused more by ethnic than religious differences.

"However, as well as having a responsibility to provide cohesion for society, religion has a responsibility to challenge society and its leaders when they are going wrong, when they are oppressing their own people or engaging in unjustified conflict with another state."

Buddhism

The Dalai Lama

"I see *all* the different religious traditions as paths for the development of inner peace, which is the true foundation of world peace. We need to ensure that different religions of the world can become powerful allies of peace. To do this, the different faiths need to develop mutual respect for and understanding of each other's beliefs and values. The world's religions can contribute to world peace if there is peace and growing harmony between the different faiths.

"It is also my belief that whereas the 20th century was a century of war and untold suffering, the 21st century should be one of peace and dialogue. As the continued advances in information technology make our world a truly global village, I believe there will be a time when war and armed conflict will be considered an outdated and obsolete method of settling differences among nations and communities. The nations and peoples of the world will soon realise that dialogue and compromise are the best methods of settling differences for mutual benefit and for the sake of our future and the future of our much ravaged and fragile planet.

"However, there can be no peace as long as there is grinding poverty, social injustice, inequality, oppression, environmental degradation, and as long as the weak and small continue to be trodden by the mighty and powerful."

Taken from the Dalai Lama's message to the Millennium World Peace Summit, August 2000.

Discussion Questions

1. What is the definition of violence?
2. Where does violence most often occur?
3. How much violence is there in America?
4. What are the rates of the various forms of violence?
5. Who is committing most violent acts?
6. What are typical victim/offender relationships?
7. What does violence do to its victims?
8. What are the most commonly cited causes of violence?
9. What role does society play in encouraging a violent culture?

Many Voices: An Introduction to Social Issues

10. What role does mass media play in encouraging violence?
11. What role does economics have in violence rates?
12. What works best to reduce violence?
13. What can parents do to reduce violent tendencies in their children?
14. What can schools do to reduce and prevent violence within their walls?

Related Readings

Akers, R. L. (1994). *Criminological theories*. Los Angeles: Roxbury.

Gill, M. L., Fisher, B., & Bowie, V. (Eds.) (2002). *Violence at work: Causes, patterns, and prevention*. Cullompton: Willan Publishing.

Gilligan, J. (1996). *Violence: Our deadly epidemic and its causes*. New York: Putnam.

Kimball, C. (2002). *When religion becomes evil*. San Francisco: Harper.

Nelson-Pallmeyer, J. (2003). *Is religion killing us: Violence in the Bible and the Qu'Ran*. Hamsburg, PA: Trinity.

Niehoff, D. (1999). *The biology of violence (How understanding the brain, behavior, and environment can break the vicious circle of aggression)*. New York: Free Press.

Rapp-Paglicci, L. A., Roberts, A. R., & Wodarski, J. S. (Eds.) (2002). *Handbook of violence*. New York: Wiley.

Richard, A. J., & Rohn, R. (1999). *Roots of violence in the U.S. culture: A diagnosis towards healing*. Nevada City: Blue Dolphin.

Ridley, M. (2003). *Nature via nurture: Genes, experience, and what makes us human*. New York: HarperCollins.

Van Hasselt, V. B., & Herseu, M. (Eds). (1999). *Aggression & violence: An introductory text*. Needham Heights, MA: Allyn & Bacon.

Zimring, F. E., & Hawkins, G. (1997). *Crime is not the problem: Lethal violence in America*. Oxford: Oxford University Press.

Related Web Sites

Center for the Prevention of School Violence: http://www.cpsv.org
Center for the Study and Prevention of Violence: http://www.colorado.edu/cspv
Minnesota Center Against Violence and Abuse: http://www.mincava.umn.edu
National Center on Elder Abuse: http://www.elderabusecenter.org
Partnerships Against Violence: http://www.pavnet.org/front.html
Stockholm International Peace Research Institute: http://www.sipri.org
United States Institute of Peace: http://www.usip.org

Related Movies/Videos

Boyz 'N the Hood (1991) with Laurence Fishburne and Cuba Gooding, Jr.
Burning Bed (1984) with Sarah Fawcett and Paul Le Mat
The Killing Fields (1984) with Sam Waterston and Hang S. Ngor
Lord of the Flies (1990) with Balthazar Getty
We Were Soldiers (2002) with Mel Gibson

MENTAL HEALTH

Herbert W. Helm, Jr.

12

Chapter Outline

Who is being described in each of the following cases?

Case A: He had been a Boy Scout, a law school dropout, a counselor on a suicide hotline, and a Republican Party worker. He had worked for the Seattle Crime Prevention Advisory Commission on a preliminary investigation into rape assaults. Like most with his disorder, he was white, intelligent, and charming. At age 42, he was electrocuted as one of the most famous serial killers in the United States. He had confessed to slaying thirty women, but there may have been another fifty. He tended to victimize beautiful and intelligent co-eds. He drank before committing acts of sexual murder (MacPherson, 1989). A day before his execution, he claimed his urges were triggered by violent pornography.

Case B: On March 30, 1981, he attempted to kill President Ronald Reagan in an effort to impress actress Jodie Foster, whom he had never met. Instead, he hit the president's press secretary, leaving the secretary mentally and physically crippled for life. He was judged to be not guilty by reason of insanity. That judgment sent shock waves throughout the country and affected how courts deal with the insanity issue. Still, under 1981 laws he can be freed if judged to be sane. Most of his psychiatrists feel he has recovered from the psychotic episode that provoked the attack on the president. However, no one who has attempted to assassinate a president has ever been released. One of his pen pals was Case A (Fields-Meyer, 1997).

Case C: By day she walks down the French Quarter in New Orleans. Looking to be in her late 40s, she appears poorly dressed and disheveled. If not homeless, she appears to live at a very low socioeconomic level. Her life appears disorganized and shattered. She yells repeatedly, "Get away from me," yet no one is near her. She appears to be hallucinating. She searches through garbage cans to see what she can find. At one she finds a cup with some drink remaining. At another she finds a bite of discarded food. She eats and drinks, then moves down the street.

Case D: He was born in the Soviet Union and worked as an engineer in an armaments factory during World War II. He was a distinguished scientist who played a vital role in the development of the Soviet hydrogen bomb. In 1975 he won the Nobel Peace Prize. Instead of living a life of luxury, he chose to fight the injustices he saw in his country. He was exiled to Gorky, a city off-limits to foreigners and under KGB guard. There, he was officially an "unperson." During one of his hunger strikes he believed that they put psychotropic drugs (medications given for mental disorders) into the food they force-fed him. This, he believed, influenced his writing of a statement concerning the ending of his hunger strike. In 1986 Mikhail Gorbachev released him without condition.

Case E: He has made millions, yet still spends many days entertaining people. He makes funny faces and tries to look dopey at times. He talks about his bad hairpiece, yet we know that not even a poor person would buy such a hairpiece. We can see that his hair "problem" is little more than the receding hairline of a middle-age man. Despite the impression he tries to give of not quite understanding what is going on, he is in control of most of his guests. He is good at getting into his guests' lives, but rarely lets them into his.

Answers:

Case A: Ted Bundy, serial killer with antisocial personality disorder.

Case B: John W. Hinkley, Jr., attempted to shoot President Reagan, judged to be insane.

Case C: An unidentified schizophrenic in the French Quarter, probably paranoid type.

Case D: Andrei Sakharov, Soviet physicist and political leader, imprisoned for views differing from that of the government.

Case E: David Letterman, showman—eccentric, or mentally disordered?

Introduction

As you consider the five cases presented above, would you say these people are behaving abnormally? Most of us have a sense of what constitutes abnormal behavior, but do the behaviors exhibited by these people fit your concept of mental disorder? Are their behaviors the result of disorganized thinking, emotional problems, or illness—or are they simply at odds with the expectations of our society? What criteria do you use in determining whether someone is behaving abnormally? How do mental disorders affect individuals and the society within which they live? These are some of the topics and questions we will explore in this chapter.

As you read this chapter, use the following questions to guide your thinking and discussions:

- How does one recognize a mental disorder? How does society define mental deviance? What is the origin (or etiology) of mental disorders?
- How should we classify mental disorders?
- What is the incidence and cost of mental disorders?
- What factors are associated with mental disorders? How and why do these factors affect our behavior?
- How should we treat mental disorders? Does society have a responsibility to treat mentally disordered individuals? Who should decide which people receive treatment?

What Is a Mental Disorder?

ISSUES: Who should define what constitutes a mental disorder? What types of behavior, thinking, or feelings must be present for a person to be considered abnormal? Should social considerations, such as the violation of social norms, play a role in the determination of abnormality?

In this section we will explore five ways of defining abnormal behavior.

1. The person is experiencing distress or dysfunction and finding it maladaptive. People often seek therapy because they are unhappy and experiencing some sort of distress. They may be suffering from depression, anxiety, a poor marriage, or some other difficulty. Whatever the reason, they seek relief from their pain. Such distress, in itself, is not evidence of a mental disorder. At one time or another, most of us experience distress over things such as financial problems, the loss of loved ones, or overwork. Since these are common problems experienced by most people at times during the course of their lives, they are not considered abnormal. But some people experience suffering and distress even when their lives would seem, by most standards, to be going fairly well (**neurosis**). This suffering can include phobias, bodily symptoms that appear to be due to physical ailments but for which no objective medical

diagnosis can be made (**somatoform disorder**), and persistent thoughts combined with the need to engage in certain repetitive acts (**obsessive-compulsive disorder**). On the other hand, people with certain personality disorders experience little distress themselves, but can cause a great deal of distress in the lives of others. In spite of the difficulties they cause others, they believe that their behavior is quite acceptable.

2. The person has lost control over some aspect of life or is in poor touch with reality. Loss of control can range from a fear or phobia to having lost touch with reality (**psychosis**). A sense of being out of control can affect people's behavior and their responses to the world around them. For example, people with a fear of snakes may attempt to maintain control by restricting certain activities. They may decide to live in a city and avoid visiting places where snakes might be found. Fear thus controls what they are willing to allow themselves to experience. The case of the lady in

New Orleans suggests someone who is out of touch with reality in that she is not responding appropriately to her external environment.

Inside the idea of control over our lives lies the issue of predictability. If your roommate treats you pleasantly on one occasion, is aloof on the next, and screams at you on another, such unpredictable behavior may lead you to believe that something is wrong. This is especially true if you cannot find a logical reason for the behavior. But seemingly illogical or unpredictable behavior may not, by itself, be evidence of a mental disorder. For example, many religions expect their devotees to talk to God or some spirit. Within their system of beliefs, it may be acceptable—and even desirable—to be overtaken by a spirit. This hardly seems predictable, but would you be willing to describe a person exhibiting such behavior as having a mental disorder?

3. The person's behavior is seen as extreme or unusual from a statistical or observational viewpoint. One way to determine whether a person has a disorder is to compare his or her feelings and behavior to those of others. For instance, when a person's intelligence and adaptive behavior falls within the bottom two or three percent of the population as a whole, we may consider him or her to be mentally retarded. Most of us exhibit a range of behaviors or experience a range of feelings that lie along a continuum of possibilities. It is normal, for example, for most people to experience feelings of depression at times during their lives and feelings of joy at other times. Problems arise when our feelings or behaviors tend to remain at an extreme (either prolonged depression or mania), or bounce from one extreme to the other (manic-depressive), and our lives become dysfunctional as a result.

We may also judge the behavior of another person or group as unusual in comparison to our own. A conservative Midwesterner walking into a New York nightclub might consider the dress and behavior exhibited there as abnormal and extreme. That same Midwesterner might find some of the behavior exhibited by the Amish—who live without electricity, work without the aid of motors, and dress in their own distinctive style—equally unusual. Yet both a New York

nightclub patron and an Amish person might consider their behavior quite normal within the context of their communities. We cannot use cultural differences alone as a basis for defining abnormality.

4. Abnormalities are labels given by professionals and used as a basis from which to treat mental disorders. In our society, some people, such as doctors and therapists, have the power to label particular behaviors as abnormal and then use that diagnosis as a basis for treatment. Such people typically go through long periods of study and training and follow carefully prescribed, objective guidelines in making their diagnoses. But we must consider that their diagnoses may often be influenced by their own—subjective—beliefs and experiences. Consider the case of a child who, because of excessive behavior, is labeled as hyperactive. The behavior may indeed be due to some disorder, but it may also be the result of inadequate restraints from parents or teachers. It may be easier to label the child as hyperactive than to deal with the environmental components.

5. The behavior is seen as a deviation from social norms. While this definition can cover some aspects noted above, such as judging "unusual" behavior, it goes further and suggests that culture or society helps determine what is normal. Under current diagnostic measures, the **DSM-IV-TR**, the American Psychiatric Association does not consider homosexuality a mental disorder. However, until the 1980s homosexuality *was* considered a sexual disorder. While homosexuality may not have changed, society's perspective may have. Societies believe that people ought to behave in certain ways, and when an individual's behavior violates those standards that person may be perceived as having a mental disorder.

There are other issues to consider when attempting to define abnormal behavior. For example, the degree to which people's behavior helps or hinders them in their daily lives can determine whether that behavior is seen as being "normal" or "abnormal." For the purpose of this chapter, however, the five concepts presented above will serve as adequate definitions. Having defined abnormality, we should now examine its origins by looking at some different perspectives on mental disorders.

Perspectives on Mental Disorders

ISSUES: Who should define what constitutes a mental disorder? Should social considerations, the determination of abnormality?

However we define mental disorders, we need to look at the origins, or **etiology,** of these disorders. Here, we will view their etiology from five perspectives: the supernatural, the psychological, the biological or medical, the sociocultural, and the myth (or social labeling) perspective. How we view the etiology of a disorder influences how we attempt to treat it. For example, those who view a disorder from a supernatural perspective might try to treat it through prayer or religious ritual. Those who take a biological perspective might try using drugs or surgery.

The Supernatural Perspective

Several ancient cultures, including the Persians, Hebrews, Babylonians, and Egyptians, believed spirits could enter a person and cause mental and physical disorders. The Greeks noted the power of Cupid's arrows. Here, an otherwise normal individual could be smitten with love by a shot from Cupid's bow. The New Testament tells of people who were brought to Jesus because they exhibited behaviors that were attributed to demonic possession. It was common for some cultures to see humans as the battleground for good and evil. Not only were physical and psychological illnesses attributed to outside forces, but so were other occurrences in their lives, such as floods, droughts, and imprisonment.

Here are just a few examples of cases in which people believed that outside forces affected human behavior and well being:

- Abnormal behavior, such as delusions, hysteria, and mania, has been attributed to witchcraft during the Middle Ages and at Salem, Massachusetts.
- Our word *lunatic* comes from the idea that during given lunar phases some people go crazy.
- During the rise of the AIDS epidemic in the 1990s, some discussed the idea of sin and punishment. AIDS was seen as a result of abhorrent behavior of homosexuals that resulted in divine punishment (Barlow & Durand, 1999).

Treatments follow what one believes about the supernatural etiology. People treating someone whom they believe is possessed by a demon, witch, or spirit will likely use some type of exorcism, ritual, incantation, prayer, or even ritualistic (or actual) death. Here are two examples from the Old Testament:

"Israel's first king, Saul, was said to be troubled by evil spirits and was treated with calming music.… David took the harp and played it…Saul was refreshed and was well, and the evil spirit departed from him" (I Samuel 16:14–23). However, abnormality was sometimes interpreted as divine punishment for disobedience. Nebuchadnezzar, King of Babylon, was said to be stricken with *lycanthropy* (the belief that one is a wolf) as divine retribution for his boastfulness (Daniel 4:28–33). The king had to live in the wild until, after acknowledging God's power, his reason was restored, and he was reinstated (Nietzel et al., 1998, p. 5).

People who believe in the power and effectiveness of prayer believe in a supernatural model. While it may not be their only perspective, they are asserting that a powerful force exists outside them.

The Psychological Perspective

An early precursor to modern psychological views of mental disorders was that of *moral therapy*—the belief that the mentally ill should be treated humanely. The idea arose from several reformers who felt the mentally ill should not be treated like animals, chained, or have their blood let. They should be treated as if they were sick, and the treatment should address their emotional and psychological problems.

While there are several psychological perspectives on the etiology and treatment of mental disorders, there is a basic focus on treating individuals rather than punishing them for their "sins." In the foundation chapters we reviewed many explanations of human behavior. Here we will look at just a few examples.

The **psychodynamic** or psychoanalytic approaches, starting with Freud, focus on the stress of development and the power of the unconscious. While Freud focused heavily on sexual development, later theorists focused on several other issues, including social ones. The role of therapy in the psychoanalytic approach is to treat unconscious processes and the suffering they bring.

The **learning** approaches examine the roles that reinforcement and punishment play in shaping our behavior. Social learning theory considers how our observations of the behavior of others play a role in shaping our behavior. Abnormal behavior is learned. If the environment is what creates disturbance, then it can be restructured to alter abnormal behavior.

The **humanistic** approaches believe we are basically good. However, society and people we value put conditions of acceptance on us. In order to gain that acceptance, we block certain behaviors and so limit the ways in which we might grow. Therapy is aimed at creating a situation of unconditional positive regard that allows for personal growth to occur.

These, and other, psychological theories have taken the role of sin and devils out of the realm of abnormal behavior. Treatment from this perspective can include various forms of psychotherapy. These psychotherapies are usually talk- or behavior-oriented (or combine elements of both) and follow the school of thought from which they arose.

The Biological or Medical Perspective

One of the more powerful models of abnormal behavior today is the biological or **medical perspective**. In this model, abnormal behavior is felt to have a biological cause, or to result from a medical illness. If the brain and its nervous system control our thoughts and emotions, it must be responsible for our behavior. Disordered behavior is therefore the result of abnormal brain chemistry. These dysfunctions could be at the levels of the neurotransmitters or hormones, or they could arise from dysfunctions within the brain or other parts of the nervous system. This is the *disease* model of abnormal behavior.

The phenomenon of witchcraft and the Salem trials is an example of how the etiology of abnormal behavior may be viewed from more than one perspective. Instead of a supernatural perspective, Caporael (1976) argues that, as a result of the damp weather, people around Salem could have been exposed to ergot fungus in their rye. This fungus produces lysergic acid,

which is a hallucinogen. When eaten, this hallucinogen affects the human nervous system, causing unusual behaviors that people who believe in a supernatural perspective might interpret as evidence of witchcraft.

The medical model seeks to find the biological roots of disorders. Studies of familial patterns, and of the similarities and differences between twins raised separately or together, try to determine the role played by our genes. The case of the Genain quadruplets—all of whom developed **schizophrenia**—presents strong evidence for a genetic basis or predisposition for the disorder (Rosenthal, 1963). Neurotransmitters, such as serotonin and dopamine, have been studied and linked with disorders such as depression, schizophrenia, anxiety, and others. Biological structures, such as the limbic system, are involved in our emotions, memory, hunger, and thirst. These examples indicate the role biology plays in our behavior.

If a disorder is believed to be of biological origin, then the treatment needs to focus on the individual's physiology. In the medical model, the person is seen as a patient who is ill and in need of an expert, such as a medical doctor. Several treatments are used, including electroconvulsive therapy (ECT), drug therapies, and psychosurgery. This approach does not adequately consider the roles of culture, society, or the environment.

The Sociocultural Perspective

The sociocultural approach says that to understand abnormal behavior we must consider the social and cultural factors involved. It sees society and its external elements, such as socioeconomic status, social policies, and race and gender bias, as causing abnormal behavior. The society, not the individual, is viewed as the problem.

Holmes (1997) noted three ways sociocultural factors can affect abnormal behavior. A society or culture can determine *what* is abnormal, the *level* at which it is abnormal, and the *nature* of abnormal behavior. For example, a culture usually decides what is "normal" sexual behavior, and this definition may change over time. It will also decide at what "level" a disorder exists. Stores like Victoria's Secret sell lingerie that can enhance sexual arousal. This is considered normal in our society. However, if this became the main way for an individual to become sexually aroused, that person would be considered to have a **fetish**. The "nature" aspect is described in this chapter under the section on culture and abnormal behavior. Here, a culture may influence the symptoms of a disorder such as Koro (genital retraction syndrome).

While there may not be a true "therapy" for this approach, one can deal with abnormal behavior by either conforming to a society's expectations or changing that society's views of what is considered abnormal. However, it is difficult to remove the label of "mental illness" once it is given (Nevid et al., 1997).

The Myth or Social Labeling Perspective

In 1960, Thomas Szasz stated that mental illness did not exist. The concept of illness comes from the medical model, and suggests that there has to be some physical or neurological deficit. Szasz made the distinction between a deficit of the brain, such as a visual deficit affecting sight, and a belief of the mind. One may have unusual beliefs or behaviors arising from aspects of political or religious systems, but those beliefs do not constitute an "illness."

Szasz contended that if a person does not behave in ways prescribed by society, or acts in ways the society considers illogical, that person may be judged to be mentally ill. But what is the illness? Here, one person is making a judgment that another person has a mental symptom. In other words, the person gets a social (and perhaps mental) label for behavior that is not acceptable for that society. It is a deviation from some social norm.

Szasz maintained that labeling deviant, dangerous, or self-destructive behavior as mental illness distracts from an understanding of such behavior. Moreover, this type of invidious labeling leads to some innocent people being deprived of their freedoms, such as in involuntary psychiatric interventions. In other situations, such as in the case of would-be presidential assassin John Hinckley, it allows individuals to avoid being held responsible for their actions, even to the point of exculpation of heinous crimes (Vatz & Weinberg, 1993, p. 62).

We live in a complex—and not always harmonious—world. Throughout their lives, people face problems and conflicts. But while their conflicts may often be psychosocial or ethical in nature, the illness model views the remedies in terms of medical measures. Szasz feels that the belief in mental illness is "real" in the same way that the belief in witches was "real." He does not want to offer a new therapy, but to reevaluate the phenomena we call mental illness. We should see it as the struggles people face in their lives. However, Vatz and Weinberg (1993) point out that if we no longer see these phenomena as mental illness, it may affect things like the insanity plea and third-party reimbursements for medical illness.

Classification Systems

ISSUES: Do we have the right to classify someone else's behavior as abnormal? If so, what cluster of behaviors, thoughts, and feelings should constitute a diagnosis? If we don't have classification systems, what should we use to determine abnormal behavior? Without classification systems, how are professionals to study and communicate about various disorders?

There are two major classification systems for mental disorders: the 10th edition of the International Classification of Diseases (ICD-10), which classifies mental and physical disorders, and the text revision of the fourth edition of the *Diagnostic and Statistical Manual of Mental Disorders* (DSM-IV-TR). The American Psychiatric Association produces the DSM-IV-TR, which is the major classification system for mental disorders used in North America by mental health professionals. The ICD-10, produced by the World Health Organization (WHO), is used by the rest of the world. The DSM-IV-TR (2000) points out that individuals who worked on the two systems attempted to "coordinate their efforts." However, psychiatric diagnosis is based mostly on

Categories of DSM-IV-TR Classification

Disorders Usually First Diagnosed in Infancy, Childhood, or Adolescence

These disorders are usually brought to attention from infancy to adolescence. However, some may not be diagnosed until adulthood. The range of problems can include areas such as developmental issues, learning disorders, communication disorders, and attention-deficit and disruptive behavior disorders. Examples include Mental Retardation, Attention-Deficit/Hyperactivity Disorder, and Autistic Disorder.

Delirium, Dementia, Amnesic, and Other Cognitive Disorders

These disorders are generally believed to develop later in life and present changes from a previous level of functioning. These disorders may have factors such as aging, medical conditions, and being substance induced. An example is Dementia of the Alzheimer's Type.

Mental Disorders Due to a General Medical Condition Not Elsewhere Classified

The displayed mental symptoms are believed to be based on a general medical condition. This is demonstrated by a physical examination, the client's history, or a laboratory assessment. An example: Personality change due to a brain tumor.

Substance-Related Disorders

These disorders include the use of various drugs such as alcohol, cocaine, and amphetamines. They also include the side effects one can get from medications and exposure to toxins. Substance intoxication, abuse, and dependence are addressed. Examples include Alcohol Dependence, Cocaine Withdrawal, and Inhalant Intoxication.

Schizophrenia and Other Psychotic Disorders

Psychotic disorders refer to classifications that have features of hallucinations, delusions, disorganized speech, and unusual behavior. Schizophrenia is a disorder in which a person's life becomes fragmented or shattered in several areas (thoughts, behavior, etc.). Examples include Schizophrenia, Paranoid Type, and Brief Psychotic Disorder.

Mood Disorders

Also called Affective Disorders, these are disorders that affect our moods. They refer to various levels of disturbance concerning depression, mania, or both (bipolar disorder). Examples include Major Depressive Disorder, Bipolar I Disorder, and Substance-Induced Mood Disorder.

Anxiety Disorders

Anxiety disorders include fears, apprehension of the future, body symptoms of tension, and thought processes (such as obsessions) that interfere with aspects of living. Examples include Obsessive-Compulsive Disorder, Panic Disorder with Agoraphobia, and Post-traumatic Stress Disorder.

Somatoform Disorders

Based on the client's complaints about somatoform disorders, one would believe that there is a physical disorder involved. However, no organic or physical reason can be found that would fully explain the disorder. There should be a strong reason to believe that these symptoms are caused by psychological processes. Examples include Hypochondriasis, Pain Disorder, and Somatization Disorder.

Factitious Disorders

These are physical or psychological symptoms the client feigns or creates so as to play the role of the patient. In these cases there is no known benefit, such as economic gain, to the client except attention and playing the role of patient. Examples include Factitious Disorder with Combined Psychological and Physical Signs and Symptoms.

Dissociative Disorders

A disruption or "splitting off" occurs in the person's memory, consciousness, or identity. In these cases the person dissociates from the environment. Examples include Dissociative Identity Disorder (formerly known as Multiple Personality Disorder), Dissociative Amnesia, and Depersonalization Disorder.

Sexual and Gender Identity Disorders

This category includes three types of disorders: sexual dysfunctions, disturbances in the sexual response cycle, such as desire and orgasm; paraphilias, sexual arousal from unusual objects or activities; and gender identity disorder, which deals with distress concerning one's sex and cross-gender identification. Examples include Sexual Aversion Disorder and Exhibitionism.

Eating Disorders

This section has two basic eating disorders. One revolves around a refusal to maintain a minimum basic weight, and the other is a binge (and possibly purge) eating disorder. There are eating and feeding disorders of infancy or early childhood that can be found under the Disorders in Infancy, Childhood, or Adolescence. Examples include Anorexia Nervosa and Bulimia Nervosa.

Sleep Disorders

Disorders of sleep are organized into groups based on their presumed etiology. These four groups include substance-induced sleep disorders, sleep disorders due to another mental disorder, disorders due to a general medical condition, and primary sleep disorders (which are broken down into dyssomnias and parasomnias). Examples include Primary Insomnia and Nightmare Disorder.

Impulse-Control Disorders Not Elsewhere Classified

Failure to resist impulses and temptations is the essential feature of these disorders. There is usually a building of tension prior to the act and a feeling of relief following. Examples include Kleptomania, Pyromania, and Intermittent Explosive Disorder.

Adjustment Disorders

With this, the mildest of the disorders, a person has a maladaptive reaction, either behavioral or emotional, to a stressor. The distress is beyond what would normally be expected. Should the stressor terminate, it is expected that the person would return to previous levels of coping within six months. Examples of subtypes include With Depressed Mood, With Disturbance of Conduct, and Unspecified.

Personality Disorders

These disorders involve personality traits or characteristics that become pervasive, maladaptive, and inflexible. Because these traits are exaggerated and depart from what is expected in the culture, the person is likely to have distress and problems in various aspects of life such as work and relationships. Examples include Histrionic, Narcissistic, Dependent, and Obsessive-Compulsive.

Other Conditions That May Be a Focus of Clinical Attention

While these conditions may be the focus of clinical attention, the victims may not have mental disorders. If they do, it is not related to the problem, or, if related to the problem, it is severe enough for clinical attention. Examples include Mental Disorder Affecting Medical Condition, Parent-Child Relational Problem, Physical Abuse of Child, Malingering, and Religious or Spiritual Problem.

Source: DSM-IV-TR, 2000

descriptive aspects. Overall, there appears about a 68% concordance (agreement) rate between the ICD-10 and the DSM-IV. Disorders such as **dysthymia**, depression, substance dependence, and generalized anxiety disorder have concordance rates above 75%. Diagnoses such as **post-traumatic stress disorder** and harmful substance use or abuse have concordance rates at or below 35% (Andrews, Slade, & Peters, 1999).

In this chapter we will focus on the diagnostic system of the DSM-IV-TR. Any classification system should be concerned with issues of both reliability and validity. Reliability indicates that different mental or physical health professionals could look at the same client and give the same diagnosis. Validity asserts that the diagnosis should be not only reliable, but valid, or correct, as well. In other words, if three psychologists saw the same client and each assigned a diagnosis of dysthymic disorder (a type of depression), there would be good reliability. However, if the client really had an anxiety disorder, such as generalized anxiety disorder, there would be poor validity, since the diagnosis was incorrect. Barlow and Durand (1999) note the following concern about the reliability and validity of both the ICD-10 and the DSM-IV: "they very strongly emphasize reliability, sometimes at the expense of validity" (p. 84).

Incidence and Cost of Mental Disorders

ISSUES: Labeling a particular behavior as a disorder incurs certain costs for a society. Conversely, once a behavior involves costs for a society, it will be labeled as a disorder. How then, should we determine the costs of a disorder? How much cost should be allowed before a society takes steps to deal with those behaviors?

This section will look at a few of the incidences and costs of mental disorders. It should be noted that current statistics are difficult to obtain, as it takes awhile to collect and organize them. Also, this type of data is difficult to collect and compile due to the large population and the diversity of organizations providing services. The following points on prevalence, taken from the National Institute of Mental Health (http://www.nimh.nih.gov/publicat/numbers.cfm, 2005), portray the state of mental health/illness in the United States:

- "An estimated 22.1 percent of Americans ages 18 and older—about 1 in 5 adults—suffer from a diagnosable mental disorder in a given year."
- "Approximately 18.8 million American adults, or about 9.5 percent of the U.S. population age 18 and older in a given year, have a depressive disorder."
- "Nearly twice as many women (12.0 percent) as men (6.6 percent) are affected by a depressive disorder each year. These figures translate to 12.4 million women and 6.4 million men in the U.S."
- "In 2000, 29,350 people died by suicide in the U.S."

- "More than 90 percent of people who kill themselves have a diagnosable mental disorder, commonly a depressive disorder or a substance abuse disorder."
- "Four times as many men as women die by suicide; however, women attempt suicide two to three times as often as men."
- "Approximately 19.1 million American adults ages 18 to 54, or about 13.3 percent of people in this age group in a given year, have an anxiety disorder."
- "Females are much more likely than males to develop an eating disorder. Only an estimated 5 to 15 percent of people with anorexia or bulimia and an estimated 35 percent of those with binge-eating disorder are male."
- "The mortality rate among people with anorexia has been estimated at 0.56 percent per year, or approximately 5.6 percent per decade, which is about 12 times higher than the annual death rate due to all causes of death among females ages 15–24 in the general population."

The following points about cost are taken from the National Mental Health Association (http://www.nmha.org/shcr/community_based/costoffset.pdf, 2005) and begin to portray the costs of mental health/illness in the United States:

- "The total yearly cost for mental illness in both the private and public sectors in the U.S. is $205 billion. Only $92 billion comes from direct treatment costs, with $105 billion due to lost productivity and $8 billion resulting from crime and welfare costs. The allocation for the cost of untreated and mistreated mental illness to American businesses, the government and families has grown to $113 billion annually."

- "Depression ranks among the top three workplace problems. Clinical depression alone costs the U.S. $43.7 billion annually. This includes workplace costs for absenteeism and lost productivity ($23.8 billion), direct costs for treatment and rehabilitation ($12.4 billion), and lost earning due to depression-induced suicides ($7.5 billion)."

In an article on the prevalence and treatment of mental disorder from 1990 to 2003, Kessler et al. (2005) noted: "The prevalence of mental disorder did not change during the decade (29.4 percent between 1990 and 1992 and 30.5 percent between 2001 and 2003…), but the rate of treatment increased. Among patients with a disorder, 20.3 percent received treatment between 1990 and 1992 and 32.9 percent received treatment between 2001 and 2003….Overall, 12.2 percent of the population 18 to 54 years of age received treatment for emotional disorders between 1990 and 1992 and 20.1 percent between 2001 and 2003…" (p. 2,515).

Had different sources been used, it is likely that these figures would differ to some degree. While we may not know the exact numbers, these figures point to the fact that a great many people suffer from some degree of mental disorder and that those disorders extract a significant cost on our society. For more detailed information, visit the websites mentioned above.

Factors Associated with Mental Disorders

ISSUES: Why do you think various factors are related to mental disorders? Are the factors a consequence of the etiology or are they simply associated with the disorder? If the factors are not caused by the etiology, what causes them? Why do you think some factors are more related to various disorders than other factors?

When studying "factors associated with mental disorders," we are not saying that the factors are causing the mental disorders; experimental studies are needed to make cause-and-effect statements. We mean that there seems to be some relationship, or association, between these factors and mental disorders. While we may not know what causes these disorders, we should be aware of the associations and our perceived explanations of these disorders. It should also be understood that several factors (age, ethnicity, and gender, for example) might be involved for any given individual.

Gender

Despite earlier studies suggesting that women have higher rates of mental illness, Sachs-Ericsson and Ciarlo (2000) found no real difference in the rates of psychiatric disorders between men and women. They suggested that differences detected in the earlier studies might have been the results of systematic biases. They did find that some disorders were gender specific, that is, occurring more often in one gender than the other. There are important and major differences when we look at the ratio of males and females for many of the diagnostic categories in the DSM-IV-TR. There are diagnoses—such as Female Orgasmic

Disorder or Premature Ejaculation—that are, by definition, restricted to one gender. Table 12.1 gives examples of sex ratios for several diagnoses as listed in the DSM-IV-TR (2000).

In her article on gender and psychiatry, Jimenez (1997) argued that our conception of mental disorders in women comes from our beliefs about the effect their reproductive systems have on them. This belief has been used to maneuver their behavior to current social norms. This concept of behavior and the reproductive system can be seen as far back as the Egyptians and Hippocrates. Hippocrates gave us the term *hysteria,* from which comes the term **histrionic,** which is the Latin word for "actor." Usually applied to women, this term is used to describe overly sentimental, excessively emotional, manipulative, and attention-seeking individuals. Hippocrates thought hysteria resulted when a women's uterus was wandering throughout her body in search of conception. Depending on where it was, it could cause physical symptoms such as blindness and paralysis. Marriage and fumigation of the vagina were seen as possible cures (Barlow & Durand, 1999).

From 1880 to 1882 Josef Breuer worked, using hypnotherapy, with Bertha Pappenheim, a client who exhibited a number of hysterical symptoms. He discussed his work with Freud, and together they came up with a psychologically oriented theory of hysteria. They came to believe that "hysterics suffer from reminiscences"—memories of emotionally painful experiences—that have somehow been excluded from consciousness. As long as such memories remain forgotten, the emotion associated with them is "strangulated" or bottled-up and converted into physical energy,

taking the form of a physical symptom. When the memory is recovered through hypnosis, the emotion can be felt and expressed, and the symptom disappears" (Hunt, 1993, p. 174).

Freud's theory of repression and sexual abuse was re-examined in the late 1980s and 1990s under the idea of repressed memories of sexual abuse. We will look at the relationship between sexual abuse and mental disorders in the next section.

Borderline personality is another disorder more likely to be diagnosed in women, who make up about 75% of the cases. While there is no single characteristic that defines a borderline, the key feature is that of a widespread pattern of impulsivity, along with instability of moods, interpersonal relationships, and self-image. Jimenez (1997) sees the borderline and dependent personality disorders as diagnoses that society uses to indicate how women should behave in the post-feminist era. As gender roles have changed and women gained more freedom, these diagnoses placed restrictions on expressions of sexuality and manipulation of men. While Jimenez may or may not be correct about these diagnoses, we should be aware that society's views of what constitutes appropriate gender behavior influences medical science and the diagnoses of mental disorders.

As another example, consider the DSM-IV's view of gender and orgasmic disorder (Hartung & Widiger, 1998): "For a diagnosis in women, the clinician must consider whether their orgasmic capacity is less than would be reasonable for their sexual experience.…No such qualifications are made for the diagnosis in men" (p. 267).

Table 12.1: Sex Ratios on a Variety of DSM-IV-TR Diagnoses

Diagnosis	Sex Ratio male:female
Attention-Deficit/Hyperactive Disorder	2:1 to 9:1
Rett's Disorder	Females only
Hallucinogen Use and Intoxication	3:1
Panic Disorder with Agoraphobia	1:3
Conversion Disorder	1:2 to 1:10
Dissociative Identity Disorder	1:3 to 1:9
Borderline Personality Disorder	75% female
Breathing-Related Sleep Disorder	2:1 to 4:1

Gender differences can also be seen in use of medications, called **psychotropic drugs,** used to treat mental disorders. For example, the antipsychotics, which are used to reduce a psychosis, work better for women at a lower dose. However, women are at a greater risk of *tardive dyskinesia*, a movement disorder resulting from long-term use. When tests are given to help establish tolerance and drug dosages, women are often excluded. This is despite the knowledge that higher levels of fat (adipose tissue) and other factors, such as the use of oral contraceptives, can affect the elimination time of some drugs (Dawkins, 1999).

We have looked at how society may have diagnoses that help control aspects of female behavior. Similar arguments could be made for male behavior with diagnoses such as oppositional disorder, **narcissist,** and antisocial **personality disorders**. What seems important is that, while there may be gender differences in diagnoses, we not allow gender bias to dictate the conception and application of these diagnoses.

Age

Age is a factor in certain diagnoses. Mental retardation is a developmental disorder that occurs before the age of 18. Personality disorders are enduring patterns of behavior and are therefore seldom diagnosed before late adolescence or early adulthood. **Dementia** generally occurs in older adults. In this section we will discuss differences that appear within categories and how age may be related to various aspects of a given diagnosis.

Robins et al. (1984) found, when looking at the lifetime prevalence of 15 DSM-III diagnoses, that those older than 65 had the lowest rates, while those between 25 and 44 years old had the highest. "In every site [a setting where research data have been collected], the group 25 to 44 years old significantly exceeded the next older group with respect to drug abuse and dependence, major depressive episode, manic episode, and antisocial personality. In every site, the group 45 to 64 years old exceeded the oldest group with respect to major depressive episode, manic episode, alcohol abuse and dependence, and panic disorder. Drug abuse and dependence is the only disorder significantly higher in the youngest group than in the group aged 25 to 44 years, and this is found only in one site" (p. 954).

In 1991, a national survey (http://www.ctclearinghouse.org/FactSheets/fmental.htm) found that younger people were more likely to experience a mental disorder. Within the prior year, 27% of 15- to 24-year-olds were likely to have had a mental disorder. Anxiety disorders and affective disorders accounted for about 21% and 14%, respectively, of these disorders.

As an example of the relationship between age and a diagnosis, let us consider depression. One aspect is *cohort effects*. This means that a group of individuals who are born around one time period may have a different rate of illness than a group born at another time. In a sample of first-degree relatives of probands (family members who have the disorder under investigation) with an affective (mood) disorder, Klerman et al. (1985) found a progressively higher rate of depression throughout the 20th century. They also found that there was an earlier age of onset with each generation, and that the disorder was consistently more common in women than in men. It is estimated that by the year 2020, major (unipolar) depression will be second only to cardiovascular disease as the most debilitating disease in the United States. Figure 12.1 shows the prevalence of major depression at various ages of onset ("Spirit of the Age," 1998).

There are many diagnostic similarities in mood disorders across various age groups. However, these disorders may manifest themselves differently at different ages and between genders. Younger adolescents were more apt to be diagnosed as having disruptive behavior disorders, perhaps because depression is more likely to be acted out at younger ages. Older adolescents were more likely to be diagnosed as having dysthymia, an ongoing type of depression (Lewinsohn et al., 1993). Another study found that adolescents with depression also had a 42% chance of having another psychological disorder. While the rate was similar for boys and girls, boys were more likely to have a disruptive disorder, whereas girls were more likely to have an eating disorder. In adults, there was more likely to be a second diagnosis of substance abuse (Peterson et al., 1993). After age 65, the gender difference disappears. While just as many women are depressed, there is an increase in the number of depressed men (Wallace & O'Hara, 1992).

For further statistics on disorders and age, particularly among children and older adults, visit http://www.nmha.org/infoctr/didyou.cfm.

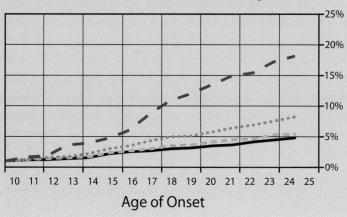

The Generation Gap

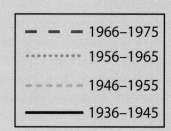

- – – – 1966–1975
- ·········· 1956–1965
- - - - - 1946–1955
- ——— 1936–1945

Age of Onset

Figure 12.1: Life prevalence of major depression in the U.S. population.

Race

Williams and Harris-Reid (1999) conducted an overview of research on race and mental health. They found little difference between African Americans and whites, especially in major classes of disorders. However, African Americans appear to have lower rates of affective disorders (depression) and substance abuse (alcohol and drug abuse). While the data was not clear, they also found that Hispanics appear to have higher rates of major psychiatric disorders than whites. A lack of studies dealing with the mental health of Asian Americans and American Indians made it difficult to draw any conclusions about those groups.

It should be noted that studies based on treatment rates are methodologically flawed. This fact, combined with the varying criteria used in different studies, makes these types of comparisons difficult.

Robins et al. (1984) found psychiatric rates between African Americans and others to be modest and rarely statistically significant. However, there may be misdiagnoses because of race. For example, elderly African American males with depression are often misdiagnosed as having schizophrenia (Harper, 1996).

A study of children in the rural South attempted to disengage the issues of race, poverty, and inner city residence, since they are correlates with psychiatric diagnosis. Diagnostically, no racial differences were noted between non-poor white and black children. Racial differences were found among poor children, with poor white children showing more oppositional disorders, conduct disorders, and emotional problems—particularly depression (Costello, Keeler, & Angold, 2001).

There may be differences in relationship to treatment issues, including the use of mental health services (Marc P. Freiman Agency, 1997). Among young adolescents, African American females and males received treatment at about one-third the rate and half the rate, respectively, of Caucasian males (Cuffe et al., 1995). The judicial system also appears to be a source of ethnic bias. It was found that courts tend to order psychological services more for Caucasians in foster care than they do for African Americans and Hispanics (Garland & Besinger, 1997).

Generally speaking, well-educated, unmarried white women between the ages of 24 and 44 who have recently had a psychiatric disorder are most likely to use mental health services of all types. African American men, with lower income and less education, are most likely to use public mental health services (Swartz et al., 1998).

Socioeconomic Status

Meeks and Murrell (1997) studied 364 older adults living in a community setting with severe mental illness. The average age of this group was 54, and around a third of the sample had a diagnosis of **schizoaffective disorder**. They examined the relationship between economic and social conditions and psychiatric disorder. When compared to a non-psychiatric sample, this sample had fewer economic resources and less-stable residences. In the psychiatric sample, 71% had annual incomes of less than $10,000, whereas in the non-psychiatric sample nearly 40% had incomes more than $10,000 per year. Individuals in the non-psychiatric sample were more likely to own their own homes (80% vs. 48%) and to have lived in them longer (a median of 16 to 18 years versus eight years).

Diagnosis also made a difference on some factors. Schizophrenics had less education and were more impoverished. For example, there was an average 75% unemployment rate for schizophrenic or schizoaffectives compared with a 40% unemployment rate for those diagnosed as having unipolar affective disorder. "Diagnosis was clearly related to the majority of other variables examined, including sex, age, living situation, types of significant relations, income, employment, education, marital status, and network size among sociodemographic variables. Generally speaking, pathology associated with schizophrenia, whether found in schizophrenia or schizoaffective disorder, was associated with poorer success in life in a number of domains and with poorer outcome" (p. 306).

One theory that attempts to explain the relationship between lower socioeconomic levels and disorders such as schizophrenia is the **social drift** (or social selection) **hypothesis**. This theory states that individuals with disorders drift towards the lower end of the socioeconomic strata. This can be compared to a **social causation hypothesis,** which would say that being at the low end of the socioeconomic strata is etiologically associated with the disorder. A study by Turner and Wagenfeld (1967) found that around 36% of the schizophrenics they studied had experienced downward mobility compared to their fathers, whereas 26% of the non-schizophrenics had experienced downward mobility. This, and other data, left them little doubt that social drift contributed heavily to an over-representation of schizophrenics in the lower socioeconomic strata. Freeman (1994) also sees the social drift as the explanation for schizophrenia and lower socioeconomic strata.

Weich and Lewis (1998) used a fairly large sample in the United Kingdom to study the issue of whether poverty and unemployment may be risk factors for common mental disorders, or delay recovery from them. Their findings suggest that, while unemployment and poverty are not associated with the onset of common mental disorders, they increase their prevalence by delaying recovery. They found that financial strain was associated with both the onset and the length of the episodes of common mental disorders. They felt this might be attributed to the amount of worry, or pessimism, present in the face of financial hardships. While unemployment was not related to increases in psychiatric morbidity, more than twelve months of poverty and financial strain were.

Urban vs. Rural Life

While about a quarter of the U.S. population lives in rural or smaller urban areas, most studies of people with severe mental disorders have been done on those living in large urban areas. Dottl and Greenly (1997) found rural-urban differences in symptomatology, diagnoses, and vocational functioning. They found that rural clients have more psychiatric symptoms, including bizarre behavior, but are less likely to be diagnosed with an organic brain syndrome, schizophrenia, or schizoaffective disorder. Rural clients are also less likely to be involved in vocational activities such as competitive employment. However, they did note that their sample consisted mostly of Caucasians, and cautioned against generalizing it to other groups. While a Danish study (Mortensen et al., 1999) found the highest risk of schizophrenia to be associated with a history of a parent or sibling having schizophrenia, it was also found to be related to place and season of birth. "Among the other risk factors for schizophrenia, the strongest was an urban place of birth. As compared with persons born in rural areas, those born in the capital (Copenhagen) had a relative risk of 2.40…, those born in provincial cities with more than 100,000 inhabitants or in suburbs of the capital had relative risks of approximately 1.6, and those born in towns with more than 10,000 inhabitants had a relative risk of 1.24" (p. 605).

Similarly, a study of over 7,000 subjects found that the level of psychotic and psychosis-like symptoms increased as the level of urbanization increased. The authors of the study proposed that the social environment—including elements like the degree of deprivation and social isolation—created childhood development liabilities that could lead to psychosis in adults (van Os et al., 2001).

Urban-rural differences exist in age, gender, marital status, and adjusted income. Rural clients tended to be older women who had been married at some point in their lives. A higher percentage of unmarried males were found in urban settings. This particular subset is more likely to use drugs and alcohol, show aggression, and be in trouble with the law. When income was adjusted to reflect differences in the cost of living between urban and rural areas, clients living in the most densely populated county had only about half the amount of income compared to those living in other counties (Greenley & Dottl, 1997).

A comprehensive review (Webb, 1984) found that the rural-urban variable was of little value in identifying consistent, substantive differences in psychiatric disorders between the two settings. "It is inadequate to define an area, a city, or suburb, or farm, and expect that the population that lives in that environment will manifest differential degrees of impairment just because they reside there" (p. 245). As Marsella (1998) pointed out, "The etiological role of urbanization for mental disorders and social deviancy remains ambiguous. Different pathological conditions can result in similar pathologies, and similar pathological conditions can result in different pathologies across rural-urban borders" (p. 632).

While this may be true, a study by Hope and Beirman (1998) shows how there may be differences within the proportions. This study found that while the relative proportion of children showing externalized behavioral problems were similar in rural and urban settings, there were differences in the settings. Children in rural areas were more likely to have home-only patterns, while children in urban areas were more likely to have school-only patterns. This suggests that rural teachers may be better able to suppress negative influences, or that denser congregations of at-risk children may have a greater effect in urban areas.

Sexual and Physical Abuse

It is difficult to acquire an accurate estimate of the frequency of sexual abuse. This is due in part to such issues as how sexual abuse is defined, differing methodologies used by researchers, and the level of willingness of victims to report cases of abuse. For example, a review of 166 studies dealing with sexual abuse of boys noted widely ranging estimates of 4% to 76%, based on the definitions and samples used (Holmes & Slap, 1998). In a review of 16 non-clinical North American samples, it was found that 22.3% of women and 8.5% of men had been sexually abused. This is consistent with popular views. When restricting analysis to those samples with 60% response rates or better, the estimates were 17% for women and 8% for men (Gorey & Leslie, 1997).

While it may be difficult to make accurate estimates, it is clear that there are both personal and social costs associated with abuse.

Physical and sexual abuse has been associated with several disorders and adjustment issues. Garnefski and Diekstra (1996) found a number of differences in the reactions of boys and girls to sexual abuse. As one would expect, sexually abused boys and girls reported more problems than non-sexually abused children. Sexually abused adolescent boys reported the most problems. More suicidal thoughts and behavior, emotional and behavioral problems, and addiction-risk behaviors were reported in sexually abused boys than in either non-sexually abused boys or sexually abused girls. Sexually abused girls reported the combination of aggressive or criminal behavior and suicidality about 13 times more often than non-sexually abused girls. Victims of sexual abuse were also more likely to have experienced physical abuse (which was reported in about 55% of the cases involving females and 72% of the cases involving males). For adolescents, physical abuse is linked as a risk factor in the development of disorders such as drug abuse, major depression, and conduct disorders (Kaplan et al., 1998). Lang (1997) looked at college women who had been abused before the age of 18 and found they were less secure, less trusting, and had poorer social adjustment and interpersonal functioning. However, in that study, these factors did not seem to affect academic success and achievement.

Sexual abuse and physical abuse also appear to be related to a number of diagnostic disorders. In a study by Herman et al. (1989), 81% of subjects with definite borderline personality reported major childhood trauma. These borderlines also reported physical abuse (71%), sexual abuse (67%), and serious domestic violence (62%). Sexual abuse and physical abuse have also been associated with anxiety disorders; adult sexual functioning; posttraumatic stress disorder; possible hormonal, immunological, and developmental differences; and with adolescents becoming more suicidal, depressed, and sexually active (Stein et al., 1996; Wyatt, Guthrie, & Notgrass, 1991; Rowan et al., 1994; DeAngelis, 1995). A study of female adult twins found that the risk of developing a psychological disorder increased as the level of childhood sexual abuse increased (from non-genital to genital to intercourse). There were positive associations with major depression, generalized anxiety disorders, panic disorder, bulimia nervosa, and alcohol and drug dependence. The highest associations were with bulimia and alcohol and drug dependence (Kendler et al., 2000).

Using **dissociative identity disorder** as an example, let us see how abuse affects a mental disorder and the types of social issues it can create. As early as the 1920s, childhood trauma was thought to be a contributor to dissociative states. Ross et al. (1990) found a history of sexual abuse or physical abuse—or both—in more than 95% of the cases they studied involving individuals with multiple personality disorders (now called dissociative identity disorder). In a sample of subjects who had committed murder and were diagnosed with dissociative identity disorder, it was found that not only was abuse noted, but that the subjects either underreported or had accompanying amnesia concerning the abuse (Lewis et al., 1997). This study challenges the idea that it takes overt knowledge of abuse for behavior to be affected.

Freud brought the concept of repression into mainstream psychology. This suggested that there were aspects of our personality that were not conscious and yet had powerful effects on our behavior. The idea of repressed memories of abuse and incest was the main focus of Bass and Davis's book *The Courage to Heal.* Such symptoms as depression, eating disorders, marital problems, or just vague feelings could be signs that one had been molested as a child. This soon became the "Bible" of those who had survived (Hotherstall, 1995). Jaroff (1993) noted that thousands, mostly women, came forward with accusations of being sexually molested. Therapists, in a number of cases, convinced these patients that they had "dissociated" and gave them a diagnosis of multiple personality disorder. Up to that time, and with the publication of *Sybil* in 1973, the diagnosis had been fairly rare.

Sybil is the story of a girl who, because of abuses, ends up with 16 personalities. Following her death, *Newsweek* ran an article that questioned whether Sybil had really split into 16 different personalities: "A psychiatrist who worked with the patient he will refer to only as Sybil says that she was a 'brilliant hysteric,' highly hypnotizable and extremely suggestible. The doctor, Herbert Spiegel…believes Sybil adopted personalities 'suggested' by Wilber as part of the therapy, which depended upon hypnosis and heavy doses of sodium pentothal" (Miller & Kantrowitz, 1999, pp. 67–68).

We have considered two aspects in this section: 1) that physical and sexual abuse are linked with mental disorders, and 2) that the psychological idea of repressed memories can lead to a sociological event where thousands believe they are victims. This event has led to lawsuits, in which some people were convicted on the repressed memory.

Elizabeth Loftus (1993a), considered an expert on repressed memory, suggests a more balanced approach. She believes therapists should be careful about what they "suggest" to their clients. Clients may begin to believe the new thoughts, without questioning their validity. These new thoughts may lead to new behavior and suicidal thoughts. It is not currently possible to tell which memories are false and which are true without outside corroboration. Caution is needed. We certainly want to identify and deal with incidents of physical and sexual abuse; but at the same time, we do not want to unjustly accuse innocent people. As Loftus (1993b) noted: "As important as it is to minimize the devastation that befalls an innocent person, it is, of course, important too to correctly identify genuine criminals and punish them appropriately.…Misidentifications create a double horror: The wrong person is devastated by this personal tragedy, and the real criminal is still out on the streets, probably committing further crimes" (p. 550).

Religion

There is interest and controversy in the relationship between religion and mental health. Historically, this relationship has ranged from religious organizations persecuting the mentally ill to being among the first to offer them help and support (Koenig & Larson, 2001). With the cutbacks in mental health coverage, Andrews (1995) has argued that there has been a toppling of the traditional hierarchy of therapy options. Typically, psychiatrists had been placed at the top of the hierarchy, with human service workers at the bottom. With this toppling of traditional services, there has come a serious challenge from organized religion. This ranges from medical doctors believing faith is a factor in coping with life-threatening illness to congregation-based counseling centers.

Batson, Schoenrade, and Ventis (1993) analyzed a large number of studies on religion and mental health and noted that if one only looked at the totals (of positive, none, or negative relationships), one would find a weak to negative relationship between religious involvement and mental health. On closer examination, however, a different picture began to emerge. The three groups considered were the *extrinsic (or means) dimension*, the *intrinsic (or end) dimension*, and the *quest dimension*. They defined the means-oriented people as those who use religion for their own ends, such as security, socialization, or status. While these individuals may turn to God, it is not done with the giving up of self. End-oriented people embrace religious commitments and attempt to internalize and live their religion. Quest-oriented people take an open-ended question approach to religion. These individuals realize they will not know final truth, and see the search for that truth as a quest.

When analyzed along these dimensions, means-oriented people were not found to have a positive relation between personal religion and mental health. In fact, they showed negative correlations in a number of areas relating to mental health. Most notably, they were more prone to worry and guilt, inappropriate social behavior, loss of personal competence and control, inflexibility, and being closed-minded. End-oriented individuals had positive associations with health, appropriate social behavior, freedom from worry, personal competence and control, and unification and organization of personality. Quest-oriented individuals had positive associations with being open-minded and flexible and having greater personal competence, control, and self-acceptance.

In examining the interactions of religion with mental health, Koenig (1998) found a complex relationship between religion and depression and anxiety. While the relationship between religion and psychosis has not been adequately researched, it is thought that patients' religious beliefs affect the expressions of their symptoms. These include **hallucinations, delusions**, and behavior. One of the research problems here is the inverse, cross-sectional relationship between mental health and religion. Does being religious increase mental distress, or do distressed people turn to religion to find comfort (Koenig & Larson, 2001)?

Koenig and Larson conducted a review of 850 observational studies on the relationship of religion and mental health. They found that about half of the observational studies on that topic showed lower levels of anxiety or fear and about two-thirds of the studies found less depression or its symptoms among those who were more religious. However, about 14.5% of the more religious had greater anxiety. Concerning the relationship between suicide and religiousness, 84% of the studies found that the more religious had either negative views or lower rates of suicide. Showing strong positive connections with mental health were well-being and life satisfaction, less substance abuse, and social support. Religion has been used to rationalize prejudice, and negative associations were found with certain types of distress as well as stressors revolving around personal failure. Koenig and Larson note: "Religion may restrict and impede personal growth and foster rigid, narrow thinking. For many patients who find their way to psychiatrists' offices, religion may be distorted or used in a maladaptive way to defend against necessary personal change. Nevertheless, *on the balance*, it appears that religious beliefs and practices rooted within established religious traditions are generally associated with better mental health, higher social functioning, and fewer self-destructive tendencies" (p. 72).

The sacred often gives people spiritual support and solutions when other answers are not very convincing. Certainly religion has played the role of supplying external structure and a sense of cohesion for people whose lives are falling apart (Koenig, 1998).

For the issue of mental abnormality and prophetic ecstasy, see the boxed article by Dr. Greig, which is sure to stimulate ideas.

Prophetic Ecstasy
by A. Josef Greig

"Mental abnormality," up to a point, does not disturb me. Growing up on an Indian reservation in Wyoming, where unusual mental states are achieved through peyote and vision quests are not considered unusual or antisocial, experiences have helped me learn a great deal about what is considered real or at least crucial and important in life.

Electrochemical states of the brain that diverge from the "normal" or "healthy" are quite natural. It would be risky to attribute them to an "immaterial substance" or demon. Yet discriminating against "bizarre" mental behavior is itself dependent on some all-encompassing understanding (metaphysics) of the nature of reality. "Normality" would seem, then, to be a philosophical and social judgment on what occurs in nature, regardless of whether in a larger scheme "abnormality" might have a necessary function. If what occurs in nature is the criterion for normal, we have to be careful when we define some behavior or physical state as abnormal.

Normality would seem to be appraised by the way societies arise and come to understand themselves. Some societies are less likely to make judgments about what nature offers them, while others, particularly within the Western tradition, seem dedicated to shaping, manipulating, and altering what is an apparently "mindless" nature.

Those cultures which practice mind alteration—inducing visions and trances by music, dehydration, sleep deprivation, self-hypnosis, contemplation, and hallucinogenic drugs—would hardly consider the effects of oxygen deprivation, delirium, and hysteria abnormal, or as being a part of a natural world which should be subdued or purged. Even recognizable insanity is sometimes given a respectable status. Whether these particular mental states contribute anything to society is dependent on the judgment of that society. In the Western tradition, what such mental states offer society is a question to be investigated by phenomenological studies.

Western society has largely been formed with a religious component offered by Judeo-Christianity. This religious tradition contains various instances of revelations from God through visions and ecstatic states of mind. For the purpose of this analysis I will concentrate on two areas of such psychic phenomena within this tradition: Hebrew prophecy and religious experiences, especially those investigated by William James in his book, *Varieties of Religious Experience*, and by J. Lindblom, in the first three chapters of his book, *Prophecy in Ancient Israel*. In addition, I will draw upon the study of the *mysterium tremendum* by Rudolph Otto in *The Idea of the Holy*.

There has been some denial that the "great" prophets of the classical period functioned by any form of altered mental states such as hysteria, or ecstasy, to produce visions. Rather, it is argued, they illustrated lessons from descriptions of objects they could see at the time they were prophesying, or created symbols to clarify the meaning of their message. There may be some virtue in discriminating among prophets on this basis. Indeed, a type of discrimination against ecstatics may be found in the Deuteronomistic histories of the Hebrew Bible itself. But in its more modern version, it reflects a kind of rational prejudice against the non-rational ecstatic from the start.

Some have suggested that a few of the "great" prophets exhibited such unusual behavior that it is difficult to deny their "abnormality." They have declared that Ezekiel, because of his dumbness and paralysis, should be diagnosed as having been given to catalepsy. Karl Jaspers, *Hesekiel, Eine pathographische Studie*, and Hans Heimann, *Prophetie und Geisteskrankheit*, described the prophet as suffering from paranoia and schizophrenia. However, Walter Eichrodt, *Ezekiel*, retorts that these analyses do not contribute anything to the genuine understanding of the prophet.

James also reflects such a position. In *The Variety of Religious Experience* he recounts the popular pathological explanations of the behavior of people such as George Fox, founder of the Quakers, St. Teresa of Avila, and Saint Francis of Assisi. These paragons of virtue, evaluated from a materialistic medical perspective, were all considered to be degenerate or psychopathic, despite their esteemed moral and sociological contributions to the world.

How, then, shall we relate to "prophetic abnormality"? First, we have to be skeptical of the canons of "normality." From the acceptance of what the proper chemical balance of the brain is, to the assessment of more external phenomena caused by mental activity, normality is a prejudicial term from the outset. It is the result of human judgment, which is subject to the influence of many factors.

That is not to say that there is no neurological abnormality, but that many human beings seem to fear what they cannot predict and control. Perhaps the fear of chaos is a relative attribute of human behavior. If a quantity, or quality, of disorder is natural to the world, then we might question our pathological fear of it. Might this be a carryover of fear of the demonic?

Second, prophetic insight rests on a "heightening" of experience, a kind of mysticism that provides an avenue to "truth," and produces a heightened sensitivity to current moral and social conditions and their outcomes. At times during these mystical states, colors seem brighter and images clearer, and joy and fear are raised to exhilarating and terrifying levels, respectively.

In *The End of Science*, John Horgan tells of a mystical experience he claims to have had. As a writer for *Scientific American* and a skeptic of religion, Horgan unabashedly declares his experience "pathological." It differs from most mystical experiences of faith, because rather than expressing a "vital" insight, he interprets it cynically. He sees it as an insight into God's fear that He cannot know the future because the future doesn't exist. Therefore the thought arises in God's mind that He might not be immortal and that He might die. This is a "straw man" argument, since God's omniscience does not depend on His being able to know something that doesn't exist.

Yet we may ask if the "mischievousness" (if not maliciousness) of this interpretation does not disqualify Horgan from being assessed positively as we have done with figures like Fox and St. Teresa, whose moral virtues were so compelling that people trusted putting their very souls (and—in the case of the Quakers—their money) in their hands. I will not question whether his mystical experience is genuine, but inasmuch as it strikes at the very core of ontology (what is most real), it functions to heighten Horgan's own fear of alienation and non-existence. This could be put to good use in a study such as that of James, which looks at the consequences of mystical experience from a pragmatic point of view.

Rudolph Otto argued that religious experience begins with a particular state of mind encountering the wholly "other." The result is a "dread" or "fear" which he calls the mysterium tremendum. One might recall the vision of the prophet Isaiah and his response to the mysterium tremendum in his vision of the altar, "Woe is me, for I am undone." The visionary encounter of fear immediately progresses to a feeling of moral inadequacy and repentance. It is repentance that leads to salvation and the expression of joy. The Hebrew Bible is replete with these kinds of elated utterances.

The movement from fear to moral apprehension and reasoning contrasts with the non-rational, ecstatic experience itself. Thus, ecstatic experience and moral reasoning move the prophetic figure toward the divine and away from the demonic, which is most adequately encompassed in the non-rational experience of "terror." However, in each case, a heightened experience, made possible by a particular state of mind, produced the insights, both demonic and divine.

Therefore, there would seem to be grounds for discrimination among persons with "abnormal" neurology, but not necessarily on the grounds that they have such unusual experiences; rather, it is on the basis of whether they are making an acceptable (in the case of Judeo-Christianity, a critical-moral) impact on the community of which they are an indispensable part—and that question cannot be answered by studying phenomena alone.

Culture and Mental Disorders

ISSUES: Do people from diverse cultures have the same or different cognitive structures? If they have different cognitive structures, how might this affect their mental disorders? How should culture-bound syndromes be interwoven with traditional classification systems?

One issue that should be addressed in a pluralistic text is whether, and how, culture affects our view of mental health or disorders. Culture is often defined as the values, beliefs, perceptions, attitudes, and behaviors of a group or society. These thoughts and behaviors are passed from one generation to another and are used to help that group deal with their perceived issues and problems. As noted by López and Guarnaccia (2000), behavioral problems and mental illness are bound to the social world.

Castillo (1997) noted that a belief in the psychic unity of the brain led to the idea that anthropology had little impact on mental illness. "That is, it was assumed that all people have the same basic brain structure and, therefore, universally have the same basic mental processes. Even if all people do not think the same thoughts, it was assumed that they think in the same basic way" (p. 5).

This was different from the concept that arose in the 1970s of cognitive schemas, which suggested that people constructed their subjective experiences. "These cultural schemas can cognitively construct a particular behavior as an episode of mental illness, whereas a different set of cultural schemas can cognitively construct a similar behavior as something normal and normative….The patient could experience the illness as one particular kind of problem, while the clinician could diagnose it as something entirely different. This is the distinction made by medical anthropologists between *illness* and *disease*" (p. 6).

This concept is recognized in the introduction of the DSM-IV (1994), which notes the challenge that can arise when a clinician from one cultural or ethnic group attempts to diagnose a member from another group. It states that a "clinician who is unfamiliar with the nuances of an individual's cultural frame of reference may incorrectly judge as psychopathology those normal variations in behavior, belief, or experience that are particular of the individual's culture" (p. xxiv). For example, the Ibido, a sub-Saharan African people, believe that if a rat is eating their crop, it is actually a witch who has turned into a rat (Haviland, 1996). A western psychologist may identify as psychotic (not in touch with reality) a person who believes a rat is a witch. However, the belief that witches are responsible for various diseases and problems is not unique to this group of people.

The United States has become a more diverse nation, and so have the belief systems of its people. This places a greater demand on counselors to be aware of the acculturation issues facing immigrants, the cultural histories of its minorities. Compared to previous editions, the DSM-IV has made more of an attempt to look at cultural differences (Smart & Smart, 1997). This includes the addition of an appendix titled "Outline for Cultural Formulation and Glossary of Culture-Bound Syndromes." A study by Shezi and Uys (1997) looked at a sample of patients who had been admitted to the psychiatric units of an Umzimkulu Hospital in South Africa. They found that 38% displayed evidence of a cultural bound syndrome. Because of these results, they felt that the cultural bound syndromes should be part of Axis I diagnoses.

With this in mind, let us look at three examples of the 25 culture-bound syndromes noted in the DSM-IV-TR.

Amok. Amok is a dissociative episode occurring in males from various cultures in Malaya, the Philippines, and New Guinea. It is characterized by a violent outburst—sometimes trancelike in nature—that leads a person to aggression and homicidal behavior. It may begin with the person becoming depressed, withdrawing, and having persecutory ideas. The DSM-IV-TR notes that it "tends to be precipitated by a perceived slight or insult." A person who goes *amok* displays behavior that could be described as that of a "wild man." Following the outburst and violence, the individual may experience a dissociative amnesia (forgetting) concerning the rage. (In the United States, the phrase "to run amok" refers to an individual going berserk or acting frenzied.)

Koro. Koro, also known as genital retraction syndrome, is usually reported in Southeast and East Asia. It is characterized as an intense anxiety involving the belief that the genitals are retracting into the body. It may result in death. While it is most common with young males regarding their penis, it may also occur with females concerning their vulva and nipples. During one "epidemic" it became a common sight to see young men in the admission rooms with chopsticks, or other mechanical instruments, tied to their penis to keep it from retracting. Treatment has included such things as reassurance and suggestion (Devan, 1987). Bartholew (1998) believes that this condition, which at times can erupt as an epidemic, can be classified as a sociological phenomenon involving mass social delusions rather than a mental disorder.

Rootwork. Rootwork—found in groups in the southern United States and in Latino and Caribbean societies—is characterized by the belief that witchcraft, hexing, and sorcery can cause illness. "Roots," "spells," or "hexes" can be put on other persons, causing a variety of emotional and psychological problems. People who believe they have been hexed may even fear death and seek out a "root doctor" (a healer in this tradition) to remove the hex (DSM-IV-TR, 2000, p. 902).

To understand the cultural significance of a disorder, one needs to place it within its cultural context. For example, Castillo (1997) has traced the idea of amok as a cultural emotion back to ancient India and later to the Malay Archipelago. There, warriors used it to enter a trance so they could fight—fearlessly and valiantly—to the end. During a battle, they were "possessed by warrior gods." Later, they often had no memory of the experience. Castillo is unclear as to when it moved from a military context into a personal one.

The Malays had a hierarchical culture, and honor and respect were important. If a man felt insulted, he might then feel a need to regain his honor and run *amok* seeking revenge. Amok, therefore, serves a number of functions. First, it provides a way to express emotions

the culture might not otherwise allow. It helps ensure that a man is treated with respect, since a perceived insult could lead to him taking aggressive action against the one inflicting the insult. It absolves the one running amok of responsibility for his actions, since they were the result of a "spirit" which had possessed him. Finally, it is a way of maintaining the dominance hierarchy of the culture.

Unless one understands the importance of the cultural schemas for a given syndrome, the syndrome loses its function and importance. "Reducing *amok* to a simplistic 'brain disease' would dehumanize the people involved, trivialize the complexity of the situation, and lead to a reductionistic style of treatment" (p. 62). As important as it is to understand the function of a disorder, one should also be aware of the means that a person or culture identifies for healing.

We are typically willing to look at syndromes that exist outside our own Western culture. However, Kleinman and Cohen (1997) argue that we are not as willing to concede the existence of syndromes within our own culture. They suggest multiple personality disorder (dissociative identity disorder), anorexia nervosa, chronic fatigue syndrome, and possibly **agoraphobia** as examples.

Using anorexia nervosa as an example, let us consider how this could be true. Anorexia nervosa is characterized by a preoccupation with wanting to be thin, an intense fear of gaining weight, a refusal to maintain body weight above a minimum normal body weight, and a distorted body image. Within Western societies it is considered "ideal" for women to be thin, as displayed from fashion magazines to movies. This could be further demonstrated by noting that when there is a strong identification with Western norms in terms of body weight, there is an increased risk for an eating disorder (Nasser, 1988).

Finally, Cheng (2001) proposes a different view of psychiatric disorders across cultures. He notes that variations seen in mental health across cultures are due mainly to how the subject presents the features and not to the frequency and nature of the underlying disorder. He believes there should be a differentiation between "illness behavior" (the subjective complaints of the client) and "objective symptoms," which should be assessed through standardized procedures.

Treatment of Mental Disorders

ISSUES: Should societies, professionals within those societies, individuals, or others determine who should, or should not, be treated for a mental disorder? Do you have to "be crazy" to seek treatment? Should an individual have the right to refuse treatment? How far should we go in institutionalizing treatment? Who should monitor the treatment?

Up to this point, we have looked at definitions of abnormal behavior, etiologies, incidence and costs, and related factors. The question then arises: "What should we do with mentally disordered individuals?" As noted earlier, the treatment one chooses should make sense from the theoretical or etiological perspective of that disorder. While this section addresses only a few of the concerns surrounding issues of treatment for the mentally disordered, we hope it will open your thinking about these issues.

Institutionalization vs. Deinstitutionalization

When thinking of a mental hospital, one may recall scenes from the film *One Flew Over the Cuckoo's Nest*. In this film, some characters demonstrate bizarre and psychotic behavior, while the behavior of others is more antisocial, or non-normative. They are locked on a ward and are being "treated" for mental illness by the medical profession. This is a portrayal of **institutionalization** in mental hospitals.

Prior to the 1970s, mental hospitals were seen as a way to treat those with severe mental disorders. It was felt that the needs of this population were too great for the average family or community to handle. Mental hospitals were designed to remove these severely disordered people from society. This was seen as the best way to "treat" these individuals, while at the same time protecting society.

After World War II, the view of mental hospitals began to change and focus shifted to community alternatives. The main reasons for the shift away from mental hospitals were to reduce costs, to avoid the negative connotations of a mental hospital, and to make use of the positive aspects of the community. In the 1950s, the introduction of antipsychotic drugs (called **neuroleptics**) dramatically helped the schizophrenic population. Between 1950 and 1990 there was more than an 80% reduction of patients in mental hospitals (Holmes, 1997).

While antipsychotic drugs do not cure schizophrenia, they can reduce psychotic symptoms such as hallucinations and delusions. As a result of these medications, many schizophrenics were placed back in their communities. But while between 60% and 70% of those taking antipsychotic medications improve, less than 30% are capable of living on their own (Nietzel et al., 1998). If the same proportion were in state hospitals now as in 1955, we would have around 900,000 people institutionalized. Instead there are fewer than 70,000. So over 800,000 who would have been hospitalized in the past are now living outside these institutions. "Where are these people? Approximately half of them are living with their families, in group homes or boarding houses, or on their own. Many of these people are doing well. Among the other half, however, approximately 150,000 are homeless on any given day, and another 150,000 are in jails and prisons, most charged with crimes directly attributable to their mental illnesses. The remainder are confined to nursing homes…" (Torrey, p. B4, 1997).

There was a strong movement towards getting patients out of mental hospitals (**deinstitutionalization**) in the late 1960s. From the judiciary perspective, there was traditionally more of a focus on the professional than the patient. This began to change in the 1960s as a number of laws began to focus on the rights of the patient. These new laws gave the patient the right to litigate, to be treated in the least-restrictive environment, to refuse treatment under certain circumstances, and to be committed for shorter periods of time (Grob, 1995).

In 1963, President John F. Kennedy signed into law the Community Mental Health Centers Act. Federal subsidies were to help in the construction of community mental health centers (CMHCs) to provide services for the mentally disordered. These services would help reduce the incidence of mental disorder and avert long-term hospitalization (Grob, 1995). Deinstitutionalization was combined with chemotherapy and community mental health centers, which became part of the Great Society programs (Burnham, 2002).

During the mid 1970s, professionals wrote about the lack of coordination between mental health professionals and the various agencies responsible for the mentally ill. But during this time deinstitutionalization was not separated from community mental health. By 1979, it was recognized that deinstitutionalization was not working, the deinstitutionalized population would be a part of our landscape, and adjustments in the mental health system would not change it. Deinstitutionalization had become a social problem, separate from community mental health.

By the 1980s, three trends were noted in the literature. First, there was a new group of mentally ill young people who were not going to hospitals. Even when hospitalized they were often given a primary diagnosis of alcohol or drug abuse, most likely masking schizophrenia. Second, it appeared that, to a substantial extent, mentally ill people were ending up in prisons. And third, attentions became focused on the broader social problem of homelessness (Burnham, 2002). The community mental health centers had failed to provide for the population for which they were intended: the severely mentally ill. This fact, combined with budgetary pressures, meant that they had not lived up to their expectations (Grob, 1995).

Problems as a Result of Deinstitutionalization

Few patients leave state mental hospitals under legal obligation to continue treatment. A number of them fall between the cracks of community-based programs and state mental hospitals. Others begin treatment with community mental health centers only to drop out later. In the past, most patients who were hospitalized for long periods were institutionalized into passivity. Basically, they did what they were told, which included complying with their treatment regime.

The newer generation of those who are severely mentally ill may have a difficult time getting into an acute-care hospital. They have an even harder time staying there for more than a short period. They have not been institutionalized into passivity, and few over the age of 30 show a strong desire to change their lives. The younger people with severe mental illnesses tend to drift away from families or other home arrangements. Once out on their own, they are more likely to stop taking their medications. They lose touch with the Social Security Administration, which makes it more difficult for them to receive their Supplemental Security Income checks (Lamb, 1998). When they become disruptive enough, they may be sent back to the state hospital. They get caught in a **revolving door syndrome** in which they shift between the community-based programs and state mental hospitals.

As federal monies dried up in the 1980s and 1990s, fewer of these people went to community mental health centers, and those who did had to pay more. It was felt that families would take care of their mentally disordered children and parents. However, these laws were enacted during a time when families were perhaps more stable and societies less cynical. Homelessness was an unanticipated outcome of deinstitutionalization (Grohol, 1998). It is estimated that around a third of the homeless have a severe mental disorder (CMHC, 1994).

Herman et al. (1998) noted that most studies on homelessness and mental illness focus on individuals with long histories of hospitalization. Their research focused on early stages of mental disorders and homelessness. Homelessness preceded first hospitalization for 15% of their subjects. They found this to be an unexpectedly high percentage considering that their subjects were young, mostly from non-urban areas, and early in their mental health disorder. This suggested that homelessness may have affected the disorder and is not simply the result of a poor hospital discharge. Deinstitutionalization may have seemed like a solution for several problems, but it has created some of its own.

Mossman (1997) looks at the other side of the issue of the "**abandonment thesis**" of homelessness and deinstitutionalization. The abandonment thesis says that the problems faced by the mentally ill, and those they create for society, could be medically remedied if it were not for deinstitutionalization. From a legal perspective, abandonment indicates that there was not a reasonable time notice between the physician and the patient "when there is still the necessity of continuing medical attention" (p. 73). Abandonment also implies an obligation to treat this person or group. In the United States, this relationship is usually seen as voluntary and under our current health system there is no universal program to pay for medical services.

Social institutions help people interpret their world. American liberalism sees a struggle between the individual and state. Strong tradition maintains that the individual has the ability to overcome social constraints. It can be argued that a mentally ill homeless person has a right to make decisions, reject the norms of society, and display symptoms of abnormal behavior without being subjected to institutionalization.

Psychiatry and institutionalization should not be a means of giving people the right of freedom, in exchange for what may be seen as control over abnormal behavior by that society. In other words, either you behave as society dictates or you will be involuntarily hospitalized. Furthermore, there is no guarantee that these individuals can be "cured" by institutionalization. Finally, it can be argued that social, economic, and political developments in the 1970s and 1980s—and not deinstitutionalization—led to the rise in homelessness during this period.

Medical Treatments

As noted earlier, the medical or biological perspective of mental disorders is one of the more powerful models today. It argues that mental disorders are the result of a medical illness, or that the disorders have a biological cause. Within this view, a number of treatments have evolved, including drug therapies, psychosurgery, and convulsive therapies, such as **electroconvulsive therapy (ECT)** and metrazol-induced seizures.

In ECT, an electric current is used to induce a seizure. Since its discovery, it has been used for a range of disorders. Sometimes ECT is used for schizophrenic patients. However, currently it is primarily used to treat mood disorders such as major depression and bipolar disorder. It may be used when drug therapies have not been effective or (since drug therapies may take weeks to take effect) when the person is imminently suicidal. A review of papers dealing with the use of ECT in acute mania found improvement or remission in 80% of manic patients. There is also indication that about 60% of those who do not respond well to traditional treatment, such as lithium and neuroleptics, have

remission with ECT (Mukherjee et al., 1994). A survey of patients with schizoaffective or depressive diagnoses found that 83% reported ECT as helpful in treating their disorder. While most of the subjects reported side effects, 79% indicated that they would undergo ECT again (Bernstein et al., 1998).

ECT may create issues of side effects and alteration of brain structure. A review of the literature found no research—including prospective studies using CT and MRI scans—that showed evidence of structural brain damage. There was indirect evidence of possible disruption of memory going from short-term to long-term memory (called consolidation). Also noted was spotty memory loss for events occurring around the time of the ECT. However, most patients reported an improvement in cognition that appears to be a result of a lessening of their depression (Devanand et al., 1994).

Psychosurgery involves the destruction (a lesion) or removal of part of the brain in order to alter behavior. Currently, it is used for cases of obsessive-compulsive disorder and mood disorders unresponsive to other therapies. The use of psychosurgery (ventromedial frontal leukotomy) on sixteen subjects with obsessive-compulsive disorder was found to significantly improve their symptoms and their psychosocial functioning. Of concern, however, was the fact that half of these subjects developed substance dependence after surgery (Irle et al., 1998). A long-term follow-up of subjects who had undergone psychosurgery (cingulotomy) for obsessive-compulsive disorder suggested that 30% to 40% of them believed they had improved because of the surgery alone. Another 10% thought the surgery may have augmented later behavioral and drug treatments. The researchers felt the data indicated that surgery is an option when more traditional methods fail to work (Jenike et al., 1991). Due to the introduction of psychiatric drugs, psychosurgery is used less often today than it was in the past.

The drug chlorpromazine (Thorazine) was introduced in 1952. This drug reduces psychotic symptoms in schizophrenics, and helped lead to deinstitutionalization. Since that time, there has been an increase in the use of psychoactive or psychotropic drugs. These drugs help alter people's feelings, thoughts, and behavior. Psychotropic drugs include antidepressants for depressions, benzodiazepines for anxieties, antipsychotics (or neuroleptics) for psychoses, and psycho-stimulants for attention-deficit/hyperactive disorder (ADHD).

For doctor office visits from 1985 to 1993–1994, there was an increase in the prescription of psychotropic drugs from 5.1% to 6.5%. ("Approximately 75,000 visits were sampled in the 1985 survey, 36,000 in the 1993 survey, and 34,000 in the 1994 survey. Between these implementation periods, NCHS decreased its physician sample size. Therefore, following NCHS recommendations, data from the 1993 and 1994 surveys were combined to establish a larger base from which to derive annual estimates" [Pincus et al., 1998, p. 527]). For individuals under the age of 18, there was an increase from 1.10 million medication visits in 1985 to 3.75 million in 1993 and 1994. Most of this upward trend has been due to the increased prescription of antidepressants, called selective serotonin reuptake inhibitors (SSRIs), such as Prozac, by psychiatrists. The only psychotropic drug to see an increase in prescription by primary care doctors was Ritalin. In 1985, stimulants were prescribed on only 1.5% of all visits, compared to 5.1% of all visits by 1994. For the ten years studied, there was a change in the pattern of use for psychotropic medications. This is especially true in relation to the use of antidepressants (Pincus et al., 1998). While there are many drugs available to treat psychological disorders, here we will discuss just two of the most well known and widely prescribed of these—Ritalin and Prozac.

Currently, some seven billion dollars of antidepressants are sold each year, and that number is expected to grow by 50% over the next five years. Prozac, the best selling and most famous antidepressant, earns its maker, Eli Lilly, $2.6 billion a year. Eighty percent of those in America diagnosed with depression are given a SSRI, such as Prozac, as the first line of treatment ("Spirit of the Age," 1998). But many are now questioning whether Prozac and other SSRIs are being over-prescribed. Despite the estimate of depression doubling since WWII, some (Schrof & Stacey, 1999) believe that Prozac is not the magic bullet against depression it was once thought to be. Prozac has side effects—including sexual dysfunction, insomnia, and nervousness—that affect about 30% of those who take it (Hellerstein et al., 1993).

Beyond the issues of side effects, we have to look at the effectiveness of SSRIs in comparison to other treatments, such as psychotherapy. Prozac does not appear to be any more effective than earlier generations of tricyclic antidepressants (Greenberg et al., 1994). And

for about 40% of depressed patients, SSRIs offer no significant relief ("Spirit of the Age," 1998).

Antonuccio, Burns, and Danton (2002) cite a number of studies which suggest that antidepressants work only slightly better than placebos, and that even this effect may be the result of methodological artifacts. They propose that part of the perception of the power of antidepressants may arise from biased publications resulting from possible conflicts of interest with the $250 billion per year pharmaceutical industry. They cite other studies suggesting that psychotherapy—of comparable efficacy to drugs—should be considered as a first approach.

Ritalin is a stimulant given to calm down individuals diagnosed with attention-deficit/hyperactive disorder. At first this may seem paradoxical: why would you give a stimulant to someone who is already overactive? But even people without a diagnosis of ADHD seem to show better concentration with low doses of these stimulants. Many questions have arisen with the increased use of Ritalin. There is debate over how well defined the diagnosis is, and how the disorder should be treated.

There has been a sevenfold increase in the production of Ritalin in recent years, and 90% of Ritalin is consumed in the United States. This raises the question as to whether the American public, school systems, and insurance companies are looking for a quick fix in dealing with children's behavior (Gibbs et al., 1998). As a result of the types of problems associated with ADHD, a panel in the United States called for clarification of the diagnosis and the long-term effects of Ritalin (Charatan, 1998).

Medication is the most used of medical treatments for mental disorders. Nietzel et al. (1998) have the following concern: "In spite of all that has been learned about drug treatment, there is still too little research on the differences in drug effects among people of different ethnic backgrounds and genders. Preliminary data suggests that antidepressant, antianxiety, and neuroleptic drugs are metabolized differently in men and women and in people of differing genetic and cultural backgrounds" (p. 555).

With the little we know about drug effects on different subpopulations, the large quantities of drugs used for mental disorders, the potential long-term side effects that they may create (many of which we are not even aware of), and the increase in use that has occurred in the past few years to deal with mental disorders, one has to wonder whether the drugs are being overused and whether other treatments could be as effective.

Psychotherapy and Self-Help Groups

Psychotherapy is a non-biological approach to treating psychological disorders. Here there is an attempt to change people's thoughts, feelings, and behavior through psychological techniques, usually involving talking. Therapists come from several theoretical backgrounds and have developed many types of psychotherapies. These include, but are not limited to, the following:

1. Psychoanalytic therapy. This insight-oriented therapy is based on the belief of unconscious memories. The goal is to bring these memories to consciousness to help people resolve their problems.

2. Humanistic and existential therapies. Humanistic therapies believe that people can take responsibility for the blocks to their personal growth, and, as a result, reach more of their full potential. Existential therapies emphasize the freedom and responsibility that people have for making their own choices, despite the anxiety that may result.

3. Behavior therapy. Here, a person's behavior is seen as the result of the learning conditions, reinforcements, and punishments experienced. Behavior therapy attempts to set up new learning conditions so that new behavior can result.

4. Cognitive therapies. Cognitive therapies take the position that disturbed behavior is the result of disturbed thinking. Therefore, as one changes one's thinking, behavior is affected. Cognitive therapy is often combined with behavioral therapies.

Therapies can occur in an individual, couples, family, or group context. One type of group setting is the **self-help group**. Unlike those mentioned above, it is usually not led by a professional and has usually arisen because of perceived need. Individuals in these groups both give and receive help. Most of these groups revolve around a problem or disorder, such as alcohol or narcotics, which these individuals have in common. A large number of the self-help groups are free. Perhaps the best known of these is Alcoholics Anonymous (AA). A number of 12-step programs have evolved from the AA concept. It is estimated that about 12 million people participate in self-help groups (Wood & Wood, 1996).

It is difficult to say why 12-step programs work. Perhaps it is the sharing of painful aspects of life with others, the conscious effort to be honest with both others and one's self, or the reinforcement of behavior and thoughts inconsistent with the undesirable behavior (Frances & Miller, 1998). Many 12-step programs claim to enhance one's spirituality. One study (Borman & Dixon, 1998) that compared a 12-step program to a non-12-step program found an increase in spirituality for participants in both programs. Similarly, an evaluation of inpatients using a treatment plan that included a 12-step program found that those who failed to report a mainstream Christian religious preference were more likely to fail (Craig et al., 1997).

Does therapy work? A meta-analysis (in which a large number of studies are compared) was done in 1980 with 475 studies. It was found that the average person who received therapy was 80% better off than those who did not engage in therapy (Smith, Glass, & Miller, 1980).

An in-depth survey by *Consumer Reports* found that more than 40% of people who rated themselves as being "very poor" and "fairly poor" at the beginning of therapy felt improvement during the course of the therapy. Those in the "very poor" category reported more improvement. The longer people stayed in therapy the better they did. Those going to mental health professionals for more than six months did better than those who went to their family physicians. Satisfaction and improvement were similar whether they saw a psychiatrist, psychologist, or social worker. Most who went to self-help groups indicated satisfaction and felt they had improved. Half of those who took drugs felt side effects. Drowsiness and disorientation were the most cited complaints. Because of the side effects many people felt that talk therapy was important. This does not imply that people would not have gotten better without any therapy (*Mental Health: Does Therapy Work?*, 1995).

The *Consumer Reports* article and a reanalysis of it by Seligman (1995) resulted in a special issue of the *American Psychologist*. A number of criticisms and issues were addressed in this issue. One major criticism was that most of the data came from only 4% of the original contacted sample (Brock et al., 1996). Jacobson and Christensen (1996) argued that the study done by *Consumer Reports* either tells us what we already know, or indicates that what is not already established in the field is questionable because of its methodology. This questionable methodology includes the use of a retrospective survey, the absence of a control group, and the unreliability of the data. Much of that *American Psychologist* issue examines the struggles of how to measure the effectiveness of therapy and how to evaluate the relative effectiveness of therapy in comparison to medications.

Conclusion

The field of mental health and disorders is large and complex. We have touched on only a few of the thoughts and issues within the field. We recommend that you enhance your personal and classroom experience by visiting web sites, finding articles, and discussing films that address the issues you have been studying. It is important to understand both the societal and personal issues that may affect your mental health.

Response

The Social Work Perspective

by Karen E. Stockton, Sharon W. Pittman, and Jan F. Wrenn

Beth Jones is referred to a psychotherapist by her family doctor because she is experiencing sadness, tearfulness, and sleep disturbances accompanied by feelings of hopelessness. The presenting symptoms under the medical model would typically lead to a DSM-IV diagnosis of depression. Such a diagnosis would most often render the treatment choice of medication, psychotherapy, or both. However, six months after diagnosis and treatment, Beth returns, reporting the same symptoms plus suicidal thoughts. How could the process have been modified to more effectively restore her to a normal level of functioning?

Depression and suicidal thoughts have complex origins. Social workers would question the adequacy of the initial assessment to determine the treatment approach, suggesting that more information be gathered in order to determine whether other factors might be involved. A more comprehensive assessment would elicit the information that two months prior to her initial treatment, Beth and her husband of 10 years had separated immediately following a move from Chicago to San Francisco. Additionally, Beth's mother had died a year prior to the separation. These personal and social losses depleted her support systems. All too often, the medical-model treatment approach limits the focus to the "identified patients," placing them at the center of the problem. Social workers argue that the long-term change in human behavior is enhanced by interventions based upon a holistic, comprehensive assessment perspective called the "ecological" or "person-in-environment" perspective.

Apart from the social perspective, other perspectives mentioned in the chapter are limited by their focus on the individual as the problem. We are a culture that has enthroned the individual (Minuchin, 1984). We have focused on individual psychotherapy as demonstrated by the emphasis of the DSM-IV manual. *The Diagnostic and Statistical Manual of Mental Disorders* (American Psychiatric Association, 1994), a volume of over 800 pages, dedicates only one and a half pages to psychosocial and environmental factors. Even though psychosocial and environmental factors are acknowledged, they are typically not a focus of treatment. Thus, treatment has often centered on being inside of the self. Minuchin (1984), describing the individual in the context of family, suggests that "this is an extraordinary feat of the imagination because 'decontexted' individuals do not exist. Life consists of growing, mixing, cooperating, sharing, and competing with others....We live our lives like chips in a kaleidoscope, always part of patterns that are larger than ourselves and somehow more than the sum of their parts" (pp. 2–3). He explains that as we look at the interior of a person, we view various scenarios—which can be dramatic, whimsical, or absurd—but carry the tantalizing feeling that they are complete. However, in kaleidoscopic images, there are hundreds of other pieces with clear or uneven edges which must be fitted together to form the overall picture of human behavior. Surely most of us have had our most significant experiences within our complex social environment (Minuchin, 1984). Therefore, the cultural paradigm of individuality betrays us by limiting or distorting our traditional assessments of individuals. Unfortunately, the pervasive, traditional assessment and categorization of mental disorders often blind clinicians to the kaleidoscopic self of the person they are seeking to help.

The ecological perspective argues that an individual's problems may be caused by a personal system, environment, or both. This view emphasizes that the psychological, emotional, and behavioral problems that are experienced by individuals are not necessarily the result of individual pathology, as the medical model suggests, and may well be the result of dysfunctions elsewhere in the ecosystems around them (Queralt, 1996). This perspective, adapted to the field of social work by Germain, focuses on the need for a comprehensive assessment of person and situation and for intervention that encompasses individual, familial, interpersonal, institutional, societal, and cultural systems (Queralt, 1996).

Holistic Approach

"Social workers must guard against unconsciously making the client's situation fit a particular theory or diagnostic category" (Sheafor, Horejsi, & Horejsi, 1997, p. 302). According to Meyer (1992), the use of the psychosocial perspective distinguishes social workers from all other mental health disciplines. As social workers know, problems clients experience often defy classification because variables including history, personality, culture, support system, and socioeconomic status may vary significantly (Austrian, 1995). Assessment in social work practice is guided by the practitioner's use of the person-in-situation context and forms the basis for ways particular social work interventions are implemented (Meyer, 1993). The major impact of the ecosystems perspective on classification systems is that it counters efforts that narrowly categorize problems. The perspective broadens the interrelatedness of case variables and depicts the dynamics between a person and his or her environment.

Leery of Labeling

As the chapter mentioned, labeling serves a significant role in diagnosing from the medical perspective on mental disorders. This disease model blames the victim and addresses the maladaptive behavior of individuals, rather than the all-too-often maladaptive societal responses to those who are different. For example, in children who are labeled ADHD, teachers and classmates often look for expected symptoms to explain acting-out behaviors. It follows that once a child is labeled, the chance of staying in mainstream programs is jeopardized. What school social workers often find, in such situations, is a home or family environment that exacerbates or precipitates these hyperactive behaviors.

The very term *mental disease* suggests that the biological perspective is problem-oriented. Yet, often the psychiatric condition could be a symptom, rather than the etiology, of the problem. The complexities suggest that diagnosis of mental disease may be a case of "which comes first: the chicken or the egg?"

The medical community appears eager to label (as in DSM-IV), partition, and sanction pathological behaviors. This is evidenced by our historical preference to institutionalize those who demonstrate abnormalities. Our society's policies toward the mentally ill were challenged and changed during the late 1960s and early 1970s. Subsequent changes in policies demonstrated the unwillingness of society to assume responsibility for the ongoing support for individuals labeled as mentally challenged or maladaptive. Exceptions to these policy changes were based upon the perception that intervention must be provided for persons who were perceived likely to harm themselves or others. Treatment for these "maladaptive" individuals usually involved psychotropic drugs or punitive judicial responses, while passive individuals without social supports were left to wander the streets and eke out a survival.

Person-in-Environment Approach (PIE)

The person-in-environment construct (also referred to in social work literature as person-in-situation) has been espoused by many social work theorists (Karls & Wandrei, 1997). More specifically, social work assessment and intervention models address the following four domains in helping those labeled as experiencing mental disorders or mental disease, or just being at odds with society. The domains are 1) personal challenges with social functioning, 2) environmental resources, 3) mental health, and 4) physical health.

Social functioning involves social roles such as family roles, interpersonal roles, occupational roles, life situation roles, and friend roles. Interactional problems may emerge, such as misuse of power, dependency, loss, isolation, or victimization. PIE assessment identifies issues related to social functioning and points toward possible solutions for increasing social resiliency.

Social workers explore the environmental resources or barriers that may be confounding to a person's well-being. Issues to be addressed are a client's access to, and ability to utilize, societal services through transactions with various social systems. Social systems that may affect a client's functioning include economy, education, legal services, mental and physical health, safety and social services, religion, and—most significantly—the support of friends, neighbors, and family. Issues of physical health are explored as they are diagnosed and treated by medical professionals. Other health issues, whether self-reported or suggested by significant others, are also important to the holistic model for enhancing the well-being of clients. The social work PIE perspective provides a system for exploring and evaluating issues related to client resiliency in coping, severity of discomfort, and the duration of a challenging or problematic experience. Social work practitioners also monitor mental health functioning, including the assessment of clinical syndromes, personality, and developmental disorders.

The profession of social work continues to emphasize the importance of client uniqueness in the context of their environments in order to adequately understand and change human behavior. Assessing individuals through the person-in-environment perspective should provide new vistas for exploring human behavior and alleviating pain.

Discussion Questions

1. Who should determine which people are mentally ill? What kinds of symptoms or behavior should be demonstrated?
2. What role should culture and societies have in the categorization of mental disorders? If that behavior is acceptable in one culture but not another, should it be seen as a disorder?
3. Various factors have been associated with mental disorders. What suggestions do you have for reducing the effect of these factors? For example, should there be diagnoses that are exclusively (or largely) designated toward one gender?
4. Have you, or a friend, ever used a mental health facility? How helpful did you find the services? What recommendations would you have for changes? What did you find the most useful? You might do a small survey of individuals you know to get their impressions.
5. How are deinstitutionalization and homelessness related? Should society protect these people or let them live by their own decisions?
6. What types of treatment programs should be given to the mentally disordered? Who should be responsible for these programs and how they are carried out? Should people be treated against their own consent?

Related Readings

Barlow, D. H., & Durand, V. M. (1999). *Abnormal psychology: An integrative approach.* Pacific Grove: Brooks/Cole Publishing Co.

Castillo, R. J. (1997). *Culture and mental illness: A client-centered approach.* Pacific Grove, CA: Brooks/Cole Publishing Co.

Greenburg, J. (1964). *I never promised you a rose garden.* New York: A Signet Book.

Hafner, R. J. (1986). *Marriage and mental illness: A sex-roles perspective.* New York: The Guilford Press.

Horwitz, A. V., & Scheid, T. L. (Eds.). *A handbook for the study of mental health: Social contexts, theories, and systems.* New York: Cambridge University Press.

Koenig, H. G. (1998). *Handbook of religion and mental health.* San Diego: Academic Press.

Szasz, T. (1994). *Cruel compassion: Psychiatric control of society's unwanted.* New York: John Wiley & Sons.

Related Web Sites

American Counseling Association: http://www.counseling.org

International Labour Organization: http://www.ilo.org

Internet Mental Health: http://www.mentalhealth.com

Mental Health Infosource: http://www.mhsource.com

National Alliance for the Mentally Ill (NAMI): http://www.nami.org

National Attention Deficit Disorder Association (ADDA): http://www.add.org

National Institute of Mental Health: http://www.nimh.nih.gov

National Institute of Mental Health, National Institutes of Health. *Statistics:* http://www.nimh.nih.gov/healthinformation/statisticsmenu.cfm

National Mental Health Association: http://www.nmha.org

National Mental Health Association, *Did you know?*: http://www.nmha.org/infoctr/didyou.cfm

Substance Abuse and Mental Health Services Administration: http://www.samhsa.gov

Related Movies/Videos

As Good as It Gets (1997) with Jack Nicholson and Helen Hunt
A Beautiful Mind (2002) with Russell Crowe and Ed Harris
Back from Madness: The Struggle for Sanity (Films for the Humanities & Sciences, 1996)

The Fisher King (1991) with Robin Williams, Jeff Bridges, and Mercedes Ruehl
Girl, Interrupted (1999) with Winona Ryder and Angelina Jolie
One Flew Over the Cuckoo's Nest (1975) with Jack Nicholson

RELIGIOUS FUNDAMENTALISM AND CULT BEHAVIOR

Derrick L. Proctor

13

Chapter Outline

- Introduction
- Characteristics of Religious Fundamentalism
- Cults
- Conclusion

An article in US News & World Report *helps to show the relationship between religious fundamentalism and cult behavior. The article states:* "The group [al Qaeda] was also more hierarchical than the CIA had believed. Bin Laden, once thought to be a figurehead, turned out to be a hands-on leader who approved al Qaeda's most ambitious attacks, including 9/11. Descriptions of the group's inner workings, with its religious dogma and blind obedience, appeared almost cultlike, with bin Laden cast as guru. As one top official put it, bin Laden seemed 'more Koresh than Napoleon'— a reference to Branch Davidian cultist David Koresh, who perished with his followers in a fiery death in Waco, Texas" *(Kaplan et al., 2003, p. 24).*

Introduction

Religious fundamentalists are found in all major religions, both Christian and non-Christian. While the specific beliefs of fundamentalists differ greatly, they are all united in their strong conviction in the correctness of their position and their desire to mold the world to their belief system. Most religious fundamentalists are not members of a cult and tend to be hard-working, honest, and productive members of society. In this chapter we will look at issues such as these:

• What are the characteristics of religious fundamentalism?

• What is a cult, and what are its sociological characteristics?

• Why would people join or leave a cult?

In today's society, religion plays a major role in people's lives and how they evaluate the world around them. Since terms like "religious fundamentalism" and "cult" are used in everyday language, it seems important to understand concepts surrounding them.

Characteristics of Religious Fundamentalism

ISSUES: What does it take to be a religious fundamentalist? What are the pros and cons of being a religious fundamentalist? Is all fundamentalism religious? What would draw a person to religious fundamentalism?

The origin of the word "fundamentalist" is traced to the early 1900s when liberal and conservative Protestants differed on how to react to modernism (Peterson, Wunder, & Mueller, 1998). The liberals made peace with the modern world and accepted many of the changes that were taking place in society. The liberals more readily accepted new beliefs—such as evolution and the acceptance of scientific inquiry—and practices, such as new morality and greater freedoms and rights for women. The traditionalist conservatives, on the other hand, wanted to maintain the status quo and chose to reject most new ideas, citing biblical explanations. The conservatives became the defenders of what they saw as the fundamentals of Christianity and therefore became known as fundamentalists.

Today the meaning of the phrase "religious fundamentalism" has evolved somewhat to include individuals who, to some degree, have one or more of the following characteristics:

- a literal interpretation of the Bible or other sacred writings such as the Koran or Talmud,
- a strong desire to return the government to a religious government and away from being a secular one,
- an ultra-conservative philosophy and beliefs, and
- a strong objection to modernism and secularism.

Other attributes that many religious fundamentalists share include a degree of isolation from the "evils" of society, a supportive network of friends and family who are also fundamentalists, and a simple, less materialistic style of living. Compared to other people who have religious beliefs, fundamentalists tend to be more conservative in their beliefs and have stronger confidence in the correctness of their position. They tend to be more involved with church activities and take religion extremely seriously.

Religious fundamentalists in the United States, in the Middle East, and elsewhere firmly believe that their way of life and their beliefs are superior to all others. Many fundamentalists try to follow the Bible or other sacred writings as best they can in a secular world. They have strong beliefs and strong faith, but are respectful of other points of view and do not try to impose their personal beliefs on others. Other fundamentalists work diligently to persuade others of the correctness of their religious beliefs and the error of all other lifestyles. Sometimes the persuasive tactics employed by people who are trying to further their religious beliefs can lead to atrocities. This can occur in any geographical location. For example, in the U.S., religious fundamentalists might bomb abortion clinics and shoot doctors who provide the abortions. In Iran, women who have had sexual relations outside of marriage may be stoned to death by fundamentalists trying to uphold their religious beliefs.

Did religious fundamentalists take part in the terrorist attacks of 9/11? Pyszczynski, Solomon, and Greenberg (2003) suggest they did. They cite characteristics of American society and characteristics of the Islamic fundamentalists that interacted to bring about 9/11. The Islamic fundamentalists abhor the American emphasis on money and materialism, sex and sexual openness, and the elevated status of women in comparison with the fundamentalist Islamic treatment of women. They also dislike the power, prestige, and successfulness of American society. Being able to attack and wound the United States in the attack of 9/11 was viewed as somewhat similar to David taking on Goliath. Although Goliath was not killed this time, he was certainly frightened and humbled.

Were those who participated in 9/11 members of a cult? As the opening statement infers, al Qaeda was a cult-like organization. Apparently it enforced many of the characteristics that are found in cults, such as total obedience, a strong religious base (fundamentalism), and a strong, charismatic leader (bin Laden). In the next section, we will look more at the characteristics of cults.

Cults

ISSUES: What is a cult? In what ways are religious cults and sociological cults similar? In what ways do they differ? What are the sociological characteristics of a cult? How many of these characteristics are needed for a group to be considered a cult? What is the difference between a fringe movement and a cult? Should an open society expect to have cults and fringe movements? How should it deal with them? What would it take for someone to join a cult? How is joining a cult different from joining another social group or movement? If joining a cult is a gradual process, how can one be aware of the process? What would make someone willing to limit his or her frame of reference? Is there a difference between joining a fundamentalist movement and a cult? If so, describe it. Why is leaving a cult difficult? What would help a person leave a cult? Why is there guilt over leaving a cult? How far should society go to help an individual leave a cult, or should it be purely an individual choice?

A common, stereotypical view of cults is that they are basically groups of religious fanatics living in functional, if not actual, isolation. Even if cultists live near other people, they keep to themselves and interact with non-cult members only when necessary or for purposes of converting them to the views of the cult.

In the last 30 years, three cults have received considerable publicity in the United States because all three resulted in the deaths of most or all of the members. In 1978, Jim Jones and his nearly 1,000 followers committed mass suicide on their ranch in Jonestown, Guyana. This cult is a good example of actual isolation. Even though the cult members had lived in Indianapolis and San Francisco at one time, all had departed for the jungle of South America a few years before their deaths. In 1993, David Koresh and his followers lived on a compound outside of Waco, Texas. The city was close enough for the members to go to when given permission by Koresh. The Koresh group is a good example of a mixture of both actual and functional isolation. They had neighbors within easy walking distance, but chose to live relatively removed from them and had little contact with others outside of their compound. The third group, Heaven's Gate, lived in a mansion in Southern California. Other homes were

a few hundred feet from theirs. This group is a good example of functional isolation only. Although people were close by, cult members had almost no interaction with them, and neighbors expressed shock when it became known in 1997 that people living so close to them had committed mass suicide.

Cults have religious and sociological characteristics. Since we usually think of cults in religious terms, we will look at the religious definition first. Walter Martin (1980) offers this definition: "A group, religious in nature, which surrounds a leader or group of teachings which either denies or misinterprets essential biblical doctrine. Most cults have a single leader, or a succession of leaders, who claim to represent God's voice on earth and who claim authority greater than that of the Bible. The cultic teaching claims to be in harmony with the Bible but denies one or more of the cardinal doctrines presented therein" (p. 16).

Raymond Corsini (1999) gives a secular definition of a cult: "1. A specific complex of beliefs, rites, and ceremonies held by a social group in association with some person (usually considered charismatic) or object (usually considered magical). 2. The group of persons associated with such beliefs, usually not considered mainstream, and often the term is used derogatorily for groups or persons (fanatically) committed to a certain belief" (p. 244).

The sociological characteristics of cults apply to religious and **secular cults** and include the following:

Authoritarian or Charismatic Leadership. Sometimes this leadership may come from one person, such as David Koresh, who attempted to control every aspect of his followers' lives. Koresh routinely required his followers to eat rather simple diets, with only certain foods allowed on certain days. He would randomly change what foods could be eaten in combination with others. He could eat or drink anything he wanted to, but exercised stringent control over the diets of his followers. On one occasion he expelled a member who had gone into town without permission and eaten ice cream. This served as a lesson to others as to what would happen to them if they violated the rules, and at the same time those who went along with these arbitrary rules became more devoted to the leader and would allow him even greater control of their lives in the future. In some cults, leadership is invested in a group or central committee. Only this group has the power to change rules and establish codes of conduct. Whether the leadership is a single person or a committee, unswerving and unquestioning obedience is expected and required. The reasoning behind this is that since this person or committee is in direct contact with some higher authority (usually God), their pronouncements are of greater urgency than the will of any individual person or even the collective will of many others. All members are to submit to the person or committee of higher authority.

Conformity of Thought. Members must allow others (the authoritarian leader or committee) to think for them and make all of their decisions. Irving Janis (1972, 1989) has termed this process *groupthink* when it takes place in organizations and leads to bad decisions. In a cult, a person known as the mindguard functions solely to keep other group members from asking questions that stem from original thoughts. When David Koresh informed the couples who were following him that husbands and wives had to live apart from each other, there was little opposition. Later, when he informed the people that he was the only person allowed to have sexual relations with the women, there was, again, little opposition. Koresh had molded their thinking over a period of time so that the members allowed him to think for them.

Superiority of Beliefs. Most people believe that their most important beliefs are better in some way than

beliefs that differ from theirs. However, a feeling of moral or religious exclusivity that makes people think they are better than everybody else is not normal. Most "normal" people have a preferred make of car that they like to drive, or places to visit on vacation, or restaurants to frequent. However, they do not feel morally superior or think that they have secret knowledge given only to them and their like-minded friends, making their choices superior to decisions of other people. The good cult member truly believes that he or she has been chosen or singled out to have superior information or insight. Frequently members talk in reverential tones about when they first received a piece of unique information. This is somewhat similar to mass delusion for the members of the cult. In religious groups this is sometimes referred to as "accepting the truth," or "wearing the Star of David," or "joining the remnant." There is little or no tolerance for those who have other beliefs. The cult member sees only one correct belief and only one way of practicing it.

Separation from Family and Friends. Many times cult members will be encouraged to break all ties with family members and friends who are not a part of the cult. Jim Jones prohibited high-school-age students who were members of his church from talking to other students at school who were not. When two girls broke this rule, they were publicly reprimanded and punished by being hit more than 100 times with a paddle. Punishment was meted out during the church service. Instead of rebelling and objecting to this treatment, the girls accepted the punishment as a sign that the leader, Jim Jones, really loved them and wanted them to make the right decisions in life. Most cult members lose contact with people outside of the cult and associate exclusively with other cult members.

Exploitation of Members' Time and Finances. Severe demands are placed on members to contribute both their time and their money to the group. At first this may be voluntary, but as time progresses, increasing demands are made for them to contribute. In the final years before moving to South America, Jim Jones required his followers to put in as much as 80 hours per week "volunteering" for the church. He also demanded a large portion of their wages or retirement checks. Eventually some people turned over to him all of their earnings in exchange for him providing them with food and shelter. Then they were able to donate even more of their time to the church. Outside of

Many Voices: An Introduction to Social Issues

cults, people frequently give of their time and money to benefit worthy causes. The differences are that the cult *demands* the financial and time commitment, and that those demands are usually far in excess of what a person would do on a voluntary basis.

Mind Control. Initially, new recruits in a cult are watched to make sure they are giving the correct responses to questions. The **self-perception theory** describes how people look at the ways in which they behave and conclude that their attitudes and beliefs must be in alignment with their actions. By gradually taking control of a person's behavior, the cult leader can also take control of the mind. The person may have food or sleep withheld for long periods while working for the group. Sometimes even going to the bathroom is not permitted until the recruit makes a positive statement about the group. Good behavior is then rewarded with the giving of food, sleep, or bathroom time. As recruits see their behavior being brought under control by the leader, they are less likely to question or challenge other demands made by the leader.

Fear of Expulsion. Members of a cult do not have a significant life apart from the cult. Over time, nothing is important to a member except for his of her function and status within the group. Group members become **deindividuated** or lose their sense of personal identity. Ties with family and friends have been broken. The member views the real world as hostile and unaccepting. Thus the leader can threaten dissenters with expulsion. This may be termed "shunning," "disfellowshipping," or "banning," and it usually works effectively to keep members in line. After all, what would they be or what would they do if the group was not there to make decisions in their lives? When a member is expelled, he or she is usually thought to be worse than those who have never joined the group and suffers harsh condemnation.

Historically, there has always been a fringe movement in religions, both Christian and non-Christian. We currently see wide variations in how the Muslim religion is practiced. In some locations it is unlawful for a woman's ankle to be uncovered. In some areas a woman must be completely covered if she is in public. Elsewhere it is illegal for a woman to drive a car. Some places do not allow women to attend school, while in others women make up half of the student population at colleges and universities. While these are rules or restrictions imposed on women, the degree to which they are believed and voluntarily conformed to by women and enforced by men is an indication of cultic or fringe practices on the part of both sexes.

The term *cult* is almost always applied to a religious group and is used almost exclusively to refer to fringe religious movements. However, there can be secular cults as well. A secular group with conditions meeting most, or all, of the seven criteria listed above would qualify as a cult. One should remember that a cult is a fringe group of a generally accepted culture or group in society. A certain member of one stamp-collecting cult spends most of his time interacting with other members in the group. They tend to see stamp collecting as the only real hobby that a normal person should have. Huge amounts of the member's time are spent attending meetings and reading books and periodicals about stamp collecting. Even greater amounts of his money are spent traveling to stamp conventions, purchasing equipment and stamps, and providing financial backing to club members who are not as wealthy as he is. Although this group does not meet all seven criteria above, it does meet five of them. This acquaintance would deny belonging to a cult, just as most cult members would not call their own group a cult. It might be more accurate to say that any group which meets a majority of the seven criteria above is a cult-like group.

Joining a Cult

People don't wake up in the morning and say to themselves, "Today I think I will join a cult." Indeed, most people in a cult would deny that they are members of one because the term has such a negative connotation. Being in a cult is a bit like being infatuated. Usually when a person is infatuated he or she thinks of it as being in love. It is only in hindsight after the relationship has ended that the person can look back and say that it was not love but only infatuation. Using the term *infatuation* to describe a current romantic relationship is almost never done because the term has a negative connotation.

Joining a cult usually takes time. The target person is frequently recruited over a period of weeks or months in escalating steps. If one person were to initiate contact with another by saying "Do you want to join my cult?" the answer would be "No!" However, most people feel much more comfortable with someone befriending them and gradually getting them involved with a group of other individuals who seem to have genuine care and liking for them.

Frequently the first step in the recruitment of a new cult member is starting a friendship with that target person. If the target is undergoing stress or some major disappointment at that time, so much the better, as he or she will be more responsive to the offered friendship. The foot-in-the-door technique is likely to be used. This means that the recruit will be asked to engage in some minor action that is positive toward the cult. This may be accepting a small gift, taking a piece of literature, visiting with other cult members, or visiting at cult headquarters. The followers of David Koresh would invite potential recruits to visit their compound. After all, they reasoned, just visiting would do no harm but would help the target to see what the group was all about. Once at the compound, the target would be befriended by many people and readily accepted by all. This technique, sometimes referred to as "love bombing," was used by Jim Jones's church. A visitor to the church on Sunday would be warmly welcomed and then during the next week receive 50 to 150 cards and letters from church members assuring the visitor that it was such a pleasure to meet him or her and how church members hoped the visitor would come again.

The next step frequently involves some public commitment or acknowledgment on the part of the target person. This may mean that the visitor does as little as stand up when guests are welcomed. The visitor may be asked what he or she likes about the group or if the members have been treating him or her well. This will be done so that all members are able to hear the target's response, which is then met by vigorous approval from the members. The target's positive comments are reinforced by members applauding, nodding their heads and smiling in approval, shouting words of encouragement and acceptance to the target, or in some other way making the target feel that he or she has been readily accepted by the group.

Traditionally, those who have joined **religious cults** in the U.S. have had a similar psychological profile. They tended to be in early adulthood, from about 18 years of age to their early 30s. They came from middle-class or upper-class families. Frequently they had recently suffered a major loss such as the ending of a romantic relationship, recently being fired, flunking out of school, or losing a relative or friend through death. In addition, such potential recruits would be cognitively grappling with their lot in life and trying to find meaning for their existence. Their emotional state would be unsettled as they actively searched for something better. These individuals may be looking for acceptance and companionship and are trying to simplify their lives. While this is a general profile, it is not accurate in all cases. Sometimes persons may be middle-aged or older. Sometimes they may be very poor. It seems that age and socioeconomic status are not as strong predictors as someone searching for something better and needing acceptance.

Since September 11, 2001, the profile of a cult member has changed considerably as America has revised its long-held views of who might be a terrorist. Terrorists have most, if not all, of the characteristics of cult members. They have some religious underpinnings, but tend to be more secular or political than most cults. Terrorist cult members tend to be more fanatical, disciplined, and secretive than most cult members. They also tend to have wives and children not active in the cult and work at blending in with the larger society.

Joining a cult is, in some ways, similar to falling in love. When falling in love, the more you get to know the other person, the more attractive he or she seems and the more blind you become to potential deficiencies. If your parents or friends try to tell you the person is not right for you, you think you know better than they do and continue with the relationship. Judgment of the recruit in a cult becomes more impaired and the recruit is frequently put into the position of having to defend the group to parents and friends. Thus the group becomes more attractive and the critics less attractive. In a romantic relationship this same phenomenon is known as the **Romeo and Juliet effect**.

When a person is being recruited, only the good aspects of the cult are revealed—much the same way any salesperson might give the most favorable information about a product or service. The friendship of other caring people is emphasized. The goodness of the cause is stressed. The ability to make a difference in the world and to find true peace and happiness is offered to the recruit. The socially strange and bizarre practices of the cult are revealed only gradually. Even within a cult there may be different levels of knowledge among the members. The more trusted members know more about the goals and aims of the cult. Gradually exposing members to the more bizarre practices of a cult helps them to appear less deviant. In psychology, we sometimes talk about the "**just noticeable difference**," or the least amount of difference that must exist between two tones or two lights in order to be able to detect a difference between them. Humans are highly adaptable creatures not only physically but psychologically as well. When a person goes from the bright sunlight into a semi-dark room, the difference is great. After a few moments one adapts and it doesn't seem so dark anymore. Likewise in social settings, we frequently compare ourselves with others. In a class when we get a test back and have 80% of the possible points, we try to compare our scores with those of other students. If we find that the other five people we compared scores with all had 90% or better, our score does not seem so good by comparison. If, on the other hand, we find that all others have scores of less than 70%, our 80% looks quite good.

If in Michigan, for example, the temperatures are in the 60s in December, people will be outside in short-sleeve shirts talking about the absolutely balmy weather they are having. A year ago there had been a foot of snow on the ground, and a few days earlier temperatures were below freezing. In comparison, this is warm weather. However, if temperatures dropped to the 60s in July, people would be commenting on how cold it was. Likewise, in a cult, members judge their own behavior and practices by comparing themselves with what the other members are doing. Their frame of reference is very limited. Remember that most cult members have been isolated from family and friends outside the cult and only have other cult members for comparison. If everyone else is doing something, it doesn't seem strange for me to do it also. This process of **social comparison** may be downward or upward. We feel better as a result of comparisons with those below us (downward comparison) or worse when we compare with those above us (upward comparison).

The gradual imposition of strange rules and practices has another advantage. The longer a person stays in the cult and participates in the unconventional behavior, the more dedicated he or she becomes and the stronger is the bond between members. Group members who have experienced much together are more cohesive than those who have experienced little together.

Do you belong to any groups that have cult-like characteristics? They might not have all seven of the characteristics, but do they have a few of them or most of them? The father in a certain family is highly authoritarian. He controls the day-to-day activities of his wife and children. He has established strict rules for behavior and does not allow any deviance from them. He and the family members believe that their way of living is superior to that of their neighbors and relatives. They have little interaction with people other than those few families that have a similar philosophy about life. Family members put in a high number of hours each week working on assigned tasks. Much of the money they make is put into a general fund administered by the father. This family has several of the characteristics of a cult but certainly would not be considered a cult. They are a little eccentric or extreme perhaps, but are not a cult.

The more closely a person identifies with a particular group and the more time a person spends with a group, the more likely it is that the group will take on cult-like characteristics. A certain football fan of the Chicago Bears has season tickets and lives for the weekend when his beloved Bears will be playing and hopefully winning. On weekends when the Bears are playing in Chicago, he and his friends drive about five hours one-way to attend the game. They usually arrive the day before the game and stay in a hotel. On game day they are at the stadium several hours early to pitch their tent for their tailgate party. On weekends when the Bears are playing outside of Chicago, he is usually able to get tickets and travels by plane or car to bask in the reflected glory of his winning team. There has never been an article of clothing with the Bears logo on it that he has not purchased. He generously gives to charities supported by Bears players and buys products endorsed by the players. Every season he spends thousands of dollars and hundreds of hours cheering his team on. He knows that the Bears are superior to every other team and will be going to the playoffs every year. And if not one year, certainly the next. He tends to eat the same foods, drink the same beverages, wear the same clothes, talk the same way, and behave the same way as his other Bear-fan friends.

Is this man in a cult? Probably not as we usually define the term. It is certainly not religious. In fact, members' behavior on Sunday is quite different from what you would anticipate in most cults. However, the group does show several cult-like practices. For example, there is charismatic leadership (the team), conformity of thought, superiority of belief (in their team), separation from family (especially on weekends), and exploitation of time and finances. Probably many of us, while not members of any cult, are members of groups that have some cult-like characteristics and dominate certain areas of our lives.

A certain group of friends became very active in a Bible study led by a lay minister. At first they met only once a week for an hour or two. Then they met twice a week and gradually increased their time until several of the members were living together. The lay minister taught about the "holy kiss" that members used in greeting each other. After some time, the leader engaged in other unholy practices with the women followers. Many of the people in the group ceased having regular contact with friends and family members. They believed that God was giving their leader more insights into the Bible than other people had been given. The way members dressed and combed their hair was similar to what the leader did. Members spent most of their free time in study and other group-sanctioned activities. Members gave large portions of their wages to the leader for him to use as he thought best.

When the group disbanded some years later, members found it difficult to adjust to the real world. The normal support system they had relied on for several years was gone. Relationships with other friends and family members were not good. For the first time in several years, some people had to make their own decisions about simple issues of living. Were these people in a cult? To the outside observer, the answer would be yes. It had all of the psychological and sociological characteristics of a cult. The people who were a part of it denied that it was a cult, as we would expect any good cult member to do.

How do the football fans differ from the "holy kiss" people? The main difference is that one was secular and one was religious. One engaged in more socially acceptable behavior than the other. Both groups were similar in the extent to which the psychological and sociological dimensions were present. They were alike in the amount of involvement of the members and their feelings of closeness to other members. Society would look at one as a cult and the other as just a group of dedicated sports fans. But in terms of personal involvement and the effect on lives of those involved with each of these groups, there are few differences.

There are similarities between fundamentalism and religious cults and secular cults. If we were to diagram the overlap, it would look something like this.

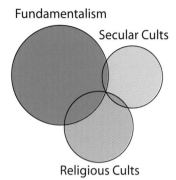

While some fundamentalists may be in religious or secular cults, most are not cult members. There may also be a few cults that overlap both secular and religious themes. The majority of cultists are not fundamentalists.

Long-term effects on a cult member include such things as dependent thinking. The person finds it increasingly difficult to make personal decisions because someone else is giving advice and encouragement to behave in a particular way. The cult member becomes further removed from society and family and friends not in the cult. Some cult members have said, "The community is my family." There is greater conformity among cult members. There is a sameness even in members' physical appearance. There is no ambiguity in life. Cult members know what is right and what is wrong, what they are supposed to do and not do, who their friends are and who their enemies are. They never have to grapple with complex issues. They know that their beliefs will not be challenged and they will not spend time thinking about issues in the real world. Their lives become deindividuated; group members have no personal identity apart from their association with the group.

Leaving a Cult

Leaving a cult is very difficult for many members. The longer people stay in a cult, the more control the cult exercises over their thinking. Former cult members frequently report that they wanted to leave the group but could not bring themselves to do so even though they knew that the cult was having a negative influence on them. Leaving a cult is also difficult because it is not a gradual break but an abrupt one. There is no social support group on the outside like there was on the inside. There will be condemnation and anger from cult members. Joining a cult is a slow, gradual process, allowing time to get adjusted to new people and expectations. Thinking about leaving may be a gradual process also, but usually there is no one with whom a member can confer. If it becomes known by the cult leader or other group members that one member is thinking of leaving, there will be increased efforts made to keep the person in the cult. And those who are trying to keep the person in the cult have much more control over that person's thoughts and behaviors now than when he or she first joined the cult.

People who leave cults physically do not always leave them psychologically, but they continue to have an attachment to the cult for months and years afterwards. Survivors of Koresh's inferno at Waco reported feeling guilty for being alive. They wondered months later if Koresh had been right after all. Likewise, cult members who ran into the jungle at Jonestown and escaped with their lives were tormented by thoughts years later that they would have been better off if they too had willingly drunk the cyanide-laced Kool-Aid that killed their closest family members and friends. Guilt is pervasive among those who do leave a cult.

Conclusion

Cults and cult-like groups are likely to increase in the future. When there is uncertainty and fear, there is greater need for having absolute answers and decreasing ambiguity. There are some questions that people can ask to determine how much control a group is exercising in their lives:

- Am I associating with these people on my own free will?
- Do members of this group all have strong similarities to each other in thinking, behavior, and appearance?
- How much of my time and money will be involved in joining this group?
- Do members of the group seek to establish a relationship with me or am I seeking to establish a relationship with them?
- Do group members consider themselves to be superior to most other people in some ways?

Response

Religious Fundamentalism as a Form of Stability

by Herbert W. Helm, Jr.

How would you respond to the following statements (use a range from "strongly agree" to "strongly disagree")?

1. We need a greater spirit of patriotism in our country today.

2. Basic skills are not given enough attention in today's schools.

3. The traditional American way of life should be maintained.

4. Law and order are breaking down in our society.

5. Society will fall apart if traditional moral values decline.

6. Radical fringe groups pose a real threat to our way of life.

7. The unemployed could help themselves much more than they do.

8. Sex education should be taught in our schools.

9. Free enterprise is the key to our economic success.

10. There should be strict laws against the personal use of marijuana.

11. Alternative lifestyles should be tolerated in our society.

12. Christian standards should be the basis of our whole way of life.

After you have thought about these statements, analyze your responses along the following dimensions:

- How conservative or liberal were your answers?
- Did your political, religious, educational, or other ideologies affect your answers?
- Did demographic variables like age, gender, or occupation play a role?

Your responses to these questions may help to define whether or not you are a fundamentalist.

The above statements were taken from an article by Knight and Chant (1990) titled "Fundamentalism: A Potential Constituency for an Australian New Right." (Some of the questions were changed by taking the word "Australia" out and substituting another word or phrase.) Their study looked at the contribution that religion, particularly fundamentalism, played in shaping the differences between "Left and Right." They found that fundamentalists were more likely to be supportive of rightist or conservative dimensions, such as keeping traditional Australian lifestyles and emphasizing "Anglo-dependent national identity" (paragraph 13). In short, fundamentalists preferred views that were culturally conservative.

The purpose of this response is to evaluate more deeply the concept in the chapter, which notes that "liberals made peace with the modern world and accepted many of the changes that were taking place in society....The traditionalist conservatives, on the other hand, wanted to maintain the status quo and chose to reject most new ideas, citing biblical explanations. The conservatives became the defenders of what they saw as the fundamentals of Christianity and therefore became known as fundamentalists."

Aikman (2003) goes further to note that "[m]any of so-called fundamentalist movements are undoubtedly hostile to much of modernity" (paragraph 8). Arguing against the book titled *The Desecularization of the World* (1999), edited by Peter Berger, Aikman goes on to question why we believe the world should be secularized. The view that the world would gradually abandon religion seems incorrect; rather, the world seems enormously religious today.

Perhaps one of the issues for many people, and one reason why religion is not dead, is that they need some guidance as to what is morally right and wrong. Fundamentalism may provide one of the solutions as it proposes a certain inerrancy (because one believes it follows scripture, or other holy writings). As van der Vyver (1996) notes: "Fundamentalism in the broadest sense may thus be said to thrive upon a belief that God sanctions attitudes and behavior developed and executed in strict obedience to what the faithful observer perceives to be holy commandments. It develops an uncompromising commitment to basic principles believed to be

eternal and immutable. It enhances a spirit of repristination: condemnation of contemporary perceptions, institutions and conduct, coupled with glorification of the past and endeavors to restore the ways of the supposedly 'good old days'" (p. 22).

Within this quote we might find two "good" reasons to be a fundamentalist—to engage in behaviors sanctioned by God and to return to the "good old days." While doing the "will of God" may have appeal to many, there is a problem with intransigent orthodoxy: "The problem with intransigent fundamentalism is, precisely, that many established or mainstream religions found their base in age-old revelations, defined and interpreted in the metaphor of an almost forgotten and mostly misconceived era of human history. Abiding by the letter of those definitions and interpretations has inevitably resulted in a certain doctrinal intransigence which has often belied contemporary values that have come to be associated with human rights and fundamental freedoms. In most cases, perhaps, doctrinal formulations predate human rights theories" (van der Vyver, 1996, pp. 29–30).

This view can lead to at least one social problem with fundamentalism: the campaigns by religious, or political, fundamentalists to clean out the "infidels and apostates." Neier (1992) points out that these fundamentalists appear to be shaping social policy at the expense of human rights. While one might think that humility and religion go together, as humility is a major part of many religions, Rowatt et al. (2002) found that as intrinsic religiousness increased, so did the holier-than-thou attitude.

Religious fundamentalism is positively associated with right-winged authoritarianism and prejudice towards minorities (Altemeyer & Hunsberger, 1992). These facts may raise the potential for fanaticism on the part of those disposed toward fundamentalism. And they raise a number of questions:

- How does one take one's faith seriously and not become a religious fundamentalist?
- Where is the line between strong faith and fundamentalism?
- Can one be a fundamentalist and not seek to clean out the "infidels and apostates"?
- Is shaping social policy part of being a fundamentalist?
- How does the world both modernize and retain beliefs that people find valuable or functional?
- What human rights exist within fundamentalism?

These, and other questions like them, are not easy to answer. Goldfried and Miner's (2002) research may help in some aspect. They note that previous research on prejudice and religious orientations have not considered, nor have they confounded, the issues of belief content and belief style. They found that it was a combination of religious orientation and style—not religious orientation alone—that predicted prejudice. They concluded that we all seem to discriminate against those whose core values are different from our own, and suggested that this understanding could help us temper our own self-righteousness and instead extend compassion to those not like us.

I leave you to consider two final questions. First, is awareness of discrimination towards others enough to alter behaviors and beliefs that keep us comfortable (the good old days) and which seem "God ordained"? If not, how should we respond to fundamentalism?

Discussion Questions

1. Do you belong to groups that have cult-like characteristics? If so, what characteristics do they demonstrate?
2. Under what conditions or circumstances is it positive for a person to be in a cult-like group or a cult?
3. What is the difference between having a hobby or some interest one enjoys and being in a cult?
4. How does a person feel and think when joining a cult in comparison with leaving a cult?
5. What can be done to prevent people from joining a cult?
6. Are people in some religious denominations more susceptible to joining a cult than people in other religious denominations? Give reasons to support your answers.
7. What, if anything, is wrong with having strong beliefs and being very dedicated to them?
8. How do religious fundamentalists view themselves?
9. Do people who join cults or fundamental religious groups differ from other people in intelligence, gullibility, street smarts, or any other characteristics?
10. Do men and women join cults or fundamental religious groups for the same reasons?
11. List and describe several secular cults or groups with cult-like characteristics.
12. What are the differences, if any, between Christian cults and non-Christian religious cults?

Related Readings

Bussell, H. (1993). *By hook or by crook*. New York: McCracken Press.
Corduan, W. (1998). *Neighboring faiths: A Christian introduction to world religions*. Downers Grove, IL: InterVarsity Press.
Gruss, E. C. (1994). *Cults and the occult* (3rd ed.). Phillipburg, NJ: Presbyterian and Reformed Publishing Company.
Martin, P. R. (1993). *Cult proofing your kids*. Grand Rapids, MI: Zondervan Publishing House.
Rhodes, R. (2001). *The challenge of the cults and new religions*. Grand Rapids, MI: Zondervan Publishing House.
Saliba, J. A. (1995). *Understanding new religious movements*. Grand Rapids, MI: William B. Eerdmans Publishing Company.
Samples, K., de Castro, E., Abanes, R., & Lyle, R. (1994). *Prophets of the apocalypse: David Koresh and other American messiahs*. Grand Rapids, MI: Baker Books.
Spong, J. S. (1998). *Why Christianity must change or die: A bishop speaks to believers in exile*. New York: HarperSanFrancisco.
Tabor, J. D., & Gallagher, E. V. (1995). *Why Waco?* Berkeley, CA: University of California Press.
Watson, W. (1991). *A concise dictionary of cults & religions*. Chicago: Moody Press.

Related Web Sites

Apologetics Index—Religious cults and sects: http://www.apologeticsindex.org
Cult Information of AFF's Cult Information Service: http://www.csj.org
Factnet—Homepage of Cults, Brainwashing, Mind Control: http://www.factnet.org
Hartford Institute for Religion Research: http://www.hirr.hartsem.edu/org/faith_new_religious_movements.html
Nurelweb—The Cults and Religion Website: http://www.ucalgary.ca/~nurelweb
The Religious Movements Homepage Project @ The University of Virginia: http://religiousmovements.lib.virginia.edu

Related Movies/Videos

The Architecture of Doom (1989) directed by Peter Cohen
My Son the Fanatic (1997) directed by Udayan Prasad
The Nostradamus Kid (1993) with Noah Taylor and Miranda Otto
People's Century: God Fights Back—The Rise of Fundamentalist Religion (1999)
Waco: The Rules of Engagement (1997) with Dan Gifford

POVERTY

Jan F. Wrenn

14

Chapter Outline

- Introduction
- What Is Poverty and How Does One Measure It?
- Who Are the Poor?
- The Effects of Poverty

- Explanations of Poverty
- Proposed Solutions to Poverty
- Conclusion

Do you know someone who is poor? What do you believe about people who live in poverty? The following myths and facts may surprise you.

Myth 1: The poor are lazy and people on welfare refuse to work.

Facts: Contrary to the stereotype that welfare recipients are lazy, the facts are that most are willing to work and even desire to work, but because of difficult circumstances (e.g., health problems, lack of childcare, lack of transportation) they are unable to do so. Some do work, but they are forced to take low-paying jobs, usually due to a minimal level of education, and they are not able to make enough to support themselves and their families.

Meet Joy, a 24-year-old Caucasian and single mother of two who went on welfare when she lost her job and had her home destroyed by fire. She says the biggest lesson she learned from being on welfare is that most people assumed she didn't want to work. She said they didn't seem to understand that she didn't have a job due to health problems. Joy wants to be more than a "statistic"—someone who lives off our tax dollars. She graduated in the top 10% of her high school class. She's studying nursing at her local community college, she's bilingual, and she knows several computer programs well (Stagg, 1999).

Meet Patrice, an African American, 25-year-old woman who had finished high school and was also taking classes toward becoming a nurse until an unexpected pregnancy with complications caused her to become dependent on welfare when she had to have complete bed rest. After her child was born, she began working part time at a hospital. However, she is not able to cover all her living costs due to low wages (Seccombe, 1999).

Myth 2: Welfare makes it profitable for women to have illegitimate babies. The argument that women continue to have children to increase their welfare checks has been controversial. Some women argue that $50 more a month is not enough to encourage them to have additional children.

Facts: It takes an average of $160,000 to raise a child from birth to age 18. The amount received from welfare is, of course, a very small portion of this total. Thus, having additional children makes a family poorer (Zastrow, 2000).

Meet Molly, a Caucasian woman with three children who attends a community college. She said: "It sickened me some of the things people were saying [in sociology class]. They were not true. You can't generalize and say that everyone is the same. 'She has babies so she can have this extra money to live on!' I don't think I've met anybody who wanted to be on welfare" (Seccombe, 1999).

Myth 3: Most welfare families are African American.

Facts: Many people incorrectly believe that the majority of welfare recipients are African American. Whites make up 37% of recipients and blacks make up 35% (Seccombe, 1999).

Meet Amy, a 23-year-old Caucasian mother of one child, who will graduate with a bachelor's degree next year and plans to get a master's degree. She said, "It's a very humiliating experience being on welfare and being involved in the system. You are treated as though you are the scum of the earth. A stupid, lazy and nasty person" (Seccombe, 1999).

Myth 4: Most welfare recipients are cheaters and frauds.

Facts: A national survey found that one out of every 20 recipients received a check for which he or she was ineligible. Because determining eligibility is often a complicated process, most of the errors were identified as honest mistakes made by state and local workers or by welfare recipients (Zastrow, 2000).

Meet Coreen, a bright, ambitious 21-year-old who, although she never thought she'd find herself on welfare, had to rely on it temporarily due to an unplanned pregnancy. Acting contrary to welfare guidelines, she worked 30 hours a week at a fast food restaurant, believing it was the only way she would be able to survive financially. The guidelines for receiving assistance do not allow for such work hours, gifts, or other ways of subsidizing income, thus making it extremely difficult for some to be completely compliant with all regulations and still meet their needs. Many on welfare find that the amount of assistance provided is inadequate to cover basic needs (Seccombe, 1999).

Introduction

Maria and Carlos Valesquez live in a large northeastern inner city. Both are in their early thirties and they have five children, ages 2 to 13. Carlos is a construction worker who is not always able to find work easily. Maria works as a waitress in a restaurant, except when she can't find childcare for her younger children. The family's combined annual income of $16,000 is well below the poverty level, which, for a family of seven, is $26,710 per year. After paying rent ($475) for their two-bedroom apartment, they must pay for bus fare, utilities, and necessities for the children. Little money is left to buy food. Last winter the children missed several days of school because they didn't have proper clothing to keep them warm. Carlos and Maria grew up living in poverty, and both dropped out of school in junior high in order to work and help support their families. Though they are hard workers, it is nearly impossible to find higher paying jobs that will provide health insurance, due to their limited education (Heffernan, Shuttlesworth, & Ambrosino, 1997).

Defining poverty by looking at the Valesquez family is easy to do. They do not have adequate income to provide for the needs of their family. They lack food, clothing, and health insurance, and their house is too small for their family. Their household income is judged as inadequate by a specific standard. What is this standard and how is it determined? The "poverty line" is the level of income that the federal government considers sufficient to meet basic requirements of food, shelter, and clothing. It is determined by assessing current costs of these necessities for a family and setting a dollar amount that would supply them. This dollar amount varies in relation to the number of members in the household. For example, a family of four whose income is below $18,400 lives in poverty, whereas for a family of seven, the poverty line is $27,820 (U.S. Government Federal Register, 2003).

What Is Poverty and How Does One Measure It?

ISSUES: What types of issues should be taken into account when defining poverty? Should there be income equality in the United States? If not, is there a limit to how large the gap should be between various family incomes? Should the government provide assistance to those defined as living in poverty? Do people "choose" poverty by earlier choices they have made in life (e.g., marrying young, not studying in school, or pursuing too little education)?

There are some problems with the ways in which we define poverty. Two methods generally used are the absolute approach and the relative approach. The absolute approach asserts that a certain level of goods and services are necessary for a family's wellbeing. Those who do not have this level of wellbeing are considered poor. Disagreements exist as to what level of goods and services are needed for a family's wellbeing. What is the "minimum" standard for health, comfort, and happiness?

The relative approach defines a person as poor when his or her income is substantially less than the average income of the population. For example, anyone whose income is in the lowest one-fifth (or tenth) of the population is regarded as poor. This method does not describe how these people are actually living, compared with those with higher incomes. The federal government has generally chosen the absolute approach in defining poverty: the poverty line is adjusted each year as costs of necessities change. In 2003, the government set the poverty line at $18,400 for a family of four (see Table 14.1 for poverty guidelines; U.S. Government Federal Register, 2003).

As with the Valesquez family, adults without an adequate income are unable to obtain adequate medical care, due to not having insurance benefits. They are unable to buy fresh fruits and vegetables because they are too expensive; they eat mostly beans and rice, which are cheaper. Often they are unable to get milk for their children. The children stay home from school some days during the winter due to lack of heavy clothes or coats and boots.

Tom and Mary Smith, who have two small children, ages two and four, confront even more difficult circumstances. Tom works in a factory and Mary is a homemaker. Recently their home was destroyed by fire, and with no insurance (with such a low income, they needed to use money for food and clothing for their children instead), they are now forced to live in their 15-year-old van. They have no extended family to provide assistance and are worried about the approaching winter.

Income Inequality

Since 1982, *Forbes* magazine has annually published a list of the 400 wealthiest individuals in the United States. The 2005 list (Miller, 2005) shows that the collective worth of these people climbed from $125 billion to $1.3 trillion. This is the third consecutive year in which the rich got richer, with increased real estate and oil prices contributing to the fortunes of several individuals. The disparity between the very wealthy and those living in poverty can be seen in the staggering incomes of corporate executives, entertainers, and sports figures. For example, *CNN/Sports Illustrated* provides a list of current baseball contracts, with an average annual salary of $12.5 million.

In the United States, the rich are getting richer, while the poor continue to grow poorer. With this income disparity, it is not surprising that welfare programs are losing the battle against poverty. Another

Table 14.1: 2003 Federal Poverty Guidelines

Number of People in Family	Gross Yearly Income
1	$ 8,980
2	$12,120
3	$15,260
4	$18,400
5	$21,540
6	$24,680
7	$27,820
8	$30,960
Each additional person add	$ 3,140

Source: Adapted from U.S. Government Federal Register, Vol. 68, No. 26, February 7, 2003, pp. 6,456-6,458.

way to view the extent of income equality is to look at the census data on the income earned by different "quintiles" or fifths of households. In 1998, the lowest fifth of U.S. households averaged $9,223, and the second lowest fifth averaged $23,288. Half of all households earned less than $38,885. By contrast, the top fifth of households averaged $127,529 (Page & Simmons, 2000). The wealthiest 20% of households in the United States receive nearly 50% of all income, and the poorest 20% receive less than 5% of all income (Karger & Stoesz, 1998). See Table 14.2 for a comparison of households earning less than $10,000 and those with more than $100,000 adjusted for inflation in 2000.

Table 14.2: Income and Benefits in 2000 Inflation—Adjusted Dollar

Households	Number	Percent
Less than $10,000	10,030,633	9.5%
More than $100,000	12,695,390	12.1%

Source: Census 2000 Supplementary Survey Summery Tables.

Who Are the Poor?

ISSUES: What groups or classes of people are most likely to live in poverty? Why do you think this is so? Should some of these groups get better services from the government? What would you base your decision on? What is your image of the poor?

According to the U.S. Census Bureau (2004), 24.7% of blacks and 10.8% of whites live in poverty. In recent statistics, those younger than 10 had a higher poverty rate than any other age group, and New Mexico, Mississippi, and Arkansas had the highest poverty rate (17.1% each) in 2001 (U.S. Census Bureau, Current Populations Survey, 2002). Here we will discuss people who are more vulnerable to poverty than are others.

One-Parent Families

A female heads the majority of one-parent families, and 37% of female-headed families are poor, compared with 12% of families with two parents. Many women face poverty after a divorce and have problems such as lack of adequate employment, insufficient job training, and poor education skills; they also have childcare concerns (Mauldin, 1991). Discrimination in the workplace is another problem for single-parent families (Scanlan, Watson, McLanahan, & Sorenson, 1991).

Children

The child poverty rate in the U.S. is substantially higher than that of most other major western industrialized nations. In 2003, 16% of children (almost 12 million) lived in poverty. More than four million of those were under the age of six (National Center for Children in Poverty, 2003). Thirty percent of African American children and 29% of Latino children live in poverty. Sadly, 7% of America's children live in extreme poverty because their families have incomes less than half that of the poverty line.

Immigrant children are twice as likely to be poor as native-born children. Of children living in two-parent families, immigrant children are almost four times as likely to be poor as native-born children. Children living in homes where one or both parents work may still be at risk of living in poverty (National Center for Children in Poverty, n.d.). "Between 1995 and 2000, the percentage of poor children living in working poor families rose steadily from 32 percent to 43 percent, before falling to 40 percent in 2001" (Child Trends, 2003).

Young children are more likely to be poor than any other age group. The poverty rate for children under three years of age was 80% higher than the rate for adults or the elderly in 2000 (National Center for Children in Poverty, 2002). These 2.1 million poor

Many Voices: An Introduction to Social Issues

children under the age of three face a greater likelihood of impaired development due to increased exposure to multiple factors associated with poverty. Some of these risk factors include inadequate nutrition, environmental toxins, diminished interaction due to maternal depression, trauma and abuse, lower quality childcare, and parental substance abuse.

Nearly 40% of all children under age three lived in poverty or near poverty in 2000. Children who live with single mothers are more likely to be poor than those with married parents (National Center for Children in Poverty, 2002). Poor children are more likely to experience difficulties at school (Parker, Greer, & Zuckerman, 1988) and, as adults, to earn less and have more unemployment (Duncan & Brooks-Gunn, 1997).

The Elderly

Several factors are associated with poverty and the elderly, including the fact that they have fixed and limited sources of income. The U.S. Government Census Bureau (2001) indicates that 10% of those over 65 are often dependent on social security benefits, meager pensions, or assistance programs for their basic needs. They are often unable to look for ways to bolster their income due to eligibility standards for receipt of assistance. Other problems include poor housing, lack of medical care, poor nutrition, and lack of transportation (Johnson & Schwartz, 1997).

The elderly are vulnerable to increased health care costs and often are forced to spend large amounts of money on medication. From age 70 till death, individuals with no functional limitations have medical expenses estimated to be around $136,000, while those with at least one daily living limitation have an estimated cost of $145,000. Males have higher yearly expenditures, but due to shorter life expectancy have overall lower costs; blacks have similar expenditure levels, but lower life expectancy than whites (Lubitz, Cai, Kramarow, & Lentzner, 2003). Depending on their work history, women are less likely to have a pension or retirement income. When elderly women become poor, they will remain poor because marriage and employment may not be options to escape poverty (O'Hare, 1996).

There are often complications related to health care for the elderly person living in poverty. Physicians often misdiagnose their conditions due to receiving minimal special training in the unique medical needs of the elderly. Also, physicians often prefer not to treat the elderly due to reimbursement limits for their care set by Medicare (Zastrow, 2000).

People of Color

Members of minority groups are disproportionately likely to be poor (Rodgers, 2000). In his popular 1987 book, *There Are No Children Here*, Alex Kotlowitz writes about a family of five living in low income housing in Chicago. The family members are in constant fear of gang violence. Though cramped and unsafe in their apartment, they do not have enough money to move from the neighborhood. They cling to the hope of a better life, but are unable to overcome the tremendous obstacles that confront them on a daily basis. Black families are at greater risk of experiencing economic hardship than families of any other ethnic group. The economic conditions of black Americans have been linked to a history of oppression and discrimination (Staples & Johnson, 1993).

Geographic Variations in Poverty

Rural areas are more often home to people with higher incidences of poverty than are urban areas. In rural areas, wages are low, unemployment is high, and often work is seasonal. People in rural areas tend to be made up of those who are married, employed, elderly, and disabled. They are less likely to be children or members of a minority group. They are also less likely to receive public assistance than people in urban areas (Johnson & Schwartz, 1997).

Some decaying cities in the Northeast and Midwest have large urban slums with many poor people. Poverty is also extensive on Native American reservations and among migrant workers who travel from one location to another in order to earn a living (Zastrow, 2000).

The Working Poor

Millions of Americans with full-time working family members are poor. Being employed does not guarantee escape from poverty. In the mid 1990s, the working poor were almost equally distributed among cities, suburbs, and rural areas. Most (62%) had graduated from high school, most were white, and about half were married (O'Hare, 1996).

Some argue that the working poor are lazy and that if they worked harder and longer they would not be poor (Schiller, 1994). However, studies have shown that most of the working poor would remain poor even if they worked 40 hours a week, 52 weeks per year. At the end of the 1990s, a minimum wage earner, paid $5.15 per hour, would earn $10,300 per year. The poverty threshold for one person is $9,645 and for a couple is $12,334 (U.S. Census Bureau, 2004). Thus, working more hours is not a solution to poverty because the problem involves low wages or jobs that do not provide full-time employment (Kim, 1998).

This group, unfortunately, is usually not eligible for most assistance programs due to their inability to meet income requirements. Also, some of the working poor want to avoid the stigma attached to such programs and thus do not apply for food stamps. Sometimes farmers are considered part of the working poor. Even if they own land, they may be unable to provide adequate income to meet their basic needs (Johnson & Schwartz, 1997).

The Underclass

Although there is no generally acceptable definition of the underclass (Sjoquist, 1990), they may be broadly identified as working-age adults with low income, little formal education, and a weak attachment to the labor force. The term *underclass* means much more than just being poor. Studies have focused on causes of growing concentrations of poverty, causes of the persistence of poverty, and neighborhood poverty and its relation to deviant behavior patterns (Buttrick, 1990).

Two broad explanations describe why the underclass exists. The first is that some people are the victims of societal changes that cause neighborhoods to deteriorate and economic opportunities to evaporate. Thus, the group known as the underclass reflects changing employment opportunities and other events over which they have no control (Wilson, 1987). The opposing explanation categorizes this group on the basis of their behaviors (Ricketts & Sawhill, 1988).

Our Images of the Poor

In his book *Upon Whom We Can Depend: The American Poverty System*, J. Gordon Chamberlain discusses a study by Yale University political scientist Martin Gibens, which found that although white Americans make up 67% of the nation's poor, blacks make up 56% of the poor pictured in major news magazines. He also found that the news magazines fueled the stereotype that the poor are lazy, showing only 15% of the poor as working, though census data show that 51% of the poor actually work. In a 1994 *New York Times/CBS* poll, 47% of high school dropouts, 59% of high school graduates, and 48% of college graduates believed that most poor people are black (Chamberlain, 1999). See Table 14.3 regarding poverty in the United States for the years 1994 and 2004.

Table 14.3: Poverty in the United States: 1994 and 2004

	Below Poverty 1994		Below Poverty 2004	
	Number (in thousands)	Percent	Number (in thousands)	Percent
Total People	38,059	14.5	36,997	12.7
White	25,379	11.7	25,301	10.8
Black	10,196	30.6	9,000	24.7
Hispanic	8,416	30.7	9,132	21.9
Asian & Pacific Islander	974	14.6	1,209	9.8

Source: U.S. Census Bureau, 2004.

Many Voices: An Introduction to Social Issues

The Effects of Poverty

ISSUES: How do you think other people would perceive you if you were poor? What are the effects of poverty, and which bother you the most? Who should deal with the homelessness issue—the government (federal, state, or local), religious organizations, or the individual? Should there be socialized medicine so that people have more equal access to heath care? How should the justice system respond to poverty?

Stigma

Amy, a 23-year-old mother of one, describes her feelings about being on welfare: "It's a very humiliating experience being on welfare and being involved in the system. You are treated as though you are the scum of the earth. A stupid, lazy and nasty person. How dare you take this money. It's a very unpleasant experience. I'd avoid it at all costs. But unfortunately, I can't avoid it right now" (Seccombe, 1999, p. 59).

Dawn, a welfare recipient, says, "I'm embarrassed about being on welfare." She told her children that they should not be happy to be receiving a welfare check (Seccombe, 1999).

Seccombe, in her 1999 book *So You Think I Drive a Cadillac?* concluded that the stigma surrounding poverty is deep and widespread. The welfare recipients she interviewed revealed that they are very well aware of their stigmatized status and all have been victims of negative comments from others. These experiences make the individuals feel devalued as persons, and lead to a decline in self-worth. Seccombe found that the women she interviewed used one or more strategies to try to cope with the feelings aroused by the stigma attached to their status: 1) expressing denial, 2) distancing themselves from other women on welfare, 3) valuing their role as a mother (particularly as a single parent), and 4) blaming external forces and insisting that being on welfare was not their fault.

Housing and Homelessness

The Cochran family lost their $350-a-month apartment in Columbus, Ohio, when the rent was increased by almost 50%. Mrs. Cochran was six-months pregnant and had to stop working. The Cochran family included a ten-year-old and an eight-year-old, and Mr. Cochran's $230-a-week take-home pay was not enough to support the family. They could not find a place to live that was within their budget. They had no choice but to go to a shelter for homeless families, where they slept together in one room for a week. For the next four weeks they were shuttled each night to various motel rooms provided by an agency working to help homeless families. Despite being hardworking, they, like others who are considered the "working poor," are unable to provide for their own basic needs (Cole & Corliss, 2003).

The Christian family, with four children ages four to fourteen, became homeless after Mr. Christian lost his job when the business closed. Mrs. Christian's income was inadequate to provide for the family. They sold their belongings and resorted to begging. Mrs. Christian said, "We went from doing fine one day to being homeless" (Stein, 2003, p. 55).

Homelessness is a social problem that has received increased media attention over the last two decades. There are many reasons why people are forced to live on the streets, in vehicles, or in shelters made from cardboard and other temporary materials. Sudden loss of a home through fire, the loss of a job, or health problems may leave families destitute. If fortunate, they are able to regain some financial security after a few months. For others, though, homelessness is a chronic problem that they have no hopes of changing. Individuals may suffer from mental illness or substance abuse, or they may have escaped a violent home and have no options other than seeking shelter on the streets. Physically disabled individuals may be homeless because their benefits do not provide enough income for permanent housing. The elderly are sometimes faced with this same dilemma, as are some immigrants (Schmolling, Yonkeles, & Burger, 1997).

Breakey (1987) has described another category as

"situationally homeless"—those whose situations have changed, forcing them to give up their homes. Situations include unemployment, spousal or child abuse, and eviction or urban redevelopment. Women and their children are disproportionately represented in the homeless population (Hagen, 1990) due to low income, unemployment, underemployment, and family violence. Even though there are shelters in many cities to accommodate homeless people, they are inadequate in meeting all the existing needs of the thousands of homeless individuals. Many families with inadequate incomes are forced to live in cramped conditions, often in unsafe areas. Some live in unhealthful conditions without proper sanitation and water. One major problem is lack of affordable, clean, safe, and adequate-sized housing. This is due to increases in costs of rental units, increased utility costs, lack of moderate and lower priced housing, and lessened governmental help in providing adequate housing (Karger & Stoesz, 1998). The need for housing assistance exceeds existing federal resources. The growing demand for affordable housing is caused in part by the number of single individuals and elderly who live alone. A problem is the percentage of their income that those in poverty are forced to pay for shelter (Johnson & Schwartz, 1997). Often people living in poverty are in substandard housing that higher income families have rejected. In urban areas, the elderly and people of color, particularly Latinos and African Americans, inhabit housing that has deteriorated. Problems include inadequate heat, broken light fixtures, leaking toilets, cockroaches and rats, broken windows, and overcrowded rooms (Zastrow, 2000).

Health Care

The poor are negatively impacted by the health care system. Because gaining access to health care is often difficult and cumbersome, they often wait too long before seeking help (Beeghley, 1983). Due to nutritional deficits, lack of affordable health care, and stresses related to living in poverty, many poor individuals have health concerns which interfere with their ability to secure or keep a job. This is particularly true of single mothers. Seccombe (1999) found that of the 47 welfare recipients she interviewed, nearly one third of them suffered from health problems, including asthma, depression, high blood pressure, and back pain. She also reported other data that indicated that many welfare recipients

are in poor health. Because of the lack of medical care, children of single mothers are more likely to suffer from both chronic and acute illnesses (The Children's Defense Fund, 1994). These conditions are often caused by prenatal and postnatal factors, such as the mother's poor nutrition, stress, smoking, and drug use.

Access to the health care system is directly related to socioeconomic class and race. For example, life expectancy for white males is about eight years longer than that for African American males (Kornblum & Julian, 1998). Being in a lower social class has been shown to be a factor for higher rates of illnesses. The poor are seriously ill more frequently and for longer periods of time. This is often due to their inability to afford high-quality medical care (Zastrow, 2000).

The Justice System

When the poor are unable to attain economic or occupational success through usual legal means, some resort to street crime in order to provide some means of support. The justice system is organized in a way that perpetuates the relationship between crime and poverty; it dehumanizes offenders while they are in jail or prison and severely restricts their options afterwards. Emphasis is placed on the victims of crime in poor neighborhoods and then such areas become known as unsafe. The poor are not able to control their own environments. The focus on the poor and their criminal behavior takes attention away from the illegal acts of the upper class. Thus, the criminal justice system helps to perpetuate a class of impoverished people (Beeghley, 1983). What kinds of crimes do poor individuals commit? Beeghley (1983) reports that they usually rob people on the streets in an attempt to attain cash or other valuables. These crimes are frightening and receive special attention by the criminal justice system. Thus, Beeghley concludes that poor people are more likely to be arrested and found guilty, and usually they are given longer prison sentences. The facts are generally true regardless of a person's actual guilt or innocence. While people who work as professionals are able to use computers to embezzle funds or commit similar illegal acts, the poor have no access to these options. They are more likely to acquire a gun and rob people on the streets.

Psychological and Social Impact

Economic factors such as unemployment and low

income have a negative effect on the emotional well-being of individuals and families (Adler et al., 1994; Klebanov et al., 1994; MacFadyen et al., 1996; Takenchy, Williams, & Adair, 1991). Studies show a relationship between economic strain and distress, including increased levels of anger, hostility, depression, anxiety, and poorer physical health (Hamilton et al., 1990; Keith, 1993; Kessler, House, & Turner, 1987; Krause, 1987; Peirce et al., 1994). Social costs include negative impacts on relationships (e.g., marital, parent-child, friendships) through strain and disruption in social activities, support, and networks (Voydanoff, 1990). Economic stress decreases family satisfaction and cohesion (Voydanoff, 1990), and the greater the perceived economic hardship, the poorer the family relationships (Gomel et al., 1998). Adults experiencing economic difficulties may have increased problems with parenting (Takenchy et al., 1991). The consequences of poverty on children include greater levels of depression, more impulsive and antisocial behaviors (Takenchy et al., 1991), and diminished self-esteem (Ho et al., 1995).

Explanations of Poverty

ISSUES: What factors cause or contribute to poverty? How can you explain the existence of poverty in a wealthy country? How does a capitalist economy help or hinder the issue of poverty? Is poverty functional for a country?

In 1999, the United Nations Human Development Report indicated that the United States had the worst level of poverty (16.5%) of the 17 industrialized countries. This is based on a combination of factors, including the survival rate, literacy rates, long-term unemployment, and the proportion of people living on less than half the median income (http://www.wsws.org/articles/1999/aug1999/un-a06.shtml).

Why does poverty exist in a nation that has so much wealth? How can there be so many hungry and homeless people when many others live in extreme wealth? Dozens of possible factors may cause or contribute to poverty, including these:

• High unemployment
• Poor physical health
• Physical disabilities
• Emotional problems
• Large families
• Lack of employable skills
• Low educational level
• Racial discrimination
• Female head of household with young children
• Labeled "convict" or "crazy"
• Living in a geographic area where jobs are scarce
• Divorce
• Desertion or death of a spouse
• Sex discrimination
• Underemployment
• Low-paying jobs

Although this list is far from exhaustive, it gives us an idea of the complexity of trying to resolve the problem of poverty (Zastrow, 2000). Two of these causes—unemployment/underemployment and feminization of poverty—will be further described below.

Unemployment/Underemployment

In a market economy, people are expected to work and earn an income to meet their needs. However, the labor market fails to provide for the basic needs of all people. Some who could work must depend on social welfare programs for economic support (Karger & Stoesz, 1998). This may lead to stigma, frustration, poor self-esteem, and other emotional and physical problems (Brenner, 1984). The unemployment rate is officially based on the proportion of the labor force that is not employed. This rate, however, does not include discouraged workers who want jobs but have given up looking (Page & Simmons, 2000).

Brenner (1984) found a strong relationship between unemployment and emotional problems. Divorce and suicide rates are higher, and health problems increase because of unemployment. Long-term unemployed persons often exhaust their savings, sell their homes, and become recipients of public aid. A few, particularly young people, turn to crime (Zastrow, 2000).

Some groups have chronically high unemployment rates, including African Americans, Latinos, teenagers, women, older workers, the unskilled, the semi-skilled, and people with disabilities. High unemployment for African Americans and Latinos is partly due to racial discrimination (Zastrow, 2000).

High rates of unemployment often lead to under-employment. This occurs when people are forced to accept jobs below their level of skill due to the unavailability of jobs for which they are qualified. College graduates, for example, may take positions as clerks just to be employed (Zastrow, 2000). The results of underemployment include insufficient wages, lessened satisfaction, diminished self-esteem related to the job, and inability to provide for the family (Johnson & Schwartz, 1997).

Feminization of Poverty

Women as a group are more likely to be poor than are men (Rotella, 1998). Shortridge (1989) has established that women are twice as likely to be poor within their lifetimes as are men. If a woman is divorced, a teen mother, or over 65, she is likely to be living in poverty (Appleby, Colon, & Hamilton, 2001). Women earn less than men do for the same amount of work. Married women earn less than their husbands do and single women who are head of their households have an income which is lower than that of equivalent families headed by men (McBride-Stetson, 1997). In the United States, more than 12 million women work full-time jobs that pay wages below the poverty line. Many more women than men are part of the working poor. Twenty years ago women made 64 cents for each dollar a man earned. In 2003 women made 75 cents for each dollar earned by a male, but this figure had decreased from almost 77 cents in 2002 (McKay, 2004).

A social trend affecting the lives of women is the changing family structure. The marriage rate is declining and the number of single mothers is increasing. Thus more and more women are trying to manage their homes and families alone. Often they are forced to work at lower-paying jobs due to lack of skills and/or education. The feminization of poverty can be blamed in part on government programs that stipulate insufficient alimony and child support, and fail to enforce child support orders. Many politicians do not recognize how policy issues are detrimental to women's welfare. They believe that government support rewards laziness and family breakup. The assumption is that the poor are lazy and choose welfare over jobs (Appleby, Colon, & Hamilton, 2001). Researchers found that women have been forced to frequent soup kitchens, live in inadequate housing, and sometimes stay in violent relationships due to a lack of other options (Mishel & Schmitt, 1995).

The Functions of Poverty

Poverty is dysfunctional to the poor and the affluent. However, the poor provide some functions that are helpful to the non-poor, including the following (Zastrow, 2000; Chamberlain, 1999):

- They do unpleasant jobs that others do not want to do, such as cleaning hotel rooms.
- They purchase poor quality goods that otherwise would not be sold.
- They serve as symbolic opponents for some political groups and as constituents for others.
- They provide opportunities for some to practice their "Christian duty" in helping others.
- They do work that serves others—caring for children, checking out groceries, serving fast food, cleaning homes, and sewing clothes.

Theories for the Existence of Poverty

The functionalist perspective is one view for why poverty exists. Proponents of this theory blame dysfunctions in the economy for the poverty seen among so many people. One such dysfunction is rapid industrialization, which has caused some workers who lack needed skills to seek alternate jobs paying low wages. This perspective also blames the welfare system, arguing that changes need to be made to improve assistance for those in need. Some functionalists believe that poverty becomes a problem when it no longer performs the function of motivating people to contribute to society.

The conflict perspective states that poverty exists because of the power structure. It says that the working poor are being exploited, receiving low wages so their employers can earn more and live in affluence. Wealthy people tend to value the ideology of individualism and believe poverty and unemployment result from lack of effort rather than other factors. However, they may contribute to charitable programs for the poor and feel they have done "good deeds."

Finally, the interactionist perspective suggests that poverty is subjective and proponents compare poverty in a relative sense. For example, poor people in this country are much better off than people in third-world countries. This theory emphasizes the psychological effects of being poor in a wealthy nation, and interactionists believe that those living in poverty begin to think of themselves as failures. They are stigmatized and may turn to drugs and crime to obtain material possessions (Zastrow, 2000).

See Chapter 20, "From Social Problems to Policies," for more information on theories of poverty.

Proposed Solutions to Poverty

ISSUES: What do you see as viable solutions to poverty? Can it be eliminated? If so, what consequences would this have? If not, how would the consequences differ? Do you see the "haves" giving to the "have nots," and under what conditions? How much do you think they will be willing to give? Do solutions revolve around re-cutting the pie (or that which already exists) or creating different pies (avenues which do not exist)?

Although much study and many debates have addressed the possibilities for eliminating poverty, it continues to be a high-priority political agenda item. Many Americans believe the government has done little to find solutions to poverty and that it has been wasteful, inefficient, and bureaucratically rigid in its attempts to do so. Widespread cynicism exists about the motives of officials, their desire to help ordinary people, and their competence. There is also skepticism about what laws and policies can actually accomplish (Page & Simmons, 2000).

Of the major western industrialized nations, the United States has been the most conservative about social welfare policy. Americans believe that everyone should have the opportunity to succeed, that opportunity is bountiful, and that failure usually reflects personal shortcomings. Public surveys usually show that although Americans are sympathetic toward the poor, they are not comfortable with welfare programs (Rodgers, 2000). Some people believe that such programs are wasteful and that they reward, support, and encourage indolence and even immoral behavior (Bobo & Smith, 1994). Many believe that assistance should be given only to those who cannot be expected to support themselves. This philosophy has shaped the establishment and evolution of the American welfare system (Rodgers, 2000).

After the Great Depression, which began in 1929, one-fourth of the nation's adult men were unemployed, millions of people lost their homes, and thousands stood in bread lines each day (Rodgers, 1979). In 1935, President Franklin D. Roosevelt proposed and Congress passed the Social Security Act, establishing assistance programs for those who were outside the labor force. At the time this legislation was passed, it was a radical step for the government to undertake. Several changes were later made to the program:

- 1961: Aid to Families with Dependent Children was amended to allow states to provide support for families in which both parents are unemployed.
- 1964: Food stamp program was established.
- 1965: Medicare and Medicaid programs were enacted.
- 1971: Congress adopted national standards for the food stamp program.
- 1972: Supplemental Security Income Act (SSI) was passed (Rodgers, 2000).

The major public assistance programs thus included aid to families with dependent children, and also included food stamps, Medicaid, and Supplemental Security Income (SSI).

Aid to Families with Dependent Children (AFDC)

From 1935 to 1996, AFDC was the core cash-welfare program for poor families with children. Its original intent was to help mothers afford to stay home with their young children (Zastrow, 2000). This program was phased out after welfare reform legislation was passed in 1996.

Food Stamps

In 1964 food stamps were established on a pilot basis that was expanded nationwide in 1974. The program was designed to help low-income families purchase foods for a nutritionally adequate diet. Participating families must contribute 30% of countable income to food expenditures, and food stamps supplement that amount to provide a low-cost, nutritious diet. The food stamp benefit varies by family size and can be used only to purchase food items. To be recipients of food stamps, able-bodied adults must register for work, accept any suitable job offer, fulfill job training requirements, and not resign without good cause or reduce work hours to below 30 hours per week (Rodgers, 2000).

Medicaid

The Medicaid program was added to the Social Security Act by amendment in 1965. It provides medical assistance to low-income people who are aged, blind, or disabled; families who receive "Temporary Assistance to Needy Families" (formerly AFDC); and some pregnant women and their children. Each state administers its own Medicaid program, within federal guidelines.

Supplemental Security Income (SSI)

Passed by Congress in 1972, the SSI program became effective in 1974. It is a guaranteed income program for the aged, disabled, and blind. The program was designed to provide a national minimum-level income for this select group. If the aged, disabled, and blind have less income than the guaranteed amount, SSI pays the difference. SSI provides over six million recipients with cash benefits each month. The income level, which is guaranteed for recipients, is adjusted yearly. In 2003, SSI provided assistance for an eligible individual of up to $552 a month (http://www.thearc.org/afcsp/appealsfull.htm).

By the early 1990s, costs of federal and state welfare programs were in excess of $300 billion. Although millions of Americans received valuable assistance, some programs were criticized as being flawed. Additionally, there was little evidence that poverty was being prevented, or that those receiving benefits were able to escape poverty. This assessment led President Bill Clinton to propose the Personal Responsibility and Work Opportunity Reconciliation Act (PRWORA) of 1996 (Rodgers, 2000). Listed here are some of the provisions of this welfare reform:

- Welfare programs were turned over to states by providing block grants to states.
- A cap was placed on welfare spending by limiting the amount given by the federal government.
- Grants are distributed to states on the basis of predetermined criteria.
- States must continue to spend at least 75% of funds they contributed to welfare programs in 1994.
- States are encouraged to be innovative in designing their welfare policies.
- Adult welfare recipients are required to begin work within two years.
- Block grant funds can be awarded to adults for only five years.

Many more specific provisions are related to this welfare reform. In contrast to the Social Security Act of 1935, the 1996 Welfare Reform Act placed federal spending for several major welfare programs on a yearly basis and turned welfare administration over to the states (Rodgers, 2000).

The PRWORA changed the focus of welfare in America. It emphasized helping most able-bodied poor to enter the job market. Some states have been slow in making changes to their programs, but others have been inventive. How have these changes impacted poor families? We do not have conclusive evidence, but data suggest that most adults formerly receiving welfare are not working forty hours a week, and most are living in poverty or just above the poverty line. There are clearly pros and cons of the PRWORA.

The last part of the 20th century showed dramatic growth in single-parent families and women in the job market. Yet many people do not have health insurance and struggle to provide for their families (Rodgers, 2000). Does the government want to help? Should it help? Although there is disagreement about the government's involvement, possible solutions include extending public assistance, reducing causes of poverty, reducing unemployment, and tax reform. DiNitto (1995) defined social welfare policy as "anything a government chooses to do, or not do, that affects the quality of life of its people" (p. 2).

Extending Public Assistance

In her interviews with welfare recipients, Seccombe (1999) found three strengths of the welfare system:
- Some recipients would literally be out on the streets without it.
- Medicaid, the medical insurance provided for those in poverty, was especially appreciated, because otherwise many people would not be able to afford medical treatment.
- Voluntary programs designed to help women transition off welfare were very helpful.

Weaknesses of the welfare system were also noted in Seccombe's book:
- Welfare does not provide enough money for a family to meet basic necessities.
- Services are delivered inappropriately.
- Benefits are eliminated prematurely.

Several social insurance programs are financed by taxes on employees and/or employers:
- Medicare: provides health insurance for those over age 65.
- Old Age Survivors Disability and Health Insurance (OASDHI): partially replaces the income of those who retire or become disabled.
- Unemployment Insurance: provides benefits to workers who have been laid off or, in certain cases, fired.
- Worker's Compensation Insurance: provides income and assistance for medical expenses related to injuries sustained on a job.

Public assistance programs are paid from general government revenues and are financed from taxes on personal income and property. Benefits from these programs are viewed as charity, and individuals applying for assistance must meet specific eligibility requirements (Zastrow, 2000).

Reducing Causes of Poverty

Many factors cause or perpetuate poverty. Among them are some that could be addressed by laws or programs. Possible solutions include:
- Laws to end racial and sex discrimination

- Programs to curb alcohol and drug abuse
- Higher-quality education programs in impoverished areas
- Sex education and family planning services
- Expanded public housing program
- National health insurance program
- Financial counseling for families
- Provision of jobs (Zastrow, 2000)

The women interviewed by Seccombe (1999) are not opposed to welfare reform. They believe the system needs to be changed. Eager to work, they need help in finding well-paying jobs, support for education and childcare, and medical benefits. All of these women want a system based on positive incentives that offer support and encouragement, rather than a punitive system. They do not want to stay dependent on the welfare system, but need help getting off assistance.

Reducing Unemployment

Systemic barriers to employment for welfare-dependent heads-of-household have been documented; they include lack of training, shortage of jobs that pay a livable wage, lack of childcare, and transportation problems. Psychological barriers are also problematic. Single-parent welfare recipients often feel disempowered, helpless, overwhelmed, and anxious. Often their living patterns are unstable and have included low self-esteem, fear of the unknown, lack of role models, poor education, and weak employment histories. Many suffer from depression and some have come from violent homes (U.S. Department of Labor, 2001).

Seccombe (1999) found that some people on welfare face severe obstacles to employment, including poor physical health or deep-rooted psychological problems. Research conducted by participants at the University of Michigan found that many single mothers have problems with physical health, substance dependence, domestic violence, and child care responsibilities that make steady work difficult. They also found that these problems can be overwhelming when combined with lack of education, work experience, and work skills. Additionally, these women often face discrimination and harassment in the workplace (Danziger et al., 2001).

To reduce unemployment, we must find ways to provide more jobs that pay a wage on which a family can live. We must also look at the systemic and psychological barriers that confront so many, and create solutions that specifically address these barriers.

Tax Reform

For more than three decades, economists have been advocating the use of the tax system instead of the welfare system to help alleviate poverty. The Earned Income Tax Credit (EITC) has been offered as a policy solution to many pressing economic concerns. Two benefits of using this system for transferring income to the poor are high participation rates and low administrative costs (Liebman, 1998). The majority of dollars given through EITC are to taxpayers at or above the poverty level. Programs that use the standard welfare budget constraint give most of the money to households with little other income. The EITC appears to be an effective way to assist workers with low wages.

Another proposal suggests progressive taxation. That is, high-income people would pay greater percentages in taxes than low-income people. This argument for progressive taxation is based on the assumption that people with high incomes can pay a proportionally higher percentage of their incomes than those with much less money. Critics of this proposal argue that higher progressive tax rates might reduce the amount of income available to be taxed, and may reduce overall welfare benefits (Page & Simmons, 2000).

Conclusion

Many suggestions are offered to explain why poverty exists. One is that individuals are ultimately responsible for their own economic well-being; people who are motivated to work will be able to provide for themselves and their families. In contrast, a social structural perspective assumes that poverty is a result of economic and social imbalances within our society, including the emphasis on capitalism, a changing economy, and the concern that the welfare system perpetuates poverty (Seccombe, 1999).

Poverty in this country often includes poor dietary intake, severely impoverished living conditions, greater susceptibility to health and emotional problems, shorter life expectancies, and fewer opportunities socially, economically, or educationally (Zastrow & Kirst-Ashman, 2001).

Possible solutions to the problem of poverty must include helping those with no education or job skills to obtain them, and creating jobs for all who want to work. Seccombe (1999) suggested the following strategies to help alleviate poverty:

- Enhance work by increasing the minimum wage to at least $8 per hour.
- Create viable and important public works jobs.
- Expand the Earned Income Tax Credit (EITC).
- Provide medical insurance to all families without it.
- Subsidize childcare to make it affordable.
- Allow workers to keep a portion of their food stamps and housing benefits.

Seccombe (1999) found from her study that the poor generally want to get off welfare. They simply do not have the supports in place to do so. Much is being done to help those in poverty; however, much more remains to be done.

Response

Give a Man a Fish...

by Timothy E. Spruill

Definitional Problems

Numerous difficulties exist when attempting to define poverty. The first definition cited—inadequate income to provide for the needs of the family—hinges on the ability to define the term *needs*. The extremes of this subjective term may suggest a lack ranging from basic necessities (food, shelter, clothing) to material comforts (air-conditioning, health insurance, television). All definitions hinge on personal opinion.

It is even more ironic that the federal government, legendary for fiscal irresponsibility, should determine what income is sufficient to meet basic requirements. To what extent does their calculation take into account individual variations in ability to manage and budget resources? In *Hitting the Lottery Jackpot: State Governments and the Taxing of Dreams,* David Nibert (2000), an associate professor of sociology at Wittenberg University in Springfield, Ohio, points out that lower-income groups are the segments of the general populace that spend a much higher percentage of their income on lotteries than others.

Another definitional problem stems from the fact that the U.S. Census Bureau's poverty thresholds do not vary geographically, despite the fact that wages paid for the same job class vary considerably from location to location. For example, the median income of a "Crater/Packer I" in Anchorage, Alaska, is $25,431, whereas the same worker in Greenville, Mississippi, earns $19,486—a 24% variation annually (http://www.salary.com).

Even taking a purely objective statistical approach to defining poverty has drawbacks—the most obvious being how many standard deviation units from the mean one draws the poverty line. In addition, the question of whom to include in the comparison sample is critical. When compared with the rest of the world, even the poorest American is well off. This is well illustrated by James Wolfenson (2000), author of *The Other Crisis,* who said: "Today, across the world, 1.3 billion people live on less than one dollar a day; 3 billion live on under two dollars a day; 1.3 billion have no access to clean water; 3 billion have no access to sanitation; 2 billion have no access to electricity." If the goal is to attack poverty, it would seem that America is the last place to focus the effort.

Clearly there are those even in America who are unable to meet the most basic needs without financial assistance, primarily due to factors outside their control such as significant physical/emotional disability. At the same time, there are many others who could perform a productive role in society given the proper training and reinforcements. Most unfortunate of all, others continue to fraudulently "milk" the system.

Current overly simplified definitions fail to adequately encompass the wide range of factors that contribute to poverty.

Causes of Poverty (or Wealth, for That Matter)

The best approach to any question of causality is a "systems theory" approach that includes analysis from all of the following perspectives: theological/moral, philosophical, sociological, and biological. I will limit my arguments primarily to the psychological perspective. This is not intended to suggest that this perspective is inherently superior to the other views. However, since key differences exist from one human being to the next, the science of psychology has much to contribute to this subject.

Because psychology as a distinct discipline arose largely out of the identification and measurement of individual differences, it seems like an appropriate starting point for discussion about causal factors. Few, if any, credible experts would argue that we all enter this world with equal talents and abilities. Fortunately, psychology has begun to move beyond its early, extremely narrow definition of intelligence as reflected only in verbal and analytical skills. Many "intelligences" have been recognized, including linguistic, logical/mathematical, musical, spatial, body-kinesthetic, interpersonal, intrapersonal, and, most recently, naturalist abilities (individuals who can discern patterns in nature) (Gardner, 2000).

Any explanation of the causes of poverty or wealth has to take into consideration the wide range in which natural abilities express themselves from person to person. While society does not equally value each of these abilities, and there is some variation in the potential for reward, all of these talents, if recognized and supported by the environment, represent the potential for productive, rewarding contributions to society. Also, such factors as timing, opportunity, and motivation clearly moderate the effects of raw ability. Those with limited talents will have to compensate with motivation and determination. Yet a sense of personal fulfillment can be gained in even the simplest of tasks.

Research from the field of psychological learning theory is also highly relevant to a discussion of causality. What follows is a brief summary of the relevant findings from operant conditioning, social learning theory, and cognitive-behavioral theory.

The fundamental principle behind operant conditioning states that reinforced behaviors are strengthened such that they occur more frequently. Since money is a universal reinforcer, those behaviors which lead to acquisition of currency will be strengthened. This is the essential basis for token economies (a behavior modification program that uses generalized reinforcer in the form of a token), a highly effective approach to changing behaviors. The principle explains why those who apply hard work, natural talent/ability, and ingenuity in their efforts to "build a better mouse trap" reap financial rewards. It also can explain why some turn to the government and seek to obtain the designation of Social Security Disability or to qualify for welfare benefits such as food stamps. In each case, there is tangible reinforcement in the form of currency.

While working in physical medicine and rehabilitation, I often treated those who had been neurologically or physically injured as a result of an accident. The purpose of such treatment is to help rehabilitate patients with psychological and cognitive deficits and/or compensate for them in ways that allow the patients to return to as normal a lifestyle as possible. Without exception, when these patients are involved in pending litigation, their progress is minimal if measurable at all. Persons with similar injuries, whose financial settlements will not be diminished if they recover lost function, consistently recover faster and more completely. A clear conflict of interests is present when recovered function will invariably result in a reduced financial settlement or award. This illustrates the power of financial rewards as a universal reinforcer.

Another example drawn from my clinical experience involved a man in his mid-thirties who had recently been diagnosed as HIV positive. Prior to the diagnosis, he worked as a building superintendent in New York. He found it very satisfying and derived a great deal of self-esteem from being a productive member of society. As his disease progressed, he was encouraged by a well-meaning healthcare professional to seek Social Security Disability. Once on disability, with the checks arriving, he had little purpose in life and found his emotional health spiraling downward towards clinical depression. Lack of employment resulted in a diminished sense of self-worth. When I suggested vocational rehabilitation as a means of returning to a productive role, his affect immediately brightened. After a few minutes, he interrupted me to ask if returning to work would mean an end to the disability payments. When I answered yes, I could see his enthusiasm wane. He failed to follow up with vocational rehabilitation.

Reinforcement also plays a role in another current phenomenon in America—the trend toward "victimization." Individuals are increasingly encouraged (reinforced) to view themselves as victims of their circumstances; as a result, personal responsibility for their actions, as well as any personal control over future events, are sacrificed in the process. One glaring example of this reinforcement is seen in people who have chosen to live in regions designated as flood plains. When the inevitable cycle of flooding destroys their homes, they are granted federal funds to rebuild (often in the same location) rather than to relocate in an area safe from flooding.

The leading social learning theorist, Albert Bandura (1997), stated that "People can exercise influence over what they do" (p. 3). He calls this "human agency." This is not the only causal factor; rather, he identifies three major classes of determinants. The relative strength of the three factors varies for different activities and circumstances. Human agency is a part of the internal Personal factors, which include cognitive, affective, and biological events. The other two factors are external **E**nvironmental events and **B**ehaviors. These three sets of determinants interact with and influence one another, as the diagram below illustrates.

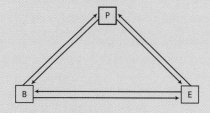

Bandura believes the key to positive change lies in a personal factor he refers to as *self-efficacy*. He defines this as "beliefs in one's capabilities to organize and execute the courses of action required to produce given attainments" (Bandura, 1997, p. 3). He cites numerous studies showing that as individuals' perceptions of their self-efficacy improve, positive changes in behavior result.

Translating this to poverty at the individual level, Bandura would argue that one major element absent in the poor is a sense of self-efficacy. Welfare systems have unintentionally reinforced this lack of belief in one's capabilities. An implicit message accompanies extended institutionalized financial support to the economically disadvantaged individual: "You lack the capabilities to organize and execute the courses of action required to produce financial independence." Notice that this is the exact opposite of the definition of self-efficacy.

Bandura's views are consistent with the central premise of cognitive-behavioral theory. This position argues that rather than antecedent events directly causing a certain behavior or outcome, it is the individual's belief about the meaning of those events that influences the subsequent behavior. If, for

example, I believe that my financially destitute condition as a car sales person is the direct result of stupidity on my part and that stupidity cuts across all my ability levels and will not change, I may stop attempting to actively better my condition. Such a view is the direct result of a "pessimistic" attributional style, according to Martin E. P. Seligman (1990), since it is characterized by what he calls the three "P's." This style is **P**ersonal because I see the problem as within myself, **P**ervasive since I view myself as inherently deficient in all types of abilities, and **P**ermanent because I see it as a condition that will never change. If, instead, I take the position that my current status is due to external circumstances such as an economic recession, which is generally a temporary phenomenon, or if I see the problem as a lack of ability related specifically to sales, Seligman would credit me as having the attributional style of an "optimist."

Research using Seligman's Attributional Style Questionnaire (ASQ) has repeatedly shown that optimists outperform pessimists. In the creation and validation of the ASQ, high scores have been found to reflect an optimistic attributional style, whereas low scores depict a pessimistic attributional style. In two closely related studies, Seligman and Schulman (1986) hypothesized that the tendency to explain bad events by internal, stable, and global causes increases the odds of quitting when bad events happen. This prediction was tested in an actual work setting with sales agents for life insurance, individuals who frequently experience bad events. Explanatory style, as measured by the ASQ, correlated with and pre-

dicted the performance of the sales agents. In a cross-sectional study of 94 experienced agents, individuals scoring in the top half of the ASQ sold 37% more insurance in their first two years of service than those scoring in the bottom half. In the related prospective one-year study of 103 newly hired agents, individuals who scored in the top half of the ASQ when hired remained in their job at twice the rate and sold more insurance than those scoring in the bottom half of the ASQ. These two studies support the claim that a pessimistic explanatory style leads to poor productivity and resignation when bad events are experienced in an actual workplace.

What Should Be Done about Poverty?

The question regarding what should be done about poverty depends on several factors. First and foremost, it assumes that something *can* be done to eliminate poverty. A statistician might liken the goal of eliminating poverty to that of having everyone be "above average" economically speaking. Periodic attempts by our government to elevate the economic status of the poor by raising the minimum wage illustrate the impossibility of equal distribution of wealth in a capitalistic society. Such an event has an immediate "ripple effect" such that the costs of goods and services increase to the same extent that the minimum wage is raised. It is as if the entire compensation scale were adjusted upward.

So what has happened to the poverty rate in America over time? Since the advent of Franklin D. Roosevelt's "New Deal," and continuing with Lyndon B. Johnson's

"Great Society," organized governmental efforts have attempted to significantly reduce, if not eliminate, poverty. "In 1992, President Clinton promised to end welfare as we know it" (http://clinton5.nara.gov/WH/EOP/nec/html/2000SotuBookFinal.html). Seven years later, in his 1999 State of the Union Address, Clinton stated that we had "the smallest welfare roles in 30 years" (http://www.infoplease.com/t/hist/state-of-the-union/212.html). Was Clinton's announcement the result of his having finally solved the problem of the poor? Not so. The 1999 poverty rate of 11.8% was not that different from the record-low rate of 11.1% set in 1973 (http://www.census.gov/income/histpov/hstpov2.lst, 11/24/03). Rather, Clinton's announcement may reflect an acknowledgment that previous efforts on the part of the federal government have not accomplished their goals.

Setting aside the above arguments as to whether it is possible to significantly impact the extent of poverty, and assuming instead that we can make a measurable difference, at what level should efforts be organized? It would appear that the key phrase in "the end of welfare as we know it" is "as we know it." The federal government, having tired of poor results, has simply shifted the task along with some funding from the federal to the state level. The George W. Bush administration attempted to take it even further towards the grassroots by suggesting that federal funding be extended to private, church-affiliated charities. For years, these institutions have found ways without government financial support, but primarily through private contributions, to assist the poor in meeting basic needs such as food, shelter, and sometimes re-entry into the workforce. This attempt has not been without considerable controversy, including, at times, objections from church leaders who fear the attachment of government "strings" to any federal funding.

Meanwhile, back at the federal level, ongoing interest seeks to address the needs of the poor in ways other than issuing welfare checks. The primary example is the movement for the federal government to fund the healthcare needs of the poor. Many believe that access to healthcare is a fundamental human right.

So what are the basic human rights? One of our nation's founders, Thomas Jefferson (1776), defined them as follows in the Declaration of Independence: "We hold these truths to be self-evident, that all men are created equal; that they are endowed by their Creator with inherent and inalienable rights; that among these are life, liberty, and the pursuit of happiness; that to secure these rights, governments are instituted among men, deriving their just powers from the consent of the governed; that whenever any form of government becomes destructive of these ends, it is the right of the people to alter or abolish it, and to institute new government, laying its foundation on such principles, and organizing its powers in such form, as to them shall seem most likely to effect their safety and happiness."

On December 10, 1948, the General Assembly of the United Nations (1948) extended the range of rights beyond life, liberty, and the pursuit of happiness to include the following:

Article 3: "Everyone has the right to life, liberty and security of person."

Article 25: (1) Everyone has the right to a standard of living adequate for the health and well-being of himself and of his family, including food, clothing, housing, and medical care and necessary social services, and the right to security in the event of unemployment, sickness, disability, widowhood, old age or other lack of livelihood in circumstances beyond his control. (2) Motherhood and childhood are entitled to special care and assistance. All children, whether born in or out of wedlock, shall enjoy the same social protection.

This more modern international statement of basic rights seems to fit the current beliefs of many Americans. But is healthcare a basic human right? Leonard Peikoff, PhD, in a speech given at a Town Hall meeting on the Clinton health plan, argued that healthcare is *not* a right. Peikoff (1993) believes that there are moral issues at stake in answering this question. He stated that our rights to life, liberty, property, and the pursuit of happiness all share one common element. They are rights to action, not to rewards from other people. These basic American rights impose no obligations on other people but that of not blocking the attainment of goals. The system guarantees us the opportunity to work for what we want—not that it will be supplied without personal effort. Peikoff goes on to say that the so-called right to healthcare is no different than if the government were to declare a universal right to food, a vacation, or a haircut, free of charge, without personal action but simply as handouts from a benevolent government.

320

Many Voices: An Introduction to Social Issues

Is There a Solution?

Where does the solution to poverty lie, if not in expanding our definitions of basic human rights and moving to a more socialistic society where means are increasingly shifted from those who produce to those who do not? The ancient Chinese proverb holds the answer: "Give a man a fish and you feed him for a day. Teach a man to fish and you feed him for a lifetime" (Tripp, 1976). Many experts suggest that educational level is the single most important correlate of poverty/wealth. International statistics clearly indicate that the larger the percentage of children in school, the greater the national and hence individual wealth.

We must find more effective ways of reinforcing the individual pursuit of education. At the same time, the frequency of those behaviors that result in indigent status should be reduced and eventually eliminated through extinction (the removal of reinforcement). This will involve doing what behaviorists call a "functional analysis" of the reinforcements that currently exist in "dropping out" of the educational system. The system will then need to be modified so as to increase the rewards for staying in school and diminish the rewards for dropping out.

One possible approach would be to legislate that all youth, up until the age of 18, must either be 1) in a traditional high-school setting where course work is directed towards preparation for college; 2) in a vocational training program where specific skills are acquired, leading to proficiency in a trade; 3) working full-time; 4) engaged in a national work program; or 5) an active member of the military. These choices would preclude "hanging out" at the mall, or otherwise engaging in nonproductive behavior. They would also require that we rethink the concept of a two-track system of education, which was previously abandoned by American educators in favor of the idea that everyone should attend college. Finally, greater attention would need to be paid to developing valid assessment tools to assist in guiding individuals toward the areas of their personal interests, strengths, or intelligences.

Social learning theorists such as Bandura would argue that efforts should focus on developing a greater sense of self-efficacy in our young people. This is not to be confused with the recent educational movements focusing on "self-esteem." Bandura clearly distinguishes between the two movements. "[S]elf-efficacy is concerned with judgments of personal capability, whereas self-esteem is concerned with judgments of self-worth" (1997, p. 11). Hence it is possible for people to enjoy high self-esteem because little is demanded of them. This distinction explains how American high-school students can rank lower than their European and Japanese counterparts on administered standardized tests of math and science skills, yet still maintain the belief that they possess superior skills in these areas. It seems as though the bar has been lowered for our students. Research has shown that in ongoing pursuits, perceived self-efficacy predicts both the goals people set for themselves and their attainment of those goals, whereas self-esteem affects neither personal goals nor performance (Mone et al., 1995).

Bandura recommends that students be encouraged to compare their progressive skill improvement with esteemed, proficient role models. Performance tasks should be structured in ways that ensure progressive mastery and bring out the best of each student's capabilities. Students are taught to view their own skill at any point in time as a snapshot of the process of growth rather than a fixed indication of basic ability. Working with groups of students whose skills are more homogenous than heterogeneous reduces the potential for negative peer comparisons. It helps to support an optimistic personal appraisal despite an individual's current minor deficiencies in skill relative to peers.

Seligman and his associates (http://www.positivepsychology.org.htm, 11/24/03) have been attempting to answer the following two questions: Can optimism be taught in our schools, and what will be the effects? Two ongoing studies address these questions directly—the Penn Optimism Program (POP) and the Penn Enhancement Program (PEP). In POP, students are taught techniques from cognitive therapy. They identify negative beliefs and interpretive styles, examine evidence for and against negative beliefs, and generate more realistic alternative interpretations for problems. Students also learn techniques for assertiveness, negotiation, relaxation, and decision-making. In PEP, students discuss topics relevant to interpersonal relationships during the middle and high school years. Discussions focus on setting goals and identifying values, foundations of self-esteem, friendships, and dealing with peer pressure. The POP and PEP are both brief interventions, lasting for only 12 two-hour sessions. Students meet in groups of approximately eight to ten, which are led by school teachers and guidance counselors trained by developers of the intervention programs.

Up to this point, POP and PEP have been compared only to non-intervention-control students. Relative to controls, those students who participated in POP or PEP were significantly more optimistic in their interpretations of events, and experienced greater reduction and prevention of depressive symptoms. Middle-school students whose parents enroll them in the project are randomly assigned to POP, PEP, or a no-intervention control. Follow-up extends for three years beyond the end of the intervention so as to reveal the long-term effects of the prevention programs on students' adjustment, including academic achievement, optimism, self-worth, depressive symptoms, and episodes of depression. Researchers hope to be able to determine the mediators responsible for any prevention effects that are found.

The cognitive behaviorists have also set a new course for the field of psychology. Seligman (http://www.positivepsychology.org.htm, 11/24/03) has launched a major research initiative aimed at empirically establishing a taxonomy of "virtues," or positive attributes. The goal of "positive psychology," as he has termed this rapidly expanding movement, is "to discover and then apply psychological knowledge acquired in scientific research to solve real-world problems, alleviate suffering, and help individuals and institutions achieve a high quality of life." Seligman points out that for most of the 20th century, psychologists focused largely on understanding and healing psychological ailments within a disease model. The new field of positive psychology focuses instead on understanding and building the best things in life. At the individual level, positive psychology is about character strengths, including the capacity for love and work, courage, compassion, resilience, hope, creativity, social skills, integrity, self-knowledge, impulse control,

future-mindedness, and wisdom. This new research thrust has obvious implications for efforts at combating poverty, for it is out of this initiative that psychologists might soon discover the reasons why some individuals are able to excel despite unfavorable environmental barriers.

Until we have further answers from the field of positive psychology that can be integrated into our educational system, we need to further reverse the trend of depending on our governmental institutions. As the family unit has eroded, and as our society has become more mobile, we have increasingly depended on our government to assume responsibility for providing for the poor and sick among us. There was a time, in our distant past, when these duties were the responsibility of the immediate, if not the extended, family. If we cannot reestablish the role of the family, then perhaps local communities can come together to address these problems rather than look to what has become an impersonal, bureaucratic system staffed by well-meaning yet overworked and under-appreciated individuals.

Discussion Questions

1. In a nation of such staggering wealth, how can we explain the extent of the poverty that also exists?
2. Choose one or two groups of individuals who are most vulnerable to the possibility of living in poverty—such as women, children, the elderly, and people of color—and discuss some of the reasons why these groups are more at risk than the general population.
3. What do you think could be done to improve the lives of the working poor? What are the best methods you can think of for eliminating poverty?
4. How does situational homelessness differ from chronic homelessness? Explain the consequences of each.
5. Why is stigma such a problem for those living in poverty?
6. What are some ways in which the feminization of poverty could be alleviated?
7. Discuss two of the myths of poverty. Explain whether you believe them, or have in the past, and what could be done to change them.
8. Which proposal for addressing the problems of poverty do you believe would be most effective? Explain your answer.
9. If poverty is functional, should it be eliminated? Explain your answer.

10. Does the welfare system help or hinder impoverished people? Explain your answer.
11. What types of assistance should the poor receive?

Related Readings

Ehrenreich, B. (2001). *Nickel and dimed: On (not) getting by in America.* New York: Metropolitan Books.

Hays, S. (2003). *Flat broke with children: Women in the age of welfare reform.* Oxford: Oxford University Press.

Jencks, C. (1994). *The homeless.* Cambridge, MA: Harvard University Press.

Rodgers, H. (2000). *American poverty in a new era of reform.* Armonk, NY: M. E. Sharpe.

Seccombe, K. (2006). *So you think I drive a Cadillac? Welfare Recipients' Perspectives on the System and Its Reform.* 2nd ed. Boston: Allyn & Bacon.

Related Web Sites

Department of Health and Human Services—Homelessness: http://aspe.hhs.gov/progsys/homeless/index.shtml

Homelesspages: http://www.homelesspages.org.uk

Institute for Research on Poverty: http://www.ssc.wisc.edu/irp

Institute on Race and Poverty—Research, Education, and Advocacy: http://www.umn.edu/irp

Joint Center for Poverty Research: http://www.jcpr.org

National Alliance to End Homelessness: http://www.naeh.org

National Center on Poverty Law: http://www.povertylaw.org

National Law Center on Homelessness and Poverty: http://www.nlchp.org

National Resource Center on Homelessness and Mental Illness: http://www.nrchmi.samhsa.gov

U.S. Census Bureau, Poverty: http://www.census.gov/hhes/www/poverty.html

U.S. Department of Health and Human Services—Poverty Guidelines, Research, and Measurement: http://aspe.hhs.gov/poverty

World Bank Poverty Net Home—Resources and Support to Alleviate Poverty: http://www.worldbank.org/poverty

Related Movies/Videos

City of Joy (1992) with Patrick Swayze and Pauline Collins

Country (1989) with Jessica Lange and Sam Shepard

The Fight in the Fields: Cesar Chavez and the Farmworkers' Struggle (1996)

The Grapes of Wrath (1940) with Henry Fonda and Jane Darwell

Ironweed (1988) with Jack Nicholson and Meryl Streep

Les Miserables—The Dream Cast in Concert (1998) directed by John Caird

RACE

Nancy J. Carbonell

15

Chapter Outline

In 1991, two attractive, friendly, well-groomed men, of the same age and with the same level of education, who had graduated from the same school, were sent to a Midwestern town and were individually followed for a day by a film crew. The catch? One man was white; the other was African American. Diane Sawyer, from ABC-TV, set out to see if there continued to be evidence of racism in the U.S. The results, caught on tape with hidden cameras, were surprising to some (the whites) and confirming to others (the African Americans). In all situations, the white young man was better treated than the black young man. When the white man asked for directions to get around town, people were extremely helpful, actually going out of their way to point out where to go. When the black man asked for directions, he received a brief response from some and was ignored by others. In the stores the white man received good service, while his African American friend was avoided, and in some cases watched closely. They both were sent to buy a car, rent an apartment, and get a job in this town. At the car dealership the white man was offered a lower price, with a lower down payment and better financing; he obtained an apartment in a complex which had just recently turned the African American away because there were supposedly no vacancies; and he received a job offer at a place where his African American friend was turned down. The experiences of these two young men were as different as could be. Both were asked, "Would you like to live in this town?" The white man said yes, while the African American said no. The white man experienced the town as a friendly, accepting, and nice place to live, work, and start a family. To the African American it represented a cold, unfriendly place, full of avoidance, suspicion, and discrimination. Two men, two races, two different worlds...

Introduction

Today, the world has never seemed smaller. The World Wide Web, television, radio, technology, and efficient modes of travel have all contributed to this phenomenon. Images of what is happening around the world are seen on TV the very day the news breaks. A trip to India, Spain, or Chile is common fare. The financial ups and downs of the Japanese Nikkei stock market affect the stock markets in other countries, and the changes in the rainforests of Brazil affect the weather in other parts of the world. Within the United States, the impact of globalization is seen in how multiethnic the faces of Americans have become. Walk down the street of any major city and you will see people with varied ethnic facial features, skin color, hair texture, accents, religions, and dress—all of whom are American citizens. Many families contain at least one parent or grandparent who speaks with an accent or was born outside of the United States. Knowing how to relate effectively to different ethnic groups and cultures is a must in today's world. Whether one works in a hospital, schoolroom, business, or court, the issues of cultural variety and differences often arise. Is it any wonder that there is a push in all college professions to address the multicultural aspects of today's society, and that learning to speak Russian, Spanish, or Arabic can greatly enhance a college degree earned in any area of study?

Unfortunately, as many of us know, possibly by experience, racial diversity is not always well received. Our newspapers and history books tell of horrendous acts of injustice and discrimination performed by one ethnic group on another simply because of differences in skin color or how one's last name was pronounced. From the ethnic cleansing attempted by the Nazi regime, to that more recently waged by Saddam Hussein on the

Kurdish people in Northern Iraq, one can read of inexplicable acts of racial hatred.

Even here in the United States, where we pride ourselves on a democracy that recognizes the equality of all people, racism has been and continues to be an ugly mark on our past and present. From the earliest treatment of the American Indian to the prejudicial conduct toward the many "minorities" that followed, prejudice and racial discrimination have been unjustly practiced. In June of 1998, for example, James Byrd, Jr., a 49-year-old African American living in Jasper, Texas, was walking home after spending some time at his niece's bridal shower. He was offered a ride by three white men in a truck, and then was mercilessly beaten, chained to the back of the pickup, and dragged for two miles. The men had ties to a local white supremacist group, and killed James Byrd because he was black. Racial injustices such as this abound. Hate and misunderstanding have led many people not only to murder those who are different from them, but also to refuse others housing, jobs, an education, or even a seat on a bus because of ethnic heritage.

Why does this happen? Can anything be done about it? How can we deal with our own prejudices? Before we evaluate these issues, there are others we must consider first: What are racism, prejudice, and discrimination? How did prejudicial attitudes develop? How are they maintained?

In this chapter we will first define the concepts frequently reflected in discussions of racism, prejudice, and discrimination. Second, we will briefly review how particular prejudicial attitudes developed in the United States. Third, we will discuss how racial discrimination has affected various ethnic minorities in the United States and their integration into our society, and take a look at what it is like to be white in this country. Finally, we will explore ways to reduce the patterns of ethnic prejudice and discrimination in the United States.

Definitions of Terms and Racial Issues

ISSUES: How does one define one's own or others' race or ethnicity? Are racism, discrimination, and prejudice the same thing, or do they differ? Should racial assimilation or acculturation be the goal within the United States? Is pluralism possible in a nation that has a large diversity, and if so how? Is affirmative action for one group discrimination for another?

Race is a concept often used to categorize people according to their distinct physical characteristics—focusing on skin color, body shape and size, hair color and texture, and facial features such as the shape of the head, lips, nose, or eyes. The implications of such biological differences, which are often given erroneous social or political meanings, are now deemed by many to be meaningless. Research on skin color, for example, has taught us mostly about the functions of melanin, the primary dark pigment found in skin, and that skin-color variation is more a function of ultraviolet light on the human body than anything else. For example, studies have found that skin color, on the average, is darker the closer one lives to the equator, and lighter the closer one lives to the poles. The skin's lighter or darker pigment, therefore, helps humans survive in a world with differing levels of ultraviolet light (Cohen, 1998). Anthropologist Mark Cohen (1998) challenges us to see the fact that the term "race" is often misused to increase the racial divide and tensions between people. He suggests that "Most of our folk classification of people and 'races' depends on three or four highly visible distinctions such as skin color, the shapes of eyes or nose or lips, the texture of hair, or the length of limbs. But human beings vary in thousands of ways, many of them far more important than those" (p. 13). He also forewarns us: "Classifying people by color is very much like classifying cars by color. Those in the same classification look alike, superficially (if you ignore the detailed differences), but the classification tells you nothing about the hidden details of construction or about how the cars or the people will perform. For the most part, one biological variation cannot be predicted from the presence of another....More important, most human variation has nothing to do with either noses or skin colors" (p. 12). Many scientists now reject the concept of race and have chosen to speak of **populations** when referring to groups of people (Zack, 1998).

Ethnicity is how we classify individuals who share a common ancestry. They have the same customs and traditions in religion, food, dress, and nationality that are passed on from generation to generation.

Culture is a broader category than race or ethnicity in that it includes any group of people who share common lifestyle characteristics, which include socioeconomic status, geographic location, and sexual orientation.

Racism is behavior, what one says or does, that is motivated by the belief that some people are superior to others because of their racial characteristics. In the past, even scholarly works perpetuated this racist belief. For example, Steinberg (2001) shares that in the 1911 version of the *Encyclopaedia Britannica*, under the listing "Negro," one finds the following entry: "...the negro would appear to stand on a lower evolutionary plane than the white man....Mentally the negro is inferior to the white....[T]he remark of F. Manetta, made after a long study of the negro in America, may be taken as generally true of the whole race: 'the negro children were sharp, intelligent and full of vivacity, but on approaching the adult period a gradual change set in. The intellect seemed to become clouded, animation giving place to a sort of lethargy, briskness yielding to indolence....' On the other hand negroes far surpass white men in acuteness of vision, hearing, sense of direction and topography....For the rest, the mental condition is very similar to that of a child, normally good-natured and cheerful, but subject to sudden fits of emotion and passion during which he is capable of performing acts of singular atrocity..." (*Encyclopaedia Britannica*, 1911, vol. 19, pp. 344–345, quoted in Steinberg, 2001, p. 30).

In Melvin Steinfield's book, *Cracks in the Melting Pot* (1970), one sees how effectively racism was used to "justify" the actual injustices committed by one race on another. He reprints an editorial written for the *New York Evening Post* just before the Mexican-American War of 1848 when the nation was interested in overtaking the Mexican territories that now comprise Arizona, California, Nevada, New Mexico, Utah, part of Colorado, and Texas: "The Mexicans are *Indians*—Aboriginal Indians....They do not possess the elements of an *independent* national existence. The Aborigines of this country have not attempted, and cannot attempt to exist *independently* along side of us. Providence has so ordained it, and it is folly not to recognize the fact. The Mexicans are *Aboriginal Indians*, and they must share the destiny of their race" (p. 74).

Racism has also been used to discourage certain racial groups from achieving legal privileges, financial gain, financial aid for education, the right to live in certain neighborhoods, or marriage between members of different ethnic groups. Racism does not exist in a vacuum, but rather is enacted and reinforced through social, cultural, and institutional practices that endorse the hierarchical power of one racial group over another. Racism is a combination of racial prejudice and discrimination.

Racism comes in two forms. Overt racism is easily noticed and takes the form of direct behavioral action or offensive remarks. Covert racism is more subtle and hidden, and is often denied and discounted.

Prejudice is an attitude of positively or negatively "pre-judging" another in a categorically predetermined way. Unlike other attitudes, prejudicial ones are rigid and very resistant to change, even in the face of rational evidence. Thus it is extremely difficult to change once one develops an attitude towards another person.

Discrimination is the overtly unequal treatment of people on the basis of their membership in a certain social group. It is a behavior that is often seen when one group or person openly treats another as inferior simply because of race; this was the case in the southern states when whites and blacks had different bathrooms and drinking fountains because of their obvious differences in skin color.

Racial minority groups consist of people who share certain inherited biological characteristics, such as light skin or eye folds. As with race, these distinctions are purely social and carry no significance with regards to meaningful biological or genetic differences. A group may or may not be a numerical minority, but the defining feature is a lack of social, political, and economic power that is enforced by the majority group.

Ethnic minority groups are composed of people who share common cultural features, such as food, history, language, religion, land of origin, and traditions. A group's cultural heritage often continues to be influential even as members enter a different culture. This was well demonstrated in the movie *My Big Fat Greek Wedding*, in which the protagonist was keenly aware of how her Greek heritage (as seen in family reunions, food, and house decor, among other details) made her feel odd and different from her American-born friends.

Acculturation has to do with learning about another culture, and often includes learning to speak the language, to appreciate new food and customs, and to adopt the values of the culture. Obviously, one can become acculturated only if one has contact with the majority group and wants the acculturation to occur. Another important factor is whether the minority group is warmly accepted by the larger cultural group. Those who are rejected by the host culture will find acculturation difficult at best.

Assimilation occurs when one becomes integrated into a new culture to the point of being one with it. The term "melting pot" reflects a form of assimilation. In the United States, the white, Anglo-Saxon Protestant tradition dominates the culture. Often those populations who have assimilated well are treated as traitors to their ethnic origin by those who strive to keep their original traditions and identities alive. Hispanics who appear well assimilated into today's culture have been referred to, in a pejorative way, as "coconuts," brown on the outside, yet white on the inside. Assimilated Asians have been called "bananas," yellow on the outside and white on the inside. And African Americans who assimilated well have been referred to as "Oreos," black on the outside and white on the inside.

Again, people are assimilated into a new culture only if they are in contact with a majority group they desire to join. Experience shows that those who are well received by the larger culture have an easier time assimilating than those who are rejected by the host culture.

Marital assimilation, also known as amalgamation, occurs when members of different ethnic or racial groups marry or live together and give birth to a child. In the United States, although it is common to find marriages between people of different ethnic heritage, interracial marriages are still not common or always well accepted by the families of origin.

Racial profiling occurs when a person is suspected of being a criminal because of his or her ethnic origin.

Racial profiling was at work when thousands of Japanese Americans were placed in internment camps after the bombing of Pearl Harbor. It was also more recently seen after 9/11 when many people who looked Palestinian were suspected of participating in the heinous acts of terrorist Osama Bin Laden and his followers. Members of ethnic groups often complain that they are frequently stopped and questioned by the police, and treated as violators of some law, simply because of their skin color.

Segregation is the physical separation of people on the basis of certain identifiers in the workplace, school, neighborhood, or any social arena.

In **pluralism**, racial and ethnic groups maintain their distinctness while respecting each other. Mutual respect and social equality are enjoyed for all and by all in pluralistic societies. In Switzerland there are four distinct ethnic populations: Swiss German, German, French, and Italian. They are officially recognized, and mutual respect is shown between them. Because these four ethnic groups speak three different languages—German, French, and Italian—all three languages are represented in the media and used for all public services, including education.

Affirmative action often involves policies that address and put into place guidelines and procedures that aid in correcting institutional discrimination. Affirmative action programs have helped to open up job opportunities and educational experiences that would have otherwise excluded minority groups. Affirmative action policies have not been well received by all, however. Many white males, in particular, contend that affirmative action now infringes upon their rights, and makes them pay for past discriminations. Some white men have felt that doors closed on them because lesser-qualified minority candidates were given certain work or educational opportunities and financial aid, not offered to them, just because they were white and male. How fair is it, they contend, that today's white males have to "pay for" the suffering of those who were unjustly treated in the past? Kivel (1995) points out, however, that when one looks at the average income levels of white men, it is evident that they continue to be overrepresented and paid more in all categories than people of color. While minority group members are underrepresented in the job market in proportion to their numbers in society, "white men are tremendously over-represented in almost any category of work that is highly rewarded except for professional athletics" (p. 175).

Racial Prejudice and Discrimination in the United States

ISSUES: How does history help define racism? How are racism and fear related? How did racism become such a big issue in our country? Is racism a one-way street? What role do the media play in racism?

Citizens of the United States have been proud to proclaim that they live in the land of the free that provides freedom for everyone. Unfortunately, history books, including recent ones, reveal just how difficult it has been to attain real freedom for many now living in the U.S. The struggle against prejudice and discrimination has been long and hard, and extremely painful. From the American Indian, to the African American, and to the multitude of Hispanics seeking ways to fit in to this society, it appears that many in the United States have had a particularly hard time. Steinhorn and Diggs-Brown (2001) point out that one of the biggest challenges to our society is how differently the races perceive what is currently happening. Whites, for example, believe that the civil rights gains of the 1960s largely ended the problem of discrimination in America. Many think that Dr. King's dream of integration is within reach. Many believe that blacks now have the same opportunities as whites. Blacks, on the other hand, see discrimination as more subtle, yet very much present and ongoing. "When blacks see discrimination, whites see equal opportunity. When blacks say civil rights, whites say special interests. When blacks support affirmative action, whites label it quotas, preferential treatment, and reverse discrimination. And where blacks see racism, whites respond that they are being overly sensitive..." (Steinhorn & Diggs-Brown, 2001, p. 34).

Historical Causes of Racism

Steinberg (2001), in *The Ethnic Myth: Race, Ethnicity, and Class in America*, believes that the racial tension often seen in the United States has its roots in the different roles each of the ethnic groups took on in the early days after the nation's founding: some

were conquered, others were conquerors. Many came as laborers, while others were brought as slaves. He writes: "Ethnic [pluralism] in America has its origins in conquest, slavery, and exploitation of foreign labor. Conquest, first, in the case of Native Americans who were systematically uprooted, decimated and finally banished to reservation wastelands; and second, in the case of Mexicans in the Southwest who were conquered and annexed by an expansionist nation. Slavery, in the case of the millions of Africans who were abducted from their homelands and forced into perpetual servitude on another continent. Exploitation of foreign labor, in the case of the tens of millions of immigrants who were initially imported to populate the nation's land mass, and later to provide cheap labor for industrial development" (p. 5).

Today's society has benefited from many positive values in having such a diverse mix, and many minorities who have come to this country to begin a new life have reaped the benefits of an affluent society (Steinberg, 2001). Yet Steinberg (2001) also reminds us that immigrants often were victims of maltreatment by this very society. He suggests that only by understanding the negative conditions in which America's ethnic diversity developed are we able to understand the roots of the racial tensions that continue today.

Approximately 99% of those who colonialized early America were British, white, English-speaking Protestants (Steinberg, 2001). "Non-English colonials were typically regarded as aliens who were obliged to adapt to English rule in terms of both politics and culture" (p. 8). Because of the settlers' sheer numbers, English became the favored language, and their culture dominated. Steinberg points out that unlike the colonization of other countries, such as India and those found in Asia, colonists coming to British America found a lot of land and few indigenous people to "be exploited by the colonial power" (p. 6). They obtained, by any method, the cheap labor needed to build the new country. Some were bound by contracts to work for another, or given a free trip to America to begin a new life in exchange for seven years of labor, and others were involuntarily taken from their countries of origin to work as slaves.

As time revealed, it was "economic necessity rather than a principled commitment to the idea of America as an asylum" for foreigners (Steinberg, 2001, p. 11) that made our founding fathers uncomfortably tolerate the immigration of so many different ethnic groups to the United States in those early days. Early American leaders expressed concern about allowing "foreigners" to come over to this new world and live here. Madison Grant, an activist who sought to curtail immigration in the early twentieth century, compiled statements of warning from the founding fathers in his publication *The Founders of the Republic on Immigration, Naturalization, and Aliens*. He quotes Benjamin Franklin as saying: "Why should the Palatine boors be suffered to swarm into our settlements, and, by herding together, establish their language and manners, to the exclusion of ours? Why should Pennsylvania, founded by the English, become a colony of aliens, who will shortly be so numerous as to Gemanize us, instead of our Anglifying them…?" (Grant, 1928, p. 26, cited in Steinberg, 2001, p. 11).

And he quotes George Washington as saying: "My opinion, with respect to immigration, is that except of useful mechanics and some particular descriptions of men or professions, there is no need of encouragement, while the policy or advantage of its taking place in a body (I mean the settling of them in a body) may be much questioned; for, by so doing, they retain the language, habits, and principles (good or bad) which they bring with them" (Grant, 1928, p. 90, cited in Steinberg, 2001, p. 12).

These prejudices reflected the attitudes of many early Americans. All who were not white Anglo-Saxon Protestants were treated with tremendous suspicion, prejudice, and discrimination from the start. It is important to recognize how these attitudes helped determine how the "minorities" were and are treated here in the United States. Discriminatory attitudes affected all elections, all policies, and all areas of life from the founding of this country all the way to the present.

It would be too simplistic, however, to blame the presence of prejudice and discrimination entirely on what happened in the days of our founding fathers. Other theories of how racism, prejudice, and discrimination develop have been suggested. The major ones will be explored here.

Frustration-Aggression Model

Some believe that prejudice has arisen throughout the ages because of deficiencies in the human personality and the *very* "unsavory nature of man himself" (Daniels & Kitano, 1970, p. 17). One such theory, known as the **frustration-aggression model**, holds that it is common for everyone to feel frustrated from time to time, and that this frustration leads to an aggressive blaming of others. This behavior is referred to as scapegoating, and tends to feed on racist prejudicial attitudes. For example, suppose that a white male arrives late to his doctor appointment. Although he left work too late to get there on time, he tells the doctor he was late because of "those stupid foreign taxi drivers" who kept getting in his way. The "foreign taxi drivers" are the scapegoats, blamed for his lateness, even though they had nothing to do with it. Here we can see how the frustration-aggression cycle is used to support racial intolerance.

Stereotyping

Another source of prejudice and discrimination is **stereotyping**. Throughout the world, it is common for people to form sweeping impressions of a population, and then define the whole group by overgeneralizations. It is common to label all American Indians as drunks, all Mexicans as illegal wet-backs, all residents of the Appalachia as hillbillies, all Jews as shrewd, all Italians as Mafiosos, all Arabs as terrorists, all blacks as welfare recipients, all Polish as dumb, and so forth. Many believe that such stereotypes would disappear if people had enough contact with racially diverse groups. Snyder (1995), however, found through research that despite people's best intentions, their initial impressions of others are not easily changed and are often shaped by preconceived assumptions. He and his colleagues determined that these assumptions are reinforced by the behavior of both prejudiced people and the targets of their prejudice. He goes on to say, "if people treat others in such a way as to bring out behavior that supports stereotypes, they may never have an opportunity to discover which of their stereotypes are wrong" (p. 375). He recognizes the challenge that we face to free victims of the constraining and damaging false stereotypes that are placed on them by others in society.

Racism, the Media, and the English Language

Literature has shown that language often reflects and maintains society's beliefs, stereotypes, attitudes, and prejudices. In some instances, the prejudice is blatantly signaled, as in the words "nigger," "chink," and "spic." At other times, racial slurs are more indirect or hidden. Moore (1995) discusses how in the movies and in children's books one finds the use of "white" to symbolize what is positive and "black" as negative. The good guys tend to wear white and the bad guys are dressed in black, for example. He also points out that prejudice is evident in the words used to describe historical events. The fact that Columbus "discovered" America underscores the lack of acknowledgment that the Native Americans had "discovered" it before he. Also, the terms "victory," "massacre," and "conquest" are frequently used to describe what the self-proclaimed heroes (the white men) achieved in overcoming the enemy (the Native Americans). Moore explains how this usage represents a Eurocentric (white European) perspective, using loaded words to tell the story from one's biased point of view. This was demonstrated again during the Iraqi conflict when U.S., British, and Australian troops entered Iraq in order to overthrow the Saddam regime. For example, on CNN, one of America's most popular news channels, one would hear reporters refer to the allies as the "coalition troops," whereas these same troops were referred to as "the invaders" on the Arab channels. Here each side revealed a different political slant.

Racism and Fear

Our list of what contributes to racism would not be complete without the role fear has played in perpetuating racism in the United States. Have you ever found yourself avoiding an elevator because a black person walked in just before you? Have you ever clutched your purse tighter when a Hispanic walked by? Or have you ever suspiciously eyed people just because of

their ethnicity? Fear is at the root of all these behaviors, and is spawned by the tales of danger and violence that we are constantly being fed in the news. Kivel (1995) believes this fear is what was used back in the days of slavery to justify the whites' brutal treatment of the slaves. By maintaining an "illusion of danger," the white slave owners "were able to justify the harshness of their treatment, and to scare other white people into supporting their subjugation" (p. 55). He also suggests that society needs "to recognize just how deeply we have been trained to fear and distrust people of color and how much that fear guides our behavior, because that fear is easily manipulated by politicians, the media or corporate leaders" (p. 58).

Is it any wonder, then, that African American and Latino males are often suspected of crimes and murders? Society "expects" them to be dangerous and is quick to suspect them of untold crimes, often on the basis of racial profiling. This has led to many unfair sentencings and other injustices within our judicial system. For example, when Susan Smith reported her two young boys missing, she said they had been kidnapped by an African American, and she almost got away with it. It was not until enough evidence was gathered that her lies were revealed and the horrible truth shown that she, herself, had drowned them by driving her car into a river! How telling that she chose to scapegoat an imaginary African American male!

Shaheen (1995) suggests that the current "bogeyman" on American television is the Arab. Until we received images of young Palestinian children being hurt by the horrors of war, little humanity was afforded the Arabs, who were portrayed as either billionaires or bombers, but rarely as victims. And when the federal building in Oklahoma City was destroyed, many believed the bomber was from an Arab terrorist group. Many were shocked to learn that the culprit was an all-American white man.

Most likely each of these perspectives has contributed to the type of prejudice experienced in the United States at this time. But whatever the reason, it appears to be built "*basically [on a] false premise— that all whites are superior to all nonwhites*" (Daniels & Kitano, 1970, p. 11). Before we address what can be done about prejudice, let us first look at how it has affected the various racial populations here in the United States.

Prejudice and Minority Groups: An Overview

ISSUES: What types of prejudice have different minority groups experienced? Why do you think different minority groups have experienced different (or the same) types of prejudice? Should slavery reparations be made generations later? Should Native Americans receive better reparations than they have been given so far? What impact will Latino Americans have by becoming the largest ethnic group in America? What effect will people of mixed heritage have on racial issues?

Native Americans

The first ethnic people to experience prejudice and maltreatment by the early American colonialists were the native Indians. Although they had migrated from Asia years earlier, the "claim that 'Columbus discovered America' [was] symptomatic of an enduring colonialist mentality that" denied their very existence (Steinberg, 2001, p. 13). At first, the new settlers felt compelled to negotiate and purchase land from the natives, but it soon became the practice to just take the land they wanted. With time, the colonialists rationalized that the Native Americans were not as "human" as they, but rather savage and beast-like, entitling them no rights to the land upon which they lived. Miller (1974), in his book *This New Man, The American,* reported that the colonialists held that "savages have no particular propertie in any part or parcell of that country, but only a generall residencie there, as wild beasts have in the forests" (p. 171). Gradually, over many years, the natives were killed or chased off the land they once owned since the whites' weapons were superior. They won few wars and lost many, and with each loss treaties were written up exchanging more land for promises that their rights to the remaining land would remain unchallenged (Steinberg, 2001). But the promises were soon broken, as whites desired more and more land in the great expanding west after the Revolutionary War. By the 1800s, entire tribes of Indians were forced to live on reservations, often situated in unpopulated places that lacked the natural resources that would have provided farming or grazing land. "The plight of the Indian west of the Mississippi River was only a sad, monotonous duplication of what had happened east of it—warfare, broken treaties, expropriation of land, rebellion, and ultimately defeat. No sooner were the eastern Indians dropped down on the plains than the United States discovered the natural resources of the West. Miners and settlers were on the move, emigrant trains rumbled across the plains, and once again the aim of the frontiersman was to get the Indian out of the way" (Farb, 1978, p. 242).

Guns were not the only weapons used to get rid of the native Indians. Churchill (1994) recounts the genocidal methods used to exterminate them, reporting that "in 1763 Lord Jeffrey Amherst ordered a subordinate to distribute items taken from a smallpox infirmary as 'gifts' during a peace parley with Pontiac's Confederacy....Upwards of 100,000 Indians died of smallpox in the ensuing epidemic" (pp. 31–34). Although we have often heard that many Native Americans died from diseases, few of us ever imagined that these diseases were introduced intentionally and systematically! By the 1900s, due to genocide, disease, and economic hardship, the Native American population fell from approximately fifteen million indigenous people at the time of Columbus to around two million (Jaimes, 1992).

Land continued to be taken from the Native American people "well into the twentieth century," a practice that continues to be at the heart of many tensions between whites and the Indian population (Steinberg, 2001, p. 20). Even the barren lands of the reservations, where the Indian people were finally "corralled" to live, have been sought after by large companies hoping to gain access to newly discovered great mineral wealth, which includes coal, uranium, and oil. And for those who continue to live on the reservations, life is grim and marked by high rates of poverty. Along with this low socio-economic status are found high levels of suicide, homicide, depression, school failure, family violence, diabetes, infant mortality, and tuberculosis (Bachman, 1992).

Within the past decade, things have begun to look brighter for the American Indians. Thanks to their ability to form cohesive communities, which keep alive their traditions and customs and instill greater ethnic pride, they have also been able to achieve better political and legal representation. As of late, they have won important judgments which have, for example, returned 300,000 acres of prime land in Maine, the right to fish in the Great Lakes, and the legal rights to open gambling casinos on reservations (Hess, Markson, & Stein, 1995). The casinos have brought huge profits to formerly poverty-stricken tribes, while providing thousands of new jobs for the native Indians (Johnson, 1993).

African Americans

The plight of the African American has been studied more and documented better than that of any other minority group in the United States. Many would agree that they have sustained, perhaps, the most prejudice and discrimination of all. Their arrival as slaves, the inhumane treatment they received on the plantations, the lack for many years of freedom to become landowners or work for their own financial gain, and the various other struggles they have always faced, at all levels, have placed them at a brutal disadvantage. Steinberg (2001) tells how fearful the North was, even after the Civil War, that the Negroes would invade their part of the land. "These fears were especially pronounced among ordinary laborers, many of them immigrants, who found themselves in competition for jobs with the small black population living in northern cities. This was particularly true of Irish immigrants, who rapidly became as racist as any segment of northern society simply because they competed with blacks for jobs at or near the bottom of the occupational ladder" (p. 177).

Steinberg goes on to explain that the immigrants of those days were not the only ones to fear the "Negro invasion" in the North. Even the then Democratic Party of Pennsylvania denounced their rivals, the Republicans, as "…the party of…crime…that seeks to turn the slaves of the Southern states loose to overrun the North and enter into competition with the white laboring masses, thus degrading and insulting their manhood by placing them on an equality with Negroes in their occupations is insulting to our race, and merits our most emphatic and unqualified condemnation" (p. 179).

Although the Civil War freed the slaves, the years that followed showed slow and painful progress for blacks, producing only modest gains. Even after World War II, prejudice and discrimination were, unfortunately, still alive in the United States. Dudziak (2000), in her book *Cold War Civil Rights,* reminds us of the differential treatment African Americans continued to experience, even for those who served their country during World War II. While in the armed services, the Negro soldiers were segregated from their white counterparts in many ways. They often slept in different barracks and ate at different times than the white soldiers. Even their call to duty varied. The African American soldiers were often asked to work in service areas, while the white soldiers were asked to engage in the more sought-after combat jobs. Many blacks served and fought in the battlefields of Europe, risking their lives for the freedom of many. Yet, as Dudziak (2000) points out, once they returned home they had to deal with the same racism and prejudice directed at them before the war. It was as if society, particularly in the South, did not want to let them forget their "racial inferiority." During this time, many Negro veterans suffered injustices including horrific lynchings that were highly organized and geared at "putting them in their place."

Many changes would occur after World War II. For one, the world seemed to become a smaller place. Many realized how much foreign countries affected each other, and an obligation to look out for one another seemed to develop. With this new sense of responsibility, the rest of the world believed that the United States had to do something about racial unrest and Americans became more aware and concerned as to how other nations saw them. Gunnar Myrdal (1944), a Swedish sociologist, identified this contradiction between racism and the ideology of democracy as the "American dilemma." Although most Americans would say that they believed in the creed that "all men were created equal," with equal rights to freedom and fair opportunity, many outside of the U.S. pointed out that this did not exist in real life. The social injustices recognized by the rest of the world were appalling to many. Pearl Buck reported that many old enemies of the U.S. were actually happy to see these ugly cracks appear so publicly in what they felt was an artificial image of the "wonderful, democratic" United States. She noted: "Every lynching, every race riot, gives joy to Japan. The discriminations of the American army and navy and the air forces against colored soldiers and sailors, (…) are of the greatest aid today to our enemy in Asia, Japan. 'Look at America,' Japan is saying to millions of listening ears. 'Will white Americans give you equality?'" (Buck, 1942, p. 29).

We are told that even the Soviet Union rushed to expose the injustices of the United States. Dudziak (2000) found an article in a Soviet newspaper entitled "The Tragedy of Coloured America," which reported: "It [the U.S.] is a country within a country. Coloured America is not allowed to mix with other white America, it exists within it like the yolk in the white of an egg. Or, to be exact, like a gigantic ghetto. The walls of this ghetto are invisible but they are nonetheless indestructible. They are placed within cities where the Negroes live in special quarters, in buses where the Negroes are assigned only the back seats, in hairdressers where they have special chairs" (p. 93).

These observations were shocking to the world, and embarrassing to the U.S. government. Myrdal (1944) identified the challenge laid before this nation in *An American Dilemma: The Negro Problem and Modern Democracy:* "In this War the principle of democracy had to be applied more explicitly to race. Facism and nazism are based on a racial superiority dogma…and they came to power by means of racial persecution and oppression. In fighting fascism and nazism, America had to stand before the whole world in favor of racial tolerance and cooperation and of racial equality" (p. 1,004).

The United Nations also proved to be invaluable in putting pressure on the U.S. to work on these incongruities. In 1947, the National Association for the Advancement of Colored People (NAACP) drafted a letter and sent it to the United Nations Commission on Human Rights. It explicitly discussed the bad treatment of the African American in the United States and claimed that racism harmed the nation as a whole. E. B. DuBois, the main contributor to this letter, stated

in *An Appeal to the World* that "It is not Russia that threatens the United States as much as Mississippi; (…) Internal injustice done to one's brothers is far more dangerous than the aggression of strangers from abroad" (p. 380).

Although the United Nations ultimately decided not to act directly on the petition, it did arouse a lot of interest in the international world as to what was actually happening in the U.S. with regards to its treatment of the African American. The world's attention, however, was enough to make U.S. officials sufficiently uncomfortable to push the racial issue to the political forefront. Soon, two court decisions were made: one was to desegregate the military, and the second was to desegregate schools (with *Brown v. Board of Education)*, both in the early 1950s.

As the African Americans and their supporters gained attention, civil rights reform was called for by many in the 1950s and 1960s, and civil unrest extended throughout the country. The number of demonstrations grew. In 1963, President Kennedy responded by calling for landmark civil rights legislation: "Today we are committed to a worldwide struggle to promote and protect the rights of all who wish to be free. And when Americans are sent to Viet-Nam or West Berlin, we do not ask for whites only. It ought to be possible, therefore, for American students of any color to attend any public institution they select without having to be backed up by troops (…) We preach freedom around the world, and we mean it, and we cherish our freedom here at home, but are we to say to the world, and much more importantly, to each other that this is a land of the free except for the Negroes; that we have no second-class citizens except Negroes; that we have no class or cast [sic] system, no ghettoes, no master race except with respect to Negroes?" (1964, p. 469).

The signing of the Civil Rights Act in 1964 was the next great step towards fighting discrimination in the United States. Although it was a bill whose development came about because of the plight of the African American, it has proven to be important for other ethnic groups as well. The bill not only prohibited racial discrimination in the employment of individuals and in the availability of public accommodations, but it also denied federal funds to government agencies that permitted discrimination. The rest of the world applauded its passage, which was seen as true evidence that the United States was progressing towards needed social change. The next big step was taken with the Voting Rights Act of 1965, and the Civil Rights Act of 1968, which prohibited housing discrimination of any sort.

Although these documents were written in the hope of reducing racism, much work was still left to be done. The unrest and anger spawned by the discrepancy between the laws of the land and the racial inequality that remained led to riots in the 1960s in Los Angeles and Detroit, as well as to the assassination of key national leaders—Malcolm X in 1965, and Martin Luther King, Jr., and Robert F. Kennedy in 1968. Similar anger led to further riots in L.A. when police beat Rodney King in 1992. The infamous O. J. Simpson trials revealed a racial divide. In 1999 came outcries against the perceived racially instigated shooting by the New York City police of Guinean immigrant, Amadou Diallo, as he stood unarmed in the doorway of his home.

In comparison with the experience of other urban minorities, the isolation of blacks was more intense and took place over a longer period of time. Kivel (1995) points out: "We have not yet fully acknowledged as a society the extent of the devastation that white people perpetrated on West African civilization and on African Americans in this country during the period of slavery. We don't talk about the horrors of the Middle Passage, the systematic attempt to eradicate African culture, and the everyday participation of common white folks in supporting slavery. (…) We don't talk about the benefits of slavery to white people. Most of our families did not own slaves. Most of our families did participate in and benefit from slavery, even if our foreparents arrived here after slavery ended. Immigrants benefitted from the presence of a group of people that had less respect and status than they did…" (p. 122).

Although they comprise about 12% of the population, African Americans remain disadvantaged along many dimensions of social stratification (Hess, Markson, & Stein, 1995). They continue to witness that business owners prefer to hire white immigrant workers, who may not even speak English proficiently, rather than black people. Although most of the best athletes in basketball are black, very few ever reach manager status. Blacks also continue to experience injustices in getting home loans and in the area of education, and are discriminated against in stores and restaurants (Feagin, 1991; Massey & Denton, 1993; Neckerman & Kirschenman, 1991).

One of the latest strategies being pushed forward by various African American leaders is what is known as **slavery reparations**. This movement calls for the U.S. government to repay African Americans for the pain and indignity of slavery as a way to compensate for the historic wrongs allegedly committed by the government and private corporations (Tracinski, 2001). Many African American citizens feel that they are still experiencing the lingering effects of their ancestors being treated as laboring animals. They also argue that other groups have been paid for their unjust treatment (the Jews and the Japanese Americans during WWII) and, thus, so should they be. Those in favor argue that such reparations would help repair the racial tensions between blacks and the U.S. government, encourage forgiveness, and promote healing. They feel this would show that the U.S. government was finally apologetic for having enslaved their ancestors, and thus paid the consequences.

However, many are against reparations. First, they argue, the government would enter into economic hardship if it had to make such payments. Second, even though reparations were paid to Jews and Japanese Americans, all payments were made to living victims, not to their descendants. And as Thernstrom (2000) pointed out, slavery disappeared from our country in 1865, roughly six generations ago. No American alive today ever had to live in involuntary servitude in the United States. Third, it is argued that paying one racial group would create resentment among other racial groups, who might seek reparations as well (Woodley & Horn, n.d.). And fourth, how would one pay all the African Americans whose ancestors were both white and black? Would a person who is 1/8th African American receive 1/8th of the total reparations? Who would be able to make such decisions and who would determine what was fair or not fair? And, as Williams (2001) asked, "Are the millions of Europeans, Asian and Latin Americans who immigrated to the U.S. in the 20th century responsible for slavery, and should they be forced to cough up reparations money?" What about descendants of Northern whites who fought and died in the name of freeing slaves? Should they cough up reparations money for black Americans? What about non-slave-owning Southern whites, who are a majority of Southern whites—should they be made to pay reparations?" (pp. 1–2). What do you think?

Latino Americans

The Latino Americans are now considered the largest ethnic group represented in the United States. This population is made up of a variety of subgroups, and perhaps one of the most racially diverse groups of all. Their roots can be traced back to the explorers who came from Spain and Portugal and who then intermarried and intermixed with the native people in North and South America, Central America, and even the Philippines. These native groups included the Arawak, Mayas, Aztecs, Incas, and the African Americans who were brought involuntarily to the Caribbean. Novas (1994) reminds us that the racial diversity of the Latino people is old and connected to war and political movements over many decades.

Due to differences in the Latinos' histories, countries of origin, and circumstances of emigration to the United States, each subgroup differs greatly from the others. Members of different groups tend to prefer different foods, but all are proud of their heritage, and it is a high priority to share it with their offspring. The children who are educated in the United States tend to assimilate into American culture more easily than their parents (Hess, Markson, & Stein, 1995, p. 185). In general, greater prejudice and discrimination are directed towards Latinos who not only have darker skin but also have more common and recognizably Spanish-sounding names.

Within the last decade, Latino Americans have enjoyed a surge of growth and popularity within the entertainment world. Latino American entertainers, such as Gloria Estefan and Jennifer Lopez, are known and beloved by many. And, interestingly enough, T.V. cable programs in Spanish, such as Telemundo, are now enjoying better ratings than the major English-speaking broadcasting companies, including ABC, NBC, and CBS.

The largest Latino subgroup consists of Mexican Americans, also known as Chicanos (male) and Chicanas (female). They are predominately Catholic, and many continue to speak Spanish within their families and communities. It has been found that the experience of Chicanos/as in the United States depends greatly on how dark their skin is and/or whether they have Native American features or not. Those who look European American seem to experience the least prejudice and discrimination. Although the stereotype of the Mexican is of a farm worker or illegal alien, about 90% live in cities and the majority are legal residents of the United States.

The Puerto Ricans make up the second largest subgroup of Latinos. Since Puerto Rico is a U.S. territory, they have been American citizens since 1917. Puerto Ricans are characterized by a mixture of Spanish, Indian, and African ancestry. They continue to experience racial and ethnic barriers to high school and college graduation, and have low representation in the arts, and little political influence or community control. The high school dropout rates remain too high, and statistics show that many remain unemployed. Almost half of the families are headed by a single parent (Hess, Markson, & Stein, 1995).

The third largest group consists of Cuban Americans. For various reasons, they have enjoyed better assimilation into the American culture than the other subgroups. First, being of European Spanish descent, they tend to have features that are white European in nature. Second, many arrived with the support of the United States government, and they tend to be relatively conservative in their politics, supporting an end to the Castro regime. And third, the majority of Cuban Americans arrived in the United States better educated and wealthier, thus giving them more resources for success from the start (Hess, Markson, & Stein, 1995).

Asian Americans

The variety of Asian Americans is as great as their many distinct cultures and different languages. This group is comprised of at least a dozen different subgroups: Chinese, Japanese, Filipino, Korean, Asian Indian, Southeast Asian, Vietnamese, Hawaiian, Malaysian, and other Asian Pacific Islanders. Although they make up less than 3% of the population, they are the fastest growing minority group in the United States (Lee, 1991). "While the Japanese-American group remained relatively stable in the 1980s, the Indochinese more than tripled" (Lee, 1991, p. 39). According to Hess et al. (1995), in general Asian Americans are considered to be the "model minority group." On the whole, they fulfill the American Dream by obtaining a good education and achieving great financial security. They are seen as good students in academics and music, and can be found among the most accomplished professionals in all walks of life, from physicians to computer scien-

Many Voices: An Introduction to Social Issues

tists. Lee (1991) points out, however, that although the achievements of the Asian American population seem impressive, the economic and social reality is far more complex. She states: "Focusing on averages and success stories misses an equally striking case of Asian 'over-representation': at the bottom of the barrel. Although Asian Americans are three to five times as likely as whites to be engineers and doctors, they are also two to four times as likely to work in food services or textiles. Many of the poorest Asian Americans are undocumented or paid under the table at sweatshops or restaurants: their incomes are likely to be under-represented by official figures" (p. 40).

Lee also suggests that the stereotype of being the "successful minority" actually hurts any Asian American group that is disadvantaged. Not only are they overlooked and denied benefits other struggling minority groups enjoy, but the image of being the "super-minority" creates unreasonable expectations and interracial tensions. It is important to recognize that each subgroup has a different past to contend with, which has created variation in how the different groups live and eventually assimilate into the greater population here in the United States.

Hess and colleagues (1995) recount that the Chinese first arrived by force in the mid-nineteenth century, charged with helping build the transcontinental railroad. Their beginnings in this new land were tough. They were not allowed to bring their families from China, become citizens, or marry American citizens, making naturalization impossible for many years to come. In the early days, Chinese communities were all male, and often were filled with gambling, drug use, and prostitution. By 1965, when the restrictive immigration laws were revised, many were able to become citizens, bring their families to the U.S., and manage their own establishments. Their large numbers formed Chinatowns in many big cities, which in turn created tourist interest and financial gain for this population. They opened restaurants, specialty stores, and laundries that helped establish financially stable communities. All this, together with their strong belief in learning, has led many young Chinese Americans to do exceptionally well in the academic and professional worlds. Of course, as is common for all populations, some have had a harder time, and most new immigrants live in poverty and are often exploited, working long hard hours at low wages.

The history of Japanese immigration, according to Hess et al. (1995), began differently than for the Chinese because they were able to emigrate along with their wives, thus allowing their American-born children to become U.S. citizens by birthright. Many found their niche on the West Coast and became great farmers and gardeners. Hess and colleagues (1995) describe how in 1941 this population was stripped of their land, treated as untrustworthy, and rounded up in detention camps following the Japanese attack on Pearl Harbor. Their land was then soon taken over, without compensation, by their white neighbors, leaving the Japanese Americans without a means to make a living. The American Japanese were eventually freed from internment camps after the war, and were able to relocate and enter better paying white collar jobs. Finally, in 1988 Congress approved legislation leading to a formal apology to the Japanese Americans for their forced detention as well as a token tax-free payment of $20,000 to each of the surviving victims.

Many other Asian groups did not immigrate to the United States until further policy changes were made in the 1980s. This brought an influx of people from Southeast Asian countries, such as Cambodia, Thailand, Laos, and Vietnam, as well as Asians from Korea, the Philippine Islands, and India (Hess et al., 1995). While the Filipinos/as recently overtook the Chinese to become the largest single Asian group, the number of Asian Indians and Koreans has continued to grow steadily (Lee, 1991). Hess and colleagues point out that while the Southeast Asians and Koreans have come to the United States with little education, poor English proficiency, and minimal job skills, the Filipinos/as and the Asian Indians have come with better educational credentials and technical skills that allow them to assimilate more easily and move up into better jobs and higher levels of economic success much more readily.

Interestingly enough, the Asian Americans as a group have found their niche by buying small businesses. Compared to other minority groups, the Asian Americans have a high rate of business ownership. For every 1,000 Asians or Pacific Islanders, 54.8 own their own business, compared to 12.5 for blacks and 17 for Latinos per every 1,000 (Lee, 1991). Lee also points out that while opportunities are provided, "small businesses are difficult to run" and "particularly vulnerable to business cycles, with higher than average failure rates" (p. 43).

People of Mixed Heritage

As the United States becomes a nation of people of mixed heritage, it is becoming common for people to answer, when asked about their origin, that they have backgrounds of three or four different nationalities. Being part this and part that, or 1/4 of this, 1/4 of that, and 1/2 of another, is common. Today, most people considered "white" are of mixed heritage, along with the majority of African Americans, and all Latinos/as and Filipinos. Kivel (1995) says that the challenge is great for millions of people of mixed heritage in our society since racial identity continues to be a crucial determinant of one's opportunities in life. It used to be that one drop of African American blood was enough to put someone in the category of being African American. Now, because of ever changing definitions of who is white and who is not, it is becoming harder to distinguish neat categories for everyone.

Even for those who profess not to be racist, the thought of their white offspring marrying people of color may bring about shudders and protests. Not keeping one's racial heritage "pure" seems to be the major objection to interracial marriages. Likewise, the fear of interracial relationships and their effect on the offspring has often been used to justify persecution and discrimination against interracial couples. Interestingly enough, though, it has never been proven that the majority of biracial children end up being gravely affected for not belonging to any particular racial group, that they suffer from poor self-esteem, or that they find life extra hard (Root, 1992).

Some may believe that mixing the races will eventually lead to the elimination of racism as racial differences become harder to distinguish. Kivel (1995) warns us, however, that unless white power and privilege are done away with, people with lighter skin color, regardless of racial heritage, will be more highly valued than those with darker skin.

Being White in the United States

ISSUES: What is it like being white in America? (Respond to this question from both sides, assuming you are white and assuming you are not.) Do whites have as much freedom to respond to racial issues as other groups? Why or why not? How should whites respond to racial issues? What changes do you see happening in the future as the United States becomes less white?

In many of the books that address the multicultural dynamics in the United States, either historically or in the present, a section often left out is one that discusses what it is like to be a white person in the United States. Although there has never been a genetic or biological basis for the concept of whiteness, Kivel (1992) notes: "In more recent historical times in western Europe those with English heritage were perceived to be pure white. The Irish, Russians and Spanish were considered darker races, sometimes black, and certainly non-white. The white category was slowly extended to include northern and middle European people but still even fifty years ago definitely excluded eastern or southern European peoples, such as Italians, Poles, Russians and Greeks. In the last few decades, although there is still

prejudice against people from these geographical backgrounds, they have become generally accepted as white in the United States" (p. 17).

What is it like to be white and what are some of their feelings about how whites are perceived by minority groups?

One reaction white people have been known to have with regard to the issue of race is perplexity. "Why are they so angry at me? I've never done anything to them!" Although such reactions are seen by members of minority groups as incredibly naive, it is important to recognize that white people and people of color do not experience the world in the same way. To be white in the United States, where the commercials showing what is All-American feature white actors, is to feel rather comfortable with one's race. Although many white families struggle in other ways, race is just not an issue. As the story at the beginning of this chapter showed, to be white is to be welcomed almost anywhere. This is a part of life for whites, and not often reflected upon as something only they are privileged to experience.

Professors have noted a "Here we go again!" on the part of white students in class when minority students address the prejudicial treatment they and their families sustain in everyday life. "Why can't they just get on with their lives?" some ask. "Why do they continually bring it up?" "I never had a part in them coming as slaves. I didn't have anything to do with what happened back then!" or "Maybe if they would stop whining and blaming the whites for where they are today, they'd succeed in life!" "I have to work hard at everything I accomplish, so why can't they?" "If the Chinese can succeed, why can't the blacks?" After watching the devastating fall of the World Trade Center, one psychology student candidly admitted, "You know, as a psychologist I'm supposed to be understanding of different cultures. But right now I'm so angry at those terrorists I'm not sure I want to know more about them....I just want to hate them." The array of emotions behind each of these comments is varied, personal, and intense, often spurred by personal experiences.

Another common reaction for many white people is to feel that they are not able to participate fully in conversations about race without being labeled racist. In their talk, in society, at school and work, the white population feels that they must always show openness and acceptance to all ethnic groups and must never say anything negative about them. Some also feel that behavior which would be interpreted as racist if undertaken by whites is often deemed acceptable if performed by an ethnic minority member. For example, in institutions that seem to uphold racial and cultural separation by mere tradition or history—like colleges or universities, residence halls, and student unions—the special recognition given to black students at graduation, and the organization of African-American clubs, are seen as progressive. Minority leaders who openly express anti-white hatred and extreme bigotry are applauded and supported. Some consider this to be "reverse racism."

Joe Matthews (n.d.), a white male student at Harvard, interviewed a dozen white students in order to "get a handle on a group of students who are becoming more aware of their unique place in the multicultural universe"

(p. 2). He found that the complaints of these Harvard students sounded strikingly similar to the grievances raised by the minority students on campus. One student felt that being made to feel uncomfortable as a white male by minority groups may actually be of help. He stated: "The fact that more white males are aware of their white maleness could turn out to be good. (...) They talk about an understanding gap between how whites and blacks see the world. But maybe by facing racial stuff ourselves, by being 'dissed' and made uncomfortable, we're learning to feel what it's like for minorities. And maybe that process will give us common understanding" (p. 3).

Another white male student shared a situation that he experienced at a school cafeteria. He had gone there alone and sat down to eat at the end of a table at which a group of six black students were already sitting. When he sat down, the black students stared at him with a look implying that he did not belong there. Feeling uncomfortable, he decided to pick up his tray and find another seat. As he rose to leave, he heard one of the black students say, "Bye, whitey," while the rest of them giggled and laughed. He felt he had been singled out because of his color. "You'd think people who are subject to racism themselves would be more sensitive" (p. 3), he said.

The majority of the students interviewed felt they had no place to air their complaints without being branded racist or troublemakers. "Minorities are taught to speak up, and it's just assumed that they're always right because they're experts or something," said one student. "I could be a smart guy, but since I'm white I supposedly don't understand the first thing about people or race relations," he added (pp. 4–5). When questioned further, he said that he thought the attitude on campus about race was good because it kept ignorant people from saying "stupid things." "They have to stop and think. But there also needs to be a climate where individuals, students, can have honest discussions about how they feel about race. And we don't have such a climate" (p. 4).

We must spend more time talking about what it means to be white in the United States, instead of *only* focusing on what it means to be a minority in a white-dominated culture. Perhaps by allowing all races to discuss openly how skin color can affect one's daily life on the streets, in the stores, in the classroom, and at work, a deeper understanding of who we are and how we experience this world will be reached. Greater understanding often leads to more empathy, better insight, and tolerance.

The Effects of Prejudice, Racism, and Discrimination

ISSUES: How does racism take a toll on our society? Are we trained to scapegoat various minorities or groups? If so, how and why? Do you think it is possible to honestly discuss racial issues? Why or why not?

To members of a minority group, prejudice, racism, and discrimination lead to low self-esteem, depression, anxiety, and physical illness. It limits their access to necessary and desired resources, and impinges on their freedoms and rights. Kivel (1995) highlighted five ways in which racism takes its toll on our society. First, he suggested, it forces one to give up traditional languages, foods, music, and rituals in order to assimilate into the mainstream of American society. Such variety actually would bring cultural richness to our country. Second, racism hurts us because, in an attempt not to tell the ugly truth about how the past is tinted with racist thought and action, half-truths and lies are told, distorting what is real and hiding damaging belief systems. Third, racism affects our interpersonal relationships. Friendships become strained, families have feuds, and co-workers struggle with disagreements due to tensions produced by racism. We have seen riots, unjust killings and sentencings, and the lifelong stinging effects of crime, violence, and poverty because of racism. Fourth, racism has distorted our sense of danger and safety. Not only have we as a society avoided addressing our own issues honestly, but we have been trained to scapegoat minorities for the troubles society faces as a whole. This has led only to further alienation and destruction. And fifth, because we as a country are unable to practice what we preach, that is, uphold and carry out the ideals of our democratic creed in real life, cynicism and pessimism have developed, leading us all to witness further apathy, blame, despair, self-destructive behavior, and acts of violence.

The Initiative on Race: How to Fight Racism in the 21st Century

ISSUES: What methods should be employed to reduce racism? What strengths and weaknesses do you perceive in the methods you suggested? Why would/should the majority group give up its political power? Is affirmative action still needed or viable? Should free market (unqualified individualism) or some type of racial preferences determine rights and privileges? Why?

In 1997, under the administration of President Clinton, an advisory board convened to identify specific ways to help reduce racial tensions in the United States. The initiative was called "One America in the 21st Century: Forging a New Future." The seven-member panel was tasked with examining race, racism, and the potential for racial reconciliation in America by using a process of study, constructive dialogue, and action.

Board members spent 15 months traveling from coast to coast, talking to thousands of Americans of different ethnic origins about how race and racism had impacted their lives. Their report to President Clinton was finally completed in September, 1998, and can be found at the following web address: http://clinton4.nara.gov/media/pdf/PIR.pdf.

The report stated that since the population in the United States will consist of approximately 58% white, 25% Hispanic, 14% black, 8% Asian Pacific American, and 1% American Indian and Alaska Native by the year 2050, the thousands of interviews held contributing to this report reflected the diversity and major concerns of the American people. The board identified several major areas to be addressed in order to achieve "One America in the 21st Century." These areas included continued commitment to the study and causes of racial reconciliation; support for multicultural education; development of programs for the youth of America; a need to support affirmative action; development of diversity training in the workplace; exposure of police misconduct towards minorities and work to eliminate it; and confrontation of conflicts between different minority groups, not only between whites and the various minority groups.

Let us now explore in greater depth how American society and the government have dealt with some of these areas, such as education, affirmative action, political support, and diversity training.

Multicultural Education

Multicultural education focuses on the need to reflect the country's diversity in all areas of the school curriculum. It is used to dispel stereotypes and identify prejudicial practices that attack and weaken the images and rights of minorities. For years, schools taught history from a biased, white, protestant, European perspective, for example. Honest accounts of what happened in the past are valuable since greater understanding can be achieved by knowing how our present day is shaped by what happened years ago.

The President's advisory board suggested several areas in which multicultural education could be enhanced. First, it could be improved by providing ethnic celebrations and discussions on the diversity of our nation, as well as by paying tribute to Americans who come from different racial and ethnic backgrounds. By

actually engaging in the traditions of other people, we all learn to appreciate everyone's heritage better. Second, schools are encouraged to develop programs in ethnic studies, hold multicultural events, and support study-abroad programs. More dialogue between ethnic groups needs to occur in the classroom and communities about such topics as ethnicity, racism, prejudice, and discrimination.

Third, the board suggested that the public be educated as to how certain stereotypes are erroneously perpetuated on the big and little screens. Their study found that many of our attitudes, beliefs, and opinions about race are significantly shaped by what we read and by what we watch at the movies and on television. For example, when looking at portrayals on the evening news, it became evident that local newscasts tended to treat black suspects and victims of crime more pejoratively than whites in the same categories. They suggested that this practice could cultivate an exaggerated sense of conflict between blacks and whites in the political arena.

Related to this, it would help to seek more ethnic diversity in all media. For example, the President's advisory board found in their research that all three non-white populations were sorely underrepresented as experts on local news broadcasts on television, while at the same time a significant overrepresentation was noted among white professionals.

Affirmative Action

Affirmative action has been defined as "any action taken to ensure, or affirm, equal opportunity for oppressed or previously disadvantaged groups" (Hooks, 1991, p. 128). Because this policy has affected decisions regarding who may enter certain colleges and obtain certain jobs, the debate on the fairness of such an action has continued for years. In their report, the President's advisory board found that while Americans of all races felt that equal opportunity for all citizens was an important concept to uphold for the good of our nation, they also found that no other issue divided the American population as much as affirmative action. Walkins (1995), on the pro side, suggested that affirmative action was the result of an honest look at how things work in America. He said: "As amply documented in the 1968 Kerner Commission report on racial disorders, when left to their own devices, American institutions in such areas as college admissions, hiring decisions and loan approvals had been making choices that discriminated against blacks. That discrimination, which flowed from doing what came naturally, hurt more than blacks: It hurt the entire nation, as the riots of the late 1960s demonstrated. Though the Kerner report focused on blacks, similar findings could have been made about other minorities and women" (p. 1).

On the other hand, Canaday (2001) believes that affirmative action actually hinders civil rights, causing us to continue treating individuals differently on the basis of race. He argues that it is just another form of discrimination (in that it promotes preferences and denies opportunity to individuals because they are members of the "nonpreferrred group" (p. 121), and it actually leads both whites and nonwhites to doubt the abilities and competencies of the minorities. He also points out that not only does this hurt us as a nation, but we are fooling ourselves: "Racial preferences are frequently justified as a measure to help low-income blacks. But the evidence is compelling that the beneficiaries of preferential policies are overwhelmingly middle-class or wealthy. For the most part, the truly disadvantaged have been unable to participate in the programs that grant preferences" (p. 121).

Du Pont (n.d.) observed that supporters of affirmative action tended to fall on two distinct sides of this issue, depending on their political position: "Today's Conservatives believe the colorblind principle of merit is the fairest way to treat individuals. Today's Liberals take the view that merit is unfair to minorities, who must be given an advantage in the present to make up for the discrimination they suffered in the past. This view has the support of many of America's institutions—governments, corporations and philanthropic organizations—since it gives them a politically correct way to atone for the unfairness of yesterday" (p. 2).

The advisory board, after polling the Americans interviewed, found that the majority of this country's citizens were in favor of affirmative action and felt that it was a good way to equal the playing field. The board felt that the nation should not only support this policy, but also do what it could to improve public discourse on the subject and help the public understand the value of affirmative action as a tool for achieving racial equality.

Political Support

The President's advisory board for "One America in the 21st Century" also recognized the need to rally the support of leaders in the community, whether corporate, religious, or governmental, in order to make racial reconciliation a reality. It is necessary to provide mentors for the younger generation and focus on ways to develop youth leadership, to increase the numbers of those experiencing academic success, and to find ways to prevent violence. Board members believed that no one group would be able to succeed without the support, either moral or financial, of all the entities—all striving for the same goal. A call to increase minority representation in the government and seek minority leadership in the community was also made.

Diversity Training in the Workplace

The President's advisory board also suggested diversity training in order to reduce prejudice and discrimination in the workplace and in police/community relationships. Diversity training involves educating workers and managers on the differences among diverse ethnic groups in order to increase understanding among all peoples. It is hoped that such training would eliminate the tensions that negatively affect relationships between workers, workers and managers, and/or police and the community.

The board also identified two actions as necessary for reducing racial tensions: 1) help the Equal Employment Opportunity Commission promptly resolve disputes in the workplace; and 2) support better training and more drastic disciplinary action for police officers who continuously violate the civil rights of others. This second issue was a particular concern of all those interviewed, in all states, coast to coast.

Education Issues

Several issues pertaining to education of the different ethnic groups were identified during the advisory board's investigation. The first issue was the controversy of whether to offer bilingual education, especially for the Hispanic population. Today the Hispanics rival blacks as the nation's largest minority group (Cobb & Kimberly, 2002). Ascher (1993) pointed out that many of the changes needed in the schools of today are due to changes in school diversity. She states: "Since 1980, eight million immigrants have arrived in the

U.S., bringing two million students into the nation's schools. These newcomers have changed American schools from biracial to multiracial, multicultural, and multilingual institutions. While the percentage of non-Hispanic whites has dropped significantly, both the percentage and ethnic diversity of nonwhite students have increased.…Recently, the great influx of immigrant children has brought into new focus the potential conflict between school desegregation and bilingual education, as children whose native language is not English have had to be placed either in language segregated environments or integrated into mainstream classes without the benefits of special language instruction" (pp. 1, 3).

Advocates point out that without bilingual education opportunities, Hispanic children find it hard to succeed in school. Since they do not understand the language of instruction, Hispanic students fall behind academically only days after the start of the school year (MacSwan, 2001). Garcia (1988) points out that many of the students arriving in this country have had limited schooling, and, thus, limited literacy ability in their own mother tongue. Because they do not have sufficient first-language skills, learning the second language is even harder for these students. Many have pointed to studies with large national samples that have found that children in bilingual programs do better than those taught exclusively in English.

However, some believe that the best thing society can do for these children is to place them in "English immersion classes." This is where the children are taught only in English from the very beginning (Geyer, 2001). They too point to studies that support the successes of such programs. The debate is still ongoing.

Another issue pertaining to education has to do with desegregation and integration. Many blacks and whites believed that if their children "went to school together and got to know each other as human beings, cooperation and brotherhood would follow" (Cose, 1997, p. 72). They also hoped that by placing children of various ethnic origins in the same school, an equitable educational opportunity would be available for all children. Sinclair and Tharp (1998) briefly review how the meaning of desegregation changed throughout the decades: "In the 50s, desegregation meant calling out federal troops to ensure that a few black students could enter white schools without injury. In

the 60s, desegregation meant giving civil rights organizations the authority to sue school districts for noncompliance with federal court orders to desegregate. In the 70s, desegregation meant busing—usually black students—to outlying districts. In the 80s, desegregation meant the incredible transformation of the South from the most absolutely segregated region of the country into the most integrated region of the country. In the 90s, desegregation…has come to mean the end of *de jure* desegregation and the beginning of *de facto* resegregation, as federal courts have renounced busing…" (p. 1).

In the 21st century, desegregation is no longer seen as the answer for equalizing the academic performance of minority and white students. "Vouchers, charter schools, even single-race or single-gender schools look like attractive alternatives for many black and Hispanic parents whose children on average perform below the level of whites" (Cobb, 2002b). Edwin Darden, an attorney with the National School Board Association, observed that people are now asking if the benefit of one minority child sitting next to a non-minority child is going to magically change the academic experience of the minority child. He believes the short answer is no (cited in Cobb, 2002b). Test scores continue to be lower for the minority students than for the white students in the same school. Interestingly enough, the latest trend appears to be towards segregation. Latest U.S. Census figures show that many well-off minority members are moving into new neighborhoods where they can be with others of their own race, maintain their ethnic identity with people of similar cultural experiences, and form a majority instead of remaining a minority (Serrie, 2001).

A third area of concern involved ensuring that minority children were receiving the education and aid needed to enhance their chances of succeeding in the career world, while not labeling them negatively by using unfair evaluations. Cobb (2002a) quoted Gary Bledsoe, president of the Texas conference of the NAACP, as saying, "You hear everyone talking about educating the kids. No one is talking about integration. That's not even on the radar screen anymore" (p. 1). A 1998 survey conducted by the Public Agenda Foundation showed that 80% of black parents and 88% of white parents believe raising academic standards and achievement are more important than integration (Cobb, 2002a).

Conclusion

As this chapter shows, we still have a lot to do as a nation when it comes to equal treatment and opportunity for all humankind. Finding ways to change prejudicial attitudes and beliefs must begin with the commitment to fight racism by parents, teachers, schools, churches, and communities. Making a conscious effort to get to know people of other races; to support institutions that promote racial inclusion (in the workplace, on T.V., in the movies, etc.); to participate in community efforts to reduce racial discrimination and increase the equal treatment of all people; to initiate constructive dialogue on race in the schools, churches, and communities; and to become advocates for improving race relationships are just some of the ways we can all confront the prejudice, racism, and discrimination that handicap us all.

Response

The Elimination of Racism

by Rudolph Bailey

This chapter on race and multicultural issues is a sympathetic treatise on the issue of race in America. I use the word "sympathetic" to note that there are many "scientific" and factual writings that are not helpful to race relations. Race is so ingrained in the American psyche that there is no way that this society can be "colorblind." In order for racism to be eliminated, a number of changes must be made. I was hoping for more of these suggestions than were given in the chapter. These suggestions need to be aimed at specific problems rather than simply reflecting a wish for a general attitude change. They might include funding the integration of housing and schools under a different formula. Actions must be taken that will directly address the problem, and Americans must agree to some type of social engineering in which one attempts to change or engineer a social problem via the use

of the legal system or the manipulation of culture. Of course, social engineering happens every day, but people are reluctant to plan and talk about it with regards to solving long-standing problems.

Individuals like Dr. Carbonell must continue writing sympathetically about racism and multicultural issues. Those who hold power in this country must be convinced that compensatory measures must be taken in order to change a long-standing system of racism, segregation, and discrimination. The United States Congress must write laws to make this country officially multicultural (as did Canada). Laws on discrimination must be strengthened to include severe penalties, compensations, and ease of prosecution. School funding by local property taxes must be replaced by a system that ensures that schools in poor neighborhoods get the best teachers, with adequate supplies

and good buildings. A system of affirmative action must be designed that provides opportunities for compensatory education (with high standards) and job training for oppressed minorities (as the U.S. military already does) (Moskos, 1986).

There is enough good discussion about whether racist motives should be compensated (Levin, 1987, and Brooks, 1987, are two good examples). Many of these discussions surround the issue of whether discrimination is against individuals or groups (Cahn, 2002). It is necessary to recognize that in America today when one African American is discriminated against, for example, many other African Americans feel that this is a discrimination against the "race." The legal and theoretical discussions that surround affirmative action policy at the University of Michigan many times miss the mark by starting with people's belief systems and actions. If people believe and act as though they are mistreated when one of their identified groups is discriminated against, then we must start at that point and address the buildup of consequences of that belief. In the meantime, we can change that belief system if all races become enraged by individual discrimination, no matter the race of the person being discriminated against. In other words, discrimination against any one person will not be tolerated by all peoples. Until society becomes "colorblind," colorblind policies cannot be implemented. Therefore, affirmative action, although not perfect, should be continued (see Ezorsky, 1991, for arguments in favor of this position). It is necessary to remember that affirmative action provides professionals to serve the underserved, the people who feel the greatest effects of racism (Cantor, Miles, Baker, & Barker, 1996). Affirmative action as an instrument of racial integration needs to be emphasized because it is more easily accepted than affirmative action as a means of redressing old harms (Anderson, 2002). Anderson also argues that it would be acceptable for states to use affirmative action to redress private sector discrimination.

Massey and Denton (1993) wrote a very persuasive book to show that residential segregation is the source of continuing black socioeconomic disadvantage. Although residential segregation is a multi-factored problem, it is perpetuated by real estate agents and landlords who in subtle ways ensure that the status remains unchanged. One must also acknowledge that much segregation is enhanced by the choices made by the segregated groups. In other words, people now feel more comfortable living in neighborhoods with people of the same race. Desegregation will take a consorted effort on all sides. Minorities will have to insist that real estate agents show them homes in white neighborhoods. Penalties can be put in place for real estate agents who fail to do so. Whites should stay in neighborhoods when minorities move in and should buy homes in black neighborhoods. These actions will do more to revitalize poor neighborhoods than any other actions. However, they will not happen because someone says they should. There must be some type of incentive. For example, the government can declare many of the old inner-city houses to be historic sites, and spend money revitalizing them and declaring the residents their trustees. Such action will create incentives for whites to move to those neighborhoods. It will solve a multitude of problems, such as falling property values, poor access to public services such as schools, and social and cultural isolation.

Kennedy (1997) wrote a comprehensive assessment of racial discrimination in law enforcement. The consequence is differential protection of racial groups from crime, racial profiling, differential arrest rate and prosecution, and differential application of the death penalty. Until watchdog groups are set up and law enforcement individuals are held accountable, such practices will continue. Watchdog groups will at least make individuals less inclined to carry on these practices. They can be given the power to bring suits against individuals and/or to recommend the firing of public individuals. These groups should be headed by multicultural fair-minded individuals who have a long history of fighting for social justice.

As long as schools continue to be funded partly by the local property tax base, schools in districts with low property values will be under-funded. Black neighborhoods tend to have less expensive homes and thus black schools tend to be under-funded. In order to solve this problem, states must pass laws that require a different way of funding education. It takes extraordinary effort to produce good students in under-funded schools. When we consider the fact that many students in neighborhoods with under-funded schools are disadvantaged in other ways (due to the lack of books to read and have read to them, poor nutrition, poor sleeping habits, and a host of other disadvantaging circumstances), we cannot expect good results.

In order to eliminate affirmative action at universities, we must solve the pre-school and grade school problem of unequal education. This can be done by providing all new mothers in poor neighborhoods with individualized training in how to interact with and read to newborns (taking this training and carrying out these responsibilities can be a requirement for receiving social assistance) and by providing adequate schooling and proper out-of-school supervision for children. These actions might not fit American capitalist ideals; however, there are many young mothers on social assistance in this country. Different thinking is needed on this issue.

Education is an important issue in the fight against racism and discrimination, but what education? What should be included in the curriculum? Who determines the curriculum? Whose perspective should be considered? These important questions are not impossible to answer. If the objective is to raise the profile of different racial groups, to promote cultural understanding, and to bring about a valuing of the accomplishments of various racial groups, then literature which does so would be used. One must find educators and educational programs to reach these goals. The starting place must be at the grade school level. Thus, publishers of children's curricula must become part of the process.

Many of the above suggestions do not fit political and cultural thinking in the United States. However, we must either find ways of solving the race problem or stop talking about it. Giving attention in print to these situations without solving social problems will only continue the frustration that is felt by many people on all sides of the issue.

Discussion Questions

1. Is it possible to be free of prejudice? Have you ever met anyone who was?
2. Are *you* prejudiced? If so, what are some recent instances in which you behaved in a prejudiced way? If not, how do you know that you're not prejudiced?
3. If a close friend or family member were to make a prejudiced comment, would you protest? Why or why not? What about a stranger or acquaintance—would you respond in that situation?
4. Are stereotypes ever a good thing? Have you ever tried to get people to stereotype you, either positively or negatively?
5. Which forms of prejudice are most socially acceptable, and which are least acceptable? Why are some forms more acceptable than others?
6. When, if ever, is it best to remain colorblind to race and ethnicity? When, if ever, is it best to celebrate multicultural differences? Do the goals of colorblindness and multiculturalism conflict with each other?
7. What do you think the most difficult aspect is of being a racial, ethnic, or religious minority member? What is the most difficult aspect of being a majority group member?
8. In general, which forms of prejudice seem to be declining over time, and which forms seem to be persisting or increasing?

(Questions taken from http://www.understandingprejudice.org/teach/stereosb.htm)

Related Readings

Anderson, E. (1994, May). The code of the streets. *The Atlantic, 273,* 80–94.
Cahn, S. M. (2002). *The affirmative action debates* (2nd ed.). New York: Routledge.
Elorsky, G. (1991). *Racism and justice: The case for affirmative action.* Ithaca, NY: Cornell University Press.
Loury, G. (2002). *The anatomy of racial inequality.* Cambridge, MA: Harvard University Press.
McGary, H., Jr. (1977). Justice and reparations. *Philosophical Forum, 9,* 250–263.
Zack, N. (1995). *American mixed race: The culture of microdiversity.* Lanham, MD: Roman and Littlefield.
Zack, N. (1998). *Thinking about race.* Belmont, CA: Wadsworth.

Related Web Sites

The Balch Institute for Ethnic Studies: http://www.balchinstitute.org
The Geography of Race in the United States: http://www.umich.edu/%7Elawrace
The National Association for the Advancement of Colored People (NAACP): http://www.naacp.org
Research Supporting Affirmative Action in Higher Education: http://www.umich.edu/%7Eurel/admissions/research
The Sociology of Race and Ethnicity: http://www.trinity.edu/~mkearl/race.html
Understanding Prejudice: http://www.understandingprejudice.org

Related Movies/Videos

American History X (1998) with Edward Norton and Edward Furlong
Barbershop (2002) with Ice Cube and Cedric the Entertainer
The Color Purple (1985) with Danny Glover and Whoopi Goldberg
Crash (2004) with Sandra Bullock
The Joy Luck Club (1993) with Tamlyn Tomita and Rosalind Chao
Jungle Fever (1991) with Wesley Snipes and Annabella Sciorra
Malcolm X (1992) with Denzel Washington and Angela Bassett
Men of Honor (2000) with Robert De Niro and Cuba Gooding, Jr.
Mississippi Burning (1988) with Gene Hackman and Willem Defoe
My Big Fat Greek Wedding (2000) with Nia Vardalos and John Corbett
Spanglish (2002) with Adam Sandler

INFANTS, CHILDREN, AND ADOLESCENTS

M. Catherin Freier and Ronald D. Morgan

16

Chapter Outline

"Youth comes to us wanting to know what we propose to do about a society that hurts so many of them." Franklin Delano Roosevelt, 1936

"Throughout the world future generations of children and families will be much more interrelated. In order to protect the future for one child, we must protect it for all." T. Berry Brazelton & Stanely I. Greenspan, 2000, p. 182

Introduction: Case Illustrations

Tanesha's Story

Tanesha is a two-year-old toddler who is going to live for the first time with her biological mother. Tanesha is described as being overactive, noncompliant, and inattentive. She appears to change who she is attached to frequently and is often more friendly to strangers than to her caregivers. She does not talk and appears not to listen well.

Tanesha's mother is of African American descent and it is not known who the child's father is. In order to feed and clothe her two other children, Tanesha's mother occasionally worked as a prostitute. She was arrested for prostitution and possession of drugs and was serving a jail term when Tanesha was born.

Tanesha was exposed to methamphetamines, marijuana, and alcohol in utero as her mother was taking these drugs during her pregnancy. Tanesha was a fussy infant who had trouble feeding and required an oxygen monitor during episodes when she would stop breathing. Since many foster parents were afraid to take a child on a machine, it was difficult to find a home for Tanesha. Tanesha has lived in six foster homes since her birth.

Tanesha's mother has completed her jail term and a drug treatment program. Since her mother has followed through with her court-ordered treatments, Tanesha may now go home to live with her. While

Tanesha has had some limited visits with her mother, she does not know her well. Tanesha cries when she sees all of her belongings put into a box. She tearfully goes with her caseworker to the car to be taken to her mother's apartment.

Sallie's Story

Sallie is a seven-year-old Caucasian girl who is on the rehabilitation ward of a children's hospital. Sallie looks very small for her age and has a very wobbly walk. Sallie was admitted to the hospital approximately six months ago. At the time of admission she was malnourished, could not walk, was significantly developmentally delayed in all areas, and was both hypersensitive and hypervigilant in relation to her environment.

Sallie had been locked in her room for most of the first six years of her life. She had been tied to her bed or potty-chair during most of her waking hours. Her grandfather had seen her as an embarrassment since she had a congenital syndrome that made her slightly delayed in her overall development. He instructed Sallie's mother, his daughter, to keep Sallie locked in her room. Sallie saw people or heard them talk only when they brought her food. She was a child who suffered from severe neglect and abuse.

Sallie's family was fairly well known in their quiet, friendly, but not close neighborhood. While the neighbors had seen Sallie when she was an infant, no one had seen her in several years. No one had ever questioned the family on Sallie's whereabouts. In fact, when Sallie reached school age, no one wondered why she was not waiting for the school bus with the other neighborhood children.

Sallie's mother, desperate for money, wanted to get some state assistance to help out with family expenses. Thus she took Sallie with her to the Social Service Agency to see how and what she might be eligible for since she had a handicapped child. The worker at the agency noticed Sallie's physical symptoms of malnourishment and her apparent inexperience and fear of everything in her environment. As a result of an immediate investigation, Sallie was taken to the hospital and her mother and grandfather were charged with child endangerment.

While Sallie could not walk or speak and was easily overwhelmed since everything was new to her, she did have a sense of curiosity. It was this curiosity that allowed her to make significant gains in her development. At the time of her discharge to a foster home, she was walking unsteadily, pointing to things she wanted, and smiling at familiar persons.

Pete's story

Pete is a 16-year-old boy who has just gotten out of the psychiatric hospital after a three-day stay for slashing his wrist with a butcher knife, severing nerves and tendons in his left hand.

Pete is the son of a Vietnamese mother and an American serviceman. He lived with his mother in Saigon until he was two years old. Upon her death he came to the United States to be adopted by an American family. He was apparently abused (burned and beaten) in this family, so he was removed to a foster home for several months before being placed with his current adoptive parents at age two.

Although always somewhat reserved and uncommunicative with his adoptive parents, Pete initially did well in his new surroundings. He was a bright and quite beautiful little boy who was sought out by other children from the time he started school. He always got along well with his friends, but his relationship with his parents was stormy, and they described him as the most difficult of the four children they had adopted.

By the time he was in junior high, Pete was hanging out with a group of kids who skipped school to smoke marijuana, considered nihilism a way of life, shoplifted beer from the local market, and disparaged the values of their parents and teachers. Pete's grades began dropping and he got into trouble for shooting squirrels with his BB gun, blowing up mailboxes with firecrackers, and getting into fights at school.

When Pete was 14, his adopted parents separated, and he elected to stay with his father rather than move out of state with his mother and siblings. After that, his misdemeanors escalated and he and his friends were arrested for stealing a neighbor's car to go joyriding. By the time he was 15 and in his second year of high school, Pete was absent more days than he was in school. He was using several different types of drugs and was generally angry with his father most of the time, so he was referred for counseling. Shortly thereafter he slashed his wrists.

When seen by the counselor following his hospitalization, Pete said he did not intend to kill himself when he slashed his wrists. He said he had been using LSD with some of his friends and heard a police siren. So he would not be arrested again, Pete said, he slashed his wrist and then lost consciousness. He denies being depressed but said his life is pointless and it makes no difference whether he lives or dies.

These case illustrations raise questions about the society in which children grow up.

Shared Social Issues for Infants, Children, and Adolescents

ISSUES: How does societal policy affect children? When is it okay for society to take children away from their parents? Do society's etiquette rules say that it is okay for me to question how my neighbor, friend, or family member treats their child? When should I mind my own business and when should I care about a child being disciplined? Should cultural views or individual value systems supersede societal policy? Who should advocate for children? Who is to blame for "problem" children? Are some children really born as "throw away kids"? Is there anything I can do? Are my attitudes toward children positive and do they motivate me to become involved in their defense? How does violence affect children? Are some types of violence worse than others for children? Who should be responsible for the types of violence children are exposed to? Does children's grief differ from that of adults? If so, how? Who should advocate for children?

The idea that children should be a particular and important focus of society is, surprisingly, rather recent. That children are unique and face their own socialization issues is a relatively new concept. Recognizing that children not only deserve attention but also require distinct considerations is even newer. Further, most attempts to address children as an indispensable part of society have used what may be termed "downward" perspectives. In other words, the concerns or issues that were seen as important for adults were applied to children without modification or consideration that their issues may be different from adults. In effect, the child was seen as a miniature adult with no real uniqueness other than size.

Social Issues for Youth: Historical Perspectives

One of the first attempts to look specifically at the social issue of children was actually due to society's need to discriminate among them. It was economically necessary to distinguish between the "normal" child and the "retarded" child in order to determine who could benefit from school and who could be institutionalized. In 1905 in France, Alfred Binet developed the first psychometric test for children, which assessed for mental retardation. This scale came to the United States in 1910 and the current version is called the Stanford-Binet. It was during the 19th century that labor laws were put into place, thus providing children with a childhood. Prior to this, children were considered small adults and made to work without a real "childhood." The importance of childhood had not been understood or promoted.

From a behavioral health perspective, it was Sigmund Freud in the early 1900s who first gave credence to the importance of childhood. While he did not do therapy with children, he recognized that many of the social issues that he was dealing with in his adult clients actually stemmed from their childhoods. As a result of this recognition, other theorists, researchers, and clinicians began to get information directly from children about their experience of childhood. More and more professionals and adults in general became aware that most issues of socialization are rooted in life experiences of early childhood.

It took many more years before the United States organized and funded child advocacy groups. "…[T]he impetus for child advocacy as a means of rectifying discrimination against children came in 1969 in the report of the Joint Commission on the Mental Health of Children with the support of the 1970 White House Conference on Children. A confluence of currents led to the subsequent endorsement of "child advocacy" (Westman, 1991, p. xix). This effort promoted attention to the fact that there was a shortage of children's mental health services. In addition, activist groups, particularly from minority groups, and government committees further supported a focus on child mental health. Furthermore, "there was growing interest in the prevention of mental illness, which was seen as extending beyond the boundaries of health care to penetrate the very fabric of society and as involving a range of ecological, sociological, cultural, psychological, and biological factors" (Westman, 1991, p. xx).

However, many of these efforts, while based on good intentions, actually decreased the importance of family and child-parent relationships. In 1974, Maria Montessori highlighted what she termed the "universal prejudices" against children. She emphatically pointed out the mistakes of a society that has determined that adults know what is best for children and always "act for their good." She pointed out the errors of this kind of thinking. It was believed that children must be taught to learn, overlooking their inherent, insatiable curiosity; that children's minds are empty, overlooking their rich imaginations; and that children do not work, overlooking their creative play (Montessori, 1974).

Whether it is the Baby Boomers, Baby Busters, Generation Xers, or the newly named Generation 9-11, one thing is for certain: they must understand that not only are children an important part of society, but they are also dependent upon it. Society does shape its youth. In this section of the chapter we will discuss some of the shared social issues of infants, children, and adolescents. The following sections will address social issues from a developmental perspective. Finally we will briefly discuss our collective and individual responsibility to children.

Family Systems

This chapter will not cover the larger societal issue of the family; however, it is necessary to underscore the importance of the family in the lives of children. Further, it is important to remember that, according to a sociological perspective, economic productivity depends on strong families. Families are often the cornerstone in the foundation of social issues for children. In the following paragraphs we will offer an overview on how the composition of the family impacts the child's social development and, more specifically, how early attachment is related to one's social development throughout life.

Composition

Family composition plays an important part in young children's understanding of socialization and will affect social interactions and perceptions throughout their lives. With over half of all marriages ending in divorce and many women having children out of wedlock, single parenting has become a norm in family composition. Further, it is more likely that the woman will be the single parent, resulting in many children who have little or no opportunity to have a male role model. According to the 2000 census, only 20% of children in the United States live with married biological parents. Researchers and clinicians have been expressing concern regarding the socialization of children when a parent, particularly the father, is absent (Garbarino, 1999).

In recent decades, parents have also had difficulty adjusting to role reversals. Due to economics there are several variations of working parent families. Thus, many parents have experimented with child rearing roles, which have often resulted in more confused parenting.

There are many instances of extended family care, in which several different family members, including the biological parents, may share the primary care-giving role. Further, the increasing number of children who are wards of the court or who are involved in a child protection agency indicates that many children are in non-kinship homes and may live in many different homes during the course of their childhoods. It is not uncommon for children by the age of four or five to have lived in up to six or eight different homes.

Obviously, family composition and the number of times it changes is a foundation layer of the child's socialization process.

Attachment

The ability to trust one's environment, which provides children the courage to explore the world, comes from a basic connection, called attachment, to a trusted adult.

Bowlby (1989), one of the primary theorists of attachment, stipulated that attachment characterizes humans "from the cradle to the grave."

Much research demonstrates that the nature and quality of attachment developed between an infant or young child and a primary caregiver significantly impacts the child's socialization process and quality of relationships throughout life. Three attachment styles have been described:

- *Secure:* a healthy attachment where the child can explore the environment due to a secure base, usually the mother.
- *Insecure:* poor attachment where the child is afraid to explore the environment even in the presence of the mother.
- *Disorganized:* random attachment where the child may appear more welcoming to strangers than to the caregiver; the child avoids intimate or long-term relationships.

As they get older, children who do not feel attached or do not develop a sense of connectedness to their caregivers or families will search for belonging in other areas. Due to the overwhelming number of fragmented families and communities, more children have become involved in gangs, even at young ages. Other children withdraw and find a sense of belonging by identifying with entertainment figures or other teen icons. Isolated or detached children are attracted to figures who emulate what they are feeling inside, often negative or depressed emotions, resulting in children identifying with many negative social influences. With the increase of child access to the Internet, these icons are even more readily available. Sometimes Internet groups develop that support and propagate this connectedness, often promoting a very negative socialization process.

Thus attachment is the scaffold on which children build their social experiences. Attachment is key to understanding what children will choose to identify with and how they will experience and impact their social world.

Value Systems

Children's socialization occurs through the values they are taught at a very early age. What, when, where, why, and how things are appropriate are developed in the context of society at large and from families and caregivers. While the family composition and attachment provide a base from which social learning takes place, the mechanisms or learning tasks are those in the value systems the child encounters. An example of how encompassing and far-reaching this learning is can be taken from the tradition of the Lakota Indians. They hunted for food, which was essential for their survival. It was of great importance that nothing interfered with hunting, including noises that might scare away the prey. Thus, during the first few hours after an infant was born, the mother would hold her hand across its mouth almost to the point of suffocation every time it would try to cry. If this were done consistently in those first few hours of life, the infant would never cry again. While this was done for survival, it taught a broader concept of the extreme importance of silence and the value and wisdom that silence carries. Thus the belief systems carried by our culture and subcultures, such as religion, provide influential training and learning in socialization.

Role of Culture and Religion

Culture and religion are two aspects of society that make a significant impact on the values and mores of

Religion can play an important role in a child's socialization. Here two boys admire the glow of the menorah in their celebration of the Jewish festival Hanukkah.

the child. It is the culture of the majority that expresses the role of society to the child and influences the child in direct or indirect but always powerful ways through economics, opportunity, education, and policy. As Matsumoto and Juang (2004) note: "One aspect of childhood that is probably constant across cultures is that people emerge from this period with a wish to become happy, productive adults. Cultures differ, however, in exactly what they mean by 'happy' and 'productive.' Despite similarities in the overall goals of development, cultures exhibit a tremendous degree of variability in its [sic] content" (p. 133). Thus socialization, in which the child learns and internalizes the rules of society, is culture dependent, and this learning begins in the first moments of life.

While parents are the main socialization agents, particularly for the family culture, the child will learn the broader culture from siblings, extended family, friends, teachers, and peers. An example of culture and values is that "American parents and teachers are more likely to consider innate ability more important than effort; for the Japanese and Chinese, however, effort was far more important than ability.…Americans are more likely to attribute the cause of the problem to something they cannot do anything about (such as ability)" (Matsumoto, 2000, p. 189). In another study, American mothers of preschoolers reported less interest in academic skills and more importance on building their child's self-esteem, while the Chinese mothers conveyed a high value on education and on their direct involvement in making their child successful (Chao, 1996).

Cultural influences through socialization have also been linked to cognitive development in children. Lev Vygotsky (1986–1934) was a Russian developmentalist who viewed cognitive development as a socially mediated process that may vary from culture to culture. Vygotsky's sociocultural theory focuses on how culture—values, beliefs, customs, and skills—is transmitted to the next generation. This helps us to understand that the wide variations of cognitive competency are impacted by what is emphasized or valued in each culture. Sociocultural theory, which emphasizes that children acquire their ways of thinking from their parents/caregivers and adult community, reveals that children in every culture develop unique strengths that are not present in other cultures.

In addition to the major culture or even the family culture, religion will play an important part of the child's socialization. Religion is a powerful socialization mechanism not only in terms of its belief system but also through the community it creates. While religion has been a difficult concept for sociologists to define (Stark, 1989), they have recently given much more credence to its impact on societies, communities, families, and individuals. Central to the impact of religion on the socialization process of children has been that it provides meaning. Meaning-making has been seen to impact physical and behavioral health as well as connection to one's community; typically, religious values provide the motivation to be a productive and positive contributor to society. According to Jim Garbarino, the core of the youth violence problem is a spiritual crisis: "They often have a sense of 'meaninglessness,' in which they are cut off from a sense of life having a higher purpose. By the same token, they often have difficulty envisioning themselves in the future. This 'terminal thinking' undermines their motivation to contribute to their community and to invest their time and energy in schooling and healthy lifestyles. Finally, they often have lost confidence in the ability and motivation of the adults in their world to protect and care for them. The shallow materialist culture in which we live undermines spirituality and exacerbates these problems. According to research reviewed by psychologist Andrew Weaver, non-punitve, love-oriented religion institutionalizes spirituality and functions as a buffer against social pathology" (foreword to Freier, 1999b, p. 5).

Role of Society

Society creates the collective attitude by which we view children. Children are dependent upon society for the resources necessary for survival, growth, development, and nurturance, as well as for the laws that will protect these resources. One of the most telling things about a society is the number of its children who live in poverty. In the United States, 16% of children are living in families where the household incomes are below the poverty threshold, according to the Forum on Child and Family Statistics (2001). This not only has implications for survival but also indicates a potential lack of opportunities and negative societal influences that children may encounter.

While there is significant diversity in terms of the economic advantages young people grow up with, all of them are exposed to and often enticed into negative lifestyles that are promoted as making them important: "…our society presents young people with adults who model greed on Wall Street, deceit in government, and hypocrisy in the pulpit. The media offer a backdrop of sex, violence, hot cars, and fast foods. Commercial interests view the young as prime targets for exploitation. Adults who are not personally affected parents protest the costs of public education and child health programs, the location of children's group homes in their neighborhoods, and workplace accommodations to parents and young children. Nowhere does there seem to be a political or economic motive for presenting children with models of trustworthy adults" (Westman, 1991, p. xvii).

Society has a responsibility for the protection of its children. While there is much debate over who knows what is best for children, there are laws that can implicate anyone who physically, sexually, emotionally, or otherwise tries to harm them. These laws are not comprehensive nor do they protect children from all potentially harmful situations. There have been challenges to society when there is a question of whether our policies may actually be harmful to some, many, or all children. One area of current controversy has been the excessive use of medication by children in America. This issue has as its main focus the legal use of medications to treat behavior in children. The controversy over if and when it is appropriate to medicate a child for not behaving according to society's norms will probably continue for some time, since both sides include parents, professionals, and lawmakers, all thinking they have the best interests of the child in mind. Further, many others aware of the debate fall along a continuum of beliefs rather than on one side or the other, making it less likely that many potentially influential persons (e.g., parents) will become informed or get involved. This current controversy is a good example of the multiple levels of society that can determine the lives of children. Economics, politics, laws, drug companies, the medical profession, behavioral health professions, and parents all have significant stakes in the outcomes of this debate.

Exposure to Violence and/or Abuse

There are four types of violence to which children are exposed: media, community, domestic, and self. In terms of abuse, there are at least four types of abuse that are inflicted upon children and can cause serious consequences for them: physical abuse, emotional abuse or negative home atmosphere, sexual abuse, and neglect. **Child abuse** can be defined as the violation of trust and boundaries, perpetrated by adults charged with protecting a child (Giles-Sims, 1985).

Abuse is tragic and affects children of all ages. Studies report that children in the first year of life suffer more abuse (and more fatal abuse) than in any other one-year period in their development (U.S. Department of Health & Human Services, 2000). Thus violence and/or abuse can impact children's overall development and certainly their social development very early in life. The experience of trauma will affect and perhaps even direct the socialization process.

Primary Sources of Exposure to Violence

Home: Domestic or family violence is the most underreported kind of violence in our nation. According to the American Institute on Domestic Violence (2001), there were an estimated 5.3 million acts of violence in homes each year (AIDV-USA). Look at your watch and sit in silence for the next 30 seconds. In the time that you were just sitting in silence, three children in the United States were abused. Domestic violence is a pervasive public health concern for all communities. Abuse and violence do not respect society's boundaries and know no geographical or economic limits.

The father figure initiates a large proportion of domestic violence. At times, the mother or maternal figure becomes frustrated and may also begin to abuse the children. In terms of abuse charges, however, mothers are now being charged with neglect of their children for not protecting them from the abuser or removing them from homes in which they witness abuse. More and more state laws around the United States stipulate that children be removed from the care of their mothers when their mothers neglect to take them out of the home where they were witnesses of violence. One reason for this more aggressive legal approach is the issue of safety. In homes where spousal abuse is present, children are at high risk for abuse themselves. "Our legal enforcement agencies also tell us that there has been a dramatic increase in the number of 911 calls made by children for help for violence in the home. Children are reaching out for help when the adults in the home are not taking the steps to do so" (Freier, 1999a, p. 52). These laws also reflect the concerns of health professionals who have studied how witnessing violence affects children. Children who witness violence show no physical signs of harm and are often overlooked. They do, however, suffer from symptoms similar to children who have been abused emotionally and behaviorally. This often includes attachment difficulties, depression and anxiety, acting out behaviors (impulsiveness and hypervigilence), and/or social isolation and withdrawal.

Data are available showing that children who witness violence in the home identify along gender lines with their parents' relationship. Thus it is very likely that when children witness abuse, boys become abusive as adults and girls become victims (Jaffe, Wolfe, & Wilson, 1990). Further, "harsh and continual physical punishment by parents has been implicated in the development of aggressive behavior patterns. Physical punishment may produce obedience in the short term, but continued over time it tends to increase the probability of aggressive and violent behavior during childhood and adulthood, both inside and outside the family. These findings suggest a cycle in the development of aggressive behavior patterns: Abuse at the hands of parents leads children to think and solve problems in ways that later lead to their developing aggressive behavior patterns and to their continuing cycle of violence" (Becker-Lausen et al., 1995).

Community: Community violence receives the most press and is becoming more and more frequent in many areas. Child perpetrators of community violence are also a significant social concern. A study done in a Boston community health center found that one in 10 children before the age of six had witnessed a severe act of violence (stabbing/shooting)—half in the home and half on the streets. The average age of the children in this study was two and a half (Finkelhor & Browne, 1985). Community violence has had recent surges in rural as well as urban communities, with the events frequently occurring on school grounds.

Self-Violence: One of the most tragic consequences of society's impact on children is when their response is to take their own lives. As a result of the toxic influences in the media, community, and, most importantly, abusive and chaotic home environments, the rate of children who commit or contemplate suicide has also been increasing. Children are not only striking out at others, but are also harming themselves as a response to their life situations (Freier, 1999a).

Secondary Sources of Exposure to Violence

Media: The most common indirect exposure of violence to children is through the media. Children who watch three hours of television a day see an average of 230 violent acts each week. Media violence can seriously affect children, causing psychological problems for them. For example, when the "Nightmare on Elm Street" movies were released, featuring "Freddy Kruger," a character who traumatized children through their dreams, there was a noticeable increase in child therapy referrals. As a result of viewing these movies, many children developed sleep disorders and feared falling asleep. "Professionals and committed public officials have sought ways to counteract the negative impact of television that are consistent with the First Amendment. Their efforts have led to limited successes. The U.S. federal government now requires broadcasters to provide at least 3 hours per week of educational programming for children" (Berk, 1999, p. 386).

Media influences on children are not limited to television. Children are bombarded with violent images in movies (at home and at the theater) and on the Internet. If you ask young people if their parents know what they are exposed to in the media, the overwhelming response is an emphatic "no." In fact, many children indicate that their parents would be shocked if they knew what they were exposed to. What about you? Did your parents know what you were exposed to? Do they now?

Re-traumatization

Re-traumatization occurs when a particular act of violence is witnessed again, either directly or, more often, indirectly. For example, students who were victims of the Columbine High School shooting in Littleton, Colorado, in 1999 may have experienced traumatic symptoms including flashbacks as a result of watching another school shooting incident in San Diego, California, on television two years later. Often the re-exposure, even if indirect and geographically distant, can cause children to be re-traumatized. This re-traumatization can be triggered by repeated violence in the home or community, nationally or globally.

Grief and Loss

Children grieve and mourn after trauma and/or loss. Often as a society we do not allow children to grieve and deny them the opportunities to do so. Since loss, especially death, is so difficult for adults to deal with, society has propagated myths of childhood grief in order to avoid having to face or address it (Freier, 1998). Some of these myths include:

- Grief and mourning are the same experience. However, grief is the feeling of loss and mourning involves the behaviors exhibited as a result of the grief.
- A child's grief and mourning are short in duration.
- There is a predictable and orderly stage-like progression in the experiences of grief and mourning.
- Infants and toddlers are too young to grieve and mourn.
- The grief and mourning of adults surrounding bereaved children do not have any impact on them.
- The trauma of childhood bereavement always leads to a maladjusted adult life.
- Children are better off if they don't attend funerals.
- Children who express tears are being weak and harming themselves in the long run.
- Adults should be able to instantly teach children about religion and death.
- The goal in helping bereaved children is to get them over grief and mourning (Wolfelt, 1983).

There are many factors that affect how loss and trauma determine the grief and consequently the socialization process of the child. These include:

- The age of the child
- The developmental stage and cognition level of the child
- The age of the person who died or nature of the loss
- The nature of the death
- The nature of the relationship between the child and the person who died or left
- The child's support system
- The mental, physical, and spiritual health of the child
- The child's religion or cultural beliefs about death
- The child's previous exposure to loss
- Society's expectations of the child.

Physical/Cognitive Impairments

Sometimes what is lost can be the child's physical or cognitive functioning. Then children must not only grieve their own loss of functioning but must take on the new role of reacting to how society treats children with a handicap or developmental delay.

Development and Grief

Both the developmental level and the chronological age are crucial factors for a child's understanding about death. Box 16.1 is a brief description of how children understand death at different ages.

Child Advocacy

As discussed above, children are dependent upon society for their social development. While this is a natural developmental process it begs the question, "Is child advocacy necessary?" "For most children, life unfolds without the need for special professional or public concern. For many, however, the intricate and fragmented legal, health, education, and welfare systems are their only hopes for a reasonable chance to succeed in life. Unfortunately, these systems lack coherent means for applying the principles of child advocacy to the lives of these vulnerable children" (Westman, 1991, p. xi). So if child advocacy is necessary, whose job is it?

The question of whether Americans really like children is supported by the substantial numbers of children who experience an array of preventable burdens. America has a high rate of infant mortality, low rankings in academic achievement, and a high rate of poverty (Goetting, 1994). Children are often caught between family, legal, educational, social, and political systems. In order to be effective and appropriate for the child, an agency must be inter-collaborative and have the best interest of the *child* in mind. In order to know what it means to have the best interests of the child in mind, we must understand how society impacts children differently at different developmental stages.

Box 16.1: Developmental Understanding of Death

Birth–2 years
- Concept: There is no cognitive concept but there will be an emotional feeling of loss if the person who died was a caregiver.
- Issue: The infant will respond to the emotional effect of losing the caregiver and may miss the person who died.

2–3 years
- Concept: The toddler has heard of the concept of death but does not see it as final or understand what it means.
- Issue: If the loss was of a caregiver, then separation is the key issue.

3–5 years
- Concept: Children understand that death means someone doesn't breathe or have a heartbeat; it is a result of injury or accident. It is seen as a departure or sleep and is associated with lack of movement.
- Issue: Injury to parts of the body.

5–11 years
- Concept: Death is real and it happens but not necessarily to everyone. There is a fascination with the process of death and decomposition. There are concrete perceptions based on observable facts.
- Issue: When there is a loss, the child will fear the death of a caregiver.

11 years–Adult
- Concept: Death is real and permanent. Death happens to everyone, even me.
- Issue: Fear of one's own death.

Social Issues of Infants and Young Children

ISSUES: How do infants organize their behavior? How do the roles of mothers and fathers differ in early parenthood? Why do you think there is a fairly high infant and young child mortality rate in an industrialized country like the United States? How is an infant socialized?

The primary feature of infants and young children (ages 0 to 5) is their total dependence on caretakers for psychological and physical survival. As a result, an attachment to the caregiver is of central importance. An infant's behavior toward its mother influences the way in which the infant organizes behavior toward other aspects of the environment (Ainsworth, 1983).

Thus the social issues significant to this age group are pivotal to their caregivers. The following is a list of the significant social issues often affecting children in this age group:
- Prenatal and postnatal influences
- Importance of the caregiver and the parent/infant dyad

- Key developmental issues
- Social/environmental influences

Each of these areas will be discussed in more detail to understand better what children in this age group face as they go through the developmental process.

Prenatal and Postnatal Influences

One of the first developmental milestones that can affect the long-term outcome for infants and children is the extent to which the mother developed the maternal role, and its quality. Maternal role attainment has been seen as a critical milestone in that not only does it affect the mother's physical and mental health, thus affecting infant outcome, but it also affects longer-term social issues, such as whether the mother will keep her child, abort her pregnancy, or give up her child for adoption. Many social influences and values will significantly impact her decision. In addition to the physical and psychological changes, the mother must make lifestyle and relationship changes in order to optimize the likelihood of a healthy baby. During pregnancy there may be fear and depression regarding the outcome. Complicating this, depressed women often have higher rates of obstetric complications. The adjustment of the mother to her pregnancy is also impacted by how she views herself as a potential mother, how her culture views her, and whether or not she has a sufficient social support system. Thus, significant maternal and pregnancy risk factors include medical complications, substance use, teenage pregnancy, and lack of environmental resources, including food, shelter, and support.

Recent public health initiatives in the United States identify the improvement of maternal and infant health outcomes as a national priority. Prenatal care is emphasized in these initiatives as a crucial intervention for reducing the risks of adverse outcomes. Frequently, access to health care due to monetary or geographic limitations has been a significant barrier to prenatal care. In a study examining women from Puerto Rico who lived in the mainland United States, researchers found that while monetary and transportation problems were a barrier to prenatal care, secrecy, consideration of abortion, and women's lack of awareness that they were pregnant were also considered barriers to prenatal care (Oropesa et al., 2000).

While fathers may have less pressure from society to attain a paternal role, they too, if they are aware of the pregnancy, will need to determine if the pregnancy is desired and if and what role they will play in the mother's and infant's lives. There has been some movement on the part of society to influence men to become more involved in parenting, if not by their presence then by mandated child financial support. The father's response to parenthood often involves responding to and supporting the emotional changes in the mother, potentially changing their lifestyle and their roles in the relationship. While roles for parents are changing, traditionally fathers were primarily concerned with the financial responsibility of having a child.

Infant Risk Factors and In Utero Substance Exposure

There are four different risks that can affect infant outcome and development. First, there is established risk, when there is a known etiology and when a child is born with a syndrome (e.g., Down Syndrome) or HIV

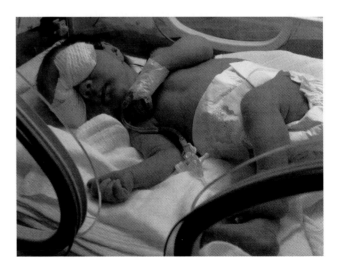

An ill infant girl lies under an ultraviolet lamp.

infection. Second, there is environmental risk, which is related to the quality of mother/infant interaction and hence infant stimulation. Third, there is biological risk, in which the fetus or infant is exposed to potentially noxious events such as an intraventricular hemorrhage or lack of oxygen. Fourth, there can be a combination of risk factors, which can be called a double jeopardy (Aylward, 1997).

Perinatal drug exposure, which occurs when a mother ingests drugs during her pregnancy, significantly impacts an infant's development and socialization trajectory. While there is more risk of medical complications, including prematurity, for these infants, there are also long-term developmental consequences. These infants are often irritable, with rapid mood changes. They can be hard to comfort and may have poor weight gain and tremors or other gross motor problems. They are very disorganized in their response to the environment, which often makes socialization a difficult and negative process. While perinatal drug exposure is a problem in all societies, advantaged or disadvantaged, infants who are most often negatively targeted by society are those who live in poverty or are members of minority groups. It has been suggested that anywhere between 5% and 24% of all children born in the United States are born with in utero drug exposure. One investigation cited a prevalence rate of 5.2% of delivering mothers (Slutsker et al., 1993). Many of these children will grow up in poor economic conditions, which are associated with an increase in accidents and family violence. It is not uncommon for these children to be homeless or to live in multiple homes with many different caregivers.

Mortality

It is tragic that mortality is a significant concern for infants and young children. Infant mortality in the United States is at a rate of 7.2% and young children (ages 1–4) have a mortality rate of 35%. The leading cause of death in infants and young children is non-accidental trauma or abuse. Other significant causes of death in young children include cancer, birth defects, homicide, heart disease, and pneumonia, according to The Forum on Child and Family Statistics (2001). Further, according to the National Clearinghouse on Child Abuse and Neglect (2005), an estimated 1,500 children died in 2003 due to abuse or neglect and 79% were under the age of four.

Homicide: There has been little examination of the social correlates directly pertaining to infant homicide. A study done by Smithey (1998) found that as the age of the infant victim increases, the level of violence used to fatally injure the child also increases. In addition, as the level of relational intimacy decreases, the level of violence used to fatally injure the infant increases. Another study found that when infant homicide occurred at the hands of the mother, it was the result of a culmination of predisposal factors evolving from the mother's socialization experience (i.e., abusive parents, sexual abuse and trauma, parental substance use, and abusive partners) and precipitating factors stemming from economic deprivation (absence of the infant's father and adverse living conditions) (Smithey, 1997).

SIDS: Sudden Infant Death Syndrome, or SIDS, is the leading cause of death for infants between the ages of one month and one year. It has been defined as "the sudden death of an infant less than one year of age that remains unexplained after a thorough case investigation, including a complete autopsy, examination of the death scene, and review of the clinical history" (Horchler & Morris, 1997). While there is no known etiology for SIDS, risk factors include maternal smoking, low birth weight, prematurity, infections, and perinatal drug use. In June 1992, The American Academy of Pediatrics Task Force on Infant Positioning and SIDS (1992) published a recommendation that healthy full-term infants should be placed laterally or on their backs to sleep, as this has been associated with a decrease in the prevalence of SIDS.

Society: Society has a direct impact on the mortality of young children since it is the responsibility of society to protect its youngest and most vulnerable citizens. It is evident that in this respect society has failed, since children in this age period account for the most significant number of deaths, with the leading cause being abuse perpetrated by adults. Further, it has been shown that welfare directly and indirectly affects infant mortality rates. States with higher welfare benefit levels also had lower infant mortality rates. In addition, homelessness has also been linked to high infant mortality rates, according to the Forum on Child and Family Statistics (2001).

Importance of the Caregiver and the Parent/Infant Dyad

The caregiver is at the crux of infant development and is the single most important factor in infant socialization. Thus, how the caregiver views the infant and the caregiver's ability to provide the necessary environment and interaction to the infant is crucial. It is estimated that 30% of pregnancies in America are unintended. Further, it has been determined that unwanted pregnancy is associated with low levels of well-being and physical health in the mother (Barber et al., 1999).

The mood of the mother is also an important socialization and developmental factor for infants. It has been found that maternal depression negatively affects infants as early as in the first year of life. Often a dysregulation is noted in the infant behaviorally, physiologically, and biochemically (Lundy et al., 1999). This means that the infant does not learn social interaction and also physically changes to mimic the depression of the mother. Mothers who are depressed or have problems regulating their affect are seen to act in one of two predominant styles. They either become withdrawn or intrusive, providing either inadequate or too much stimulation for their infants. Single mothers and those with few social supports are at higher risk for depression.

The mother's own history may have a significant impact on how she relates to her child. She may have a history of being abused. It is not uncommon for the birth of a baby to make a mother remember and have to deal with previous events of trauma or abuse. The mother may have lost a child before, making her less attached to or overprotective of this baby.

In the typical and expected interactions between the infant and the mother, the infant stimulates protective urges in the mother and the mother stimulates adoration from the infant. This interaction contributes to attachment, trust, and the infant's sense of self. Infants arouse in their caretaker images of innocence, hope, and promise for the future. Thus, in addition to what the mother brings to the relationship, it is important that the baby also contributes to the relationship. More important than either the mother or the infant will be the match between the two and the interaction between them.

An infant brings its own temperament to the situation. Some infants are easygoing and can adapt to change quickly. Others may be slow to warm up and still others can have a difficult or fussy temperament (see Box 16.2 for a description of the various temperaments). In addition to their affective or behavioral qualities, some infants have medical complications and physical difficulties, which will result in another level of need and socialization.

The match between the mother and the infant or toddler is based on how well they can negotiate both of their needs into a relationship. Obviously, confidence in the maternal role and an understanding of infant and toddler development are key to a positive outcome and healthy socialization for them both.

Key Developmental Issues

As stated above, the prerequisites for cognitive and social development in infancy are security and attachment. Trust will invite and encourage exploration of the environment, which will provide the sensory experiences that facilitate learning. Erik Erikson, a major developmental theorist, posited that basic trust and autonomy grow out of warm, supportive parenting and reasonable expectations for impulse control during the second year (Erikson, 1950).

The infant will explore the world through sensory modes: hearing, seeing, proprioception (feeling your

---

Box 16.2: A Model of Temperament

- Easy child: A child who quickly establishes regular routines in infancy. The child is generally cheerful and adapts easily to new situations or experiences.
- Slow-to-warm-up child: A child who may be inactive; shows mild, low-key reactions to environmental stimuli; is negative in mood; and adjusts slowly to new experiences.
- Difficult child: A child who is irregular in daily routines, has difficulty with new experiences, and tends to react negatively and intensely.

Source: Thomas & Chess, 1977

---

body move in space), smelling, touching, and tasting. The infant is undefended and basically trusting, which is developmentally appropriate. Infants are known to turn to their mother's voice over any other voice at birth and will turn to the smell of their mother's milk over any other breast milk.

Toddlers are in the process of actively exploring their world. They too are undefended and basically trusting of their environment. Thus, because they have only a very simple thought process, they will confuse fantasy and reality. They also have a distorted sense of time so that one hour, tomorrow, or next month have little meaning.

Social Cognition

Social cognition is the process by which individuals develop the ability to monitor, control, and predict the behavior of others. It is learned by engaging in mutual exchanges with others, essentially by sharing experiences. In the second half of the first year of life, infants learn that others are "like me" and that they can learn from them. During this time infants also learn that they too can affect their world. Social knowledge occurs when infants learn that they are agents of social exchange, as are other people, and that they can share and direct each other's experiences (Rochat & Striano, 1999).

There are three basic categories of social exchange:
- Feelings: perception of specific private experiences—pain, hunger, or frustration
- Affects: general mood or perceived private tone—background to feelings and emotions—diffuse and fluctuate on a continuum
- Emotions: observable (public) expressions of feelings and affects—communicating what is experienced privately; behavioral expressions of pain, joy, disgust, sadness, surprise, and anger

Most parents demonstrate a natural talent for highly sophisticated interactional skills with their infants. They naturally and importantly echo the affects and emotions that arise in interaction with their young infants and toddlers. If infants do not learn the components of social exchange, they may be deprived of the opportunity to develop prosocial behaviors, empathy, and moral judgment (Rochat & Striano, 1999).

Some theorists believe that all the basic emotions are present in the first few weeks of life and can be directly inferred from facial expressions, such as happiness, interest, surprise, fear, anger, sadness, and disgust. Others regard the emotional life of the newborn as quite limited, with only the capacity to approach pleasant stimuli and to withdraw from aversive stimuli. This position is less popular. What we do know is that infants and toddlers rely on trusted persons' emotional reactions to decide how to respond in a situation. This is called **social referencing**. Learning to practice self-control and to resist an impulse to engage in socially disapproved behaviors begins in a limited level around 18 to 24 months of age. Lack of parental or caregiver understanding of this limited capacity is often the precipitator of abuse. Parents often abuse children who do not obey them. This typically centers around expectations of toileting, feeding, and behaviors that are too advanced for the child. Around the age of three, children start to take the perspective of others and begin to predict how another person might feel.

Thus, key to the development of infants and toddlers are experiences with primary caregivers, attachment, and environmental conditions.

Social/Environmental Influences

Infants and toddlers are more dependent on their immediate social environment than children at any other age. They are the trusting recipients of cultural and societal decisions. Further, whether a caregiver is supported by the society will have a significant impact on the infant's or toddler's living conditions and even life expectancy.

Society may be indirectly harmful to infants and toddlers, depending on how it views their parents. Society can aversely affect children if it feels the mother is too old or too young; uses drugs, smokes, or drinks alcohol; is poor; or is a member of a minority group. Furthermore, society can also have a direct negative influence on an infant or toddler depending on how it may view the infant's disability, facial anomaly, or behavior.

Social Issues of Childhood

ISSUES: How do the physical changes that children go through affect their overall social development? What would you consider to be a good balance between adequate parental involvement and influences from outside, in order to produce normal childhood development? What are the overall effects of single parenting? What recommendations would you have for "latchkey kids"? What makes school success so important in childhood?

The primary feature of childhood (ages 6 to 12) is the transition from family as the main influence to that of school and peer group. Because of this, the number of other influences on the child becomes multifaceted. The following is a list of the significant social issues often affecting the children in this age group:

- Key developmental issues
- Parental influences
- School adjustment (e.g., attendance and appropriate conduct)
- External influences (e.g., music, television, movies, video games, drugs, and teen idols)
- Peer relationships

Each of these areas will be discussed in more detail to clarify what children in this age group face as they go through the developmental process.

Key Developmental Issues

One of the key developmental issues for children between the ages of six and twelve is how their bodies change so dramatically. Each year there are significant changes that the child physically goes through that put the focus on body image. This can have either a negative or positive influence on children, depending on their ability to adjust in a healthy manner to the changes. In children where these changes occur more rapidly, there is a greater chance of poor adjustment. The opposite is true as well; if the child develops more slowly than normal, then healthy adjustment may not occur.

As girls adjust to the body changes that begin occurring around age nine or ten, family environment has a significant impact on body image and weight control practices. A positive affirming relationship with the primary caregivers is a chief indicator of how a young girl will view her body image. If a girl's mother is overly concerned about weight issues, then there is a higher probability that the girl will be as well. Exposure to violence either in the home or in initial dating practices elevates the probability that girls will become involved in some type of weight control practices (Thompson, Wonderlich, Crosby, & Mitchell, 2001). The pressures of society to be thin only add to the desire to control one's weight. Girls with weak impulse control are also at greater risk for initiating weight control practices that can lead to an obsession with body image. When weight gain first occurs in pre-adolescent girls because of changes related to puberty, there is often alarm and a feeling of "I'm going to become overweight." At that point they may try to diet and feel a sense of accomplishment if they are actually able to lose some weight. Unfortunately, if weight loss is sustained, then maintaining the new weight, or even losing additional weight, can become a preoccupation at that point (Finelli, 2001). This preoccupation can develop into an eating disorder.

Often boys' adjustments to body image at this age can be quite the opposite of girls. As they enter puberty, boys are often overly focused on gaining weight, especially as it relates to building muscle. Again, societal pressures for boys to develop big muscles in order to fit in and be desirable are extremely influential. Those boys with weak impulse control and poor family role models are at greater risk for developing an obsession with body image. A boy's self esteem and confidence in himself is often affected when too much focus is on body image. A balance between accepting who they are becoming as they go through puberty and what they want to be is an important developmental issue for boys in this age group.

Another growing problem for American children in regards to body image is obesity. The prevalence of childhood obesity within the United States between 1999 and 2001 has been estimated to be 31% (Hedley et al., 2004). Obesity in children is of economic concern in American society because of the enormous amount of health care costs. In addition to lack of exercise and poor nutrition, depression and poor self-esteem are becoming a concern for obese children. A sedentary society, excessive television viewing, and Internet surfing are also blamed for the etiology of obesity in children (Sallis & McKenzie, 1991).

Another key developmental issue is the heightened sexual awareness that often occurs before a child enters puberty. A significant amount of this awareness comes from repeated exposure to various media that reinforce a certain look one must have to be sexually attractive. Children are often bombarded with messages that sexual attractiveness is tied to everything from how to dress to what to eat and drink. Children are being told at a younger and younger age that they need to look or act a certain way in order to be desirable. The onset of puberty is also occurring at a younger age, especially in girls (Cobb, 1992).

Parental Influences

Although parental influence is important throughout a child's development, it is affected by outside entities when a child begins school. Such areas as gender role attitudes, household labor, and religious participation can all be affected and sometimes even altered by outside influences (Cunningham, 2001). Often one of a parent's biggest worries is that regardless of the way children are taught at home there is always the possibility that outside influences will sway their thinking. Some parents more than others have a difficult time allowing their children to spend significant time outside the family. This becomes harder for a parent to control as the child becomes more involved in school and social activities. If a child doesn't have a parent or parents who are involved in his or her life, or if the child lives with foster parents or in an institutional setting such as a group home, influences often come from other sources, such as peers or other adult figures. Often an adult can serve as a mentor or positive role model for a child who doesn't have an actively involved parent. This adult could be a teacher, coach, youth pastor, or anyone else who becomes a positive role model for a child.

Even with children who have parents who care for them, there is an increasing number who are left unsupervised for part of the day. These unsupervised children are often referred to as "latchkey kids" and may spend part of a day at home without a parental or other adult figure. It is during these unsupervised times that children are at a higher risk for deviant behavior. Incidents of drug and alcohol abuse, sexual involvement, and even criminal activity are all significantly higher among latchkey kids. In her study on delinquency, Haynie (2001) researched the need for parental structure in a child's life. She found that parents need to provide a structured environment for when they can be with their children in order to prevent negative or even deviant behavior from occurring.

Children raised in a single-parent home may spend more time alone or away from their parent. If the single parent is the only provider for the family and working long hours, there is less time for a healthy parent-child relationship. Often an older child will be left at home to care for younger siblings because a single parent is at work. This older child might even assume the role of a parent when left to supervise younger siblings, which can cause role confusion within the family.

Approximately 50% of children in the U.S. live in a family with divorced parents. They often are presented with a number of issues related to the dynamics of divorced parents, such as which parent they primarily live with, parent re-marriage, step and/or half siblings, moving, and feelings of guilt for being at fault in relation to the divorce.

Children without parents or positive adult role models can be susceptible to negative peer influences such as gangs, drugs, and other delinquent behaviors. Gangs have been an increasing risk for children over the past ten years, especially in urban settings. Most gangs are non-adult sponsored, self-determining groups that are involved in some sort of youth violence (Short, 2001). Often children at age ten or eleven look outside the home for acceptance and a feeling of belonging, a feeling that a gang may provide for them. If they don't find influences that are positive in their lives, they are at a higher risk for involvement in negative or even destructive behaviors.

Studies show repeatedly that parental involvement while a child is young is essential in preventing deviant behavior later on (Simons et al., 2001). Difficult behavior in childhood often leads to deviant adolescent behavior if parental interventions aren't successfully implemented. Even though a parent's role changes as a child goes from childhood to adolescence, it doesn't mean the level of involvement should be lessened. Children of all ages need to feel that their parents are a constant source of strength and support to them. Working out the degree of involvement each child needs is the part that most parents find to be a challenge. There are those who believe that children's heredity is perhaps more important in defining who they will become than the type of parenting they receive. Harris (1998), in fact, dismisses the importance of children learning from their parents, stating, "children cannot learn how to behave by imitating their parents." She goes on to say that most of the things children see their parents doing are things they as children cannot do, such as driving cars, lighting matches, and coming and going as they please, so there can't be as much role modeling occurring as once was thought (Harris, 1998).

School Adjustment

Children are expected to be able to control their behavior at school. They need to understand the importance of following classroom rules and respecting their teacher or else face consequences for aberrant behavior. As children learn to adapt to their school environment, they begin to feel more comfortable in it. They learn the basic expectations of conduct, from not hurting anyone to respecting those in their school family. Children either adapt to the school setting early on or experience difficulty adjusting to their new environment. Many studies have been done to look at how children adjust to the school setting. Most have focused on children's perceptions of how they feel they fit into the school environment and whether they perceive school as a successful experience.

Many experts agree that for children to be successful they need to feel that their lives are going well in at least two of the three following areas: 1) family and home life, 2) school functioning, and 3) peer relationships. Obviously, it would be optimal if children felt all three of these areas were going well for them, but the majority of children will still be successful if they are functioning satisfactorily in at least two of those three areas. If a child feels that only one of these three areas is going well, there is a greater chance that he or she won't be successful. Unfortunately, more and more children

in today's society feel that none of those three areas are going well in their lives and see themselves as lost or, as some have termed, "throwaway kids." Some child advocacy experts question whether the United States as a nation really values children when so many of them don't live in their homes, don't do well in school, and have few or no social skills. These situations are seen as preventable burdens, yet substantial numbers of children remain in these dire straits (Goetting, 1994).

External Influences

Children today are influenced by various external entities more than in other times in history because of the amount of environmental exposure to which they are subjected. Through advertising alone, children are bombarded with messages about what is popular. Advertisers are aware that more and more young people are becoming a significant segment of their consumers. How much does media exposure on how to look or what to buy or eat or drink affect a child socially? Is the impact on a child of watching television and movies greater than parental influence? These questions have no clear-cut answers, but many studies show that children who are already at risk for deviant behavior are definitely more susceptible to negative media influences (Trzcinski, 1992). For instance, children at risk are more likely to commit an aggressive act after seeing a violent movie than children not considered to be at risk. Children who don't have positive adult role models are more influenced by figures in the entertainment and sports fields. They want to mimic behaviors that they see these figures involved in, which can often be misinterpreted into something that becomes negative or even deviant.

Peer Relationships

Many different influences determine how successful a child is in developing friendships. The ability to make and sustain friendships is molded at a young age by family members in such areas as dependency, caring, and overall trust issues. If a child's experiences with a peer group were negative at a young age, this can often carry over into poor relationships in later years. Examining the underlying structural properties of friendships is essential in understanding peer influence on a child (Haynie, 2001). A peer group influences every child in different ways, but children who have strong relationships with their parent(s) are usually less likely to be swayed by their friends toward deviant behavior.

A child's social behavior often mimics that of one or both parents but can also be a learned skill that can improve as he or she grows and matures. Children who initially feel successful in social relationships will probably continue to be good at forming friendships. If a child feels from an early age that he or she isn't very good at establishing friends, that can have a downward spiraling effect through childhood and even into adolescence.

Social Issues of Adolescence

ISSUES: What are the most significant social issues facing today's adolescents? Who do you think are more important in influencing adolescents—parents or peers? Why? Does your answer differ depending on the issue, and if so, how? What affects career choice for adolescents?

During the often misunderstood developmental phase of adolescence, many different factors affect the make-up of today's teenager. Regardless of where they live or go to school, adolescents face key developmental issues, external influences, peer relationships, and decisions about the future.

Key Developmental Issues

The developmental issues facing most adolescents revolve around their identity, peer group, and self-esteem. The challenge for most teenagers is to discover who they are and, based on that, how they fit into society. The subject often examined about the teenage years is the impact of social influences on adolescents' self-esteem and ultimate ability to understand who they are. As teenagers individuate from their parents' influences, it is important to consider what influences play a key role in their lives. The degree to which these influences have a bearing on a teenager's search for identity is somewhat different for each adolescent. In fact, the length of time it takes adolescents to discover their identity and transition to adulthood has increased over the past ten years (Furstenberg, 2000). According to Furstenberg (2000), a number of factors are involved in delaying the transition from adolescence to adulthood, including peer group relations, biological influences, employment experiences, and increased autonomy at a younger age. However, teenagers who were raised in a strong family system will be less influenced by these other factors. This is especially true when teenagers were raised with solid family values and hence developed belief systems that influenced their decision-making.

External Influences

Adolescents, just like children, are impacted by external influences. Several key factors are particularly troubling social issues that have a negative effect on a significant number of today's adolescents. O'Hare (1999) did a survey called "Kids Count," which identified these key factors to be 1) an absent father; 2) an uneducated mother; 3) household income below the poverty level; 4) lack of health insurance; and 5) family reliance on some form of public assistance. O'Hare (1999) also reported that over 9.2 million youth lived in families who were affected by three or more of these detrimental factors. He further stated that adolescents living under any of these high-risk conditions are 26 times more likely to drop out of school than teenagers from families with none of these factors.

The question is often asked as to which age group is most susceptible to external influences, and the answer is related to how each individual child or adolescent is affected by various influences. Adolescents are often perceived as being easily influenced to become involved in negative behavior (Lashbrook, 2000). Whether these negative influences result from peer pressure or if it is simply that teenagers can be easily swayed is certainly subject to debate. Teenagers are targeted commercially for everything from what music to listen to, to what food to eat, to what clothes to wear. Adolescents, who are easily influenced for whatever reason, are strongly affected by what they hear and are likely to behave in ways that they think helps them fit in. Music, video games, television, and movies that promote violence, drugs, and even the occult will affect those adolescents who are already at risk for deviant behavior. Garbarino (1999) called these influences "social toxicity," and reported that youth at risk are much more susceptible to them. Adolescents who are at risk were defined by Garbarino (1999) as "lost," and he said there are three main causes for it: 1) they become detached from society's spiritual and cultural underpinnings, 2) they gravitate to peer groups that reinforce their own sense of righteous indignation, and 3) they are surrounded by cultural images that validate their feelings. When these at-risk adolescents commit acts of violence at school or in their neighborhoods, they are part of a social issue that can have an impact on everyone.

Adolescents are exposed to drugs and alcohol both at school and in their neighborhoods. They get mixed messages from society about whether it's okay to use some drugs, or a minimal amount of alcohol, or none at all. Often messages promoting drug and alcohol use are heard in music that many adolescents listen to. Those adolescents who are already considered to be at risk are more susceptible to using drugs or alcohol. Adolescents who don't feel good about themselves or who have past abuse or trauma issues will often use drugs or alcohol to "numb" how they feel. Recreational drug use can quickly turn to heavy use, as the adolescent likes this feeling of being invulnerable to the harshness of reality. The trend of drug use among teenagers hasn't changed much in the last decade and continues to be an extremely difficult social issue. Most experts agree that the problem won't be resolved until a greater emphasis is put on preventative and intervention programs focused on children and adolescents throughout their school experience.

In addition to using drugs and alcohol, other risky behaviors, including sexual activity, may be prominent in an adolescent's social life. Above and beyond the social consequences of substance use and sexual promiscuity are the physical consequences of poor health and sexually transmitted infections, including HIV/AIDS infection. Now in its third decade and having claimed the lives of over 40 million people, HIV has become a young person's disease in that over half of all new HIV infections occur in youth between the ages of 15 and 24. Further, the majority of all new infections occur by means of heterosexual transmission. Thus, HIV/AIDS infection is one of the most serious social issues of adolescents (UNAIDS, 2000).

Peer Relationships

Most adolescents will say that friendships are most important to them. Research has shown repeatedly that who teenagers associate with is more important than what they might be actually doing. To be connected socially is more important to most teenagers than how they are doing academically in school or what they hope to do in the future. When adolescents have questions or concerns about various issues in life, they often turn to their peer group. The sense of self that develops within the family setting prepares teenagers for friendships outside of it (Cobb, 1992). Typically, adolescents gain a sense of who they are through what may appear to be insignificant encounters with their peers. The question asked by parents and teachers alike is, "what makes an adolescent's peer group so important?" Teenagers often respond that "my friends accept me for who I am," which makes perfect sense because their plea is "accept me with all my imperfections." This is especially true for the adolescent with low self-esteem who is looking for acceptance. Most adolescents just want emotional support, intimacy, and advice from their friends. They want to feel they can trust someone with their thoughts and feelings. When adolescents have difficulty making or sustaining friendships, they look at other alternatives. Unfortunately, peers who are involved in gangs or the drug culture can be appealing to adolescents who struggle to make friends, because they will accept anyone who participates in the desired deviant behavior. One of the main reasons an adolescent joins a gang is to feel acceptance and belonging which that type of peer involvement provides. An adolescent who joins a gang gives up a part of his or her identity and becomes involved in deviant behavior, but is willing to do so in order to be accepted by a peer group.

It has also been found, according to Cobb (1992), that adolescents often see more than their present selves reflected by their friends. Often teenagers will imagine themselves as other than who they are, so they can set goals, rehearse new roles, and plan various ways of attaining them. This type of image may include more than the roles the adolescent is refining, extending to the adult roles they will soon grow into. Sometimes adolescents imagine themselves in roles completely different from who they are, like the introverted teen pining to be the most popular person at school. Often, adolescents who have difficulty making friends are the ones showing more social incompetence. These adolescents have trouble assessing a peer situation and then adapting accordingly. They may also have difficulty responding appropriately to a peer's behavior, as they are unsure how to proceed. Sometimes teenagers having difficulties socially simply need to learn appropriate social skills in order to improve how they cope with their peer group (Cobb, 1992).

Social competence is most noticeable among teenagers in the dating scene. Adolescents who tend to be socially incompetent have greater difficulty participating and being successful in dating relationships. Most adolescents begin the dating process between the ages of 12 and 16, with girls dating at an earlier age than boys. Many social issues are played out in dating scenarios—who does the asking, who pays for the date, whether they should open doors for each other, and so on. Dating can cause the teenager to feel nervous and even apprehensive at times, although most report that it is usually an enjoyable experience. Teenagers who aren't socially competent tend to feel nervous about dating and will often not participate in it because they fear it will turn out badly.

Often the biggest social concern for adolescents in developing and establishing relationships is peer pressure. Many studies have been done on the overall effect of peer pressure among teenagers (Cobb, 1999). The perceived demand to act and think just like their friends is a significant pressure felt by many adolescents, especially those with low self-esteem or social incompetence. The young adolescent is usually most affected by peer pressure. As teenagers mature and become more sure of themselves, the pressure to conform to their peer groups lessens. Research on peer pressure shows that with age and maturity most adolescents become better at thinking for themselves and less reliant on friends for decisions.

Decisions about the Future

Middle to late adolescence is a time of decision making about what will follow high school graduation. It is important to look at the various influences that have a bearing on future decisions that adolescents will make. As discussed previously, it is often a peer group that influences decisions about the future. Teenagers will often choose a college or job to match a friend's decision. This is especially true when the adolescent is undecided about what to do after high school. In other words, the more undecided an adolescent is about the future the more inclined he or she is to mimic what someone from a peer group is going to do.

According to Cobb (1999), many factors, especially gender and ethnicity, affect decisions about what type of career an adolescent will decide to pursue. Many adolescents won't even consider certain careers because they haven't seen individuals of their gender or ethnicity in those particular occupations. Another issue that affects an adolescent's decision about the future is socioeconomic level. If adolescents have too narrow a view of what career choices they may have, then their options become almost self-limited.

One of single biggest decisions an adolescent will make about the future is whether to pursue an occupation or go on to college after high school. A number of factors influence that decision, including family history, geographical area, academic success in high school, and socioeconomic level and peer group. The number of teenagers going to college has steadily increased over the past decade, and that trend is expected to continue in the future.

Saving Our Children— What You Can Do

ISSUES: What can be done for children at individual, community, state, and federal levels? What do you consider the most important issues for children? Since there are so many "nontraditional" families, how can the family help children?

Unfortunately, there continues to be a striking number of tragedies involving our youth. Children are often killed in homes and schools, areas thought to be the safest for our children. The reality that all children are at potential risk to perpetrate harm or to be victims of crime affects us all. As a result of the tragedies, there have been many efforts to raise awareness of the needs of our youth or, more typically, to expose the "warning signs" indicating those youth who are at risk of harming others. This is done with an earnest hope for a better world for our children. As discussed in a monograph by the senior author, "One of the problems of identifying risks is that along with identification come blaming and release from individual responsibility. If the risk is guns, then let those who distribute or condone guns take the blame and do something. If the risk is the media, then let Hollywood or the entertainment industry take the blame and change their products. If the risk is poor parenting, then let the parents take the blame and assume responsibility for their children. While all of these are significant areas of concern, targeting them as the risk does nothing to save our children. Saving our children is a task that is much more multifaceted and requires the active involvement of each of us.

"We live in a fragmented society, a society in which a neighbor is often someone you don't know well and a 'good' one does not interfere. Community, defined by Webster as 'people with common interests living in a particular area,' now more typically represents a location rather than a unified group of people. Common purpose and common interest rarely define community today. We know from professionals who do relief work in areas of strife, such as war-torn Bosnia or Kosovo, that the most vulnerable groups to suffer in any fragmented community are the elderly and the children. So it is in our nation where community no longer carries with it

the responsibility and availability for others, that our youth are our most vulnerable citizens" (Freier, 1999b, p. 6). Thus, it is the responsibility of adults to advocate for children and to ensure that children have a healthy and safe environment in which to grow and learn.

How Do We Make Our Communities Healthy for Kids?

"For all of us concerned with the well being of children, the important question obviously becomes what types of steps foster cohesive, safe, reflective communities in comparison to unsafe, polarized, fragmented, and/or suspicious ones" (Brazelton & Greenspan, 2000, p. 163). Identifying and implementing community approaches for child welfare and safety are essential. This was discussed in a monograph by one of the authors of this chapter: "While there are things we can and need to do individually with children, our goals for our children also need to be set on the broader community level. We need to make our communities a safe place for all children. The interventions we carry out need to address both sides of the coin—promoting healthy communities and healthy children. We must work individually with the child and collectively with the community.

"A first step in this task of uniting children and community in a positive way requires that we find out how children view their community. A colleague of mine had seventh-grade children write something about themselves and include a few sentences on what they thought about their neighborhood. Here are a few of their responses in regards to their neighborhood: 'My neighborhood is not violent. And they don't do drugs.' 'My neighborhood is peaceful and no one kills each other and no drug dealers.' 'My neighbors are all old and mean. Whenever I go and play outside, they come out and start yelling at me. But I don't listen and keep on playing. My town sucks, it is all poor.' 'I don't know about my neighborhood. I usually go bike riding.' 'In my neighborhood, there are a lot of guys that drink and do drugs. Some live next door to me and they are always outside smoking.' Even those children who indicate that they live in a nice neighborhood do so in the context of there not being violence or drug use there. Other children report an unfriendly environment and many others talk of dangerous situations in their neighborhood. Very few children describe their neighborhood as a child-friendly place where adults and programs are available to them.

"Children need places that are 'Child friendly.' Places which allow them to rub shoulders with positive adult role models. Even those children we call 'bad kids' would join in these places of pro-social behavior if that is where their peers are. We need to be involved in our communities so that they become child-friendly with programs that youth have access to and input into. Many of our communities do have effective programs in which we work together to keep dangerous persons out and, in many cases, we have reduced crime. What is called for now is communities to work together to keep children in productive programs and prevent crime. Communities with programs that allow for active involvement for children of all ages, interacting with each other and adults, can bring our fragmented society into a united neighborhood. Studies that address substance abuse and youth violence reveal that community collaboration with the child and their family is the more effective intervention. Communities that develop tutoring or mentoring programs provide positive places for children to be. There are many venues or groups in our communities which can work together to effect these positive experiences for our youth.

"Many youth are isolated from caring and consistent adult relationships. In many communities, older adults are, in particular, an untapped resource for mentoring our children. Older adults are the fastest-growing segment of the population, and many seek opportunities for continued productive activity and meaningful human contact. Intergenerational experiences are very important for all involved. As older adults we can benefit from companionship and the ability to pass on our experiences. The child in relationship with an older adult has the opportunity to feel supported, connected, and be provided with a 'future' orientation. Older adults have the ability to make a significant difference and they need to be involved in 'Saving Our Children.' Youth will—and do—respond to the older adult and, in turn, many older adults are willing to be available to the youth.

"Thus, we need to ensure that communities are set up to facilitate intergenerational experiences by providing places, transportation, and programs in which these relationships can occur.

"We need to work alongside our educational systems. Children spend a majority of their time in the school system, and we need to become involved in supporting current programs and using our skills and experiences to assist in developing new ones. In many of our secondary education systems, teens float from class to class without a 'home' room of peers and an adult to connect to, thus making teens feel more alone and alienated, a significant problem which can also make it more difficult for anyone to notice potential risk factors. Having a teacher or community volunteer to assist with an opening and closing class each day would allow for our teens to feel more connected to us and to each other.

"Another area of great concern is that of literacy. Each of us can assist the educational system in promoting and educating to increase the literacy levels of our children. Statistics reveal that children with lower literacy are at higher risk for delinquency.

"We need to become involved and help develop creative ways in which children can feel connected in school which, in turn, connects them to their community.

"Our involvement could help to make current after-school programs accessible and affordable to a larger number of children. Volunteering to be involved in these programs or learning from educators how to develop programs for youth in the community could make a large difference for many children. In a poll by *Newsweek* (May 10/99) 56 percent of Americans polled reported that teens do not have enough places to go to help them stay out of trouble. Statistics have shown that the highest crime perpetrated by youth occurs in the late afternoon and early evening.

"The time period after school and before any adults are home to monitor children is a crucial time for our so-called 'latchkey' children. We need to find ways to eliminate these times where children are left alone and have no adult connections. The business and educational communities need to communicate with each other

Many Voices: An Introduction to Social Issues

for the sake of our children. Perhaps time schedules need to be altered so that they are more compatible or youth need to be incorporated into programs in the business community.

"The athletic community must also be encouraged to provide activities to meet the physical needs of our youth. Athletic centers, parks, and health clubs can all be resources that fill an important need for children. Programs like YMCA and YWCA need to be encouraged and supported by the community. We need to be involved in programs where children interact with adults around physical activity, such as those centers that have become available to youth for basketball games, etc. Physical exercise through team sports and individual workouts would do a lot to promote a healthier child, mentally and physically; however, our involvement is necessary to make this possible.

"Further, our religious communities need to be urged to promote positive activities for youth. Church community members can play a critical role in planning, recruiting, implementing, and evaluating youth programs. Churches are ideal social systems from which to launch prevention efforts for our youth. The church community has a unique ability to develop creative programs to meet a variety of youth needs, as it has within in it a diverse group of professionals and laypersons, at all age levels. As reported by Dr. Garbarino in his book *Lost Boys,* research has shown that children who are raised in non-punitive religious communities are buffered from social toxins. More church communities need to follow those that have set up mentoring programs, substance abuse programs, youth activity programs, etc. A spiritual community that can provide place, activity, purpose, and adult connection can go a long way in promoting healthy child development.

"We must look at our communities to see if they are child-friendly, to address how our kids are responding to existing programs, and to work on ways to get more people involved. We need to have communities that are places of viable social relationships rather than geographical boundaries. The goals of community-based programs for our children are to provide healthy adult relationships for children, to make the community a place of positive child activity and, when necessary, to assist in linking children and their families to professional services. Our communities can be healthier places for our children because of us!" (Freier, 1999b, pp. 12–16).

Conclusion

Society shapes our children and their future. Thus it is the responsibility of each of us individually to make a difference collectively. Educating ourselves on current social policy that affects youth, finding out what is available in our communities, being a part of community youth groups, or helping to develop new ones can make a significant impact on young people. Since by working with the individual we can have an effect on the group, we must take the step to connect with young people and have them teach us what they need and how we can make a positive difference in their lives.

Response

Connecting

by Robin Butler

The need for physical and emotional connection with a significant other has been well established. While severely deprived infants may die, severely deprived older children and adolescents may become disconnected from their parents and society. We have witnessed the outcome of this disconnection in accounts from the Columbine and Middleton school shootings. These incidents did not happen overnight and might have been prevented if intervention with the offenders (often originally the offended) had occurred early in the downward cycle.

In western culture we have made theoretical and philosophical advances in terms of how we view the needs of children. However, the question still arises: *In practice, how far have we come in meeting the actual needs of children?* This question refers not only to the children in the lower economic strata who have obvious basic physical issues, but also to "day-care orphans," middle and upper-class "latch key kids," children in boarding/military/specialty schools that serve to indoctrinate, and children in regular educational institutions that have been given the job of raising today's youth. Many of these youth have more than enough in terms of economic privilege. Ironically, and perhaps as a natural consequence of the material excesses, these children suffer a severe poverty of human connection and thus of the "soul."

But just how does one achieve connectedness and the resulting benefits?

- Can a child call an 800 number and get human connectedness?
- Will going to the mall attach children to their society?
- Which teen idol promises to bond with them?
- Which drug will make them believe they are fixed?
- Which investment portfolio does one put faith in to ensure safety in today's unpredictable world?

Religion can be described as a powerful mechanism for socialization and our spiritual nature, which is considered to be a fundamental component, if not the essence, of what makes us unique as human beings. This has been what most religions have attempted to satisfy. The literature defines a healthy spirituality as one in which the individual has a sense of purpose, meaning, hope, and a connectedness to a higher power and to one's fellow humans. The personal connectedness that can result from religion is thought to be one of its beneficial effects.

Myriad studies have confirmed the efficacy of spiritual interventions to heal biopsychosocial illnesses. Parents and other significant caregivers have the potential to be powerful mentors in facilitating the crucial exploration and development of that spiritual core so necessary for connecting and finding hope, meaning, and purpose in the lives of our youth. The most effective method for accomplishing this is through role modeling. Unfortunately, this cannot be done by those who are spiritually bereft themselves or, in other words, trying to give from an empty cup. Spiritual growth is a lifelong process, and as with mental health we all move back and forth upon a continuum, ideally progressing towards health. But as this is a dynamic process, our focus on our own spiritual growth and development is as important as promoting that of our children, especially as they tend to emulate behavior far more often than they follow verbal instruction.

Unfortunately, our current culture creates substantial challenges to meeting this goal. In our extremely competitive world of fast food, fast cars, and even faster computers, can we make *meaningful* connections? Can relationships with their complexities, inherent risks, and required time investments compete with the transitory "quick-fix" alternatives that are currently used to satisfy our spiritual hunger?

Our children today are very aware of their existential plight. Gone is the innocence of childhood. Realism in the various media has provided our youth an early awakening to the knowledge of good and evil. The significant increase in teenage suicide and, even in small children, the prevalence of ADD, ADHD, depression, anxiety, and other conduct disorders herald the "Future Shock" that Alvin Toffler (1971) referred to in the second half of the 20th century. He predicted that, as our culture moved into the information age and technology advanced, we would continue to escalate our pace until we reached a point where the human organism could no longer adapt. He went on to describe some of the sequelae that we are witnessing today. Included were a global sense of disorientation and stress, which would eventually lead to an incapacity in individuals and institutions to make wise adaptive decisions. Toffler predicted the breakdown and fragmentation of the nuclear family, as we have witnessed, and Toffler has since reconfirmed in his later publications "Third Wave" (1981) and "Powershift" (1990).

While working with suicidal youth, I have noted their perception that very few adults in their lives seem to be aware of, or care about, the void they experience. This contributes to their sense of rage, ultimate hopelessness, helplessness, and eventually their sometimes final attempt to be heard and understood…or to be connected with. The nihilism that today's youth are embracing could be considered what well-known psychiatrist R. D. Laing would call a "sane reaction to an insane world." Another validation of this concept comes from James Gabarino (1999) who shares his insight in his book, *Lost Boys*, after working extensively with forensic boys. He purports

that the spiritual void experienced by today's youth, especially boys, is a primary factor in the increase in psychopathology and the resulting sociopathology.

When a void exists, it demands to be filled, and like a black hole it will consume the less than cautious seeker of meaning. A preamble to suicide may be to seek out this connectedness with those youth and/or adult(s) who share one's own sense of nihilistic outrage. Such sources may be some of the popular cultic groups, dark/shock rock music, and literature in which existential angst, rage, and various other antisocial themes and behaviors are almost celebrated. When parents were outraged by Marilyn Manson's music and lyrics, he noted that if teenagers had their parents, they wouldn't need what he had to offer. Sadly, there is a great measure of validity in that statement.

The more bizarre and intensely stimulating "entertainment" varieties provide both a sense of connectedness and an adrenaline-like rush with a temporary "high" similar to that produced by amphetamines. Without this rush, the teenager's mood plummets. Youth have in confidence reported being "addicted" to some of the most deviant and violent music and literature out there, "because it makes me feel alive for awhile."

This "fix" provides a short-lived escape from lives of desperation but can also activate internal rage and result in violent behaviors directed at others. The prevalence of a variety of mood altering, addictive, and easy-to-procure drugs contributes to the downward spiral. The current interest in vampires, witches, and other gothic/occult themes is an

excellent metaphor for the internal state of affairs for many of our youth (e.g., the living death).

Even the phenomenally popular and ostensibly benign Harry Potter series revolves around the plight of a pre-adolescent child abused by parental figures who seeks out special powers to cope with his situation by joining a school for witches to develop his inherent supernatural powers. Is this the appropriate ideology to instill into the mind of a child who is seeking identity, meaning, and purpose as a part of his or her normal psychosocial development stage? Are we oblivious or blissfully ignorant because we need another quick fix? Is the answer teaching our children that their salvation is in how to cast spells, brew concoctions, and try other sundry witchcraft techniques to cope with, or perhaps to control and/or seek vengeance upon, those they perceive as a threat? Some parents are so disconnected from their children that they applaud the series because it gets their kids to read. I suppose graphic pornographic material would also enhance and motivate reading in adolescent children. The adrenaline rush would produce the stimulation that would most likely enhance their reading experience, but what is the potential harm to relationships that will be a result of this kind of indoctrination to the most potentially intimate of all experiences? How long will it be until we are so busy and/or desensitized to this reality that we welcome that solution to our children's resistance to reading? Will it be just another "quick fix" to our increasingly complex problem?

Even positive activities can be perceived by youth in a negative manner. One young man told me that his parents enrolled him in a variety of extracurricular activities so that they wouldn't have to spend time with him. Regardless of the truth of that claim, the fact that he perceives it as such is an important issue for his family to explore. What do you suppose the parental response would be to a comment like that if the child had the audacity to actually confront the parent?

Children are a wise investment choice. These actual and potentially disenfranchised youth are the adults who will be making decisions in all of our futures. When we've all reached a point where we need assistance, guidance, and care, having become more and more vulnerable and having lost a lot of control over our immediate environment, will our children be there or even be interested in "connecting" with us, or would euthanasia be a quicker fix? The question is not fear of euthanasia, but whether a connection between children and parents would create a better society, one with less disconnection and loss of emotional ability to connect.

What can we do? CONNECT. Make and take every opportunity to connect with kids, formally or informally. Start with your own children and reach out. If you don't have children, volunteer to mentor a needy child in some way. The opportunities are endless and the need is incredible. Even brief transitory interactions can have a powerful effect if the child felt authentically connected with and cared for. Youth can spot insincerity, so going through the motions to assuage guilt won't count and may do more harm than good. Youth who are severely depressed will often relate that the one thing keeping them hanging in there instead of hanging themselves is a certain person who connected with them enough to give them a thread of hope for a better future. Be that person. It starts with one...it starts with you.

Discussion Questions

1. What are some of the unique sociological issues involving children?
2. How has the historical view of children impacted social policy?
3. Who is responsible for child advocacy?
4. What are some important sociological influences on infancy?
5. How is attachment related to sociological issues of infants, children, and adolescents?
6. How important is parenting, especially to a motivated child who is succeeding in school and with a peer group?
7. At what point do negative influences begin affecting an adolescent?
8. What factors in an adolescent's life qualify him or her to be considered at risk?
9. What factors help make an adolescent or child resilient?
10. What should society do to help children and adolescents become successful adults?

Related Readings

Garbarino, J. (1999). *Lost boys: Why our sons turn violent and how we can save them.* New York: Free Press.
June-Cerza, K. (1990). *Teenagers talk about grief.* Grand Rapids, MI: Baker Book House.
Westman, J. C. (1991). *Who speaks for the children? The handbook of individual and class child advocacy.* Sarasota, FL: Professional Resource Exchange, Inc.

Related Web Sites

Assets: The Magazine of Ideas for Healthy Communities and Healthy Youth: http://www.search-institute.org/assets/index.htm
Children, Youth & Family Consortium (CYFC): http://www.cyfc.umn.edu

Connect for Kids: http://www.connectforkids.org
Creative Partnerships for Prevention: http://www.cpprev.org/contents.htm
Division of Childhood and Adolescence (Canada): http://www.phac-aspc.gc.ca/dca-dea/main_e.html
Early Warning Timely Response: A Guide to Safe Schools—Department of Education: http://www.ed.gov/offices/OSERS/OSEP/earlywrn.html
Human Services Policy: Children and Youth: http://www.aspe.hhs.gov/hsp/hspyoung.htm
KidsSource online (part of NICHCY): http://www.kidsource.com/NICHCY
The National Information Center for Children and Youth with Disabilities (NICHCY): http://www.nichcy.org
National Network for Family Resiliency: Building family strengths to meet life's challenges: http://www.nnfr.org
National School Safety Center: http://www.schoolsafety.us
Office of Juvenile Justice and Delinquency Prevention: http://ojjdp.ncjrs.org
Resilience in Action: http://www.resiliency.com
U.S. Department of Health and Human Services, The Administration for Children and Families, Research & Publications: http://www.acf.dhhs.gov/research.html

---

Related Movies/Videos

About a Boy (2002) with Hugh Grant
Finding Forrester (2000) with Sean Connery and Rob Brown
Good Will Hunting (1997) with Robin Williams and Matt Damon
Simon Birch (1998) with Ian Michael Smith and Joseph Mazzello
This Boy's Life (1993) with Robert De Niro and Ellen Barkin
What's Eating Gilbert Grape (1993) with Johnny Depp and Leonardo DiCaprio

FEMINISM

René Drumm

Suffrage parade, New York City, May 6, 1912.
Library of Congress, Prints and Photographs Division, LC-USZC4-5585 DLC

Chapter Outline

- Introduction
- Women and Economics
- Women and Education
- Women and Family Life
- Reproductive Rights

- Sexual Issues
- Women and Spirituality
- Conclusion

Is feminism still a social issue in the United States today? Hasn't the fight for equal rights for women been won? Would not this chapter on feminism be better off in a history book than in a book dealing with contemporary social issues? Before you draw any hasty conclusions, take the quiz below.

True or False:

- *The proportion of earned income that females enjoy is about equal to that of men, largely because of laws demanding equal pay for equal work.*
- *Men and women are represented in fairly equal proportions among the poor in the U.S.*
- *The worth of household labor and childcare has skyrocketed in the last decade, bringing new respect and value to this aspect of traditional women's roles.*
- *The more children women have, the lower their earnings will probably be; however, the opposite is true for men.*
- *In terms of high educational attainment, women in the U.S. do better than those in all other nations.*
- *Women in the U.S. experience a disproportionate amount of sexual violence compared to U.S. men and to women in other countries.*
- *Most feminists in the U.S. would prefer to do away with men and eliminate the problem of inequality altogether.*
- *With the rise and recognition of Hillary Clinton, the political power of women in the U.S. has become known throughout the world as exemplary.*
- *Women of all races and social classes generally agree on the important issues to tackle in promoting women's rights in the U.S.*
- *Where inequities still exist, women could overcome them easily if they would simply organize themselves as women did in the 1800s to win the right to vote.*

There are three true answers. Which ones? Continue reading to find out.

Introduction

What is **feminism**? There are so many definitions that it would probably take a whole chapter simply to quote them. A few are offered here for you to think about as we begin exploring the ways feminism has impacted society.

- "The most basic definition of *feminism* is the conviction that women really do inhabit the human realm and are not 'other,' not a separate species" (Gross, 1996, p. 16).
- Feminism involves "certain ways of thinking and of acting that are designed to achieve women's liberation by eliminating the oppression of women in society" (Freeman, 1990, p. 72).
- "Feminism is a route by which all women and men, men and women can live with more courage and a fuller consciousness to face their own strengths and weaknesses, with more courage and a fuller opportunity for growth and participation in society, and with more courage to develop a fuller sense of personal freedom" (Brookner, 1991, p. 12).
- "For me, feminism is not a movement of women against men. It's a way of thinking that allows all of us to examine the harmful role sexism plays in our personal lives and public world and to figure out what we can do to change this. It's a movement that creates space for the spirit and for being a whole person" (bell hooks as quoted in Jones, 1995, p. 188).

Of these definitions, which ones make the most sense? Which ones do you identify with? Are there some definitions that invite you to say, "If that is true,

I'm a feminist"? Are there others that invite you to say, "I'm not a feminist!"? Could some of the definitions include men as feminists?

As you read this chapter, think about how these ideas fit with your own developing definition of feminism. In addition, try to identify how the definitions reflect typical concerns of women that distinguish feminism as a contemporary social issue.

Feminism Today

Feminists today, as in times past, have both agreed and vehemently disagreed about issues that touch women's lives. Elizabeth Cady Stanton and Susan B. Anthony led the National Woman Suffrage Association, while two other women, Lucy Stone and Julia Ward Howe, headed the more conservative American Woman Suffrage Association. Although both organizations formed in 1869, they did not unite for about 20 years because of differences. As in those of early groups, different philosophies exist among feminists today.

Historical Perspectives

Historically, feminism is talked about in terms of "waves" or movements. Various types of feminism have been noted throughout the history of the movement. The first feminist movement centered on voting rights for women. People who were in favor of women voting were known as suffragists. The women's suffrage movement was closely tied to the anti-slavery or abolitionist movement. In 1837, the first national Anti-Slavery Convention of American Women met in New York City. This was the first national assemblage of women for the purpose of collective action without the help or administration of men (Blankenship, 1990). Several years later, in 1848, the first woman's rights convention was held in Seneca Falls, New York. This meeting, attended by over 100 people (men weren't invited, but attended anyway), is often remembered as initiating the women's rights movement (Cullen-DuPont, 1996). As it turned out, winning the right to vote was not easy. Several years after the Seneca Falls Convention, women got tired of waiting for the laws to be changed and some took matters into their own hands. In 1872, in one of the most famous cases of civil disobedience, Susan B. Anthony attempted to vote in Rochester, New York. As a result, she was fined $100 (which she refused to pay) and was tried and convicted of voting illegally

(Blankenship, 1990). Almost 15 years after Susan B. Anthony's death, the 72-year struggle for women's right to vote ended when Congress in 1920 passed the nineteenth amendment to the Constitution.

Following the passage of the nineteenth amendment, women were hopeful that all of the rights and privileges afforded to men would naturally follow the right to vote. Because of this expectation, many groups that worked so hard for women's rights disbanded (Simon & Danziger, 1991). It was not until the 1960s, in conjunction with the civil rights movement, that feminist issues again surfaced. The injustices suffered by racial minorities angered women and drove them to become involved in activism. Anger at social injustice continues to be a motivating emotion that leads women to action today (Hercus, 1999).

Social action in the mid-twentieth century was spurred on, in part, by the actions of one woman in Montgomery, Alabama. In 1955, Rosa Parks, a black woman, refused to give up her seat and move to the back of the bus. She was arrested. This one brave act is often credited with touching off the bus boycott the following year that was directed by Martin Luther King (Simon & Danziger, 1991).

Fighting for civil rights such as sexual and racial equality and raising awareness of economic and political injustices became the focal point of this second wave of feminism, best known as the **Women's Liberation Movement**. In 1966, Betty Friedan organized the National Organization for Women (NOW), which was to become America's best-known women's rights organization (Cullen-DuPont, 1996). In the 25 years that followed, NOW was active in legal activism that challenged many types of sex and employment discrimination. NOW also endorsed the Equal Rights Amendment (ERA). The ERA proposed that men and women should have equal rights and that those rights should be constitutionally protected. Although Congress passed the ERA in 1972, thirty-eight states were required to ratify the amendment. In 1982, time ran out for the amendment to be ratified; it was still three states short of approval (Cullen-DuPont, 1996).

The third wave of feminists are primarily under age 30 and are characterized by their break with the past. The "third wavers," as they are called, differ from the previous generation in that they view individual rights and differences as paramount. This contrasts with second wave feminists, who stressed sisterly unity. In addition,

Many Voices: An Introduction to Social Issues

third wave feminists have not shown as much interest in the economic and political injustices that were so important to second wave feminists (Bulbeck, 1999).

Researchers are examining third wavers' views by conducting studies with college females. Studies show that while most college women identify with some of the goals of feminism, their views of feminism vary greatly. At one extreme, some women view feminism as negative, filled with man-hating, masculine-type fanatics. On the other hand, some college women see feminists positively working to fulfill their own goals. Most college women find their place in feminism somewhere between these two extremes (Alexander & Ryan, 1997), often within the context of causes. Women have made a great deal of progress in such things as combating domestic violence and promoting equal job opportunities. And while women will fight for feminist causes, some do not want to identify with feminism itself (Brookner, 1991).

Types of Feminism

Feminist authors discuss liberal feminism, socialist feminism, radical feminism, psychoanalytical feminism, lesbian feminism, revolutionary feminism, black feminism, and cyberfeminism (Lown, 1995; Luckman, 1999). Each type of feminism has its own philosophy, strategies, tactics, and political agenda.

The three predominant feminist theoretical perspectives continue to be liberal, socialist, and radical feminism (Freeman, 1990). Working for reform, **liberal feminists** seek social and legal changes that support equal opportunities for women. They believe that society must change its patterns of sex-role socialization, which will enable more egalitarian gender relationships. **Socialist feminists** see social class differences (caused by the capitalist system) as the basis of gender discrimination. Those in power (i.e., men) exploit women in order to maintain their positions. Socialist feminists promote revolutionary approaches to change, such as abolishing the capitalist and patriarchal systems.

Radical feminists focus on sexual and fertility issues at the heart of feminism. It is primarily through sexual and procreative relations at home that women experience male dominance. Radical feminists would like to develop a culture for women that is separate from men through revolutionary means (Freeman, 1990).

Cultural Issues in Feminism

Feminism has been criticized as a movement predominantly of and for middle- and upper-class white women. Among African American women, studies show that, in general, racial issues outweigh issues of gender inequality. While African American women support feminist ideology, they have concerns about focusing on gender issues (Hunter & Sellers, 1998). According to one writer, feminism is "still an F word to many Black woman" (Jones, 1995, p. 187). An award-winning African American feminist writer, bell hooks, noted: "Many Black women whom I talk to opt not to use the term [feminism] solely because they feel Black men won't approve of it—or because they don't want to be associated with anything that reads as an affirmation of White women.…It isn't as important that people claim the term feminism at an initial stage. What is important is that Black women begin to claim a critique of sexism. Male domination in any form—be it discrimination on the job or abuse at home—hurts. Sexism hurts" (Jones, 1995, p. 187).

Culture plays an equally important role in forming attitudes toward feminism among Mexican American females. Studies indicate that mothers of Chicana high school students promoted traditional male/female roles but also shared a feminist ideal with their daughters regarding their futures. For example, mothers spoke of self-reliance, family planning, the importance of higher education, and maintaining personal independence. As these young women developed their own sense of womanhood and its relationship to feminism, their cultural traditions remained an important part of its evolution (Marsiglia & Holleran, 1999).

Women and Economics

ISSUES: Why is economics an issue for women any more than for men? Aren't employers required by law to offer equal pay for equal work? How could job discrimination exist when the law works the same for everyone? If women want to get ahead, shouldn't they just enter a field proven to earn more money?

Equal Pay for Equal Work?

Since 1963, when the Equal Pay Act became law, employers and employees in the U.S. have been struggling with the question, "What does equal pay for equal work really mean?" In its most restrictive sense, it means that if McDonald's has an opening for a french-fry fryer, McDonald's is required by law to pay the fryer the same wage whether a male or female is hired for the position. This sounds good; the issue, however, is much more complex. What happens when the jobs are not identical? In 1981, the Supreme Court, using Title VII of the Civil Rights Act of 1964, prohibited wage discrimination even when the jobs were similar, but not exactly the same. This also sounds good and should take care of the problem of pay inequity. So, how do we know that the law isn't working as well as intended?

The Wage Gap

Overall, women earn only 72% of men's earnings annually. This figure comes from U.S. Census Bureau statistics and was arrived at by dividing the annual income for women by the median annual earnings for men. The median income in 1999 for male full-time employees was $36,476, compared with $26,324 for women. This means that for every one dollar that a man earned, a woman only earned 72 cents. The gap widens when race is introduced as a factor.

Table 17.1 lists median annual earnings of year-round, full-time workers in 2001. The figures in the table indicate that people of color and white women all earn less than white men when working fulltime. The large differences in annual earnings indicate that Hispanic and black women are subject to double discrimination based on gender and race. These data point to the need to address not only gender issues, but issues of racism as well.

Table 17.1: 2001 Median Annual Earnings of Year-Round, Full-Time Workers

	Men	Women
White	$40,118	$30,134
Black	$31,463	$26,654
Hispanic	$25,000	$21,525

Source: U.S. Census Bureau Annual Demographic Survey, Table PINC-10

While the U.S. is still grappling with gender and racial pay equity, the trends are not all bleak. In fact, over the past few decades, the wage gap has narrowed (Blau, 1998). In 1970, women could expect to make only 59 cents for every dollar that men earned, whereas today that percentage is much higher. In addition to narrowing the wage gap, there are other indicators that women are making progress economically. For example, more women are working than ever before. Female participation in the labor force increased 23 percentage points over the past 25 years (Blau, 1998). More women in the work force create more opportunities for women to advance economically.

Men's Work/Women's Work

Women are also making headway in the types of jobs for which they are hired. Traditionally, opportunities for men and women have been segregated into "jobs for men" and "jobs for women," which places them in different and unequal jobs. The problem here is that employers value men's work more highly than women's work, which is reflected in higher wages for men. These artificial differences do not make sense when examined logically. For example, a neighbor has a lawn to mow and a two-year-old to care for. The neighbor hires 13-year-old twins, a boy and a girl who live next door, to do these tasks. As

Many Voices: An Introduction to Social Issues

we would expect, the boy tackles the lawn-mowing job. The neighbor has a new ride-on mower and the boy is happy to try it out. The girl takes the baby-sitting job. In your mind's eye, imagine the afternoon activities of each adolescent. Try to put yourself in each twin's place. At the end of the afternoon, the neighbor returns and the twins get paid. Table 17.2 shows a possible employment summary for the two jobs.

It's obvious that the necessary responsibility level and skills are far greater for the babysitter. In fact, if the babysitter does not do her job well, an ultimate consequence could be the death of the child. The skills involved in taking care of a child far exceed the skills needed to mow a lawn, yet lawn mowing remains a service that has higher compensation rates than babysitting. In addition, the pay differences are tremendous—$20.00/hour vs. $3.00/hour. This difference is primarily due to society's designation and valuation of "women's work."

Comparable Worth

When whole classes of jobs are undervalued because society views them as "women's work," it distorts fair compensation. Comparable worth means that people should be compensated similarly when performing jobs with equivalent skills, responsibility, work conditions, and effort (Simon & Danziger, 1991).

Researchers point to job segregation as the primary reason the pay gap continues (Reskin & Padavic,

1994). This is why the concept of comparable worth is so important. When employers are required to examine issues of skills, responsibility, and effort instead of who is performing the work, there will be more chances for women to be compensated fairly in the workplace.

In spite of reluctance from employers to move toward comparable worth compensation, women are making headway. The trend today suggests that the job segregation problem is lessening. More women are entering traditionally male occupations with the result appearing to be greater economic opportunities for women (Blau, 1998). While this method of reaching for greater pay is helpful, it does not address the need for women in traditional female occupations to be fairly compensated.

Women and Poverty

While some women enjoy greater economic opportunities by moving out of traditionally female occupations, a great number of women live in poverty. Women in the U.S. today are at a higher risk than men of being in poverty. In fact, women and children in single-parent families account for the greatest number of poor people in the U.S. (Miller, 1994, p. 44). When racial factors are considered, the risk becomes even greater. "[B]lack and Hispanic single mothers suffer poverty rates 50 percent greater than those of their white counterparts" (Tobias, 1997, p. 229).

Table 17.2: Employment Summary for Male/Female Summer Jobs

Job	Total Pay	Time Invested	Skills Needed	Consequences if Not Done Properly
Mowing Lawn	$10.00	½ hour	• Sit on lawnmower • Turn on mower • Drive mower in straight lines on grass	• The neighbors might say, "Their lawn looks awful!"
Babysitting	$9.00	3 hours	• Food preparation • Distraction techniques • Ability to re-direct negative behavior • First aid training • Ability to give comfort • Ability to entertain person with a 15-minute attention span • Diaper changing	• The child could go hungry • The crystal lamp might break • Temper tantrums may erupt • The child might bleed to death • The child might cry all afternoon • The child might become bored and take every toy out of the toy box • Severe diaper rash

Women and Education

ISSUES: In your experience, have male and female students been treated differently in the classroom? How might culture impact women in the educational system? If more and more women enter higher education, how might that impact the educational system?

The apparent educational equality most Americans enjoy today has not always existed. In 1841, Oberlin College graduated its first woman from a "literary" course, one that was not as "difficult" as the courses of study offered to men. The female students had to perform all of the domestic chores for the male students: washing their clothes, cleaning their rooms, and serving meals. In addition, women could not recite in public or work in fields with male students. From 1925 to 1945, medical schools adopted a quota allowing only 5% of the admissions to be female. Many colleges, including Columbia and Harvard Law School, would not even consider female candidates (Blankenship, 1990).

College students scanning the classroom horizon would probably not notice many differences today between the male and female student's quality of education. Both genders are free to sit in the front or back sections of the classroom. Both males and females ask questions and answer questions posed by the professor. Typically, some students are prepared for class and others not. So, if there are no visible differences, how is education an issue of concern for women today?

In many ways, females fare quite well in terms of educational attainment in the U.S. For example, males and females attend high school in nearly equal proportions. In college, women surpass men's participation, making the U.S. one of the best places on earth for women's higher educational opportunities (Nussbaum, 1999).

On the other hand, researchers have some pointed criticism of the educational system's service delivery when it comes to educating female and male students. Research supports the fact that girls and boys have very different educational experiences. How can this be when they are taught together? Doesn't our instructional system ensure that girls and boys are getting the same education?

Consider the following research findings: Science teachers graded work lower when they thought a girl had produced it (Spear, 1984). In terms of everyday teacher interaction in class, males are given more attention than females by being questioned, cued, or prompted (Byrne, 1993; Einarsson & Granstrom, 2002); school counselors are more likely to advise girls than boys to avoid taking math and science (Marini & Brinton, 1984). Science teachers elaborate more on male responses in large-group discussions of scientific concepts compared to female responses (Jones & Wheatley, 1990; She, 2001) and appear to take a student's argument on a position more seriously when a male poses the argument (Lemke, 1990).

Culture also plays a role. For example, Native Americans value learning through oral traditions and histories preserved primarily by women. This type of traditional learning has the effect of empowering females. In most U.S. schools, however, such learning experiences are not valued, reducing the power of Native American women (Almeida, 1997).

In addition to gender discrimination and cultural insensitivity in the classroom, feminists are concerned about the structure of the educational system itself. For example, although women account for between 75% and 83% of the teachers in elementary settings, they hold only 3% to 7% of the jobs as district superintendents (Glass, 1992; National Center for Education Statistics, 2004). Among university professors, females were more likely to report being addressed as "Ms." or "Mrs." rather than "Dr.," as compared to male professors (Kelly & Stanley, 1999). This finding may indicate a status difference, from the students' perspective, between male and female professors.

What if more women had greater status and held more leadership positions in the educational system? After an extensive review of the literature on feminist leadership in the educational system, one writer concludes: "Above all, a repeated theme in almost all of this literature is that many women are relational leaders, that is, leaders who strive to get to know students, teachers, and other members of the school community. Based on having good knowledge of others, relational leaders see themselves in relationships that are facilitative of others' efforts rather than in control" (Grogan, 1999, p. 521).

Regardless of the gender difficulties within the educational system, education itself is good for women. In fact, one of the biggest problems concerning women and education occurs when women do not stay in school.

Research points to a sharp decline in women's status among less educated women and particularly among high school dropouts (Blau, 1998). Women's future earning potentials depend, in large part, on education in a field that will keep them out of poverty.

Economics is not the only reason that education is especially important for women. Research indicates that education plays a protective role in relation to domestic violence. In terms of victimization, high school dropouts experience higher rates of violence across education categories. Among female college graduates, this trend is reversed, establishing a considerably lower rate of violence (Blau, 1998).

Women and Family Life

ISSUES: How much do you believe the saying, "A woman's place is in the home"? Should women be expected to take on the role of primary caregivers of children? What are some of the difficulties women face as they enter the workforce? Who is responsible for stopping domestic violence? What is it that makes women's reproductive rights so controversial in our society today?

Balancing Work and Family

Research reveals that female-based poverty comes about largely because of the challenges of combining family duties with work responsibilities (Blau, 1998; Tobias, 1997). "[T]he fact that women still are expected to perform most unpaid housework and child care constrains women's access to employment and their productivity within it" (Nussbaum, 1999, p. 135). Child care and household tasks continue to be seen as primarily women's obligations (Reskin & Padavic, 1994). Women do far more household work than men and experience that difference as unfair (Pittman & Teng, 1999; Sanchez & Kane, 1996; Tingey, 1996). This perception of unfairness is found across racial lines (John & Shelton, 1995). While researchers indicated that the trend toward unequal housework had been changing, at least one study casts doubt on that change (Press & Townsley, 1998). Some scholars imply that women prefer to engage in household work and that if researchers would stop interpreting household duties as drudgery, there would be no problem (Ahlander & Bahr, 1995).

Unfortunately, there is no research evidence to support this claim (Riley & Kiger, 1999). In fact, quite the opposite is true (Baker, Kiger, & Riley, 1996). In studying women's attitudes over the past 25 years, researchers note that women are consistently unsatisfied with doing the majority of the housework (Robinson & Milkie, 1998).

Just how unsatisfied women are with doing household tasks may be determined by the types of tasks. Research indicates that the type of household job predicts how distressing it may be to perform (Barnett & Shen, 1997). For example, people reported as distressing jobs that have to be done at a certain time, such as planning and preparing meals, buying groceries, and doing laundry. Jobs that could be done with fewer time pressures were not as stressful, such as car repair, taking out the garbage, and caring for plants and the yard. It appears that the daily demanding and repetitive household chores are most often the source of difficulties for women (Sanchez & Kane, 1996).

In addition to housework, women are also primarily responsible for most of the management tasks, such as organizing and planning for family events and providing childcare (Mederer, 1993; Walzer, 1996). It is interesting to note, however, that women do fewer of all of these types of tasks in a second marriage (Sullivan, 1997). It appears that women gain experience in negotiating housework from a previous marriage or cohabiting relationship that they use to reduce their own housework participation.

As more women entered the workforce, they also continued to bear the responsibilities of traditional female roles, creating two full-time jobs instead of one. This phenomenon became known as the "**double day**" or the "second shift" (Hochschild & Machung, 1989). Employers have been reluctant to hire and/or promote women because of their divided loyalties, causing further declines in employment opportunities (Reskin & Padavic, 1994). In fact, research shows that women's earnings are directly influenced by the number of children they have (Korenman & Newmark, 1992). As the number of children in a family increases, the amount of women's earnings generally decreases. For men, the opposite is true (Blau, 1998). One possible explanation for this disparity could be differences in how men and women perform status enhancement work. Status enhancement involves one person in a relationship helping the other with job advancement. Typically, women will more often engage in status enhancement work than men (Pavalko & Elder, 1993). For example, when a man offers to host a birthday dinner for the boss, it is often his wife's duty to manage and prepare for the event. In this way, the man gets credit at work for what his wife does at home and his standing in the company is enhanced.

Because of their strong sense of obligation to home duties, women are seen as less productive in the workplace. When women appear less involved in the company because they have children, they are less likely to be promoted. These women are seen as being on the "mommy track," an invisible barrier to advancement because of family commitments.

Unfortunately, researchers hold out little hope for this dynamic to change rapidly. In research conducted among college women about combining career and family life, the author noted pessimistic attitudes for positive adjustment in uniting marriage and work. These students believed that women are rarely able to successfully combine career and family (Goldin, 1990). In another study, the researcher looked at how college students anticipated work-family conflict. This research suggests that females anticipate more work-family conflicts than do males (Livingston et al., 1996).

The U.S. government has not been active in trying to alleviate these stresses for women. Many countries compensate women (and men) for the roles they play in child rearing through paid family leave and other programs. "The United States is the only Western industrialized country that does not have a system of Children's Allowances, payments to families to help defray the cost of child rearing" (Miller, 1994, p. 51). This lack of governmental support for women may contribute to increased stress levels in families. Carrying the burden of caretaker of the family may also leave women especially vulnerable to other social problems, such as domestic violence.

Domestic Violence

Domestic violence, marital or spouse abuse, wife battering, and partner violence are all aggressive acts that occur between people in an intimate relationship. While domestic violence literature sometimes includes violence toward children, those studies will not be included here. The focus will remain on adult men and women who are married or cohabiting.

What Makes Domestic Violence a Feminist Issue?

Why is domestic violence of particular concern to feminists? Some history may be helpful in providing a context for understanding how domestic violence became a feminist issue. In the 1960s, several forces converged that led to an increased social awareness of domestic violence. First, there was a resurgence of social activism and feminism. Women began talking to each other in encounter groups about their experiences of being abused by husbands and partners, which decreased the isolation that they felt. They began to view domestic violence as a social problem as well as a personal one.

In response to their new awareness of the magnitude of the domestic violence problem, feminists were active in creating battered women's shelters and rape crisis centers. About the same time, academic researchers became interested in studying domestic violence and its effects on marriage. Researchers found that violence was a substantial factor in divorce (Levinger, 1966; O'Brian, 1971), which was also seen as an increasing social problem. Mental health professionals began writing about domestic violence, which was rampant among their clients and patients (Cummings et al., 1981; Walker, 1979). Domestic violence was clearly seen as a women's issue because women were the primary activists in promoting awareness and social action. In addition, women were recognized as the primary targets of domestic violence, and thus as the benefactors of activism.

Types of Abuse

Domestic violence takes three primary forms: emotional, physical, and sexual. Emotional abuse includes such acts as belittling, constantly criticizing, threatening harm, making efforts to control behavior, making accusations, and showing outward contempt for the other person. For example, one man felt it was important for his wife to stay at home all day, every day, while he was away at work. The couple lived in a mobile home on property in a rural area. The man ensured that his wife would stay at home by wrapping duct tape around every window and the outside door when he left. She was a prisoner in her own home. A more severe type of emotional abuse includes the destruction of property and pets. One man killed his wife's dog after he accused her of loving the dog more than him.

Sexual abuse occurs when one partner uses the other for sexual gratification without her (or his) consent. A survivor of domestic sexual abuse told of being out in a wooded area of a farm with her husband and his brother. She recalled the men drinking while they were cutting logs for their wood-burning stove. They began "talking dirty," which made the wife feel uncomfortable. Soon her husband took off his shirt, began unbuckling his belt, and said, "All this talk has put me in the mood, how about you bro'?" He then grabbed his wife and forced her to have sex while the brother watched. The husband then offered her sexual services to the brother.

Physical abuse includes slapping, kicking, biting, choking, and punching. This type of violence is so commonly portrayed in the media that no additional explanations or examples are necessary.

How Much Violence Is There?

Just how widespread domestic violence is remains unknown. Domestic violence usually occurs in the privacy of a home. Most people are ashamed and embarrassed that battering happens in their households, which leads to underreporting. According to the U.S. Department of Justice (1999), about half of the incidents of intimate violence experienced by women are reported to the police. In addition, measurements differ greatly depending on how domestic violence is defined. The following statistics may help to gauge the proportion of domestic violence from a variety of sources.

- Approximately 1.3 to 5.3 million women are physically assaulted by an intimate partner annually in the United States (Tjaden & Thoennes, 2000; CDC, 2003).
- Females are five to eight times more likely than males to be victimized by an intimate partner.
- From 1993 to 2001, victimization by an intimate accounted for about 20% of the violence experienced by females, and about 3% of the violent crime sustained by males (Rennison, 2003).
- In 2000, approximately 1,687 murders were attributable to intimates; nearly three out of four of these had a female victim (Rennison, 2003).
- About 30% of female murder victims are killed by their intimate partners.
- Women ages 16 to 24 experience the highest per capita rates of intimate violence.

Hospital emergency department data show that women are about 84% of those seeking hospital treatment for an intentional injury caused by an intimate assailant.

Why Do Women Stay?

One of the first questions people ask about domestic violence is, "Why does the woman stay? If things are so bad, why doesn't she just leave?" This question is male-biased and presumes that it is the woman's responsibility to solve the problem. The better question to ask is, "Why do men hit their wives? Why doesn't he just stop?" This question is more appropriate because it places the responsibility for violence on the aggressor rather than the victim. However, since this chapter focuses on feminism, it will highlight the multiple forces that keep women in battering relationships. Identifying these forces has helped feminists recognize specific areas in which women can be educated and empowered to leave hurtful relationships.

Forces That Keep Women in Battering Relationships

Children: Women often stay in abusive relationships "for the sake of the children." Society promotes the belief that children should be raised with their fathers. Women do not want to see their children raised in a "broken home," stigmatized by others (Dobash & Dobash, 1979; Butts-Stahly, 1999).

Beliefs in Traditional Male/Female Roles: Throughout history, the man has been perceived as the "head of the household," the provider for the family, the adult "in charge." In the not-so-distant past, women were the legal property of their husbands. Therefore, traditional thought leads people to see it as appropriate for men to discipline their wives (Sewell, 1994). Other traditional views of sex roles promote sexism and a "natural" excuse for abuse, such as women being submissive, nurturing, and passive while men are dominant, strong, and active (Hutchings, 1994).

Love: Contrary to what may seem logical, abused women can and do love their partners. When a man who has recently beaten a woman says "I'm sorry" and cries, begs for forgiveness, and swears that he will never again hit her, she wants to believe him. An abusive man is often very sorry and contrite after an attack. He is quite convincing that it will *never* happen again. This is the caring, sensitive man that the woman fell in love with and it is very difficult for her to turn and walk away.

Economics: Women, in general, are more financially dependent than men. In addition, many men who batter do not allow their partners to work, which increases their dependence. When women who have been in battering relationships are asked, "Why don't you leave?" they frequently reply, "Where can I go? How would I get there? What will happen to me and my children if we do leave?"

Isolation: Women in battering relationships often do not have many opportunities to develop networks of support—people they can call on when they need help. In the example of emotional abuse above, the woman's husband would not allow a phone in the house and she was locked in all day. The only times she was allowed out were either when they went someplace together or after he came home when she was expected to get groceries or do the laundry. Even among employed women, abusive men use isolation to keep them in their place.

For example, a man will call his wife at work several times a day to see if she is still there and what she is doing. He may show up at the workplace and let her co-workers know that they should keep their distance. Under these or similar circumstances, it is very difficult to build connections with the outside world.

Fear: Most women in battering relationships are very afraid of their spouses. Wives have seen their husbands follow through on small threats of violence. They have no reason to doubt all of the threats. It is typical for an abuser to threaten his wife with a variety of violent acts if she hints at leaving. For example, he may say, "If you leave, when you come crawling back, then you'll really get it." Or, "If you leave, I'll find and kill you." "I'll kill you and the kids." "I'll kill your parents, your sister, her husband and kids."

Self-Blame: A battered spouse is told so frequently that all of the trouble in the family is her fault that she begins to believe it. Typically, the abuser will make a statement like, "Now you've gone and done it," implying that the violence is caused by the victim when she tries to ward off a fight or defend her position. One woman, after coming into a women's shelter, told the worker, "It's really all my fault. I served low-fat mayonnaise instead of regular mayonnaise for his sandwich. I know he likes regular, so I should have gone to the store before he got home. That's why he beat me. I should have given him what he likes."

Forces That Help Battered Women Leave

Children: You will notice that the heading "Children" appears both in the list of forces that keep women in battering relationships and among the forces that help women leave. "The most common reasons given by women for leaving their husbands, or staying with them, or returning to them are related to children" (Dobash & Dobash, 1979, p. 148). When women become concerned that the spouse abuse will progress to child abuse, it sometimes serves as the catalyst for their leaving.

Law Enforcement: While research findings are mixed, it appears that alerting the legal system helps reduce domestic violence recurrence (Sherman & Berk, 1984; Tolman & Edleson, 1995; Zorza, 1993). "Over one half of perpetrators appear to cease their violent behavior during the 6-month to 1-year period following identification of the violence by law enforcement or other community agencies" (Hamby, 1998, p. 255).

One factor that helps explain the impact of arrest is the action taken by law enforcement following arrest. Research indicates that when offenders were arrested and jailed, the expected frequency of subsequent aggression was reduced by 30% (National Institute of Justice, 2001).

Unfortunately, women frequently do not perceive police intervention as helpful. One study found that battered women saw police as among the least helpful professionals (Hamilton & Coates, 1993). According to the U.S. Department of Justice (1999), the most common reasons given by victims for not contacting the police were that they considered the incident a private matter, they feared retaliation, or they felt the police would not be able to do anything. The most helpful responses came from professionals who believed the victims' stories and helped them make safety plans.

Another aspect of law enforcement intended to help battered women is a **restraining order** from the court system making it illegal for the perpetrator of abuse to make contact with the person seeking the order. The purpose of the restraining order is to keep the abuser away from the victim, offering the victim relief from the abuse. Research on the effectiveness of restraining orders has shown both positive and negative outcomes (Hamby, 1998). Evidence shows that women could not count on restraining orders alone to keep them safe.

Women's Shelters: **Women's shelters** are places in the community where women and their children can go to escape violence. A women's shelter provides temporary housing for women who need a safe place to stay before or after an abusive episode. Shelters also usually offer advocacy services to help women negotiate the legal and social service systems.

An important goal of women's shelters is to keep women and children safe, both temporarily during the crisis period and in the long term. Long-term safety is addressed by developing a safety plan for women who choose to return to their situations. A safety plan is a detailed outline of steps to take when a woman senses danger. For example, it is important that a potential victim keep extra money and car keys handy, positioning herself near an exit for a quick escape. Another important feature of a safety plan is to inform others about the plan, such as neighbors or family members, who will know what to expect and how to best help if a crisis should arise (Hamby, 1998).

Women who have been in abusive relationships find shelters beneficial on a personal level (Hamby, 1998). Women who have used shelters report that it was a helpful experience when compared to other domestic violence services. However, shelters are not intended to stop domestic violence and generally do not have as a success indicator numbers of women who have left their violent situations. Therefore, research has not shown shelters to be successful when effectiveness is associated with numbers of women leaving their violent situations (Strube, 1988). More research is needed to evaluate the effectiveness of shelters for the users of their services.

Activism: One promising approach used in conjunction with shelters is the development of **coordinated community action models** (CCAMs). CCAMs are community coalitions generally put together by domestic violence programs to facilitate a coordinated response to domestic violence within a given community. Women's advocates work with community organizations, services, and programs to coordinate efforts in reducing domestic violence. Community coalition members meet on a regular basis to mobilize as many community resources as possible. "(CCAMs) are the best model currently available for service provision" (Hamby, 1998, p. 257).

This type of activism highlights advocacy for women, which has historically been a way to achieve progress on many feminist issues. "The feminist battered women's movement has been widely credited with creating public awareness of wife abuse as a social problem, establishing safe places for victims of intimate violence, working to eliminate gender bias in the law, and creating equal protection for battered women" (Gagne, 1996). The success of activism is apparent in stabilized rates of violence. While there are good reasons for feminism to continue promoting violence-free homes, there is room for encouragement. Unlike many other social problems, it appears that the rates of domestic violence are not on the rise (Blau, 1998).

Reproductive Rights

ISSUES: How much control should the government put on contraceptive information? Do you favor the current abortion laws of your country? What issues do they solve, and what issues do they create? If you changed the abortion laws of your country, how would that affect society and the individuals in it? Who should decide the laws concerning abortion (government, religion, women, men, etc.)? How much say should the father have concerning abortion?

In contrast to the social problem of domestic violence, the issue of reproductive freedom is an intensely personal issue for most women. Collectively, women have had to fight for their reproductive rights in order for them to be legally protected.

Contraception

With contraceptive methods as commonplace today as chewing gum, it is hard to imagine a society without the right to offer information about contraception. Yet in the early 1900s a great debate raged between the feminists and the anti-suffragists regarding the right to understand and use contraceptives. The contraceptive issue at that time was seen as a moral one. Those who opposed birth control considered childbirth a miracle that should not be interfered with in any way. It was "wrong" or immoral to try to control the number of children a woman could bear.

In 1873, Congress passed a law that prohibited mailing obscene materials, which included contraceptive information. This statute, known as the **Comstock Law**, became a model for many state laws prohibiting contraceptive information from being distributed (Cullen-DuPont, 1996). Margaret Sanger, a nurse in New York City, became a leader in promoting women's right to knowledge about contraceptives. Sanger studied birth control in clinics abroad, and when she returned she fought against laws that prevented contraception information from being dispersed (Blankenship, 1990). Sanger founded the National Birth Control League in 1914. Mary Coffin Dennett became its leader the following year. Both women challenged the Comstock Law by publicly attempting to distribute contraception information through the post office. Dennett was arrested in 1928 for mailing sex education materials to youth and church organizations. Her appeal took two years and the Comstock Law was overturned in 1930. This time the court allowed for accurate sexual information to be shared as long as it was not "indecent" (Cullen-DuPont, 1996). While this event led many states to ease contraceptive information restrictions, it wasn't until 1965 that the United States Supreme Court decision did away with state restrictions.

Abortion

Until the mid-1800s, abortion was legal in the United States. Fetuses were not protected until the fifth or sixth month, when "quickening" occurred. "Quickening" refers to the baby's movement in the womb felt by the mother (Simon & Danziger, 1991). By 1900 all states had passed anti-abortion laws. These laws came about primarily through the efforts of physicians to regain control from midwives and other practitioners, known as "irregulars," whose medical practices were growing. "Irregular" doctors included midwives, nurse practioners, and abortionists who did not attend medical school, but who performed medical procedures. "The 'irregular' physicians, who were entering medical practice in increasing numbers…stood in sharp contrast to physicians who became concerned about losing their practices if women went to irregular doctors for abortions and continued to seek their advice for other medical needs" (Simon & Danziger, 1991, p. 108).

It wasn't until the 1960s that the issue of abortion resurfaced. In addition to promoting the civil rights movement and the sexual revolution, women's rights advocates started working toward abortion rights. Abortion rights organizations helped educate people about abortion and referred women to illegal abortionists. These activists worked through state legislatures to begin repealing abortion laws. In 1967, Colorado passed a law granting limited abortion rights. A few other states followed, including California, Hawaii, and New York (Simon & Danziger, 1991). It wasn't until 1973, in the U.S. Supreme Court decision *Roe v. Wade*, that abortion rights were granted in all states as part of a woman's right to privacy. Since that time, women's rights to abortion, once broadly defined, have been limited through legislation, court decisions, and administrative actions (Kennedy, Davis, & Taylor, 1998). In fact, in 1989 attorneys for the George H. Bush administration asked the Supreme Court to overturn *Roe v. Wade* (Blankenship, 1990). This attempt was unsuccessful; however, state challenges to the *Roe v. Wade* decision are undertaken regularly.

What was getting an abortion like before *Roe v. Wade*? The following narrative was taken from court proceedings in the trial of an abortionist. Rickie Solinger (1994, p. 338) reported in *Extreme Danger: Women Abortionists and Their Clients before Roe v. Wade*: "A woman in Missouri, like many others all over the country in these pre-*Roe* years, did not know where she was going, even after she was well on her way to the 'office' of the abortionist....All she knew was that she was supposed to stand in a certain doorway at eight on Saturday evening, April 28, 1956. When she got to the place, a few minutes before eight, she found three other women already there, anxious, waiting, and pregnant. A little after eight, a red-haired woman walked up to the huddle of waiting women, counted noses, and escorted them to a nearby parking lot. She told them to get into a blue and white Cadillac parked there. The redhead got into the driver's seat. Before she pulled out of the lot, she leaned over and took four pairs of sunglasses out of the glove compartment. Each pair had dark paper pasted over the lenses. She handed a pair to each of the women and told them to wear the glasses so that they would never know where they had been. Then the driver told her passengers to squat on the floor of the car.

"On both Saturday night when she was dilated with a catheter and Sunday morning when her uterus was scraped, Mrs. Black (a pseudonym) was blindfolded after she had been put on a padded kitchen table and her feet placed in stirrups. When the abortion was over, Mrs. Black slept a bit. Then she woke and dressed.

All four of the women who had arrived together the night before were taken down to the basement and resupplied with dark glasses. The red-haired woman told them to crouch again on the floor of the car where they stayed until, all together, they were left at a bus stop at the city limits."

Another story is of an abortion rights activist in the 1960s whose roommate in college (whom we will call Jane) became pregnant: "Once the pregnancy was confirmed, her choices seemed stark: Her boyfriend had left her, the shame and stigma of a home for unwed mothers seemed out of the question, and an illegal abortion seemed the only remaining option....The abortion was a nightmare, as were so many in that era. She was met on a street corner in Mexico by a taxicab driver, aborted without anesthesia, and unceremoniously dumped, shivering and retching, on still another street corner" (Luker, 1994, p. 98).

In spite of the horrors of illegal and unsafe abortions, the debate continues about whether or not abortion should be a legal option for women. During this era of legalized abortion, it is difficult to imagine the desperation that drove women like Mrs. Black and Jane to pursue abortion, and yet such historical accounts abound. Is it possible that times have changed so much that if abortion were to become illegal, women would somehow feel less desperate? Is it realistic to think that women today, like Jane and Mrs. Black, would not seek illegal and unsafe means of terminating a pregnancy if they felt so compelled? If women *will* have abortions regardless of the legal status of the procedure, why does the debate continue with such force? One possible answer could be that women themselves are divided about the issue. It appears that women on each side of the abortion question have very distinct approaches to life, not just to abortion.

In a study of over 200 pro-choice and anti-abortion activists, Luker found the women to be fundamentally different types of people with opposing worldviews and lifestyles. Table 17.3 below summarizes some information that Luker (1994) found to describe the "average" activist.

Given these differences, it seems unlikely that women will take a united approach to abortion rights. Perhaps the best we can hope for is increased understanding of the issues each woman faces within her own value, cultural, and belief system.

Table 17.3: Demographic Profile of Pro-choice and Anti-abortion Women

Demographics	Pro-Choice Women	Anti-Abortion Women
Average age	44	44
Marital status	married	married
Age at marriage	22	17
Number of children	1 or 2	3 or more
Employment status	employed	unemployed
Spouse's employment	professional	low-income white collar
Family income	$50,000 +	$30,000
Education	college graduate	high school graduate
Parent's education	college graduate	high school graduate
Church attendance	rarely	at least once a week
Views on gender	See men and women as fundamentally equal and basically similar in regard to rights and responsibilities for family, home, and work. Therefore, when motherhood is an involuntary activity, inequality is a likely result.	Believe that men and women are intrinsically different. Men are best suited to the public world of work, and women to the private world of rearing children, managing homes, and caring for husbands.
Views on contraception	Believe that a good contraceptive method is one which is safe, non-distracting, and pleasant to use. Contraception is not a moral issue.	Are opposed to most contraceptives. A substantial number use periodic abstinence, or natural family planning, as their only form of fertility control, rejecting other methods of contraception on moral and social grounds.

Sexual Issues

ISSUES: How big a problem is sexual assault for women in the United States? Can men be raped? Is rape more a societal problem or an individual problem? Who is responsible for date rape? If a friend of yours was raped, what would you do and say? In general, is it sex discrimination if a joke derides a particular gender? Given the factors that seem to increase sexual harassment, in what types of jobs might women be most subject to sexual harassment?

Sexual issues are important to feminists because women are sexually more at risk than men (Nussbaum, 1999). This section discusses two social problems of special concern to women: sexual harassment and sexual assault.

Sexual Harassment

Sexual harassment has traditionally been defined as unwanted sexual advances, requests for sexual favors, or displays of other verbal or physical behaviors of a sexual nature. One turning point in identifying sexual harassment as a social problem came when Anita Hill accused Clarence Thomas, a Supreme Court nominee, of sexually harassing her during a former working relationship. Anita Hill's accusations brought national attention to the issue of sexual harassment because many people did not expect it in upper echelon work settings. Sexual harassment is not confined to the workplace, which is why we discuss it here with sexual issues rather than with workplace concerns. Sexual harassment happens in schools, the military, the court system, between tenants and landlords or professionals and clients, and in other social settings.

Sexual harassment is illegal. Prohibited by Title VII of the U.S. Civil Rights Act, sexual harassment is a form of sex discrimination, a violation of a person's civil rights. Legally, sexual harassment takes one of two forms—"quid pro quo" and through exposure to a hostile work environment. "Quid pro quo" means "this for that." In other words, a person in power such as an employer or teacher asks or coerces the person with less power (an employee or student) to perform sexually in exchange for something such as continued employment, a raise, or good grades. A hostile work environment, on the other hand, exists when the person with less power is subjected to sexually abusive surroundings that interfere with the person's productivity.

Quid pro quo activities involve a type of harassment that researchers have identified as sexual coercion (Fitzgerald & Hesson-McInnis, 1989). People who engage in sexual coercion promise rewards or threaten punishment for participating in sexual activity. Many people think of this type of behavior as "typical" sexual harassment. For example, a boss hints to his secretary that if she would just be a bit "friendlier" she might get a pay raise. Researchers have identified two other ways a hostile work environment may be created: through gender harassment and unwanted sexual attention (Fitzgerald & Hesson-McInnis, 1989). Gender harassment occurs when people make sexist comments or behave in a way to insult, degrade, or embarrass the other person on the basis of sex. For example, a male who says to another male when the company hires a woman, "I hear we're getting another bleeder" (referring to the fact that women menstruate), is engaging in gender harassment. Unwanted sexual attention covers a broad range of behaviors, from pressing up against another person to rape.

Prevalence

The extent of sexual harassment is difficult to measure. Researchers report that from 42% to 92% of people are subject to sexual harassment in a given year (Sev'er, 1999; Risley-Curtiss & Hudson, 1998; Firestone & Harris, 1999). The wide range is due to sampling strategies, definitions of sexual harassment, and population characteristics. For example, among school children, researchers agree that about 85% of girls and 76% of boys reported experiencing some form of sexual harassment in school (Fineran & Bennett, 1999; Kopels & Dupper, 1999). However, job-related sexual harassment figures vary widely. In a study of female lawyers, researchers found that nearly two-thirds of the subjects in private practice and almost 50% of those in corporate or public agency settings related either experiencing or observing sexual harassment by male superiors (Laband & Lentz, 1998).

What Tends to Increase Harassment?

Research indicates that both personal and structural (environmental) characteristics may put people at risk for sexual harassment. In terms of personal characteristics, studies show that when a young, unmarried woman is in a job where a man of higher rank is older, has more education, is married, and is rather unattractive, she is at high risk of being a target of sexual harassment (Hendrix et al., 1998; Gutek, Cohen, & Conrad, 1990; Littler, Seidler-Feller, & Opaluch, 1982). Another personal characteristic that may tend to increase harassment is race. While study outcomes vary, it appears that women of color may be more frequent targets of harassment, with the harassment taking more severe forms (Murrell, Frieze, & Frieze, 1995). Particularly vulnerable are single African American women with incomes at or below the poverty level (Wyatt & Riederle, 1995). Additionally, women of color are less likely to be believed when they do report sexual harassment (Murrell, 1996).

Research also points to several personal characteristics of men that tend to increase sexual harassment. In one study, the number-one predictor for inflicting sexual harassment was harboring hostility toward women in general. Other personal characteristics included lack of acceptance of women as equals and negative masculinity. Negative masculinity is characterized by arrogance, greed, boastfulness, hostility, selfishness, and cynicism (Rosen & Martin, 1998). Along with negative masculinity, men who described themselves as socially and sexually dominant expressed more dominant non-verbal behaviors when interacting with a subordinate female (Murphy, Driscoll, & Kelly, 1999).

Age also appears to be a personal characteristic that may contribute to sexual harassment. Several studies note that older men are more likely to be unaware of sexual harassment and to tolerate it when they become aware (Ford & Donis, 1996; Padavic & Orcutt, 1997). In terms of victimization, researchers note that women who are under the age of 44 are more frequent victims (Maypole, 1986).

In addition to personal characteristics, structural characteristics—the particular features of a workplace or environment—may increase sexual harassment. One of the most basic structural features that predicts the increase of sexual harassment is an environment that consists predominantly of men. The more contact women had with men in an environment dominated by men, the greater the risk for sexual harassment (Gutek et al., 1990; Gruber, 1998). This risk may exist because of the differences in toleration levels in men and women. Women are much less tolerant of sexual harassment then men (Ford & Donis, 1996).

Effects of Sexual Harassment

Sexual harassment negatively affects both victims and organizations in a number of ways. Women who are targets of sexual harassment tend to experience guilt, shame, anxiety, irritability, tension, and hostility, and will often suppress these feelings instead of dealing with them in healthy ways (Gutek & Koss, 1993; Richman et al., 1999). Often these feelings lead to depression, post-traumatic stress, diminished emotional well-being, sleeplessness, increased drinking and drug use, and cigarette use (Richman et al., 1999).

Sexual harassment affects women's work habits, making them take time off, ask for transfers, and leave the job (Gutek & Koss, 1993). Research indicates that women who have been sexually harassed have lower overall job satisfaction and often express an intention to quit (Laband & Lentz, 1998). Companies in which sexual harassment is unchecked experience low employee morale, lower productivity, increased employee turnover and absenteeism, and may face financial penalties (Jameson, 1997; Knapp & Kustis, 1996).

Barriers to Stopping Sexual Harassment

In spite of the negative effects sexual harassment has on victims and companies, and the great cost to society, it has been a difficult crime to inhibit. Court cases concerning sexual harassment have made it clear that it is the responsibility of the victim to show that the behavior 1) was unwanted, 2) resulted in economic loss, and 3) inflicted some form of psychological suffering.

Several factors complicate meeting these criteria. First, sexual harassment victims fear retaliation and are reluctant to report the offense. In most cases, sexual harassment happens when the victim is alone with the perpetrator, making the facts hard to substantiate. In addition, the harassing person is usually on a higher level with more power, and people tend to believe the person with more power. Even when others may be aware of the harassment, in some settings there is a conspiracy of silence, such as a "good old boys" network, traditions of academic freedom, faculty tenure, and military "closing ranks" that inhibit verification (Leitich, 1999; Kasinky, 1998).

Women also often have very personal reasons for reporting or not reporting sexual harassment. In general, family relationships play a vital role in women's decisions about what to do. Research indicates that a woman who feels that her family deserves compensation for the suffering that the harassment caused is more likely to take legal action. On the other hand, some women see their families as too valuable to risk participating in a contest

Equal Employment Opportunity Commission Guidelines for Sexual Harassment

Unwelcome sexual advances, requests for sexual favors, and other verbal or physical conduct of a sexual nature constitutes sexual harassment in several situations:
- Submission to such conduct is made explicitly or implicitly a term or condition for employment.
- Submission to, or rejection of, such conduct is used as the basis of an employment decision.
- Such conduct has the purpose or effect of unreasonably interfering with an individual's work performance, or creating a hostile or intimidating or offensive environment.

Many Voices: An Introduction to Social Issues

over rights. In this case, they are less likely to report the harassment or take other actions. Family factors appear more important in the decision-making process than in how severe the harassment was or the amount of legal aid that was available (Morgan, 1999).

Preventing Sexual Harassment

While sexual harassment is a difficult crime to combat, research indicates that there are many ways that it may be reduced. Organizations interested in curbing sexual harassment should do several things:

- Carefully define the behaviors that could constitute sexual harassment.
- Post federal and state guidelines on sexual harassment for easy access to employees (*Journal of Accountancy*, 1997).
- Develop a strong policy stating that sexual harassment will not be tolerated.
- Communicate the sexual harassment policy clearly to all constituents.
- Implement a variety of proactive strategies, such as required training sessions and educational programs, to help people recognize and confront sexual harassment (Gruber, 1998).
- Develop grievance and reporting procedures that are effective, timely, and easily accessible (Jameson, 1997).
- Maintain appropriate employment liability insurance to provide coverage for the costs associated with lawsuits resulting from harassment (*Journal of Accountancy*, 1997).
- Investigate complaints (informal as well as formal) as soon as possible (Aikin, 1999).
- In some situations, it may be best not to allow the accused individual to return to the workplace until all charges have been resolved.

Sexual Assault

Sexual assault is a social problem that feminists take very seriously. Particularly in the United States, the magnitude of the problem of sexual assault exposes societal complacency toward women's vulnerability. In fact, according to one researcher, the United States may lead the world in sexual violence (Nussbaum, 1999). Consider these research findings:

- Sexual assault is one of the most rapidly growing violent crimes in the United States (Dupre, Hampton, & Meeks, 1993).

- 14 to 25% of all females may experience rape or attempted rape in their lifetimes (Koss, 1993; Tjaden & Thoennes, 2000).
- 1,871 rapes occur each day (National Center for Victims of Crime, 1992).
- Yearly estimates of rape run from 130,000 to 700,000 depending on the definitions of rape and sampling strategies (National Center for Victims of Crime, 1992).
- Only a small percentage (6 to 16%) of rapes are reported to police, which contributes to the wide variation in yearly estimates (National Center for Victims of Crime, 1992; Rickert, Wiemann, & Vaughan, 2005).
- Most women are raped by someone they know. Only about 27% of rapes are perpetrated by an unknown assailant (U.S. Department of Justice, 2003; Heise, 1993).

While some of these findings have been challenged in terms of methodology (Gilbert, 1998), researchers do not deny that the problem remains significant in the United States.

Types of Rape

Researchers and clinicians have classified several types of rape to help identify intervention and prevention strategies that may be helpful in understanding the problem of sexual assault. These are stranger rape, acquaintance and date rape, marital rape, and gang rape.

Stranger Rape

Sexual assault by a perpetrator who is unknown to the victim is known as *stranger rape*, the only type that many people recognize. An example of stranger rape is when a woman leaves the office at the end of the day, heads for the parking lot, and is forced by a stranger to get into his car. Then the stranger drives the woman to a secluded area and rapes her. In many stranger rapes the woman is also beaten up, stabbed, or otherwise injured, leaving physical as well as emotional scars. Unfortunately, society tends to believe women are not raped unless they are physically assaulted into submission. Research indicates that when women are physically hurt as well as raped, the rapist is more likely to be charged with the crime. One study reported that the more injuries a woman had as a result of rape, the more likely it was that charges would be brought against the suspect (McGregor, Le, Marion, & Wiebe, 1999). The victim is more likely to be believed and protected when she is physically hurt than if she is "simply raped."

Acquaintance and Date Rape

When the victim knows the rapist, the attack is referred to as *acquaintance* or *date rape*. From the statistics cited above, it is evident that the vast majority (about 70% to 75%) of rapes are perpetuated by a person known to the victim. In fact, in one study, 96% of the victims knew the perpetrator and nearly half of the women said they were in love with him (Nussbaum, 1999). Yet, in spite of these findings, society appears reluctant to call sexual assault "rape" when the victim knows the offender. This reluctance is evident in the conviction rates and prison sentences of acquaintance versus stranger rapists. Research comparing the prison sentences of convicted rapists who knew their victims with rapists who did not know the victims found that stranger rapists received longer sentences (McCormick & Maric, 1998). This gives the message that if you're going to rape someone and get caught, it's better that you rape someone you know. This finding offers evidence that society condones rape to some extent when the rapist is known to the woman. It perpetuates the myth that women are to blame for rape because they were conflicted about saying "no," they were inappropriately dressed, or they invited sex and changed their minds.

Marital Rape

Some of the most difficult rape situations involve a woman who is married to the rapist. In terms of num-

bers of times assaulted, marital rape survivors experience the highest victimization rates. Some marital rape survivors experience more than 10 assaults in a six-month period (Mahoney, 1999). Multiple victimizations are key to understanding subsequent problems of marital rape. Researchers found that women who suffered more assaults had more risk factors for homicide and were more depressed. In terms of physical health, the marital rape victims experienced a greater number of adverse overall health and gynecological symptoms (Campbell, 1999).

Marital rape victims appear to have difficulty in seeking help. One study indicates that marital rape survivors did not seek help as often as other victims did from the medical community, police, or other agencies (Mahoney, 1999).

Gang Rape

Gang rape occurs when two or more people rape the same victim. In gang rape situations, not all offenders necessarily have sexual relations with the victim. The other participants may include those who threaten or use force to make the victim submit. Usually a group leader initiates the rape and encourages others to participate (Porter & Alison, 2004).

The victim of gang rape may experience more humiliation than individuals who experienced a single-assailant rape. Because more individuals watched, participated, or knew what was going on and did nothing to stop it, the victim sometimes feels more helpless. People involved in the attack sometimes brag about their conquest, which adds to the humiliation of the victim.

Suggestions for Avoiding Date Rape (Powell, 1991; Crooks & Baur, 1993)

It is important for every woman to become aware of what may increase the likelihood of rape so that she can do everything in her power to avoid being a victim. The following are suggestions for avoiding date or acquaintance rape:

- Set sexual limits early by communicating them to your date.
- Be vehement in your refusal of sexual advances by speaking firmly and making eye contact.
- Stay sober. Most rapists and victims used drugs or alcohol prior to the rape. In addition, when rapists and victims drank, the severity of sexual victimization increased (Ullman, Karabatsos, & Koss, 1999).
- Date in group settings and in public places that are not isolated.
- Watch for any behavior in a date that appears controlling or dominating.
- Listen to your inner wisdom if you have feelings that a person may not be safe.
- Avoid behavior that others may interpret as sexually teasing or seductive.

Many Voices: An Introduction to Social Issues

Suggestions for the Rape Survivor

- Call for help.
- Get to a medical facility and tell the professionals there that you've been raped. They will know what to do.
- Have a friend meet you at the hospital with fresh clothing. The police may need to take what you're wearing as evidence.
- Resist the urge to shower or clean up in any way. You may be destroying evidence.
- Do not blame yourself. Rape can happen to anyone.
- Talk to someone you trust about what has happened. It helps.

Myths about Rape

- *Women like it; they are asking for it.* Nothing could be further from the truth. Research documents overwhelming evidence that women experience negative reactions from being raped (Nussbaum, 1999). Women do not like it. A related myth is that women who are raped were just asking for trouble. With no other crime is the victim accused of causing the violation. Rape should be no exception.

- *Women cry rape to get back at a guy for a bad date.* Again, there is no support for this. The reluctance among women to call unwanted sexual contact "rape" may contribute to its vast under-reporting. Of 65 rape victims in a sample of college seniors, the majority did not classify their experience as rape even though their description of the event met the definition of felony rape under state law (Schwartz, 1999).

- *If a man spends money on a woman, she "owes" him sexual favors.* Societal attitudes about male/female relationships contribute to this myth. People believe that if the woman got something in return, the "debt" is paid. The truth is, when it is not consensual, sex in exchange for a nice dinner is rape.

- *Women who are raped while intoxicated are not emotionally or psychologically distressed.* In one survey, nearly all victims, those drinking as well as those not drinking, reported being affected by the rape (Schwartz, 1999).

Effects of Sexual Assault

Whether or not they have been directly affected, all women are victims of the societal problem of sexual assault. This victimization manifests itself through fear. Because sexual assault is rampant in the United States, many women live in fear. While women tend to be victims of fewer crimes than men overall, they have a greater fear of victimization. Research examining this fear points out that sexual assault may represent a master offense for women, increasing their fear of other crimes (Ferraro, 1996).

Women who are sexually assaulted experience grave emotional and sometimes physical consequences. One survey found a substantial positive correlation between the experience of force and general unhappiness. Women who have been sexually assaulted tend to experience greater unhappiness in life (Nussbaum, 1999). This generalized unhappiness may lead to increased attempts at suicide, one of the most serious effects for women who are sexually assaulted. Women who had a history of sexual assault were six times more likely to make suicide attempts than women without such background (Davidson, 1996).

While suicide attempts represent the greatest threat in the aftermath of rape, ongoing emotional difficulties are common. According to the National Center for Victims of Crime (1992), nearly one-third of all rape victims develop rape-related posttraumatic stress disorder (PTSD). Rape survivors with PTSD often feel helpless and vulnerable and re-experience the rape in their minds. Even though the survivor tries not to relive the incident, the memory comes flooding back. In these sudden and uncontrollable memories, called flashbacks, the woman feels very much like the rape is happening at that moment. During flashbacks, women may experience a physical reaction, becoming highly alert or hyper-vigilant. Flashbacks often happen at night, causing sleep disturbance, which leaves the survivor constantly tired.

Women who have been raped and experience PTSD symptoms usually show some signs of social withdrawal. They feel emotionally anaesthetized. This numbing sometimes makes survivors avoid any thoughts or feelings that could spark memories of the attack. Wanting to feel nothing for fear of feeling the deep emotional pain that comes with rape may cause women to self-medicate with drugs or alcohol. The National Center for Victims of Crime (1992) indicates that rape survivors have a 13.4% greater probability of experiencing major alcohol problems and are 26 times more likely to have serious drug abuse problems.

In addition to emotional problems, sexual assault victims encounter many physical problems as well. When women are treated for sexual dysfunction, menstrual pain, or menstrual bleeding, research reports that they have a history of sexual assault at about twice the rate of women who do not have gynecological problems (Schreck, 1999). Besides medical and physical problems, women who have been sexually assaulted may experience other health risks such as an increase in smoking (Acierno & Kilpatrick, 1996).

Societal Bias against Rape Victims

Society has a double standard regarding rape. Rape victims have had to answer questions that victims of other crimes would not even be asked. The following account dramatizes this double standard through dialogue between a victim of a holdup and the defendant's lawyer.

The "Rape" of Mr. Smith (Morrissey, 1975)

"Mr. Smith, you were held up at gunpoint on the corner of 16th & Locust?"

"Yes."

"Did you struggle with the robber?"

"No."

"Why not?"

"He was armed."

"Then you made a conscious decision to comply with his demands rather than to resist?"

"Yes."

"Did you scream? Cry out?"

"No, I was afraid."

"I see. Have you ever been held up before?"

"No."

"Have you ever given money away?"

"Yes, of course—"

"And did you do so willingly?"

"What are you getting at?"

"Well, let's put it like this, Mr. Smith. You've given away money in the past—in fact, you have quite a reputation for philanthropy. How can we be sure that you

weren't *contriving* to have your money taken from you by force?"

"Listen, if I wanted—"

"Never mind. What time did this holdup take place, Mr. Smith?"

"About 11 p.m."

"You were on the streets at 11 p.m.? Doing what?"

"Just walking."

"Just walking? You know that it's dangerous being out on the street that late at night. Weren't you aware that you could have been held up?"

"I hadn't thought about it."

"What were you wearing at the time, Mr. Smith?"

"Let's see. A suit. Yes, a suit."

"An *expensive* suit?"

"Well—yes."

"In other words, Mr. Smith, you were walking around the streets late at night in a suit that practically *advertised* the fact that you might be a good target for some easy money, isn't that so? I mean, if we didn't know better, Mr. Smith, we might even think you were *asking* for this to happen, mightn't we?"

"Look, can't we talk about the past history of the guy who *did* this to me?"

"I'm afraid not, Mr. Smith. I don't think you would want to violate his rights, now would you?"

What Helps Victims of Sexual Assault?

One of the first things a woman who has been sexually assaulted can do to help in her recovery is to tell a supportive person about what happened. Research indicates that women who told friends or relatives about their sexual assault found it helpful (Ullman, 1996; Neville & Pugh, 1997). On the other hand, women who told professionals, predominantly male professionals (such as clergy, police, or physicians), reported the experience as not helpful (Ullman, 1996). This reluctance to talk to professionals is especially true among African Americans (Neville & Pugh, 1997). When women feel they are clearly not to blame for the attack, they are more likely to tell someone. For example, when the offender had used alcohol prior to the assault, women tended to tell someone about it much sooner (Ullman, 1996). When women delay telling a supportive person about the sexual assault, they are at higher risk for negative psychological outcomes (Saunders et al., 1992).

In addition to talking to a supportive person about the assault, greater spirituality appears to help survivors cope. Women who reported spirituality playing a greater role in their lives after an assault felt an elevated sense of well-being. The opposite was true, however, among women who did not report increased spirituality. They experienced significantly depressed well-being (Kennedy et al., 1998).

Women and Spirituality

ISSUES: Is there a biblical reason that women have inferior status? In the perfect world of gender equality, how might the religious world be different? How might worship services change? How might church leadership change? Would there be any differences in the types of services that churches offer?

From the inception of the women's movement, feminists have challenged traditional, institutionalized religion. Elizabeth Cady Stanton studied organized religion and declared it to be a major source of women's inferior status. As a result of her study, she wrote *The Woman's Bible*, which was published in 1895 (Blankenship, 1990).

Feminists have many concerns about organized religion and its impact on women. One problem involves basic concepts of and about "God," which are closely connected with "maleness." In fact, in most representations God is male. The underlying message to a woman is that since she is not like God, she must have a subordinate role. That role is "to serve him [God], as she is expected to serve the needs, works and concerns of men at the secular level" (Gidlow, 1990, p. 414).

Another challenge that organized religion encounters from feminists is the charge of unequal treatment of men and women. A major study of religion and women concluded that "none of the major world religions—Judaism, Christianity, Islam, Buddhism, Hinduism, and the East Asian philosophical traditions of Confucianism and Taoism—treat women and men equally" (Gross, 1996, p. 106). Feminists have criticized world religions for valuing men over women, promoting men's experience as the "norm" without considering women's experience, portraying God in predominantly masculine metaphors, and using the Christian message to support violence against women (LaCugna, 1993). "Without a doubt, the church has perpetuated the concept that the suffering servant is the holiest person of all. Women and minorities have been encouraged to be suffering servants, thereby achieving absolution" (Schaef, 1992, p. 173).

While feminists often see traditional religions as perpetuating a male dominant/female submissive paradigm, they recognize that spirituality is an important component in women's lives. Spirituality offers women direction and meaning in life. Therefore, it is not religion itself that feminists protest, but the position women are often assigned in the religious world. "To the feminist, women and men are full partners in the human enterprise, not one a potentate and the other a helpmate. Not one the image of God and the other the temptress of the human race. Feminist spirituality bridges the isolation of both women and men and gives both of them a chance finally, finally, to be whole" (Chittister, 1998, p. 157).

One phenomenon bridging the gap for women in religion is that more and more women are studying theology. Overall, about 30% of the students in seminary are women, though many denominations will not ordain them (Lampman, 1998). Feminist theologians have searched for historical accounts of female religious leaders and writers and they have criticized the patriarchal aspects of theology such as male superiority, which tradition says reflects God's will. One goal of Christian feminism is to uncover the deep hurt that patriarchy has caused for both men and women and work toward invalidating the connections between patriarchy and theology. "A fundamental principle of feminism is that both women and men share fully in human nature and that neither is superior to the other. Neither men nor women can claim to be closer to God or more perfectly created in God's image…" (LaCugna, 1993, p. 2).

In addition to women becoming involved in the systematic study of religion, female clergy are finding new approaches to ministry. Many enter specialized tracks such as prison and hospital ministries because more traditional tracks are less available to them. Thus, female clergy are moving some denominations to increase their definitions of ministry through outreach work (Lampman, 1998).

Female clergy and Christian feminists work together to broaden the definition of religion to focus on spirituality. For example, to some feminist Christians, following religious teachings means highlighting love for others. "[T]he biblical tradition reveals spiritual maturity as an experience of deep and inclusive love" (Conn, 1993, p. 245).

One feminist Christian writer shared her vision for women and spirituality: "Feminist spirituality says that in the end we will be judged on the companionship story of Genesis 2. We need a new relationship with animals. We need to immerse ourselves in creation with new respect. We need to come to see ourselves as one more creature dependent on all the others more than they are dependent on us. We need a new sense of enoughness, a new sense of limits, a new sense of interconnectedness with all of life that makes slaughter unthinkable and the destruction of the species impossible. We need to live more simply, take up less space on the earth, and realize the functions of the rest of life so that creation may re-create itself. We need to convert dominion to companionship and patriarchy to feminism before creation itself is in danger from a patriarchy that has admittedly taken science, business, and technology to unparalleled heights but has become pernicious in the process because its tenets are flawed at the core" (Chittister, 1998, p. 167).

Feminists who write about spiritual issues often expound on the importance of peacemaking and relationships. It is important to feminists to emphasize the interconnectedness of the universe, the interplay of the environment, and the individual as a unified whole. For feminists, spirituality involves the responsibility of humanity to foster relationships that are mutually beneficial to all, not just the most powerful.

Conclusion

As this chapter ends by discussing postmodernism, we again ask, "What is feminism?" It is with this question that postmodern thought most pointedly challenges the feminist movement. Postmodernism is a philosophical perspective proposing that there are multiple versions of "Truth." Thus, a postmodernist perspective would hold that one overarching explanation is not sufficient to account for women's experiences in the world. This means that we can no longer say, "Women need…, women want…, women expect…" and be accurate. There are too many different experiences and realities that require acknowledgment to make such sweeping statements. Consequently, it is more difficult to define feminism under postmodern thought than ever before, especially if we are to include every conceivable viewpoint. In fact, because of the rise of postmodernism, one writer describes a "battle" being fought among feminists over what feminism is and whom it represents (McLaughlin, 1997). Because of differing perspectives, there seems to be no common banner under which women unite.

Women who prefer traditional feminist perspectives to postmodern approaches believe that differences among women should be minimized in favor of the larger issues at stake. One feminist writer declared that the differences among women may not be significant considering that they are arising at a time "when women perform two-thirds of the world's work, receive five percent of the world income, own less than one percent of the world land; when in the United States every seven minutes a woman is raped, every eighteen seconds a woman is battered…" (Allen, 1989, p. 41). In other words, women have more similarities and common issues than differences. Indeed, research supports that some issues pertaining to women appear almost universally. For example, there is a far-reaching movement toward more egalitarian gender role attitudes among women regardless of individual circumstances (Harris & Firestone, 1998).

Postmodern philosophies recognize the importance of perspective. When we assume any one perspective, we accept a grand overall viewpoint. Once a viewpoint is constructed or developed, something of importance is left out. Individual realities and needs are abandoned in favor of a dominant, privileged perspective. For example, most students who have studied American history can recount a story about the Pilgrims landing at Plymouth Rock. But how many students know that, approximately 30 years before, the first baby born to English colonists in the New World was a girl? In 1587, Virginia Dare was born to Elenor White Dare and Ananias Dare in Roanoke Island, North Carolina (Blankenship, 1990). Historians allow important other realities to become invisible when they propagate a predominant viewpoint.

Feminist researchers and writers are working to bridge the gap between the feminist movement and postmodern thought (McLaughlin, 1997; Pennell & Ristock, 1999). These writers emphasize the importance of seeing a continuum along which feminism and postmodernism meet. They suggest that women should not have to choose between the idea that "a united feminism is the only way to advance women's causes and, therefore, individual differences must be minimized" or "women are so different that no one movement can possibly be meaningful." Instead, they suggest that through careful questioning of "What is left out?" along with "Where do we agree?" women may gain enough solidarity to once again move feminism forward as a vital social issue worthy of inclusion in a textbook other than a history primer.

Response

Equality or Alternative Platform?

by Herbert W. Helm, Jr.

In a review of the book, *Flux: Women on Sex, Work, Kids, Love, and Life in a Half-Changed World*, Karen Lehrman (2000) begins with this paragraph: "In the past couple of years, debates over gender have receded into the realm of the boring. Just mouthing the word 'discrimination' can snuff out the liveliest of dinner parties. Feminism is dead; long live a happy, healthy postfeminism. After all, with very few exceptions, women now have the option to do whatever men can do" (p. 30).

In her analysis of the book, Lehrman notes that women are still struggling with the same issues of identity, sexuality, and self-esteem that they did twenty years ago, all the while trying to balance work and family.

In this response I will not question whether or not there has been less than equality in regards to issues that females have faced. This has been true for a number of groups. However, I would like to evaluate the question of equality and what may be perceived as the failure of feminists to get their message to mainstream America, to both females and males.

Tough questions include who is a feminist and what is she about? At one end of the spectrum, one might think of the woman who doesn't shave, wears flat-bottomed shoes, and espouses the negative values that men bring into society. They believe the adage that "A woman without a man is like a fish without a bicycle." At the other end may be the feminists who are "'elite' professionals

who mistreat their secretaries, 'elite' over-educated careerists who can't empathize with their female underlings, and 'elite' designer-clad achievers who patronize and even disdain the 'average' woman" (Faludi, 1996, paragraph 2). Of course, there is the vast "middle ground," which seems just as difficult to define, making questionable its goals and messages.

Kersten (1991), in "A Conservative Feminist Manifesto," found herself having little in common with those who call themselves feminists. "Reduced to its essence, their feminism often seems a chip on the shoulder disguised as a philosophy; an excuse to blame others for personal failures..." (paragraph 2). She expresses gratitude to a system that has allowed reform to be possible, rather than anger toward injustices of the past. The most rewarding and challenging job she has found is that of raising her children. However, she also notes the "frustration and isolation" that can go along with being a full-time parent. How did isolation become part of the role of a full-time parent, and why are females the traditional full-time parents? In order to answer these questions, we need to consider the history of marriage and economics.

In preindustrial times, economics brought people to marriage, not personal psychological reasons. Marriage was contracted on the basis of the effect it would have on assets, particularly agricultural land. When the industrial revolution occurred, wealth became based upon industry more than on land, and marriage was no longer the means for redistributing wealth. While social status and finances still played a role in marriage, other elements such as psychological compatibility and physical attractiveness were influential.

In preindustrial times, a couple may have owned a small farm or cottage industry, and the work was divided among the members of the family, including children. With the exception of small children (under five years old), it was not deemed to be the mother's role to nurture the children. It was assumed that the knowledge and skills of the father would be passed to the sons, and those of the mother to daughters. The Industrial Revolution changed this lifestyle to one in which the father left home to work and the mother was left to run the domestic household. The father might be removed from interaction with his family, except for on Sundays.

This economic change resulted in husbands having all the economic power. Less than 10% of married women worked outside the home, for this suggested the husband was not able to care for his wife. While the Industrial Revolution released people from the tedious labor of the field, it created a new social structure (Hafner, 1986) that resulted in less economic power for women. At the same time, children became the domain of women, and isolation became part of full-time parenting.

Iannone (1995) notes how far some feminists, like Betty Friedan, have taken this issue of isolation and housewives. The extreme analogy made by Freidan is between the housewife and the millions who faced death in concentration camps. As those who "adjusted" to the concentration camps lost their human identity, so could the American housewife who adjusted to her role. Mothers could be reduced to child-like preoccupations, lose adult frames of reference, lack outside stimulation, and, in denying the reality of their situation, become prisoners of their minds. All this would result in the symbolic genocide of young mothers, and dehumanize their children. Iannone cautions about such exaggerations and falsehoods, which contemporary feminists have used to advance their cause; she feels that today's woman has more privilege and power than ever. She does not see how American women can be compared to prisoners of the Nazis, women of the Middle Ages, or even third-world women. Some of the opportunities that have come to women have been the result of "patriarchal" constructs like medicine and technology.

Although more women are working outside the house than before, various groups of feminists still want more freedom and equality. We are left with the question, "What about the children?" In addressing this issue, Iannone (1995) points out: "the real reason that women seem to have so much time today to give to jobs and careers, leading them to decry what they see as female subjugation in past eras, is that as a society we have managed to convince ourselves that children no longer require the care and attention it was once thought they did. Far from being an established truth, however, the spread of this idea has been accompanied in our country by a worsening of children's lives on every count—poorer academic performance and higher rates of teenage pregnancy, venereal disease, accidents, suicide, homicide, mental illness" (paragraph 27).

I am not suggesting that child raising is a female responsibility. But children are the real losers as society attempts to readjust the roles of the sexes. There seems to be little indication that the average male does as much childcare or housework as women do. The result is that many women who work outside the home have taken on more responsibilities as they have gained greater freedoms. With greater freedom and responsibility comes the issue of how to redefine oneself. Does one basically stay with the traditions of the past or, as Gloria Steinem said to graduating seniors at Smith College, "Now you are becoming the men you once would have wanted to marry" (as quoted in Eakin, 2001, paragraph 4).

Linked to this issue is the question, What do women (and men) want, and do they want the same thing? Lehrman (2000) found in Peggy Orenstien's book, *Schoolgirls: Young Women, Self-Esteem, and the Confidence Gap*, that the single women interviewees wanted a relationship, and that the older they became the more desperate this issue became. It appeared that the adage about women needing men like a fish needs a bicycle just was not true. This concept did not match biological reality.

Meanwhile, what about the needs of younger women? Today, teenage girls receive many messages. Fields (1998) notes the following: "The most glaring error of modern feminism was encouraging the ascendancy of the nutty idea that the sexes are more alike than different. We are made dramatically aware of that difference in adolescence. When girls should be competing aggressively with boys in academics they are told to exploit their sexuality in the same way the boys try to....We refuse to give the girls the distinctions they need to forge their female identities as different from boys" (p. 48).

A girl doesn't know whether she should be a corporate woman, a Pulitzer prize winner, a stay-at-home mom, Miss America, or just worry about the pimple on her face (Kuczynski, 2001). While for women the model of work roles may be that of corporate America, a girl's model is likely to be her mother. If older women are confused about their roles, why would we believe that younger ones are any less confused?

The major issue in this chapter is equality. But is equality what feminists really want? Equality demands that everyone be treated alike. The phrase that Kersten (1991) uses is "uniform standards of equality and justice" (paragraph 28).

At times I question whether believers in most "isms" want equality, or just a larger piece of the pie. Someone who really wanted equality would demand it across the board and not just on issues that seemed beneficial mostly to one group. To illustrate this, let's look at a few examples:

- In the U.S., males have to sign up for selective service when they turn eighteen, but females do not. While this may have little consequence in times of peace, it can drastically change the issues of roles and duty during times of war. Currently, only one gender is "required" to serve. The fight for pure equality would require the demand for an equal standard, regardless of sex. However, going to war is not something most people want to do, much less be required to do, unless they think it is highly justified. Is it correct to demand equal rights in pay but not in citizenship duty?

- When a classified ad says, "women and minorities encouraged to apply," does it reflect an inequality that feminists would fight to resolve? Or do they believe that advantages are justified in the context of "adjusting the injustices of the past"? Who then determines when there has been enough adjustment? For example, there are now more females than males getting Ph.D.s in psychology. Does this mean we should now favor male applicants?

- Another inequality is in the number of men who get equal access to or custody of children following a divorce. But this inequality begins much earlier. Feminists,

and laws, state that sex should be consensual. If it isn't, the male can be charged with rape and incarcerated. After the birth of a child, the male can, and should, be held responsible for helping raise that child. Unfortunately, the most courts can do at times is make this a financial responsibility. However, from the time of conception to the time of birth, the father has no legal rights. The decision whether to have an abortion can be made by the female alone. This often is done under the rhetoric of "my body, my rights." Where is the idea of "our zygote" or "our fetus"? Where is the idea of an equal union? Where are the equalities for the male?

As long as feminists fight for rights that are beneficial mostly for them, do they really expect others to take their messages of equality seriously? Though many other examples could be given, one by George F. Will (1999) appears in *Newsweek*, in which he discusses the work by Diana Furchgott-Roth and Christine Stoba, authors of "Women's Figures: An Illustrated Guide to the Economic Progress of Women in America": "In combating the idea that women make 74 cents for every dollar men make, thus perpetuating the idea of discrimination, they indicate that the differences are negligible and the result of women's choices.

"Between 1960 and 1994 women's wages grew 10 times faster than men's, and today, among people 27 to 33, women who have never had a child earn about 98 cents for every dollar men earn. Children change the earning equations.... The 'adjusted wage gap,' adjusted for age, occupation, experience, education and time in the work force, is primarily the product of personal choices women make outside the work environment" (p. 84).

Many women who have had children will choose a lower paying job for the flexibility that it gives them with child rearing. Earning differentials are frequently due to the choice of different career paths. Also addressed in Will's article is the "glass ceiling" (an invisible ceiling that blocks women from progressing up a hierarchy) which may reflect the small number of qualified women. This may be changing as more women than men are now "pouring from the educational pipeline."

It would be no easier to paint a picture of who men are and what they want than it would be to paint a picture that included all women. It seems that we are left not only trying to understand each other, both within our genders and without, but also determining how to meet each other's needs while meeting our own. I am not foolish enough to think I can solve something that complex. But an "us vs. them" mentality will not help in forging the answers. It's easy to yell "discrimination" and "equality"; it's harder to work for and find answers that further humanity.

Discussion Questions

1. If you were going to revitalize the feminist movement, what would you do and why?
2. Should feminists package their message so that it is more appealing to males and mainstream women? If so, how?
3. Have males been able to transcend the role of breadwinner? Should they? (This includes the belief that when things go wrong economically it is their fault and their responsibility to fix the problem.)
4. If men are making more money than women, should anything be done to even out pay inequities?
5. While laws can legislate against discrimination at work, they cannot legislate who does the dishes at home. How should couples work out new roles in an evolving society?
6. Why does the fashion industry seem to have more influence over young women than do feminist issues?
7. Women are often associated with children and childcare. What evidence do we have that society does not value the work of caring for children? If men were more involved in childcare, how might society's view change?
8. What do women need to do to make progress in balancing work and family life? How might these changes affect men? How might they affect businesses?
9. How large a role do the media and entertainment industries play in keeping violence a glamorized aspect of American culture? How might this figure into the issue of domestic violence?
10. Why does the abortion controversy continue to rage in the United States? What are some current events that indicate new life in the debate?
11. How should college administrations become involved in curbing date rape?
12. How closely does the analogy of the person being robbed or mugged at gunpoint reflect the phenomenon of rape? Discuss any differences you see in that analogy.
13. Is it ever all right for a teacher to ask a student out on a date? At what point does a relationship between a teacher and student become sexual harassment?
14. What types of interpretations were people making from the Bible that might have prompted Elizabeth Cady Stanton to write *The Woman's Bible* in 1895?
15. In looking at the postmodern view that it is more important to recognize the voices of many women than "women" with one voice, how can women ever unite? What would women gain if they put some of their differences behind and focused on their similarities? What might they lose?

Related Readings

Duplessis, R. B., & Snitow, A. (Eds.) (1998). *The feminist memoir project: Voices from women's liberation.* New York: Crown.

Lerner, H. G. (1985). *The dance of anger: A woman's guide to changing the patterns of intimate relationships.* New York: Perennial Library.

Lerner, H. G. (1989). *The dance of intimacy: A woman's guide to courageous acts of change in key relationships.* New York: Perennial Library.

Meyerowitz, J. (Ed.) (1994). *Not June Cleaver: Women and gender in postwar America, 1945–1960 (Critical perspectives on the past).* Philadelphia, PA: Temple University Press.

Related Web Sites

Distinguished Women of Past and Present: http://www.distinguishedwomen.com
feminist.com: http://www.feminist.com
Feminist Majority Foundation Online: http://www.feminist.org
National Organization for Women: http://www.NOW.org
Women Online Worldwide: http://www.wowwomen.com
Women's Resources: http://www.wwwomen.com

Related Movies/Videos

Divine Secrets of the Ya-Ya Sisterhood (2002) with Sandra Bullock, Ellen Burstyn, and Ashley Judd
First Wives Club (1996) with Goldie Hawn, Diane Keaton, and Bette Midler
Fried Green Tomatoes (1991) with Kathy Bates
Nine to Five (1980) with Jane Fonda, Lily Tomlin, and Dolly Parton
Something to Talk About (1995) with Julia Roberts and Dennis Quaid
Steel Magnolias (1989) with Sally Field, Julia Roberts, and Dolly Parton

ECONOMIC MARKETS AND GOVERNMENT MANDATES

18

Chapter Outline

- Introduction
- Defining Terms
- Economic Forms
- Relationship of Government Mandates to Economic Markets

- The Chicken and Egg Debate—Which Comes First?
- Conclusion

Should the government break up a company that has become an icon of success?

Anyone would have had to be asleep during the last decade not to read and hear debates about the government's antitrust case against Microsoft's dominance. In 2002, a federal judge approved most of the antitrust settlement provisions, which "...would prevent Microsoft from participating in exclusive deals that could hurt competitors; require uniform contract terms for computer manufacturers...and require that the company release some technical data so software developers can write programs for Windows that work as well as Microsoft products do" (CNN Money, http://money.cnn.com/2002/11/01/technology/microsoft_remedy). Regardless of what you think about the settlement, you have to ask yourself at what point a government should become involved in the private business sector.

Shouldn't having the world's largest software company in your country be good for your economy? What if there have been concerns that it has flexed its muscles to reduce competition? As Chris Taylor (1998) said in Time, *"Signing exclusive contracts is all very well, legally speaking, if you control 10% of a particular market. Increase your share to 30%, and your exclusionary practices may attract the attention of the Feds. Control half the market or more, and you should hear klaxons blaring every time you twist a rival's arm. With a 97% share, and 120 high-priced lawyers in its employ, Microsoft can hardly play dumb on this score."*

It seems that the harder large companies like Standard Oil (which once controlled about 95% of the U.S. oil market) and Microsoft work to gain market shares, the tougher the government gets. Hence there must be some type of dance going on between these entities. If you were running the government or a powerful business, how would you orchestrate the dance? There must be times when companies like Microsoft or Standard Oil (when it was essentially a monopoly) are playing fairly. How should a government decide when these companies are to society's benefit or not?

Introduction

From earliest colonial times and throughout the settling of the Wild West, government actions and business decisions took place in characteristic isolation. The Pennsylvania legislature deliberated on measures that the politicians envisioned would affect only Pennsylvanians; likewise, small-town grocers stocked supermarket shelves with food preferences of local customers.

But the thaw of the nearly half-century-long Cold War (1945–1990) dissolved not just military barriers, but ended economic, political, and social isolation as well. Prevailing ideologies of self-sufficiency and detachment were replaced by a spirit of cautious cooperation and synergism. Former isolationist practices were now viewed as impeding rather than expanding business markets and preventing political alliances necessary to combat mutual enemies such as piracy along trade routes. Local and international focus shifted to a commonly held belief that the collaboration of corporations and leagues of nations might produce more for the common good than could be achieved by their individual parts.

Ethnicity and culture, language, and religious beliefs have long been used to distinguish groups of people from one another. However, politics and economics could be used to create common bonds that would benefit individuals and nations. In 1776, Adam Smith, in *The Wealth of Nations,* hypothesized that indeed elements of politics and economics should be joined, no longer solely for the enrichment of the elite, wealthy, or ruling class, but for the betterment of the nation and all its citizens. Smith envisioned economics as enhancing one's ability to earn money and acquire land; politics would guarantee protection from having one's property confiscated by feudal lords and the freedom of movement from place to place as one chooses, and would establish courts to deal fairly with aggrieved parties.

The primary focus of this chapter is on the benefits and the downsides of a free-market economy and a constitutionally representative democracy. We will explore how these two elements interact with one another in order to produce synergistic effects, and in what ways they disrupt each other's activities. Most importantly, we will consider ways to harness the strengths found in both economics and politics, thereby deriving the highest returns from these two systems on behalf of individuals, society, the nation, and the world.

Defining Terms

ISSUES: What were the various types of governments and economic policies in the 18th, 19th, and 20th centuries? Why do most of these forms no longer exist? What national and individual goods are derived by cooperation among nations? Might there be appropriate times for nations to retreat momentarily into isolationism?

It is crucial to begin this discussion by describing those characteristics ascribed to a **democratic rule** and a **free-market economy** because, although commonly used, these terms carry a variety of sometimes dissimilar meanings. While defined further in the chapter, democratic rule refers to political systems in which the majority rule, while there are still minority rights. A free-market economy is one in which buying and selling can be carried out with minimal governmental involvement, with no limitation to price, and without restrictions on who participates in the process.

Forms of Governance

Until the end of the 19th century, most governments fell under two broad rubrics. The first was *monarchical* or *inherited rule.* No one other than those of family lineage could ascend to the throne. A second form was that of *imperial rule,* in which governance was gained and advanced by military conquests. Thus, national wealth and power were reserved exclusively for those of either bloodline or military command. These rulers, in turn, extended authority to a favored few as a reward for their loyalty. Any consideration given citizens by political

leaders was limited to ways in which the nation's subjects might enhance the standing and continued rule of those in power—by increasing agricultural and industrial production, by forced surrender of their property and possessions, or by conscription into government service, including the military. Citizens received neither rights nor privileges.

Beginning in the 20th century, a distinctly different form of governance emerged—**communism**. Unlike the traditional familial reigns or military dictates, this new national authority rested solely on ideology. Through the combined order of the people, a common and beneficial effect would result and the nation would prosper.

Mao Zedong, China's communist leader, declared the principle, "from each according to his ability [to work and contribute], to each according to his need" (Dreyer, 2000, p. 4). In other words, people were expected to work to their maximum capacity and contribute fully of their energy and earthly possessions. In return, they would be assured of having their needs met. Like a family holding assets in common, so the nation was to operate. Working collectively, each would share equally in the rewards. Communist theorists and officials declared that by this communal way of living, existing disparities between the rich and poor would be erased. The touted principle of "equality" was intended to reach beyond pure politics and economics with the ideological goal of purging an individual's psyche, replacing selfishness with greater dedication to the society as a whole, until a utopian socialist system would be attained. However, the people quickly learned that slackers in the group received the same reward as those who fervently labored. Thus, the motivation to participate rotted in the hearts of individuals and society. In spite of its professed ideology, communism had much in common with monarchical and imperial rules; the wealthy and powerful Communist elite were the only ones to realize gain.

Furthermore, in spite of communism's pledge that its citizens would possess a vital and participative role in the government, central authorities held on firmly as the ultimate decision-makers, encroaching upon every aspect of citizens' lives: who would marry whom, the number of children allowed, career choices and place of employment, community, and the apartment in which each lived—even controlling with whom one spoke and the content of that conversation. No one was allowed to think independently of the government; neither were individuals allowed to act unless instructed to do so by the government. Ultimately, this "command politics," micro-managing an entire population, exhausted government resources, eventually leading to its collapse and demise.

Although there are many more ways by which to govern a nation, the fourth and final approach this discussion addresses was espoused by the English political philosopher John Locke. Locke held that all people, not just royalty, possessed God-given rights that should not be under the domination of, nor usurped by, any human-instituted government. As he put it, *all* individuals possess guaranteed individual rights to "life, liberty, and property" (Curtis, 1981). Locke further held that persons constituting society would establish a contract with a few qualified individuals to represent and govern the nation collectively in those matters which citizens by themselves would not be able to manage. Examples of appropriate government intervention include coining a national currency and maintaining a national army. If, however, government exceeded the conditions of its authority or ignored its duty, then citizens would have the right and obligation to break this "social contract." Locke considered appropriate actions against any government violating the terms of the contract with its citizens to be everything from replacing officials to overthrowing the government.

It was not until the writing of the United States Constitution in 1787 that Locke's principle of "natural and unalienable rights" was fully embraced as a foundation of government, the "grand experiment" of all time. The concepts of "natural rights" and "social contract" proved particularly attractive to those who experienced the oppressive rule of that time. Democracy came to be a form of government in which people's rights were firmly embedded in a living constitution. Democracy presents itself as a national forum of many voices, not the singular sound of those in power. Finally, democratic governance is not to function for its own benefit, but rather its existence is meant to empower all of society. These covenants of democracy will be explored in greater detail throughout this chapter as they relate to the nation's economy. But it is important that we now define the various forms of nations' economies.

To further explore John Locke's treaties on government, see http://www.iep.utm.edu/l/locke.htm. You can also join a lively campfire chat about Locke's theories on the following web site: http://killdevilhill. com/lockechat/shakespeare1.html.

Economic Forms

ISSUES: Compare and contrast how Microsoft's founder and multi-billionaire Bill Gates would have faired if his computer designs and resulting income had been made under a monarchy, an imperial rule, communism, or a democracy. One can find a wide range of government involvement in the economy, from a total "hands off" approach to that of a dominating force. What different styles have economies taken over time? Describe the economic continuum ranging from "laissez-faire" to that of a "command economy."

One of the earliest forms of commerce from the ninth to the fifteenth centuries in Europe was that of **feudalism**. In this state, service was compelled of **serfs,** or peasants, by the landowners. The treatment serfs and tenant farmers received was closely akin to that of indentured servitude—a service in which an individual enters an unbreakable work contract for a given period of time in exchange for something else, such as room and board, training, or passage to another country. Most, if not all, the yield produced by these serfs or bondsmen—whether in raising crops or livestock, building construction, or hand manufacturing—was for the sole enrichment of the ruling class.

Based on a system of trade and **barter**, feudalism was eventually replaced in the 1800s by **mercantilism**. The underlying principle of this new, more cash-oriented society was that government held the power to grant coveted favors to those in the commercial arena. Examples of preferential treatment and prized rewards afforded the business community included exclusive rights to markets or the granting of monopolies. Under mercantilism, any accumulation of wealth realized by businesspeople was viewed by government officials to be the direct result of political protections. Thus, the government expected hefty remunerations (kickbacks) in return for benefits afforded. Unlike the feudal system, which benefited only the ruling power-elites, this new system consisted of business-government alliances. However, the economy remained subservient to the state.

Understandably, a revolutionary spirit arose among society's business class—the conviction that economic rewards should be realized directly and exclusively by those whose efforts produced the financial gains. Out of people's growing discontent under mercantilism arose two distinctly different ideologies.

One concept, originating with political thinkers such as Karl Marx in the late 1800s, was that of **socialism**. Closely aligned with communist thought, socialism espoused equality for all. Every man, woman, and child living in communes would contribute skills to the national labor pool. Each would be provided housing, meals, schooling, day care, and whatever else might be needed to free them from worry or want so that all might devote their full energies to the nation's work. Moreover, so as not to leave the fate of agricultural and manufacturing production to individuals or groups, the government positioned itself as sole determiner of such matters as what crops should be grown and materials produced, when plantings and harvest should occur, and the assignment of individual laborers to each of the tasks. The government set production goals for each of the work units, dictated the methods of distribution, and set the prices to be charged on all the goods and produce.

While similar to mercantilism in its power, socialism asserted the goal of benefiting the masses. Socialism seemingly included the people more integrally as part of the political-economic equation. Yet, as with communism, the sheer weight of government involvement with every business decision minimized efficiency in accomplishing any given task. The constant emphasis on uniformity failed to acknowledge and maximize the varying training and skill levels of laborers, geographic differences, and varying weather conditions for crops. Neither would socialist theorists concede the fact that certain elements of the human condition cannot be altered by government dictates—that the heart and soul of individuals are self-directed.

A counterbalancing theory, advanced by the Scottish economist Adam Smith, held that private initiative should rule the economy. Government involvement should be minimal to non-existent both at the local agriculture and industrial levels (microeconomics) and at the ascendant national (macroeconomic) level. According to Smith, persons should be left to pursue their own economic initiatives without any interference from government, nor from any other power aside from the business owners themselves. Further, Smith proposed, entrepreneurs should be the full beneficiaries of any economic success they might achieve, as well as the bearers of any failures. This type of system, known today as **capitalism** or a **free-market economy**, was designed to encourage open competition among those choosing to participate. Resources—be they land, labor, or capital—would be acquired and utilized solely at the owner's discretion.

The primary difference between socialism and capitalism is the level of the government's involvement in the economy. There is a full range of national policy related to the economy, spanning these two extremes of the continuum.

Adam Smith advocated for a government that would assume a "laissez-faire" stance, allowing the economy to self-regulate. If industry had an idea for a new product, which went into production but failed to attract buyers, then production would cease. Conversely, if there was high demand for a particular product, then there would be a resulting increase in production for the manufacturer, along with a drop in price for the consumers due to the production of mass quantities. These adjustments to either cease or increase production were envisioned by Smith to be possible without any directives or intervention by the government.

Smith's approach to the economy was widely accepted and practiced by many in the free world until the Great Depression of the 1930s. Because of mass unemployment and the plummeting of the nation's economy, economist John Maynard Keynes argued the necessity of government intervention in the economy. Keynes held that, for the most part, the economy could operate well by itself, but that there were certain times when government involvement was crucial to the viability of the nation's overall health. Action would be mounted from outside the business world during a national recession or depression, or during times in which harm might possibly come to consumers due to market inequities. Some economists called on governments to establish anti-trust laws, thereby preventing artificially created shortages or price-gouging brought about from lack of competition. Still other economists saw the need for more stringent action by government in order to monitor and regulate industries.

From Adam Smith's "laissez-faire" style of the government's relating to the economy, to that of John Maynard Keynes's encouragement of government issuing antitrust and regulatory policies to make useful adjustments to the economy, we now move to a third style on the continuum, that of a **mixed economy**. This is when the market is owned partly by the private sector and in part by the government. Some theorists, nations, and trades argue the appropriateness of proprietorship by the government of certain industries. It might be that no one in the private sector is interested in owning a specific industry, so the government might have to step in and create the service. Another reason for government ownership of industry would be in cases where the function, if in private hands, might compromise the nation's security, such as the military. A third reason for considering government as part investor and owner of the economy would be to assist fledgling industries until such time as they can establish themselves in the competitive market.

Completing the economic continuum, on the extreme left of the spectrum is socialism, as discussed earlier in this chapter. Sometimes known as "command economy," directives for the economy come not from shareholders, a board of directors, nor consumers, but from the government.

The overwhelming consequence of these traditional political economic experiments is that the vast majority of the 191 member-states constituting the United Nations have opted for some form of a constitutionally representative democracy in combination with a free-market economy. These preferred forms seem to be the obvious choices considering the freedoms and openness afforded to individuals by each. What might come as a surprise to some observers is that these two mutually complementary concepts of democracy and capitalism at times compete and conflict with one another, unable to comfortably share the same space. We will explore the interrelationship between democratic and capitalistic structures and the impact they have on various elements of people's lives.

You can learn more about various economic recommendations of Adam Smith by going to the website for the Adam Smith Institute: http://www.adam-smith.org. You can join a discussion forum and live chat regarding Adam Smith's business philosophy at http://businessphilosophy.com/business/AdamSmith-business/mobydick.html. John Maynard Keynes was interviewed for the purposes of reporting to U.S. President F. D. Roosevelt. Read excerpts of that interview at http://newdeal.feri.org/misc/keynes1.htm. And you can debate the concepts of capitalism, communism, and socialism at http://www.thefence.com.

Relationship of Government Mandates to Economic Markets

ISSUES: Would you agree with Ronald Reagan's concept of "trickle-down economics" that when those higher up the economic ladder are enriched by any transaction, a positive gain flows down to all those on the lower rungs, thereby benefiting everyone? How do various forms of governance (democratic, communistic, etc.) and economies (free-market, socialistic, etc.) impact one another—for good or for ill?

It might be helpful to use terms applied to the natural world to best represent the relationship of democracy and a free-market economy. The three naturally occurring conditions we will explore are **mutualism**, **commensalism**, and **parasitism**.

Mutualism

Mutualism is a biological condition found among organisms that actively contribute to the existence and survival of one another. Whether naturally occurring or by artificial fusion, two organisms establish a close association and an exchange of benefits.

A good example of this concept is apparent in the relationship of termites and their intestinal protozoan. Termites feed on wood, but have no enzymes to digest the wood. The protozoan in termite intestines are able to break down the wood cells (cellulose) into sugar, using some of it for their own metabolism, but leaving ample nutrition for the termite. Should these protozoan in the termite be killed, the termite soon would die as well (Johnson, 1969).

Similarly, there exists mutuality between democracy and the economy. Both systems exalt knowledge, intuition, and common sense as the fundamental principles to support their actions. Democracy and free markets place great emphasis on the license to communicate freely. Likewise, both seek to minimize the threat of national discord and external aggression. Democratic principles provide the economy with a sturdy foundation of personal freedoms and liberties on which to establish itself. Specifically, business leaders and corporations find economic growth more readily achievable when governmental rules of "how the game is to be played" are already established. Government authority or influence might extend from such tasks as defining property rights to building infrastructure such as roads, railways, and shipping docks; rules of how commerce among states is to be conducted extend to the fostering of trade agreements between nations. Governments also facilitate the exchange and conversion of international currencies when purchases are made. Through nationally established court systems and legislation, participants can trust that binding decisions between private parties will be enforced and appeals heard when there is a perceived violation of rights.

So what, you now ask, does the free-market economy contribute in return for the benefits it receives from democratic governance? For one thing, under capitalism, individuals have opportunities to pursue income-generating activities by which to free themselves from financial worry or anxiety. Financially secure, people are then freed for "higher pursuits" such as community building, political participation, and activities that enrich the mind, body, and soul. Ultimately, the economic sector assures the financial viability of a democracy. When segments of society must, from time to time, seek government aid—be they welfare recipients, veterans, the aged, ill or disabled, or farmers who have suffered a seasonal drought—it is taxes collected from free-market operations that bear a large portion of the relief costs. Thus, the more productive the economy, the more taxes become available to both support those in need and sustain the government's viability.

Elements of mutualism found between democracy and free-market capitalism are not without difficulty or strain, primarily because these two societal organisms hold differing objectives. Consider the following: free-market economies promote self-interest, while democracy promotes the interest of the group; free-market economies seek to realize immediate returns from activities and investments, while democracy seeks to insure long-term gains. Free-market economies function as a result of private initiatives instead of public debates fostered by democratic governance. Finally, the highest pursuit of free-market economies is that of material prosperity and gain as contrasted to the democratic values of "life, liberty, and the pursuit of happiness."

Yet, for all of these differences, there is a high degree of mutualism, which serves as the basis for a strong alliance between democracy and a free-market economy. As noted economist Milton Friedman summarized at a 1982 Chicago symposium, "The idea that there may be an inescapable connection between capitalism and democracy has recently begun to seem plausible to a number of intellectuals who once would have regarded such a view not only as wrong but even as politically dangerous"(Friedman, 1982, p. viii). Such thinking is nearly universally held by the current generation of academicians, politicians, and economists.

Commensalism

A second analogy drawn from the natural world that portrays relationships between politics and the economy is that of **commensalism**. This association is one in which two organisms live closely aligned to each other; yet, while one partner enriches the other, that giving is not returned, although the non-reciprocating member of the alliance is neither unfriendly nor hostile. Unlike mutualism, in which both parties benefit from the association, only one party profits with commensalism.

An example of commensalism is bacteria that take up residence on our skin. A human's outer epidermal layer provides a place for certain bacteria to attach and benefit from the host site. In limited quantities, the bacteria are of no threat to their human host, yet neither do they contribute to the host. Only the bacteria benefit from this relationship.

The remora fish is another example of commensalism. This small fish hitches a ride by attaching itself to the underside of a shark. From time to time, the fish detach themselves to rummage through the fragments of the shark's meal and find food for themselves. Then they reattach themselves to continue their journey. The shark provides transportation and meal scraps, yet the remora fish contributes nothing to its gracious host.

Much the same way as bacteria and remora fish seek a sponsor, so also do free-market economies attach themselves to democratic governments, thereby deriving benefits while pursuing their primary objective of self-reward. The government accommodates by making loans to small businesses, offering subsidies as a way to protect financially threatened sectors of the economy, creating legislation that serves to reduce unfair competition, and targeting federal and state taxes by which to extend infrastructures that will benefit the business community.

Parasitism

A third conceivable result of the association of democracy and capitalism is that of **parasitism**. A parasitic relationship is a negative one in which one of the partners lives at the expense of the other, resulting in a negative consequence, even death. The infestation of humans with tapeworms is a prime example. Early on, the association appears non-threatening; yet over time the tapeworm comes to subsist at the expense of the host, eventually destroying its benefactor.

Might there be ways in which democracy exerts debilitating effects on a free-market economy? Democracy's strong tendency to involve everyone slows the decision-making process. Delays mean missed opportunities for markets. Majority rule and special interest groups are also democratic threats to the economy. Democracy's focus on the collective society compounds problems for potentially free and independent markets, whereas capitalism values the individual as producer, merchandiser, and purchaser of goods and services. Moreover, democracy's preeminent goal of equity is often at odds with the capitalist's underlying concept of efficiency. Thus democracy, by its efforts to be thoroughly deliberative, equitable, and all-inclusive, has the potential of zapping the vitality from a free-market economy.

Most worrisome to free-marketers, however, is when democratic governments exert martial rule, grabbing hold of the economy, even if only temporarily. One such memorable time in U.S. history was during the stock market crash and subsequent Great Depression of 1929 to 1933. Franklin Delano Roosevelt responded to the nation's financial pain by formulating the New Deal. By legislative and executive measures, Roosevelt set up a welfare system for the first time, created a national retirement program (Social Security), instituted oversight of banking practices, offered housing to the homeless, and organized work units in an effort to shrink the more than 25% unemployment rate.

Another such occasion for the government's intrusion into the economy was during America's involvement in World War II. In late April 1942, President Roosevelt submitted to Congress a program by which the government would take control of the economy. A plan known as the General Maximum Price Regulation was put into place, effectively fixing all prices for the duration of the war. As the President put it, "You do not have to be a professor of math or economics to see that if people with plenty of cash start bidding against each other for scarce goods, the price of these goods goes up" (Goodwin, 1994, p. 339). Furthermore, the entire manufacturing facilities of the auto industry were brought into the national armaments program, reconfiguring factories from producing pleasure vehicles to supplying war-time transports for weapons. Drastic action by the Office of Price Administration rationed cars and trucks on hand to government, police, fire departments, and doctors.

These measures taken by Roosevelt breathed life back into the American economy and brought relief to a war-torn Europe. Yet, extending the President's dominance of the nation's economy beyond these periods of crises might have resulted in devastating consequences to the free-market economy. In fact, some businesspeople went so far as to suggest that Roosevelt was attempting to institute a permanent form of socialism in the United States (Goodwin, 1994). Free markets are typically self-reliant, acting independently of government assistance. Conversely, under "command economies," the state is involved in the daily operations of commerce. Of paramount concern is that too close a connection between government and markets can threaten the stability and very foundation of the political regime. Citizens, disgruntled over delays or deficits in governmental provisions of food, housing, and employment, may well resort to protests, strikes, and riots as expressions of their displeasure.

To complete the picture, we must also inquire whether capitalism has the power to exert parasitic domination over a democracy. Earlier discussion suggested that the free market enjoys fashioning its own rules, resisting all efforts to be regulated, standardized, or overseen either by governmental or consumer watch-dog groups. As far as possible, free markets seek independence from all governance save their own.

Unlike democracies, which exist solely by the will of the governed, capitalist economies clasp tightly to their independence, entering into, abiding within, and exiting the system on an individual "at will" basis. The autonomous nature of free markets can be seen when a favorite family restaurant closes, doubles in size, relocates to a finer neighborhood, or becomes part of a national chain, all without any notice or input from its customers. It is seemingly impossible for customers and democratic governments to influence or exert control upon a business.

Most confusing to democratic and capitalistic relations is the fact that wealth wields power. This power, held by a few prosperous businesspeople and investors, can result in monopolies and cartels; taken to its extreme, however, this power can dominate a segment that seeks to govern. Such powers carry the potential for abuse that democracies seek to prevent—abuse to the environment or to a particular workforce or segment of society. Exploitation of workers or world resources is done to realize economic gain without regard to the long-term effects on society.

Many Voices: An Introduction to Social Issues

The most subtle, albeit unintentional, parasitic effect of free-market economies on a democracy occurs during times of prosperity. A strong economy lulls the nation into complacency. Citizens come to feel less urgent about participating in government or continuing to hold the governing power accountable for its actions. Prosperous times may also engender a resistance to change, new systems, or needed regulations.

The impact of those with wealth and its powers extends beyond national borders, exerting international influence. Aid and loans given by transnational corporations to developing nations, even if given with the most altruistic motives, may ultimately serve little more than to confirm and fortify the developing nation's often militaristic or absolutist ruling party, thereby weakening any local initiatives for popular sovereignty.

The Chicken and Egg Debate— Which Comes First?

ISSUES: What benefits are derived and what problems are encountered as developing nations first establish a free and open government and then expand the economy? Would it be better to develop democracy and a free-market economy simultaneously? How would you advise an authoritarian government as it considers opening market opportunities while denying any representative, constitutionally based freedoms to its citizens?

Throughout this chapter we have highlighted two democratic processes that contribute significantly to an enterprising economy: granting individual freedoms and insuring political stability. We have come to appreciate the significance of a vibrant economy in sustaining democratic forms of government. So, the paramount question routinely posed by developing nations is this: Should nation-building begin by establishing an open and democratic political system, or should developing a free-market economy precede all other efforts?

Doubtless, granting people a voice in the political process will garner strong support for the government, and yet, unless individuals realize a marked and immediate improvement in their standard of living, they will become discontent with the rule and political instability will most likely result. On the other hand, if the self-interests of a capitalist economy are allowed to predominate in the nation's development process, then collective democratic ideals may have difficulty taking root. Governance might well become the handmaiden of the wealthy. With which foot, then, should nations

lead in this most delicate dance—with the more immediate gratification realized from a spirited market economy or with the more sustained and equitable soul of a free and open society?

Historically, nations have chosen one of three developmental paths. First are those nations which purposefully determined to create a constitutionally based, fully participative republic within which capitalism was then encouraged to flourish. The United States serves as an example of taking this path to independence and modernization. Relatively few nations have taken the second path to modernization, one in which democratic rule and capitalist markets are instituted simultaneously. Perhaps it is because of the inordinate national energies required to work on two major elements of society simultaneously that few pursue this path. Japan's situation following World War II serves as an excellent case study of a nation having followed this second course. The third path affecting the country's modernization and development, typically taken by authoritarian nations, is that of developing the economy along capitalist lines while continuing to exercise rigid and constraining forms of governance. We have selected the People's Republic of China as one nation that chose this third path.

Let's then briefly consider each of these case studies—the United States, Japan, and the People's Republic of China—by analyzing the economic and political gains or losses resulting from the developmental path pursued by each nation.

The United States

While some of England's subjects immigrated to America intent on commercial gain, the vast majority sought relief from oppressive restrictions placed on individual freedoms by Great Britain's monarchy. In particular, the colonists had experienced curtailment of certain personal religious, economic, and political freedoms. They imagined that moving a distance of two months by ship from the motherland would naturally limit Great Britain's domination in their lives. So initially, these adventurers and faith-seekers graciously accepted British oversight of the thirteen colonies until King George III and his Parliament imposed a series of taxes on the New World.

These taxes were to help pay for costs incurred during England's Seven Year War with France. The new settlers in America felt that they should not be held responsible for the costs of a war in which they had no stake. More importantly, they objected to the process of taxation in which they were offered neither voice nor vote. As Thomas Jefferson reflected during one of the debates in the House of Burgess, "Great Britain has no more right to put its hand into my pocket, without my consent, for money, than I have to put my hand into your pocket without your permission." Thus the American settlers felt it necessary to resist this form of tyranny. They gave vent to their discontent through a series of embargoes against British goods, culminating with the American Revolutionary War. Colonists who had previously considered themselves loyal British subjects now responded to a call for self-rule.

This new experiment of self-governance was designed not only to throw off the excessive and unwelcome burdens imposed by the British, but also to offer respect for individual freedoms. In the Declaration of Independence, Thomas Jefferson proclaimed that the responsible role of government would be to "form a more perfect union, establish justice, insure domestic tranquility, provide for the common defense, promote the general welfare, and secure the blessings of liberty to ourselves and our posterity." These broad goals originated with the great British political philosophers, including John Locke.

Locke claimed that all persons possess certain "natural rights," granted not by government, but rather by the Creator Himself. It thus stood to reason that these rights could not be violated, neither by government nor by other individuals. Locke described natural rights as "the right to life, liberty and property."

To the concept of "natural rights," Locke added a second: that political power originates with and remains with the people. This theory, known as a "social contract," is one in which government serves at the direction of its citizens and only for as long as the people think justified (Porter, 1997). Should the majority of citizens feel that the government has failed to meet its intended purposes, or has not been responsive to the people, then several avenues are available by which the social contract can be revisited: replacing officials during regularly scheduled elections, holding recall elections, or even overthrowing the government.

The designers of America's political system consisted mostly of aristocrats who were financial giants of their day. Yet, interestingly, they began crafting this new government, not by laying down economic policy to insure their fortunes, but rather by spelling out individual freedoms and delineating limitations on government. Look at the seven Articles of the U.S. Constitution and its twenty-seven Amendments. They call for essentials of freedom: to assemble together, to enter into open discourse, to have the right to due process under law, to be tried by one's peers, and to face accusers and have others speak favorably on one's behalf. While these and the other freedoms included in the Constitution frame a democracy, it is easy to see how these same legal assurances are essential for an open and competitive system of commerce. Individually assured freedoms would quiet the loud voice of cartels, monopolies, and factions contending for group rights that might well overrun the rights of individuals. By assuring democracy, the Founding Fathers felt confident that they had laid the foundation necessary for all aspects of life—religious, political, social, and economic.

Many Voices: An Introduction to Social Issues

Japan

The development of modern Japan began after the devastations of World War II. Allied forces imposed certain post-war conditions on Japan's propensity to dominate other nation-states, known as hegemony (Hayes, 2001). First, if Japan wished to sustain its sovereignty, it had to function as a constitutionally based, democratic form of government. Second, the economy must shift from being nationally owned to being one operated primarily by the private sector. These two measures altered the nation's system from one of domination, at home and abroad, to one of inclusiveness by means of citizen participation.

This is not to ignore the fact that other war settlements enhanced Japan's national and economic standing. To illustrate, one condition of surrender was that Japan was prohibited from producing or engaging in any future military actions. This measure, in effect, freed the country to focus largely on becoming a nation of economic rather than military might. Likewise, restraining Japan from any armament production resulted in a cost shift in the national budget away from the former military allotments towards maintaining the nation's infrastructure, doubtlessly providing key resources for the nation's economic recovery.

The simultaneous development of Japan's democratic government and free-market economy effectively knit the nation's politics with its business sector into a common sharing of interests and goals. Business-friendly policies designed by the government support private corporate growth, even to the point of protectionism. In turn, the free market contributes to national development and investment. Crafting a political framework of individual freedoms, while at the same time allowing for independent business holdings, has generally resulted in relationships of loyalty and support among politicians and corporate officials rather then attitudes of distrust, competition, and secrecy so typically manifest in other nations' governments and private sectors. As Japan's experience demonstrates, the joint development of democracy and capitalism has certain distinct advantages.

The People's Republic of China

The People's Republic of China (PRC) is a hybrid system of economics and governance. Until recent times, the nation operated under a Soviet-style centrally planned economy directed exclusively by the central government. The Communist Party's control of the economy was rigidly maintained until 1978 when China's leader, Deng Xiaoping, promoted entrepreneurial thinking as a means of stimulating the nation's bleak financial performance.

This new-found business opportunity led to the establishment of "special economic zones" (Spence, 1990), areas in which Hong Kong-style capitalism operated inside the PRC without government interference or restraint. In short order, these economic initiatives embraced by Deng have become living testaments to the power of capitalism. Referred to as "Socialism with Chinese characters" (Dreyer, 2000, p. 331), these local endeavors are being replicated across the nation, leaving China's official platform of communism seemingly irrelevant in light of the sweeping free-market gains.

Following closely on the heels of this first economic liberalization, Deng replaced the old collective system of agriculture with one of household responsibility (Dreyer, 2000). This measure effectively semi-privatized production. Economic rewards would accrue to the individual rather than to the collective group and in direct proportion to one's labors.

The third element of Deng's Five Year Plan was in granting managers of state-owned enterprises greater authority for the daily operations, along with ultimate responsibility for the plant's performance. Those operations not found to be financially profitable would either be closed or privatized. Deng made it clear that government would no longer support losing propositions.

In adamant tones, China's Communist leaders expressed concerns about adopting Western-style capitalism. But Deng's response was that it didn't matter "whether the cat is white or black as long as it catches mice." In other words, China's first entrepreneurial leader was declaring that a system could be called anything at all as long as it produces a healthy national economy. However, these revitalizations of China's national economy are now making demands on its political system. These economic demands call for establishing legal protections of inventions and other property rights, requiring the government to assist with interstate and international trade involving treaties, and nationally funding compulsory education to insure a better-prepared labor force.

By whatever name one chooses to call it, China's free-market economy is dragging its reluctant political partner to dance to the music the economy wishes to play. This "economics first" approach is finding the stagnant government politically unprepared to address the needs and concerns of an energized, decentralized economic power. The strains will prove challenging to the current governmental structure.

Discussion of Japan's economic relationship with the government can be explored further at http://www.freetrade.org/pubs/pas/tpa-003.html. A report in *Time* on Deng Xiaoping's reforms on behalf of China is found at http://www.time.com/time/archive/preview/from_search/0,10987,1101850923-142530,00. html (September 23, 1985). Another website detailing China's modern economy is http://www.gwu.edu/~econ270/Taejoon.html. The U.S. State Department maintains a website of countries' economic policies and practices at http://www.state.gov. Another informative location on the Internet regarding economic and policy research is http://www.cepr.net. And for further study of the differences between Asian, American, and European economic systems, go to the Atlantic Monthly Magazine's website: http://www.theatlantic.com/politics/ecbig/whatecon.htm.

Conclusion

Elements of democracy and a liberal economy are both essential for vibrant societies. Democracy benefits from having an active and growing economy as part of its make-up. After all, writes Alexander Hamilton, "Money is, with propriety, considered as the vital principle of the body politic; as that which sustains its life and motion and enables it to perform its most essential functions" (Rossiter, 1961, p. 188 – Hamilton #30). Just as important to the success of any developed nation, we have seen, the financial standing of a society is sustained by the underpinnings of a secure democracy. As James Madison reminds us, justice is the end, the basic essential of life and the ultimate purpose of government (Rossiter, 1961 – Madison #51).

Response

The Triumph of Free Markets

by Malcolm B. Russell

An ancient Greek or Roman, miraculously restored to life and set down in Manhattan just two hundred years ago, would not have been overwhelmed by businesses and society around her. Certainly, ships now boasted far more sails, brought into view with a telescope. The money was stamped a little more finely, and books provided a remarkable benefit for readers. Large buildings meant that people could gather indoors for important meetings or to worship God. All in all, though, these things could be taken in stride—just like the fact that male wrestling was no longer done in the nude. Certainly, the standard of living was not much changed in 1,700 years.

A few decades later, sometime in the mid-1800s, this relatively stable standard of living began to change, for the United States of America entered a long era of economic growth. Although hard economic times continued to alternate with prosperity, generation after generation grew richer than their parents, at the modest increase of 1.4% per year. But compound interest has its marvels, and today per capita income for the United States stands at about $25,000. Without that compounded growth, it might amount to $7,000 at current prices.

Whether you ever thought about those figures, economic growth made it possible for you to

Many Voices: An Introduction to Social Issues

buy a fast-food meal for less than an hour's work, or, if you were very careful, a set of clothes for about a day's minimum wage. Economic growth—a greater output of goods and services per person—means that consumers gain the ability to buy more of the nice things in life after they purchase the essentials. Fifty years ago, groceries cost 25% of the typical family income; today (helped somewhat by smaller families) the figure is only 11%. As long as we share in it, economic growth gives us more options.

So far as economists can tell, this great burst of economic prosperity is unique in world history, though it is not unique to the United States. It also occurred in a number of other countries that brought together the same minimum essentials: elementary education for nearly all; the right to enjoy private property without arbitrary government interference or seizure; tax rates low enough to encourage people to seek profit; access to the growing level of technology; and the freedom to buy, sell, advertise, sign contracts, and travel. It seems no accident that politically these nations adopted growing political freedoms and democracy, while economically they left individuals and businesses free to respond to markets.

One way to categorize nations considers their rules for producing and exchanging the things their people make and the services they provide. In the modern world, all nations lie on a continuum between two extremes. At the right end, in free markets, individuals and companies agree among themselves about what to buy and sell, and at what prices; government plays no direct role. At the left end of the contin-

uum, the government decides what society needs and orders the farms, factories, and other organizations to produce it. These are known as command, or Centrally Planned Economies (CPEs), and they have always suffered the loss of some individual freedoms. For a short period of time, rapid economic growth also occurred in many of them, but they proved unable to adapt to the needs of high-technology information societies. The Soviet Union and Eastern European CPEs collapsed around 1990, bringing down their Communist political systems with them.

Markets have existed for thousands of years because individuals attempted to live more easily by exchanging what they made fairly efficiently for things less easy to produce. Nevertheless, over the centuries philosophical, religious, and social ideas often condemned trade and wealth: Plato proposed that the ruling class abandon them, while Aristotle defended private belongings mostly on practical grounds. Judaism, Christianity, and Islam joined many thinkers in condemning the payment of interest, and the foremost medieval Christian scholar, St. Thomas Aquinas, created the theory of "just price" that could make it a sin to charge too much for an item, even if the buyer willingly accepted the price. Society also limited what people could use: one intriguing set of laws common to most countries prohibited individuals from dressing in the styles of their superiors. If you were a peasant, beware of adopting the styles of a lawyer or nobleman. Flaunting wealth like that could quickly lead to fines or imprisonment.

The flood of silver and gold from the New World, the Protestant

Reformation that divided Europe, and the resulting wars helped create in the 17th and 18th centuries a new set of ideas about business and trade that we now lump together under the label **mercantilism**. Wars required professional soldiers, and kings needed money to pay them. Paper money was still a novelty, so money really meant gold and silver coins. Spain enjoyed mountains of treasure from Mexico, Peru, and other colonies, but most European countries could only obtain these precious metals by selling foreigners goods worth more than the products they bought with the proceeds. Mercantilism aimed to increase that inflow of gold and silver. It therefore involved a great deal of government interference with the economy. Unless they were raw materials to be processed for export, imports were taxed heavily or prohibited entirely. Some companies received monopolies to compete more effectively abroad, while patents, monopolies, and subsidies favored domestic companies. So while the American frontier family farmed, hunted, and exchanged local goods quite free from government interference, merchants and shipping companies faced distinct limitations on trade. It was not just any tea the Bostonians improperly tossed into the bay: it was tea aboard ships of the East India Company, which had a monopoly on selling tea in Britain and the colonies.

Always an invitation to smuggling and evasion, mercantilism met its intellectual doom in the writings of Adam Smith, David Ricardo, and other economists of the late 18th and early 19th centuries. Their writings were probably as influential as the American Declaration of

Independence; like that document, they also demanded greater freedom. In particular, Smith laid the foundations of modern economics by noting six key points:

- We can accomplish more if we specialize in doing just part of the work that needs to be done. Economists call this the "division of labor." In the straight pin factory Smith studied, by dividing the work into specialized tasks, a group of workers could produce about 4,800 pins apiece per day. By contrast, a relatively skilled individual who attempted to work alone could only hope for about 20 pins per day (Smith, 1986).

- However, workers at the pin factory hardly wish to live on the pins they produce. Like others, after all, they desire food, housing, and fancy Mediterranean vacations. So specialized production inevitably involves exchange. In turn, money makes exchange practical.

- *The Wealth of Nations* also introduced the modern understanding of why people bother to make pins—or for that matter bake bread or butcher meat. Medieval thinkers assumed that people did their jobs to help society, operating in a way comparable to the organs of a body. Smith pointed to a much more worldly motive: "It is not from the benevolence of the butcher, the brewer, or the baker that we expect our dinner, but from their regard to their own interest. We address ourselves, not to their humanity but to their self-love, and never talk to them of our own necessities but of their advantages. Nobody but a beggar chooses to depend chiefly upon the benevolence of his fellow-citizens" (Smith, 1986).

- Unlimited self-interest turns into greed. Smith recognized that religion and morality fail to stop some people from taking advantage of others. Likewise, he distrusted governments to do the job. But in one of his greatest insights, he recognized that self-interest can be trusted to keep prices fair—the self-interest, that is, of eager competitors in free markets. A baker cannot charge the highest price that a hungry consumer would pay for a loaf of freshly baked bread if a competing bakery found it quite profitable to underprice the first baker. By combining self-interest and competition, Smith explained the operation of a market, a system of economic exchange that required very little government regulation.

- But even Smith recognized that markets could fail, particularly if traders and merchants conspired to set prices, or if competition were removed by the creation of a monopoly.

- Although markets usually work best *without* government intervention, in fact they depend crucially on the government. Most business deals will fail unless the government provides a national currency, educates at least some of its citizens, creates laws that define contracts, punishes those who break them, and maintains order in the streets. The streets themselves, defense from foreign invasion, weights and measures, a post office, public health rules, and other government activities are also important for prosperous markets.

The free market ideas fit well with the newly industrializing society in Britain, where iron furnaces, textile mills, canals, and steam engines were changing the landscape. The entrepreneurs needed freedom to operate, freedom that meant escaping the traditional regulations of guilds. These associations of producers (e.g., candle makers, bakers, or weavers) controlled prices, set quality standards, excluded new competitors, and attempted to block new technology. The guilds lost the battle, and during the mid-19th century reformers across Europe combined the democratic ideas of Locke, an increasing sense of national identity, and the free-market ideas of Smith. By the end of the century, in most countries they had replaced the old ruling cliques of aristocrats and wealthy landlords with political parties more sympathetic to business and urban interests.

Although the Industrial Revolution undoubtedly brought riches to many and cheaper products to millions, the less fortunate suffered atrocious living and working conditions. In 1848 the murmurings of discontent over the plight of the working class found tremendously powerful voices to condemn the free market system. In the *Communist Manifesto*, Karl Marx and Frederich Engels called the working classes to revolution: "The workers have nothing to lose but their chains. They have a world to gain. Workers of the world, unite!"

A towering intellect embittered by the conditions of the working class, Marx expounded in his theoretical works why the free market system must fail. The Industrial Revolution and market freedoms had separated workers from real psychological involvement in their work, he argued, and reduced them to simple hired labor to be discarded when no longer productive or needed. Emphasizing the roles of financial investors and wealth, Marx labeled the system "capitalism" rather than a free market. To the satisfaction of an increasing number of followers, he also argued that capitalism carried the seeds of its own destruction. Companies would exploit their workers so greatly that, as a whole, society would not buy the products they had produced. Nations would stagger from economic depression to recovery and then to greater depression, until workers and the many unemployed would finally revolt, overthrow capitalism, and establish common ownership of the farms and factories. Socialism would result, then communism, guided by Marx's rule: "From each according to his abilities, to each according to his needs."

The collapse of Czarist Russia during World War I provided the circumstances to avoid decades of suffering under capitalist rule. Far less industrialized and far more agricultural than Western and Central Europe, Russia hardly fit Marx's model of a workers' revolution. However, Vladimir I. Lenin, leader of one branch of the Russian Marxists, argued that a highly disciplined political party could serve as a vanguard and seize power before capitalism deteriorated. Under Lenin's orders, the Bolsheviks (later renamed the Communists) seized power in the October 1917 Revolution. Banks and large industrial firms were seized by the new government, large agricultural estates were broken up, and individual farmers gained the land they cultivated.

Under the revolution, the state seized the farmers' harvests, urban housing, and industrial output as needed. Not surprisingly, this initial attempt at economic organization failed: Farmers had no motive to produce bumper crops if everything they did not need for survival would be seized. The system also lacked a way to balance what the state wanted to collect with what factories and farms could actually produce. After the war, Lenin backtracked by adopting the New Economic Policy (1922). It retained state ownership of heavy industry like steel and oil refineries, but relaxed control over private farming and trade.

After the rise to power of Josef Stalin, in 1929 economic policy took a vastly different turn. Anxious to industrialize and to weaken the more successful farmers who sought prosperity rather than communism, Stalin seized farms or forced them into "collectives" that were largely state-controlled. Trade and industry were virtually completely nationalized, and Stalin initiated a new device to control production and distribute it: central planning.

Based in part on the mathematical models of Russian economists, central planning started with estimates of what the Soviet Union's industries could produce. The Communist Party set its goals for output during the next five years, and the planners then attempted to reconcile the likely supplies of inputs (raw materials and semi-finished goods) with the various needs. A tractor, for example, might include 500 pounds of iron and steel. Therefore an annual goal of one million tractors required 250,000 tons of iron and steel delivered to the tractor factories. The central planners likewise considered other major uses of iron and steel in construction, railroads, ship building, defense, and trucking. The total required output of perhaps 40 million tons would be divided up among the various steel mills. In turn, the mills would receive from coal and iron mines the raw materials required to meet their quotas of output.

The planners then reconciled the sources of supply with the projected uses. If, after allowing for reasonable increases of production over a period of time, the existing steel mills could produce only 36 million tons, the planners faced a choice: cut the use of steel somewhere or expand the industry.

All these calculations required a huge bureaucracy and great limitations on personal freedom to accomplish what markets achieved almost automatically. But the central planners could not rely on market signals to know where to increase production and where to cut it. Prices no longer signaled anything: the central planners dictated the prices for the steel, and the central plan's bank credited the mill with funds to pay its workers. Managers concentrated on increasing output, especially by greater use of machinery paid for by the state.

Anxious to strengthen the Soviet Union's economy, Soviet planners generally set the country's goals high. During the 1930s, the Great Depression struck every major economy except the Soviet Union, throwing millions out of work, shutting factories, and causing grave economic harm. In Detroit, New York, Manchester, and Berlin, the unemployed lined up at soup kitchens. By contrast, visitors carefully escorted around the Soviet Union reported shortages of workers. Central planning enabled the Soviet Union to become a major industrial nation in a few years, practically overnight compared with the decades required in Britain and the United States. Central planning invested in mines, factories, giant dams, and the railroads. However, it required citizens to accept low wages at the time with the promise of a wealthier society later. From 1930 through the 1960s, except for the war years, the Soviet economy consistently grew faster than the United States economy.

In the 1970s, however, central planning began to lose the symbolic race with capitalism over faster GDP growth. As survival became less the issue than a better life, Soviet citizens desired the same appliances and technology found in Western countries. However, the sheer number of items made planning very difficult, even with computers. (Without computers, according to one calculation, eventually all men in the country would plan, leaving women to accomplish the actual production). Quality increasingly became another issue, because factories anxious to achieve a plan's targets learned that shoddy goods for consumers (except defense industries) usually met the target. Great shortcomings marked the service sector: it was almost impossible to find good restaurant meals, repairs on anything, well-maintained buildings, and grocery stores that stocked fresh food.

Much less visible, but as challenging, was the sheer inefficiency of management. Perhaps—the figures were debatable—the Soviet Union was growing slightly faster than the United States. But to do so required applying about 40% of production

to investment in machinery, buildings, and so forth, while America invested only about 15% and enjoyed consuming the difference. The failure of central planning undoubtedly contributed to the collapse of communism, because despite television sets that hardly worked, "liberated" workers clearly saw themselves much poorer than the unfortunate workers exploited by capitalism. The Soviet Union sent the first man to orbit the earth, but pizza was unavailable in Moscow.

Of course, free market economies also faced significant economic problems during the 20th century. The century opened with businesspeople attempting to manipulate markets by agreeing to set prices high rather than compete for customers. "Robber Barons" like John D. Rockefeller went much further; for example, he conspired with a railroad to receive a kickback on every load of oil his competitor shipped. This sort of market abuse spurred the Progressive movement, and led to federal regulation of commerce (1887), public health, and monopolistic trusts (the 1890s and during Theodore Roosevelt's presidency, 1901–1909).

In fact, government regulations frequently failed to meet their promise, often because industry insiders came to dominate the very agencies established to regulate them. However, increasing competition from outside narrowly defined industries proved far more effective at keeping prices down. A solitary railroad stretching across the prairies might possess great monopolistic powers and charge some customers far more than others. It might even manipulate or evade regulations. But when national highways and long-dis-

tance trucks arrived, it would have to compete for customers.

Capitalism's great crisis, the depression of the 1930s, occurred for rather different reasons too complex to summarize conveniently. However, under President Franklin D. Roosevelt, the United States attempted to combat the depression in ways that often interfered with free markets. The National Industrial Recovery Act of 1933, for example, attempted to set prices and allowed companies to collude in setting them. Fortunately the Supreme Court ruled it unconstitutional. In the end, most of the New Deal's economic changes were less destructive to economic freedom; rather they sought to regulate markets where competition alone had failed to work and to extend assistance to the poorest. Bank failures and the stock market had clearly prepared the way for the Great Depression; both institutions now faced greater regulation. Banks, at least, also reaped greater stability because a government agency guaranteed the saving and checking accounts of millions of customers. Other prominent New Deal changes included a national minimum wage law, greater rights for labor unions, and social security.

Today, economists dispute the effectiveness of Roosevelt's policies, but most agree that it was only lavish defense spending for World War II that finally ended the Great Depression. (After all, in December 1941 the U.S. unemployment rate still exceeded 10%.) In the postwar world, concern about another possible depression focused great attention on macroeconomic policy, particularly the use of monetary policy (influence over interest rates and the money supply) and fiscal policy (changing the levels of taxes or government spending) to guide the Gross Domestic Product to levels high enough to avoid severe unemployment.

In general, American economic policy after 1960 accepted the importance of free markets, but regulated them to achieve social goals such as worker safety, racial nondiscrimination, and a cleaner environment. "Industrial Policies," where the government would pick important growth industries and aid them with subsidies and other favors, were not adopted, despite the great economic success of Japan where they were tried. After the decade of economic stagnation in Japan, such policies are now largely discredited for other countries, and it seems unclear that they even contributed significantly to Japanese success during the years of prosperity.

By the beginning of the new millennium, the American experience with free markets had led scores of countries around the world to lower taxes, abolish regulations, reduce barriers to foreign trade, and generally liberate their economies from government control. Although China remained a communist dictatorship, its centrally planned industries fell in significance (many also seemed to fail) and a rapidly expanding private sector propelled the economy forward. Only North Korea and Cuba maintained centrally planned economies. For many developing nations, corruption and favoritism emerged as greater problems to markets than open government control.

After WWII through the work of international organizations like the World Trade Organization (WTO) and its predecessor, the General Agreement on Tariffs and Trade, barriers fell on trade between nations. As countries reduced taxes and regulations that had limited imports, world trade flourished, growing far faster than most major economies. To its credit, world trade brought greater competition and more efficient production. It reduced monopoly power in many industries and spurred economic growth in many countries.

Therefore it came as something of a shock when demonstrators in the late 1990s began to attack meetings of the WTO and other gatherings of international policymakers. The critics of world trade rarely speak with a united voice, but in general they pictured globalization as a threat, not a benefit. In this backlash, opponents of "globalization" desire to halt and even reverse the spread of free markets for several reasons. Large corporations seem to benefit most from greater freedom to trade, while ordinary workers and their communities bear the costs of unemployment. Other protestors fault "unfair" labor practices in poor countries, while intellectuals in many parts of the world condemn the American cultural influence that seems to accompany the global exchange of ideas and goods.

In the 19th and 20th centuries, the concept of free markets triumphed over alternative economic ideologies within countries. As the 21st century advances, possibly the increased wealth and riches produced by free markets will persuade people around the globe that competition and self-interest work best under conditions of international free trade. Alternatively, the antiglobalization demonstrators, despite their internal contradictions, might succeed in convincing us that free markets involve culture and society as well, and should be limited by the borders of our country.

Discussion Questions

1. Compare a free-market economy with a socialistic economy.
2. How does a free-market economy work?
3. How does democracy work?
4. How does capitalism work?
5. Discuss democracy's impact on capitalism and vice versa.
6. What elements of politics and economics could be used for the betterment of the nation and all its citizens?
7. Discuss different methods governments have used to relate to commerce.
8. What are concerns that Karl Marx and others had concerning free markets and capitalism?
9. What are the social issues or problems behind different theories of governing and commerce?
10. Randomly select a nation from each continent. Assess the form of government and economy for each of the five nations. Next, consider the relationship between power politics and the market. Discuss how the government might be enhanced by a change in the economy; conversely, explore how the economy might become more vibrant with another system of government. A website such as The World Factbook 2002 may be useful: http://www.odci.gov/cia/publications/factbook.
11. Global issues such as the environment and e-commerce via the Internet are erasing the drawn boundaries of nations. What impact will this have on governance and on national identity?

Related Readings

Blair, J. P., & Reese, L. A. (Eds.). (1998). *Approaches to economic development: Readings from economic development quarterly*. Thousand Oaks, CA: Sage.

Friedman, M. (1982). *Capitalism and freedom*. Chicago: The University of Chicago Press.

Friedman, M., & Friedman, R. (1990). *Free to choose: A personal statement*. San Diego: Harvest Books.

Gilpin, R. (1987). *The political economy of international relations*. Princeton, NJ: Princeton University Press.

Gosling, J. J. (2000). *Politics and the American economy*. New York: Addison Wesley Longman.

Heilbroner, R. L. (1999). *The worldly philosophers: The lives, times, and ideas of the great economic thinkers* (revised 7th ed.). New York: Touchstone.

Heilbroner, R., & Milberg, W. (1998). *The making of economic society* (10th ed.). Upper Saddle River, NJ: Prentice Hall.

Isk, R. A. (2000). *Managing world economic change: International political economy* (3rd ed.). Upper Saddle River, NJ: Prentice-Hall.

Miller, R. L., Benjamin, D. K., & North, D. C. (1999). *The economics of public issues* (11th ed.). Reading, MA: Addison-Wesley.

Schwartz, E. (1995). *ECON 101 ½*. New York: Avon Books.

Schwartz, H. M. (2000). *States versus markets: The emergence of a global economy*. New York: St. Martin's Press.

Toruno, M. (2003). *The political economics of capitalism* (2nd ed.). Cincinnati: Atomic Dog.

Related Web Sites

Bureau of Democracy, Human Rights, and Labor: http://www.state.gov/g/drl

Foundation for Economic Education (FEE): http://www.fee.org

National Endowment for Democracy: http://www.ned.org

Political Science Resources on the Web: http://www.lib.umich.edu/govdocs/poliscinew.html

Richard Kimber's Political Science Resources: http://www.psr.keele.ac.uk

Related Movies/Videos

Antitrust (2001) with Ryan Phillippe
The Big One (1998) with Michael Moore (II)
Hoffa (1992) with Jack Nicholson and Danny DeVito
The Insider (1999) with Al Pacino and Russell Crowe
Power of Attorney (1991) with Rae Dawn Chong
Wall Street (1987) with Michael Douglas and Charlie Sheen

POPULATION AND MIGRATION

Ken R. Crane

19

Chapter Outline

- Introduction: How the Changing Population Affects Our Lives
- Population Issues in the Industrialized World

- Public Policy and Unintended Consequences
- Conclusion

Yolanda lives in a Midwestern city and works as a database manager. Yet her childhood was not nearly as comfortable as her life is now. Her father was born in Mexico, and her mother in south Texas. As a child, she traveled with her family as they migrated to Ohio each summer to work the tomato fields and canneries. In the winter they would return to their home in the Rio Grande Valley of Texas. Wherever she was, she went to school. Living conditions were rough sometimes: bad housing, cold showers, and no privacy. Yet they endured, and eventually settled down in another state. Yolanda managed to graduate from high *school and landed a job as database manager for a migrant education program. How did migration shape the lives of Yolanda and her family? Yolanda attributes much of her success to her parents' insistence that she attend school wherever they happened to be living. Some of her siblings, however, did not do as well and dropped out before finishing high school. For Yolanda, as for many people around the world, migration is a fundamental fact of life. As we will see in this chapter, migration has a profound impact on people and dramatically alters the faces of communities that are the destinations of immigrants.*

Introduction: How the Changing Population Affects Our Lives

ISSUES: How many people is the world capable of supporting? What kind of world (i.e., living styles) do we want to live in? Would a "zero population growth" policy be best for the Earth? If so, how would you propose creating that policy? What is the relationship between economic growth, modernization, birth rates, and the rise of cities?

This chapter asks a very fundamental question: How do we improve our understanding of the human condition through the analysis of **population processes**— such things as migration and population growth or decline? How do these processes shape the structure of our society? We will look at how an understanding of common, yet life-changing, events such as birth, death, and migration is vital to our understanding of human society.

The study of population is called **demography**, and demographers are considered the experts in this science. However, demographers who wish to comprehend the deeper psychosocial processes within which population changes occur draw on many other disciplines, such as sociology, anthropology, and psychology. After all, population events are conspicuous and regular events. Haven't we all experienced the joyous birth of a new family member, the wrenching death of a relative or friend, and the disorienting task of relocation? These events have personal and social relevance, as evidenced by the secular and religious attention to birth, aging, and death (Goldscheider, 1971). Demography looks at these processes not as isolated events, but as cumulative processes influencing the structure of human societies.

Demographic processes not only impact our lives but are themselves affected by the structure of society (Goldscheider, 1971). The quality of life in a community—the educational and income level of its citizens—influences birth rates, death rates, and migratory patterns.

Demography and Demographics

The science of demography has many applications for marketing and government planning. The application side is referred to as **demographics**, as in "dude, get me the demographics on snowboarders in Seattle." Demographics inform us of important characteristics of a population of a particular city, state, and county, such as age, socio-economic status, race and ethnicity, and migratory patterns. Marketing often targets a particular "demographic" (e.g., women professionals making $80,000 a year).

Most demographers and social scientists who do demographic studies are concerned with more than just numbers. They want to know, for example, not only that the fertility rate in Kenya is six, but also to understand *why* families in Kenya want an average of six children. In addition, what does it mean for the country of Kenya (economically and socially) that more than half of the population is under the age of twenty? Social demographers want to see the people behind the numbers. It is hoped, as you learn to apply demographic analysis to the world around you, that you will not neglect the deeper understanding of the social processes behind the numbers.

The "People Bomb"

I remember attending with my older sister one of the first Earth Day celebrations back in the early 1970s. There was a lot of new and hip terminology being kicked around back then, such as **ZPG** (**zero population growth**). The most environmentally sound family policy was to have no more than two children per family (thus slowing the growth of the country's population). As a fifteen-year-old environmentalist, I went around zealously converting my friends to ZPG.

The excitement about ZPG was sparked by a book written by Stanford University biologist, Paul Ehrlich, called *The Population Bomb* (1968). Ehrlich predicted that disaster would befall the planet as early as the 1970s if we allowed the world's population to grow at its current rate. The logic behind his argument was that the world was becoming increasingly crowded; we were running out of food and resources, impoverishing ourselves, and polluting our fragile planet. Therefore, he argued, we must act with urgency to quell population growth, or face certain disaster. Ehrlich and others were trying to prove that the biggest environmental problem is population growth, pointing out that the recent increase in population, when viewed over the course of human history, was truly unprecedented, and that the consequences, if left unchecked, would be disastrous.

All experts agree that the current rate and scale of population growth is truly unprecedented. According to the noted demographer and scientist Joel Cohen (1995), 80% of the increase in the number of people living on the planet has occurred in this century, which represents less than 1% of human history. In 30 A.D., the world's population was about 250 million. It took another 1,650 years for it to double to 500 million. Since 1930, when the population was 2 billion, it has increased more than two and half times to over 6 billion. The increase in the last decade of the 20th century exceeded the total population in 1600 (an increase of 1 billion per decade, and 250,000 people per day in the 1990s). In case it is hard to relate to a billion people, Cohen describes what it could look like: "If a billion people spaced 38 centimeters (15 inches) apart...formed a straight line, then, ignoring such minor physical constraints as gravity and the hazards of outer space, the line would go from the Earth to the moon..." (p. 19).

Ehrlich's predictions about certain disaster, however compelling, are less convincing in light of the fact that the 1970s were not marked by mass pestilence and starvation (perhaps the real disasters were in the form of disco and polyester!). Ehrlich was considered a **"Neo-Malthusian"** because his warnings echoed those of Thomas Malthus, an English clergyman and professor who lived at the turn of the 18th century in the post-Enlightenment era of great optimism. In 1803, Malthus wrote a very pessimistic tract in which he expounded the *natural law of population*, which argued that, while food is necessary, passion between the sexes (and hence baby production) is a more powerful impulse (especially for the masses). The result is that population growth will inexorably outstrip food production.

Ehrlich and his collaborators (1993) argued that the global food production system, through its mismanagement of natural resources, is depleting future agricultural capacity. A central concept is that of "nutritional carrying capacity": the maximum number of people who can be provided with an adequate diet at any given time without undermining the planet's capacity to support people in the future. While cultural and technological innovations may increase food production over the short term, environmental pollution and other degrading practices will, over the long term, deplete essential, nonrenewable resources, and hence will reduce the planet's nutritional carrying capacity.

Ehrlich laid considerable blame on the social, political, and economic institutions that facilitate mismanagement of resources and distort the free market. This argument supports the growing awareness that hunger is primarily a function of social inequality. Ehrlich also agreed with others that reducing poverty would help the situation, because if the poor had more purchasing power it might stimulate food production.

Even though there is presently enough food to feed the world on a vegetarian diet, Ehrlich draws no comfort from this fact. As countries modernize, meat consumption increases. Most experts agree with Ehrlich that any future dramatic increase in food production worldwide such as the **green revolution** of the 1960s and 1970s is unlikely. Too many biophysical constraints exist (e.g., land conversion and water shortage). We are getting the same bad news about fisheries. A green revolution would require too high a usage of water, pesticides, and fertilizers. Even when these are applied (as in Japan and the Philippines for rice), the results are mediocre. It seems a threshold has been reached. Some possibilities for increasing food production are not ruled out, such as bioengineering and reducing storage loss. Also, if less grain was used for feed, it would free up as much as one third more grain for human consumption.

Ehrlich argued that we need to take action now, and the ultimate solution is to reduce population growth—fewer babies means fewer problems. Ehrlich's main departure from Malthus is his view that it is not that population growth will simply outstrip the supply of food, but that people are destroying the Earth's future ability to produce food through environmental pollution, ozone depletion, UV-B radiation, and global warming. Ehrlich's later arguments (Ehrlich & Ehrlich, 2005) put more emphasis on the impact that the wealthier inhabitants of the world have through their greater demand on resources. Quoting from a 1993 statement by the Union of Concerned Scientists, Ehrlich argues that certain populations consume resources at an unsustainable rate: "The magnitude of the threat...is linked to human population size and resource use per person. Resource use, waste production and environmental degradation are accelerated by population growth. They are further exacerbated by consumption habits..." (p. 8). Ehrlich's description of the effects of population growth on the environment is seen by some as a gross oversimplification. They argue that bad economic policies lead to poverty in rural areas, which is the main driving force behind high fertility rates, which lead to higher population growth, which intensifies stress on the natural resource base, which leads to more poverty, ad infinitum. They also argue that he underestimates the effect of local actions taken by people and organizations to mitigate environmental problems, such as the reforestation movements in Africa spearheaded by rural women.

How Many People *Can* the Earth Support?

When Ehrlich wrote *The People Bomb* in 1968, there were 3.5 billion people living on the planet. After only three decades the world's population now stands at 6.5 billion, with some 76 million added annually since 2000 (U.N., 2005). Some demographers and scientists predict that the Earth's human population, growing at current rates, will hit nine to ten billion sometime in the 21st century before leveling off (see Ehrlich et al., 1993; U.N., 2005). They predict that such a scenario could have drastic consequences in the form of massive environmental problems caused by an intensification of modern agricultural practices, which pollute the environment with their heavy use of pesticides and fertilizers, and which lead to the loss of valuable topsoil. In addition, food production requires water, and there is concern that adequate irrigation may be a major constraint on food production. Ehrlich believes that we cannot feed a growing world population without further undermining the very life-support system of the planet. Geographer Vaclav Smil (1994) counters this claim by suggesting that human beings are ingenuous enough to extract from the biosphere enough food to support healthy and vigorous life for a population of 10 billion. Smil claims that the obstacles to feeding the planet are not insurmountable, and that we can find ways to mitigate the burden that agriculture puts on the ecosystem (2000, 2002). He makes the following points regarding the food vs. population dilemma:

- Food production estimates are probably low.
- What a person actually needs to function may be overestimated (some people can exist on fewer calories per day).
- If we correct current inefficiencies in agronomic practices, including fertilizer uptake, reduced irrigation waste, and reduced post-harvest losses, we could feed an additional 2 to 3 billion people.
- Diets lower in meat would be more energy efficient (and healthier).
- The nations of the world could produce enough food for 11 billion if agriculture was more efficient and if rich nations were willing to reduce or re-channel energy consumption away from leisure into agriculture.

Bongaarts (1994) points out that much depends on the political factor, that is, the capacity of governments to implement the necessary improvements and reforms. Joel Cohen (1995), a scientist and mathematician who has studied the world's population growth extensively, analyzed many predictions and has come to the conclusion that it all comes down to human choices. The answer to the question of "How many people can the Earth support?" depends on what *kind* of Earth people want to live on. He stresses that the outcome of the future depends on people making some very tough choices. People will have to make decisions that curtail their high level of consumption, perhaps becoming vegetarians, or trading the car for a bicycle, or having fewer children. But he is ultimately hopeful that people will realize that their choices about family size and consumption do matter and will act in the interest of the planet. Ehrlich

and others have a more pessimistic outlook, claiming that we live under the illusion that science and technology will be able to deal with whatever population problems may surface: "Science and technology might eventually permit 12 billion people to live sustainable on Earth, but in the style of a factory chicken. Is that a desirable goal?" (Ehrlich & Ehrlich, 2005:11). While there is intense debate about whether an additional 3 or 4 billion people will exhaust the earth's capacity to sustain life, there is widespread agreement that the earth's population will finally stop growing around the middle of the 21st century. In the next section we will examine why demographers make this prediction.

Demographic Transition Theory

The huge, and truly unprecedented, "explosion" in the world's population in the last century was driven primarily by decreases in mortality rather than increases in fertility. Dramatic decreases in death rates were due to improved health care practices, including vaccinations and new ways of controlling infectious diseases, particularly in low-income countries. Where mortality rates are lower than birth rates, there is a **natural increase** in population. If birth rates are higher than death rates worldwide, then the world experiences population growth. The peak in the world's population growth rate occurred between 1965 and 1970, when it grew at an annual rate of 2.1%. In the 1970s birth rates finally started to fall faster than death rates, meaning that the rate of growth was beginning to decline. Even if fertility rates fall to the same level as mortality rates, a country's population would continue to grow because of something called **population momentum**. Earlier high fertility rates have created unusually large numbers of women of childbearing age.

There is presently enough food in the world to feed the population on a vegetarian diet, but any future dramatic increase in food production worldwide is unlikely, according to experts.

Many Voices: An Introduction to Social Issues

Demographers have identified a pattern called **demographic transition**, in which birth rates decline as economic growth and modernization take hold of a given society. Lower mortality rates come first, which lead to a temporary increase in population growth. But this is soon followed by lower fertility rates. For example, in 1800, the birth rates in the United States were higher than in any country today. Eventually, birth rates began to match lower mortality rates. The **total fertility rate (TFR)** is now slightly above two, which is generally thought to be the level of births in the U.S. needed to maintain the present level of population. Unfortunately for this theory, the transition in the economically poor countries, especially sub-Saharan Africa, has not happened as quickly as the experts predicted. The exact reason for this is complicated, but it is related primarily to socioeconomic conditions. For example, birth rates are lower where the gap between rich and poor has been narrowed, as in Kerala State (India), and they are also lower where the literacy rate for women has increased.

What this means for the future is that the poorest countries will continue to have the fastest growing populations, while the wealthiest countries will have below-replacement-level fertility rates (and thus their population will decrease). Sub-Saharan Africa and southern Asia have the highest birth rates in the 21st century. Ninety-five percent of the population growth will take place in the poorest countries; and by 2050, two-thirds of the world's people will live in the poorest countries (U.N., 2005; Ehrlich & Ehrlich, 2005). The greatest burden, then, of the "people bomb" will continue to be borne by those countries already having difficulty meeting the needs of their existing population.

Despite the regional variation of the demographic transition, it will continue to happen in all countries, leading to an eventual leveling out of the world's population by the middle of the 21st century. Predictions vary from 7.7 billion at the low end to a higher estimate of 11.7 billion, depending on how fast or slow birth rates decline, and estimating the impact of such things as the HIV/AIDS epidemic, which could reduce the total population by 200 million by 2050 (U.N., 2005; Ehrlich & Ehrlich, 2005).

The Interplay of Culture and Policy

If governments believe that population growth is a problem, what can they do about it? Who can dictate on such personal matters as reproduction and family size? In considering many of the population issues affecting our world and society, we have to look at the interplay of culture and public policy. Governments and their agents do indeed promote the use of birth control and **family planning** to their citizens. In reality, however, official slogans have very little impact since there are usually other factors that override what governments want to dictate. Heavy-handed government measures, such as the forcible sterilizations imposed by Indira Gandhi's government in India, are generally counterproductive. It is more likely that people's decisions about family size and migration are not made in direct response to government policy. There is even evidence that **China's "One Child" policy** is secretly ignored in many rural parts of the country (NOVA, 1984). In Kenya, fertility rates have declined and the country's population is no longer growing at 4% per year as it was in the 1980s, but this has more to do with land shortages than with family planning programs. The religious component of culture is also a powerful influence in family planning; witness how the **Hutterites** of North America, who in the past did not believe in artificial birth control, had the highest fertility rates in the world (Hostetler & Huntington, 1996).

Public policy can be an effective means of curbing population growth in two ways. Improvements in the education of women and in reproductive health care can indirectly affect positive family planning choices. As the educational status and health situation of women improve, birth rates tend to decline. Public policy also plays an effective role when it responds to human preference. When people already want to have fewer children, governments should respond by providing greater access to contraceptives along with instructions on how to use them.

Urbanization and the Rise of Cities

Population growth in some countries has had a major impact on another demographic phenomenon, the rise of cities. Urbanization used to be driven primarily by people migrating from rural to urban areas, usually because new opportunities were emerging in cities. Now the growth of cities in many countries is due not only to migration but also to the high birth rates within the cities themselves, particularly in low income countries. Those countries with the highest population growth are also those where the largest urban centers are emerging.

Urbanization is the transformation of a society from **rural** to **urban**. An urban place is a spatial concentration of people who organize their lives around non-agricultural activities. It was assumed by early sociologists (Tonnies, [1887] 1988) that urban people also perceived the world differently and behaved according to a different set of rules. Rural life was communal and major choices were strongly influenced by family, tradition, and religion. Urban life subsequently liberated one from the constraints of traditional life. No longer did everyone in the village know your business. A person could now choose relationships based upon mutual interests, not because parents or relatives approved. These somewhat oversimplified images of urban life reflect suspicions that urban life undermined moral values and weakened social ties, causing people to retreat within themselves (Simmel, [1905] 1950; Wirth, 1938).

According to Simmel, the crowded bustle of urban life caused people to retreat within themselves. Human interaction became reduced to calculated exchanges based on material benefit. Aversion and calculation prevented people from really caring about their neighbors. Overall, the downside of urban life was its emotionally alienating character—relationships were impersonal and instrumental; one felt isolated, withdrawn, fragmented, even while surrounded by masses of humanity (who felt equally isolated).

Later observers of urban life began to see more than just the dark side, and discovered tight-knit communities with strong ties to kin and friends, like urban villages. Whyte's (1981) study of Italian-American communities found that people in cities had a strong sense of identification and loyalty to the neighborhood and its inhabitants. More recent studies of new immigrant communities in cities (see section on immigration) have also identified tight-knit communities bounded together by ties of culture and family.

Cities have been around a long time, but until the 19th century most people still lived outside of cities. A shift occurred in the 19th century as some European societies became more urban than rural, with a majority of their populations living in urban centers. One explanation is that economic development is more efficient when concentrated in cities. During the industrial revolution, people migrated toward employment opportunities expanding in the cities.

The United States is experiencing a restructuring of its urban population. In the 1960s, people began moving away from the older cores of cities into suburbs. This out-migration was facilitated by interstate highways and housing subsidies for suburbanites. Then shopping malls moved economic activity into the suburbs. Over the last two decades, a different kind of community has arrived on the urban horizon known as the **edge city** (Garreau, 1991). Created at the periphery of older cities, these former suburbs have jobs, markets, and housing all in dense concentrations.

Some cities have become truly globalized as international centers of trade, finance, and culture. Urban growth is now fastest in **low-income industrializing countries**. In 1950, six of the top ten cities were in the United States, Europe, or Japan. By 1994, only three were in those regions. Furthermore, the size of cities has increased drastically. Lagos had about 1 million people in 1950, and is estimated to have about 24 million by 2015. Tokyo, the largest city in the world, had 6.2 million in 1950, but could have 28.7 million by 2015. It is likely that, by 2007, half the world's population will live in cities (United Nations, 2004). The consequences for developing countries are ominous. Demands for services in these huge and rapidly expanding urban centers, such as sewage disposal, garbage collection, schools, and roads, cannot be met fast enough, and put a tremendous strain on poorer countries.

Population Issues in the Industrialized World

ISSUES: What population issues are facing the United States? Is an aging population really something to worry about? How are recent immigrants different from earlier waves of immigrants? What is the impact of current immigration on traditional American communities? Do you agree with the current immigration policies? Why or why not?

America's "Gray Dawn"

"The challenge of global aging, like a massive iceberg, looms ahead.…Lurking beneath the waves, and not yet widely understood, are the wrenching economic and social costs that will accompany this demographic transformation—costs that threaten to bankrupt even the greatest of powers…" (Peterson, 1999).

So far the debates about population problems have centered around the potentially devastating impact of an additional three billion people on the earth's resources and its life support systems and what to do about it. However, in the United States there seems to be much more alarm raised about the opposite trend—low birth rates and its growing population of people living past retirement. This trend is often called the **graying of America**, an aging population with spiraling health costs and the looming crisis these present in terms of the nation's ability to pay for them through the Medicare program. Low fertility rates have already caused the populations of Germany and Russia to decrease. If fertility trends continue, some eastern European countries and Russia could have 20% to 50% fewer people in 2050, while Japan's population could decrease by 14%. In addition to the strain this puts on social programs for the elderly, there is the additional concern about the labor force and shrinking markets.

Some countries, such as the United States, continue to grow because of liberal immigration policies. This presents an interesting population dynamic. In the 1980s, three social scientists—David Hayes-Bautista, Jorge Chapa, and Werner Schink—studied the available demographic data on Latinos in California and wrote a book called *The Burden of Support* (1988). In it, they deal with the implications of a young, increasingly Latino population that is supporting an aging, largely Caucasian population.

In California, as in the United States as a whole, lower **birthrates** and longer **life spans** mean that the average age of Americans is increasing. At the same time, immigration from Latin America and higher birth rates among Latinos are causing a change in the ethnic composition of the population, primarily among younger **age sets**. California is one of several states where Latinos will become the majority of the population in the near future.

What are the critical implications of this kind of population dynamic? The first has to do with the **dependency ratio**, especially the makeup of those who are supporting the older population. In California, an increasingly greater proportion of the active workforce is Latino (mostly of Mexican and Central American origin). But most of this population works in low-paying service jobs (for example, as migrant farm workers, hotel maids, dishwashers, domestics, or in low-skilled manufacturing). Combined with this trend is the disturbing fact that Mexican youth have some of the highest high school dropout rates. The problem is that as the dependency ratio increases, it is the Latino population that is increasingly shouldering the burden of supporting the aging population. But this raises the question of how a low-paid, less educated workforce can support such things as Social Security and Medicare as those funds are being drained by an aging population.

The intersection of age structure and immigration illustrates the interconnectedness of demographic processes—that fertility and migration are interrelated events. As the world's population continues to grow in countries least able to absorb them, and economic globalization accelerates, it is inevitable that the migration of people for jobs and security will be primary concerns. The next section looks specifically at the impact that international migration is having in the United States.

Immigrant America

Between 1965 and 2000, about 30 million people immigrated into the United States. The proportion of immigrants in the population has reached 20%, exceeding the historical high set at the turn of the century when millions came from Europe seeking religious freedom and economic opportunity (Portes & Rumbaut, 2001). During the 1990s, somewhere between 700,000 and 900,000 legal immigrants entered the United States annually (depending on how efficiently applications were being processed) (Portes & Rumbaut, 1996). The Census Bureau estimates that 13.3 million of the foreign-born residents immigrated since 1990 (Millard & Chapa et al., 2004).

Up until 2003, admission to the United States was handled by the **Immigration and Naturalization Service** within the Department of Justice. Immigrant visas are now granted through the newly established Bureau of Citizenship and Immigration Services within the Department of Homeland Security (DHS). Other INS functions are now performed by the Bureau of Customs and Border Protection, and the Bureau of Immigration and Customs Enforcement.

Who are these **new immigrants**? By looking at one year's admissions we can get a quick profile (USDHS, 2005). In 2004, the DHS states that it granted legal residence to 946,142 people. Charts and tables give us a profile of these immigrants, such as region (Figure 19.1), country of origin (Table 19.1), and the basis for their being granted legal status in this country (Figure 19.2).

These "new immigrants" reflect a tremendous diversity, both within themselves and in contrast to the current population of the United States. The collective experience of the turn-of-the-century migration was significantly different from the current "new" immigration in several ways. Although they came from numerous European countries, which reflected many different ethnic backgrounds, these immigrants were in some ways less diverse, both internally and in contrast to the native population, than the current migration that hails primarily from Asia and Latin America (see Figure 19.1 and Table 19.1). Changes in immigration policies led to a long hiatus after the 1920s, during which very little replenishment of those groups took place. The current immigration is characterized by constant replenishment, and all indicators suggest it is bound to continue (Massey & Golding, 1995).

The policy that helped set this in motion is the **Immigration and Nationality Act of 1965**. This act abolished a quota system, established in the 1920s, based on the proportion of nationality groups already in the United States, and thus had favored applicants from Western Europe (England, Germany, and Ireland) (Portes & Rumbaut, 1996). The new act abolished nationality and race of ancestry as basis for admission, technically giving all countries a chance to apply for its quota of visas. However, the act also gave preference to relatives and those with special occupational skills (see Figure 19.3). Although the 1965 act also put a first-time cap on entries from the Western Hemisphere such as Latin American countries, which made it more difficult for Latin Americans to apply for immigrant visas, the flow of immigrants from Mexico and Caribbean nations continued to increase due to family unification provisions, transnational networks, and labor demand (Massey & Goldling, 1994; Portes & Rumbaut, 1996).

Half of all the immigrants in the U.S. are from Latin America, the largest group being of Mexican origin. The rapid growth of the number of immigrants from Mexico in the 1980s and 1990s is due to a combination of economic and social factors:

- *Economic:* The devaluation of the peso, and the inability of the Mexican economy to keep up with their own "baby boom," combined with a strong demand for inexpensive labor in the United States, stimulated the ongoing northward migration.
- *Social Networks:* Simultaneously the social pathways linking families and friends in both countries became stronger. These pathways serve as conduits of information and resources that decrease the costs and risks of migration for each successive family member.
- *Status Adjustment:* In 1986, more than a million undocumented Mexican workers were granted permanent status under an amnesty program. Family

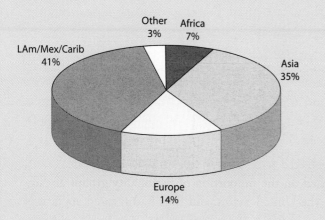

Figure 19.1: Region of origin for FY 2004
Source: *DHS Yearbook of Immigration Statistics for 2004.*

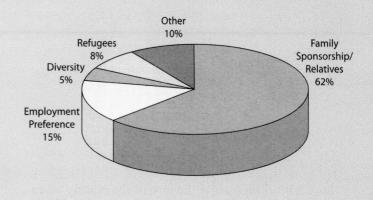

Figure 19.2: Major reasons for admission for 2004
Source: *DHS Yearbook of Immigration Statistics for 2004.*

Table 19.1: Countries of Origin 2004
(top 10 sending countries):

Country	Percent of Total
Mexico	18.5
India	7.4
Philippines	6.1
China	5.4
Vietnam	3.3
Dominican Republic	3.2
El Salvador	3.1
Cuba	2.1
Colombia	2
Korea	2

Source: *DHS Yearbook of Immigration Statistics for 2004.*

reunification provisions made it easier to secure visas and citizenship for family members.

Mexican immigration is illustrative of the principle of **cumulative causation**, where migration eventually creates an internal momentum that perpetuates it. As Massey puts it: "The range of social contacts in the network expands with the entry of each migrant, thus encouraging still more migration and ultimately leading to the emergence of international migration as a mass phenomenon" (Massey et al., 1990, p. 5).

Immigrant Origins and Types

Within the diversity of immigrant experiences, immigrants fall into four broad types or categories—laborers, professionals, entrepreneurs, and political refugees (Portes & Rumbaut, 1996).

Labor Migrants

The United States has a long history of recruiting workers from abroad. As the United States expanded and industrialized during the latter 19th and early 20th centuries, the Chinese and Irish built its roads and railways. It was a common saying that "an Irishman was buried under every railroad tie" (Takaki, 1993). Mexicans were recruited from early in the century to work the mines and farms of the Southwest. The value of Mexican agricultural labor was apparent during World War II, when the **Bracero** guest worker program was established to guarantee manpower for U.S. agriculture. The Bracero program actually increased in the 1950s, during which time U.S. authorities also deported a million allegedly undocumented workers (Garcia y Griego, Weeks, & Chande, 1990), illustrating the inconsistent government policy toward immigrant labor. American agriculture continues to rely heavily on labor recruited from Mexico (especially fruit and vegetable production).

The burgeoning service industries (restaurants and hotels, for example) and semiskilled manufacturing (such as in the garment and textile industries) depend on immigrants for much of their workforce. Immigrant laborers tend to have low levels of education and to come from low-income communities and families. Hotel workers from Mexico and the West Indies are one example.

Labor migrants frequently have a specific purpose for venturing from home and family: "'My family needed money for planting and food' or 'I came to

work and send my parents money'" (Chavez, 1998, p. 29). In addition to family needs, they may see their sojourn as necessary for securing additional capital for a business venture. For these reasons they are called **target earners** (Chavez, 1998).

Professionals

Contradicting the cherished notion that immigrants come to the U.S. because they are poor is the fact that 17% of immigrant visas in 2001 were granted to professionals who had skills in short supply in the United States (USDOJ, 2003). Immigrants of this type tend to be highly educated, come from affluent families, and live in suburbia (Portes & Rumbaut, 1996). Examples are the large numbers of nurses who continue to be recruited from India and the Philippines, and the engineers and software developers from Pakistan, India, and Israel who were in particularly high demand during the 1990s. American companies argue that they need to be able to recruit certain highly skilled workers from abroad in order to stay competitive, and are active in lobbying the government to maintain provisions in immigration laws that will allow foreign skilled professionals to obtain work permits.

Entrepreneurs

The entrepreneurial immigrants are the most highly visible, due to their concentration in enclaves such as Koreatown in Los Angeles or Little Havana in Miami. These immigrants have used networks of friends and family, pooled resources, and savings from their home countries to start new businesses (Light & Bonacich, 1988). Many of these tend to be small businesses catering to the ethnic market. Most come under the visa provisions for skilled or professional workers, family unification, or the 10,000 visas per year for individuals who invest $500,000 and create five new jobs. The entrepreneurial class of immigrants creates niches in the economy (for example, Koreans control the wig retail outlets) and often revitalizes lagging industries and urban centers.

Refugees

Traditionally, the United States has been a haven to those fleeing governments that oppressed them for political or religious reasons. During the Cold War (from about the early 1950s to the late 1980s), the United States provided asylum for those leaving

Many entrepreneurial immigrants tend to start small businesses catering to the ethnic market.

Communist regimes such as in Cuba, Eastern Europe, and the Soviet Union. Geopolitical relationships between the U.S. and other countries also create flows of immigrants into the United States. After the Gulf War, hundreds of refugee families from Kurdistan and Iraq were resettled in the United States. And the largest groups of refugees in recent history have been the Vietnamese, following the defeat of South Vietnam by the communist North Vietnam in the mid 1970s, and Cubans who found themselves losers in Fidel Castro's revolutionary takeover in Cuba. Since the Cold War, refugees have continued to come for political and religious reasons. In the 1990s, Jews from the former Soviet Union were the largest group admitted under this provision. In 2001, 10% of immigrants in the U.S. were admitted as refugees, the largest group being from Bosnia (Patrick, 2002).

The United States routinely accepts more refugees for **resettlement** than any other country in the world. For example, in 2000 over 70,000 refugees were resettled (the next largest number was in Canada, which accepted about 7,000). The mandated **ceiling** for resettlement varies, depending on foreign policy considerations. For example, in response to the Balkan crisis, the resettlement ceiling was raised to over 140,000. Since the early 1990s it has declined by half to 70,000 (Patrick, 2002).

Controversies Surrounding Immigration

Alejandro Portes and Ruben Rumbaut, two sociologists who have spent much of their careers studying immigrants in the United States, have observed: "Never before has the US received so many immigrants from so many different countries, from such varied and economic backgrounds, and for so many compelling reasons.…The new immigrants are changing fundamentally the ethnic and racial composition and stratification of the American population, and perhaps also the social meaning of ethnicity and race" (1996, p. 1).

We have just outlined the reasons for the magnitude of immigration in this era. Immigration does not happen by random choices of people outside a given country's borders—rather, it stems from a complex combination of policy decisions, politico-economic relationships between countries, and cultural-familial ties between communities. Furthermore, one thing is certain: it has generated heated debate about the economic, social, and security consequences for American society. These concerns express themselves in different ways at local, regional, and national levels. Local communities can react negatively when they have received large numbers of immigrants who are culturally and linguistically different from the native population (see Crane & Millard, 2004). Some states and local communities, especially along our borders, have voiced concerns about the additional economic burdens placed on them by growing immigrant populations. At the national level, the debate centers on security risks of both legal and undocumented immigrants from certain regions of the world, as well as on fears that the number of immigrants (especially non-European) is too high.

Changing Ethnic Composition of the United States

The U.S. is an extremely diverse country by the world's

standards. Historically, the U.S. has been shaped by people who came from Africa, Latin America, and Asia, as well as from all parts of Europe (Takaki, 1993). The change in immigration policy over the latter half of the past century has accelerated the growth of the Latino and Asian populations. For example, Latinos are presently the largest "minority," comprising 12.5% of the U.S. population (U.S. Bureau of the Census, 2000), a 58% growth since the last census. It is projected that by the year 2050 Latinos will constitute 25% of the population. These same projections show that Americans of European descent will no longer be in the majority, that there will be as many "people of color" (those of non-European descent, see Figure 19.3). This is already a reality in cities such as Los Angeles, and will be happening in some states well before the year 2050.

Fears of Ethnic Separatism

Why do some people find these projections alarming? There are some who believe that immigration will change the essential core values of American civilization. According to Hardin (1995), "When we admit a Sikh or a Muslim, for instance, we are admitting more than a human body. We are admitting a person imbued with cultural values that are *significantly different* from our own" (p. 138, italics added).

Taking Hardin's point a step further, Brent Nelson (1994) argues that concentrations of immigrants have the possibility of influencing the mainstream culture in their vicinity to adopt foreign values, what

he labels "reverse assimilation." His views reflect the fear that immigrants will irrevocably change America—its complexion, its religions, and its culture. The end result, it is feared, will be a fragmentation or "Balkanization" of America into a disunity of ethnic pluralism, similar to what happened to Yugoslavia in the 1990s.

In historical perspective, America is always in the process of being re-created by diverse peoples from far-flung places who have become American. That is only part of the picture, for all those who have come to America have been likewise changed in the process. The **Children of Immigrants Longitudinal Study (CILS)** illustrates this reality. By the time the youth of immigrant parents graduate from high school, only 15% are still bilingual and most prefer to speak English (Portes & Rumbaut, 2001). The study reveals a pattern of segmented assimilation, in which immigrant youth adapt to various layers of American society in different ways, depending on the context of reception, family resources, and the presence of an ethnic community. Immigrant youth who acculturate more slowly to America have fewer problems in school and display less deviant behavior. Thus we should not see it as a threat when immigrants hold on to their language and culture, and when youth have strong ethnic communities to support them along the road to adulthood. There are more problems when immigrant children Americanize rapidly, especially when this causes family conflict and loss of parental control.

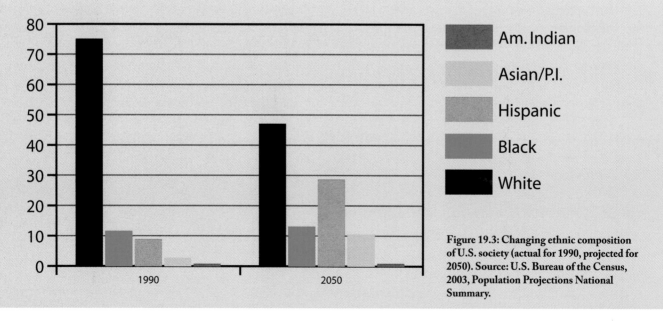

Figure 19.3: Changing ethnic composition of U.S. society (actual for 1990, projected for 2050). Source: U.S. Bureau of the Census, 2003, Population Projections National Summary.

Many Voices: An Introduction to Social Issues

Case Study in Demography: Latinos in the Heartland

The experience of Ligonier, Indiana, illustrates the fears that some have about the impact that immigration can have on communities. "With a population of about 4,000, Ligonier appears to be one of the cities or towns in northeast Indiana most affected by the growth of the Latino population," observed the local press. Below is a description of how the Latino community grew dramatically during the 1990s, and the reactions that followed (Crane & Millard 2004).

When the Dominguez family (pseudonym) settled in Ligonier in the mid 1970s, only about 12 Mexican-American families lived there. But people like Jose Morales had been giving Ligonier a good reputation to friends and relatives in other parts of the country. It was through his friend Jose that Ignacio Ambriz heard about Ligonier and decided to move his family, including nine children, to this small peaceful town in the heartland. Ligonier was considered a place where "dreams have come true" for the Latino families who had settled there.

The trickle of families who joined the pioneers became a wave in the late 1980s and early 1990s. Mexican workers from the pioneer families had by this time already proved themselves as model workers. Some of these long-term employees were asked by companies to recruit additional workers, and they did, bringing friends and relatives from Mexico, the border region, and other parts of the United States. Since housing was in short supply, many rented second-story apartments in the downtown business district, making them particularly visible.

In January of 1993—the same year in-migration of Latinos became more noticeable—a new mayor took office. The mayor began his tenure by having to confront a mounting series of complaints directed to his office regarding certain behaviors and practices of the now substantial and highly visible Mexican population—loud music, loitering, and slaughtering of goats in backyards (see Figure 19.4).

In 1995 the mayor lost his re-election bid because he was considered too "welcoming" to the new immigrants. Tensions ran very high for several years. After a difficult period of tension and adjustment, the town eventually achieved a kind of equilibrium. The school system, law enforcement, and local government had to adapt to the changes brought about by the arrival of hundreds of new persons of Mexican descent seeking to better their lives in the Midwest. While the newest mayor admits there are problems—including language barriers, building code violations, illegal immigrants, and drugs—there is a general feeling that the "situation" has improved. Most attribute it to efforts (started by the mayor who was not re-elected) to educate newcomers about ordinances and local norms, as well as attempts to bring about mutual understanding. White residents who originally complained seem to have conceded the permanent existence of a large Mexican community in the center of Ligonier.

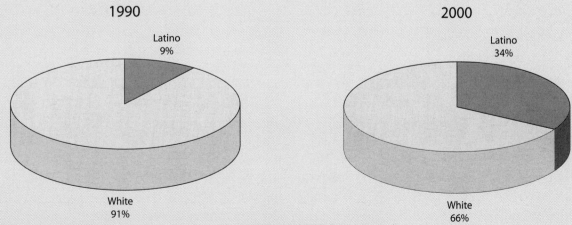

Figure 19.4: Comparisons of Latino population in Ligonier from 1990 to 2000 (U.S. Census Bureau)

Each year, thousands of immigrants go through citizenship classes, swearing allegiance to defend the Constitution and the nation's laws. Luedtke (1992) argues that there is solid evidence that immigrants adhere just as much to the core values that have historically characterized America as do its citizens. These values, after all, have nothing to do with accent, religion, or dietary preferences. America was not founded on a common language, religion, or ethnic identity, but rather on a common set of democratic, political ideals—freedom of religion and expression, equal opportunity, all encapsulated in the Constitution and the Bill of Rights. Immigrants may adhere to traditions, religions, and languages that are different from the mainstream, but they defend just as strongly as non-immigrants the core ideals on which this country was founded.

Impact on Communities

Much of the attention in the immigration debate has been focused on cities and states that have been the primary destinations of new immigrants, such as Los Angeles, Miami, and New York. But the impact of immigration on small, rural communities may be more dramatic and intense than it is on urban communities. In the 1990s, many smaller, rural communities experienced dramatic changes in the ethnic makeup of the population. A group of researchers who studied the growth of Latino communities in the rural Midwest found that for some communities it was the defining issue of the decade (Chapa & Millard, 2004). This possibility is illustrated by the case study from Indiana (Crane & Millard, 2004). While adding 1,000 immigrants in a decade may mean nothing in New York, for Ligonier, Indiana, it means that a third of the town is now Latino.

There are many concerns about immigrants, both legal and illegal. Some fears have been expressed about immigrants not becoming like "us" and bringing with them "strange" non-Christian religions. Even in heartland states like Indiana, small rural towns are experiencing a much greater ethnic diversity. As we saw from the Ligonier example, communities find this kind of change difficult. Established residents feel threatened by the cultural difference of newcomers, and complain that the newcomers do not want to learn English or obey local laws, and that they must be "illegals." Immigrant newcomers sense the hostility directed at them

and keep to themselves, further "evidence" that they don't want to fit in. Older Latino residents feel caught in the middle, as do those who attempt to bridge the gap between both groups. Hundreds of communities in the South and Midwest are learning how to cope with similar changes.

Economic Impact

The argument that immigrants are a drain on the economy is based on a belief that they annually cost the government about 44 billion dollars over what they contribute in the form of taxes (Huddle, 1994). Some studies show, however, that the amount that immigrants take in the form of government resources (food stamps or bilingual programs) is overestimated (Fix & Passel, 1994). Undocumented immigrants tend to avoid encounters with government agencies for fear of deportation. Some immigrants will return to their own country for such things as childbirth (Chavez, 1998). Likewise, tax collections are usually understated. Immigrants pay not only sales tax but income tax (even illegal immigrants pay social security taxes). The widely repeated claim that immigrants are a drain on the welfare system is not true for the nation as a whole. In fact, welfare rates of non-refugee immigrants (refugees are granted government support as part of the Refugee Act) are lower than that of non-immigrant residents (Fix & Passel, 1994). We have already seen that the new immigrants are a more highly educated group than in the late 19th and early 20th centuries. For the new immigrants who arrived post 1965, their level of college attainment is equal to the resident population, and those immigrants in the professional and managerial class exceed the resident population (Portes & Rumbaut, 1996).

There is some evidence that immigrants depress wages for resident workers in some low-wage jobs. This depends, however, on how the economy is doing overall (Fix & Passel, 1994). During recessionary periods, for example, economic opportunities for African Americans who live in areas of high immigration are reduced, but they are increased during periods of economic growth. This is because immigrants create jobs by starting businesses, and buy and consume goods and services. The other economic benefit is that they provide a de facto guest worker program (Chapa & Millard, 2004; Massey et al., 2002).

Some professions have depended on professionals from abroad to meet labor demand. In the case of nurses, there is no evidence that foreign nurses replace resident nurses (Fix & Passel, 1994). However, it is possible that continued reliance on foreign nurses may reduce efforts to train and recruit nurses in the resident population. The recruitment of foreign nurses may also decrease the rate at which salaries and working conditions improve for nurses.

Research does not support the claim that immigration hurts job prospects for resident minority groups. The group whose job prospects are most negatively affected are immigrants who recently preceded them—that is, the most recent arrivals will have fewer job opportunities because they have to compete with a large number of immigrants who are already in the job market (Fix & Passel, 1994).

Very little attention in the public debate is given to the economic benefits of immigration. Certain sectors of the economy (such as the textile industry and agriculture) could not survive without a large supply of relatively cheap, often immigrant, labor. By helping these "transitional" industries survive, immigration prevents jobs from leaving communities. Furthermore, immigrants create jobs through new business ventures and investment. As mentioned above, 10,000 visas are granted annually to entrepreneurs who start new businesses and create jobs.

Illegal Immigration

Immigration reform was at the top of the agenda in the fall of 2001 when President-elect George W. Bush met with the President-elect of Mexico, Vicente Fox. Fox was concerned about Mexican citizens who had been working in the United States illegally for many years, some of whom risked their lives each year crossing and re-crossing the southern border. There were plans to continue a dialogue between the two leaders about immigration between the two countries which share a long border and many economic and political interests, even a discussion about an amnesty for undocumented Mexicans in the U.S. and a freer and more open border between the two countries in the future. Then the terrorist attacks of 9/11 changed the course of this dialogue, replacing it with concerns of lack of border security and possible entry points for those who wish to harm the United States.

The increasingly common perception that the situation is out of control has prompted groups like the "Minuteman Project" to send volunteers to patrol the border crossings between Arizona and Mexico. The group's founder claims that it is "a grassroots effort to bring Americans to the defence of their homeland" which is "devoured and plundered by the menace of tens of millions of invading illegal aliens" (BBC, 2005). The governor of New Mexico declared a state of emergency in 2005, citing the "violence directed at law enforcement, damage to property and livestock, increased evidence of drug smuggling, and an increase in the number of undocumented immigrants" (CNN, 2005).

Undocumented or illegal immigrants come from all parts of the world. According to the Immigration and Naturalization Service, the five countries with the largest number of illegal residents in the United States are Mexico, El Salvador, Guatemala, Canada, and Haiti, with Mexico being the single largest (59% of the total). During the 1986 amnesty program, 70% of those granted legal status were Mexican (Reimers, 1992). Based on data released by the U.S. Census Bureau, the INS has estimated that the number of illegal residents in the United States as of January 2000 was 7 million (U.S. Department of Justice, 2003). Estimates from 2001 put the number of undocumented Mexican immigrants alone at 4.5 million (Chapa et al., 2004; Lowell & Suro, 2002). The INS also believed that each year the number of undocumented immigrants in the U.S. increased by about 275,000, 41% through overstaying the terms of their visas (U.S. Department of Justice, 2001).

The experience of being an undocumented immigrant is fraught with legal difficulty, hostility, and vulnerability to exploitation (Portes & Rumbaut, 1996). Crossing the borders involves physical risks, robbery, rape, accidents, and death (Chavez, 1998). In March 2002, eighteen Mexicans died from dehydration while traveling in the desert (McInroy, 2003). Whatever their origins, "their lack of legal status, unfamiliarity with American customs and institutions, and frequently lack of fluency in English make them vulnerable in the labor market" (Reimers, 1992, p. 226). Most undocumented immigrants fill low-paying and low-status jobs, in which they have little recourse if employers exploit them. For this reason, those in favor of an amnesty program say it is time to extend to them the rights and protections of the citizens. After all, it is argued, they have been productive and law abiding residents in this country for years, providing a de facto guestworker program (Chapa et al., 2004).

Complaints about illegal immigrants are similar to those made against immigrants in general—that they are a drain on the country's scarce resources. Furthermore, some argue, amnesty programs are unfair to those who are applying for citizenship through regular channels. They also fear that amnesty programs will only increase the flow of undocumented migrants from countries like Mexico. More recently, concerns about the undocumented revolve around national security risks.

Public Policy and Unintended Consequences

ISSUES: Do governments actually have control over the movement and flow of people? How can a country meet its economic (job) and political needs and still control the flow of people going in and out? Do you believe there will always be a movement of people from poorer countries into richer ones? If so, how do you think that affects both countries?

At first glance, it may seem as if governments can actually have some influence over the movement of peoples: they can police borders and deny or grant visas to whomever they wish. However, policymakers have not been able to predict the actual consequences of immigration laws. These laws can be effective in regulating who is allowed into the country. But those laws have often been subservient to economic, political, and military relationships with certain countries that ultimately determine who has access to visas.

We have also seen that what shapes the destinations of immigrants into the U.S. are **social networks**—relationships with family and friends across borders. The **Immigration Reform and Control Act of 1986** was partly a response to criticism of lax policy regarding undocumented workers. The resulting law, however, did not take into account the social network multiplier effect of its actions. Granting amnesty, and eventual citizenship, made it possible for family members to be brought to the U.S. over and above legal quotas (Portes & Rumbaut, 1996). Rather than diminishing the flow of immigrants into the U.S., the act probably increased the flow of people, both documented and undocumented, across the U.S. border.

Immigration policy continues to be shaped by the strong demand for labor by powerful economic entities in the U.S. This is why both the Immigration Reform and Control Act of 1986, and Proposition 187 in 1994, which denied any form of social or educational services to undocumented immigrants, were written so as to not effectively obstruct employment of the undocumented. Close analysis of Proposition 187 (Chavez, 1998) reveals that it is based on the assumption that undocumented immigrants are attracted to the health and welfare benefits in the U.S. It is clear from research, however, that those concerns are secondary to economic motivations.

Conclusion

While demographers specialize in studying population, many people, including sociologists, anthropologists, geographers, and political scientists, also study populations and population trends. Government planners and business marketers are constantly trying to understand the demographics of groups of people at all levels from individual communities to countries as a whole. An understanding of patterns of migration, family size, age, and ethnicity contributes to a better understanding of human behavior.

Looking over the history of the world's population growth, we are in a truly unique period in history. We add more people per decade than existed on Earth in the year 1600. The yearly growth of population was at its high point in the late 1970s, and has tapered off since then. But many less economically developed countries of the world are still experiencing rapid growth, which contributes to the process of urbanization.

It is important to see the connection between the two main issues in this chapter—world population growth and migration. The majority of immigrants to the United States are from regions and countries (such as the Philippines, Central America, India, Pakistan, and China) that have experienced high rates of population growth in the recent past. These lower-income countries tend to have younger populations, meaning that a greater percentage of their population is between the ages of 15 and 40 (people of working age seeking jobs) than higher-income countries. This follows a global pattern of migration from lower-income countries with young populations to post-industrial economies with older populations. Some countries are caught in the middle. Mexico, for example, not only sends many emigrants north, but receives many immigrants of its own from its neighbors to the south, such as El Salvador and Guatemala.

The two most significant population trends in the United States are that the population is growing older, and that record-high levels of immigration from Latin America and Asia are changing the complexion of our society. The two issues intersect in California, where there is an aging resident population and a young and rapidly growing Latino population. Previous hot-button issues about immigrants refusing to assimilate or negatively affecting the economy have been preempted by the war on terrorism and new concerns about America's security. Immigration laws and border policies have come under scrutiny, as have certain nationalities associated with terrorist activity.

World Population Growth and International Migration

by Isidore Flores

In simple terms, world over-crowding will lead to population control through war, famine, disease, or family planning. As the world's population grows, there is increased demand for living space, food, and raw materials—all of which are finite resources. If we do nothing to control population, the physical limits of the world will do it for us. Discussions of how many people the planet can support and how that number might be reached do not change that fact. Whether larger or smaller, there is a limit, and we are better off putting in place family-planning structures sooner rather than later because people are suffering the effects of overpopulation now.

Overpopulation. One can consider the Japanese, who have learned to live close together with very little personal space, as an example for arguing that the world can sustain many more people. But what has happened because of the tight space situation? As the population has grown, the demand for living space has also grown. Japan's economy became disproportionately supported on the demand for more and more living space, and that, in turn, increased land values more and more. They are now suffering a long, chronic recession triggered when land in Tokyo got so expensive that real estate values could not be sustained. Hence, the quality of life in the country which has one of the top three economies in the world isn't what it used to be.

Japan, the U.S., and the countries of Western Europe, for example, enjoy excellent infrastructures due to their well-evolved economies. What happens to poorer countries that cannot afford extensive and inclusive public health systems like water treatment facilities? They cannot sustain larger populations (in comparison to the richer countries) without increases in significant outbreaks of life-threatening diseases.

The Japanese experience also shows how the need for natural resources by a growing population can lead to war. Japan depends on the importation of fuels because it has no naturally occurring oil or gas deposits. As its population and economy grew, fuel imports became more and more critical. Feeling its oil imports threatened, Japan entered WWII partly to secure those supplies.

Famines are nothing new, but an increasing population can increase their frequency and severity. When populations were relatively small, a year of bad crops could be offset by surplus from a previous year. As populations grow and take up more agricultural space for housing and infrastructure while needing more agricultural produce, food surpluses and overproduction capacity become less of a buffer against problems brought on by the vagaries of nature or human-caused environmental assault. What once would have been a glitch in the food supply could quickly become a famine.

Immigration. There are virtually no places left in the world where an ethnic group can live in its own autonomous territory. The Balkan region, with its historically rooted animosities, gives us an example of ethnic groups that resist living together peacefully and go to war with each other when their populations grow and spill over into neighboring territories.

A result equally as disastrous can occur when countries push back their borders to gain greater land area to accommodate population growth. A good example is what our own country did in what it calls the Mexican War of 1845. The U.S. attacked Mexico and expropriated two-thirds of its land area for no other reason than to increase its territory for its growing population at the expense of a militarily weaker neighbor. Much of the existing population in this area was killed, terrorized into fleeing south, or forcefully evicted from the lands they owned because the protections against these actions written into the Treaty of Guadalupe Hidalgo that ended the war were, for the most part, ignored by all levels and branches of government.

In an ironic twist and due to population pressures, Mexicans are spilling back across the present-day border to repopulate some of those expropriated areas with a population culturally similar to that which was formerly there. A common scenario involves farming families in northern Mexico who can no longer subdivide their land among their children because to do so would render the resulting parcels too small to sustain a viable livelihood from farming. Most of their children are faced with seeking agricultural work somewhere else, or joining those who look for some other type of work in urban areas. Many choose to migrate north of the border without documents (i.e., illegally), where skilled agricultural workers can earn more than in Mexico. Many of them join the streams of migrant farm workers that spread north all the way to the Canadian border. When their work is done, they travel back south, crossing the border to spend the winter at home. Some stay in areas this side of the border, such as in south Texas or Florida, thinking it easier to escape notice by posing as residents rather than trying to evade immigration officials while trying to cross back over the border the following year.

The numbers of undocumented workers who remain in the United States is affected by the unemployment rate here. When it is higher, fewer can find work to sustain them over the winter. When it is lower, there are more employment opportunities. In the 1980s it was estimated that 15% to 20% of people in the farm worker migrant stream were undocumented. Things began to change as the economy improved in the early 1990s. The unemployment rate began to drop. This phenomenon, coupled with the growing trend of establishing meat packing plants in rural areas close to cattle feed lots and other livestock operations, provided the opportunity for many U.S. citizens who did migratory farm work to "settle out" of the migrant stream and take permanent, year-round jobs in those plants. This left a labor shortage in the agricultural, migrant labor stream that was filled by undocumented workers. In the 1990s, the number of undocumented workers doing migratory farm work grew to 80% in some areas of the Midwest.

The U.S. has long depended on new immigrant labor to fuel its ever-expanding economy. The American Dream promises that you can pull yourself up the socioeconomic ladder if you work hard enough. As people become better skilled and start climbing, new people are needed for those bottom-rung positions. Successive waves of immigrants have been refilling those positions without pause for the entire history of this country. It is doubtful that the tide of undocumented immigrant labor can be stemmed given the widespread support among employers who depend on cheap immigrant labor, even after the World Trade Center tragedy (and related events) of September 11, 2001. It is more likely that attempts to legalize their status through a modern-day "Bracero" type program (that made it legal in the 1960s to hire agricultural workers from across the border) will overcome any large-scale attempts to deport illegal workers or keep new illegal workers out.

Let us not lose sight of the fact that at some point, immigration and fertility rates will inflate the population of this country to the point where the physical limits are approached. If we do not incorporate population controls into our socio-cultural milieu, our country will suffer the same sorts of disruptions to our quality of life and social order as any other country in this increasingly overpopulated world.

Discussion Questions

1. Concerning the history of the world's population, why is this current period of time significant?
2. Why is it disadvantageous for a country to have either a predominantly "young" or predominantly "old" population?
3. Do you think we are headed for certain disaster because of population growth, or do you think people are resourceful enough to avoid catastrophe?
4. What is the "new immigration," and in what way is it different from the previous wave of migration at the turn of the 19th century?
5. There is wide agreement that immigration is indeed changing America. But what do you think about Brent Nelson's claim that America's core values are being changed in a negative way?
6. Many employers want fewer restrictions on immigrants, not more. What would happen if immigration laws restricted visas for foreign nurses? How would that affect wages and working conditions for nurses, or affect health care costs? Who would be the winners or losers in that policy change?
7. Is the Ligonier case evidence that people's worst fears about the "Balkanizing" effects of immigration are coming true? Are immigrants undermining the cultural values of small communities?

Related Readings

Birdsall, N., Kelley, A. C., & Sinding, S. (Eds.). (2003). *Population matters: Demographic change, economic growth, and poverty in the developing world.* New York: Oxford University Press.

Chapa, J., & Hayes-Bautista, D. (1988). *The burden of support.* Berkeley, CA: University of California Press.

Cohen, J. E. (1995). *How many people can the Earth support?* New York: W. W. Norton.

Ehrlich, P. R., & Ehrlich, A. H. (1990). *The population explosion.* New York: Simon and Shuster.

Gold, S. J. (1992). *Refugee communities: A comparative field study.* Thousand Oaks, CA: Sage.

Gold, S. J. (1995). *From the workers' state to the Golden State: Jews from the former Soviet Union in California.* Boston, MA: Allyn and Bacon.

Gold, S. J., & Rubaut, R. (Eds.). (2002–2004). *The new Americans: Recent immigration and American society.*

Massey, D. S., Durand, J., & Malone, N. J. (2002). *Beyond smoke and mirrors: Mexican immigration in an era of economic integration.* New York: Russell Sage.

Millard, A., & Chapa, J. (Eds.). (2005). *Apple pie and enchiladas: Latino newcomers and the changing dynamics of the rural Midwest.* Austin, TX: University of Texas Press.

Portes, A., & Rumbaut, R. (1996). *Immigrant America: A portrait* (2nd ed.). Berkeley, CA: University of California Press.

Portes, A., & Rumbaut, R. (2001). *Legacies: The story of the new second generation.* Berkeley, CA: University of California Press.

Rothenberg, D. (1998). *With these hands: The hidden world of migrant farmworkers today.* New York: Harcourt Brace.

Simon, J. L. (1996). *The ultimate resource.* Princeton, NJ: Princeton University Press.

Smils, V. (2000). *Feeding the world: A challenge for the twenty-first century.* Cambridge, MA: MIT Press.

Related Web Sites

Center for Immigration Studies: http://www.cis.org
Immigration History Research Center: http://www.umn.edu/ihrc
Immigration Index: http://www.immigrationindex.org
The Immigration Superhighway: http://www.theodora.com/is.html
Migration Information Source: http://www.migrationinformation.org
Office of Immigration Statistics (OIS): http://www.Uscis.gov
Population Division, Department of Economic and Social Affairs, United Nations: http://www.un.org/popin
Population Reference Bureau: http://www.prb.org
United Nations Population Fund (UNFPA): http://www.unfpa.org/index.htm
U.S. Bureau of the Census: http://www.census.gov

Related Movies/Videos

Avalon (feature on Polish immigrant family)

Between Two Worlds (documentary on Korean American youth)

Blue Collar and Buddha (documentary on refugees and community reception)

China's Only Child (NOVA documentary on population control programs in China)

Double Happiness (feature on Chinese immigrant family)

El Norte (Feature on Refugees from Guatemala)

Food or Famine (documentary on population growth)

Geronimo: His Story (documentary on illegal immigrants in California)

The Great Wall (feature on Chinese Americans)

Human Tide (documentary on population growth)

Mi Familia/My Family (chronicles three generations of a Mexican American family)

Natives: Immigrant Bashing on the Border (documentary on U.S./Mexico immigration issues)

Tales from Arab Detroit (documentary on young Arab Americans)

FROM SOCIAL PROBLEMS TO POLICIES

Héctor Luis Díaz

20

Employment agency. San Francisco.
Library of Congress, Prints & Photographs Division, FSA-OWI Collection, LC-USF34-016164-D

Chapter Outline

The Great Depression: A Story of Suffering, Enlightenment, and Transformation

The crash of the United States stock market in October 1929 marked the beginning of the Great Depression in this country. During the years that followed, one out of every four persons in the nation became unemployed and one out of six received government assistance in order to survive. Many people were willing to work in exchange for food, but in spite of that they remained unemployed, poor, and hungry. Shantytowns covered the landscape of America and soup kitchens became commonplace. The incidence of suicides skyrocketed because many were unable to cope with their sudden poverty. Riots and strikes were frequent. The political and economic crisis threatened the stability, security, and cohesiveness of the nation (Axinn & Levin, 1982).

For more than a century, most Americans had adhered to an ideology according to which it was wrong for the federal government to become involved in social welfare. It was believed that governmental assistance to people in need would promote dependency, drain the national treasury, violate states' rights, and destroy the moral fabric of society (Axinn & Levin, 1982). Before the Great Depression crisis, many believed that the economy was self-regulating and that most economic problems would correct themselves if left alone. It was also believed that economic prosperity was a sign of divine favor. Consequently, poverty was believed to be the result of a flawed character, sinfulness, and/or lack of God's blessing. The Great Depression, however, proved that wrong. Many people who had been considered honest, law-abiding, hard-working, religious, good

citizens were willing to work in exchange for food but still were unable to become employed. The realization that for the most part poverty is the result of systemic economic factors rather than individual immorality or lack of virtue paved the way for reform and recovery (Axinn & Levin, 1982; Trattner, 1989).

In 1933 Franklin Delano Roosevelt became president of the United States, inheriting a country that was almost at the point of economic and political collapse. He came into office with a new vision and a new value system. He believed that it was not only acceptable for the federal government to help the poor directly but also that it was the government's moral, civic, and God-given responsibility to do so. Under his administration a massive strategy for economic recovery was developed, called "the New Deal." The three primary goals of this new strategy were "relief, recovery, and reform." Food, clothing, and housing were made available to people in need of these basic human necessities. New laws were enacted that provided protections to the poor, social programs were created, and the federal government became the nation's largest employer. During the 1930s and early 1940s the federal government engaged in numerous public works projects that enabled it to hire more than three million workers. Jobs that provided steady incomes allowed people to spend money and in this way give a boost to the economy (Axinn & Levin, 1982; Trattner, 1989).

Many historians and social scientists strongly believe that had it not been for the vision and intervention of Franklin Delano Roosevelt, the United States would not exist today as the powerful leading nation that it is.

Introduction

Social scientists and other individuals interested in promoting the welfare of societies often wrestle with the issue of how to respond to social problems. This textbook, for instance, has clearly illustrated how social issues are conceptualized by professionals and academicians from different disciplines, and has described some of their proposed responses to such problems. Unfortunately, sometimes we spend an excessive amount of time identifying and assessing social problems while not investing enough time and energy in devising strategies for responding to those problems in rational, efficient, effective, and accountable ways. The purpose of this chapter is to encourage the reader not to remain satisfied with simply documenting the existence of social problems but to go one step further and devise appropriate courses of action for responding to them.

This chapter provides the accountable professional with a logical model that can be used to develop social policies. The proposed model for policy-making, in essence, requires the decision-maker, before recommending any course of action, to review the practicality of available options as well as the historical, theoretical, and value contexts of the social issue under consideration. The model also encourages the policy practitioner to analyze the political and financial feasibility of any proposed policy. The extent to which we gather useful and scientific information to inform our decisions will determine whether we adopt a **rational/behavioral**, **incremental**, or **criteria-based** approach to policy-making (Dobelstein, 1990).

The **rational/behavioral** approach to policy-making relies on the largest possible amount of empirical data (research). This approach is very thorough, carefully analyzing and evaluating each policy alternative. Because of its comprehensive and detailed nature, the rational/behavioral approach is often impractical for the policy-maker who must wrestle with a large number of policy proposals. On the other hand, the **incremental** model of policy-making requires very little data. It is primarily concerned with marginal benefits associated with possible choices. The incremental approach often becomes a process of trial and error. A variety of strategies are tried, and the combination of those strategies that works becomes the policy. This approach seems too unscientific for many people. Finally, the **criteria-based model** represents a compromise between the rational and the incremental approaches. It allows the policy-maker to evaluate different alternatives while taking key values under consideration (Dobelstein, 1990).

The social problem of poverty has been selected as an example to illustrate how the proposed model can be implemented. Before we begin our discussion, some time will be devoted to identifying the criteria a problem must meet in order to be considered a social problem, and to defining and explaining the concept of policy.

Social Problems

Social policy-makers concern themselves with the amelioration of social rather than personal problems. For this reason, it is important for social welfare students and professionals to know the criteria a problem must meet in order to be considered a social problem.

According to Zastrow (1992), a **social problem** is one that affects a significantly large group of people, that elicits consensus regarding its existence, that is recognized as such by individuals in positions of power, and that can be solved or ameliorated only through collective action.

Is poverty in the United States a social problem? Let us look at the facts. By 1997 an estimated 36.5 million Americans were considered to be poor according to federal guidelines (DiNitto, 2000). The public at large as well as people in positions of power agree that poverty is a pervasive social problem. This is evidenced by the constant enactment of federal and state laws intended to assist and protect the poor, as well as by the creation of programs intended to meet their most basic needs. The fact that government officials, churches, volunteers, and human service organizations are constantly intervening in an attempt to ameliorate this problem indicates their recognition that no individual is able to solve the problem alone. It seems evident that this problem can be solved only through collective action. On the basis of Zastrow's criteria, poverty should be considered a social problem in the United States.

Social Policies

Numerous definitions have been provided in an attempt to explain what **social policies** are. They include the following elements, by J. P. Flynn (1992, p. 19):

- A formal or informal expression of goals or valued ends
- A statement of desired ends with an indication of selected alternative means
- Ordering of priorities
- An organizing principle
- A standing plan
- A decision made or not made
- A position taken, implicitly or explicitly
- The outcomes of social choice about who gets what, when and how
- Information ordered in a system

A simple definition of policy is *a position adopted in relation to a social problem along with a corresponding plan of action.* Policy-making is analogous to decision-making. The process is called policy-making only in those situations in which the decisions made or not made affect a significantly large group of people.

The Historical Context of Poverty

Throughout history, several strategies have been followed in an effort to deal with the problem of poverty. It is very important to know about previous efforts in order to avoid the pitfalls of our predecessors and learn from their experiences.

In the year 1780 B.C., the famous Code of Hammurabi was written (http://sacred-texts.com/ane/ham/index.htm). As reflected in this code, the Babylonian ruler Hammurabi became concerned with the poor and the needy in his kingdom. As a result, he incorporated laws into his famous code aimed at protecting the poor, women, and children (Trattner, 1989). These laws prevented many people from starving but did not eradicate poverty.

In ancient Israel a similar concern existed. It was extremely difficult for women to survive financially without the protection and support of men. For this reason, Jewish laws required men to marry the widows of their deceased brothers (Karger & Stoesz, 1998). This practice made sense within the context of Jewish culture and traditions. Today, it would be extremely difficult to enforce such a practice in the United States since it would be perceived as an infringement on the rights of widows and on the freedom of men and women to choose their spouses.

The leaders of ancient Israel also adopted a practice intended to prevent the starvation of the poor. All farmers were required to leave one-sixteenth of their crops behind to enable those deemed worthy to harvest the crops for themselves (Dolgoff, Feldstein, & Skolnik, 1993; Karger & Stoesz, 1998). This practice assumed that the poor only need food, that those in need of food are able to go get it, and that the pool of poor people is small enough to be fed with leftover crops. In the United States today the poor represent approximately one-eighth of the population as opposed to one-sixteenth; they need a lot more than food; and many of them are children, elderly, or disabled, and consequently are physically unable to obtain needed resources.

The Greeks and the Romans provided allowances for those disabled, distribution of grain for the needy, and institutional care for the unfortunate. Later, during the Middle Ages, feudalism became widespread throughout Europe and other parts of the world (Trattner, 1989). Feudalism helped prevent the starvation of the poor; nevertheless, it did not attempt to eradicate poverty. On the contrary, it perpetuated poverty and was extremely oppressive. According to Trattner (1989), feudalism imposed "strong measures of constraint on individual freedom" (p. 4). Others have stated that the relationship between serfs and landlords was characterized by a constant struggle for independence (http://www.newadvent.org/cathen/06058c.htm).

In colonial America, a very low percentage of the population needed public assistance for their subsistence. This was understandable because those in need were very unlikely to migrate from Europe, and many people in such conditions who took the risk of coming to America died during the trip. For the most part, only those who were willing and able to adhere to the principles of hard work and **rugged individualism** settled in the American colonies. Cases of extreme poverty represented rare exceptions to the norm. Cases of people in need were handled on a case-by-case basis. The church often assumed responsibility for assisting the poor. In other instances, these cases were handled individually by residents in town meetings. During these meetings decisions were usually made to auction off the poor to neighboring farmers, apprentice out children, place the poor in private homes at the public's expense, or send the poor to privately owned **almshouses**. Loafers were indentured, expelled from town, whipped, or jailed. When poor strangers attempted to settle in a community, they were often warned not to stay, or they were sent back to their place of origin at the town's expense (Trattner, 1989).

Strategies used during colonial times in the United States attempted to manage poverty without addressing the causes of it and would not be appropriate in 21st-century America for obvious reasons. By 1997 the poverty rate in the United States was 13.3% (DiNitto, 2000). This equaled 36.5 million people, totaling more than the populations of many countries. The poor can no longer be aided on a case-by-case basis, and cities and states in the country cannot adopt policies to expel all poor people from their communities. The poor have to live somewhere. Finally, no policy to whip or jail poor people would be enforceable because it would be contrary to our societal values and laws.

The industrial revolution in Europe provoked a drastic change in the socioeconomic structures of the countries that experienced it. The creation of factories and the emergence of higher paying jobs motivated a mass migration from rural areas to urban centers. This led to the decline of feudalism and to the emergence of big cities (Trattner, 1989).

The high population density of the new cities brought a series of social problems with it. Epidemics were common and acts of crime significantly increased. Due to the higher cost of urban living, both husbands and wives were forced to get jobs outside of the home and, as a result, many children were left unsupervised. This contributed to an increase in juvenile delinquency. People who migrated to the cities left their extended families behind in the rural areas. This represented a big loss of support systems that were very much needed, particularly during times of tragedy or illness. Long hours of factory work led to an increase in on-the-job accidents, job-related illnesses, and deaths. Consequently, many more widows and orphans could be found in the cities than in rural areas.

In the early 1300s, England fell victim to the bubonic plague, which killed approximately one third of the work force. The resulting shortage of laborers led to instability in the job market and to inflation because laborers kept moving around in search of better and higher paying jobs (Trattner, 1989).

For many centuries the family, the church, and local communities had been responsible for meeting the needs of the poor. But the magnitude of these social problems made government intervention necessary during the 14th century. This led to an increase in the power of the state and facilitated a systemic response to poverty. For instance, in 1349 the Statute of Labourers was enacted in England. This law set maximum wages for given types of jobs, imposed travel restrictions on workers, and forced the unemployed to accept any job offered to them. In 1531 a new piece of legislation outlawed begging by able-bodied individuals (Trattner, 1989).

In 1601 the **Elizabethan Poor Laws** emerged in England in an attempt to address the problem of poverty more effectively. These laws are very significant to people in the United States because many of the principles contained in them still regulate aid to the poor in this country. These laws represented a well organized and discriminating effort to deliver social assistance only to those who really needed it. The laws made a distinction between the **deserving** and the **non-deserving poor** by classifying each individual as a child or woman, a non-able-bodied person, or an able-bodied person. As these categories suggest, only children, women, and non-able-bodied people were eligible for public assistance. The Elizabethan Poor Laws also introduced the concept of **less eligibility**, which indicated that those receiving governmental aid should receive less public assistance than the earnings they could gain working full-time at minimum wage. This, of course, was intended to serve as an incentive to people receiving public aid to get jobs (Trattner, 1989; Dolgoff, Feldstein, & Skolnik, 1993; Axinn & Levin, 1982). The greatest problem with trying to implement these guidelines was that they ignored macroeconomic factors. The principles contained in these laws assumed that there were jobs available for every person who was able-bodied and that it would be best for the economy to have zero unemployment. Today, however, economists recognize that a capitalistic economy like that of the United States does not have a job for every person who is willing and physically able to work. They also know that no country can sustain full employment over long periods of time without causing serious problems to the economy.

According to Esping-Andersen (1990), genuinely sustained full employment has been very rare even within the international community of nations. Only Norway, Sweden, and Switzerland have been able to consistently secure unemployment levels below 3% throughout the complete post-war era. In a capitalistic system, the challenge is even greater. The functioning of the United States economy at near to full capacity would lead to inflation and other economic problems. This would create a shortage of laborers and raw materials, and an imbalance between the economy's supply and demand (Todaro, 2000). As a result of full employment, prices and wages would spiral out of control. Another issue that policy makers must consider is that full employment would alter the balance of power in American society by creating a more powerful and influential working class. It has been argued that full employment would represent an obstacle to balanced national economic growth (Esping-Andersen, 1990).

The Great Depression was one of the most significant events of American social welfare history and represents a historical and ideological turning point. As a result of it, millions of people realized that poverty was not necessarily associated with laziness, flawed character, or immorality. The people of the United States learned that poverty can result from macroeconomic factors beyond the control of any individual. These realizations paved the way for the emergence of the American **social welfare state**. A social welfare state exists when the government creates a formal system of policies, programs, and services to respond to the needs of the most vulnerable in society. From then on, many honest, law-abiding, and religious Americans believed that it was acceptable, appropriate, and ethical for the federal government to assist the poor directly (Trattner, 1989).

Today, most members of the Republican party seem to adhere to the ideology that prevailed before the 1930s, while most Democrats tend to adhere to the new ideology that emerged during that devastating and traumatic decade (Pierson, 1994; Karger & Stoesz, 1998). The fact that conflicting ideological views are maintained along party lines becomes understandable, in part, when we look at the composition of both parties and the constituencies that they are trying to satisfy. The typical member of the Republican party is a white middle- or upper-middle-class male while the typical member of the Democratic party is a middle-class or poor person from a minority group. Since all politicians need to satisfy the needs and expectations of their constituents in order to stay in power, Republican administrations tend to emphasize foreign relations, the military, and corporate welfare during their tenure while Democratic administrations tend to give more priority to domestic social problems and assistance to the poor (DiNitto, 2000).

Theoretical Context of Poverty in the United States

Theories describe, explain, and predict social and other phenomena. Their ability to predict depends on the accuracy or validity of their explanations. Consequently, the understanding and acceptance of the cause-and-effect relationships that a theory proposes will dictate appropriate courses of action. In this section, we examine three sociological theories that have been used to explain the causes of poverty in the United States. The primary purpose of this section is to demonstrate how any chosen theoretical framework can influence and guide our decision-making.

Functionalist Perspective

Functionalism is a macro sociological theory often used to describe societal functioning in the United States. This theory views society as a very organized system regulated by shared values, norms, and beliefs. A primary concern of this conceptualization is to make sure the system works as effectively and efficiently as possible. For this reason it is highly concerned with stability and balance. According to functionalism, social problems occur when society or a portion of it becomes disorganized. Such disorganization, it is argued, may be a consequence of rapid social change and a "cultural lag between technological changes and our adaptation to them" (Zastrow, 1992, p. 23).

Functionalists argue that poverty is a result of the dysfunctions of the economy. Institutions and people in general may not be able to cope with rapid industrialization and as a result many are left behind. Training centers may provide students with obsolete knowledge and skills, and consequently they are unable to become employed. Supporters of functionalism also contend that poverty results from the dysfunction of many government programs intended to help the poor, since many of these programs are not adequately designed, funded, or implemented (Zastrow, 1992).

Many functionalists view poverty and economic inequality as functional. By this they mean that poverty as an institution makes it possible for society to function. They do not say that poverty is moral or desirable, but simply that it plays important functions for society. Sullivan et al. (1980, p. 30) has identified eleven functions that the poor carry out on behalf of the rich and the rest of society. These may be described this way:

- They are available to do unpleasant jobs no one else wants to do.
- Their activities subsidize the more affluent (for example, they perform domestic service for low pay).
- They help create jobs (for example, social workers provide services for the poor).
- They purchase poor-quality goods that otherwise could not be sold.

- They serve as examples of deviance that are frowned on by the majority and thereby support dominant norms.
- They provide an opportunity for others to practice their "Christian duty" of helping the less fortunate.
- They make mobility more likely for others because they are removed from competition for good education and good jobs.
- They contribute to cultural activities (for example, by providing cheap labor for the construction of monuments and works of art).
- They create cultural forms (for example, jazz and blues music) that are often adopted by the affluent.
- They serve as symbolic opponents for some political groups and as constituents for others.
- They often absorb the cost of change (for example, by being the victims of high levels of unemployment that result from technological advances).

An immediate and logical outcome of adopting a functionalist perspective would be a reluctance to work toward the eradication of poverty. According to this theory, doing so would cause a state of societal imbalance and disorganization. Consequently, society would not be able to function as it currently does. Without a doubt, the financial empowerment of the poor would alter the balance of power in our country. Many people view the logic behind the functionalist perspective as immoral. We should remember, however, that sociological theories do not provide a picture of how things should be but rather are a valid description of social and behavioral phenomena. Politicians and other people in positions of power in this country are well aware of the systemic implications of financially empowering the poor. This might explain why our traditional political parties do not seem totally committed to the eradication of poverty and why many of our current policies have the impact of perpetuating dependency instead of promoting financial self-sufficiency.

Policy makers wishing to support functionalism will be likely to formulate policies intended to control the poor and maintain them "in their place." Their policies will emphasize charity more than empowerment and socioeconomic development. Others may use functionalism as a way to describe and explain the dynamics of American society while finding in it the motivation to work for significant social change.

Many Voices: An Introduction to Social Issues

Conflict Perspective

A second theory that has been used to explain the causes of poverty in the United States is the **conflict perspective**. Conflict theorists view society as made up of opposing groups with varying levels of economic and political power. According to them, poverty exists because people in positions of power want it to exist. The more powerful groups in society benefit from maintaining the deprivation and oppression of others and engage in practices designed to keep people poor. Just like functionalists, they prefer charity to empowerment and socioeconomic development. They recognize that in order for the poor to have more, they themselves would have less. According to this perspective, poverty becomes a social problem when the poor realize that their condition is primarily the result of unfairness and social injustice and decide to do something about it (Zastrow, 1992).

Conflict theorists believe that the best way to deal with poverty as a social problem is to create awareness among the poor, who will respond by becoming organized and politically active. In their opinion, the poor should become empowered and be able to lobby in order to impact legislative and policy-making processes.

Conflict theorists believe that good things can result from conflict. For instance, a conflict between labor and management may lead to better working conditions for laborers; a conflict between husband and wife may lead to a more satisfying marital understanding; and even a war may lead to better relations between nations and/or better intergroup relationships within a country. Conflict theorists view conflict as a normal and inevitable part of life. For this reason, they contend that our objective should not be to avoid conflict at all costs, but to learn to manage it to everybody's advantage.

The implications of adopting this perspective for policy-making seem evident. Policy-makers may take positions or recommend courses of action that conflict with societal norms, values, and traditions. They may also challenge the power of elite groups and may question the justice of societal, political, and economic institutions.

Interactionist Perspective

The third and final theory that will be discussed is the **interactionist perspective**. According to interactionist theorists, poverty is relative and subjective. All people can be viewed as rich or poor depending on whom we compare them to. Interactionists believe that poverty is also a matter of shared expectations. They view this social problem as originating not from the societal system but from the individual. They believe that many people are poor because they have low self-esteem and low expectations.

Interactionists believe that the social problem of poverty will be resolved if we eliminate the stigma associated with it and help improve the self-esteem of the poor. They argue that the poor will be able to escape poverty once they are convinced that they can accomplish more in life. Adopting this way of thinking will help maintain the status quo since it makes it possible to blame the victim while freeing government and elite groups from all responsibility (Zastrow, 1992).

Policy-makers adhering to the interactionist perspective often formulate policies intended to change the individual while ignoring the systemic causes of poverty. They are likely to adopt an incremental approach to policy-making and will never challenge the system or current economic and political paradigms.

Value Context of the Policy-Making Process

Policy-making is a value-laden endeavor. When faced with alternative courses of action for responding to a social problem, policy-makers choose the option that is most consistent with their personal, religious, professional, and cultural values. Of course, policy-makers in elected positions also take the value preferences of their constituents into account.

Authors such as Masters and Friedman have discussed the way dominant values may influence the policy-making process (http://www.cencomfut.com/social_values.htm). In this section, however, we concentrate on John Tropman's typology and conceptualization of American values given that his book (Tropman, 1989) has become a classic on this topic. In his book, Tropman discusses the American values of **work**, **mobility**, **status**, **independence**, **individualism**, **moralism**, and **ascription**, as well as their implications for policy-making.

The way Americans view **work** has been highly influenced by **Calvinism** and the **Protestant work ethic**. According to this belief system, we have all been called by God to engage in whatever work we do. It follows, then, that if God called us to our jobs, we will honor Him if we excel in our professions or vocations. Furthermore, financial success is viewed as an inevitable outcome of our professional or vocational success. Work is important for Americans because it provides social status, meaning, and a way to earn a living. At the same time, work is considered to be a source of virtue and worth (Tropman, 1989).

Our understanding of the value and meaning of work greatly influences our attitude toward the poor and toward social welfare policy. What would be an implication of believing that professional and financial success are signs of divine blessing and favor? What, then, would be the meaning of being poor? According to the Protestant work ethic, people are poor because they are morally flawed, and as a result God cannot bless them.

Policy-makers who adhere to the Protestant work ethic tend to blame individuals for their conditions. They argue that in order to escape poverty the poor simply need a moral and spiritual transformation. This position ignores the systemic causes of poverty and the fact that in the United States there is not a job for every person who is willing and able to work.

It is interesting to note that according to Catholic theologians, such as Saint Francis of Assisi, there is virtue in poverty, while according to Calvinist Protestantism there is virtue in wealth. Catholic theology views the love of money as the source of all evils and it encourages people to detach themselves from worldly and material things in order to attain a higher degree of spirituality. Calvinistic Protestantism, on the other hand, views poverty as a curse and financial success as a sign of God's blessing and approval (Giddens, 1976; Tropman, 1989; Reese, 1980).

Dominant American attitudes toward work suggest that all able-bodied individuals in America should be gainfully employed. Most economists, however, agree that it is not possible for most countries to sustain full employment over long periods of time (Esping-Andersen, 1990). If the economy were to function at 100% capacity, there would be a shortage of laborers and of raw materials. If every able-bodied person had a job, people wanting to create new industries would have nobody to hire. As a result, employers would have to compete with one another for laborers and wages would skyrocket. This would lead to inflation and other serious problems for the economy. Economists agree that the U.S. economy needs a pool of unemployed people who can be used to supply new industries with employees, the military with soldiers, and employers with new workers when former employees go on strike.

Many people become unemployed because they lack marketable skills, and sometimes they are between jobs. This is called **structural unemployment**. Economists recognize that a certain level of unemployment is necessary and inevitable in a capitalistic economic system (Murray, 1984; Karger & Stoesz, 1998). Some argue that a four or five percent unemployment rate is equivalent to full employment. It would be very difficult, however, to convince the millions of unemployed Americans of that assertion. If the cause of unemployment is structural and systemic, why do we blame the unemployed for being unemployed and the poor for being poor? Why is there so much stigma associated with being poor? The social stigma associated with welfare dependency, poverty, and unemployment likely originates in the particular way that Americans view work.

Americans also value **mobility,** a concept tied to the idea of independence. As a society we value moving up, moving to, and even moving away (Tropman, 1989). Mobility is associated with the idea of progress in general. In American society even running away is often viewed positively. This is especially true when running away from something negative or harmful. **Social mobility, social metabolism**, and **social velocity** are three concepts associated with the American value of mobility. Social mobility refers to movement or progress over time. Social metabolism has to do with the rate of exchange between two statuses, and social

Many Voices: An Introduction to Social Issues

velocity refers to the speed of progress or movement. Because of this social and cultural value, most policy makers in the United States refuse to formulate policies that restrict people or limit their freedoms.

Status is a third American value. This concept encompasses a person's position in society as well as the prestige associated with the position. Status has added meaning when we realize that American society is achievement oriented. Money, education, and occupation can be viewed as predictors of status, while power and prestige can be viewed as indicators of status. However, Tropman (1989) has chosen to identify power and prestige as dimensions of status, rather than predictors or indicators. The perceived powerlessness of the poor in America can be explained by the fact that they often lack all of the five dimensions of status: money, education, occupation, power, and prestige.

American policy-makers tend to formulate policies that favor individual efforts to attain higher social status, especially through business, education, or occupation. They try to accomplish this, however, without challenging or threatening the existing socioeconomic system. Whether policy makers are politically conservative, liberal, or radical will determine the way they approach the value of status. Conservatives prefer to maintain the status of the various social and ethnic groups in the United States. Liberals argue that everybody should try to better themselves, but gradually and while complying with all the rules. Radicals, in turn, advocate major structural changes that would threaten the status of all powerful groups in America.

Americans highly cherish the value of **independence,** or freedom from external controls and constraints (Tropman, 1989). This love for independence is expressed through the freedom to choose, freedom to move, freedom to marry or stay single, and so on. Independence requires a high degree of self-confidence and self-reliance. Americans understand, however, that total freedom from external controls is not always possible. For this reason, whenever dependency is inevitable they prefer situations of **interdependency,** which assumes symmetry in a relationship and implies sharing as well as giving and taking. The American respect for freedom, for instance, has led federal courts to decide that mentally ill people are also entitled to liberty and freedom of choice and that they should not be hospitalized against their will. According to the courts, they have the right to adequate treatment as well as the right to refuse treatment (Zastrow, 1992). American policy-makers, in general, are very reluctant to formulate policies that threaten freedom or independence.

Individualism as an American value is often confused with independence; however, it refers not to freedom but to a position in the social structure, emphasizing the individual as a unit of analysis. Americans celebrate individual accomplishments, blame individuals for their misfortunes, and try to change the individual rather than the system in an effort to bring about social change. In the U.S., for instance, one family member could be rich while other members are not, sons and daughters are encouraged to move out of their parents' homes as soon as they are 18 or 21 years old, elderly parents are often placed in nursing homes when their deteriorating health is perceived as a burden to the family, and individuals are encouraged to undergo a moral and psychological transformation in an attempt to solve social problems.

The sixth American social value identified by Tropman (1989) is **moralism.** Moralism should not be confused with **morality.** Morality is an adherence to moral principles, while moralism refers to using moral arguments to oppress and discriminate against people. Morality is constructive and redemptive while moralism is destructive. Moralism has three distinct components: judgment, assigning responsibility or fault, and stating what ought to be done.

One biblical passage, John 8:3–11, clearly illustrates the difference between these two values. A woman caught in the act of adultery was brought to Jesus by a group of law-abiding citizens, who stated that according to law she must be put to death. Jesus responded that anyone in the group who was free of sin should feel free to throw the first stone. After the accusers were caught in their hypocrisy and had left, Jesus told the woman that He did not condemn her either and that she should go away and sin no more.

In this example we can clearly see that the primary purpose of the law-abiding and moralistic accusers was not to help the woman but to destroy her. Jesus did not deny the fact that she had sinned; however, His handling of the situation demonstrated that His primary objective was to uplift her and to redeem her. Jesus did not judge and assign fault, but rather proposed a very edifying course of action.

Ascription is the last of Tropman's social values. This concept describes the process through which we assign or take away value from people, events, qualities, or characteristics. People from European backgrounds are usually ascribed more importance in the United States than Blacks and Indians, for example, who tend to be underestimated. People tend to consider themselves superior to others on the basis of nationality, race, culture, socioeconomic class, and other characteristics. The belief that certain groups of people are superior to or better than others because of any given characteristic impacts decisions about the allocation of resources. Without a doubt, ascription influences our beliefs about who is and who is not worthy of opportunities, resources, and privileges.

According to Tropman (1989), our position in relation to cultural values determines how we resolve various dilemmas. For instance, our ideas about work impact our understanding of who is or is not worthy of societal privileges. Our attitude toward mobility may determine whether we choose to assist the poor, the mentally ill, and the racially different within the mainstream or at the margins of society. Our views towards status may motivate us either to lump people into broad categories or to see them as unique. Our commitment to the value of independence may motivate us to value internal controls over external controls. Individualism is likely to motivate us to conduct micro instead of macro analyses and interventions. Our adherence to moralism will motivate us to promote punishment instead of compassion. Finally, ascription for the most part will motivate us to value white people more than others. Tropman's analysis reveals the relevance of cultural values to the policy-making process.

Policy Formulation

The previous sections have illustrated the importance of exploring the historical background of a social problem, including prior successful and unsuccessful attempts to deal with it. Furthermore, they have pointed out the importance of having a theoretical frame of reference to guide our decision-making, as well as the pertinence of understanding the values behind our policy preferences. At this stage, we should be prepared to make an informed decision—that is, to take a position and recommend a course of action. Depending on whether we are conservatives, liberals, or radicals, we may choose to ignore the plight of the poor, or to provide them with charity to prevent them from starving while keeping them poor. We may make interventions aimed at promoting their economic self-sufficiency or seek a complete transformation of our economic and political system.

Before developing a strategy to ameliorate a targeted social problem, the accountable policy-maker must be concerned with the political as well as the financial feasibility of the policy under consideration. He or she must determine whether the proposed policy is consistent or in conflict with existing laws or policies, and must understand the political environment or sensitive circumstances surrounding key players. He or she must consider whether explicit attention is being given to minority or other vulnerable groups. The intended and likely unintended effects of the policy must be identified. Among other things, the policy maker must be able to articulate how the proposed policy is expected to contribute to social justice.

Policy positions are usually operationalized through human service programs or some other type of social intervention. In some instances, however, the policy position taken in relation to an issue or problem is one of indifference or inaction. This was exemplified by the response of President Hoover in the late 1920s to the economic crisis the country was facing (Trattner, 1989). He decided to do nothing, believing that the natural forces of the economy would correct the situation. As history shows, his policy of inaction greatly contributed to one of the greatest economic crises our country has ever experienced.

In a vast majority of cases, however, social policies require that a service or other type of intervention be provided. In such situations, the policy-maker must consider the financial feasibility of the proposed intervention. The accountable professional must consider alternative interventions and weigh the required costs of each likely outcome. More specifically, he or she must estimate the cost-effectiveness, cost-benefit, and the cost-utility of each alternative.

Cost-effectiveness

Cost-effectiveness (CE) measures the cost of providing a unit of service or of any intended output. Of course, the primary objective of calculating CE is to produce the desired effect with minimum effort, cost, and waste (Burch, 1996). This requires adding up all costs associated with the desired output, including the cost of such things as human resources, publicity, equipment, supplies, and information, and then dividing the total cost by the number of output units—units of service or products of any program or intervention. For example, output units for an employment program may be the number of job placements completed per month. For other programs they may be the number of persons counseled per month or the number of child adoptions completed per year.

The calculation of CE can be approached two different ways. One is called the "fixed utility" approach. The policy-maker knows the desired output in advance and seeks to find the least expensive way to elicit it. The second approach is called "fixed budget." In this case, the policy-maker knows how much money he or she wants to spend and then tries to determine how to get the most out of the money already budgeted for a particular purpose. For example, under the fixed utility approach the policy-maker may know in advance that 100,000 people need to be placed in jobs. The policy-maker will try to devise a program that will accomplish this goal at the lowest possible cost per placement. Under the fixed budget approach, the policy-maker may know in advance that he or she has $1,000,000 to create a job placement program and will design a program intended to place the largest possible number of people in jobs.

Cost-benefit

Cost-benefit analysis "measures input cost per unit of economic utility" (Burch, 1996, p. 287). It involves assigning a dollar value to all financial and non-financial resources invested in an intervention and looking at what was gained. This helps determine whether the intervention was worth the effort. The calculation of cost-benefit measures the gains and losses of the intervention in dollar terms, and aggregates them to find out whether there was a net gain or a net loss. For example, a job training program costing $100,000 may have provided training to 500 people, of whom 100 were able to obtain jobs. The question is whether adding 100 new people to the workforce is enough of a benefit in exchange for the $100,000. The worst possible scenario under this type of analysis would be one in which the number of unemployed people in the targeted group increased after the job training program.

Cost-utility

Finally, **cost utility** is concerned with nonfinancial indicators of things believed to be good or desirable. Cost utility deals more with outcomes than with outputs. It is concerned, for instance, with the financial cost associated with achieving levels of satisfaction, political correctness, and family unity. Cost utility analysis is applied to intangible benefits. For instance, when considering a $100,000 investment, a cost-utility analyst would try to answer such questions as these: "Following the implementation of the job training program, is the city mayor more popular?" And "did the job training program have a positive impact on the behavior of voters and on the mayor's reelection?" Politicians would be very willing to invest $100,000 and more in programs likely to help their reelection even if the actual number of program beneficiaries was not very large.

The responsible and accountable policy-maker engages in cost-effectiveness, cost-benefit, or cost-utility analysis as a way of avoiding day dreaming, budget deficits, wasteful use of financial resources, and loss of support from constituents.

Individuals responsible for operationalizing and implementing social policies must also concern themselves with the **evaluability** of the programs and interventions they create. In other words, they must ensure that among other things program objectives are time-sensitive, worded in terms of observable behaviors, and measurable. Those responsible for the creation of programs or interventions must also ensure that program goals and objectives are consistent with the organization's philosophy and mission (Gabor, Unrau, & Grinnell, 1998).

Policy Evaluation Approaches

Accountable policy-makers and other professionals must ensure that the outcomes of the policies they propose and implement are measured. This way they can know if their target populations were reached and if their policies brought about the desired changes. Policies, however, can be evaluated only through the programs or interventions that result from them. The assumption is that if the program was effective, the policy was also effective. This is a risky assumption. A program evaluation may suggest that there was no positive outcome resulting from the intervention. However, in reality the problem may have been that the program was ill conceived or poorly implemented. Using **nonexperimental research designs** for program evaluation may also result in distorted findings and may lead people to believe that the intervention was not worth the effort when in reality it was. Nonexperimental research projects do not rely on random samples or include experimental and control groups. The absence of these characteristics makes it difficult if not impossible for researchers to control for factors that may influence the study findings, besides the intervention. Several limitations are associated with using empirical methods for policy evaluation. However, a greater risk would be not to engage in any evaluation process. In spite of the margin of error of research studies, they are likely to provide more valid pictures of what has transpired than no formal evaluation at all.

Ginsberg (2001) has identified multiple approaches that can be used for program evaluations. The quantitative and qualitative evaluations he recommends include satisfaction studies, needs assessments, single-system studies, utilization studies, empowerment evaluations, fraud and abuse detection, case studies, and journalistic evaluations.

Other Policy-Making and Policy-Analysis Models

This section briefly introduces various models found in the literature, which can be used to formulate and analyze social policies.

Chambers and Wedel (2005) have developed a model for social policy analysis that includes the social problem context, the judicial context, the historical context, the social program, and the policy system. Analyzing the social problem context includes defining the problem, identifying the ideological perspective behind it, analyzing possible causes, and identifying gainers and losers. On the other hand, analyzing the social program and policy includes identifying goals and objectives, eligibility criteria, form of benefit or service, service delivery system, and the adequacy of financing. Chambers's model has become widely known and used, and the book in which he shares his model is now in its fourth edition.

Dobelstein (1990) has described a five-stage model for policy-making. In the first stage, issues of public concern or social problems are identified. In the second stage, different policy-making units engage in the policy-making process. These units include executives, legislatures, administrative agencies, courts, and private sector organizations. Policy-making processes differ from one policy-making unit to the other. Executives usually make a decision after exploring the range of policy options available to them. Legislatures take the policy proposal through a series of committees and hearings that require a significant amount of negotiation and compromise. Courts formulate policies in the process of interpreting the law, and administrative agencies formulate policies through discussions in staff meetings. In the third stage, policies are adopted. In the fourth stage, programs are designed, and, in the fifth stage, policies are executed. The type of information needed varies from one policy-making unit to the other and may include the range of policy options, what constituent or interest groups exist, who the winners and losers are, legal aspects, competing values, policy-specific data, and program-specific data.

Jansson (1994) has developed and proposed a model for policy-making that identifies a series of tasks. These tasks include agenda-setting, problem-defining, proposal-writing, policy-enacting, policy-implementing, and policy-assessing. All of these tasks are carried out while taking into account contextual factors that may present constraints or opportunities. Agenda-building is the process through which policy practitioners persuade decision-makers to include policy issues in their agendas. Problem-defining refers to analyzing the "definitions, causes, nature and prevalence of specific problems" (Jansson, 1994, p. 71). Proposal-writing describes the development of solutions by policy-makers. Policy-enacting is the process of getting policy proposals approved. This includes trying to eliminate barriers to policy implementation. Finally, policy-assessing refers to the responsibility policy practitioners have for evaluating the programs their policies create. They would have a very hard time justifying the existence of any policy without some hard evidence of its effectiveness.

DiNitto (2000) has provided a model for rational policy-making as well as a model for political policy-making. According to her, in an ideal situation policy-makers should follow a rational approach that calls for identifying and defining a particular social problem, identifying associated societal values, identifying and considering all possible alternative policies, understanding the consequences of the proposed policy for various societal groups, conducting a cost-benefit analysis for each alternative, and selecting the policy that maximizes net values.

However, DiNitto highlights the fact that things usually do not work in ideal ways. According to her model for political policy-making, rarely do most people agree on any social value. It is extremely difficult to define social problems due to inconsistent perceptions and definitions. It is hard to calculate costs for intangible things such as dignity, or to predict the outcomes of policies. Power and influence tend to blur social values, policy-makers are most motivated by self-interest, and government bureaucracies tend to create barriers to the policy-making process. For these reasons, policy-makers often find themselves forced to engage in a process of incrementalism. In other words, very frequently they must settle for small changes to existing policies or targeted problems.

Conclusion

When faced with a challenge or social problem, policy-makers are first influenced by their political ideologies and by their value systems, as well as by the value systems of their constituents. Such values and ideologies usually determine what the policy-maker will try to accomplish. For instance, the belief that poverty is functional, the fault of the individual, and a natural part of a system mandated by God would most likely motivate policy-makers to ignore the plight of the poor or to provide them with charity in order to prevent their starvation. On the other hand, the belief that poverty is an inevitable byproduct of our capitalistic economic system might motivate decision-makers to formulate policies intended to ameliorate socioeconomic inequities and promote the empowerment and economic self-sufficiency of the poor. Radical thinkers might in

turn feel motivated to try to replace our economic system altogether.

A historical review of the social problem of poverty, including prior attempts to deal with it, helped reveal what strategies have been effective or ineffective. An analysis of the policies of the ancient peoples of Israel and the Roman Empire, for instance, shows that they were effective in preventing the starvation of many people; however, they were ineffective in reducing, ameliorating, or eliminating poverty as a social problem. Experiences in England during the 1500s and early 1600s clearly illustrate that high proportions of poverty and human need often cannot be properly handled by the family, the church, or the local community. In such cases, government intervention is not only desirable but absolutely necessary. The Great Depression in the

United States revealed, for instance, that poverty can be caused by systemic factors beyond the control of any individual. It also showed that poverty is not necessarily tied to issues of morality or unwillingness to work. One of the lessons learned from President Roosevelt's response to the Great Depression is that accountability at all levels is absolutely necessary when formulating social policies and implementing the human service programs that result from them. Many problems, including wasteful spending, resulted from the mismanagement and corruption associated with many social welfare programs created during the 1930s and the 1960s (Karger & Stoesz, 1998). Another lesson learned from analyzing the American experience is that poverty as a social problem has never been eradicated from the United States, one of the richest countries in the world, in spite of the programs of the New Deal in the 1930s and the War on Poverty during the 1960s. Accountable policymakers must consider why poverty as a social problem still persists in our society.

Our theoretical frame of reference also plays a vital role in our policy-making efforts. For example, adhering to a functionalist perspective may cause us to blame the system for the problem of poverty, while adopting an interactionist perspective may motivate us to blame the victim. It is obvious, then, that our theoretical perspective will determine whether we seek micro or macro changes.

Policy-makers inevitably must consider the political feasibility of any options at their disposal. For example, the current political climate of the United States does not allow policy-makers to completely ignore the needs of the poor; that would be political suicide. Thus political conservatives in the U.S. do not dare eliminate the welfare system in spite of the fact that for the most part they disagree with it and blame individuals for their problems.

A second policy option is that of providing charity to the poor in the form of income transfers and **residual welfare programs** at the taxpayer's expense. Residual welfare programs are those that are only available to an identifiable minority group meeting strict eligibility criteria. There is usually social stigma attached to receiving benefits from such programs because those eligible for assistance are poor. This strategy has come under fire in recent years since it is perceived to promote laziness and dependency. Critics have pointed out that other alternatives are to provide no government

assistance to the poor, or to empower the poor through economic development programs and education. The first alternative would make such critics very unpopular and prevent their election to public office, while the second would alter the balance of power in society and in the process threaten the control of conservatives.

This chapter proposes the formulation of social policies and the implementation of programs oriented toward the socioeconomic development and the self-sufficiency of the poor as a strategic response to the social problem of poverty in the United States. Critics rightly argue that we cannot turn every poor person into a professional or business person. Nevertheless, we should allow the talents, intelligence, and motivation of the poor to determine who becomes a business person, who becomes a professional, and who decides to enter different trades, instead of letting institutional biases determine who can gain access to opportunities and resources. The socioeconomic development of the poor and efforts aimed at their empowerment will most likely receive support from **public interest groups** and opposition from **special interest groups**. Special interest groups usually attempt to protect the profits of businesses and corporations while public interest groups try to promote the overall well-being of society without being concerned about financial profits.

Finally, the radical option of replacing our political and economic system is not really viable for policymakers and will not be discussed by people in positions of power. Any person proposing such an alternative will be immediately stigmatized and labeled as unfit to be a public service official in the United States or any other country. It seems evident that the only viable options for modern policy makers in the U.S. are to provide charity to the poor through income transfers and residual welfare programs, and to promote the socioeconomic development of the poor through entrepreneurship and/or education. Strategies aimed at empowering the poor socially and economically are likely to face a lot of resistance because of the implications of these options for those who are currently in power. This helps us understand why American society throughout its history has chosen the way of charity.

The accountable policy-maker will always need to know the cost associated with delivering a particular unit of service, the overall cost associated with a particular policy outcome, and the cost associated with obtaining fewer tangible benefits, such as higher levels of constituent satisfaction or of popularity. Finally, due to ethical, practical, and political reasons, policy-makers should always formulate policies and implement programs that can be empirically evaluated and are likely to perform as expected. The policy-maker failing to do so will soon be out of business.

Discussion Questions

1. How should social policy be applied to the social issues discussed in this text, or should it? Which social issues should be left to the individual or market rather than to social policy?
2. When should the government step in and create social policy? Are there times it would be better if it didn't? If so, when?
3. In your view, which is more important—cost-effectiveness, cost-benefit, or cost-utility—and why?
4. What values of society are most important in driving policy-making?
5. Could social policies create more problems than they solve, and how?

Related Readings

Dolgoff, R., Feldstein, D., & Skolnik, L. (2003). *Understanding social welfare* (6th ed.). New York: Longman.

Johnson, L. C., & Schwartz, C. L. (1997). *Social welfare: A response to human need* (4th ed.). Boston: Allyn and Bacon.

Popple, P. R., & Leighninger, L. L. (2004). *The policy-based profession: An introduction to social welfare policy for social workers* (3rd ed.) Boston: Allyn and Bacon.

Sullivan, T. J., & Thompson, K. S. (1994). *Introduction to social problems* (3rd ed.). New York: Macmillan (pp. 157–193).

Related Web Sites

Center for Law and Social Policy (CLASP): http://www.clasp.org

Gateway to Social Policy and Development: Website of the Division for Social Policy and Development, Department of Economic and Social Affairs, United Nations: http://www.un.org/esa/socdev

Moving Ideas—Electronic Policy Network: http://www.movingideas.org

Social Policy Virtual Library: The International Social and Public Research Information Gateway: http://staff.bath.ac.uk/hsstp/world3-menu.htm

The Urban Institute: A Nonpartisan Economic and Social Policy Research Organization: http://www.urban.org

GLOSSARY

abandonment thesis: the belief that the problems faced by the mentally ill, and those they create for society, could be medically remedied if it were not for deinstitutionalization and the abandonment they experienced.

accommodate: in Piaget's theory, it is the modification of a cognitive structure (a scheme) via new information, which can occur when a current cognitive structure fails to work.

acculturation: learning about another culture, which often includes learning to speak the language, to appreciate new food and customs, and to adopt the values of the culture.

acute: medical treatments that are severe but of short duration.

addiction: the condition of a person who is dependent on a substance and uses it compulsively.

adultery: engaging in sexual intercourse outside of marriage with someone other than a lawful spouse.

affirmative action: policies that address and put into place guidelines and procedures that aid in correcting institutional discrimination.

age sets: people grouped or ranked by age, particularly useful in analyzing the age structure of a population.

agonism: a drug that mimics the effect of a given neurotransmitter.

agoraphobia: an anxiety disorder that involves fear and panic symptoms when away from home, or in a situation where escape may be difficult.

almshouses: institutions utilized mostly in the United States and England during the 17th through 19th centuries to take care of the poor.

alternative schools: schools created within the public school system for at-risk students.

analytic psychology: the psychoanalytic movement developed by Carl Jung, also known as Depth Psychology or Archetypal Psychology, which looks at deep forces, such as the collective unconscious, and how they motivate behavior.

animism: the religious belief in functioning spirits or life forces that operate in the natural world through plants, animals, or other elements and have an impact on events in society and personal life.

anomie theory: the concept promoted by Robert Merton which asserts that a state of normlessness is caused by undermining norms of traditional values and focuses upon the disjoint between socially acceptable goals and the approved means of reaching those goals.

antagonism: a drug that blocks the effect of a given neurotransmitter.

anthropology: the study of humankind.

antisepsis: the destruction of the growth and multiplication of microorganisms to prevent infection.

archaeology: the study of early humans through an investigation of their material remains.

archetypes: inherited tendencies or images which predispose us in how we shape our experiences.

arousal theory: the idea of motivation suggesting that a given individual has an optimal level of arousal to engage in a given behavior.

artifact: an object made by human beings.

ascription: American cultural value that describes the process through which value is taken away or assigned to things, people, or events.

asepsis: the process of removing pathogenic microorganisms or protecting against infection by such organisms.

assimilation: becoming so integrated into a new culture that a person becomes one with it.

attributional theory: an idea about motivation which notes that people want to attribute a cause for their successes or failures.

auletrides: a class of Greek prostitutes higher than the dicteriades who were entertainers and used seductive acts in their performances and often engaged in sexual behaviors with members of the audience.

authoritarian: favoring blind submission to authority.

bacillus anthracis: a well-known species pathogenic to humans, which causes anthrax. It derives from bacillus which is a genus of bacteria of the family bacillaceae. All species are rod-shaped, sometimes occurring in chains.

barter: to trade by exchanging goods or services without using money.

Big Five: a trait theory that looks at behavior through five domains—openness, conscientiousness, extraversion, agreeableness, and neuroticism.

bioterrorism: the use, or threatened use, of biological agents to promote or spread fear or intimidation upon an individual, a specific group, or the population as a whole for religious, political, ideological, financial, or personal purposes.

birthrates: the number of live births per year, sometimes divided by the midyear population.

bisexuality: the attraction to and/or the sexual engagement with both males and females, regardless of one's own gender.

borderline personality: a disorder including a widespread pattern of impulsivity, along with instability of moods, interpersonal relationships, and self-image.

Bracero: the program of recruitment of Mexican workers established during WWII and ending in 1964 which guaranteed labor supply for U.S. agriculture.

brothel: a place where clients go to attain the services of a prostitute.

Calvinism: a religion of the reformation emphasizing that people were predestined to be saved or lost and that the primary virtue which testified for salvation was to work, thus the origin of the *Protestant work ethic*.

capitalism: see *free-market economy*.

case study: a descriptive type of research in which a "case" or individual is studied in-depth to gain insight or to make inferences about a situation or behavior.

ceiling: the maximum number of people allowed to immigrate under certain categories such as employment, family unification, and refugee resettlement.

celibacy: abstinence from any form of sexual activity.

charter school: a school sponsored by a public school body which can hire its own teachers, develop its own academic program, and be held to a minimum accountability standard.

child abuse: The violation of trust and boundaries, perpetrated by adults charged with protecting a child.

Children of Immigrants Longitudinal Study (CILS): presently the most comprehensive sociological study of immigrant children and families, conducted in San Diego and Miami.

China's "One Child" policy: The official policy of the People's Republic of China that monitors women of childbearing age and penalizes families for having more than one child.

chronic: medical treatments marked by long duration or frequent recurrence.

church: a religious organization that is highly integrated into the established social norms and value system of the wider society.

classical conditioning: also called Pavlovian conditioning, it is learning which occurs by pairing a conditioned and unconditioned stimulus until the conditioned or neutral stimulus elicits the response which is attached to the unconditioned stimulus.

cognitive dissonance: a negative, tension-filled state which occurs when there is inconsistency between cognitions and behavior, or between two cognitions.

cognitive theory: the idea that motivation has purpose and is goal-directed, encouraging people to be actively involved in thinking, explaining, or giving attributions to their behavior.

cohabitation: living together in a sexual relationship, especially when not legally married.

collective unconscious: for Jung, the deepest layer of unconsciousness which contains the collective memories of the common experiences shared by all people of preceding generations.

commensalism: a close association or union between two kinds of entities, in which one is benefited by the relationship and the other receives neither benefit nor harm.

communism: a political ideology in which the government exercises control over employment, wages, the economy, housing, entrance into college, even marriages, with the goal to eliminate disparities that occur in open societies and systems.

comparative method: a methodology used to compare and contrast customs and practices found in different societies.

complex: a group or set of ideas, feelings, and memories that hold together and come from both personal experiences and a core behavior pattern that is inherited.

Comstock Law: a law passed by Congress in 1873 that prohibited mailing obscene materials, which included contraceptive information.

conditional positive regard: a position which says that in order to receive love, one should engage in ways of thinking and acting that are approved by parents and society.

conditioned response: in classical conditioning, the response that has become conditioned to the neutral (conditioned) stimulus.

conditioned stimulus: the neutral stimulus in classical conditioning.

conflict perspective: a sociological theory that views society in terms of a series of groups in conflict but asserts that conflict is not necessarily bad and that thus our goal should not be to avoid conflict but to manage it to everybody's advantage.

conflict theory: a perspective in sociology that views society as a series of conflicts between social groups vying for political and social dominance.

constructivism: a child-centered approach, also called discovery learning, which seeks to make available an environment that is responsive to the child so that the child can determine when and where he or she will learn from it.

control group: the group in an experiment that does not receive the treatment, and to which the treatment group is compared.

coordinated community action models (CCAMs): community coalitions generally put together by domestic violence programs to facilitate a coordinated response to domestic violence within a given community.

coprophilia: gaining sexual gratification or excitement from contact with feces.

correlation: a statistical method that describes the relationship between variables.

correlation coefficient: a numerical value that describes the relationship of variables (.00 being no relationship and 1.00 indicating a perfect relationship).

cost-benefit analysis: the process of assigning a dollar value to all financial and non-financial resources invested in an intervention and looking at what was gained in an attempt to determine whether the intervention was worth the effort.

cost-effectiveness (CE): calculation of the cost of providing a unit of service or of any intended output.

cost utility: calculation of the cost associated with obtaining non-financial indicators of goodness or desirability.

criteria-based model: an approach to policy making that attempts to maximize benefits based on agreed-upon values.

cult: a religious group that emphasizes new teachings, most of which come from a human leader.

cultural and social anthropology: the study of culture and social structures.

cultural relativism: a principle that requires people to be judged by the cultural standards of their own societies.

culture: any group of people who share common lifestyle characteristics which are passed on to members of the group, including values, beliefs, and behaviors.

cumulative causation: creation of social pathways between communities—the more they are transversed the easier it becomes for each successive person to migrate.

defense mechanisms: means used by the ego to distort our reality so that we are not conscious of our intra-psychic conflicts.

deindividuated: the feeling of being anonymous or just like everyone else in a group—having no personal identity apart from membership in a certain group.

deinstitutionalization: the movement to get the mentally disordered out of institutions, such as mental hospitals, and have them cared for in their communities.

delusion: a psychotic symptom revolving around a bizarre or unreal thought.

demand characteristics: cues in an experimental setting which may bias how a subject responds, typically with the subject responding in ways which support the hypothesis of the research.

dementia: a cognitive disorder of gradual onset, usually occurring in the elderly, which affects memory, thinking, and disorientation.

democratic rule: a political system governed by the people, in which there is majority rule yet minority rights with equality of opportunity for all.

demographic transition: a pattern in which modernization leads temporarily to an increase in population followed by an eventual equilibrium between mortality and fertility rates.

demographics: the application of statistical data about a population to practical uses in marketing and government planning.

demography: the social-scientific study of population and the dynamics of fertility, mortality, and migration.

denomination: a church-like religious organization that is tolerant of other religious groups, many of which coexist peacefully in a given society.

dependency ratio: the ratio of working to non-working people.

dependent variable: the variable being measured in an experiment so as to determine how it being affected by the independent variable.

descriptive statistics: statistical methods that help describe characteristics of the data.

deserving poor: people considered unable to work because they are children, the elderly, sick or handicapped, or women caring for small children.

developmental theory: a perspective suggesting that individuals and families change over time in stages.

dicteriades: literally the "whores of the brothel," they were considered the lowest ranking prostitutes in the hierarchy of prostitutes in the Greek culture.

discrimination: the overtly unequal treatment of people on the basis of their membership in a certain social group.

dissociative identity disorder: formerly known as the multiple personality disorder, it involves more than one personality, or fragments of a personality, within the same person, which affects his or her behavior.

double day: also known as the "second shift," it is the idea that as more women entered the workforce, they also continued to bear the responsibilities of traditional female roles, creating two full-time jobs instead of one.

drive-reduction theory: the idea that all organisms have the goal of homeostasis and try to achieve and maintain balance or equilibrium.

DSM-IV-TR: the text revision of the fourth edition of the *Diagnostic and Statistical Manual of Mental Disorders*, a classification system of mental disorders produced by the American Psychiatric Association.

dualism: the view that there is both a mind and a body—both a mental and a physical reality.

dysfunctional: pertains to any phenomenon that undermines the stability or survival of a system of which the phenomenon is a part.

dysthymia (dysthymic disorder): a chronic less severe depression, lasting at least two years for adults.

ecclesia: a religious group so integrated into the dominant culture that it is difficult to tell where one begins and the other leaves off; also called a government sponsored or state religion.

ecological theory: the belief that humans develop within the context of four systems: the microsystem, mesosystem, exosystem, and macrosystem.

edge city: a community formed out of suburbs that has jobs, markets, and housing all in dense concentrations.

ego: in Freud's levels of consciousness, the psychic structure of the personality that develops from the id to deal with the external environment while operating on the reality principle.

electroconvulsive therapy (ECT): treatment in which an electric current is used to induce a seizure, especially used for mood disorders such as major depression and bipolar disorder.

Elizabethan Poor Laws: laws enacted in England in the early 1600s in an attempt to regulate poverty. These laws introduced the concepts of deserving and non-deserving poor as well as the concept of less eligibility.

empiricists: individuals who believe that our knowledge is gained from experience.

end-stage renal disease: end-stage kidney failure that occurs when the kidneys' function has been reduced to less than 10% of normal function and they can no longer perform life-sustaining removal of waste and water from the body.

epidemiology: the study of the nature, cause, control, and determinants of the frequency and distribution of diseases, conditions, injury, disability, and death in human populations.

ethnic minority groups: people who share common cultural features, such as food, history, language, religion, land of origin, and traditions. A group's cultural heritage often continues to be influential even as members enter a different culture.

ethnicity: the classification of individuals with a common ancestry who share customs and traditions in religion, food, dress, and nationality that are passed on from generation to generation.

ethnocentrism: the belief that one's culture is superior to all others.

ethnography: a research method used especially in anthropology to describe what is occurring in a culture.

etiology: the study of the causes and origins of diseases.

evaluability: a quality of a social program which makes it possible to be evaluated.

exhibitionism: the need to expose one's genitals to unsuspecting others for the purposes of sexual gratification.

existentialism: a philosophical orientation that emphasizes freedom, authenticity, meaning in life, and the uniqueness of the individual, in face of the human predicament and its absurdities.

experiment: a type of research in which the researcher will manipulate one or more variables and measure the effect on one or more other variables, used to determine cause and effect.

experimental group: the group that receives the treatment in an experiment.

experimenter bias: behavior by the researcher which may unintentionally bias the results of an experiment.

extrinsic motivation: motivation that comes from without, encouraging certain behaviors because of the benefits they bring to a person.

extroversion: the state of being more concerned with the outer world of people and events than with one's own thoughts.

family cohesion: a feeling of emotional closeness among people or an experience of being nurtured and loved in a family.

family flexibility: the ability to change the power structure, roles, and rules of a family as necessary.

family planning: programs that respond to a wide variety of reproductive needs, often focusing on education and access regarding contraception, but varying according to the cultural climate of a particular society.

family sociology: the branch of sociology that studies the family.

feminism: a movement towards women's liberation and a belief advocating that women and men have equal rights.

feudalism: An all-encompassing political, economic, and social system based entirely on land holdings and the obligatory relation of vassal (or bondsman) to that of the lord. In exchange for working the property without wage (a form of slavery) and total allegiance to the lord, the vassal received protection.

fetish: a paraphilia in which an inanimate object is used to achieve sexual gratification.

fictions: subjective beliefs which guide people in their attempts to reach an ideal.

field experiment: an experiment done outside the laboratory in a natural setting.

flushing response: following alcohol consumption, a flushing of the face, neck, and upper chest, along with symptoms such as dizziness, pounding of the head, and nausea.

folkways: norms that carry the lightest sanctions when violated.

free-market economy: any market in which buying and selling can be carried out with minimal government involvement, no limitation to price, and without restrictions as to who participates in the process.

frotteurism: the sexual pleasure gained from rubbing up against an unsuspecting other, often a stranger in crowded places.

frustration-aggression model: a theory advocating that it is common for everyone to feel frustrated from time to time, and that this frustration leads to aggressively blaming others for one's own plight.

functional finalism: the concept developed by Alfred Adler which suggests that there is an ideal that we want ultimately to reach—a final functional goal.

functionalism: macro sociological theory that views society as a very organized system regulated by shared values, norms, and beliefs; primarily concerned with whether a society as a system works effectively and efficiently, the theory focuses on stability and balance, asserting that social problems occur when society or a portion of it becomes disorganized.

generalization: the process of taking results, or observations, and applying them to subjects beyond the study.

generalized other: a role in which an individual is capable of measuring his or her behavior against that of others and acting according to the expectations of others.

gestalt: a German word meaning "form" or "shape," which is used to describe the whole of something.

graying of America: the trend of the average American becoming increasingly older, with more of the population concentrated in older age sets.

green revolution: dramatic increases in food production during the 1960s and 1970s, particularly in low income countries with rapidly growing populations such as Mexico, India, Pakistan, Indonesia, and the Philippines.

hallucination: a psychotic symptom in which the sensory experience does not match reality, such as hearing voices that are not there.

harm reduction methods: methods or techniques that place an emphasis on reducing behaviors that are causing harm to the individual, without focusing on total abstinence.

health maintenance organization (HMO): a prepaid health plan that provides comprehensive health-care services for a specified group or members at a fixed cost or through pre-paid periodic payments. It entitles members to services of participating hospitals, clinics, and physicians.

health service organization (HSO): an organization that provides medical health promotion and preventive care activities related to diagnosis, treatment, therapy, and rehabilitation.

hetaerae: the highest class of Greek prostitutes who were often very educated, talented, and respectable women who would, in addition to providing sexual favors, engage in intellectual conversations with their clients.

heterosexuality: the attraction to and/or the sexual engagement with members of the opposite sex.

histrionic: a term coming from the Latin word for "actor" which is used to describe a person who is overly sentimental, excessively emotional, manipulative, and attention-seeking.

homogeneous: of the same or similar nature or kind.

homosexuality: the attraction to and/or the sexual engagement with members of the same sex.

human adaptability: the study of the relations between humans and their physical environments.

humanism: a philosophical orientation that emphasizes human interests, ideals, and dignity, and focuses on issues of freedom, personal growth, and self-fulfillment.

humanistic approach: a system of psychology, or approach to therapy, that focuses on the uniqueness of individuals, conscious choice, and fulfillment of human potential.

Hutterites: a Protestant group from the same European religious context as the Amish and Mennonites, who live communally in the northern plains states of the U.S. and in central Canada; Hutterite women used to hold the record for the highest fertility rates.

hyperlipidemia: the presence of excess fat or lipids in the blood.

hypersexuality: an insatiable desire for sexual activity, which adversely affects everyday functioning.

hypertension: abnormally high blood pressure and especially arterial blood pressure.

hypothetico-deductive thinking: the ability to set up a hypothesis and deduce, through logical consequences, whether it is true.

hypoxyphilia: literally "the love of lack of oxygen," used in reference to deriving sexual pleasures from oxygen deprivation.

id: in Freud's levels of consciousness, the psychic structure of the personality present at birth which is the driving force of the personality, consisting of our drives and instincts and operating on the pleasure principle.

idiographic: a research approach that involves studying a single subject for a long time period, called a longitudinal study, in order to determine the reason behind particular actions.

Immigration and Nationality Act of 1965: the policy that abolished nationality and race of ancestry as the basis for admission to the U.S.

Immigration and Naturalization Service: an agency of the U.S. government which processed requests for visas according to immigration laws and was replaced by the newly formed Bureau of Citizenship and Immigration Services.

Immigration Reform and Control Act of 1986 (IRCA): a law which combined amnesty for undocumented immigrants who met certain conditions with harsher penalties for employers who knowingly hired undocumented workers.

incentive theory: the idea that external or environmental factors pull us toward a given goal or behavior.

incest: sexual contact between an adult and a child who are close blood relatives.

incremental model: an approach to policy-making that relies on little empirical data. It is a process of trial and error in which policy-makers keep using whatever works, and stop using whatever does not work. Whatever works eventually becomes the policy.

independence: American cultural value characterized by freedom from external controls.

independent variable: the variable manipulated in an experiment so as to determine its effect on the dependent variable.

individual psychology: the school of psychology founded by Alfred Adler that viewed individuals as an indivisible whole, who were goal oriented and had a drive to compensate for feelings of inferiority.

individualism: American cultural value characterized by emphasis on the individual as a unit of analysis.

inferential statistics: statistical methods that allow us to infer or draw a conclusion about a population from a sample.

instinct theory: the belief that an organism behaves the way it does because it has no other choice due to inborn or genetically determined patterns of behavior that are rigid, inflexible, and fixed.

institutional differentiation: a process in which institutions, including religious institutions, become separate in function from one another and take on specialized roles.

institutionalization: the use of institutions, such as mental hospitals, to treat individuals with more severe forms of mental disorders.

interactionism: a sociological perspective that focuses on mezzo level group and individual micro level human interaction, emphasizing human creativity in the development and modification of human institutions which are seen not so much as controlling human development but rather resulting from human interaction.

interactionist perspective: a macro sociological theory that views poverty and other social problems as something relative and subjective. Interactionists believe that most social problems are a matter of shared expectations originating not from the societal system but from people's low self-esteem and low expectations in life.

interdependency: a balanced and reciprocal level of dependence between two or more entities.

interview: a type of survey research method in which data is gathered by directly talking to the subject.

intoxication: a reversible substance-specific disorder that results from ingesting or exposure to a substance, typically affecting moods, thinking, judgment, and psychomotor and interpersonal behavior.

intrinsic motivation: motivation that comes from within, encouraging behaviors because of the joy or pleasure they bring to a person.

introversion: the state of being more concerned with the inner world of one's own thoughts than with the external environment of people.

just noticeable difference: the smallest amount of change between two stimuli that a person can detect.

Kama Sutra: a first-century Hindu Sanskrit text about both a physiological and social description of lovemaking, erotic pleasures, and related topics.

key informant: an individual who acts as a guide to help an ethnographer learn about a culture.

latent functions: those consequences of social actions that are unintended and unexpected.

learning: a relatively enduring change in attitudes, beliefs, and values, as well as an actual or potential change in behavior resulting from an interaction with the environment/your experiences.

learning disability: a condition when a discrepancy between ability and academic performance exists due to processing disorders rather than mental retardation, emotional disturbance, or environmental disadvantage.

lesbian: originally from the Greek island of Lesbos associated with female homosexuality, the term refers to a female homosexual.

less eligibility: the principle regulating social welfare in the United States and England according to which the amount of public assistance a person receives should not be greater than the amount of money the same person could earn if working full time at a minimum wage.

liberal feminists: people seeking social and legal changes that support equal opportunities for women who believe that society must change its patterns of sex-role socialization, which will enable more egalitarian gender relationships.

life space: all the influences or psychological facts that act upon a person's behavior at a given time.

life span: the maximum age to which any human being can live.

linguistic determinism: the idea that language directs our thoughts.

linguistic relativity: the idea that different languages frame reality differently.

linguistics: the study of language.

locus of control: a person's attribution of control as either internal or external. You can believe that your life is controlled by you (an internal locus of control), or you can believe that it is your environment, chance, or others (an external locus of control) that are in control.

looking-glass self: Charles Horton Cooley's idea that we come into being through a three-phase process: we imagine how we appear to others, we interpret the reactions of others to us, and we develop a self-concept.

low-income industrializing countries: countries in Asia, Africa, and Latin America with low per-capita incomes whose economies are still based primarily on industry or agriculture.

managed care system: any health-care delivery system—such as an HMO, another type of doctor-hospital network, or an insurance company—that acts as an intermediate between the person seeking care and the physician; it manages both the delivery and the cost of care in such a way that expenses, quality, utilization, and operations are controlled.

manifest function: the stated purpose for a behavior.

marital assimilation: an integration, also known as *amalgamation*, that occurs when members of different ethnic or racial groups marry or live together and give birth to a child.

masochism: sexual pleasure derived from pain inflicted upon oneself.

master status: a status which seen as more important than all the other statuses held by an individual.

medical perspective (also called "disease model"): a view which looks at etiology from a biological perspective; it would treat abnormal behavior as a medical illness, looking for dysfunctions in the brain and nervous system.

mercantilism: a system under which government stockpiled treasure gathered from conquests and colonies and in which government controlled all aspects of economic activity in order to increase the wealth and power of the system.

mixed economy: a style of government in which the market is owned partly by the private sector and in part by the government.

mobility: American cultural value that cherishes the ability of individuals to move up, move to, and/or move away.

modernism: a belief that scientific reasoning and research provide the correct way to evaluate what works best in a society.

monism: the view that only mind or only body exists—either a mental or a physical reality.

monogamy: the condition of being married to only one other person.

monotheism: the belief in only one God.

moralism: American cultural value concerned with making judgments of other people, assigning fault, and indicating what ought to be done. Moralism often represents the use of moral arguments to oppress and discriminate against people.

morality: an adherence to moral principles.

morality principle: the operating principle of the superego, it sets the moral standards and is composed of the ego ideal and the conscience.

mores: informal but serious social standards of moral conduct that carry stronger sanctions than do folkways.

mutualism: a relationship that proves to be of mutual benefit to both, or all, organisms involved.

narcissist personality disorder: a disorder of personality characterized by grandiosity, feelings of superiority, lack of empathy, and issues of power.

natural increase: the net increase in human population by subtracting the total deaths from the total births.

naturalistic observation: a descriptive research method in which the subject is unobtrusively observed in a natural setting.

nay-sayer: a person who disagrees with almost anything appearing on a questionnaire.

necrophilia: fantasizing about or engaging in sexual behavior with a corpse.

Neo-Malthusian: the view, similar to that of Thomas Malthus, that high rates of population growth are a grave threat to the life support systems of the planet.

neurochemical: chemical processes and phenomena related to the nervous system.

neuroleptics: a group of antipsychotic medications which help reduce symptoms such as hallucinations and delusions.

neurosis: a category of disorders that includes individuals who are in basic touch with reality but experience distressing emotional or behavioral symptoms (perhaps due to unconscious elements of anxiety and conflict, as was thought by Freud).

new immigrants: the primarily Latin American and Asian immigrants who have come to the U.S. since the changes in immigration laws in 1965.

nomothetic: a research approach that involves studying large numbers of subjects to note what is happening to the "average" person in the group and determine a general reason for behavior.

non-deserving poor: poor people who are mentally and physically able to work.

nonexperimental research designs: research designs that do not require the use of experimental and control groups, thus making it difficult if not impossible for researchers to control for many intervening factors that may provide the researcher with invalid or distorted findings.

nonparticipating providers: providers in managed care that have not entered into a contract with a managed-care health plan to render services under a group subscriber agreement.

norm: any way of behaving or rule of conduct that is conventional in a given community.

normlessness: a lack of socially accepted rules for determining appropriate and inappropriate behaviors.

norm-referenced test: a test in which the performance of the subject taking it is compared to the norms (standardized test results) of a relevant sample.

nuclear family: a family unit consisting of a mother and father and their children.

object permanence: occurring during the sensory-motor stage of cognitive development, it is the idea that an object is present even when it cannot be seen.

observational learning: learning that occurs by observing what a model does and the outcomes of that behavior.

obsessive-compulsive disorder: a disorder of obsessions, or intrusive repetitive thoughts, and compulsions, or repetitive behaviors.

operant conditioning: a type of learning that occurs when an organism operates (behaves) its environment and is rewarded for that behavior, increasing the odds that it will perform that behavior again.

opponent-process theory: the theory of motivation suggesting that there can be two opponent processes in which one emotion is expressed (e.g., fear) while the other is suppressed (e.g., relief). If fear is lost, then relief is expressed.

parasitism: a symbiotic relationship of two kinds of organisms in which the parasite benefits while the host is harmed.

pathology: a condition of the organism that gives rise to suffering—usually implies an abnormal or disordered condition of the body or its parts.

patriarchal: of or relating to a society governed primarily by men.

pedophilia: literally "love of children," referring to any form of child sexual abuse or incest.

Perinatal drug exposure: Occurring when a mother ingests drugs during her pregnancy, such exposure significantly impacts an infant's development and socialization trajectory.

personality: a relatively stable pattern of behavior, thoughts, or feelings that predispose a person to act in a given manner.

personality disorders: disorders characterized by a lifelong pattern of deeply ingrained maladaptive behavior (also known as "character disorder").

physical anthropology: the study of humankind through an investigation of their biological origins, evolutionary development, and genetic diversity.

placebo effect: when subjects show a change in the hypothesized direction of the dependent variable, even though they have not received any amount of the independent variable.

pleasure principle: the operating principle of the id which seeks the immediate gratification of the instincts, and immediate removal of any tension, without regard for the world around.

pluralism: the diffusion of power among many interest groups, preventing any single group from gaining control.

polygamy: the condition of having more than one spouse at one time.

population: a group of people who have at least one characteristic in common.

population momentum: the continual growth of a population even if fertility rates decline due to the large number of women of childbearing age.

population processes: the demographic processes of fertility (birth), mortality (death), and migration.

pornography: derived from the Greek word "pornographos," meaning "the writing of harlots," this term may refer to a variety of written, photographic, or motion picture media illustrating sexual or erotic behaviors for the purposes of arousing sexual excitement.

position preference: a response style in which a person chooses a particular answer because of its location on a list.

postmodernism: a perspective resting on the premise that at least many, if not all, values, norms, and beliefs have equal value and cannot be verified by empirical scientific analysis.

post-traumatic stress disorder: an anxiety disorder that can occur following a traumatic incident in which a person keeps reliving the trauma and the anxiety symptoms revolving around it.

preferred provider organization (PPO): in managed care, a specialized health-care delivery organization formed by hospitals, physicians, medical groups, or health plans that negotiate fee schedules with insurance companies, thus becoming preferred. With such a medical plan, members receive more coverage if they choose health care providers approved by or affiliated with the plan.

prejudice: a rigid attitude of positively or negatively "pre-judging" another in a categorically, predetermined way, even in the face of rational evidence.

profane: whatever is not sacred; the ordinary and mundane.

prostitution: the act of providing sexual favors for money or other consideration.

protestant work ethic: a moral value which suggests that work is a good in and of itself, and may be a sign of salvation. According to this view, many people are poor because they are morally flawed, and as a result God cannot bless them.

psychoanalysis: a form of therapy, originally developed by Freud, that seeks to discover the unconscious motives behind people's behavior.

psychodynamics: a system of psychology, or approach to therapy, coming out of Freudian thought that stresses the role of unconscious conflict.

psychology: beginning as a study of the soul or mind, psychology is now seen as the scientific study of mental processes and behavior.

psychomotor stimulants: drugs that have one effect in common: they stimulate transmission at synapses that use the neurotransmitters norepinephrine, dopamine, or serotonin as a transmitter.

psychopathology: the study of the origin, development, and manifestations of mental or behavioral disorders.

psychosis: a category of disorders affecting individuals who have a severe distortion of reality, including hallucinations and delusions.

psychosurgery: surgery involving the destruction (a lesion) or removal of part of the brain in order to alter behavior.

psychotherapy: a non-biological approach to treating psychological disorders, attempting to change people's thoughts, feelings, and behavior through psychological techniques, usually involving talking.

psychotic: affected by psychosis (mental disorder that interferes seriously with the usual functions of life).

psychotropic drugs: medications used to treat mental disorders.

public interest groups: groups or entities that usually lobby to promote the well-being of the public at large.

p-value: the level of probability that samples have come from the same group (or population).

qualitative: pertaining to data that varies in categories, names, or kind and is expressed so.

quantitative: pertaining to data that varies in amount (sometimes called measurement) and can be expressed in a numerical form (numbers).

quasi-experiment: a research design which is much like an experiment, except that the subjects are not randomized (usually due to ethical or inherent reasons).

race: any one of the categories into which the world's population can be divided on the basis of inherited physical characteristics such as skin or hair color.

racial minority groups: people who share certain inherited, biological characteristics. A group may or may not be a numerical majority, but the defining features are a lack of social, political, and economic power, which is enforced by the majority group.

racial profiling: when a person is suspected of being a criminal because of his or her ethnic origin.

racism: behavior, demonstrated by what one says or does, that is motivated by the belief that some people are superior to others because of their racial characteristics.

radical feminists: people who focus on sexual and fertility issues at the heart of feminism. They would like to develop a culture for women that is separate from men through revolutionary means.

randomization: the process of dispersing variables in a study so that each person from a population has an equal chance of landing in any of the groups being studied.

rational/behavioral model: an approach to policy-making that requires the largest possible amount of empirical data and a thorough analysis of all available policy options. This approach is usually very costly and time consuming and is often impractical for the policy-maker who must wrestle with a large number of policy issues and/or proposals.

rationalists: individuals who believe that one must use reason to gain knowledge or understand truth.

reactivity: a condition in which subjects will alter their behavior when they know they are being studied.

reality principle: the operating principle of the ego which seeks to find rational and logical ways to satisfy the id that can be safely secured in the external environment.

religion: a system of beliefs and practices oriented to the sacred.

religious cult: a religious group having a strong leader with considerable control of the members' time, money, and thought processes which the members gradually give up over a period of time. See also *cult* and *secular cult*.

religious fundamentalism: a movement or attitude by followers of a religion stressing that their sacred writings are to be interpreted literally, typically with an adherence to a set of basic beliefs that are considered orthodox.

representativeness: how much a sample resembles, or is representative of, the general population.

resettlement: a strategy for settling refugees in another region when their lives are at risk.

residual welfare programs: government programs intended to help the poor that are only available to easily identifiable minority groups of people meeting very specific eligibility criteria.

response rate: in survey research, the number of surveys returned by respondents.

response style: a manner in which a subject responds to a question, regardless of its content.

restraining order: an order from the court system that forbids one person (e.g., the perpetrator of abuse) from making contact with the person seeking the order (e.g., the victim).

retrospective data: data collected on a subject, based on his or her (or others') memory of past events or behavior.

revolving door syndrome: the movement of mentally disordered people back and forth between the mental hospitals and their community mental health resources as a result of deinstitutionalization.

ritual: a practice which is carried out in a formal and set way as a means of honoring the sacred (e.g., baptism, worship service, etc.).

Roe v. Wade: a 1973 U.S. Supreme Court decision that granted abortion rights in all states as part of a woman's right to privacy.

roles: the expectations, behaviors, obligations, and privileges attached to a status.

Romeo and Juliet effect: a phenomenon regarding a romantic relationship in which the more other people try to separate the two lovers, the more attractive the lovers seem to each other.

rugged individualism: American cultural value that emphasizes individual effort.

rural: pertaining to less densely populated spaces traditionally organized around agricultural enterprises.

sacred: anything extraordinary, beyond the mundane, which inspires reverence, awe, and fear (the transcendency of God, the cross of Christ, church building, etc.).

sadism: sexual pleasure derived from inflicting pain upon or humiliating someone else.

sample: a set of subjects drawn from the population.

Sapir-Whorf hypothesis: the theory developed by American researchers Edward Sapir and Benjamin Whorf which states that we come to embrace a particular way of thinking about and perceiving the world through our language.

schizoaffective disorder: a psychotic disorder that is characterized by a combination of major mood disorders and schizophrenia.

schizophrenia: a psychotic disorder that can be characterized by a deterioration of social and occupational functioning and can have a combination of delusions, hallucinations, disorganized speech, motor functioning, and affect.

sect: a religious organization that has defected from another such organization and tends to exist in some tension with the wider society.

secular cult: similar to a religious cult but lacking religious overtones, beliefs, and practices. The individual member is still totally devoted to the cult beliefs and practices and is usually separated in some way from the more mainstream society. See also *cult* and *religious cult*.

segregation: the physical separation of people on the basis of certain identifiers in the workplace, school, neighborhood, or any social arena.

selective perception: the tendency to see what one wants to see when doing research, especially in a natural setting.

self-help group: a group, such as AA, that meets because of a perceived need (such as a problem or disorder) and is usually led by a nonprofessional.

self-perception theory: a theory suggesting that a person observes his or her own behavior and concludes that he or she must be in agreement with something just because he or she is doing it.

serf: a person in servitude, bound to his/her master's land and transferred with it to a new owner.

sexual abuse: a situation in which a sex act is forced upon a person against his or her will, sometimes with the use of threats and coercion.

sexual harassment: unwanted sexual advances, requests for sexual favors, or displays of other verbal or physical behaviors of a sexual nature in the workplace.

simple supernaturalism: the religious belief in a general supernatural force, without a specific god or force, that influences the natural world.

slavery reparations: a movement calling for the U.S. government to repay African Americans for the pain and indignity of slavery as a way to compensate for the historic wrongs allegedly committed by the government and private corporations.

social causation hypothesis: a theory which states that being at the low end of the socioeconomic strata is etiologically associated with the disorder of the individual.

social cognition: The process by which individuals develop the ability to monitor, control, and predict the behavior of others.

social comparison: the process of comparing ourselves with other people to determine how we are performing in relationship to how they are performing.

social construction: the creation of meaning within the social context.

social desirability: the tendency to respond to questions in ways that make the interviewee look good.

social drift hypothesis: also known as the social selection hypothesis, this theory states that individuals with disorders drift towards the lower end of the socioeconomic strata.

social exchange theory: a perspective suggesting that society is composed of individuals who are participants in bargaining for life's rewards.

social metabolism: the rate of exchange between two statuses.

social mobility: movement or progress over time.

social networks: relationships based on kinship or friendship through which information and resources are accessed, and which help shape migration patterns.

social policy: a position adopted in relation to a social problem along with a corresponding course of action.

social problem: a problem that affects a significantly large group of people, that elicits consensus regarding its existence, that is recognized as significant by individuals in positions of power, and that can be solved only through collective action.

social referencing: when infants, toddlers, or others rely on trusted persons' emotional reactions to decide how to respond in a situation.

social roles: the behaviors that we expect from someone who holds a given social position.

social solidarity: the natural order in a society.

social velocity: the speed of social progress or movement.

social welfare state: a system of policies and social programs intended to promote the well being of society.

socialism: an ideology that society is organized without class distinctions so that every person produces according to his or her ability and consumes according to his or her needs.

socialist feminists: people who see social class differences (caused by the capitalist system) at the basis of gender discrimination. They promote revolutionary approaches to change, such as abolishing the capitalist and patriarchal systems, in order to achieve a balance in power.

society: a group of people living in a structured community.

socio-demographic research: information about a person—including age, gender, education level, and sometimes income—that is often used by sociologists to describe basic characteristics about a population being studied (e.g., old or young, primarily male or female, educated or uneducated).

sodomy: any form of "abnormal" or atypical sexual behavior, including but not limited to anal sexual intercourse.

somatoform disorder: a mental disorder with physical complaints that look like a medical condition, but cannot be fully explained by biological factors, substance use, or another mental disorder.

special education: education that is specifically designed, and individualized, for individuals with disabilities or special needs.

special interest groups: groups or entities that usually lobby to promote their own profits or self interests.

specific learning disability: a learning disability in a specific area or basic psychological process such as spoken or written language, or math calculations, which can affect oral and/or written expression, listening and/or reading comprehension, basic reading skills, and math calculation and/or reasoning.

spurious: an artificial relationship between two variables which is created by another variable.

standardized tests: tests which have a standardized, or uniform or spelled out, manner in which to give, score, and interpret the test and testing procedures.

standards-based education: a movement to create standards within the school system regarding what teachers teach and what students learn; seen as a way to raise the education standards and usually includes a fair amount of testing.

statistical significance: a case in which the results of research are unlikely to have occurred by chance and suggest that the null hypothesis (a hypothesis of no difference) should be rejected.

statistics: mathematically based methods that make data of samples more understandable.

status: American cultural value that encompasses the ideas of a person's position in society as well as the prestige associated with such position.

status set: the sum of the statuses or positions that an individual occupies in society.

stereotyping: a source of prejudice and discrimination that arises when people form sweeping impressions of a population, and then define the whole group by these overgeneralizations.

stimulus-response (S-R) learning: learning that occurs because a stimulus becomes conditioned to or associated with a given response.

striving for superiority: taking feelings of inferiority and striving to become superior or perfect.

structural functionalism: a perspective that focuses on the interplay of the family subsystem with other institutions in society.

structural unemployment: a level of unemployment believed to be the result of dysfunctions in the economy due to people not having the knowledge and skills needed by the market, people being in transition between jobs, and the slowing down of the economy often caused by the rising of the interest rates by the Federal Reserve Bank.

substance: a medication, an abused drug, or a toxin.

substance abuse: a maladaptive pattern of substance use leading to significant adverse consequences within a 12-month period. Unlike substance dependence, abuse does not include compulsive use, withdrawal, or tolerance.

substance dependence: a maladaptive pattern of substance use that includes cognitive, behavioral, and physiological symptoms.

substructure: the fundamental institution.

superego: in Freud's levels of consciousness, the psychic structure of the personality that develops out of the ego and is determined by the social and moral codes of that society; operating on the morality principle, its main goal is perfection.

superstructure: an institution based on a more fundamental one.

survey: a descriptive type of research which collects data via questionnaires or interviews.

symbolic interaction theory: a perspective that views humans primarily as cognitive beings who are influenced and shaped by their interactive experiences with others.

taboo: something forbidden and/or unacceptable in a society, carrying the strongest sanctions.

tabula rasa: the mind as a blank slate, as the empiricists considered it, upon which experience writes ideas.

target earners: immigrants who come initially to earn money for specific needs with the intent of returning home after their economic needs are fulfilled.

theism: the religious position that directs its principle belief towards a supreme being or beings.

tolerance: the process of becoming habituated to a substance (drug), and, therefore, having to increase the amount in order to achieve the original effect.

total fertility rate (TFR): an estimate of the number of children a woman in a given society can be expected to have over the course of her childbearing years.

traditional family: a family that holds beliefs and follows practices that are based on their culture and customs which are passed from one generation to another.

traits: aspects of personality that are relatively enduring.

transcendent idealism: the classification of religion that focuses upon ideas and sacred principles of thought and conduct as opposed to beings such as spirits or gods.

transience: instability, sometimes from moving frequently.

transvestism: the experience of gaining sexual pleasure by dressing up in the clothes of the opposite sex.

unconditional positive regard: the idea that one should accept, love, support, and value people even if their behavior is not agreeable to us.

unconditioned response: in classical conditioning, the response that normally occurs to the unconditioned stimulus.

unconditioned stimulus: in classical conditioning, the stimulus that naturally creates a given response.

urban: pertaining to a spatial, usually dense, concentration of people who organize their lives around non-agricultural activities.

urbanization: the transformation of a society from rural to urban.

urophilia: gaining sexual gratification or excitement from contact with urine.

values: our ideas of what is good or bad, worthy or unworthy, desirable or undesirable.

voyeurism: a strong urge to watch unsuspecting individuals when they are undressing or are engaging in sexual activity.

willingness to respond: a response style based on a subject's willingness to respond to a question, such as a willingness either to take a risk or to proceed conservatively.

withdrawal: a substance-specific syndrome that occurs after the cessation of, or reduction of, a substance that has been used heavily for a long time, affecting important areas such as social and occupational functioning.

Women's Liberation Movement: the second wave of feminism that fought for civil rights such as sexual and racial equality and raised awareness of economic and political injustices.

women's shelters: places in the community where women and their children can go to escape violence, especially when women need safe temporary housing after an abusive episode. Shelters also usually offer advocacy services to help women negotiate the legal and social service systems.

work: American cultural value representing the belief that people are called by God to engage in a specific type of employment and that financial success is the result of moral virtue and God's blessing, while poverty and unemployment are seen as signs of being morally flawed.

yea-sayer: a person who agrees with almost anything appearing on a questionnaire.

Yerkes-Dodson Law: the theory that performance on tasks of varying difficulty is affected by an individual's level of arousal.

zero population growth (ZPG): a strategy introduced in the 1970s for achieving an equal balance between births and deaths, usually by families having no more than two children.

zoophilia: fantasizing about or engaging in sexual behavior with a non-human animal.

REFERENCES

Preface

Farrelly, F., & Brandsma, J. (1974). *Provocative therapy*. Fort Collins, CO: Shields Publishing Co.

Chapter 1: Foundations of Sociology

Berger, P. L. (1967). *The sacred canopy: Elements of a sociological theory of religion*. New York: Doubleday.

Dawson, L. L. (1998). Anti-modernism, modernism and postmodernism: Struggling with the cultural significance of new religious movements, *Sociology of Religion, 59*(2): 131–156.

Durkheim, E. (1950). *The rules of sociological method*. New York: The Free Press.

Goffman, E. (1959). *The presentation of self in everyday life*. Garden City, NY: Doubleday.

Henslin, J. M. (1995). *Sociology: A down-to-earth approach* (2nd ed.). Boston: Allyn & Bacon.

Henslin, J. M. (2005). *Sociology: A down-to-earth approach* (8th ed.). Boston: Allyn & Bacon.

Maines, D. R. (2001). *The faultline of consciousness: A view of the interactionism in sociology*. New York: Walter de Gruyter.

Marx, K., & Engels, F. (1969). *The Communist manifesto*. Baltimore: Penguin. (Originally published in German in 1848.)

Mead, G. H. (1934). *Mind, self, and society*. Chicago: University of Chicago Press.

Merton, R. (1949). *Social theory and social structure: Toward the codification of theory and research*. Glencoe, IL: Free Press.

Merton, R. (1968). *Social theory and social structure* (2nd ed.). New York: Free Press.

Mills, C. W. (1959). *The sociological imagination*. New York: Oxford University Press.

Parsons, T. (1951). *The social system*. Chicago: Free Press.

Perdue, W. D. (1986). *Sociological theory: Explanation, paradigm, and ideology*. Palo Alto: Mayfield.

Sapir, E. (1921). *Language: An introduction to the study of speech*. New York: Harvest Books.

Schwalbe, M. (1998). *The sociologically examined life: Pieces of the conversation*. Mountain View, CA: Mayfield Publishing Company.

Stone, R. (Ed.) (1998). *Key sociological thinkers*. New York: New York University Press.

Sullivan, T. J. (1998). *Sociology: Concepts and applications in a diverse world* (4th ed.). Needham Heights, MA: Allyn & Bacon.

Turner, M. E., & Maryankski, A. (1979). *Functionalism*. Menlo Park, CA: Benjamin/Cummings.

Whorf, B. L. (1956). *Language, thought, and reality: Selected writings of Benjamin Lee Whorf* (John B. Carroll, ed.). Cambridge, MA: Technology Press of the Massachusetts Institute of Technology.

Williams, R. M., Jr. (1965). *American society: A sociological interpretation* (2nd ed.). New York: Knopf.

Chapter 2: Foundations of Psychology

Bandura, A., & Walters, R. H. (1963). *Social learning and personality development*. New York: Holt.

Erikson, E. H. (1963). *Childhood and society*. New York: W. W. Norton.

Festinger, L. (1957). *A theory of cognitive dissonance*. Evanston, IL: Row Peterson.

Fogiel, M. (Ed.). (1994, c1980). *The psychology problem solver* (rev. ed.). Piscataway, NJ: Research and Education Association.

Frankl, V. E. (1984). *Man's search for meaning*. New York: Washington Square Press.

Goldberg, L. R. (1993). The structure of phenotype personality traits. *American Psychologist, 48,* 26–34.

Haney, C., Banks, C., & Zimbardo, P. (1973). Interpersonal dynamics in a simulated prison. *International Journal of Criminology and Penology, 1,* 69–97.

Hebb, D. O. (1955). Drives and the CNS (conceptual nervous system). *Psychological Review, 62,* 243–254.

Hergenhahn, B. R. (1990). *An introduction to theories of personality* (3rd ed.). Englewood Cliffs, NJ: Prentice Hall.

Hergenhahn, B. R. (1992). *An introduction to the history of psychology* (2nd ed.). Belmont, CA: Wadsworth.

Hergenhahn, B. R., & Olson, M. H. (1997). *An introduction to theories of learning* (5th ed.). Upper Saddle River, NJ: Prentice Hall.

Herrnstein, R. J., & Murray, C. (1994). *The bell curve: Intelligence and class structure in American life*. New York: The Free Press.

Hull, C. L. (1943). *Principles of behavior*. New York: Appleton-Century-Crofts.

Kalat, J. W. (2002). *Introduction to psychology* (6th ed.). Pacific Grove, CA: Wadsworth Thomson Learning.

Koffka, K. (1935). *Principles of Gestalt psychology*. New York: Harcourt, Brace, & World.

Lefton, L. A. (2000). *Psychology* (7th ed.). Boston: Allyn & Bacon.

Lepper, M. R., Greene, D., & Nisbett, R. E. (1973). Undermining children's intrinsic interest with extrinsic rewards. *Journal of Personality and Social Psychology, 28,* 129–137.

Lewin, K. (1935). *A dynamic theory of personality: Selected papers.* New York: McGraw-Hill.

Maslow, A. H. (1970). *Motivation and personality* (2nd ed.). New York: Harper & Row.

McCrae, R. R., & Costa, P. T., Jr. (1987). Validation of the five-factor model of personality across instruments and observers. *Journal of Personality and Social Psychology, 52,* 81–90.

McDougall, W. (1908). *Introduction to social psychology.* London: Metheun.

McDougall, W. (1923). *Outline of psychology.* New York: Scribner.

Omrod, J. E. (1999). *Human learning* (3rd ed.). Upper Saddle River, NJ: Prentice Hall.

Pavlov, I. P. (1927). *Conditioned reflexes: An investigation of the physiological activity of the cortex* (G. V. Anrep, Trans.). London: Oxford University Press.

Piaget, J. (1970). *Genetic epistemology* (E. Duckworth, Trans.). New York: Columbia University Press.

Pulaski, M. (1980). *Understanding Piaget: An introduction to children's cognition development.* New York: Harper & Row.

Rogers, C. R. (1966). Client-centered therapy. In S. Arieti (Ed.), *American handbook of psychiatry* (Vol. 3). New York: Basic Books.

Rotter, J. B. (1954). *Social learning and clinical psychology.* Englewood Cliffs, NJ: Prentice Hall.

Skinner, B. F. (1938). *The behavior of organisms.* New York: Appleton-Century-Crofts.

Solomon, R. L. (1980). The opponent-process theory of acquired motivation. *American Psychologist, 35,* 691–712.

Stagner, R. (1988). *A history of psychological theories.* New York: Macmillan.

Tolman, E. C. (1932). *Purposive behavior in animals and men.* New York: Appleton.

Vaihinger, H. (1924). *The philosophy of "as if": A system of the theoretical, practical and religious fictions of mankind* (C. K. Ogden, Trans.). New York: Harcourt, Brace & Company.

Wahba, M. A., & Bridwell, L. G. (1976). Maslow reconsidered: A review of research on the need hierarchy theory. *Organizational Behavior & Human Performance, 15*(2), 212–240.

Weiner, B. (1980). *Human motivation.* New York: Holt, Rinehart & Winston.

Yerkes, R. M., & Dodson, J. D. (1908). The relation of strength of stimulus to rapidity of habit-formation. *Journal of Comparative Psychology and Neurology, 18,* 459–482.

Chapter 3: Foundations of Anthropology

Chagnon, N. (1977). *Yanomano—The fierce people.* New York: Holt, Reinhart and Winston.

Davis, W. (1985). *The serpent and the rainbow.* New York: Warner Books.

Gordon, P. (2004). Numerical cognition without words: Evidence from Amazonia. *Science, 306,* 496–499.

Gribbin, J., & Cherfas, J. (2003). *The first chimpanzee.* New York: Barnes & Noble Books.

Lee, D. (1950). Lineal and nonlineal codifications of reality. *Psychomatic Medicine, 12,* 89–97.

Levi-Strauss, C. (1963). *Structural anthropology I.* New York: Basic Books.

Pinker, S. (1994). *The language instinct.* Harmondsworth: Penguin.

Whorf, B. (1941). The relation of habitual thought and behavior to language. In L. Spier, A. I. Hallowell, and S. S. Newman (Eds.), *Language, culture, and personality: Essays in memory of Edward Sapir.* Menosha, WI: Sapir Memorial Publication Fund.

Chapter 4: Research Methods

American Psychiatric Association (2000). Diagnostic and statistical manual of mental disorders (4th ed., text revision). Washington, DC: American Psychiatric Association.

Bodley, J. H. (1994). *Cultural anthropology: Tribes, states, and the global system.* Mountain View, CA: Mayfield.

Haviland, W. (1990). *Cultural anthropology* (6th ed.). Fort Worth: Holt, Rinehart and Winston.

Hothersall, D. (1995). *History of psychology* (3rd ed.). New York: McGraw-Hill.

Hunt, M. (1993). *The story of psychology.* New York: Anchor Books.

Lord, J. (2000). Really MADD: Looking back at 20 years. *Driven Magazine.* Retrieved November 28, 2003, from http://www.madd.org/aboutus/0,1056,1686,00.html

Mooney, L. A., Knox, D., & Schacht, C. (2000). *Understanding social problems* (2nd ed.). Belmont, CA: Wadsworth.

Myers, A., & Hansen, C. H. (2002). *Experimental psychology* (5th ed.). Pacific Grove, CA: Wadsworth.

Scarpetti, F. R., Andersen, M. L., and O'Toole, L. L. (1999). *Social problems.* New York: Addison-Wesley.

Chapter 5: Education

Abbott, J. (1997). 21st century schools. *The Education Digest, 10,* 11–15.

Aiex, N. K. (1994). *Home schooling and socialization of children* (EDO-CS-94-07, June 1994). Bloomington, IN: ERIC Clearinghouse on Reading, English, and Communication Digest #94.

Alexander, K., & Alexander, M. D. (1992). *American public school law* (3rd ed.). St. Paul, MN: West.

Alexander, K., & Alexander, M. D. (2001). *American public school law* (5th ed.). Belmont, CA: West/Thompson Learning.

Arnold, M. L. (1998). Three kinds of equity. *The American School Board Journal, 5,* 34–36.

Bai, M. (1999). Anatomy of a massacre. *Newsweek, 5,* 25–31.

Barber, B. R. (1997). Public schooling: Education for democracy. In J. I. Goodlad & T. J. McMannon (Eds.), *The public purpose of education and schooling* (pp. 21–32). San Francisco: Jossey-Bass.

Barclay, J. D. (1999). Chalk talk—Fiscal accountability under the Individuals with Disabilities Education Act: How do we ensure the money is spent on handicapped education and related services? *Journal of Law and Education, 28*(2), 327–333.

Bell, J. D., & Whitney, T. (1998). A for adequate, F for funding. *State Legislatures, 24*(3), 24–29.

Berkowitz, A. (1992). College men as perpetrators of acquaintance rape on campus: A review of recent research. *Journal of American College Health, 40,* 175–181.

Berman, S., Davis, P., Koufman-Frederick, A., & Urion, D. (2001). The rising costs of special education in Massachusetts: Causes and effects. In *Rethinking special education for a new century.* Retrieved October 1, 2001, from the Thomas B. Fordham Foundation Web site: http://www.edexcellence.net/library/special_ed/index.html

Binge drinking high on campuses (1999, June 4). *Apples for Health, 1*(1). Retrieved October 1, 2001, from http://www.apples-forhealth.com/binget.html

Bizar, M. (2001). Standardized testing is undermining the goals of reform. Retrieved October 1, 2001, from the North Central Regional Educational Laboratory Web site: http://www.ncrel.org/mands/docs/4-2.htm

Bolt, D., & Crawford, R. (2000). *Digital divide: Computers and our children's future.* New York: TV Books.

Bracey, G. W. (1998). The eight Bracey report on the condition of public education. *Phi Delta Kappan, 80*(2), 112–131.

Buchen, I. H. (1999). Business sees profits in education: Challenging public schools. *The Futurist, 33*(5), 38–43.

Buechler, M. (1997). Charter schools so far. *The Education Digest, 9,* 60–63.

Bumstead, R. A. (1979, October). Educating your child at home: The Perchemlides case. *Phi Delta Kappan, 61,* 97–100.

Bureau of Justice Statistics (1995). Criminal victimization in the United States. Washington, DC: U.S. Department of Justice.

Carbo, M. (1996). Whole language vs. phonics: The great debate. *Principal, 75*(3), 36–39.

Carnine, D. (2000). Why education experts resist effective practices (and what it would take to make education more like medicine). Retrieved September 8, 2001, from the Thomas B. Fordham Foundation Web site: http://www.edexcellence.net/library/carnine.html

Center for Education Reform (2000). *School Choice Today.* Retrieved October 19, 2001, from http://edreform.com/pubs/choice1.htm

Center for Education Reform (2000, September). *Nine lies about school choice: Answering the critics.* Retrieved October 28, 2001, from http://www.edreform.com/pubs/ninelies2000.htm

Clinton, B. (1997, June 4). *IDEA '97 Speeches—Remarks by the President.* Retrieved October 27, 2001, from http://www.ed.gov/policy/speced/leg/idea/speech-1.html

College binge drinking kills. (1999). Retrieved from About.com on October 28, 2001, from http://alcoholism.about.com/library/weekly/aa990922.htm

Collins, J. (1997, October 27). How Johnny should read. *Time, 150*(17), 78–81.

Cook, J. (2000, July 25). Rising math scores suggest education reforms are working. Retrieved October 7, 2001, from RAND Web site: http://www.rand.org/hot/Press/naepscores.html

Cookson, P. W., & Shroff, S. M. (1997). School choice and urban school reform. *Eric Clearinghouse on Urban Education,* RR93002016.

Cullen, R. (2001). Special education at Coles Elementary. In *The evolution of the federal role: In rethinking special education for a new century.* Retrieved October 1, 2001, from the Thomas B. Fordham Foundation Web site: http://www.edexcellence.net/library/special_ed/index.html

Damon, W. (1995). *Greater expectations: Overcoming the culture of indulgence in America's homes and schools.* New York: The Free Press.

Demitchell, T. A. (1997). The legal confines of school reform. *The School Administrator, 54*(10), 28–31.

Ellis, A. K., & Fouts, J. T. (1997). *Research on educational innovations* (2nd ed.). Larchmont, NY: Eye on Education.

FairTest (2001). Retrieved October 17, 2001, from http://www.fairtest.org

Farkas, S., Johnson, J., & Duffett, A. (1994). Different drummers. In *First things first: What Americans expect from the public schools.* New York: Public Agenda.

Finn, C. E., & Amis, K. (2001). *Making it count: A guide to high-impact education philanthropy.* Retrieved October 7, 2001, from the Thomas B. Fordham Foundation Web site: http://www.edexcellence.net/philanthropy/making_it_count.html

Forgione, Jr., P. S. (1998a). *Achievement in the United States: Progress since A Nation at Risk?* Retrieved October 7, 2001, from the National Center for Education Statistics Web site: http://nces.ed.gov/Pressrelease/reform

Forgione, Jr., P. S. (1998b). *Violence and discipline problems in U.S. public schools: 1996–1997.* Retrieved December 21, 1999, from the National Center for Education Statistics Web Site: http://nces.ed.gov/Pressrelease/violence.html

Friedland, S. (1999). Violence reduction? Start with school culture. *The School Administrator,* 14–16.

Fuchs, L. S. (1995). *Connecting performance assessment to instruction: A comparison of behavioral assessment, mastery learning, curriculum-based measurement, and performance assessment.* ERIC Digest E530. Reston: VA: Clearinghouse on Disabilities and Gifted Education. (Eric Document ED381984)

Gardner, H. (1998). Are there additional intelligences? The case for naturalist, spiritual, and existential intelligences. In J. Kane (Ed.) (1999), *Education, information, and transformation: Essays on learning and thinking.* Upper Saddle River, NJ: Prentice-Hall.

Gates, B., with Hemingway, C. (1999). *Business @ the speed of thought: Succeeding in the digital economy.* New York: Warner Books.

Glenn, C. L. (1998). Public school choice: Searching for direction. *Principal,* 10–12.

Goldberg, M., & Harvey, J. (1983). A nation at risk: The report of the National Commission on Excellence in Education. *Phi Delta Kappan, 80*(1), 14–18.

Goodlad, J. I., & McMannon, T. J. (Eds.). (1997). *The public purpose of education and schooling.* San Francisco: Jossey-Bass.

Greenwald, R., Laine, R. D., & Hedges, L. V. (1996). The school funding controversy: Reality bites. *Educational Leadership,*

53(5), 78–79.

Gregory, R. J. (1992). *Psychological Testing: History, Principles, and Applications*. Boston: Allyn & Bacon.

Gregory, R. J. (2004). *Psychological Testing: History, Principles, and Applications* (4th ed.). Boston: Allyn & Bacon.

Harris, J. R. (1995). Where is the child's environment? A group socialization theory of development. *Psychological Review, 102*(3), 458–489.

Hess, R. M., & Brigham, F. I. (2001). How federal special education policy affects schooling in Virginia. In *Rethinking special education for a new century*. Retrieved October 1, 2001, from the Thomas B. Fordham Web site: http://www.edexcellence.net/library/special_ed/index.html

Horn, W. F., & Tynan, D. (2001). Time to make special education "special" again. In *Rethinking special education for a new century*. Retrieved October 1, 2001, from the Thomas B. Fordham Web site: http://www.edexcellence.net/library/special_ed/index.html

Horton, J. L. (1999). Discipline under IDEA. *The School Administrator, 10*, 30–35.

http://www.nea.org/annualmeeting/raaction/images/resolutions2005-2006.pdf (n.d.), 2005–2006 NEA Resolutions. Retrieved December 20, 2005.

Hughes, J. O., & Sandler, B. R. (1987, April). *"Friends" raping friends—Could it happen to you?* (Project on the Status and Education of Women, Association of American Colleges). Retrieved October 19, 2001, from http://www.cs.utk.edu/~bartley/acquaintRape.html

Jensen, A. R. (1981). *Straight talk about mental tests*. New York: The Free Press.

Jones, L. V. (1999). *National tests and educational reform: Are they compatible?* Retrieved September 29, 2001, from the Policy Information Center, The Educational Testing Service Network Web site: http://www.ets.org/research/pic/jones.html

Kantrowitz, B., & Wingert, P. (1999, May 10). Beyond Littleton: How well do you know your kid? *Newsweek*, 36–38.

Kolderie, T. (1998). What are the alternatives? *Principal, 5*, 5–8.

Koss, M., Gidyez, C., & Wisniewski, N. (1987). The scope of rape: Incidence and prevalence of sexual aggression and victimization. *Journal of Consulting & Clinical Psychology, 55*, 162–170.

Kupper, L. (Ed.). (1996). The education of children and youth with special needs: What do the laws say? *News Digest, 15* (ND15). Retrieved November 2, 2001, from the National Information Center for Children and Youth with Disabilities Web site: http://www.nichcy.org/pubs/newsdig/nd15txt.htm

Ladner, M., & Hammons, C. (2001). Special but unequal: Race and special education. In *Rethinking special education for a new century*. Retrieved October 1, 2001, from http://www.edexcellence.net/library/special_ed/index.html

Levinson, E., & Mineo, B. (1998). *The two faces of technology in special education*. Retrieved October 18, 2001, from Converge Magazine Web site: http://www.convergemag.com/Publications/CNVGNov98/specialed/specialed.shm

Lipsky, D. K., & Gartner, A. (1998). Taking inclusion into the future. *Educational Leadership, 56*(2), 78–81.

Louv, R. (1990). *Children's future*. Boston: Houghton Mifflin.

Lyman, I. (1998, January). Policy analysis: Homeschooling—Back to the future (Cato Policy Analysis No. 294). Retrieved October 28, 2001, from Cato Institute Web site: http://www.cato.org/pubs/pas/pa-294.html

McDonnell, L. M., McLaughlin, M. J., & Morison, P. (Eds.). (1997). *Educating one & all: Students with disabilities and standards-based reform*. Washington, DC: National Academy Press.

McGroarty, D. (2001). The little-known case of America's largest school choice program. In *Rethinking special education for a new century*. Retrieved October 1, 2001, from http://www.edexcellence.net/library/special_ed/index.html

National Center for Education Statistics (12 September 2001). *Mathematics 2000 major results*. Retrieved January 23, 2004, from http://nces.ed.gov/nationsreportcard/mathematics/results

National Center for Education Statistics (2001). *Homeschooling in the United States: 1999*. Retrieved January 23, 2004, from http://nces.ed.gov/pubs2001/HomeSchool

National Center for Education Statistics (2001). U.S. Department of Education. *Expenditures for public elementary and secondary education: School year 1998–99* in Statistics in Brief (March 2001), NCES 2001–321.

National Center for Education Statistics (2003). *Reading*. Retrieved January 23, 2004, from http://nces.ed.gov/nationsreportcard/reading/results2003/raceethnicity.asp

National Center for Education Statistics (December, 2005). *Revenues and expenditures by public school districts: School year 2002–03*. Retrieved January 6, 2006, from http://nces.ed.gov/pubsearch/pubsinfo.asp?pubid=2006312

National Center for Education Statistics (2005). *Internet access in U.S. public schools and classrooms: 1994–2003*. Retrieved March 2, 2006, from http://nces.ed.gov/surveys/frss/publications/2005015

National Center for Education Statistics (n.d.). *Dropping out and disabilities*. Retrieved January 23, 2004, from http://nces.ed.gov/pubs/dp95/97473-6.html

Odden, A. R. (1995). Critical issue: Redesigning school finance: Moving the money to the school. Retrieved January 23, 2004, from http://www.ncrel.org/sdrs/areas/issues/envrnment/go/go300.htm

O'Shea, L. J., O'Shea, D. J., & Algozzine, B. (1998). *Learning disabilities: From theory toward practice*. Columbus, OH: Merrill.

Palmaffy, T. (2001). The evolution of the federal role. In *Rethinking special education for a new century*. Retrieved October 1, 2001, from the Thomas B. Fordham Web site: http://www.edexcellence.net/library/special_ed/index.html

Park, J. (2003, September 29). School finance. *Education Week on the Web*. Retrieved January 1, 2004, from http://www.edweek.org/context/topics/issuespage.cfm?id=22

Parrish, T. B. (1999). Special education—At what cost to general education? *The CSEF Resource, 2*, 6–7. Palo Alto, CA: Center for Special Education Finance, American Institutes for Research. Retrieved September 23, 2001, from http://nces.ed.gov/edfin/faqs/speced_cost.asp

Phelps, R. P. (1999). *Why testing experts hate testing*. Retrieved January 18, 2006, from the Heartland Institute Web site: http://www.heartland.org/pdf/21824g.pdf, http://www.heartland.org/pdf/21824h.pdf, and http://www.heartland.org/pdf/21824i.pdf

Popham, W. J. (1999). Why standardized tests don't measure educational quality. *Educational Leadership, 56*(6), 8–15.

Popham, W. J. (2000). *Testing! Testing! What every parent should know about school tests.* Boston, MA: Allyn & Bacon.

Randall, K., & Grey, B. (2001, March 15). *A new round of school shootings in the U.S.* Retrieved September 5, 2001, from the World Socialist Web site: http://www.wsws.org/articles.2001/mar2001/shot-m15.shtml

Rape and Sexual Assault Homepage (n.d.). Retrieved January 27, 2004, from http://www.mint.net/rrs/DateRapeDrugs.htm

Rose, L. C., & Gallup, A. M. (2001). The 33rd annual Phi Delta Kappa/Gallup poll on the public's attitudes toward the public schools. *Phi Delta Kappan, 80*(1), 41–57.

School Improvement in Maryland Homepage (1997). Retrieved January 27, 2004, from http://www.mdk12.org

Shor, I., & Pari, C. (Eds.). (1999). *Education is politics: Critical teaching across differences, K–12.* Portsmouth, NH: Boynton/Cook Heinemann.

Snider, V. E. (1990). What we know about learning styles from research in special education. *Educational Leadership, 48*(2), 8–12.

Stover, D. (1997). Public funds for private schools. *The Education Digest, 63*(1), 64–67.

Synovitz, L. B., & Byrne, T. J. (1998). Antecedents of sexual victimization: Factors discriminating victims from nonvictims. *Journal of American College Health, 46*, 151–158.

Thayer, Y. V., & Short, T. L. (1994). New sources of funding for the twenty-first century school. *NASSP Bulletin, 78*(566), 6–20.

The theory of multiple intelligences. (n.d) Retrieved January 27, 2004, from http://www.edwebproject.org/edref.mi.intro.html

Townleyk, A. J., & Martinez, K. (1995). Using technology to create safer schools. *NASSP Bulletin, 79*(568), 61–69.

Turnbull, H. R., III, & Turnbull, A. P. (2000). Introduction to the American Legal System. In *Free appropriate public education: The law and children with disabilities* (6th ed., pp. 3–14). Denver, CO: Love.

United States General Accounting Office (GAO) (2001, January). Student discipline: Individuals with Disabilities Education Act. Report to the Committees on Appropriations, U.S. Senate and House of Representatives, 1–32. Retrieved March 2, 2006, from http://www.gao.gov/new.items/d01210.pdf

U.S. Census Bureau (2001). *Home computers and internet use in the United States: August 2000.* Retrieved October 1, 2001, from the U.S. Department of Commerce Web site: http://www.census.gov/prod/2001pubs/p23-207.pdf

U.S. Department of Education (1997). *Special education spending.* Washington, DC: National Center for Education Statistics, Education Finance Statistics Center. Retrieved September 23, 2001, from http://nces.ed.gov/edfin/faqs/speced2.asp

U.S. Department of Education (1999–2000). *Information on public schools and school districts in the United States.* Washington, DC: National Center for Education Statistics, Common Core of Data. Retrieved September 23, 2001, from http://nces.ed.gov/ccd/quickfacts.html

U.S. Department of Education (2000). *Dropout Rates.* Washington, DC: National Center for Education Statistics, Digest of Education Statistics. Retrieved September 20, 2001, from http://nces.ed.gov/fastfacts/display.asp?id=16

U.S. Department of Education (2000, June). *Condition of America's public school facilities: 1999* (NCES 2000-032). Washington, DC: Office of Educational Research and Improvement. Retrieved October 1, 2001, from http://whitehouse.gov/fsbr/education.html

U.S. Department of Education (2001). *Libraries and educational technology* in Digest of Education Statistics. Retrieved September 8, 2001, from http://nces.ed.gov/pubs2001/digest/ch7.html

U.S. Department of Education (2002, May). *Statistics in Brief* (NCES 2002-367). Washington, DC: Office of Educational Research and Improvement.

Violence in U.S. Schools (n.d.). Retrieved October 18, 2001, from abcnews.com Web site: http://abcnews.go.com/sections/us/DailyNews/schoolshootings990420.html

Walsh-Sarnecki, P. (1999, May 3). College life is linked to drinking, poll finds. *Detroit Free Press*, 1–3.

Watson, J. G. (2001). Educational technology: A necessity for the 21st century—Why the delay? Retrieved October 1, 2001, from the Thomas B. Fordham Foundation Web site: http://www.edexcellence.net/library/watson.html

Wechsler, H. (2000). *Binge drinking on America's college campuses.* Findings from the Harvard School of Public Health College Alcohol study, 1–11.

Wolfe, P., & Brandt, R. (1998). What do we know from brain research? *Educational Leadership, 11*, 8–13.

Yell, M. L., Rogers, D., & Rogers, E. L. (1998). The legal history of special education: What a long, strange trip it's been! *Remedial and Special Education, 19*(4), 219–228.

Zappardino, P. H. (1995). FairTest: Charting a course for testing reform. *The Clearing House, 68*(4), 248–252.

Zettel & Ballard (1982). The Education for All Handicapped Children Act of 1975 (P.L. 94–142): Its history, origins, and concepts. In J. Ballard, B. Ramirez, & F. Weintraub (Eds.), *Special education in America: Its legal and governmental foundations.* Reston, VA: Council for Exceptional Children.

Chapter 6: Marriage and Family

Abaya, C. (2001). *Welcome to the Sandwich Generation.* Retrieved October 19, 2001, from http://www.TheSandwichGeneration.com

Ames, K., Sulavik, C., Joseph, N., Beachy, L., & Park, T. (1992, March 23). Domesticated bliss: New laws are making it official for gay or live-in straight couples. *Newsweek, 119*, 62–63.

Aquilino, W. S., & Supple, K. R. (1991). Parent-child relations and parental satisfaction with living arrangements when adult children live at home. *Journal of Marriage and the Family, 53*, 13–27.

Arenofsky, J. (1996). In defense of DINKs. *Phoenix Magazine, 31*(3). Retrieved November 14, 2001, from http://hometown.aol.com/childfreeaz/a_in_defense.htm

Bateson, M. C. (2000). *Full circles, overlapping lives and culture: Generation in transition.* New York: Ballantine.

Belsky, J. (1984). The determinants of parenting: A process model. *Child Development, 55*, 83–96.

Bengtson, V., & Harootyan, R., eds. (1994). *Hidden connections: Intergenerational linkages in American society*. New York: Springer.

Benokraitis, N. V. (2002). *Marriages and families: Changes, choices, and constraints*. Upper Saddle River, NJ: Prentice Hall.

Bird, G. W., Bird, G., A., & Scruggs, M. (1984). Determinants of family task sharing: A study of husbands and wives. *Journal of Marriage and the Family, 46*, 345–355.

Blackwell, D., & Lichter, D. (2000). Mate selection among married and cohabiting couples. *Journal of Family Issues, 21*, 275–302.

Blankenhorn, D. (1990). "American family dilemmas." In Blankenhorn, D., Bayme, S., & Bethke Elshtain, J. (Eds.), *Rebuilding the nest*. Milwaukee, WI: Family Service of America.

Blau, P. (1964). *Exchange and power in social life*. New York: Wiley.

Blood, R. O., & Wolfe, D. M. (1960). *Husbands & wives: The dynamics of married living*. New York: Free Press.

Bowen, G. L., Pittman, J. F., Pleck, J. H., Haas, L., & Voydanoff, P. (1995). *The work and family interface: Toward a contextual effects perspective*. Minneapolis, MN: National Council on Family Relations.

Brien, M. J., Lillard, L. A., & Waite, L. J. (1997). *Cohabitation, marriage, and non-marital fertility*. Charlottesville, VA: Thomas Jefferson Center for Political Economy, Univeristy of Virginia.

Bronfenbrenner, U. (1979). *The ecology of human development: Experiments by nature and design*. Cambridge, MA: Harvard University Press.

Bronfenbrenner, U. (n.d.). Retrieved November 14, 2001, from http://www.people.cornell.edu/pages/ub11

Brooks, J. B. (1998). *Parenting* (2nd ed.). Mountain View, CA: Mayfield.

Brooks, J. B. (1999). *The process of parenting* (5th ed.). Mountain View, CA: Mayfield.

Bumpass, L. L., & Lu, H. (1998). *Trends in cohabitation and implications for children's family contexts*. Madison, WI: Center for Demography and Ecology, University of Wisconsin-Madison.

Bureau of Labor Statistics (2005). *Labor force statistics from the current population survey: Latest numbers*. Retrieved October 4, 2005, from http://www.bls.gov/cps/#overview

Burgess, E. W. (1948, May). The family in a changing society. *American Journal of Sociology, 53*(6), 417–422.

Center on Budget and Policy Priorities (1997). *Poverty rate fails to decline as income growth in 1996 favors the affluent: Child health coverage erodes as Medicaid for children contracts*. Retrieved January 29, 2004, from http://www.cbpp.org/povday97.htm

Cherlin, A. J. (1999). *Public and private families: An introduction* (2nd ed.). Boston: McGraw-Hill College.

Cherlin, A. J. (2002). *Public and private families: An introduction* (3rd ed.). Boston: McGraw-Hill College.

Clark, K. (2000, March 30). The new midlife. *US News and World Report*, 70-83.

Clarke, J. I. (1978). *Self esteem: A family affair*. Minneapolis, MN: Winston Press.

Clarke, J. I., & Dawson, C. (1998). *Growing up again: Parenting ourselves, parenting our children*. Center City, MN: Hazelden.

Corcoran, M., Danziger, S. K., Kalil, A., & Seefeldt, K. S. (2000). How welfare reform is affecting women's work. *Annual Review of Sociology, 26*, 241–269.

Council of Program Directors in Community Research and Action. Retrieved November 19, 2001, from http://www.msu.edu/user/lounsbu1/cpdcra.html

Curtis, C. (2005, September). Couples ready for Conn. civil unions. PlanetOut Network. Retrieved November 16, 2005, from http://planetout.com/news/article.html?2005/09/30/01

DeGenova, M. K., & Rice, F. P. (2002). *Intimate relationships, marriages and families* (5th ed.). Boston: McGraw-Hill.

Demian (2005, July). Belgium offers legal marriage. Partners Task Force for Gay & Lesbian Couples. Retrieved November 16, 2005, from http://buddybuddy.com/mar-belg.html

DeNavas-Walt, C., Proctor, B. D., & Lee, C. H. (2005). *Income, poverty, and health insurance coverage in the United States: 2004*. Current Population Reports, P60–229. U.S. Census Bureau: Washington, DC.

Deutsch, F. M. (1999). *Halving it all: How equally shared parenting works*. Cambridge, MA: Harvard University Press.

Doherty, W. J. (1997). *The intentional family: How to build family ties in our modern world*. Reading, MS: Addison-Wesley.

Duenwald, M. (2002). Two portraits of children of divorce: Rosy and dark. *New York Times*, 3-26-02, F6&10.

Equality for All (2005, September). Equality California to Governor Schwarzenegger: "We'll be back!" Retrieved November 16, 2005, from http://equalityforall.com/news/press_release_09292005.php

Eshleman, J. R. (1997). *The family* (8th ed.). Boston: Allyn and Bacon.

Families and Work Institute (n.d.). Retrieved November 21, 2001, from http://www.familiesandwork.org

Fields, J. (2004, November). *America's families and living arrangements: 2003*. Current Population Reports. U.S. Census Bureau: Washington, DC. Retrieved October 2, 2005, from http://www.census.gov/prod/2004pubs/p20-553.pdf

Fields, J., & Casper, L. (2001). *America's families and living arrangements: 2000*. Current Population Reports. U.S. Census Bureau: Washington, DC. Retrieved November 16, 2005, from http://www.census.gov/prod/2001pubs/p20-537.pdf

Fowlkes, M. R. (1994). *Single worlds and homosexual lifestyles: Patterns of sexuality and intimacy*. In A. S. Rossi (Ed.), *Sexuality across the life course*. Chicago, IL: University of Chicago Press.

Galinsky, E. (1999). *Ask the children*. Scranton, PA: William Morrow and Company.

Galinsky, E. (October 10, 2001). *Working mother's keynote address presented at Working Mothers—Work-Life Congress*. Retrieved November 22, 2000, from http://www.familiesandwork.org/announce/WorkingMother.html. Reprinted with permission.

Galinsky, E. (2002). "Inside the Teenage Brain." Interview with Ellen Galinsky. Retrieved March 14, 2006, from http://www.pbs.org/wgbh/pages/frontline/shows/teenbrain/interviews/galinsky.html

Gewertz, H. (1994, Fall). *Domestic partnerships: Rights, responsibilities and limitations.* Public Law Research Institute at Hastings College of the Law. San Francisco, CA: University of California. Retrieved November 11, 2001, from http://www.uchastings.edu/plri/fall94/gewertz.html

Goleman, D. (1995). *Emotional intelligence.* New York: Bantam.

Gottman, J. (1994). *Why marriages succeed or fail.* New York: Simon & Schuster.

Gottman, J. (1997). *Raising an emotionally intelligent child: The heart of parenting.* New York: Fireside.

Gottman, J., & Silver, N. (2000). *The seven principles of making marriage work.* New York: Crown Publishers.

Hochschild, A. R. (1989). *The second shift.* New York: Viking.

Hochschild, A. R. (1997). *The time bind: When work becomes home and home becomes work.* New York: Metropolitan Books.

Hogan, D. P., & Farkas, J. I. (1995). The demography of changing intergenerational relationship. In V. L. Bengston & K. W. Schaie, eds., *Adult intergenerational relations: Effects of societal change,* 1–8. New York: Springer.

Homans, G. (1961). *Social behavior in elementary forms.* New York: Harcourt, Brace, and World.

Houlgate, L. D. (1999). *Morals, marriage and parenthood: An introduction to family ethics.* Belmont, CA: Wadsworth.

Howard, J. (1978). *Families.* New York: Simon & Schuster.

Johnston, E. (2005, June). Canadian house approves same-sex marriage. PlanetOut Network. Retrieved November 16, 2005, from http://planetout.com/news/article.html?2005/06/28/1

Kinnunen, U., Gerris, J., & Vermulst, A. (1996). Work experience and family functioning among employed fathers with children of school age. *Family Relations, 45,* 449–455.

Klein, D. M., & White, J. M. (1996). *Family theories: An introduction.* Thousand Oaks, CA: Sage.

Larsen, R., & Almeida, D. M. (1998). Emotional transmission in the daily lives of families. *Journal of Marriage and the Family, 61*(1), 5–20.

Lingren, H. G. (1983). *Building Family Strengths.* HEG78-97, Lincoln: University of Nebraska Cooperative Extension. Issued December 1995; electronic version issued June 1996. pubs@unl.edu.

Manning, W. D., & Smock, P. J. (1995). Why marry? Race and the transition to marriage among cohabitors. *Demography 32*(4), 509–520.

Markman, H., Stanley, S., & Blumberg, S. L. (1996). *Fighting for your marriage.* San Francisco: Jossey-Bass.

Merriam-Webster Collegiate Dictionary (n.d.). Retrieved January 29, 2004, from http://webster.com

Minear, R. E., & Proctor. W. (1989). *Kids who have too much.* Nashville, TN: Thomas Nelson.

National Partnership for Women and Families (2002). *Real stories: On how the FMLA allowed them to spend last days with their son—Jeffrey and Tammy Mosser (Sewell, NJ).* Retrieved November 22, 2001, from http://www.nationalpartnership.org/content.cfm?L1=6&L2=1.0&L3=6&StoryID=29

National Partnership on Work and Family (n.d.). Retrieved November 22, 2001, from http://www.nationalpartnership.org/workandfamily/workmain.htm

NoKidding! (n.d.). *What is no Kidding! all about?* Retrieved January 25, 2004, from http://www.nokidding.net

Olson, D., Russell, C., & Sprenkle, D. (1989). *Circumplex model: Systemic assessment and treatment of families.* New York: Hayworth.

Olson, D. H., & DeFrain, J. (1994). *Marriage and the family: Diversity and strengths.* Mountain View, CA: Mayfield.

Olson, D. H., & DeFrain, J. (2000). *Marriage and the family: Diversity and strengths* (3rd ed.). Mountain View, CA: Mayfield.

O'Neil, R., & Greenberger, E. (1994). Patterns of commitment to work and parenting: Implications for role strain. *Journal of Marriage and the Family, 56,* 101–118.

Pipher, M. (1996). *The shelter of each other: Rebuilding our families.* New York: G. P. Putnam's Sons.

Pittman, F. (1998). *Grow up: How taking responsibility can make you a happy adult.* New York: St. Martin's Griffin.

Pleck, J. H. (1999, Summer). Men: The scientific truth about their work, play, health and passions. *Scientific American 10*(2), 38–43.

Roman, M. (2005, June). Spain gives gay couples right to wed. Associated Press. Retrieved November 16, 2005, from http://planetout.com/news/article.html?2005/06/30/1

Same Sex Marriage in Canada (n.d.). Retrieved November 16, 2005, from http://www.ssmarriage.com/timeline.html

Schoen, R. (1999). Do fertility intentions affect fertility behavior? *Journal of Marriage and the Family, 61,* 790–799.

Schwartz, M. A., & Scott, B. M. (2000). *Marriages and families: Diversity and change* (3rd ed.). Upper Saddle River, NJ: Prentice Hall.

Shehan, C. L., & Kammeyer, K. C. W. (1997). *Marriages and families: Reflections of a gendered society.* Boston: Allyn and Bacon.

Stinnet, N., & DeFrain, J. (1985). *Secrets of strong families.* Boston: Little Brown.

U.S. Bureau of Census (2000). Retrieved November, 2001, from http://www.census.gov

Veevers, J. D. (1980). *Childless by choice.* Toronto: Butterworths.

Waite, L. J., & Gallagher, M. (2000). *The case for marriage: Why married people are happier, healthier and better off financially.* New York: Doubleday.

Waite, L. J., & Joyner, K. (2001). Emotional satisfaction and physical pleasure in sexual unions: Time horizon, sexual behavior, and sexual exclusivity. *Journal of Marriage and Family, 63,* 247–264.

Walsh, D. (2002, February). *Our brains are built for one thing at a time.* MediaWise with Dr. Dave. Retrieved January 29, 2004, from http://www.mediafamily.org/mediawisecolumns/brains_mw.shtml. Reprinted with permission.

Wikipedia, The Free Encyclopedia (n.d.a). Retrieved January 25, 2004, from http://en.wikipedia.org/wiki/Michel_de_Montaigne

Wikipedia, The Free Encyclopedia (n.d.b). *Economic effects of Hurricane Katrina.* Retrieved October 4, 2005, from http://en.wikipedia.org/wiki/Economic_effects_of_Hurricane_Katrina

References

Chapter 7: Public Health and Health Care

Ahmed, S. M., Lemkau, J. P., Nealeigh, N., & Mann, B. (2001). Barriers to healthcare access in a non-elderly urban poor American population. *Health and Social Care in the Community, 9*(6), 445–453.

Allison, D. B., Fontaine, K. R., Manson, J. E., Stevens J., & Vanitallie, T. B. (1999). Annual deaths attributable to obesity in the United States. *Journal of the American Medical Association, 282,* 1,530–1,538.

American Heart Association. (n.d.). Tobacco industry's targeting of youth, minorities and women. Retrieved December 8, 2003, from http://www.americanheart.org/presenter.jhtml?identifier=11226

Anderson, R. E. (2000). The spread of the childhood obesity epidemic. *Canadian Medical Association Journal, 163*(11), 1,461–1,462.

Bauman, A. (2002). Workplace health promotion—good science, but in public health terms, are we re-visiting the emperor's new clothes? *Australian Journal of Nutrition & Dietetics, 59*(2), 77–78.

Brandt, A., & Gardner, M. (2000). Antagonism and accommodation: Interpreting the relationship between public health and medicine in the United States during the 20th century. *American Journal of Public Health, 90,* 707–715.

Cassels, A. (2002). Bioterrorism becoming too dominant on public health agenda? *Canadian Medical Association Journal, 167*(11), 1,281.

Centers for Disease Control and Prevention (1996). Asthma mortality and hospitalization among children and young adults—United States, 1980–1993. *Morbidity and Mortality Weekly Report, 45,* 350–353.

Centers for Disease Control and Prevention—Bioterrorism (2003). Retrieved December 8, 2003, from http://www.cdc.gov/programs

Centers for Disease Control and Prevention (2005). Functional Mission Statement. Retrieved August 11, 2005, from http://www.cdc.gov/od/funcmiss.htm

Centers for Disease Control and Prevention (n.d.). John Snow (1813–1858). Retrieved December 8, 2003, from http://www.cdc.gov/ncidod/dbmd/snowinfo.htm

Centers for Medicare and Medicaid Services (2006, January 10). "Healthcare spending growth rate continues to decline in 2004." Retrieved January 16, 2006, from http://www.cms.hhs.gov

Charatan, F. (2002). Healthcare costs hit older Americans. *British Medical Journal, 324*(7,340), 756.

Colditz, G. A. (1999). Economic costs of obesity and inactivity. *Medicine & Science in Sports & Exercise, 31,* S663–667.

Coughlin, P.J., Janecek, F.J., Jr., and partners Milberg, Weiss, Bershad, & Hynes (1998). A review of R. J. Reynolds' internal documents produced in *Mangini vs. R.J. Reynolds Tobacco Company,* Civil Number 939359 – The case that rid California and the American landscape of "Joe Camel." Retrieved December 8, 2003, from http://www.library.ucsf.edu/tobacco/mangini/report

DanceSafe (2005). Dance Safe Philosophy. Retrieved August 11, 2005, from http://www.dancesafe.org/documents/about/philosophyandvision.php

DeOnis, M., & Blossner, M. (2000). Prevalence and trends of overweight among preschool children in developing countries. *American Journal of Clinical Nutrition, 72,* 1,018–1,024.

DiFranza, J. R., Richards, J. W., Paulman, P. M., Wolf-Gillespie, N., Fletcher, C., Jaffe, R. D., et al. (1991). RJR Nabisco's cartoon camel promotes Camel cigarettes to children. *Journal of the American Medical Association, 266,* 3,149–3,153.

DiFranza, J. R., & Tye, J. B. (1990). Who profits from tobacco sales to children? *Journal of the American Medical Association, 263,* 2,784–2,787.

Donatelle, R. J., & Davis, L. G. (1994*). Access to Health* (3rd ed.). Englewood Cliffs, NJ: Prentice Hall.

Duncan, D. M. (2001). Smokers told to fetter their fumes: Montgomery plans $750 fine if tobacco odors bother neighbors. *The Washington Post.* Retrieved December 8, 2003, from http://pqasb.pqarchiver.com/washingtonpost/90995676.html

Eaton, C. B., & Lapane, K. L. (1999). Effects of a community-based intervention on physical activity: The Pawtucket Heart Health Program. *American Journal of Public Health, 89,* 1,741–1,744.

Ebbeling, C. B., Pawlak, D. B., & Ludwig, D. S. (2002). Childhood obesity: Public health crisis, common sense cure. *Lancet, 360*(9,331), 473–482.

Eberhardt, M. S., Ingram, D. D., Makuc, D. M., et al. (2001). Urban and rural health chartbook. *Health, United States, 2001.* Hyattsville, MD: National Center for Health Statistics.

Ecstasy use declines as more teens recognize risks of drug (2003, February). *The Nation's Health, 33*(1), 1 and 27.

Ellen, I. G., Mijanovich, T., & Dillman, K. (2001). Neighborhood effects on health: Exploring the links and assessing the evidence. *Journal of Urban Affairs, 23*(3–4), 391–408.

Fee, E., & Brown, T. M. (2000). The past and future of public health practice. *American Journal of Public Health, 90,* 690–692.

Firshein, J. (n.d.). *What hasn't worked.* PBS online. Retrieved January 15, 2004, from http://www.pbs.org/wnet/closetohome/prevention/html/whathasnt.html

Flegal, K. M., Carroll, M. D., Kuczmarski, R. J., & Johnson, C. L. (1998). Overweight and obesity in the United States: Prevalence and trends, 1960–1994. *International Journal of Obesity and Related Metabolic Disorders, 22,* 39–47.

Frerichs, R. R. (2000). Cyber Sleuths. *UCLA Magazine 12,* 63.

Glouberman, S. (2001). Towards a new perspective on health policy. *CPRN Report.* Retrieved January 15, 2004, from http://www.cprn.com/Release/Back/btnp_e.htm

Health and Human Services—Bioterrorism (2003). Retrieved January 15, 2004, from http://www.hhs.gov/news/press

Health Care Financing Administration (2001). National health care expenditures projections. Retrieved January 15, 2004, from http://www.hcfa.gov/stats/nhe-proj

Hibbs, J. R., Benner, L., Klugman, L., Spencer, R., Macchia, I., Mellinger, A., & Fife, D. K. (1994). Mortality in a cohort of homeless adults in Philadelphia. *New England Journal of Medicine, 331,* 304–309.

Institute for Social Research at University of Michigan (n.d.).

Retrieved January 15, 2004, from http://www.isr.umich.edu

Josefson, D. (2002). Drug companies face pressure on profits. *British Medical Journal, 324*(7,329), 65.

Kassel, R. (2001). *National energy policy.* FDCH Congressional Testimony, House Energy and Commerce.

Koplan, J. P. (2001). *Testimony of Jeffrey P. Koplan.* House Subcommittee on Labor, Health and Human Services, Education, and Related Agencies.

Kraut, J. (Ed.). (1997). *U.S. code service—Lawyers edition: Aliens and nationality.* Rochester, NY: The Lawyers Co-operative.

Laing, P. (2002). Childhood obesity: A public health threat. *Pediatric Nursing, 14*(10), 14–16.

Levy, B. S. (1998). Creating the future of public health: Values, vision, and leadership. *American Journal of Public Health, 88,* 188–193.

Levy, B. S., & McBeath, W. H. (1991). Health for all: A public health vision. *American Journal of Public Health, 81,* 1,560–1,565.

Link, B. G., Susser, E., Stueve, A., Phelan, J., Moore, R. E., & Struening, E. (1994). Lifetime and five-year prevalence of homelessness in the United States. *American Journal of Public Health, 84,* 1,907–1,912.

Mangini v. R. J. Reynolds Tobacco Co., San Francisco Court Civil Case No. 939359. (1991). In Coughlin, P. J., Janecek, F. J., Milberg, Weiss, Bershad, & Hynes (1998). A review of R.J. Reynolds' internal documents produced in *Mangini vs. R.J. Reynolds Tobacco Company,* Civil Number 939359 – The case that rid California and the American landscape of "Joe Camel." Retrieved January 15, 2004, from http://www.library.ucsf.edu/tobacco/mangini/report

Marlatt, G. A. (1998). *Harm reduction: Pragmatic strategies for managing high-risk behaviors.* New York: Guilford Press.

Marwick, C. (1997). Helping city children control asthma. *Journal of the American Medical Association, 277,* 1,503–1,504.

Marwick, C. (2001). US Healthcare system too geared to acute medicine. *British Medical Journal, 322*(7,286), 572.

Mathew, C. (2001). Science medicine and the future: Postgenomic technologies—hunting the genes for common disorders. *British Medical Journal, 322,* 1,031–1,035.

Mathew, C., & Meckel, R. (1990). *Save the babies: American public health reform and the prevention of infant mortality.* Baltimore: Johns Hopkins University Press.

Matthew, D. B. (2001). An economic model to analyze the impact of false claims act cases on access to healthcare for the elderly, disabled, rural and inner-city poor. *American Journal of Law, Medicine & Ethics, 27,* 439–467.

Meyers, M. L. (2000). Protecting the public health by strengthening the food and drug administration's authority over tobacco products. *New England Journal of Medicine, 343,* 1,806–1,809.

Mokdad, A. H., Serdula, M. K., Dietz, W. H., Bowman, B. A., Marks, J. S., and Koplan, J. P. (1999). The spread of the obesity epidemic in the United States, 1991–1998. *Journal of the American Medical Association, 282,* 1,519–1,522.

Monitoring the Future (2005). Retrieved August 11, 2005, from http://www.monitoringthefuture.org

Morgan, J. (1996). *Principles of epidemiology: A practical text.* Bryn Mawr, CA: MDM Consulting.

National Institute on Drug Abuse. (2004). NIDA community drug alert bulletin—club drugs. Retrieved August 2, 2006, from http://www.drugabuse.gov/ClubAlert/ClubDrugAlert.html

National Institutes of Health (1997). *Ninth special report to the U.S. Congress on alcohol and health: Title NIH Pub. N. 97–4017.* Bethesda, MD: National Institute on Alcohol Abuse and Alcoholism.

The Nation's Health (2005, October). U.S. Census Bureau: Health care coverage continues to decline.

Noble, K. (1994, December 15). Initiative on aliens suffers its biggest setback yet. *The New York Times,* p. A18.

Oberlander, J. (2002). The US health care system: On a road to nowhere? *Canadian Medical Association Journal, 167*(2), 163–168.

Ogden, C. L., Troiano, R. P., Briefel, R. R., Kuczmarski, R. J., Flegal, K. M., & Johnson, C. L. (1997). Prevalence of overweight among preschool children in the United States, 1971 through 1994 (abstract). *Pediatrics, 99*(4): E1.

Page, P. B. (1997). E. M. Jellinek and the evolution of alcohol studies: A critical essay. *Addiction, 92*(12), 1,619–1,637.

Perkins, B. A., Popovic, T., & Yeskey, K. (2002). Public health in the time of bioterrorism. *Emerging Infectious Diseases, 8*(10), 1,015–1,018.

Pierce, J. P., Evans, N., Farkas, A. J., Cavin, S. W., Berry, C., Kramer, M., et al. (1994). Tobacco Use in California: An Evaluation of the Tobacco Control Program, 1989–1993. LaJolla, CA: University of California, San Diego.

Qureshi, M., Thacker, H. L., Litaker, D. G., & Kippes, C. (2000). Differences in breast cancer screening rates: An issue of ethnicity or socioeconomics? *Journal of Women's Health & Gender-Based Medicine, 2000, 9*(9), 1,025–1,031.

Rakich, J. S., Longest, B. B., & Darr, K. (1998). *Managing Health Services Organizations* (3rd ed.). Baltimore: Health Professions Press.

Rich, J. A. (2001). Primary care for young African American men. *Journal of American College Health, 49*(4), 183–186.

Russell, C. M., Williamson, D. F., & Byers, T. (1995). Can the year 2000 objective for reducing overweight in the US be reached?: A simulation study of the required changes in body weight. *International Journal of Obesity, 19,* 149–153.

Schneider, D., & Northridge, M. E. (1999). Editorial: Promoting the health and well-being of future generations. *American Journal of Public Health, 89,* 155–158.

Schoenbach, V. J. (1999). Historical Perspective. Retrieved August 17, 2005, from http://www.epidemiog.net/evolving/HistoricalPerspective.pdf

Shalala, D. E. (1994). U.S. Department of Health and Human Services. Preventing tobacco use among young people: A report of the Surgeon General, Atlanta: CDC.

Shannon, I. S. (1990). Public health's promise for the future: 1989 presidential address. *American Journal of Public Health, 80,* 909–912.

Smith, L. S. (2001). Health of America's newcomers. *Journal of*

Community Health Nursing, 18(1), 53–68.

Susser, I., & Stein, Z. (2000). Culture, sexuality, and women's agency in the prevention of HIV/AIDS in Southern Africa. *American Journal of Public Health, 90,* 1,042–1,048.

Tanne, J. H. (2002). Senators call for action on obesity as study quantifies link to heart failure. *BMJ: British Medical Journal, 325*(7,359), 298.

Taylor, W. R., & Newacheck, P. W. (1992). Impact of childhood asthma on health. *Pediatrics, 90,* 657–662.

Thigpen, D. E. (2003, March 3). In Chicago, Jesse on the spot. *Time, 161*(9), 52–53.

Thompson, K. M., & Glick, D. F. (1999). Cost analysis of emergency room use by low-income patients. *Nursing Economics, 17*(3), 142–148.

UNAIDS FactSheet (2004). Report on the global AIDS epidemic. Retrieved August 11, 2005, from http://www.unaids.org

United States Conference of Mayors (1998). *A Status Report on Hunger and Homelessness in America's Cities: 1998. A 30-city survey.* Retrieved August 11, 2005, from http://www.usmayors.org

U.S. Bureau of the Census (2000). *USA QuickFacts from the US Census Bureau.* Retrieved January 16, 2006, from http://www.quickfacts.census.gov

Visscher, T. L. S., & Seidell, J. C. (2001). The public health impact of obesity. *Annual Review of Public Health, 22,* 355–375.

Voelker, R. (1995). Impact of Proposition 187 is difficult to gauge. *Journal of the American Medical Association, 273,* 1,639–1,640.

Wang, G., & Dietz, W. H. (2002). Economic burden of obesity in youths aged 6 to 17 years: 1979–1999. *Pediatrics, 109,* e81.

Wendland-Bowyer, W. (2000). Graphic labels seek to convert smokers: Canada plasters the warnings over every pack sold. *Detroit Free Press,* http://www.freep.com

Wessler, J. (1998). National health care. *Social Policy, 28*(3), 37–39.

Wickizer, T. M., & Lessler, D. (2002). Utilization management: Issues, effects, and future prospects. *Annual Review of Public Health, 23,* 233–254.

Young, L. R., & Nestle, M. (2002). The contribution of expanding portion sizes to the US obesity epidemic. *American Journal of Public Health, 92*(2), 246–249.

Chapter 8: Religion

Aguirre, A., & Turner, J. (1998). *American ethnicity: The dynamics and consequences of discrimination* (2nd ed.). Boston, MA: McGraw Hill.

Allport, G. W. (1954). *The nature of prejudice.* Cambridge, MA: Addison-Wesley.

Beit-Hallahmi, B. (1991). Religion as art and identity. *Religion, 16,* 1–17.

Bronk, A. (2003). Truth and religion reconsidered: An analytic approach. Retrieved May 13, 2003, from http://www.bu.edu/wep/Papers/Reli/ReliBron.htm

Burch, S. P. (2000). Christian particularity does not depend on exclusive truth claims: Teaching enthusiastic witness in a pluralistic world. *Religious Education, 95*(3), 299–307.

Carmody, D. (1979). *Women and world religions.* Nashville: Abingdon.

Charon, J. M. (1998). *Ten questions of sociology: A sociological perspective* (3rd ed.). Belmont, CA: Wadsworth Publishing.

Doyle, P. J. (1981). *Sociological theory: Classical founders and contemporary perspectives.* New York: John Wiley & Sons.

Duke, S. (2003). The nature of right and wrong. Retrieved May 10, 2003, from http://www.thetruthpage.homestead.com/TheNatureofRightandWrong~ns4.html

Durkheim, E. (1965). *The elementary forms of the religious life* (J. W. Swain, Trans.). New York: Free Press.

Durkheim, E. (1973). Individualism and the intellectuals (M. Traugott, Trans.). In R. N. Bellah (Ed.), *Durkheim on Morality and Society* (pp. 43–57). Chicago: University of Chicago Press.

Fagan, P. F. (1996, January). Why religion matters: The impact of religious practice on social stability. Retrieved April 6, 2006, from http://www.heritage.org/Research/Religion/BG1064.cfm

Farley, J. M. (1998). *Sociology* (4th ed.). Upper Saddle River, NJ: Prentice Hall.

Fowers, B. J., & Olson, D. H. (1989). ENRICH marital inventory: A discrimination validity and cross-validation assessment. *Journal of Marital and Family Therapy, 15,* 65–79.

Groothuis, D. (2002, July). What is truth? Retrieved May 14, 2003, from http://www.leaderu.com/theology/groothuis-truth.html

Gutierrez, G. (1973). *A theology of liberation: History, politics, and salvation.* Maryknoll, NY: Orbis Books.

Hargrove, B. (1979). *The sociology of religion: Classical and contemporary approaches* (2nd ed.). Arlington Heights, IL: Harlan Davidson.

Henepola Gunaratana, B. (2001). *Eight mindful steps to happiness: Walking the Buddha's path.* Somerville, MA: Wisdom Publications.

Henslin, J. M. (1995). *Sociology: A down-to-earth approach* (2nd ed.). Boston, MA: Allyn and Bacon.

Johnstone, R. L. (1997). *Religion in society: A sociology of religion* (5th ed.). Upper Saddle River, NJ: Prentice Hall.

Jordan, Z. A. (Ed.). (1971). *Karl Marx: Economy, class and social revolution.* New York: Charles Scribner's Sons.

Kammeyer, K., Ritzer, G., & Yetman, N. (1992). *Sociology: Experiencing changing societies* (5th ed.). Boston, MA: Allyn and Bacon.

Kernberg, O. F. (2000). Psychoanalytic perspectives on the religious experience. *Journal of Psychotherapy, 54,* 452–477.

Lauer, J., & Lauer, R. Marriages made to last. In J. M. Henslin (Ed.), *Marriage and family in a changing society* (4th ed.) (pp. 481–486). New York: Free Press.

Levinger, G. (1965). Marital cohesiveness and dissolution: An integrative review. *Journal of Marriage and the Family 27*(1), 1, 19–28.

Luckmann, T. (1967). *The invisible religion: The problem of religion in modern society.* New York: Macmillan.

Macionis, J. J. (1999). *Sociology.* Upper Saddle River, NJ: Prentice Hall.

Marx, K., & Engels, F. (2002). *Marx and Engels on religion*. Fredonia, NY: Fredonia Books.

McGee, R. (1975). *Points of departure*. Hinsdale, IL: Dryden Press.

McGuire, M. B. (1997). *Religion: The social context* (4th ed.). Belmont, CA: Wadworth Publishing Company.

Mead, G. H. (1962). *Mind, self, and society*. Chicago: University of Chicago Press.

Mernissi, F. (1987). *Beyond the veil: Male-female dynamics in modern Muslim society* (rev. ed.). Bloomington, IN: Indiana University Press.

Myrdal, G. (1944). *An American dilemma: The Negro problem and modern democracy*. New York: Harper.

O'Malley, P. (1983). *The uncivil wars: Ireland today*. Boston, MA: Houghton Mifflin Company.

Pargament, K. I., & Brant, C. R. (1998). Religion and coping. In H. Koenig (Ed.), *Handbook of Religion and Mental Health* (pp. 111–128). San Diego, CA: Academic Press.

Pescosolido, B. A., & Georgiana, S. (1989). Durkheim, suicide, and religion: Toward a network theory of suicide. *American Sociological Review 54*(1), 33–48.

Peterson, R., Wunder, D., & Mueller, H. (1999). *Social problems: Globalization in the twenty-first century*. Upper Saddle River, NJ: Prentice Hall.

Pope John Paul II (1999, October 28). Address at the Interreligious Assembly, Rome. Retrieved April 11, 2006, from http://www.catholic-ew.org.uk/resource/id/id06.htm

Quinn, D. (1993, March). What the secular humanists are up to. Retrieved March 14, 2003, from http://www.ad2000.com.au/articles/1993/mar1993p13_788.html

Roberts, J. D. (1994). *The prophethood of black believers*. Louisville, KY: Westminster/John Knox Press.

Robertson, I. (1989). *Society: A brief introduction*. New York: Worth Publishers.

Smith, H. (1991). *The world's religions*. New York: HarperCollins.

Stinnett, N. (1992). Strong families. In J. M. Henslin (Ed.), *Marriage and family in a changing society* (4th ed.). New York: Free Press.

Stoen, T. (1997, April 7). The most horrible night of my life. *Newsweek, 129*, 44–45.

Thompson, W. E., & Hickey, J. V. (1999). *Society in focus: Introduction to sociology*. New York: Longman.

Troeltsch, E. (1960). *The social teachings of the Christian churches* (Vols. 1 & 2) (O. Wyon, Trans.). New York: Harper & Row.

Vroom, H. M. (1989). *Religions and the truth: Philosophical reflections and perspectives* (J. W. Rebel, Trans.). Grand Rapids, MI: Eerdmans.

Weber, M. (1958). *The protestant ethic and the spirit of capitalism* (T. Parsons, Trans.). London: Allen & Unwin.

Wentz, R. E. (1993). *Why do people do bad things in the name of religion?* Macon, GA: Mercer University Press.

Yinger, J. M. (1970). *The scientific study of religion*. New York: Macmillan.

Chapter 9: Sexuality

Albert, A. E., Warner, D. L., & Hatcher, R. A. (1998). Facilitating condom use with clients during commercial sex in Nevada's legal brothels. *American Journal of Public Health, 88*(4), 643–646.

Altman, D. (1989, November). Fear and loathing? *New Internationalist*, 201. Retrieved March 31, 2006, from http://www.newint.org/issue201/fear.htm

American Civil Liberties Union (2001). What we are and what we do. Retrieved May 23, 2006, from http://www.aclu.org/lgbt/gen/11828res20011213.html

American Heritage Editors (2000). *The American Heritage Dictionary of the English Language* (4th ed.). Boston: Houghton Mifflin.

American Psychiatric Association (APA). (1994). *Diagnostic and statistical manual of mental disorders* (4th ed.). Washington, DC: American Psychiatric Association.

Bailey, J. M., & Pillard, R. C. (1991). A genetic study of male sexual orientation. *Archives of General Psychiatry, 48*, 1,089–1,096.

Barale, M. A., as cited in Duggan, L. (1990). From instincts to politics: Writing the history of sexuality in the U.S. *Journal of Sex Research, 27*(1), 95.

Barlow, D. H., & Durand, V. M. (1999). *Abnormal psychology: An integrative approach* (2nd ed.). Pacific Grove, CA: Brooks/Cole Publishing Company.

Bieber, I., Dian, H. J., Drellich, M. G., Dince, P. R., Grand, H. G., Gundlach, R. H., Kremer, M. W., Rifkin, A. H., Wilbur, C. B., & Bieber, T. B. (1962). *Homosexuality: A psychoanalytic study*. New York: Basic Books.

Bradford, J., & Pawlak, A. (1993). Double-blind placebo crossover study of cyproterone acetate in the treatment of the paraphilias. *Archives of Sexual Behavior, 22*, 383–402.

Brewer, D. D., Potterat, J. J., Garrett, S. B., Muth, S. Q., Roberts, J. M. Jr., Kasprzyk, D., Montano, D. E., & Darrow, W. W. (2000). Prostitution and the sex discrepancy in reported number of sexual partners. *PNAS, 97*(22). Retrieved April 2, 2006, from http://www.pnas.org/cgi/content/full/97/22/12385

Briere, J. (1984). The effects of childhood sexual abuse on later psychological functioning: Defining a post-sexual abuse syndrome. Paper presented at the annual meeting of the American Psychological Association, Los Angeles, as cited in Turner, J. S., & Rubinson, L. (1993). *Contemporary human sexuality*. Englewood Cliffs, NJ: Prentice Hall.

Brill, N. Q. (1998). Is homosexuality normal? *Journal of Psychiatry and Law, 26*(2), 219–259.

Cahill, T. (2003). *Sailing the wine dark sea: Why the Greeks matter*. New York: Random House.

Carnes, P. (1989). *Contrary to love: Helping the sexual addict*. Minneapolis: ComCare.

Caron, S. L. (1998). *Cross-cultural perspectives on human sexuality*. Boston: Allyn and Bacon.

Center for Disease Control (CDC). 1998. Retrieved March 31, 2006, from http://www.cdc.gov/ncipc/dvp/fivpt/spotlite/rape.htm

Center for Disease Control (CDC). 1999. Retrieved March 31, 2006, from http://www.cdc.gov/ncipc/dvp/yvpt/datviol.htm

Cox, D. J. (1988). Incidence and nature of male genital exposure behavior as reported by college women. *Journal of Sex Research, 24,* 227–234.

Crooks, R., & Bauer, K. (1999). *Our Sexuality* (7th ed.). Pacific Grove, CA: Brooks/Cole.

Dobson, J. C. (1986). Enough is enough. In *Pornography: The human tragedy* (T. Minnery, Ed.). Wheaton, IL: Tyndale House Publishers.

Donnelly, D. A. (1993). Sexually inactive marriages. *Journal of Sex Research, 30*(2), 171–179.

Duggan, L. (1990). From instincts to politics: Writing the history of sexuality in the U.S. *Journal of Sex Research, 27*(1), 95–110.

Eccles, A., & Walker, W. (1998). Community-based treatment with sexual offenders. In Marshall, W. L., Fernandez, Y. M., Hudson, S. M., & Ward, T. (Eds.), *Sourcebook of treatment programs for sexual offenders.* New York: Plenum Press.

Farley, M., Baral, I., Kiremire, M., & Sezgin, U. (1998). Prostitution in five countries: Violence and post-traumatic stress disorder. *Feminism and Psychology, 8*(4), 405–426.

Farley, M., & Barkan, H. (1998). Prostitution, violence, and post-traumatic stress disorder. *Women & Health, 27*(3), 37–49.

Finn, Peter (1997, February). Sexual offender community notification, NIJ Research in Action. Washington, DC: U.S. Department of Justice, National Institute of Justice. Retrieved March 31, 2006, from http://www.ncjrs.gov/txtfiles/162364.txt

Freier, K. (1998). Pornography: The effects on children. *Report for the SDA General Conference Christian view of human life committee.* Pine Springs Ranch, CA.

Fritz, R. B. (1998). AIDS knowledge, self-esteem, perceived AIDS risk, and condom use among female commercial sex workers. *Journal of Applied Social Psychology, 28*(10), 888–912.

Fuchs, E. (1983). *Sexual desire and love: Origins and history of the Christian ethic of sexuality and marriage* (M. Daigle, Trans.). New York: Seabury Press.

Garner, B. A. (1995). *A dictionary of modern legal usage* (2nd ed.). New York: Oxford University Press.

Garner, B. A. (Ed.) (2004). *Black's law dictionary* (8th ed.). St. Paul, MN: Thomson/West.

Gibbons, E. (1993). *The decline and fall of the Roman Empire.* Vols. 1–3. New York: Random House.

Godbeer, R. (2002). *Gender relations in the American experience.* Baltimore, MD: Johns Hopkins University Press.

Gomes-Schwartz, B., Horowitz, J. M., & Cardarelli, A. P. (1990). *Child sexual abuse: The initial effects.* Thousand Oaks, CA: Sage.

Halperin, D. M. (1989). Is there a history of sexuality? *History and Theory, 28*(3), 257–275.

Harlow, H. (1962). The heterosexual affectional system in monkeys. *American Psychologist, 17,* 1–9.

Harnell, W. (1995). Issues in the assessment and treatment of the sex addict/offender. *Sexual Addiction & Compulsivity, 2*(2), 89–97.

Harrington, C. (2002). *Women in a Celtic church: Ireland 450–1150.* Oxford: Oxford University Press.

Hawkins, G., & Zimring, F. (1988). Pornography and child protection. *Pornography in a Free Society,* 175–197.

Hite, S. (1976). *The Hite report: A nationwide study of female sexuality.* New York: Dell Publishing.

Hunt, M. (1974). *Sexual behavior in the 1970s.* New York: Playboy Press.

Hyde, H. M. (1964). *A history of pornography.* New York: Farrar, Straus and Giroux.

Index Librorum Prohibitorum. (1999, April 8). Retrieved March 31, 2006, from http://www.slis.ualberta.ca/cap99/dheilik/index1.htm. See also "The Index of Forbidden Books" at http://www.beaconforfreedom.org/about_database/index_librorum.html

International Labour Organization (1998). *Sex industry assuming massive proportions in Southeast Asia.* Retrieved March 31, 2006, from http://www.ilo.org/public/english/bureau/inf/pr/1998/31.htm

Janus, S., & Janus, C. (1993). *The Janus report on sexual behavior.* New York: John Wiley and Sons.

Johnson, T. C. (1998). Children who molest. In Marshall, W. L., Fernandez, Y. M., Hudson, S. M., & Ward, T. (Eds.), *Sourcebook of Treatment Programs for Sexual Offenders.* New York: Plenum Press.

Kiernan, K. E. (1988). Who remains celibate? *Journal of Biosocial Science, 20*(3), 253–263.

Kinsey, A., Pomeroy, W., & Martin, C. (1948). *Sexual behavior in the human male.* Philadelphia: W. B. Saunders.

Kinsey, A., Pomeroy, W., Martin, C., & Gebhard, P. (1953). *Sexual behavior in the human female.* Philadelphia: W. B. Saunders.

Knight, D. (1982, January). Old Testament Ethics. *Christian Century.* Retrieved April 2, 2006, from http://www.religion-online.org/showarticle.asp?title=1276

Koss, M. P., Heise, L., & Felipe Russo, N. (1997). The global health burden of rape. In O'Toole, L. L., & Schiffman, J. R. (Eds.). *Gender violence—interdisciplinary perspectives.* New York: New York University Press, pp. 223–241.

Lauer, R. H. H. (1998). *Social problems and the quality of life* (7th ed.). Boston: McGraw-Hill.

Laumann, E. O., Gagnon, J. H., Michael, R. T., & Michaels, S. (1994). *The social organization of sexuality.* Chicago: University of Chicago Press.

Luria, Z. (1982). Sexual fantasy and pornography: Two cases of girls brought up with pornography. *Archives of Sexual Behavior, 11*(5), 395–404.

Malamuth, N. M. (1998). The confluence model as an organizing framework for research on sexually aggressive men: Risk moderators, imagine aggression, and pornography consumption. In R. Geen & E. Donnerstein (Eds.), *Human aggression: Theories, research, and implications for social policy* (pp. 229–245). San Diego: Academic Press.

Marks, A. (1999). Activists unleash campaign to shut down "sex tours." *Christian Science Monitor, 91*(35), 2.

Masters, W. H., & Johnson, V. E. (1966). *Human sexual response.* Boston: Little, Brown, and Co.

Masters, W. H., & Johnson, V. E. (1970). *Human sexual inadequacy.* Boston: Little, Brown, and Co.

McKibben, A., Proulx, J., & Lusignan, R. (1994). Relationships between conflict, affect and deviant sexual behaviors in rapists and pedophiles. *Behavior Research and Therapy, 32,* 571–575.

Miller, R. D. (1998). Forced administration of sex-drive reducing medications to sex offenders: Treatment or punishment. *Psychology, Public Policy, and Law, 4*(1/2), 175–199.

Minnery, T. (1986). The Surgeon General's report. In *Pornography: A human tragedy* (pp. 323–332). Wheaton, IL: Christianity Today and Tyndale House Publishers.

Monda, B. (2004). *Rejoice beloved woman: The Psalms revisioned.* Notre Dame, IN: Soren Press.

Money, J., & Lamacz, M. (1989). *Vandalized lovemaps: Paraphilic outcome of seven cases in pediatric sexology.* Amherst, NY: Prometheus Books.

Money, J., Schwarz, M., & Lewis, V. G. (1984). Adult heterosexual status and fetal hormone masculinization and demasculinization: 46, XX congenital adrenal hyperplasia and 46, XY androgen-insensitivity syndrome compared. *Psychoneuroendocrinology, 9,* 405–414.

National Coalition for the Protection of Children and Families (NCPCF) (2003). Retrieved March 3, 2003, from http://www.nationalcoalition.org/stat.phtml?ID=53. See also http://www.1wayout.org/pages/internet-pornography-statistics.aspx

National Gay and Lesbian Task Force (NGLTF). (2006). Over Three Decades of Fighting for Freedom, Justice & Equality. Retrieved May 23, 2006, from http://www.thetaskforce.org/aboutus/history.cfm

Oddone-Paolucci, E., Genuis, M., & Violato, C. (2000). A meta-analysis of the published research on the effects of pornography. In C. Violato, E. Oddone-Paolucci, & M. Genuis (Eds.), *The changing family and child development* (pp. 48–59). Aldershot, England: Ashgate Publishing.

O'Flaherty, W. D. *Hinduism.* Retrieved November 19, 2003, from http://sangha.net/hinduism.htm

O'Leary, C., & Howard, O. (2001). The prostitution of women and girls in metropolitan Chicago: A preliminary prevalence report. Center for Impact Research. Retrieved April 2, 2006, from http://www.impactresearch.org/documents/prostitution-report.pdf

Otchet, A. (1998). Should prostitution be legal? *UNESCO Courier,* 37–39

O'Toole, L. L. (1997). Subcultural theory of rape revisited. In L. L. O'Toole & J. R. Schiffman (Eds.), *Gender violence: Interdisciplinary perspectives.* New York: New York University Press.

Pattatucci, A. M. L. (1998). Biopsychosocial interactions and the development of sexual orientation. In Patterson, C. J., & D'Augelli, A. R. (Eds.), *Lesbian, gay, and bisexual identities in families: Psychological perspectives* (pp. 19–39). New York and Oxford: Oxford University Press.

Pinhas, V. (1989). Treatment of sexual problems in chemically dependent women. *The Female Patient, 20,* 27–30.

Potterat, J. J., Rothenberg, R. B., Muth, S. Q., Darrow, W. W., & Phillips-Plummer, L. (1998). Pathways to prostitution: The chronology of sexual and drug abuse milestones. *Journal of Sex Research, 35*(4), 333–340.

Potterat, J. J., Woodhouse, D. E., Muth, J. B., & Muth, S. Q. (1990).

Estimating the prevalence and career longevity of prostitute women. *Journal of Sex Research, 27*(2), 233–243.

Pritchard, J. (1969). *Ancient Near Eastern texts relating to the Old Testament.* Princeton, NJ: Princeton University Press.

Ramsey, P. (1991). Human sexuality in the history of redemption. In Babcock, W. S. (Ed.), *The ethics of St. Augustine.* Atlanta: Scholars Press, pp. 115–145.

Rinehart, N. J., & McCabe, M. P. (1998). An empirical investigation of hypersexuality. *Sexual and Marital Therapy, 13*(4), 369–384.

Robinson, T., & Valcour, F. (1995). The use of Depo-Provera in the treatment of child molesters and sexually compulsive males. *Sexual Addiction & Compulsivity, 2*(4), 277–294.

Russell, D. E. H. (1998). *Dangerous relationships—Pornography, misogyny, and rape.* Thousand Oaks, CA: Sage.

Saint Augustine (1994). *The city of God* (M. Dods, Trans.). New York: Modern Library. (Original work published 426 A.D.).

Saulnier, C. F. (1996). Sex addiction: A problematic concept. *Journal of Applied Social Sciences, 20*(2), 159–168.

Savin-Williams, R. C., & Diamond, L. M. (1997). Sexual orientation as a developmental context for lesbians, gays, and bisexuals: Biological perspectives. In Segal, N. L., Weisfeld, G. E., & Weisfeld, C. C. (Eds.), *Uniting psychology and biology: Integrative perspectives on human development.* Washington, DC: American Psychological Association, pp. 217–238.

Scarpitti, F. R., Andersen, M. L., & O'Toole, L. L. (1997). *Social Problems* (3rd ed.). New York: Addison-Wesley.

Schneider, J. P., & Schneider, B. H. (1996). Couple recovery from sexual addiction/coaddiction: Results of a survey of 88 marriages. *Sexual Addiction & Compulsivity, 3*(2), 111–126.

Schnurnberger, L. (1991). *Let there be clothes.* New York: Workman Publishing.

Scott, D. A. (1986). How pornography changes attitudes. In Minnery, T. (Ed.), *Pornography: A human tragedy* (pp. 115–143). Wheaton, IL: Christianity Today and Tyndale House Publishers.

Siegel, K., & Raveis, V. H. (1993). AIDS-related reasons for gay men's adoption of celibacy. *AIDS Education and Prevention, 5*(4), 302–310.

Sneed, C. D., & Morisky, D. E. (1998). Applying the theory of reasoned action to condom use among sex workers. *Social Behavior and Personality, 26*(4), 317–327.

Solomon, L. (2000). *Rape Treatment Seeks to Restore Normal Lives.* Retrieved September 1, 2001, from http://my.webmd.com/content/article/2789.184

Stark, R. (1997). *The rise of Christianity: How the obscure, marginal Jesus movement became the dominant religious force in the western world.* Princeton: Princeton University Press.

Stock, W. (1993). Pornography and gender alienation. Paper presented in the symposium, "Centerfold or person? Clinical implications of men's images of women's bodies," at the 101st annual convention of the American Psychological Association at Toronto, Canada, as cited in Stock, W. (1997). Sex as commodity: Men and the sex industry. In Levant, R. F., & Brooks, G. R. (Eds.), *Men and sex: New psychological perspectives* (pp. 100–132). New York: John Wiley & Sons.

References

Stock, W. E. (1997). Sex as commodity: Men and the sex industry. In R. F. Levant & G. R. Brooks (Eds.), *Men and sex: New psychological perspectives.* New York: John Wiley & Sons, pp. 100–132.

Time, Special Edition (2000–2001). The year's best lines. 157, 27, pp. 20–22.

Turner, J. S., & Rubinson, L. (1993). *Contemporary human sexuality.* Englewood Cliffs, NJ: Prentice Hall.

UNAIDS (2000). Report on the Global HIV/AIDS Epidemic, June 2000. Retrieved September 1, 2001, from http://www.unaids.org/epidemic_update/report/index.html#slides

U.S. Department of Justice (2001). Sexual Assault. Chapter 14 in *1997 Academy Text Supplement,* National Victim Assistance Academy. Retrieved May 23, 2006, from http://www.ojp.usdoj.gov/ovc/assist/nvaa/ch14sa.htm

U.S. Department of Justice (2005). Prisoners in 2004, NCJ 210677. Retrieved March 31, 2006, from http://www.ojp.usdoj.gov/bjs/pub/ascii/p04.txt

Weatherhead, L. D. (1942). *The mastery of sex through psychology and religion.* New York: Macmillan.

Webb, G. (2001). Sex and the Internet. *Yahoo! Internet Life, 7*(5), 88–97.

Weber, M. (1930). *The Protestant ethic and the spirit of capitalism* (T. Parsons, A. Giddens, Trans.). Boston: Unwin Hyman.

Weiner, A. (1996). Understanding the social needs of streetwalking prostitutes. *Social Work, 41*(1), 97–105.

Weiner, D. N., & Rosen, R. C. (1999). Sexual dysfunction and disorders. In T. Millon, P. H. Blaney, & R. D. Davis (Eds.), *Oxford textbook of psychopathology.* New York: Oxford Press, pp. 410–443.

Weinstein, E., & Rosen, E. (1988). Intrafamily sexual intimacy. In E. Weinstein & E. Rosen (Eds.), *Sexuality counseling: Issues and implications.* Monterey, CA: Brooks/Cole.

Wincze, J. P. (2000). Assessment and treatment of atypical sexual behavior. In Leiblum, S. R., & Rosen, R. C. (Eds.), *Principles and practice of sex therapy* (3rd ed., pp. 449–470). New York: Guilford Press.

Zaitoun, L. (n.d.). *More about sex in Islam.* Retrieved March, 30, 2006, from http://www.themodernreligion.com/misc/sex/sex_good.htm#more

Zuker, K. J. (1994). Gender identity, sexual orientation, and sexual behavior in women with congenital adrenal hyperplasia. In K. J. Zucker (chair), *Congenital adrenal hyperplasia: The nature and nurture of psychosexual differentiation.* Symposium presented at the meeting of the International Academy of Sex Research, Edinburgh.

Chapter 10: Drugs

Alcohol Impaired Driving. Retrieved October 2, 2005, from http://www.michigan.gov/msp/0,1607,7-123-1589_1711_4587-49577--,00.html

Alcoholics Anonymous Homepage. Alcoholics Anonymous World Services, Inc. Retrieved October 2, 2005, from http://www.alcoholics-anonymous.org

American Psychiatric Association. (2000). *Diagnostic and statistical manual of mental disorders* (4th ed., text revision). Washington, DC: American Psychiatric Association.

Anslinger, H., & Tompkins, W. (1953). *The traffic in narcotics.* New York: Funk & Wagnalls.

Anton, R. F. (2001). Pharmacologic approaches to the management of alcoholism. *Journal of Clinical Psychiatry, 62*(suppl. 20), 11–17.

Apospori, E., Vega, W., Zimmerman, R., Warheit, G., & Andres, G. (1995). A longitudinal study of the conditional effects of deviant behavior on drug use among three racial/ethnic groups of adolescents. In H. B. Kaplan (Ed.), *Drugs, crime, and other deviant adaptations: Longitudinal studies.* New York: Plenum Press.

Austin, G., & Lettieri, D. (1976). Drugs and crime: The relationship of drug use and noncomitant criminal behavior (*DHHS Publication No. ADM 77–393*). Rockville, MD: U.S. Department of Health and Human Services, National Institute on Drug Abuse.

Barlow, D. H., & Durand, V. M. (1999). *Abnormal psychology: An integrative approach* (2nd ed.). Pacific Grove, CA: Books/Cole.

Batson, C. D., Schoenrade, P., & Ventis, W. L. (1993). *Religion and the individual: A social-psychological perspective.* New York: Oxford University Press.

Baxter, B., Hinson, R. E., Wall, A., & McKee, S. A. (1998). Incorporating culture into the treatment of alcohol abuse and dependence. In S. S. Kazarian & D. R. Evans (Eds.), *Cultural clinical psychology: Theory, research, and practice* (pp. 215–245). New York: Oxford University Press.

Beckett, J., & Johnson, H. (1995). Encyclopedia of social work: Human development. In R. L. Edwards (Ed.), *Encyclopedia of social work* (19th ed., vol. 2, pp. 1,385–1,405). Washington, DC: National Association of Social Workers.

Belenko, S. R. (2000). *Drugs and drug policy in America.* Westport, CT: Greenwood Press.

Bellafante, G. (1997). The suffering of a fool. *Time 150*(27), p. 108.

Booth, J., & Martin, J. E. (1998). Spiritual and religious factors in substance use, dependence, and recovery. In H. G. Koenig (Ed.), *Handbook of religion and mental health* (pp. 176–200). San Diego: Academic Press.

Brewer, C., Meyers, R. J., & Johnsen, J. (2000). Does disulfiram help to prevent relapse in alcohol abuse? *CNS Drugs 14*(5), 329–341.

Bride, B. E., & Nackerud, L. (2002). The disease model of alcoholism: A Kuhnian paradigm. *Journal of Sociology and Social Welfare, 29*(2), 125–141.

Brown, B. S., O'Grady, K. E., Farrell, E. V., Flechner, I. S., & Nurco, D. N. (2001). Factors associated with frequency of 12-step attendance by drug abuse clients. *American Journal of Drug & Alcohol Abuse Special Issue, 27*(1), 147–160.

Brownstein, H. H. (1996). *The rise and fall of a violent crime wave: Crack cocaine and the social construction of a crime problem.* Guilderland, NY: Harrow and Heston.

Brownstein, H. H. (2000). *The social reality of violence and violent crime.* Boston: Allyn & Bacon.

Bui, K. V. T., Ellickson, P. L., & Bell, R. M. (2000). Cross-lagged relationships among adolescent problem drug use, delinquent behavior, and emotional distress. *Journal of Drug Issues, 30*(2), 283–303.

Caliber Associates (n.d.). The National Evaluation Data Services Web. Retrieved October 2, 2005, from http://www.neds.calib.com/products/pdfs/fs/140_economic_benefits.pdf

Cherrington, E. (1920). *The evolution of prohibition in the United States of America.* Westerville, OH: American Press.

Chriqui, J. F., Pacula, R. L., McBride, D. C., Reichmann, D. A., VanderWaal, C. J., & Terry-McElrath, Y. M. (2002). *Illicit drug policies: Selected laws from the 50 States.* Berrien Springs, MI: Andrews University. Supported by the Robert Wood Johnson Foundation and published by LaVigne Printing, Boston.

Coleman, J. S. (1988). Social capital in the creation of human capital. *American Journal of Sociology, 94*(supp.), S95–S120.

Collins, J. (1990). Summary thoughts about drugs and violence in the distribution of crack. In M. De La Rosa, E. Y. Lambert, & B. Gropper (Eds.), *Drugs and violence: Causes, correlates, and consequences* (NIDA Research Monograph 103, DHHS Publication No. ADM 90–1721, pp. 265–275). Rockville, MD: U.S. Department of Health and Human Services, National Institute on Drug Abuse.

Collins, J. (1993). Drinking and violence: An individual offender focus. In S. E. Martin (Ed.), *Alcohol and interpersonal violence: Fostering multidisciplinary perspectives (Research Monograph 24).* Rockville, MD: U.S. Department of Health and Human Services, National Institute on Alcohol Abuse and Alcoholism.

Cooper, C. (1997). *1997 drug court survey report: Executive summary.* Washington, DC: American University, Justice Programs Office.

The Cost of Parity for Substance Abuse Treatment. Retrieved October 2, 2005, from http://www.whitehousedrugpolicy.gov/prevent/workplace/health.html

De Li, S., Priu, H., & MacKenzie, D. (2000). Drug involvement, lifestyles, and criminal activities among probationers. *Journal of Drug Issues, 30*(3), 593–620.

Dorsey, T. L., & Zawitz, M. (1999). *Drugs and crime facts* (NCJ 165148). Retrieved October 2, 2005, from http://www.ojp.usdoj.gov/bjs/pub/pdf/dcf.pdf

Drug Strategies (1997). *Cutting crime: Drug courts in action.* Washington, DC: Drug Strategies.

Elliott, D. S., Huizinga, D., & Menar, S. W. (1989). *Multiple problem youth: Delinquency, substance use, and mental health problems (Research in Criminology).* New York: Springer-Verlag.

Ellis, A., & Schoenfeld, E. (1990). Divine intervention and the treatment of chemical dependency. *Journal of Substance Abuse, 2*(4), 459–468.

Evans, K., & Sullivan, J. M. (1990). *Dual diagnosis: Counseling the mentally ill substance abuser.* New York: Guilford Press.

Fagan, J., & Chin, K. (1990). Violence as regulation and social control in the distribution of crack. In M. De La Rosa, E. Y. Lambert, & B. Gropper (Eds.), *Drugs and violence: Causes, correlates, and consequences* (NIDA Research Monograph 103, DHHS Publication No. ADM 90–1721, pp. 8–43). Rockville, MD: U.S. Department of Health and Human Services, National Institute on Drug Abuse.

Farabee, D., Prendergast, M., Cartier, J., Wexler, H., Knight, K., & Anglin, M. (1999). Barriers to implementing effective correctional drug treatment programs. *Prison Journal, 79*(2), 150–160.

Fishbein, D. (1998). Differential susceptibility to comorbid drug abuse and violence. *Journal of Drug Issues, 28*(4), 859–890.

Gandossy, R. P., Williams, J. R., Cohen, J., & Harwood, H. J. (1980). *Drugs and crime: A survey and analysis of the literature* (NCJ 159074). Washington, DC: U.S. Department of Justice, National Institute of Justice.

Goldstein, P. (1985). The drugs/violence nexus: A tripartite conceptual framework. *Journal of Drug Issues, 15*(4), 493–506.

Goodman, N. (2002). The serotonergic system and mysticism: Could LSD and the nondrug-induced mystical experience share common neural mechanism? *Journal of Psychoactive Drugs, 34*(3), 263–272.

Hamid, A. (1998). *Drugs in America: Sociology, economics, and politics.* Gaithersburg, MD: Aspen.

Hamilton, L. W., & Timmons, C. R. (1990). *Principles of behavioral pharmacology: A biopsychological perspective.* Englewood Cliffs, NJ: Prentice Hall.

Harrell, A., Cavanagh, S., & Roman, J. (2000). *Evaluation of the D.C. Superior Court drug intervention programs* (NCJ 178941). Retrieved October 2, 2005, from http://www.ncjrs.org/pdf-files1/nij/178941.pdf

Hartmann, B. R., & Millea, P. J. (1996). When belief systems collide: The rise and decline of the disease concept of alcoholism. *Journal of Systemic Therapies, 15*(2), 36–47.

Heather, N., & Robertson, I. (1997). *Problem drinking* (3rd ed.). New York: Oxford University Press.

Hickman, T. A. (2000). Drugs and race in American culture. *American Studies, 41*(1), 71–90.

Hser, Y. I., Anglin, M. D., & Powers, K. (1993). A 24-year follow-up of California narcotics addicts. *Archives of General Psychiatry, 50*(7), 577–584.

Inciardi, J. A. (1994). *Screening and assessment for alcohol and other drug abuse among adults in the criminal justice system.* (Treatment Improvement Protocol [TIP] Series No. 7, DHHS Publication No. [SMA] 94–2076). Rockville, MD: U.S. Department of Health and Human Services, Center for Substance Abuse Treatment.

Inciardi, J. A. (2001). *The war on drugs III: The continuing saga of the mysteries and miseries of intoxication, addiction, crime, and public policy.* Boston: Allyn & Bacon.

Inciardi, J. A., Horowitz, R., & Pottieger, A. E. (1993). *Street kids, street drugs, street crime: An examination of drug use and serious delinquency in Miami.* Belmont, CA: Wadsworth.

Inciardi, J. A., McBride, D. C., & Rivers, J. E. (1996). *Drug control and the courts.* Thousand Oaks, CA: Sage Publications.

Jellinek, E. M. (1960). *The disease concept of alcoholism.* New Haven: Hillhouse Press.

Johnston, L. D., O'Malley, P. M., & Bachman, J. G. (2002). *Monitoring the future: National survey results on drug use (1975–2001).* Bethesda, MD: National Institute on Drug Abuse.

Kadden, R. M. (1999). Cognitive behavior therapy. In P. J. Ott, R. E. Tarter, & R. T. Ammerman (Eds.), *Sourcebook on substance abuse: Etiology, epidemiology, assessment, and treatment* (pp. 272–283). Boston: Allyn & Bacon.

Kalat, J. W. (2001). *Biological psychology* (7th ed.). Belmont, CA: Wadsworth.

Khantzian, E. J. (1985). The self-medication hypothesis of addictive disorders: Focus on heroin and cocaine dependence. *American Journal of Psychiatry, 142*(11), 1,259–1,264.

Kirst-Ashman, K. (2000). *Human behavior, communities, organizations, and groups in the macro social environment: An empowerment approach.* Belmont, CA: Wadsworth.

Koenig, H. G. (1998). *Handbook of religion and mental health.* San Diego: Academic Press.

Koenig, H. G., McCullough, M. E., & Larson, D. B. (2001). *Handbook of religion and health.* New York: Oxford University Press.

Kownacki, R. J., & Shadish, W. R. (1999). Does Alcoholics Anonymous work? The results from a meta-analysis of controlled experiments. *Substance Use & Misuse, 34*(13), 1,897–1,916.

Kristenson, H. (1995). How to get the best out of Antabuse. *Alcohol & Alcoholism, 30*(6), 775–783.

Kuhn, T. S. (1996). *The structure of scientific revolutions* (3rd ed.). Chicago: University of Chicago Press.

Leshner, A. (2001). *Hearing before the senate subcommittee on governmental affairs—"Ecstasy abuse and control."* Retrieved October 2, 2005, from http://www.drugabuse.gov/Testimony/7-30-01Testimony.html

Linnever, J., & Shoemaker, D. (1995). *Drugs and crime: A macro-level analysis.* Paper presented to the Society for the Study of Social Problems.

Lurigio, A. J., & Swartz, J. A. (2000). Changing the contours of the criminal justice system to meet the needs of persons with serious mental illness. In J. Horney (Ed.), *Criminal justice 2000: Volume 3: Policies, processes, and decisions of the criminal justice system* (NCJ 185529, pp. 45–108). Retrieved October 2, 2005, from http://www.ncjrs.org/criminal_justice2000/vol_3/03c.pdf

Maisto, S. A., Galizio, M., & Connors, G. J. (1995). *Drug use and abuse* (2nd ed.). Fort Worth: The Hartcourt Press.

Marin, R. (1998, February 16). Spade in America. *Newsweek Magazine, 131*(7), 73.

Marlatt, A. (2001). Should abstinence be the goal for alcohol treatment?: Negative viewpoint. *The American Journal on Addictions, 10*(4), 291–293.

Maxmen, J. S. (1986). *Essential psychopathology.* New York: W. W. Norton.

McBride, D. C., & McCoy, C. B. (1993). The drugs-crime relationship: An analytical framework. *The Prison Journal, 73*(3–4), 257–278.

McBride, D. C., Terry-McElrath, Y. M., & Inciardi, J. A. (1999). "Alternative Perspectives on the Drug Policy Debate," in J. A. Inciardi (Ed.), *The drug legalization debate* (2nd ed., pp. 9–54). Thousand Oaks, CA: Sage Publications.

McBride, D. C., Vanderwaal, C. J., & Terry-McElrath, Y. M. (2003). *The drug-crime wars: Past, present, and future directions in theory, policy, and program interventions.* The Office of Justice Programs, National Institute of Justice. Retrieved October 2, 2005, from http://www.ojp.usdoj.gov/nij

McCrady, B. S. (1990). The divine, the saturnine and the internecine: Comments on Ellis and Schoenfeld. *Journal of Substance Abuse, 2*(4), 477–480.

McKim, W. A. (1997). Psychomotor stimulants. In *Drugs and Behavior: An Introduction to Behavioral Pharmacology.* Englewood Cliffs, NJ: Prentice Hall.

McLellan, A. T., Grissom, G., Zanis, D., Randall, M., Brill, P., & O'Brien, C. (1997). Problem-service "matching" in addiction treatment: A prospective study in 4 programs. *Archives of General Psychiatry, 54*(8), 730–735.

Mill, J. S. (1979). *Utilitarianism: On liberty: Essay on Bentham.* Glasgow: Collins.

Moss, H. B. (1999). "Pharmocotherapy." In M. Hersen & A. S. Bellack (Eds.), *Handbook of comparative interventions for adult disorders* (2nd ed., pp. 652–676). New York: Wiley.

Musto, D. F. (1999). *The American disease.* New York: Oxford University Press.

National Association of Drug Court Professionals (2000). *Community policing and drug court/community courts project: A two-year progress report.* Alexandria, VA: National Association of Drug Court Professionals.

Nestler, E. J., Hyman, S. E., & Malenka, R. C. (2001). Reinforcement and addictive disorders. In *Molecular neuropharmacology: A foundation for clinical neuroscience.* New York: McGraw-Hill.

O'Brien, C. P., & McKay, J. (2002). Pharmacological treatments for substance use disorders. In P. E. Nathan & J. M. Gorman (Eds.), *A guide to treatments that work* (2nd ed., pp. 125–156). New York: Oxford University Press.

Office of National Drug Control Policy (2001). *The economic costs of drug abuse in the United States, 1992–1998.* Washington, DC: Executive Office of the President (Publication No. NCJ-190636).

Owen, P., & Marlatt, G. A. (2001). "Should abstinence be the goal for alcohol treatment?" *The American Journal on Addictions, 10*(4), 289–295.

Parker, R., & Auerhahn, K. (1998). Alcohol, drugs, and violence. *Annual Review of Sociology, 24*, 291–311.

Peele, S. (1995). *Diseasing of America.* San Francisco: Jossey-Bass.

Pihl, R. O. (1999). Substance abuse: Etiological considerations. In T. Millon, P. H. Blaney, & R. D. Davis (Eds.). *Oxford textbook of psychopathology* (pp. 249–276). New York: Oxford University Press.

Pihl, R., & Peterson, J. (1995). Drugs and aggression: Correlations, crime, and human manipulative studies and some proposed mechanisms. *Journal of Psychiatry & Neuroscience, 20*(2), 141–149.

Platt, S. (2001). Drug court experiment: Policy choice—political decision. *Maryland Bar Journal, 34*(1), 44–47.

Putnam, R. (1993). The prosperous community: Social capital and public life. *The American Prospect, 4*(13). Retrieved October 2, 2005, from http://www.prospect.org/print/V4/13/putnam-r.html

Rasmussen, S. (2000). *Addiction treatment: Theory and practice.* Thousand Oaks, CA: Sage.

Rawson, R. A., McCann, M. J., Hasson, A. J., & Ling, W. (2000). Addiction pharmacotherapy 2000: New options, new challenges. *Journal of Psychoactive Drugs, 32*(4), 371–378.

Resignato, A. J. (2000). Violent crime: A function of drug use or drug enforcement? *Applied Economics, 32*(6), 681–688.

Results from the 2004 National Survey on Drug Use and Health: National Findings. Retrieved October 2, 2005, from http://oas.samhsa.gov/NSDUH/2k4NSDUH/2k4results/2k4results.htm

Rogers, F., Keller, D. S., & Morgenstern, J. (1996). *Treating substance abuse: Theory and technique.* New York: The Guilford Press.

Rose, R. (2000). How much does social capital add to individual health? A survey study of Russians. *Social Science & Medicine, 51*(9), 1,421–1,435.

Roth, J. (1994). *Psychoactive substances and violence* (NIJ Research in Brief, NCJ 145534). Retrieved October 2, 2005, from http://www.ncjrs.org/txtfiles/psycho.txt

Royce, J. E. (1985). Sin or solace? Religious views on alcohol and alcoholism. *Journal of Drug Issues Special Issue: Social thought on alcoholism, 15*(1), 51–62.

Schmidt, L. (1995). "A battle no man's but God's": Origins of the American temperance crusade in the struggle for religious authority. *Journal of Studies on Alcohol, 56*(1), 110–121.

Schuckit, M. A. (1995). *Drug and alcohol abuse: A clinical guide to diagnosis and treatment* (4th ed.). New York: Plenum Medical Book Co.

Simpson, D. C., & Curry, S., eds. (1997–98). *DATOS first-wave findings released. Institute of Behavioral Research at Texas Christian University: Research Roundup, 7*(4). Retrieved October 2, 2005, from http://www.ibr.tcu.edu/pubs/newslet/97-98winter.pdf

Taxman, F. (1998). *Reducing recidivism through a seamless system of care: Components of effective treatment, supervision, and transition services in the community* (NCJ 171836). Washington, DC: Office of National Drug Control Policy.

Taxman, F. (2000). *Effective practices for protecting public safety through substance abuse treatment.* Unpublished report commissioned by the National Institute on Drug Abuse.

Thombs, D. L. (1999). *Introduction to addictive behaviors* (2nd ed.). New York: The Guilford Press.

Timko, C., Moos, R. H., & Rudolf, H. F. (2000). Long-term outcomes of alcohol use disorders: Comparing untreated individuals with those in Alcoholics Anonymous and formal treatment. *Journal of Studies of Alcohol, 61*(4), 529–540.

Tonigan, J. S. (2001). Benefits of Alcoholics Anonymous attendance: Replication of findings between clinical research sites in Project MATCH. *Alcoholism Treatment Quarterly, 19*(1), 67–77.

U.S. Department of Health and Human Services, National Institute of Health, National Institute on Drug Abuse. *Costs to society.* Retrieved October 2, 2005, from http://www.nida.nih.gov/Infofax/costs.html

U.S. Department of Health and Human Services (2001, December). National Institute of Health. National Institute on Drug Abuse. *Monitoring the future survey released: Smoking among teenagers decreases sharply and increase in ecstasy use slows.* Retrieved October 2, 2005, from http://www.nida.nih.gov/MedAdv/01/NR12-19.html

U.S. Department of Health and Human Services. Substance Abuse and Mental Health Services Administration Center for Substance Abuse Prevention. Retrieved October 2, 2005, from http://www.health.org/govpubs/prevalert/v5/5.aspx

U.S. Department of Justice Annual Report 2000 Arrestee Drug Abuse Monitoring. Retrieved October 2, 2005, from http://www.ncjrs.org/pdffiles1/nij/193013.pdf

U.S. Department of Justice, Office of Justice Programs, Bureau of Justice Statistics. *Prison statistics.* Retrieved September 20, 2005, from http://www.ojp.usdoj.gov/bjs/prisons.htm

U.S. General Accounting Office (1997). *Drug courts: Overview of growth, characteristics, and results* (GAO/GGD–97–106). Retrieved October 2, 2005, from http://www.ncjrs.org/pdf-files/dcourts.pdf

White, H. (1990). The drug use-delinquency connection in adolescence. In R. Weisheit (Ed.), *Drugs, crime, and criminal justice.* Cincinnati, OH: Anderson Publishing Company.

White, H., & Gorman, D. (2000). Dynamics of the drug-crime relationship. *Criminal Justice, 1,* 151–218. Retrieved October 2, 2005, from http://www.ncjrs.org/criminal_justice2000/col_1/02d.pdf

Wilson, D. J. (2000). *Drug use, testing, and treatment in jails* (NCJ 179999). U.S. Department of Justice, Office of Justice Programs.

World Bank Group. (2000). *Increasing evidence shows that social cohesion—social capital—is critical for poverty alleviation and sustainable human and economic development.* Retrieved October 2, 2005, from http://www.worldbank.org/poverty/scapital/index.htm

Wulff, D. M. (1991). *Psychology of religion: Classic and contemporary views.* New York: John Wiley & Sons.

Chapter 11: Violence

Alexander, P. C., Moore, S., & Alexander, E. R., III. (1991). What is transmitted in the intergenerational transmission of violence? *Journal of Marriage and the Family, 53,* 657–668.

All for the love of God (2002). *New Scientist, 174*(2,342), 46–50.

American Academy of Pediatrics. (2001, November). Media violence. *Pediatrics 108*(5), 1,222–1,226.

Amnesty USA (2000). *Race, rights, & police brutality in the United States of America.* Retrieved February 18, 2000, from http://www.amnestyusa.org

Aronson, E. (1992). Causes of prejudice. In R. M. Baird & S. E. Rosenbaum (Eds.), *Bigotry, prejudice and hatred: Definitions, causes & solutions* (pp. 111–124). Amherst, NY: Prometheus.

Aronson, E., Wilson, T. D., & Akert, R. M. (2002). *Social psychology* (4th ed.). Upper Saddle River, NJ: Prentice Hall.

Bandura, A. (1973). *Aggression: A social learning analysis.* Englewood Cliffs, NJ: Prentice-Hall.

Bandura, A. (1977). *Social learning theory.* Englewood Cliffs, NJ: Prentice-Hall.

Bergesen, A., & Herman, M. (1998). Immigration, race, and riot: The 1992 Los Angeles uprising. *American Sociological Review, 63*(1), 39–54.

Bettencourt, B. A., & Miller, N. (1996). Gender differences in aggression as a function of provocation: A meta-analysis. *Psychological Bulletin, 119*(3), 422–447.

Bjork, J. M., Dougherty, D. M., Moeller, F. G., Cherek, D. R., & Swann, A. C. (1999). The effects of tryptophan depletion and loading on laboratory aggression in men: Time course and a food-restricted control. *Psychopharmacology, 142,* 24–30.

Blazak, R. (2001). White boys to terrorist men. *American Behavioral Scientist, 44*(6), 982–1,000.

Blee, K. (2002). *Inside Organized Racism: Women in the hate movement.* Berkeley: University of California Press.

Brehm, S. S., Kassin, S. M., & Fein, S. (1999). *Social psychology* (4th ed.). Boston: Houghton Mifflin.

Brunschwig, J., & Lloyd, G. E. R. (2000). *Greek thought: A guide to classical knowledge* (Pierre Pellegrin, Ed., & Catherine Porter, Trans.). Cambridge, MA: Belknap Press of Harvard University Press.

Bushman, B. J. (1995). Moderating role of trail aggressiveness in the effects of violent media on aggression. *Journal of Personality and Social Psychology, 69,* 950–960.

Bushman, B. J., & Anderson, C. A. (2001). Media violence and the American public: Scientific facts versus media misinformation. *American Psychologist, 56,* 477–489.

Carlson, M. J. (2000). Family structure, father involvement and adolescent behavioral outcomes. *Dissertation Abstracts International Section A: Humanities & Social Sciences, 61*(2-A), 782.

Carlson, N. R. (1998). *Physiology of behavior* (6th ed.). Boston: Allyn and Bacon.

Centerwall, B. S. (1989). Exposure to television as a risk factor for violence. *American Journal of Epidemiology, 129,* 643–652.

Centerwall, B. S. (1992). Television and violence: The scale of the problem and where to go from here. *Journal of the American Medical Association, 267,* 3,059–3,063.

Children Now (2002). *Children and the media.* Retrieved October 29, 2002, from http://www.childrennow.org

Cloud, J., et al. (1999, May 24). What can schools do? *Time,* pp. 38–41.

Cohen, D., & Nisbett, R. E. (1997, November). Field experiments examining the culture of honor. *Personality & Social Psychology Bulletin, 23*(11), 1,188–1,199.

Colvard, K. (2002, February 9). Commentary: The psychology of terrorists. *BMJ: British Medical Journal, 324*(7,333), 359.

Commission for Racial Equality (1993). *Housing Allocations in Oldham.* London: CRE Publications.

Constitution of the United States, Amendment 2.

Cowan, G., & Campbell, R. R. (1995). Rape causal attitudes among adolescents. *Journal of Sex Research, 32*(2), 145–154.

Crowe, M., & Bunclark, J. (2000, February). Repeated self-injury and its management. *International Review of Psychiatry, 12*(1), 48–53.

Dabbs, J. M., Carr, T. S., Frady, R. L., & Riad, J. K. (1995). Testosterone, crime, and misbehavior among 692 male prison inmates. *Personality and Individual Differences, 18*(5), 627–633.

Dahlberg, L. L. (1998, May). Major trends, risk factors, and prevention approaches. *American Journal of Preventive Medicine, 14*(4), 259–272.

Davidson, R., Putnam, K., & Larson, C. (2000). Dysfunction in the neural circuitry of emotion regulation—a possible prelude to violence. *Science, 289,* 591–594.

Day, J. C., & Newburger, E. C. (2002). *The big payoff: Educational attainment and synthetic estimates of work-life earnings.* Retrieved September 1, 2005, from http://www.census.gov/prod/2002pubs/p23-210.pdf

DeMaris, A. (1987). The efficacy of a spouse abuse model in accounting for courtship violence. *Journal of Family Issues, 8,* 291–305.

Dozier, D. C. J. (1998). Attitudes, stress and use of force in selected areas of Texas law enforcement. *Dissertation Abstracts International Section A: Humanities & Social Sciences, 59*(4-A), 1,341.

Dugger, W. M., & Sherman, H. J. (1997, December). Institutionalist and Marxist theories of evolution. *Journal of Economic Issues, 31*(4), 991–1,010.

Faria Jr., M. A. (1999, July 9). More gun control, more crime. *Human Event*s, p. 10.

Federal Bureau of Investigation. (1998). *Uniform crime reports: Crime in the United States.* Washington, DC: U.S. Department of Justice.

Federal Bureau of Investigation. (2000). *Uniform crime reports: Crime in the United States.* Washington, DC: U.S. Department of Justice.

Federal Bureau of Investigation (2002a, November 15). *Statement for the record of Robert S. Mueller, III, Director, Federal Bureau of Investigation on Homeland Security before the Senate Committee on Governmental Affairs.* Retrieved September 9, 2005, from http://www.fbi.gov/congress/congress02.htm

Federal Bureau of Investigation. (2002b). *Uniform crime reports: Crime in the United States.* Washington, DC: U.S. Department of Justice.

Federal Bureau of Investigation (2005). *Uniform crime reports: Crime in the United States, 2004.* Washington, DC: U.S. Department of Justice.

Federal Communications Commission (2002). *Fact sheet.* Retrieved September 12, 2002, from http://www.fcc.gov/Bureaus/Mass_Media/Factsheets/factvchip.html

Ferguson, C. J. (2002, June/July). Media violence: Miscast causality. *American Psychologist,* pp. 446–447.

Fisher, D. (1999, Fall). Preventing childhood trauma resulting from exposure to domestic violence. *Prevent School Failure, 44*(1), 25–28.

Fowler, J. C., Hilsenroth, M, J., & Nolan, E. (2000, Summer). Exploring the inner world of self-mutilating borderline patients: A Rorschach investigation. *Bulletin of the Menninger Clinic, 64*(3), 365–385.

Gerbner, G., Gross, L., Morgan, M., & Signorielli, N. (1980). The "mainstreaming" of America. Violence profile no. 11. *Journal of Communication, 30,* 10–29.

Gergen, D. (1998, June 15). Protecting kids from guns. *U.S. News & World Report,* p. 68.

Goodman, L. A., Rosenberg, S. D., Mueser, K. T., & Drake, R. E.

(1997). Physical and sexual assault history in women with serious mental illness: Prevalence, correlates, treatment, and future research directions. *Schizophrenia Bulletin, 23*(4), 685–696.

Goodman, L. A., Salyers, M. P., Mueser, K. T., Rosenberg, S. D., Swartz, M., Essock, S. M., Osher, F. C., Butterfield, M. I., & Swanson, J. (2001). Recent victimization in women and men with severe mental illness: Prevalence and correlates. *Journal of Traumatic Stress, 14*(4), 615–632.

Hennessy, J., & West, M. A. (1999, June). Intergroup behavior in organizations. *Small Group Research, 30*(3), 361–383.

Hirschi, T. (1969). *Causes of delinquency.* Berkeley, CA: University of California Press.

Hohler, B. (1998, June 28). Klan rally bares hatred, but Jasper thwarts violence. *The Boston Globe,* A1, A16.

Holden, C. (2000). The violence of the lambs. *Science, 289,* 580–581.

Holland, C. C., Koblinsky, S. A., Lorion, R. P., & Anderson, E. (1996, June). *Homelessness and exposure to community violence: Child and maternal adjustment among urban head start families.* Poster session presented at the Head Start Third National Research Conference, Washington, DC.

Horn, J. L., & Trickett, P. K. (1998). Community violence and child development: A review of research. In P. K. Trickett & C. J. Schellenbach (Eds.), *Violence against children in the family and the community.* Washington, DC: American Psychological Association.

Inciardi, J. (2002). *Criminal justice* (7th ed.). Orlando: Hartcourt College Publishers.

Indiana University South Bend (2003, March 5). *Suicide statistics archive 1996–2000.* Retrieved September 9, 2005, from http://www.iusb.edu/~jmcintos/datayrarchives.htm

Irwin, A. R., & Gross, A. M. (1995). Cognitive tempo, violent video games, and aggressive behavior in young boys. *Journal of Family Violence, 10,* 337–350.

Jacobs, D., & O'Brien, R. M. (1998, January). The determinants of deadly force: A structural analysis of police violence. *AJS, 103*(4), 837–862.

Kaiser Family Foundation (1999, November). *Kids and media at the new millennium.* Menlo Park, CA: Kaiser Family Foundation.

Kalat, J. (2001). *Biological psychology* (7th ed.). Belmont, CA: Wadsworth/Thomson Learning.

Kellermann, A. L., Rivara, F. P., Rushforth, N. B., Banton, J. G., Reay, D. T., Francisco, J. T., Locci, A. B., Prodzinski, J., Hackman B. B., & Somes, G. (1993). Gun ownership as a risk factor for homicide in the home. *New England Journal of Medicine, 329,* 1,084–1,091.

King, K. (1999, September). 15 myths about suicide. *Education Digest,* 68–71.

Kirschner, R. H. (1997, November 8). Police brutality in the USA. *Lancet, 350*(9,088), 1395.

Klech, G. (1991). *Point blank: Guns and violence in America.* New York: Aldine de Gruyter, 158–162.

Kleck, G., & Hogan, M. (1999). National case-control study of homicide offending and gun ownership. *Social Problems, 46*(2), 275–293.

Klonsky, M. (2002, February). How smaller schools prevent school violence. *Educational Leadership, 59*(5), 65–69.

Kopel, D. B. (1996, August/September). The militias are coming. *Reason,* pp. 57–60.

Kotch, J. B., & Browne, D. C. (1999, April). Predicting child maltreatment in the first 4 years of life from characteristics assessed. *Child Abuse & Neglect, 23*(4), 305–319.

Kramer, M. (1990). The moral logic of Hizballah. In W. Reich (Ed.), *The origins of terrorism.* Cambridge: Cambridge University Press. 131–157.

Kumpfer, K. L., Olds, D. L., Alexander, J. F., Zucker, R. A., & Gary, L. E. (1998). Family etiology of youth problems. In *NIDA Research Monograph 177.* Rockville, MD: USDHHS, NIH.

Liska, A. E., Logan, J. R., & Bellair, P. E. (1998). Race and violent crime in the suburbs. *American Sociological Review, 63*(1), 27–38.

Luhman, R. (Ed.) (1992). Racial and ethnic relations. In *The Sociological outlook: A text with readings* (3rd ed). San Diego: Collegiate Press.

Marans, S., Berkowitz, S. J., & Cohen, D. J. (1998, July). Police and mental health professionals. *Child & Adolescent Psychiatric Clinics of North America, 7*(3), 635–651.

Mason, D. A., & Frick, P. J. (1994). The heritability of antisocial behavior: A meta-analysis of twin and adoption studies. *Journal of Psychopathology and Behavioral Assessment, 16*(12), 301–323.

Mason, J. O. (1993, January/February). The dimensions of an epidemic of violence. *Public Health Reports, 103*(1), 1–4.

Mazur, A., & Booth, A. (1998). Testosterone and dominance in men. *Behavioral and Brain Sciences, 21*(3), 353–397.

McBride, D. C., VanderWaal, C. J., & Terry-McElrath, Y. T. (2003, September). The Drugs-Crime Wars: Past, Present and Future Directions, in Theory, Policy and Program Interventions in Toward a Drugs and Crime Research Agenda for the 21st Century. National Institute of Justice Special Report, Washington, DC, NCJ 194616.

McCauley, C. (1991). Terrorism research and public policy: An overview. In C. McCauley (Ed.), *Terrorism research and public policy* (pp. 126–144). London: Frank Cass.

McClure, L. (1999, July). Address workplace anger early and fend off sabotage before it becomes a problem. *Workforce, 78*(7), 39.

Miles, D. R., & Carey, G. (1997). Genetic and environmental architecture on human aggression. *Journal of Personality and Social Psychology, 72*(1), 207–217.

Monahan, J. (1994, January). The causes of violence. *FBI Law Enforcement Bulletin, 63*(1), 11–16.

Morrison, J. A. (2000, October). Protective factors associated with children's emotional responses to chronic community violence exposure. *Trauma, Violence, & Abuse, 1*(4), 299–320.

Morrow-Howell, N., Becker-Kemppainen, S., & et al. (1998, January). Evaluating an intervention for the elderly at increased risk of suicide. *Research on Social Work Practice, 8*(1), 28–47.

Myers, B. J., Smarsh, T. M., Amlund-Hagen, K., & Kennon, S. (1999, March). Children of incarcerated mothers. *Journal of Child & Family Studies, 8*(1), 11–25.

Nabi, R. L., & Sullivan, J. L. (2001, December). Does television viewing relate to engagement in protective action against crime? *Communication Research, 28*(6), 802–825.

National Center on Elder Abuse. (2003). *Who are the abusers?* Retrieved August 31, 2005, from http://www.elderabusecenter.org/default.cfm?p=whoaretheabusers.cfm

National Center for Injury Prevention and Control (2002, October 28). *Suicide in the United States.* Retrieved September 9, 2005, from http://www.cdc.gov/ncipc/factsheets/suifacts.htm

National Center for Injury Prevention and Control (2005, September 6). Suicide Fact Sheet. Retrieved September 6, 2005, from http://www.cdc.gov/ncipc/factsheets/suicifacts.htm

National Commission on the Causes and Prevention of Violence. (1969). *To establish justice, to insure domestic tranquility.* New York: Award Books.

Nemecek, S. (1998, September). Forestalling violence. *Scientific American, 279*(3), 15–16.

Nicoletti, J., & Spooner, K. (1996). *Violence in the workplace.* Washington, DC: American Psychological Association.

Norris, J. A. (1998, November). Promoting social competence and reducing violence and negative social interactions in a multicultural school setting. *Dissertation Abstracts International Section A: Humanities & Social Sciences, 59*(5-A), 1,420.

O'Brien, S. P., & Haider-Markel, D. P. (1998, June). Fueling the fire: Social and political correlates of citizen militia activity. *Social Science Quarterly, 79*(2), 456–465.

Petrosino, C. (1999, February). Connecting the past to the future. *Journal of Contemporary Criminal Justice, 15*(1), 22–47.

Pinel, J. P. J. (1997). *Biopsychology* (3rd ed.). Boston: Allyn and Bacon.

Powers, T. (1971). *Diana: The making of a terrorist.* Boston: Houghton Miffin.

Reese, R. (2001). Building cultural bridges in schools: The colorful flags model. *Race, Ethnicity and Education, 4*(3), 181–207.

Reiss, A., & Roth, J. (Eds.) (1993). *Understanding and preventing violence.* Washington, DC: National Academy Press.

Rembolt, C. (1998, September). Making violence unacceptable. *Educational Leadership, 56*(1), 32–38.

Rosenberg, M. L. (1995). Violence in America. *Journal of Health Care for the Poor & Underserved, 6*(2), 102–113.

Rosenblatt, R. A. (1990, May 1). Abuse of the elderly rises dramatically. *Los Angeles Times,* p. A18.

Ross, S., & Heath, N. (2002, February). A study of the frequency of self-mutilation in a community sample of adolescents. *Journal of Youth and Adolescence, 31,* 67–77.

Roy, A. (2001, Summer). Childhood trauma and suicidal behavior in male cocaine dependent patients. *Suicide and Life-Threatening Behavior, 31*(2), 194–196.

Rudo, Z. H., Powell, D. S., & Dunlap, G. (1998, Summer). The effects of violence in the home on children's emotional, behavioral, and social functioning. *Emotional and Behavioral Disorders, 6*(2), 94–113.

Salzman, M., & D'Andrea, M. (2001, Summer). Assessing the impact of a prejudice prevention project. *Journal of Counseling & Development, 79*(3), 341–346.

Sanders, E. (2002, June 29). FTC says adult fare still marketed to kids. *Los Angeles Times.* Retrieved September 12, 2002, from http://www.childrennow.org/newsroom

Scarpa, A. (2001, January). Community violence exposure in a young adult sample. *Journal of Interpersonal Violence, 16*(1), 36–53.

Schlozman, S. C. (2002, October). The shrink in the classroom: Fighting school violence. *Educational Leadership,* 89–90.

Shihadeh, E., & Flynn, N. (1996, June). Segregation and crime. *Social Forces, 74*(4), 1,325–1,352.

Sibbitt, R. (1997). *The Perpetrators of Racial Harassment and Racial Violence.* Home Office Research Study 176. London: Home Office.

Sigler, R. T. (1995). The cost of tolerance for violence. *Journal of Health Care for the Poor & Underserved, 6*(2), 124–134.

Simons, R. L., Lin, K. H., & et al. (1998, May). Socialization in the family of origin and male dating violence: A prospective study. *Journal of Marriage & Family, 60*(2), 467–478.

Smith, A., & Ross, L. (2004). Introduction: Native women and state violence. *Social Justice, 31*(4), 1–7.

Steinhaus, R. (2002). *Young brothers convicted of father's murder.* Retrieved September 17, 2002, from http://www.courttv.com/trails/king.html

Stoff, D. M., & Cairns, R. B. (1996). *Aggression and violence: Genetic, neurobiological, and biosocial perspectives.* Mahwah, NJ: Lawrence Erlbaum.

Swinford, S. P., DeMaris, A., Cernkovich, S., & Giordano, P. C. (2000, May). Harsh physical discipline in childhood and violence in later romantic involvements: The mediating role of problem behaviors. *Journal of Marriage and the Family, 62,* 508–519.

Thompson, K. M., & Haninger, K. (2001, August 1). Violence in E-rated video games. *JAMA: Journal of the American Medical Association, 286*(5), 591–598.

Toch, H., & Lizotte, A. J. (1992). Research and policy: The case for gun control. In P. Suedfield, & P. E. Tetlock (Eds.), *Psychology and Social Policy* (pp. 223–249). New York: Hemisphere Publishing Corporation.

Tomes, H. (1995). Research and policy directions in violence. *Journal of Health Care for the Poor & Underserved, 6*(2), 102–113.

Trickett, P. K., & Schellenbach, C. J. (1998). *Violence against children in the family and the community.* Washington, DC: American Psychological Association.

Tristani, G. (2000, July 26). *Statement of FCC Commissioner Gloria Tristani on the impact of entertainment violence on children.* Retrieved September 12, 2002, from http://www.fcc.gov/Speeches/Tristani/Statements/2000

Turner, C. W., & Leyens, J. P. (1992). The effects of firearms on aggressive behavior. *Psychology and Social Policy,* 201–221.

U.S. Children's Bureau Administration on Children, Youth and Families. (2002). *National child abuse and neglect data system summary of key findings from calendar year 2000.* Department of Health and Human Services. Retrieved October 29, 2002, from http://www.calib.com/nccanch/pubs/factsheets/canstate

U.S. Constitution. The Declaration of Independence, Amendments to the Constitution. *U.S. Constitution pamphlet* (1976). Phillips Petroleum Company.

U.S. Department of Health & Human Services. (2005). *HHS reports new child abuse and neglect statistics.* Retrieved September 9, 2005, from http://www.hhs.gov/news/press/2001pres/20010402.html

U.S. Department of Justice, Bureau of Justice Statistics. (1988). *Report to the nation on crime and justice.* Washington, DC: U.S. Government Printing Office.

U.S. Department of Justice, Bureau of Justice Statistics. (2001, December 20). *Violence in the workplace, 1993–1999.* Retrieved September 9, 2005, from http://www.ojp.usdoj.gov/bjs/abstract/vw99.htm

U.S. Department of Justice, Bureau of Justice Statistics. (2005). *Corrections Statistics.* Retrieved August 31, 2005, from http://www.ojp.usdoj.gov/bjs/correct.htm

U.S. Department of Labor. (1996). Washington, DC: U.S. Government Printing Office.

U.S. Federal Trade Commission. (2000). *Marketing violent entertainment to children: A review of self-regulation and industry practices in the motion picture, music recording and electronic game industries.* Washington, DC: U.S. Federal Trade Commission.

Van Slambrouck, P. (1998, August 6). US prisons—under pressure—show increase in violence. *Christian Science Monitor, 90*(177), 1.

Weist, M. D. (2001, May). Predictors of violence exposure among inner-city youth. *Journal of Clinical Child Psychology, 30*(2), 187–198.

White, M. P. (1995). A comprehensive approach to violence prevention. *Journal of Health Care for the Poor & Underserved, 6*(2), 254–266.

Will, D. S. (1993, April). Teaching peace through debunking race. *Peace and Change, 18*(2), 182–201.

Willis, D. J., & Silovsky, J. (1998). Prevention of violence at the societal level. In P. K. Trickett, C. J. Schellenbach, & et al. (Eds.), *Violence against children in the family and the community,* Washington, DC: American Psychological Association.

Winnett, L. B. (1998, November/December). Constructing violence as public health problem. *Public Health Reports, 113*(6), 498–507.

Winslow, G. (2000, November). Capital crimes: The political economy of crime in America. *Monthly Review, 52*(6), 38–53.

Withecomb, J. L. (1997, October). Causes of violence in children. *Journal of Mental Health, 6*(5), 433–442.

Wolfe, J. A., Mertler, C. A., & et al. (1998, Spring). Do increasing adolescent suicide rates result in increasing prevention/postvention programs in Ohio schools? *Education, 118*(3), 426–439.

Woolf, L. M. (2003). *Elder abuse and neglect.* Retrieved May 9, 2003, from http://www.webster.edu/~woolflm/abuse.html

Zila, L. M., & Kiselica, M. S. (2001, Winter). Understanding and counseling self-mutilation in female adolescents and young adults. *Journal of Counseling & Development, 79*(1), 46–52.

Chapter 12: Mental Health

American Psychiatric Association. (1994). *Diagnostic and statistical manual of mental disorders: DSM-IV* (4th ed.). Washington, DC: American Psychiatric Association, 29–30.

American Psychiatric Association. (2000). *Diagnostic and statistical manual of mental disorders* (4th ed., text revision). Washington, DC: American Psychiatric Association.

Andrews, G., Slade, T., & Peters, L. (1999). Classification in psychiatry: ICD-10 versus DSM-IV. *British Journal of Psychiatry, 174,* 3–5.

Andrews, L. M. (1995). Religion's challenge to psychology. *Public Interest, 120,* 79–88.

Antonuccio, D. O., Burns, D. D., & Danton, W. G. (2002). Antidepressants: A triumph of marketing over science? *Prevention & Treatment, 5,* Article 25. Retrieved September 27, 2005, from http://journals.apa.org/prevention/volume5/pre0050025c.html

Austrian, S. G. (1995). *Mental disorders, medications and clinical social work.* New York: Columbia University Press.

Barlow, D. H., & Durand, V. M. (1999). *Abnormal psychology an integrative approach* (2nd ed.). Pacific Grove, CA: Brooks/Cole Publishing Co.

Bartholomew, R. E. (1998). The medicalization of exotic deviance: A sociological perspective on epidemic koro. *Transcultural Psychiatry, 35,* 5–38.

Batson, C. D., Schoenrade, P., & Ventis, W. L. (1993). *Religion and the individual: A social-psychological perspective.* New York: Oxford University Press.

Bernstein, H. J., Beale, M. D., Burns, C., & Kellner, C. H. (1998). Patient attitudes about ECT after treatment. *Psychiatric Annals, 28,* 524–527.

Borman, P. D., & Dixon, D. N. (1998). Spirituality and the 12 steps of substance abuse recovery. *Journal of Psychology & Theology, 26,* 287–291.

Brock, T. C., Green, M. C., Reich, D. A., & Evans, L. M. (1996). The *Consumer Reports* study of psychotherapy: Invalid is invalid. *American Psychologist, 51,* 1,083.

Burnham, J. C. (2002, August). *How the idea developed that deinstitutionalization represented failed social policy.* Paper presented at the meeting of the American Psychological Association, Chicago, IL.

Caporael, L. (1976). Ergotism: The Satan loosed in Salem? *Science, 192,* 21–26.

Castillo, R. J. (1997). *Culture and mental illness: A client-centered approach.* Pacific Grove, CA: Brooks/Cole Publishing Co.

Center for Mental Health Services (CMHC). (1994). *Mental health statistics.* Office of Consumer, Family and Public Information, Center for Mental Health Services, U.S. Department of Health and Human Services. Rockville, MD: Author.

Charatan, F. (1998). US panel calls for research into effects of Ritalin. *British Medical Journal, 317*(7,172), 1,545.

Cheng, A. T. A. (2001). Case definition and culture: Are people all the same? *British Journal of Psychiatry, 179,* 1–3.

Costello, E. J., Keeler, G. P., & Angold, A. (2001). Poverty, race/ethnicity, and psychiatric disorder: A study of rural children.

American Journal of Public Health, 91(9), 1,494–1,498.

Craig, T. J., Krishna, G., & Poniarski, R. (1997). Predictors of successful vs. unsuccessful outcome of a 12-step inpatient alcohol rehabilitation program. *American Journal of Addictions, 6,* 232–236.

Cuffe, S. P., Waller, J. L., Cuccaro, M. L., Pumariega, A. J., & Garrison, C. Z. (1995). Race and gender differences in the treatment of psychiatric disorders in young adolescents. *Journal of American Academy of Child and Adolescent Psychiatry, 34,* 1,536–1,543.

Dawkins, K. (1999). Gender differences in psychiatry: Epidemiology and drug response. *CNS Drugs, 3,* 393–407.

DeAngelis, T. (1995, April). New threat associated with child abuse. *APA Monitor, 26*(4), 1, 38.

Devan, G. S. (1987). Koro and schizophrenia in Singapore. *British Journal of Psychiatry, 150,* 106–107.

Devanand, D. P., Dwork, A. J., Hutchinson, E. R., Bolwig, T. G., & Sackeim, H. A. (1994). Does ECT alter brain structure? *American Journal of Psychiatry, 151,* 957–970.

Dottl, S. L., & Greenley, J. R. (1997). Rural-urban differences in psychiatric status and functioning among clients with severe mental illness. *Community Mental Health Journal, 33,* 311–321.

Fields-Meyer, T. (1997, September 1). By reason of insanity. *People Weekly, 48,* 88(4).

First, M. B., & Pincus, H. A. (2002). The *DSM-IV Test Revision*: Rationale and potential impact on clinical practice. *Psychiatric Services, 53*(3), 288–292.

Frances, R. J., & Miller, S. I. (1998). *Clinical textbook of addictive disorders* (2nd ed.). New York: The Gilford Press.

Freeman, H. (1994). Schizophrenia and city residence. *British Journal of Psychiatry, 164* (Suppl. 23), 39–50.

Garland, A. F., & Besinger, B. A. (1997). Racial/ethnic differences in court referred pathways to mental health services for children in foster care. *Children & Youth Services Review, 19,* 651–666.

Garnefski, N., & Diekstra, R. (1996). Child sexual abuse and emotional and behavioral problems in adolescence: Gender differences. *Journal of the American Academy of Child & Adolescent Psychiatry, 36,* 323–329.

Gibbs, N., Blackman, A., Dowell, W., Hornblewer, M., Kauffman, E., & Seiger, M. (1998, Nov. 30). The age of Ritalin. *Time, 152,* 22, 86–96.

Gorey, K. M., & Leslie, D. R. (1997). The prevalence of child sexual abuse: Integrative review adjustment for potential response and measurement biases. *Child Abuse & Neglect, 21*(4), 391–398.

Greenberg, R. P., Bornstein, R. F., Zborowski, M. J., Fisher, S., & Greenburg, M. D. (1994). A meta-analysis of fluoxetine outcome in the treatment of depression. *Journal of Nervous and Mental Disease, 182,* 547–551.

Greenley, J. R., & Dottl, S. L. (1997). Sociodemographic characteristics of severely mentally ill clients in rural and urban counties. *Community Mental Health Journal, 33,* 545–551.

Grob, G. N. (1995). The paradox of deinstitutionalization. *Society, 32,* 51–59.

Grohol, J. M. (1998, October 1). The results of deinstitutionaliza-

tion: Pointing the finger of blame. Retrieved March 7, 1999, from *Mental Health Net:* http://www.cmhc.com/perspectives/editorials/opin0998.htm

Harper, M. S. (1996, Summer). Mental health of the black elderly. *Dimensions* (Newsletter of American Society on Aging), pp. 1, 7–8.

Hartung, C. M., & Widiger, T. A. (1998). Gender differences in the diagnosis of mental disorders: Conclusions and controversies of the DSM-IV. *Psychological Bulletin, 123,* 260–278.

Haviland, W. A. (1996). *Cultural anthropology* (8th ed.). Fort Worth: Harcourt Brace & Co.

Hellerstein, D., Yanowitch, R., Rosenthal, J., Samstag, L. W., Maurer, M., Kasch, K., Burrows, L., Poster, M., Cantillon, M., & Winston, R. (1993). A randomized double-blind study of fluoxetine versus placebo in the treatment of dysthymia. *American Journal of Psychiatry, 150,* 1,169–1,175.

Herman, D. B., Susser, E. S., Jandorf, L., Lavelle, J., & Bromet, E. J. (1998). Homelessness among individuals with psychotic disorders hospitalized for the first time: Findings from the Suffolk County Mental Health Project. *American Journal of Psychiatry, 155*(1), 109–113.

Herman, J., Perry, J. C., & van der Kolk, B. (1989). Childhood trauma in borderline disorder. *American Psychiatric Association, 146,* 490–495.

Holmes, D. S. (1997). *Abnormal psychology* (3rd ed.). New York: Longman.

Holmes, W. C., & Slap, G. B. (1998). Sexual abuse of boys: Definition, prevalence, correlates, sequelae, and management. *Journal of the American Medical Association, 280*(21), 1,855–1,862.

Hope, T. L., & Bierman, K. L. (1998). Patterns of home and school behavior problems in rural and urban settings. *Journal of School Psychology, 36,* 45–58.

Hotherstall, D. (1995). *History of psychology* (3rd ed.). New York: McGraw-Hill.

Hunt, M. (1993). *The story of psychology.* New York: Anchor Books.

Irle, E. I., Exner, C., Thielen, K., Weniger, G., & Ruther, E. (1998). Obsessive-compulsive disorder and ventromedial frontal lesions: Clinical and neuropsychological findings. *American Journal of Psychiatry, 155,* 255–263.

Jacobson, N. S., & Christensen, A. (October, 1996). Studying the effectiveness of psychotherapy: How well can clinical trials do the job? *American Psychologist Special Issue: Outcome assessment of psychotherapy, 51*(10), 1,031–1,039.

Jaroff, L. (1993, November 29). Lies of the mind. *Time,* pp. 52–59.

Jenike, M. A., Baer, L., Ballantine, T., Martuza, R. L., Tynes, S., Giriunas, I., Buttolph, M. L., & Cassem, N. H. (1991). Cingultomy for refractory obsessive-compulsive disorder. *Archives of General Psychiatry, 48,* 548–555.

Jimenez, M. A. (1997). Gender and psychiatry: Psychiatric conceptions of mental disorders in women, 1960–1994. *Journal of Women and Social Work, 12,* 154–176.

Kaplan, S. J., Pelcovitz, D., Salzinger, S., et al. (1998). Adolescent physical abuse: Risk for adolescent psychiatric disorders. *American Journal of Psychiatry, 155,* 954–959.

Karls, J. M. W., & Wandrei, K. E. (1997*). Person-in-environment* system: *The PIE classification system for social functioning problems.* Washington, DC: National Association of Social Workers.

Kendler, K. S., Bulik, C. M., Silberg, J., Hettema, J. M., Myers, J., & Prescott, C. A. (2000). Childhood sexual abuse and adult psychiatric and substance use disorders in women. *Archives of General Psychiatry, 57*(10), 953–959.

Kessler, R. C., Demler, O., Frank, R. G., Olfson, M., Pincus, H. A., Walters, E. E., Wang, P., Wells, K. B., & Zaslavsky, A. M. (2005). Prevalence and treatment of mental disorders, 1990 to 2003. *The New England Journal of Medicine, 352*(24), 2,515–2,523.

Kleinman, A., & Cohen, A. (1997). Psychiatry's global challenge. *Scientific American, 276*, 87–89.

Klerman, G. L., Lavori, P. W., Rice, J., Reich, T., Endicott, J. E., Andreasen, N. C., Keller, M. B., & Hirschfield, R. (1985). Birth-cohort trends in rates of major depressive disorder among relatives of patients with affective disorder. *Archives of General Psychiatry, 42*, 689–693.

Koenig, H. G. (1998). *Handbook of religion and mental health.* San Diego: Academic Press.

Koenig, H. G., & Larson, D. B. (2001). Religion and mental health: Evidence for an association. *International Review of Psychiatry, 13*, 67–78.

Lamb, H. R. (1998). Deinstitutionalization at the beginning of the new millennium. *Harvard Review of Psychiatry, 6*, 1–10.

Lang, S. (1997). Childhood sexual abuse affects relationships in adulthood. *Human Ecology Forum, 25*, 3.

Lewinsohn, P. M., Hops, H., Roberts, R. E., Seeley, J. R., & Andrews, J. A. (1993). Adolescent psychopathology: I. Prevalence and incidence of depression and other DSM-III-R disorders in high school students. *Journal of Abnormal Psychology, 102*, 133–144.

Lewis, D., Yeager, C., Swica, Y., Pincus, J., & Lewis, M. (1997). Objective documentation of child abuse and dissociation in 12 murderers with dissociative identity disorder. *American Journal of Psychiatry, 154*, 1,703–1,710.

Loftus, E. (1993a). The reality of repressed memory. *American Psychologist, 48*, 518–537.

Loftus, E. (1993b). Psychologists in the eyewitness world. *American Psychologist, 48*, 550–552.

López, S. R., & Guarnaccia, P. J. J. (2000). Cultural psychopathology: Uncovering the social world of mental illness. *Annual Review of Psychology, 51*, 571–598.

MacPherson, M. (1989, September). The roots of evil. *Cosmopolitan, 207*(3), 272(10).

Marc P. Freiman Agency for Health Care Policy and Research and Peter J. Cunningham Center for Studying Heath System Change. (1997). Use of health care for the treatment of mental problems among racial/ethnic subpopulations. *Medical Care Research & Review, 54*, 80–100.

Marsella, A. J. (1998). Urbanization, mental health, and social deviancy: A review of issues and research. *American Psychologist, 53*, 624–634.

Meeks, S., & Murrell, S. A. (1997). Mental illness in late life: Socioeconomic conditions, psychiatric symptoms, and adjustment of long-term sufferers. *Psychology and Aging, 12*, 296–308.

Mental health: Does therapy work? (1995, November). *Consumer Reports, 60*, 734–739.

Mental health: Pay for services or pay a greater price (n.d.). Retrieved September 27, 2005, from www.nmha.org/shcr/community_ based/costoffset.pdf

Meyer, C. H. (1992). Social work assessment: Is there an empirical base? *Research on Social Work Practice, 2*(3), 297–305.

Meyer, C. H. (1993). *Assessment in social work practice.* New York: Columbia University Press.

Miller, M., & Kantrowitz, B. (1999, January 25). Unmasking Sybil. *Newsweek*, 66–68.

Minuchin, S. (1984). *Family Kaleidoscope.* Cambridge, MA: Harvard University Press.

Mortensen, P. B., Pedersen, C. B., Westergaard, T., Wohlfahrt, J., Ewald, H., Mors, O., Andersen, P. K., & Melbye, M. (1999). Effects of family history and place and season of birth on the risk of schizophrenia. *The New England Journal of Medicine, 340*, 603–608.

Mossman, D. (1997). Deinstitutionalization, homelessness, and the myth of psychiatric abandonment: A structural anthropology perspective. *Social Science and Medicine, 44*, 71–83.

Mukherjee, S., Sackeim, H. A., & Schnur, D. B. (1994). Electroconvulsive therapy of acute manic episodes: A review of 50 years' experience. *American Journal of Psychiatry, 151*, 169–176.

Nasser, M. (1988). Eating disorders: The cultural dimension. *Social Psychiatry and Psychiatric Epidemiology, 23*, 184–187.

Nevid, J. S., Rathus, S. A., & Greene, B. (1997). *Abnormal behavior in a changing world* (3rd ed.). Upper Saddle River, NJ: Prentice Hall.

Nietzel, M., Speltz, M., McCauley, E., & Bernstein, D. (1998). *Abnormal psychology.* Boston: Allyn and Bacon.

The numbers count: Mental disorders in America (n.d.). Retrieved September 27, 2005, from www.nimh.nih.gov/publicat/numbers.cfm

Petersen, A. C., Compas, B. E., Brooks-Gunn, J., Stemmler, M., Ey, S., & Grant, K. E. (1993). Depression in adolescence. *American Psychologist, 48*, 155–168.

Pincus, H. A., Tanielian, T. L., Marcus, S. C., Olfson, M., Zarin, D. A., Thompson, J., & Zito, J. M. (1998, February 18). Prescribing trends in psychotropic medications: Primary care, psychiatry, and other medical specialties. *Journal of the American Medical Association, 279*, 526–531.

Queralt, M. (1996). *The social environment and human behavior.* Boston: Allyn and Bacon.

Robins, L. N., Helzer, J. E., Weissman, M. M., Orvaschel, H., Gruenberg, E., Burke Jr., J. D., & Regier, D. A. (1984). Lifetime prevalence of specific psychiatric disorders in three sites. *Archives of General Psychiatry, 41*, 949–958.

Rosenthal, D. (Ed.). (1963). *The Genain quadruplets: A case study and theoretical analysis of heredity and environment in schizophrenia.* New York: Basic Books.

Ross, C. A., Miller, S. D., Reagor, P., Bjornson, L., Fraser, G. A., & Anderson, G. (1990). Structured interview data on 102 cases of multiple personality disorder from four centers. *American Journal of Psychiatry, 147*, 596–601.

Rowan, A. B., et al. (1994). Posttraumatic stress disorder in a clinical sample of adults sexually abused as children. *Child Abuse and Neglect, 18*, 51–61.

Sachs-Ericsson, N., & Ciarlo, J. A. (2000). Gender, social roles, and mental health: An epidemiological perspective. *Sex Roles, 43*(9–10), 605–628.

Schrof, J. M., & Scultz, S. (1999, March 8). Melancholy nation. *US News & World Report, 126*, 56–63.

Seligman, M. E. P. (1995). The effectiveness of psychotherapy: The *Consumer Reports* study. *American Psychologist, 50*, 965–974.

Sheafor, B. W., Horejsi, C. R., & Horejsi, G. A. (1997). *Techniques and guidelines for social work* practice (5th ed.). Boston: Allyn & Bacon.

Shezi, E., & Uys, L. (1997). Culture bound syndromes in a group of Xhosa with psychiatric disorders. *Curationis, 20*, 83–86.

Smart, D. W., & Smart, J. F. (1997). DSM-IV and cultural sensitivity diagnosis: Some observations for counselors. *Journal of Counseling and Development, 75*, 392–399.

Smith, M. L., Glass, G. V., & Miller, T. I. (1980). *The benefits of psychotherapy*. Baltimore: Johns Hopkins University Press.

Spirit of the age. (1998, December 12). *Economist, 349*, 113–117.

Stein, M. B., Walker, J. R., Anderson, G., Hazen, A. L., Ross, C. A., Eldridge, G., & Forde, D. R. (1996). Childhood physical and sexual abuse in patients with anxiety disorders and in a community sample. *American Journal of Psychiatry, 153*, 275–277.

Swartz, M. S., Wagner, H. R., Swanson, J. W., Burns, B. J., George, L. K., & Padgett, D. K. (1998). Comparing use of public and private mental health services: The enduring barriers of race and age. *Community Mental Health Journal, 34*, 133–144.

Szasz, T. (1960). The myth of mental illness. *American Psychologist, 15*, 113–118.

Torrey, E. F. (1997, January 13). The release of the mentally ill from institutions: A well-intentioned disaster. *The Chronicle of Higher Education*, pp. B4–B5.

Turner, R. J., & Wagenfeld, M. O. (1967). Occupational mobility and schizophrenia: An assessment of the social causation and social selection hypothesis. *American Sociological Review, 32*, 104–113.

van Os, J., Hanssen, M., Bijl, R. V., & Vollebergh, W. (2001). Prevalence of psychotic disorder and community level of psychotic symptoms: An urban-rural comparison. *Archivers of General Psychiatry, 58*(7), 663–668.

Vatz, R. E., & Weinberg, L. S. (1993). Is mental illness a myth? *USA Today Magazine, 122*(2,578), 62–63.

Wallace, J., & O'Hara, M. W. (1992). Increases in depressive symptomatology in the rural elderly: Results from a cross-sectional and longitudinal study. *Journal of Abnormal Psychology, 101*(3), 398–404.

Webb, L. (1984). Rural-urban differences in mental disorder. In H. Freeman (Ed.), *Mental health and the environment*. London: Livingstone-Church.

Weich, S., & Lewis, G. (1998). Poverty, unemployment, and common mental disorders: Population based cohort study. *British Medical Journal, 316*, 115–119.

Williams, D. R., & Harris-Reid, M. (1999). Race and mental health: Emerging patterns and promising approaches. In A. V. Horwitz & T. L. Scheid (Eds.), *A handbook for the study of mental heath: Social contexts, theories, and systems.* New York: Cambridge University Press.

Wood, S. E., & Wood, E. G. (1996). *The world of psychology* (2nd ed.). Boston: Allyn & Bacon.

Wyatt, G. E., Guthrie, D., & Notgrass, C. M. (1991). Differential effects of women's child sexual abuse and subsequent revictimization. *Journal of Consulting and Clinical Psychology, 60*, 167–173.

Chapter 13: Religious Fundamentalism and Cult Behavior

Aikman, D. (2003). The great revival: Understanding religious "fundamentalism." *Foreign Affairs, 82*(4), 188–194.

Altemeyer, B., & Hunsberger, B. E. (1992). Authoritarianism, religious fundamentalism, quest, and prejudice. *International Journal for the Psychology of Religion, 2*(2), 113–133.

Berger, P. L., ed. (1999). The desecularization of the world: Resurgent religion and world politics. Grand Rapids, MI: William B. Eerdmans Publishing Company.

Corsini, R. J. (1999). *Dictionary of psychology.* Philadelpia: Brumer/Mazel.

Goldfried, J., & Miner, M. (2002). Quest religion and the problem of limited compassion. *Journal for the Scientific Study of Religion, 41*(4), 685–695.

Janis, I. L. (1972). *Victims of groupthink: A psychological study of foreign-policy decisions and fiascoes.* Boston: Houghton Mifflin.

Janis, I. L. (1989). *Crucial decisions: Leadership in policymaking and crisis management.* New York: Free Press.

Kaplan, D., Latif, A., Ozernoy, I., Lande, L., & Ekman, M. (2003, June 2). Playing offense. *U.S. News & World Report*, 18–29.

Knight, J., & Chant, D. (1990). Fundamentalism: A potential constituency for an Australian new right? *Social Alternatives, 9*(1), 27–30.

Martin, W. (1980). *The new cults.* Ventura, CA: Regal Books.

Neier, A. (1992). Watching rights. *Nation, 254*(13), 440.

Peterson, R. D., Wunder, D. F., & Mueller, H. L. (1998). *Social problems: Globalization in the twenty-first century.* Upper Saddle River, NJ: Prentice Hall.

Pyszczynski, T., Solomon, S., & Greenberg, J. (2003). *In the wake of 9/11: The psychology of terror.* Washington, DC: American Psychological Association.

Rowatt, W. C., Ottenbreit, A., Nesselroade, Jr., K. P., & Cunningham, P. A. (2002). On being holier-than-thou or humbler-than-thee: A social-psychological perspective on religiousness and humility. *Journal for the Scientific Study of Religion, 41*(2), 227–237.

van der Vyver, J. D. (1996). Religious fundamentalism and human rights. *International Affairs, 50*(1), 21–41.

Chapter 14: Poverty

Adler, N., Boyce, T., Chesney, M., Cohen, S., Folkman, S., Kahn, R., & Syme, S. (1994). Socieconomic status & health: The challenge of gradient. *American Psychologist, 49*, 15–25.

Appealing a decision by the Social Security Administration for disability benefit eligibility. Retrieved October 4, 2005, from www.thearc.org/afcsp/appealsfull.htm.

Appleby, G. A., Colon, E., & Hamilton, J. (2001). *Diversity, oppression, and social functioning.* Boston: Allyn & Bacon.

Bandura, A. (1997). *Self-efficacy: The exercise of control.* New York: W. H. Freeman and Company.

Beeghley, L. (1983). *Living poorly in America.* New York: Praeger Publications.

Bobo, L., & Smith, R. (1994). "Antipoverty policy, affirmative action and racial attitudes." In S. Danziger, G. Sandefur, & D. Weinberg (Eds.), *Confronting poverty: Prescriptions for change* (pp. 365–395). Cambridge, MA: Harvard University Press.

Breakey, W. (1987). Treating the homeless. *Alcohol, Health, & Research World, 11*, 42–46, 90.

Brenner, M. H. (1984). *Estimating the effects of economic change on national health & social well-being.* Washington, DC: U.S. Government Printing.

Buttrick, S. M. (1990). The new poverty: Persistent, pernicious & growing. *Social Work Research Abstracts, 26*(4), 3.

Chamberlain, J. G. (1999). *Upon whom we can depend—The American poverty system.* New York: Lang.

Child Trends. (2003, February 11). "Percent of poor children living with working parents drops," Washington, DC, Child Trends News Room Press Release. Retrieved January 16, 2004, from http://www.childtrends.org

The Children's Defense Fund. (1994). *The state of America's children.* Washington, DC.

Cole, W., & Corliss, R. (2003, January 20). No place like home. *Time Magazine, 161*, 58–61.

Collected State of the Union Addresses of U.S. Presidents, William J. Clinton (1999, January 19). Retrieved October 2, 2005, from www.infoplease.com/t/hist/state-of-the-union/212.html

Danziger, S., Corcoran, M., Danziger, S., Siefert, K., Tolman, R., & Kalil, A. (2001). *Barriers to the employment of welfare recipients: Research Project.* Retrieved October 19, 2001, from http://www.ssw.umich.edu/nimhcenter/barriers.html

DiNitto, D. (1995). *Social welfare: Politics and public policy* (4th ed.). Boston: Allyn & Bacon.

Duncan, G., & Brooks-Gunn, J. (Eds.). (1997). *Consequences of growing up poor.* New York: Russell Sage.

Federal Register (2003, February 7). Vol. *68*(26), 6,456–6,458. Retrieved January 16, 2004, from http://www.ocpp.org/poverty

Gardner, H. (2000). *Intelligence reframed: Multiple intelligences for the 21st century.* New York: Basic Books.

Gomel, J., Tinsley, B., Parke, R., & Clark, K. (1998). The effects of economic hardship on family relationships among African American, Latino, and Euro-American families. *Journal of Family Issues, 19*, 436–467.

Hagen, J. (1990). Designing services for homeless women. *Journal of Health & Social Policy, 1*(3), 1–16.

Hamilton, V., Croman, C., Hoffman, W., & Renner, D. (1990). Hard times and vulnerable people: Initial effects of plant closing on autoworkers' mental health. *Journal of Health and Social Behavior, 31*, 123–140.

Heffernan, J., Shuttlesworth, G., & Ambrosino, R. (1997). *Social work and social welfare.* Minneapolis/St. Paul: West.

Ho, C., Lempers, J., & Clark-Lempers, D. (1995). Effects of economic hardship on adolescent self-esteem: A family mediation model. *Adolescence, 30*, 117–131. Retrieved September 25, 2001, from http://www.census.gov/press-release/www/2001/cb01-158.htm

Jefferson, T. (1776). *Declaration of independence.* ME 1:29, Papers 1:315. (A copy of the Declaration of Independence may be found at http://www.ushistory.org/declaration/document/index.htm.)

Johnson, L. C., & Schwartz, C. L. (1997). *Social welfare* (4th ed.). Boston: Allyn & Bacon.

Karger, H. J., & Stoesz, D. (1998). *American social welfare policy: A pluralistic approach.* New York: Addison-Wesley Longman.

Keith, V. (1993). Gender, financial strain, and psychological distress among adults. *Research on Aging, 15*, 123–147.

Kessler, R., House, J., & Turner, J. (1987). Unemployment & health in a community sample. *Journal of Health & Social Behavior, 28*, 51–59.

Kim, M. (1998). Are the working poor lazy? *Challenge, 41*(3), 85.

Klebanov, P., Brooks-Gunn, J., & Duncan, G. (1994). Does neighborhood and family poverty affect mothers, parenting, mental health, & social support? *Journal of Marriage & the Family, 56*, 441–455.

Kornblum, W., & Julian, J. (1998). *Social problems* (9th ed.). Upper Saddle River, NJ: Prentice Hall.

Kotlowitz, A. (1987). *There are no children here: The story of two boys growing up in the other America.* New York: Anchor Books.

Krause, N. (1987). Chronic strain, locus of control, and distress in older adults. *Psychology & Aging, 2*, 375–382.

Liebman, J. B. (1998). The impact of the earned income tax credit on incentives & income distribution. *Tax Policy & the Economy, 12*, 37, 83.

Lubitz, J., Cai, L., Kramarow, E., & Lentzner, H. (2003). Health, life expectancy, and health care spending among the elderly. The *New England Journal of Medicine, 349*(11), 1,048–1,055.

MacFadyen, A., MacFadyen, H., & Prince, N. (1996). Economic stress and psychological well-being: An economic psychology framework. *Journal of Economic Psychology, 17*, 291–31.

Mauldin, T. (1991). Economic consequences of divorce on separation among women in poverty. *Journal of Divorce & Remarriage, 14*, 163–177.

McBride-Stetson, D. (1997). *Women's rights in the USA: Debates and gender roles* (2nd ed.). New York: Garland.

McKay, J. (2004, September 6). "Big pay gap between men, women persists," Post-Gazette.com—A Service of the Pittsburgh Post Gazette. Retrieved October 2, 2005, from http://www.post-gazette.com/pg/04250/374143.stm

Miller, M. (2005). "The 400 Richest Americans." Forbes.com

Mishel, L., & Schmitt, J. (1995). *Cutting wages by cutting welfare: The impact of reform on the low wage labor market.* Washington, DC: The Economic Policy Institute.

Mone, M. A., Baker, D. D., & Jeffries, F. (1995). Predictive validity and time dependency of self-efficacy, self-esteem, personal goals, and academic performance. *Educational and Psychological Measurement, 55,* 716–727.

National Center for Children in Poverty (n.d.). "Immigrant children in the U.S. are growing in numbers & facing substantial economic hardships." Retrieved October 2, 2005, from http://www.nccp.org/immigrants.html

National Center for Children in Poverty (2002). "Early childhood poverty: A statistical profile." Retrieved October 2, 2005, from http://www.nccp.org/pub_ecp02.html

National Center for Children in Poverty (2003, March). "Child Poverty Fact Sheet." *Low social welfare: Politics and public policy.* National Center for Children in Poverty. Retrieved October 2, 2005, from http://www.nccp.org/ycpf_03.html

National Economic Council, State of the Union Address of President William Jefferson Clinton. Retrieved October 2, 2005, from http://clinton5.nara.gov/WH/EOP/nec/html/2000SotuBookFinal.html

Nibert, D. (2000). *Hitting the lottery jackpot: State governments and the taxing of dreams.* New York: Monthly Review Press.

O'Hare, W. P. (1996). A new look at poverty in America. *Population Bulletin, 51*(2), 1–48.

Page, B. I., & Simmons, J. R. (2000). *What government can do: Dealing with poverty and inequality.* Chicago: The University of Chicago Press.

Parker, S., Greer, S., & Zuckerman, B. (1988). Double jeopardy: The impact of poverty on early childhood development. *Pediatric Clinics of North America, 35,* 10.

Peikoff, L. (1993). *Health care is not a right.* Delivered at a Town Hall Meeting on the Clinton Health Plan. Red Lion Hotel, Costa Mesa, CA, December 11, 1993. Retrieved October 2, 2005, from http://www.bdt.com/pages/Peikoff.html

Peirce, R. S., Frone, M. R., Russell, M., & Cooper, M. L. (1994). Relationship of financial strain & psychosocial resources to alcohol use and abuse: The mediating role of negative affect and drinking motives. *Journal of Health and Social Behavior, 35,* 291–308.

Ricketts, E., & Sawhill, I. (1988). Defining and measuring the underclass. *Journal of Policy Analysis & Management, 7*(2), 316–325.

Rodgers, H. (2000). *American poverty in a new era of reform.* Armonk, NY: M. E. Sharpe.

Rodgers, H. R. (1979). *Poverty amid plenty: A political and economic analysis.* Reading, MA: Addison–Wesley.

Rotella, E. J. (1998). *Women and the American economy* (S. Ruth, Ed.). Mountain View, CA: Mayfield.

Salary.com Web site. Retrieved November 24, 2003, from http://www.salary.com

Scanlan, J., Watson, D., McLanahan, S., & Sorensen, A. (1991). Comment on McLanahan, Sorensen, & Watson's sex differences in poverty. *Signs, 16*(2), 409–413.

Schiller, B. (1994). Who are the working poor? *The Public Interest, Spring,* 61–71.

Schmolling, P., Yonkeles, M., & Burger, W. R. (1997). *Human services in contemporary America* (4th ed.). Pacific Grove, CA: Brook/Cole.

Seccombe, K. (1999). *So you think I drive a Cadillac? Welfare recipients' perspectives on the system and its reform.* Boston: Allyn & Bacon.

Seligman, M. E. P. (n.d.). *Mission statement.* The Seligman Research Alliance web page. Retrieved November 24, 2003, from http://www.positivepsychology.org/mission.htm

Seligman, M. E. P. (1990). *Learned optimism.* New York: Knopf.

Seligman, M. E. P., & Schulman, P. (1986). Explanatory style as a predictor of productivity and quitting among life insurance agents. *Journal of Personality and Social Psychology, 50,* 832–838.

Seligman, et al. Penn Optimism Program (POP) and the Penn Enhancement Program (PEP), as described at http://www.positivepsychology.org/prpsum.htm

Shortridge, C. (1989). *Women: A feminist perspective* (4th ed.). Palo Alto, CA: Mayfield.

Sjoquist, D. (1990). *A review of the literature regarding the urban underclass, Appendix B.* Unpublished manuscript.

Social inequality and poverty increasing worldwide (1999, August). Retrieved October 5, 2005, from www.wsws.org/articles/1999/aug1999/un-a06.shtml

Stagg, E. J. (1999, August 23). From the welfare rolls: A mother's view. *Newsweek, 40,* 10.

Staples, R., & Johnson, L. B. (1993). *Black families at the crossroads: Challenges and prospects.* San Francisco: Jossey-Bass.

Stein, J. (2003, January 20). The real face of homelessness. *Time, 161,* 53–67.

Takenchy, D., Williams, D., & Adair, R. (1991). Economic stress in the family and children's emotional and behavioral problems. *Journal of Marriage & the Family, 53,* 1,031–1,041.

Tripp, R. T. (Ed.). (1976). *The international thesaurus of quotations*, p. 76, no. 3. Harmondsworth, Middlesex: Penguin Books.

United Nations General Assembly, Universal Declaration of Human Rights, December 10, 1948.

U.S. Bureau of the Census, Current Population Survey, Annual Social and Economic Supplements. (2002). Poverty and Health Statistics Branch/HHES Division. Retrieved November 24, 2003, from http://www.census.gov/hhes/www/poverty/histpov/hstpov2.html

U.S. Census Bureau. (2004). "Poverty Thresholds 2004." Retrieved September 29, 2005, from http://www.census.gov/hhes/www/poverty/threhold/thresh04.html

U.S. Census Bureau Press Release. Retrieved November 24, 2003, from http://www.census.gov/hhes/poverty/povdef.html

U.S. Department of Labor. (2001). *Beyond shelter: Housing first.* In U.S. Department of Labor Welfare to Work Initiatives. Retrieved September 16, 2001, from http://www.dol.gov

U.S. Government Census Bureau. (2001). Press release. Retrieved September 25, 2001, from http://www.census.gov/Press-Release/www/2001/cb01-158.htm

U.S. Government Federal Register. (2003). *2001 HHS Poverty Guidelines 66*(33), 10,695–10,697.

Voydanoff, P. (1990). Economic distress and family relations: A review of the eighties. *Journal of Marriage & the Family, 52,* 1,099–1,115.

Wilson, W. (1987). *The truly disadvantaged.* Chicago: The University of Chicago Press.

Wolfenson, J. (1998). *The other crisis.* World Bank, October 1998. In *The reality of aid 2000.* London: Earthscan, 2000, p. 10.

Zastrow, C. (2000). *Social problems* (5th ed.). Belmont, CA: Wadsworth.

Zastrow, C., & Kirst-Ashman, K. (2001). *Understanding human behavior and the social environment.* Belmont, CA: Brooks/Cole.

Chapter 15: Race

Anderson, E. (2002). Integration, affirmative action and strict scrutiny. *NYU Law Review, 77,* 1,195–1,271.

Ascher, C. (1993). The changing face of racial isolation and desegregation in urban schools. [Electronic version.] Retrieved May 22, 2003, from http://eric-web.tc.columbia.edu/digest/dig91.asp

Bachman, R. (1992). *Death and violence on the reservation: Homicide, family violence and suicide in American Indian populations.* New York: Auburn House.

Brooks, D. H. M. (1987). Why discrimination is especially wrong. *Journal of Value Inquiry 17* (1983), 305–312. Reprinted in T. Mappes & Jane Zembaty (Eds.), *Social Ethics.* New York: McGraw-Hill.

Buck, P. S. (1942). *American unity and Asia.* New York: John Day.

Cahn, S. M. (2002). *The affirmative action debates* (2nd ed.). New York: Routledge.

Canaday, C. T. (2001). Affirmative action has hindered civil rights. In M. Williams (Ed.), *Race relations: Opposing viewpoints.* San Diego, CA: Greenhaven Press.

Cantor, J. C., Miles, E. L., Baker, L. C., & Barker, D. C. (1996). Physician service to the underserved: Implications for affirmative action in medical education. *Inquiry, 33*(2), 167–180.

Churchill, W. (1994). *Indians are us? Culture and genocide in Native North America.* Monroe, ME: Common Courage Press.

Cobb, K. (2002a). Civil rights group split as priorities are changed. [Electronic version.] Retrieved May 22, 2003, from http://www.chron.com/cs/CDA/story.hts/special/deseg/1433460

Cobb, K. (2002b). After desegregation: Part II: Districts find no easy solution for school inequity. [Electronic version.] Retrieved May 22, 2003, from http://www.chron.com/cs/CDA/story.hts/metropolitan/1433440

Cobb, K., & Kimberly, J. (2002). After desegregation: Part III: Stakes high for Hispanics to raise achievement bar. [Electronic version]. Retrieved May 22, 2003, from http://www.chron.com/cs/CDA/story.hts/special/deseg/1437298

Cohen, M. N. (1998). *Culture of intolerance: Chauvinism, class, & racism in the United States.* London: Yale University Press.

Cose, E. (1997). *Color-blind: Seeing beyond race in a race-obsessed world.* New York: HarperCollins.

Daniels, R., & Kitano, H. H. L. (1970). *American racism: Exploration of the nature of prejudice.* Englewood Cliffs, NJ: Prentice Hall.

DuBois, E. B. (1947). Contributing editor sent to the United Nations in 1947 by the NAACP entitled *An appeal to the world.* Reprinted in W. E. B. DuBois, "Three centuries of discrimination," *The Crisis, 54* (1947), 380.

Dudziak, M. (2000). *Cold war civil rights.* Princeton, NJ: Princeton University Press.

Du Pont, P. (n.d.). Colorblindness is golden: Will Californians vote to join the human race? [Electronic version.] Retrieved May 22, 2003, from http://aad.english.ucsb.edu/docs/petedupoint.html

Ezorsky, G. (1991). *Racism and justice: The case for affirmative action.* Ithaca: Cornell University Press.

Farb, P. (1968). *Man's rise to civilization.* New York: Dutton.

Feagin, J. R. (1991). The continuing significance of race: Anti-black discrimination in public places. *American Sociological Review, 56,* 101–116.

Garcia, O. (1988). The education of biliterate and bicultural children in ethnic schools in the United States. *Essays by the Spencer Fellows of the National Academy of Education,* Vol. IV, 19–78.

Geyer, G. A. (2001). Schools should not employ bilingual education. In M. Williams (Ed.), *Race relations: Opposing viewpoints.* San Diego, CA: Greenhaven Press.

Hess, B. B., Markson, E. W., & Stein, P. J. (1995). *Racial and ethnic minorities: An overview.* In P. S. Rothenberg (Ed.), *Race, class, and gender in the United States: An integrated study* (3rd ed.) (pp. 176–188). New York: St. Martin's Press.

Hooks, B. L. (1991). Affirmative action benefits minorities. In W. Dudley (Ed.), *Racism in America: Opposing viewpoints.* San Diego, CA: Greenhaven Press.

Jaimes, M. A. (Ed.). (1992). *The state of Native America: Genocide, colonization, and resistance.* Boston: South End Press.

Johnson, K. (1993). Indians' casino money pumps up the volume. *New York Times,* September 1, 1993, B1.

Kennedy, J. F. (1964). Radio and television report to the American people on civil rights, June 11, 1963, *Public papers of the presidents of the United States: John F. Kennedy, 1963.* Washington, DC: Government Printing Office, p. 469.

Kennedy, R. (1997). *Race, crime, and the law.* New York: Vintage Books.

Kivel, P. (1995). *Uprooting racism: How white people can work for racial justice.* Philadelphia, PA: New Society.

Lee, T. (1991). Racism is a serious problem for Asian Americans. In W. Dudley, William (Ed.), *Racism in America: Opposing viewpoints.* San Diego, CA: Greenhaven Press.

Levin, M. (1987). Is racial discrimination special? *Journal of Value Inquiry, 15* (1981), 225–232. Reprinted in T. Mappes & Jane Zembaty (Eds.), *Social Ethics.* New York: McGraw-Hill.

MacSwan, J. (2001). Schools should employ bilingual education. In M. Williams (Ed.), *Race relations: Opposing viewpoints.* San Diego, CA: Greenhaven Press.

Massey, D. S., & Denton, N. A. (1993). *American apartheid: Segregation and the making of the underclass.* Cambridge, MA: Harvard University Press.

Matthews, J. (n.d.). White guys. [Electronic version.] Retrieved May 3, 2003, from http://www.colorado.edu/journals/standards/V5N2/AWARD/matthews.html

Miller, J. (1974). *This new man.* New York: McGraw-Hill.

Moore, R. B. (1995). *Racism in the English language.* In P. S. Rothenberg (Ed.), *Race, class, and gender in the United States: An integrated study* (3rd ed.) (pp. 376–386). New York: St. Martin's Press.

Moskos, C. (1986, May). Success story: Blacks in the military. *The Atlantic, 257*(5), 64–72.

Myrdal, G. (1944). *An American dilemma: The Negro problem and modern democracy.* New York: Harper and Row, p. 1,004.

Neckerman, K. M., & Kirschenman, J. (1991). Hiring strategies, racial bias, and inner-city workers. *Social Problems 38,* 433–452.

Novas, H. (1994). *Everything you need to know about Latino history.* New York: Penguin.

One America in the 21st Century: Forging a New Future. The President's Initiative on Race. The Advisory Board's Report to the President. [Electronic version.] Retrieved August 7, 2006, from http://clinton4.nara.gov/media/pdf/PIR.pdf

Root, M. P. (Ed.). (1992). *Racially mixed people in America.* Newbury Park, CA: Sage.

Serrie, J. (2001). The new segregation: Ethnic identity or racism? [Electronic version.] Retrieved May 20, 2003, from http://www.foxnews.com/story/0.2933.3331700.html

Shaheen, J. G. (1995). *T.V. Arabs.* In P. S. Rothenberg (Ed.), *Race, class, and gender in the United States: An integrated study* (3rd ed.) (pp. 197–199). New York: St. Martin's Press.

Sinclair, C., & Tharp, J. (1998). The failure of the desegregation of America's public schools. [Electronic version.] Retrieved May 20, 2003, from http://horizon.unc.edu/edsp287/1998/Issue%20papers/DESEG/desegregation.html

Snyder, M. (1995). *Self-fulfilling stereotypes.* In P. S. Rothenberg (Ed.), *Race, class, and gender in the United States: An integrated study* (3rd ed.) (pp. 170–176). New York: St. Martin's Press.

Steinberg, S. (2001). *The ethnic myth: Race, ethnicity, and class in America* (3rd ed.). Boston: Beacon Press.

Steinfield, M. (1970). *Cracks in the melting pot.* Beverly Hills, CA: Glencoe Press.

Steinhorn, L., & Diggs-Brown, B. (2001). Racial harmony does not prevail. In M. Williams (Ed.), *Race relations: Opposing viewpoints.* San Diego, CA: Greenhaven Press.

Thernstrom, S. (2000). *Paying for past sins: The debate over slavery reparations.* [Electronic version.] Retrieved May 20, 2003, from http://abcnews.go.com/sections/us/TakingSides/takingsides8.html

Tracinski, R.W. (2001). *America's field of blackbirds.* [Electronic version.] Retrieved May 20, 2003, from http://capmag.com/article.asp?ID=79

Walkins, R. (1995). *Racism has its privileges* [Electronic version]. Retrieved May 22, 2003, from http://aad.english.ucsb.edu/docs/Nation-3-27-95.html

Williams, W. (2001). *Reparations for slavery arguments are loaded with contradictions.* [Electronic version.] Retrieved May 22, 2003, from http://capmag.com/article.asp?ID=299

Woodley, J., & Horn, F. (n.d.). *Hot button issue: "Reparations for slavery?"* [Electronic version.] Retrieved May 22, 2003, from http://www.paradigmassociates.org/ParadigmHotButton.html

Zack, N. (1998). *Thinking about race.* Belmont, CA: Wadsworth.

Chapter 16: Infants, Children, and Adolescents

Ainsworth, M. (1983). Infant-mother attachment. *Enfance,* 7–18.

American Academy of Pediatrics (AAP) Task Force on Infant Positioning and SIDS. (1992). Positioning and SIDS. *Pediatrics, 89,* 1,120–1,126.

American Institute on Domestic Violence (2001). Domestic violence in the work place. Retrieved May 20, 2003, from http://www.aidv-usa.com

Aylward, G. (1997). *Infant and early childhood neuropsychology.* New York: Plenum Press.

Barber, J., Axinn, W., & Thornton, A. (1999). Unwanted childbearing, health, and mother-child relationships. *Journal of Health and Social Behavior, 40*(3): 231–257.

Becker-Lausen, E., Sanders, B., & Chinsky, J. M. (1995). Mediation of abusive childhood experiences: Depression, dissociation, and negative life outcomes. *American Journal of Orthopsychiatry, 65,* 560–573.

Berk, L. (1999). *Infants, children & adolescents.* Needham Heights, MA: Allyn and Bacon.

Bowlby, J. (1989). *A secure base: Clinical applications of attachment theory.* London: Routledge.

Brazelton, T. B., & Greenspan, S. I. (2000). *The irreducible needs of children: What every child must have to grow, learn, and flourish.* Cambridge, MA: Perseus Press.

Chao, K. R. (1996). Chinese and European American mothers' beliefs about the role of parenting in children's school success. *Journal of Cross-Cultural Psychology, 27*(4), 403–423.

Cobb, N. (1992). *Adolescence: Continuity, change and diversity.* Mountain View, CA: Mayfield Publishing Company.

Cunningham, M. (2001). The influence of parental attitudes and behaviors on children's attitudes toward gender and household labor in early adulthood. *Journal of Marriage and the Family, 63*(1): 111–122.

Erikson, E. H. (1950). *Childhood and society.* New York: Norton.

Finelli, L. (2001). Revisiting the identity issue in anorexia. *Journal of Psychosocial Nursing, 39*(8), 23–29.

Finkelhor, D., & Browne, A. (1985). The traumatic impact of child sexual abuse: A conceptualization. *American Journal of Orthopsychiatry, 55,* 530–541.

Forum on Child and Family Statistics (2001). *America's children: Key national indicators of well-being.* Washington DC: U.S. Government Printing Office.

Freier, M. C. (1998). *When a parent dies: Supporting the children, an aid for caregivers.* Picking up the pieces series. (Available from Service Corporation International, 1929 Allen Parkway, Houston, Texas.)

Freier, M. C. (1999a). Family violence: The effect on children. In B. Couden (Ed.), *Understanding intimate violence.* Hagerstown, MD: Review & Herald Publishing Association.

Freier, M. C. (1999b). *Saving our children: What you can do.* Picking up the pieces series. (Available from Service Corporation International, 1929 Allen Parkway, Houston, Texas.)

Furstenberg, F. (2000). The sociology of adolescence and youth in the 1990s: A critical commentary. *Journal of Marriage and the Family, 62*(4), 896–910.

Garbarino, J. (1999). *Lost boys: Why our sons turn violent and how we can save them.* New York: Free Press.

Giles-Sims, J. (1985). A longitudinal study of battered women. In S. K. Wilson (Ed.), *Family Relations, 34,* 205–210.

Goetting, A. (1994). Do Americans really like children? *Journal of Primary Prevention, 15*(1): 81–92.

Harris, J. (1998). *The nurture assumption: Why children turn out the way they do.* New York: Touchstone.

Haynie, D. (2001). Delinquent peers revisited: Does network structure matter? *American Journal of Sociology, 106*(4): 1,013–1,057.

Hedley, A. A., Ogden, C. L., Johnson, C. L., Carroll, M. D., Curtin, L. R. & Flegal, K. M. (2004). Prevalence of overweight and obesity among US children, adolescents, and adults, 1999–2002. *JAMA 291*(23), 2,847–2,850.

Horchler, J. N., & Morris, R. R. (1997). *The SIDS survival guide.* Hyattsville, MD: SIDS Educational Services.

Jaffe, P. G., Wolfe, D. A., & Wilson S. K. (1990). *Children of battered women.* Newbury Park, CA: Sage Press.

Lashbrook, J. (2000). Fitting in: Exploring the emotional dimension of adolescent peer pressure. *Adolescence, 35*(140), 747–757.

Lundy, B., Jones, N. A., Field, T., Nearing, G., Davalos, M., Pietro, P., Schanberg, S., & Kuhn, C. (1999). Prenatal depression effects on neonates. *Infant Behavior and Development, 22*(1), 119–129.

Matsumoto, D. (2000). *Culture and psychology: People around the world* (2nd ed.). Belmont, CA: Wadsworth.

Matsumoto, D., & Juang L. (2004). *Culture and psychology* (3rd ed.). Belmont, CA: Wadsworth/Thomson Learning.

Montessori, M. (1974). *Childhood education.* Chicago: Regnery.

National Clearinghouse on Child Abuse and Neglect Information (2005). *Child Maltreatment 2003: Summary of Key Findings.* Retrieved September 7, 2006, from http://nccanch.acf.hhs.gov

O'Hare, B. (1999). *1999 Kids count survey.* New York: Free Press.

Oropesa, R. S., Landale, N. S., Inkley, M., & Gorman, B. K. (2000). Prenatal care among Puerto Ricans on the United States mainland. *Social-Science and Medicine, 51*(12), 1,723–1,739.

Rochat, P., & Striano, T. (1999). Social-cognitive development in the first year. In P. Rochat (Ed.), *Early social cognition: Understanding others in the first months of life.* Mahwah, NJ: Lawrence Erlbaum.

Roosevelt, F. D. (1936), as cited in Westman, J. C. (1991). *Who speaks for the children? The handbook of individual and class child advocacy.* Sarasota, FL: Professional Resource Exchange.

Sallis, J. F., & McKenzie, T. L. (1991). Physical education's role in public health. *Research Quarterly in Exercise Sport, 62*(2), 124–137.

Short, J. (2001). *Youth collectivities and adolescent violence.* Handbook of youth and justice. New York: Kluwer Academic/Plenum Publishers.

Simons R., Chao, W., Conger, R., & Elder, G. (2001). Quality of parenting as mediator of the effect of childhood defiance on adolescent friendship choices and delinquency: A growth curve analysis. *Journal of Marriage and the Family, 63*(1), 63–79.

Slutsker, L., Smith, R., Higginson, G., & Fleming, D. (1993). Recognizing illicit drug use by pregnant women: Reports from Oregon birth attendants. *American Journal of Public Health, 83*(1), 61–64.

Smithey, M. (1997). Infant homicide at the hands of mothers: Toward a sociological perspective. *Deviant Behavior, 18*(3), 255–272.

Smithey, M. (1998). Infant homicide: Victim/offender relationship and causes of death. *Journal of Family Violence, 13*(3), 285–297.

Stark, R. (1989). *Sociology* (3rd ed.). Belmont, CA: Wadsworth.

Thomas, A., & Chess, S. (1977). *Temperament and development.* New York: Brunner/Mazel.

Thompson, K., Wonderlich, S., Crosby, R. D., & Mitchell, J. (2001). Sexual violence and weight control techniques among adolescent girls. *International Journal of Eating Disorders, 29*(2): 166–176.

Toffler, A. (1971). *Future shock.* New York: Bantam Books.

Toffler, A. (1981). *The third wave.* New York: Bantam Books.

Toffler, A. (1990). *Powershift: Knowledge, wealth and violence at the edge of the 21st century.* New York: Bantam Books.

Trzcinski, J. (1992). Heavy metal kids: Are they dancing with the devil? *Child & Youth Care Forum, 21*(1), 7–22.

UNAIDS (2000). Report on global HIV/AIDS. Internet resource.

U.S. Department of Health & Human Services, Children's Bureau (2000).

Westman, J. C. (1991). *Who speaks for the children? The handbook of individual and class child advocacy.* Sarasota, FL: Professional Resource Exchange, Inc.

Wolfelt, A. (1983). *Helping children cope with grief.* Muncie, IN: Accelerated Development, Inc.

Chapter 17: Feminism

Acierno, R., & Kilpatrick, D. G. (1996, October). Violent assault, posttraumatic stress disorder, and depression. *Behavior Modification, 20*(4), 363–385.

Ahlander, N., & Bahr, K. (1995). Beyond drudgery, power, and equity: Toward an expanded discourse on the moral dimensions of housework in families. *Journal of Marriage and the Family, 57,* 54–68.

Aikin, O. (1999, July). Legal Checklist. *People Management, 5*(12), 23.

Alexander, S., & Ryan, M. (1997, December). Social constructs of feminism: A study of undergraduates at a women's college. *College Student Journal, 31*(4), 555–568.

Allen, J. (1989). Women who beget women must thwart major sophisms. In A. Garry & M. Pearsall (Eds.), *Women, knowledge, and reality: Explorations in feminist philosophy* (pp. 37–46). Boston: Unwin Hyman.

Almeida, D. A. (1997). The hidden half: A history of Native American women's education. *Harvard Educational Review, 67*(4), 757–771.

Baker, R., Kiger, G., & Riley, P. (1996). Time, dirt, and money: The effects of gender, gender ideology, and type of earner marriage on time, household task, and economic satisfaction among couples with children. *Journal of Social Behavior and Personality, 11*(5), 161–178.

Barnett, R. C., & Shen, Y. C. (1997, July). Gender, high- and- low schedule-control housework tasks, and psychological distress. *Journal of Family Issues, 18*(4), 403.

Blankenship, K. (1990). Rediscovering American women: A chronology highlighting women's history in the United States and update—the process continues. In S. Ruth (Ed.), *Issues in feminism* (pp. 431–443). Mountain View, CA: Mayfield.

Blau, F. D. (1998, March). Trends in the well-being of American women, 1970–1995. *Journal of Economic Literature, 36*(1), 112–166.

Brookner, J. (1991, Summer). Feminism and students of the '80s and '90s. *Art Journal, 50*(2), 11–14.

Bulbeck, C. (1999). Simone de Beauvoir and generations of feminists. *Hecate, 25*(2), 5–22.

Butts-Stahly, G. (1999). Women with children in violent relationships: The choice of leaving may bring the consequence of custodial challenge. *Journal of Aggression, Maltreatment & Trauma, 2*(2), 239–251.

Byrne, E. (1993). *Women and science: The snark syndrome.* London: Falmer Press.

Campbell, J. C. (1999). Forced sex and intimate partner violence: Effects on women's risk and women's health. *Violence against Women, 51*(9), 1,017–1,026.

CDC. Costs of intimate partner violence against women in the United States. (2003). U.S. Department of Health and Human Services, CDC. Atlanta (GA). Retrieved October 2, 2005, from http://www.cdc.gov.ncipc/pb-res/ipv.htm

Chittister, J. D. (1998). *Heart of flesh: A feminist spirituality for women and men.* Grand Rapids, MI: William B. Eerdmans.

Conn, J. W. (1993). Toward spiritual maturity. In C. M. LaCugna (Ed.), *Freeing theology: The essentials of theology in feminist perspective* (pp. 235–259). New York: Harper San Francisco.

Crooks, R., & Baur, K. (1993). *Our sexuality.* Redwood City, CA: Benjamin Cummings.

Cullen-DuPont, K. (1996). *The encyclopedia of women's history in America.* New York: Facts on File.

Cummings, E., Zahn-Wexler, C., & Radke-Yarrow, M. (1981). Young children's responses to expressions of anger and affection by others in the family. *Child Development, 52,* 1,274–1,282.

Davidson, J. (1996, October). Risk of suicide and past history of sexual assault. *American Family Physician, 54*(5), 1,756–1,758.

Dobash, R. E., & Dobash, R. (1979). *Violence against wives: A case against the patriarchy.* New York: The Free Press.

Dupre, A., Hampton, H., & Meeks, G. (1993). Sexual assault. *Obstetrical and Gynecological Survey, 48,* 640–648.

Eakin, E. (2001, January 28). Women behaving badly. *The New York Times,* p12(L) col 02 (18 col in).

Einarsson, C., & Granstrom, K. (2002). Gender-biased interaction in the classroom: The influence of gender and age in the relationship between teacher and pupil. *Scandinavian Journal of Educational Research, 46*(2), 117–127.

Faludi, S. (1996, January 1–15). Who's calling whom elitist? *Nation, 262*(2), 25–28.

Ferraro, K. F. (1996). Women's fear of victimization: Shadow of sexual assault. *Social Forces, 75*(2), 667–681.

Fields, S. (1998, February 2). Thank Heaven for little girls. *Insight on the News, 14*(4), 48.

Fineran, S., & Bennett, L. (1999, June). Gender and power issues of peer sexual harassment among teenagers. *Journal of Interpersonal Violence, 14*(6), 626–642.

Firestone, J. M., & Harris, R. J. (1999, Summer). Changes in patterns of sexual harassment in the U.S. military: A comparison of the 1988 and 1995 DOD surveys. *Armed Forces & Society, 25*(4), 614–624.

Fitzgerald, L., & Hesson-McInnis, M. (1989). The dimensions of sexual harassment: A structural analysis. *Journal of Vocational Behavior, 35,* 309–326.

Ford, C. A., & Donis, F. J. (1996, November). The relationship between age and gender in workers' attitudes toward sexual harassment. *Journal of Psychology Interdisciplinary & Applied, 130*(6), 627–634.

Freeman, M. L. (1990). Beyond women's issues: Feminism and social work. *Affilia: Journal of Women & Social Work, 5*(2), 72–80.

Gagne, P. (1996, February). Identity, strategy, and feminist politics: Clemency for battered women who kill. *Social Problems, 43*(1), 77–93.

Gidlow, E. (1990). The spiritual significance of the self-identified woman. In S. Ruth (Ed.), *Issues in feminism: An introduction to women's studies* (pp. 414–417). Mountain View, CA: Mayfield.

Gilbert, N. (1998). Realities and mythologies of rape. *Society, 35*(2), 356–363.

Glass, T. E. (1992). *The study of the American school superintendency.* Arlington, VA: American Association of School Administrators.

Goldin, C. (1990). Women's quest for equality (book review). *Industrial and Labor Relations Review, 44,* 167–169.

Grogan, M. (1999, October). Equity/equality issues of gender, race, and class. *Educational Administration Quarterly, 35*(4), 518–537.

Gross, R. (1996). *Feminism and religion: An introduction.* Boston: Beacon Press.

Gruber, J. E. (1998, June). The impact of male work environments and organizational policies on women's experiences of sexual harassment. *Gender & Society, 12*(3), 301–321.

Gutek, B., Cohen A. G., & Conrad A. M. (1990). Predicting social-sexual behavior at work: A conflict hypothesis. *Academy of Management Journal, 33,* 560–577.

Gutek, B. A., & Koss, M. P. (1993). Changed women and changed organizations: Consequences of and coping with sexual harassment. *Journal of Vocational Behavior, 42*(1), 28–48.

Hafner, R. J. (1986). *Marriage and mental illness: A sex-roles perspective.* New York: The Guilford Press.

Hamby, S. L. (1998). Partner violence: Prevention and intervention. In J. L. Jasinski & L. M. Williams (Eds.), *Partner violence: A comprehensive review of 20 years of research* (pp. 210–258). Thousand Oaks: Sage.

Hamilton, G., & Coates, J. (1993). Perceived helpfulness and use of professional services by abused women. *Journal of Family Violence, 8,* 313–324.

Harris, R. J., & Firestone, J. M. (1998). Changes in predictors of gender role ideologies among women: A multivariate analysis. *Sex Roles, 38*(3/4), 239–252.

Heise, L. (1993). Reproductive freedom and violence against women: Where are the intersections? *Journal of Law Medicine and Ethics, 21*(2), 206–216.

Hendrix, W. H., Rueb, J. D., & Steel, R. P. (1998). Sexual harassment and gender differences. *Journal of Social Behavior & Personality, 13*(2), 235–253.

Hercus, C. (1999, February). Identity, emotions, and feminist collective action. *Gender and Society, 13*(1), 34–56.

Hochschild, A., & Machung, M. (1989). *The second shift.* New York: Viking.

Hunter, A. G., & Sellers, S. L. (1998, February). Feminist attitudes among African American women and men. *Gender & Society, 12*(1), 81–100.

Hutchings, N. (1994). Sexism promotes violence against women. In K. L. Swisher & C. Wekesser (Eds.), *Violence against women: Current controversies* (pp. 33–38). San Diego, CA: Greenhaven Press.

Iannone, C. (1995, June). What moderate feminists? *Commentary, 99*(6), 46.

Jameson, F. (1997, July/August). Sexual harassment. *Journal of Property Management, 62*(4), 36–40.

John, D., & Shelton, B. A. (1995). Race, ethnicity, gender, and perception of fairness. *Journal of Family Issues, 16*(3), 357–380.

Jones, L. (1995, May). Sister knowledge. *Essence, 26*(1), 187–192.

Jones, M. G., & Wheatley, J. (1990). Gender differences in teacher-student interactions in science classrooms. *Journal of Research in Science Teaching, 27,* 861–874.

Kasinky, R. G. (1998, February). Tailhook and the construction of sexual harassment in the media. *Violence against Women, 4*(1), 81–100.

Kelly, K. J., & Stanley, L. R. (1999, December). Faculty perceptions and experiences of student behavior: Does gender matter? *Journal of Marketing Education, 21*(3), 194–206.

Kennedy, J. E., Davis, R. C., & Taylor, Bruce G. (1998). Changes in spirituality and well-being among victims of sexual assault. *Journal for the Scientific Study of Religion, 37*(2), 322–329.

Kersten, K. (1991). What do women want? *Policy Review, 56,* 4.

Knapp, D. E., & Kustis, G. A. (1996). The real "disclosure": Sexual harassment and the bottom line. In M. S. Stockdale (Ed.), *Sexual harassment in the workplace: Perspectives, frontiers, and response strategies* (pp. 199–213). Thousand Oaks, CA: Sage.

Kopels, S., & Dupper, D. R. (1999, July/August). School-based peer sexual harassment. *Child Welfare, 78*(4), 435–461.

Korenman, S., & Newmark, D. (1992, Spring). Marriage, motherhood, and wages. *Journal of Human Resources, 26*(2), 233–255.

Koss, M. P. (1993, October). Rape: Scope, impact, interventions, and public policy responses. *American Psychologist, 48*(10), 1,062–1,069.

Kuczynski, A. (2001, April 2). The age of diminishing innocence: Magazines shift focus as teenage girls seem to be maturing sooner. *The New York Times,* pC1(L) col 02 (47 col in).

Laband, D. N., & Lentz, B. F. (1998, July). The effects of sexual harassment on job satisfaction, earnings, and turnover among female lawyers. *Industrial & Labor Relations Review, 51*(4), 596–608.

LaCugna, C. M. (1993). Introduction. In C. M. LaCugna (Ed.), *Freeing theology: The essentials of theology in feminist perspective* (pp. 1–4). New York: Harper San Francisco.

Lampman, J. (1998, August 20). Choosing the seminary at a difficult time. *Christian Science Monitor, 90*(187), B3.

Lehrman, K. (2000, November 12). The new new woman. (Book Review Desk). *The New York Times,* p. 30.

Lemke, J. (1990). *Talking science: Language, learning and values.* Norwood, NJ: Ablex.

Leitich, K. A. (1999, Summer). Sexual harassment in higher education. *Education, 119*(4), 688–693.

Levinger, G. (1966, October). Sources of marital dissatisfaction among applicants for divorce. *American Journal of Orthopsychiatry, 26,* 803–807.

Littler, B., Seidler-Feller, D., & Opaluch, R. (1982). Sexual harassment in the workplace as a function of initiator's status: The case of airline personnel. *Journal of Social Issues, 38,* 137–148.

Livingston, M. M., Burley, K., Suchet, M., & Barling, J. (1996). The importance of being feminine: Gender, sex, role, occupational and marital role commitment, and their relationship to anticipated work-family conflict. *Journal of Social Behavior & Personality, 11*(5), 179–193.

Lown, J. (1995). Feminist perspectives. In M. Blair, J. Holland, & S. Sheldon (Eds.), *Identity and diversity: Gender and the experience of education* (pp. 107–121). Clevedon: Multilingual Matters.

Luckman, S. (1999). (EN)Gendering the digital body: Feminism and the Internet. *Hecate, 25*(2), 36–48.

Luker, K. (1994). Abortion and the meaning of life. In D. Wells (Ed.), *Getting there: The movement toward gender equality* (pp. 98–121). New York: Carroll & Graf Publishers/Richard Gallen.

Mahoney, P. (1999). High rape chronicity and low rates of help-seeking among wife rape survivors in nonclinical sample: Implications for research and practices. *Violence against Women, 5*(9), 993–1,017.

Marini, M., & Brinton, M. (1984). Sex typing in occupational socialization. In B. Reskin (Ed.), *Sex segregation in the workplace: Trends, explanations, remedies.* Washington, DC: National Academy Press.

Marsiglia, F. F., & Holleran, L. (1999, October). I've learned so much from my mother: Narratives from a group of Chicana high school students. *Social Work in Education, 21*(4), 220–238.

Maypole, D. (1986). Sexual harassment of social workers at work: Injustice within? *Social Work, 31*(1), 29–34.

McCormick, J. S., & Maric, A. (1998). Relationship to victim predicts sentence length in sexual assault cases. *Journal of Interpersonal Violence, 13*(3), 413–421.

McGregor, M. J., Le, G., Marion, S. A., & Wiebe, E. (1999, June 1). Examination for sexual assault: Is the documentation of physical injury associated with the laying of charges? A retrospective cohort study. *Canadian Medical Association Journal, 160*(11), 1,565–1,569.

McLaughlin, J. (1997, March). Feminist relations with postmodernism: Reflections on the positive aspects of involvement. *Journal of Gender Studies, 6*(1), 11–15.

Mederer, H. (1993). Division of labor in two-earner homes: Task accomplishment versus household management as critical variables in perceptions about family work. *Journal of Marriage and the Family, 55,* 133–145.

Miller, D. C. (1994). What is needed for true equality: An overview of policy issues for women. In L. V. Davis (Ed.), *Building on women's strengths: A social work agenda for the twenty-first century* (pp. 27–56). New York: The Haworth Press.

Morgan, P. A. (1999). Risking relationships: Understanding the litigation choices of sexually harassed women. *Law & Society Review, 33*(1), 67–93.

Morrissey, S. (1975). The "Rape" of Mr. Smith. In *Women helping women: Volunteer resource manual.* Urbana, IL: Rape Crisis Services.

Murphy, J. D., Driscoll, D. M., & Kelly, J. R. (1999, March). Differences in the nonverbal behavior of men who vary in the likelihood to sexually harass. *Journal of Social Behavior & Personality, 14*(1), 113–129.

Murrell, A. J. (1996). Sexual harassment and women of color: Issues, challenges, and future directions. In Stockdale, M. S. (Ed.), *Sexual harassment in the workplace: Perspectives, frontiers, and response strategies.* Thousand Oaks, CA: Sage.

Murrell, A., Frieze, O., & Frieze, I. (1995). Sexual harassment and gender discrimination: A longitudinal study of women managers. *Journal of Social Issues, 51*(1), 139–149.

National Center for Education Statistics. (2004). Retrieved February 15, 2004, from http://nces.ed.gov/fastfacts/display.asp?id=28

National Center for Victims of Crime & Crime Victims' Research and Treatment Center (1992). *Rape-related posttraumatic stress disorder.* Retrieved February 13, 2004, from http://www.ncvc.org/gethelp/raperelatedptsd

National Institute of Justice (2001). The effects of arrest on intimate partner violence: New evidence from the spouse assault replication program. *Research in Brief.*

Neville, H. A., & Pugh, A. O. (1997). General and culture-specific factors influencing African American women's reporting. *Violence against Women, 3*(4), 361–382.

Nussbaum, M. C. (1999). *Sex & social justice.* Oxford: Oxford University Press.

O'Brian, J. E. (1971). Violence in divorce-prone families. *Journal of Marriage and the Family, 33,* 692–698.

Padavic, I., & Orcutt, J. D. (1997). Perceptions of sexual harassment in the Florida legal system. *Gender and Society, 11*(5), 682–699.

Pavalko, E. K., & Elder, G. H. (1993). Women behind the men: Variation in wives' support of husbands' careers. *Gender and Society, 7,* 548–567.

Pennell, J., & Ristock, J. L. (1999, Winter). Feminist links, postmodern interruptions: Critical pedagogy and social work. *Affilia: Journal of Women & Social Work, 14*(4), 460–482.

Pittman, J., & Teng, W. (1999, November). Satisfaction with performance of housework. *Journal of Family Issues, 20*(6), 746–771.

Porter, L. E., & Alison, L. (2004). Behavioral coherence in violent group activity: An interpersonal model of sexually violent gang behaviour. *Aggressive Behavior, 30,* 449–468.

Powell, E. (1991). *Talking back to sexual pressure: What to say to resist persuasion, to avoid disease, to stop harassment, to avoid acquaintance rape.* Minneapolis, MN: CompCare.

Press, J., & Townsley, E. (1998, April). Wives' and husbands' housework reporting. *Gender & Society, 12*(2), 188–219.

Rennison, C. (2003). Intimate partner violence, 1993–2001. Washington, DC: Bureau of Justice Statistics, U.S. Department of Justice. Publication No. NCJ 197838.

Renzetti, C. M., & Curran, D. J. (1992). *Women, men, and society.* Needham Heights, MA: Allyn & Bacon.

Reskin, B., & Padavic, I. (1994). *Women and men at work.* Thousand Oaks: Pine Forge Press.

Richman, J. A., Rospenda, K. M., Nawyn, S. J., Flaherty, J. A., Fendrich, M., Drum, M. L., & Johnson, T. P. (1999, March). Sexual harassment and generalized workplace abuse among university employees: Prevalence and mental health correlates. *American Journal of Public Health, 89*(3), 358–364.

Rickert, V. I., Wiemann, C. M., & Vaughan, R. D. (2005). Disclosure of date/acquaintance rape: Who reports and when. *Journal of Pediatric and Adolescent Gynecology, 18,* 17–24.

Riley, P. J., & Kiger, G. (1999). Moral discourse on domestic labor: Gender, power, and identity in families. *Social Science Journal, 36*(3), 541–549.

Risley-Curtiss, C., & Hudson, W. W. (1998, Summer). Sexual harassment of social work students. *Affilia: Journal of Women in Social Work, 13*(2), 190–211.

Robinson, J., & Milkie, M. (1998, February). Back to the basics. *Journal of Marriage & the Family, 60*(1), 205–219.

Rosen, L. N., & Martin, L. (1998, August). Predictors of tolerance of sexual harassment among male U.S. army soldiers. *Violence against Women, 4*(4), 491–504.

Sanchez, L., & Kane, E. (1996, May). Women's and men's constructions of perceptions of housework fairness. *Journal of Family Issues, 17*(3), 358–380.

Saunders, B. E., Villeponteaux, L. A., Lipovsky, J. A., Killpatrick, D. G., & Vetohen, L. J. (1992). Child sexual assault as a risk factor for mental disorders among women: A community survey. *Journal of Interpersonal Violence, 7,* 189–204.

Schaef, A. W. (1992). *Women's reality: An emerging female system in a white male society.* New York: HarperCollins.

Schreck, L. (1999). Women with gynecologic symptoms are more likely than other women to have a history of sexual assault. *Family Planning Perspectives, 31*(3), 151–152.

Schwartz, M. D. (1999). Bad dates or emotional trauma? The aftermath of campus sexual assault. *Violence against Women, 5*(3), 251–272.

Sev'er, A. (1999). Sexual harassment: Where we were, where we are and prospects for the new millennium. *Canadian Review of Sociology & Anthropology, 36*(4), 469–489.

Sewell, B. D. (1994). Traditional male/female roles promote domestic violence. In K. L. Swisher & C. Wekesser (Eds.), *Violence against women: Current controversies* (pp. 19–32). San Diego, CA: Greenhaven Press.

Sexual harassment and discrimination (1997). *Journal of Accountancy, 184*(5), 8.

She, H. (2001). Different gender students' participation in the high- and low-achieving middle school questioning-orientation biology classrooms in Taiwan. *Research in Science & Technological Education, 19*(2), 147–158.

Sherman, L., & Berk, R. (1984). The specific deterrent effects of arrest for domestic assault. *American Sociological Review, 49,* 261–272.

Simon, R. J., & Danziger, G. (1991). *Women's movements in America: Their successes, disappointments, and aspirations.* New York: Praeger.

Solinger, R. (1994). Extreme danger: Women abortionists and their clients before Roe v. Wade. In Meyerowitz, J. (Ed.), *Not June Cleaver: Women and gender in postwar America, 1945–1960.* Philadelphia: Temple University Press.

Spear, M. (1984). The biasing influence of pupil sex in a science marking exercise. *Research in Science and Technology Education, 2,* 55–60.

Strube, M. J. (1988). The decision to leave an abusive relationship: Empirical evidence and theoretical issues. *Psychological Bulletin, 104,* 236–250.

Sullivan, O. (1997, March). The division of housework among "remarried couples." *Journal of Family Issues, 18*(2), 205–224.

Tingey, H., Kiger, G., & Riley, P. J. (1996). Juggling multiple roles: Perceptions of working mothers. *Social Science Journal, 33,* 183–191.

Tjaden, P., & Thonnes, N. (2000, November). *Full report of the prevalence, incidence, and consequences of violence against women research report: Findings from the National Violence against Women Survey.* Washington, DC: U.S. Department of Justice/Centers for Disease Control and Prevention.

Tobias, S. (1997). *Faces of feminism: An activist's reflections on the women's movement.* Boulder, CO: Westview Press.

Tolman, R., & Edleson, J. (1995). Intervention for men who batter: A review of research. In S. Stith & M. Straus (Eds.), *Understanding partner violence: Prevalence, causes, consequences, and solutions* (pp. 262–273). Minneapolis, MN: National Council on Family Relations.

Ullman, S. E. (1996). Correlates and consequences of adult sexual assault. *Journal of Interpersonal Violence, 11*(4), 554–572.

Ullman, S. E., Karabatsos, G., & Koss, M. P. (1999). Alcohol and sexual assault in a national sample of college women. *Journal of Interpersonal Violence, 14*(6), 603–626.

U.S. Department of Justice (1999). *Domestic violence.* Retrieved February 13, 2004, from http://www.ojp.gov/ovc/assist/nvaa99/chap8.htm

U.S. Department of Justice. (2003). *Number and percent distribution of incidents, by type of crime and victim-offender relationship.* Retrieved December 23, 2005, from the Office of Justice Programs Bureau of Justice Statistics: http://www.ojp.usdoj.gov/bjs/abstract/cvus/number of incidents745

Walker, L. (1979). *The battered woman.* New York: Harper.

Walzer, S. (1996). Thinking about the baby: Gender and divisions of infant care. *Social Problems, 43*(2), 219–234.

Will, G. F. (1999, March 29). Lies, damned lies and… *Newsweek, 133*(13), 84.

Wyatt, G. E., & Riederle, M. (1995, September). The prevalence and context of sexual harassment among African American and white American women. *Journal of Interpersonal Violence, 10*(3), 306–319.

Zorza, J. (1993). Mandatory arrest for domestic violence: Why it may prove the best first step in curbing repeat abuse. *Criminal Justice, 3,* 2–9 & 51–54.

Chapter 18: Economic Markets and Government Mandates

CNN Money. (2002). *Judge OKs Microsoft settlement.* Retrieved November 24, 2003, from http://www.money.cnn.com/2002/11/01/technology/microsoft_remedy

Cohn, T. H. (2000). *Global political economy: Theory and practice.* New York: Addison Wesley Longman.

Curtis, M. (Ed.). (1981). *The great political theories. Vol. I.* New York: Avon Books.

Dreyer, J. T. (2000). *China's political system: Modernization and tradition.* New York: Addison Wesley Longman.

Friedman, M. (1982). *Capitalism and freedom.* Chicago: The University of Chicago Press.

Goodwin, D. K. (1994). *No ordinary time.* New York: Simon and Schuster.

Gosling, J. J. (2000). *Politics and the American economy.* New York: Addison Wesley Longman.

Hayes, L. D. (2001). *Introduction to Japanese politics.* New York: M. E. Sharpe.

Johnson, W. H. (1969). *Principles of zoology.* New York: Holt, Rinehart & Winston.

Porter, J. M. (Ed.). (1997). *Classics in political philosophy.* Scarborough, Ont.: Prentice-Hall Canada.

Rossiter, C. (1961). The Federalist Papers: Alexander Hamilton, James Madison, John Jay. New York: A Mentor Book. Alexander Hamilton, *The Federalist Papers #6, 30,* James Madison, *The Federalist Papers #51.*

Smith, A. (1776). *The wealth of nations.* London: Penguin Books.

Smith, A. (1986). *The wealth of nations.* London: Penguin Books.

Spence, J. D. (1990). *The search for modern China*. New York: W. W. Norton Company.

Taylor, C. (1998, October 19). Gates in the dock. *TIME Magazine, 152*(16).

Chapter 19: Population and Migration

Bongaarts, J. (1994). Population policy options in the developing world. *Science, 263* (11 February): 771–76.

British Broadcasting Corporation (2005, March 28). BBC Web site. Retrieved September 22, 2005, from http://www.news.bbc.co.uk

Chapa, J. (2004). Latinos and the changing fabric of the rural Midwest. In J. Chapa, A. Millard, et al., *Apple pie and enchiladas: Latino newcomers and the changing dynamics of the rural Midwest*. Austin, TX: University of Texas.

Chavez, L. (1998). *Shadowed lives: Undocumented immigrants in American society*. San Diego, CA: Wadsworth.

CNN (2005, August 13). Border emergency declared in New Mexico. CNN Web site. Retrieved September 22, 2005, from http://www.cnn.com/2005/US/08/12/newmexico

Cohen, J. E. (1995). *How many people can the Earth support?* New York: W. W. Norton.

Crane, K., & Millard, A. V. (2004). En Pocas Palabras VI: The "Mexican Situation" and the Mayor's Race. In A. V. Millard & J. Chapa et al., *Apple pie and enchiladas: Latino newcomers in the rural Midwest*. Austin: University of Texas Press.

Ehrlich, P. R. (1968). *The population bomb*. New York. Ballantine.

Ehrlich, P., & Ehrlich, A. (2005). *One with Nineveh: Politics, consumption, and the human future*. Washington, DC: Island Press.

Ehrlich, P. R., Ehrlich, A. H., & Daily, G. C. (1993). Food security, population and environment. *Population and Development Review 19*(1), 1–32.

Fix, M., & Passel, J. S. (1994). *Immigration and immigrants: Setting the record straight*. Washington, DC: The Urban Institute.

Garcia y Griego, M., Weeks, J. R., & Chande, H. (1990). Mexico. Chap. 12 in W. J. Serow, C. B. Nam, D. F. Sly, & R. H. Weller (Eds.), *Handbook on international migration*. New York: Greenwood Press.

Garreau, J. (1991). *Edge city: Life on the new frontier*. New York: Doubleday.

Goldscheider, C. (1971). *Population, modernization, and social stucture*. Boston: Little, Brown.

Hardin, G. (1995). Excessive immigration undermines national unity. In *Population: Opposing viewpoints*. pp. 136–141. San Diego, CA: Greenhaven Press.

Hayes-Bautista, D. E., Chapa, J., & Schink, W. O. (1988). *The burden of support*. Palo Alto, CA: Stanford University Press.

Hostetler, J. A., & Huntington, G. E. (1996). *The Hutterites in North America*. Orlando, FL: Harcourt Brace.

Huddle, D. (1994). *The net national costs of immigration in 1993*. Washington, DC: Carrying Capacity Network.

Light, I., & Bonacich, E. (1988). *Immigrant entrepreneurs: Koreans in Los Angeles, 1965–1982*. Berkeley: University of California Press.

Lowell, L., & Suro, R. (2002). "How many undocumented: The numbers behind the U.S.—Mexico migration talks." The Pew Hispanic Center, Washington, DC.

Luedtke, L. S. (Ed.). (1992). "Making America: The society and culture of the United States." In *Immigration: Opposing viewpoints*. pp. 136–141. San Diego, CA: Greenhaven Press.

Massey, D., Alarcón, R., Durand, J., & González, H. (1990). *Return to Aztlan: The social process of international migration from western Mexico*. Berkeley: University of California Press.

Massey, D., & Goldling, L. (1994). Continuities in transnational migration: An analysis of nineteen Mexican communities. *American Journal of Sociology, 99*, 1,492–1,533.

Massey, D., & Goldling, L. (1995). The new immigration and ethnicity in the United States. *Population and Development Review, 21*(3), 631–652.

Massey, D. S., Durand, J., & Malone, N. J. (2002). *Beyond smoke and mirrors: Mexican immigration in an era of economic integration*. New York: Russell Sage.

McInroy, T. (2003, March 19). *Death in the desert: One year later*. Tucson Citizen. Retrieved March 18, 2003, from http://www.tucsoncitizen.com/local/archive/02/desert02

Millard, A., & Chapa, J., et al. (2004). *Apple pie and enchiladas: Latino newcomers and the changing dynamics of the rural Midwest*. Austin, TX: University of Texas Press.

Nelson, B. (1994). *America Balkanized: Immigration's challenge to government*. Monterey, VA: American Immigration Control Foundation.

NOVA. *China's Only Child*, 1984. PBS.

Patrick, E. (2002). *Spotlight on the US Refugee Resettlement Program*. Migration Policy Institute. Retrieved February 22, 2003, from http://www.migrationinformation.org/Feature/display.cfm?ID=5

Peterson, P. (1999). *Gray Dawn*. New York: Crown.

Portes, A., & Rumbaut, R. (1996). *Immigrant America: A portrait* (2nd ed.). Berkeley, CA: University of California Press.

Portes, A., & Rumbaut, R. (2001). *Legacies: The story of the new second generation*. Berkeley, CA: University of California Press.

Reimers, D. M. (1992). *Still the golden door*. New York: Columbia University Press.

Rumbaut, R. G. (1997). The crucible within: Ethnic identity, self-esteem, and segmented assimilation among children of immigrants. *International Migration Review, 28*, 748–794.

Simmel, G. (1950). *Sociology of Georg Simmel* (K. Wolff, Trans.). Glencoe, IL: Free Press. (Original work published 1905.)

Smil, V. (1994). How many people can the earth feed? *Population and Development Review, 20*(2), 255–92.

Smil, V. (2000). *Feeding the world: A challenge for the twenty-first century*. Cambridge, MA: MIT Press.

Smil, V. (2002). Eating meat: Evolution, patterns, and consequences. *Population and Development Review, 28*(4), 599–641.

Takaki, R. (1993). *A different mirror: A history of multicultural America*. Boston, MA: Little, Brown and Co.

Tonnies, F. [1887] (1988). *Community and society*. Rutgers, NJ: Transaction.

United Nations (1994). *Urban agglomerations*. New York: United Nations Population Division.

United Nations (Population Division). (2004). UN report says that the world urban population of three billion today is expected to reach five billion by 2030. New York. Retrieved December 20, 2005, from http://www.un.org/esa/population/publications/wup2003/pop899_English.doc

United Nations (Population Division). (2005). Population Estimates and Projections: The 2004 revision, New York: United Nations.

United States Department of Homeland Security (Office of Immigration Statistics). (2005). *Yearbook of Immigration Statistics for 2004*. Washington, DC: Office of Immigration Statistics. Retrieved September 22, 2005, from http://uscis.gov/graphics/shared/statistics/yearbook/YrBk04Im.htm

U.S. Bureau of the Census. (2000). *The foreign-born population in the United States*. Washington, DC: U.S. Department of Commerce.

U.S. Bureau of the Census. (2003). *Projections of the resident population by race, Hispanic origin, and nativity: Middle series, 2050 to 2070, NP-T5-G*. Washington, DC: U.S. Department of Commerce.

U.S. Department of Justice, Immigration and Naturalization Service. (2001). *INS releases updated estimates of U.S. illegal population*. Retrieved October 4, 2001, from http://www.USDOJ.gov/INS/public

U.S. Department of Justice. (2003). Estimates of the unauthorized immigrant population residing in the United States: 1900 to 2000. Retrieved September 7, 2006, from http://www.uscis.gov/graphics/shared/aboutus/statistics/Ill_Report_1211.pdf

U.S. Department of Justice, Immigration and Naturalization Service. (2003). *2001 statistical yearbook of the immigration and naturalization service*. Retrieved February 22, 2003, from http://www.immigration.gov/graphics/aboutus/statistics/Yearbook2001.pdf

Weeks, J. R. (1996). *Population: An introduction to concepts and issues* (6th ed.). New York: Wadsworth.

Whyte, W. F. (1981). *Steetcorner society: Social structure of an Italian slum* (3rd ed.). Chicago: University of Chicago Press.

Wirth, L. (1938). Urbanism as a way of life. *American Journal of Sociology, 44*, 1–24.

Chapter 20: From Social Problems to Policies

Axinn, J., & Levin, H. (1982). *Social welfare: A history of the American response to need* (2nd ed.). New York: Longman.

Burch, H. A. (1996). *Basic social policy and planning: Strategies and practice methods*. New York: The Haworth Press.

Chambers, D. E., & Wedel, K. R. (2005). *Social policy and social programs: A method for the practical public policy analyst* (4th ed.). Boston: Pearson/Allyn and Bacon.

DiNitto, D. M. (2000). *Social welfare: Politics and public policy* (5th ed.). Boston: Allyn and Bacon.

Dobelstein, A. W. (1990). *Social welfare: Policy and analysis*. Chicago: Nelson-Hall.

Dolgoff, R., Feldstein, D., & Skolnik, L. (1993). *Understanding social welfare* (3rd ed.). New York: Longman.

Esping-Andersen, G. (1990). *The three worlds of welfare capitalism*. Princeton, NJ: Princeton University Press.

Flynn, J. P. (1992). *Social agency policy: Analysis and presentation for community practice* (2nd ed.). Chicago: Nelson-Hall.

Gabor, P. A., Unrau, Y. A., & Grinnell, R. M., Jr. (1998). *Evaluation for social workers: A quality improvement approach for the social services* (2nd ed.). Boston: Allyn and Bacon.

Giddens, A. (1976). *Marx Weber: The protestant ethic and the spirit of capitalism*. Cambridge: George Allen & Unwin.

Ginsberg, L. H. (2001). *Social work evaluation: Principles and methods*. Boston: Allyn and Bacon.

Jansson, B. S. (1994). *Social policy: From theory to policy practice* (2nd ed.). Pacific Grove, CA: Brooks/Cole.

Karger, H. J., & Stoesz, D. (1998). *American social welfare policy: A pluralist approach* (3rd ed.). Longman: New York.

Murray, C. (1984). *Losing* ground*: American social policy, 1950–1980*. New York: Basic Books.

Pierson, P. (1994). *Dismantling the welfare state? Reagan, Thatcher, and the politics of retrenchment*. New York: Cambridge University Press.

Reese, W. L. (1980). *Dictionary of philosophy and religion*. Atlantic Highlands, NJ: Humanities Press.

Sullivan, T. J., et al. (1980). *Social problems*. New York: Wiley.

Todaro, M. P. (2000). *Economic development* (7th ed.). New York: Addison-Wesley Longman.

Trattner, W. I. (1989). *From poor law to welfare state: A history of social welfare in America* (4th ed.). New York: The Free Press.

Tropman, J. E. (1989). *American values and social welfare: Cultural contradictions in the welfare state*. Englewood Cliffs, NJ: Prentice Hall.

Zastrow, C. (1992). *Social problems: Issues and solutions* (3rd ed.). Chicago: Nelson-Hall.

CONTRIBUTORS

Talin Babikian, Ph.D., M.P.H.
Postdoctoral Fellow
UCLA

Rudolph Bailey, Ph.D.
Professor and Chair, Educational and Counseling
    Psychology
Andrews University

Alina M. Baltazar, LMSW, ACSW
Research Associate for the Institute for the
    Prevention of Addictions
Andrews University

C. Edward Boyatt, Ed.D.
Chair, Department of Administration and Leadership
La Sierra University

Todd Burley, Ph.D., ABPP
Professor of Psychology
Loma Linda University & Gestalt Associates
    Training—Los Angeles

Robin Butler, PMHNP, BC, MSN
Psychiatric Nurse Practitioner and Instructor
Loma Linda University and Behavioral Medicine
    Center

Nancy J. Carbonell, Ph.D.
Associate Professor of Educational and Counseling
    Psychology
Andrews University

Alexander Carpenter
Student
Andrews University

Jonathan R. Cook, B.S.
Doctoral Student in Clinical Psychology
University of Missouri, Columbia

Ken R. Crane, Ph.D.
Associate Professor of Sociology

Ancilla Domini College

Héctor Luis Díaz, Ph.D.
Professor and Chair, Department of Social Work
The University of Texas—Pan American

René Drumm, Ph.D.
Professor of Social Work
Southern Adventist University

Nancy L. Farrell, PsyD/Dr.PH.
Psychotherapy Service Provider
Casa Colina Centers for Rehabilitation, Pomona, CA

Isidore Flores, Ph.D.
Associate Research Scientist
School of Rural Public Health
Texas A&M University System Health Science
    Center

M. Catherin Freier, Ph.D.
Neurodevelopmental Psychologist
Professor of Psychology and Pediatrics
Loma Linda University and Children's Hospital
Associate Director, Center for Prevention Research
Andrews University

Elvin S. Gabriel, Ed.D.
Associate Professor of Educational and Counseling
    Psychology
Andrews University

Sharon A. Gillespie, M.A., M.P.H.
Associate Professor of Psychology and Public Health
Andrews University

A. Josef Greig, Ph.D.
Professor of Philosophy, Emeritus
Andrews University

Herbert W. Helm, Jr., Ph.D.
Professor of Psychology
Andrews University

Many Voices: An Introduction to Social Issues

Steve Helm, M.A.
Senior Lecturer in Management Information Systems
Wichita State University

Nicole J. Higgins
Student
Andrews University

Gary L. Hopkins, M.D., Dr.PH.
Director of Center of Prevention Research
Andrews University
Assistant Professor of Public Health
Loma Linda University

Loretta B. Johns, Ph.D.
Assistant Dean for Program Development and
    Evaluation
Loma Linda University, School of Medicine

Lionel Matthews, Ph.D.
Associate Professor of Sociology
Andrews University

Duane C. McBride, Ph.D.
Professor and Chair of Behavioral Sciences
    Department
Andrews University

Ronald D. Morgan, Ed.D.
Associate Professor of Education
University of Redlands

Dewey Murdick, M.A.
Chief Analyst of Berrien County Forensic Laboratory

Susan E. Murray, M.A., M.S., CFLE
Assistant Professor of Family Studies and Social
    Work
Andrews University

Daniel Pickett
Student
Andrews University

Sharon W. Pittman, Ph.D.
Professor of Social Work
Country Director for ADRA Guinea
Adventist Development & Relief Agency

Marciana Popescu, Ph.D.
Associate Professor of Social Policy
Director of MSA in Community and International
    Development Program
Andrews University

Derrick L. Proctor, Ph.D.
Professor of Psychology
Andrews University

William Richardson, Ph.D.
Professor of Religion and Dean, Emeritus
College of Arts and Sciences
Andrews University

Malcolm B. Russell, Ph.D.
Vice President for Academic Administration
Union College

Jane Sabes, Ph.D.
Professor of Political Science
Andrews University

Timothy E. Spruill, Ed.D.
Associate Director of Behavioral Medicine
Department of Medical Education
Florida Hospital Osteopathic Family Medicine
    Residency
Clinical Associate Professor
Nova Southeastern University

Karen E. Stockton, Ph.D., M.S.W.
Assistant Professor of Social Work
Andrews University

Judy W. Taylor, M.S.
Special Education Supervisor
Fort Worth Independent School District
Fort Worth, Texas

Joseph W. Warren, Ph.D.
Associate Professor of English
Andrews University

Jan F. Wrenn, M.S.W., ACSW
Associate Professor of Social Work
Andrews University

INDEX

Ecological
   degradation 427
   perspective 284
   theory 98
Economic man 40
Ecosystem 98, 284, 428
Ecosystems Theory 220–221
Ecstasy. *See* Drugs: ecstasy (MDMA)
ECT (electroconvulsive therapy) 261,
   280
Edge city 430
education. *See* Educational level, Multi-
   cultural education, Public schools,
   School, Special education, Testing
Educational level 62, 311, 321
Education for All Children Act 71, 73
Effects of Explicit Material 184–185
Egalitarian fallacy 90
Ego 24–26, 32, 100
Elder abuse. *See* Abuse: elder
Elizabethan Poor Laws 450
Emotional intelligence 107
Empathy 29, 107, 235, 251, 339, 362
Empiricists 19
End dimension. *See* Intrinsic dimension
Engels, Frederick 157
Environment 123–124, 127–128, 136,
   138, 146–147
Environmental degradation 254, 427
EPA (Environmental Protection Agency)
   128
Epidemiology 124–126
Erikson, Erik 31–32, 361
ESEA (Elementary and Secondary Edu-
   cation Act) 71
Ethnicity 14, 55, 80, 97, 117, 165, 209,
   220, 236, 239, 242, 266, 327, 331,
   341, 368, 405, 426, 435, 441
Ethnic minority groups 327. *See
   also* Minority: groups
Ethnocentrism 6, 41
Ethnography 64
Evaluability 457
Exhibitionism 190, 192
Existential 28–30, 91, 154, 210, 282,
   372–373
Expectancies 63, 316
Expectancy theory 21
Experiment 21, 31–32, 34, 63–64, 207,
   241, 407, 414
Experimental group 63, 241
Experimenter bias 63
Expert opinion 55
Extraversion (extroversion) 27, 30
Extrinsic dimension 273
Extrinsic motivation 21

F

Factitious disorder 263

Family
   cohesion 116
   communication 116
   flexibility 116
   planning 315, 379, 390, 429, 442
   sociology 99
   systems 116, 352–353, 366
   violence 127, 240, 310, 333, 355, 360
Fear of expulsion 293
Feminine psychology 28
Feminism
   liberal 379
   radical 379
   second wave 378–379
   socialist 379
   third wave 378–379
Festinger, Leon 22
Fetish 261
Fictions 27
Field
   experiment 64
   research 63
   theory 23
Fieldwork 41
Flushing response 209
Folkways 6
Food stamps 314
Four-humor theory 30
Frankl, Victor 30
Free-market economy 406, 409–413, 415
Free will 4
Free world 409
French Revolution 3
Freud, Sigmund 19, 24–28, 31, 151, 176,
   230, 260–261, 267, 272, 351
Friedman, Milton 411, 454
Frotteurism 192
Frustration-aggression theory (model)
   245, 247, 330
Functional finalism 27
Functionalism (Functionalist) 7
Fundamentalists 167, 289–290, 296, 298

G

Game stage 14
Gangs 10, 237, 251, 307, 353, 364, 367,
   393–394
Gardner, Howard 78, 91
Gay and Lesbian Rights Projects of the
   American Civil Liberties Union
   (ACLU) 181
Gay rights 181
Gender identity disorder 264
Generalization 59
Generalized other 14
Genetic drift 44
Genetic epistemology 33
Genetics 44, 136
Genuineness 29

Gestalt Theory 35
Goals 2000: Educate America Act 80
God 151–153, 155, 163–164, 168–169
Goffman, Erving 13, 15
Graying of America 431
Great Depression 69, 313, 409, 412,
   419–420, 447, 451, 459–460
Greed 252, 355, 391, 418
Greeks 174–175, 260, 338, 449
Grief 356
Groupthink 292
Growth and Development 44
Gun Control 250
Gutierrez, Gustavo (Father) 159

H

Habituation 22
Hallucinogens. *See* Drugs: hallucinogen
Harm reduction 133, 212, 217
Harrison Act 217
Hate crimes 236
Health care expenditures 141
Hebrews 260
Hetaerae 174
Heterosexuality 179
Hetherington, E. Mavis 118–120
HHS (Department of Health and Hu-
   man Services) 127, 129
Hierarchy of needs 29
Hinduism 163, 178–179, 397
Histrionic 267
HIV 123, 125, 127, 130, 140, 146, 177,
   179, 185–186, 188–189, 195, 197,
   208, 217, 243, 318, 359, 367, 429
Holistic approach 284
Homans, George 97–98
Homelessness
   situational 310
Homicide 238, 360
Homosexuality 174, 179–181
Hopi 49–50
Horney, Karen 28
Housing 309
HSO (Health Service Organization) 137
Human adaptability 45
Humanism 28
Hypersexuality 190–191
Hypothetico-deductive thinking 33
Hypoxyphilia 192

I

ICD-10 (International Classification of
   Disease) 262, 265
Id 24
IDEA (Individuals with Disabilities Act)
   70–71, 80, 84
Identity 32, 162, 366
idiographic technique 59

Micro-level 13
Microsoft 81, 405, 408
Middle Ages 161, 175, 260, 400, 449
Militia 245, 250
Mills, C. Wright 4
Mills v. Board of Education 69
Mind control 293
Minority
  children 343
  groups 135, 237, 307, 327–328,
      337–339, 341, 352, 360, 439
  students 79–80, 89, 339, 343
Mixed economy 409
Mixed Heritage 332, 338
Modernism 11, 15, 165, 167, 290
Mommy track 384
Monarchical rule 406–408
Monism 19
Monitoring the Future 133, 209
Monogamy 174
Mood disorder 263
Moral anxiety 25
Moral principle 455
Moral therapy 260
Moralism 216, 454–456
Morality 5, 25, 153, 166, 175, 179, 290,
    418, 455, 460
Mores 6, 86, 167, 353
Motivation
  extrinsic. See Extrinsic motivation
  intrinsic 21
Mourning 357
Multicultural education 341
Multiple intelligences 76, 78, 91
Mutualism 410–411
Mysterium tremendum 274–275

N

Narcotic Addict Rehabilitation Act 217
Narcotic Control Act 217
National Association for the Advance-
    ment of Colored People 334
National Center on Elder Abuse 235
National drug policy 13, 216, 218
National health insurance 143
National Institutes of Health (NIH) 127
Native Americans 209, 245, 329,
    331–332, 382
Naturalistic observation 59
Nature 20
Nay-sayer 60
Necrophilia 192
Negative valence 23
Neo-Malthusian 426
Neurochemical 133, 205–206
Neuroleptics 278, 280
Neuron 206
Neurosis 32, 258
Neurotic anxiety 25

Neurotic patterns of adjustment 28
Neurotransmission 206
Neurotransmitters 35, 204, 206–207, 247,
    261
New Age 167
Nicotine 203, 205. See Drugs: nicotine
No Child Left Behind Act 71
Nomothetic technique 59
Nonexperimental research designs 458
Norm-referenced tests 75, 77
Normality 180, 190, 274–275
Normal sexual behaviors 177
Norms 3, 5–11, 15–16
Nuclear family 54

O

Obesity 135–136, 364
Object permanence 33
Observational learning 34
One-parent families 306
One Child Policy 429
Operant conditioning 34–35, 215, 318
Opioid 203
Opponent-process theory 22
Organ inferiority 27
Otto, Rudolph 274–275
Overpopulation 106, 442
Overt racism 327

P

P-value 62
P.L. 94–142 71
Parallel public school systems 72
Paraphilia 192
Parasitism 410–411
parent/infant dyad 358
Parenthood 105–106, 358–359
Parochial schools 68, 74, 87
Parsons, Talcott 8–9, 11, 96
PASE v. Hannon 90
Pasteur, Louis 137
Pathologies 239, 271
Patriarchal society 174
Patterns that harm relationships 104
Pavlov 34
Pavlovian conditioning 34
Pedophilia 188, 190
Peer pressure 85, 131, 321, 366, 368
Penn Enhancement Program (PEP) 321
Penn Optimism Program (POP) 321
Pennsylvania Association of Retarded
    Citizens v. Pennsylvania 69
Perchemlides vs. Frizzle 86
Persona 26
Personal problem 55
Personal Responsibility and Work
    Opportunity Reconciliation Act
    (PRWORA) 314

Pharmacotherapy 213
Phencyclidine 203, 205
Phi phenomenon 35
Phlegmatic 30
Physical anthropology 43
Piaget, Jean 33
PIE (Person-in-Environment) 284–285
Placebo effect 63
Play stage 14
Pleasure principle 24
Pluralism 16, 166–167, 326, 328–329, 436
Polygamy 174
Population 425–429, 431–432, 438,
    441–443
Position preference 60
Positive psychology 322
Positive valence 23
Postmodernism 15–16, 153, 165–167,
    398–399
Postnatal Influences 359
Poverty
  causes 317, 451, 453
  reducing 315
  violence 244
PPOs (Preferred Provider Organizations)
    144
Prenatal influences 230, 358–359
Prescription drugs 140–141
Prevention programs 127, 130, 133–134,
    136, 250–252, 322
Profane 152, 164, 168
Profiles of Prostitutes 185
Programmatic intervention 230, 251
Prohibition 202, 217
Prohibition 217–219
Prophetic abnormality 275
Protestant work ethic 54, 454
Prozac 193, 281
Psychodynamic 180–181, 213, 260
Psychomotor stimulants 206–207
Psychosis 204–205, 258, 268, 270, 273
Psychosocial Theory 31
Psychosurgery 261, 280
Psychotherapy 282
Puberty 45, 184, 246, 363–364
Public interest groups 460
Public opinion 55, 57, 151, 252
Public schools 8, 68–69, 72, 74–75, 79,
    81, 87–88
Pure Food and Drug Act 216
Puritan moralism 216

Q

Qualified individualism 91
Qualitative 44, 55–56, 76–77, 458
Quantitative 44, 55–56, 76–77, 458
Quasi-experiments 63
Quest dimension 273
Quotas 77, 91, 329, 419, 440

T

Taboos 6, 41
Tabula rasa 19
Target earners 434
Tax Reform 315–316
Technology 6, 16, 40, 45, 47, 72–74, 81–82, 88–89, 108, 128, 137, 143–144, 165, 167, 180, 190, 243, 254, 325, 373, 398, 400, 405, 417–418, 420, 428
Temperament 361
Tenth Amendment 68
Terrorism 57, 146, 208, 237, 441
Test
　bias 90
　fairness 90
Testing 77, 89–91
Testosterone 4, 193, 246–247
The Bell Curve 20
Theism 155
The Wealth of Nations 406, 418
Thorazine 280
Throwaway kids 365
Tillich, Paul 100
Tobacco 41, 84, 123, 125, 127, 129–132, 138, 184, 205, 208, 218, 243
Tolerance 203–205
Tolman 21
Total Fertility Rate (TFR) 429
Traditional family 97
Trait 30
Transcendent idealism 156
Transience 240
Transvestism 192
Tripartite scheme 219
Trobriand 50–51
Twelve-step programs 191, 213–214, 282
Twelve steps of AA 213

U

Unconditional positive regard 29, 261
Unconditioned
　response 34
　stimulus 34
Underclass 242, 308
Underemployment 310–312
Unemployment 5, 54, 111–112, 140, 220, 245, 249, 270, 307, 310–313, 315, 320, 409, 412, 420–421, 443, 451–452, 454
Uniform Crime Report 188, 238
Uninsured 139
United Nations 311, 320, 334, 409
Unqualified individualism 91
Urban 430
Urbanization 98, 270–271, 441
Urophilia 192
Utilitarian 165, 168

V

Value system 8, 239, 447
Victorian era 176, 186
Violence
　biological 239, 245
　community 236
　criminal 237
　domestic 235
　etiology 238
　exposure 355
　family. *See* Family: violence
　forms 231, 239
　genetics 246
　homicide 238
　media 242
　police 238
　reduction 249
　regional variation 240
　school 88
　self 231

　workplace 235
Violence
　forms 231
　school 82–84, 88–89
Vocal sounds 49
Voting Rights Act 335
Vouchers 74, 87–88, 343
Voyeurism 190, 192
Vygotsky, Lev 354

W

Wallerstein, Judith S. 118–120
War on Drugs 134, 217, 224
Weber, Max 151, 158, 167
Welfare Reform 112, 314–315
White (Caucasian) 326–329, 331–333, 335, 338–339, 341, 431
Whorf, Benjamin 6, 49–50
Will to power 27
Williams, Robin 6
Willingness to respond 60
Withdrawal 203, 205
Women's Liberation Movement 378
Women's shelter 384, 386–387
Work ethic 54, 454
Worksite wellness programs 147
World Trade Organization (WTO) 421

Y

Yea-sayer 60
Yerkes-Dodson Law 22
YMCA 371

Z

Zedong, Mao 406
Zimbardo, Philip 31
Zoophilia 192
ZPG (Zero Population Growth) 426

DATE DUE